Competition Law and Environmental Protection in Europe

Europa Law Publishing, Groningen 2003

# Competition Law and Environmental Protection in Europe

Towards Sustainability?

Hans Vedder

Europa Law Publishing is a publishing company
specializing in European Union Law.
For further information please contact Europa Law
Publishing via email: info@europalawpublishing.com
or visit our website at: www.europalawpublishing.com.



Typeset in Scala and Scala Sans, Graphic design by
G2K Designers, Groningen/Amsterdam.

NUR 828; ISBN 90-76871-17-5

British Library Cataloguing-in-Publication Data
A catalogue record for this book is available from the
British Library.

This book is the result of research made possible
with the financial support from the Netherlands
Organisation for Scientific Research (*NWO*).

To Sigrid

## Preface

Having written one, I can now confirm that writing a PhD thesis invariably affects not only the hard disk of your computer (or the network for that matter) that gets clogged with megabytes of word documents, but also has repercussions on your social life. It is for this reason that I would first like to thank my wife Cynthia for her unstinting support, the Sunday morning discussions and for constantly reminding me that there is more to life than the thesis. There is indeed.

I would also like to thank my promotor, Hanna Sevenster, for having given me the chance to do this research as well as getting me involved in many other projects. You stood at the cradle of my academic career. To my former colleagues at the Centre for Environmental Law I would like to say that despite their (maybe subconscious) efforts the following is true: *je kunt de man wel uit het noorden halen, maar je kunt het noorden niet uit de man halen.* You tried hard enough.

Finally, I would like to thank the members of my reading committee: professors Bonus, Jans, Mortelmans, Slot and Vogelaar for their invaluable comments.

Of course more people were subjected to long monologues on the topic, gave me tips and insights or helped me in another way. I thank all of you.

*Hans Vedder*

Appingedam, July 2003

# Contents

# Introduction

## Introduction

This is a book about the integration of environmental concerns and EC competition law. From a legal perspective, Article 6 of the EC Treaty requires such integration.[1] This provision, albeit worded differently, was included in the EC Treaty by the Single European Act in 1987 as (then) Article 130R.[2] Ever since it was introduced, this integration principle has been the subject of legal research. Recurring themes in these investigations were the legal status of the principle and whether it entailed a preference for environmental considerations over the other policy objectives in which it was to be integrated. The integration principle was first put to practical legal use in the Court's judgment in *Titaniumdioxide*.[3] Since then, its practical legal role has primarily been confined to disputes concerning the correct legal basis. This, however, has done little to clarify either of the recurring themes mentioned above. A purely legal approach does not suffice to answer the question of what Article 6 EC is all about. Moreover, even apart from the purely legal question of what exactly Article 6 prescribes, there is a growing body of case law that concerns environmental protection requirements and competition law.

With the advent of the environmental agreement[4] as an environmental policy instrument and the ever-increasing flow of government funds for environmental purposes, the relation between the EC's competition laws and environmental protection came to the fore. How should EC competition law, in view of this integration principle, react to environmental agreements that protect the environment but also restrict competition? Similarly, we may ask how the prohibition of state aids in Article 87 EC is to be applied to cases where such aids are granted for environmental purposes but distort competition? In this connection, the precise content of the integration principle in relation to competition law becomes even more important. Environmental agreements and environmental subsidies may be very effective instruments of environmental policy. As such they may very well contribute greatly to achieving more environmental protection at lower costs. Particularly now, when the US have rejected the Kyoto

---

1 It reads as follows: 'Environmental protection requirements must be integrated into the definition and implementation of the Community policies and activities [...], in particular with a view to promoting sustainable development'.

2 At that time the text was: 'Environmental protection requirements shall be a component of the Community's other policies.' With the Treaty on European Union the provision was changed to read as follows: 'Environmental protection requirements must be integrated into the definition and implementation of other Community policies'.

3 Case C-300/89, *Commission* v. *Council* (Titaniumdioxide), [1991] ECR I-2867.

4 An environmental agreement is an agreement between different companies or between a group of companies and a public authority on an environmental matter. See, further, *infra*, paragraph 3.3.

protocol basically because of the costs involved and the effects of these costs on the competitive situation, achieving environmental protection more effectively as well as efficiently is likely to become one of the major challenges for environmental policy makers throughout the world. Completely ruling out categories of potentially effective and efficient environmental instruments, such as environmental agreements or environmental subsidies, because of their incompatibility with the competition rules, would therefore seem to run counter to the integration principle.

From a different perspective we should also recognise that competition is probably the most effective allocative mechanism known to man. Competition as the cornerstone of the free market economy has allowed economies to soar to great heights and brought us myriad innovations. Moreover, Article 4 of the EC Treaty dictates that 'the principle of an open market economy with free competition' is to be the basis of Europe's economic policy. Why not, the obvious question would seem to be, try and make competition work for the environment? Why should we not try to innovate in the area of environmental protection techniques to such an extent that costs are no longer an objection to high levels of environmental protection?

This, it is submitted, addresses the core of Article 6 EC and with this observation we have returned to what this book is all about: the integration of environmental concerns and EC competition law. Put more precisely the central question in this research is the following:

*What is the integration of environmental concerns and EC competition law required by Article 6 and has such an integration actually taken place?*

The question thus asked is actually twofold. Firstly, what *should* be and secondly what *is* the role of environmental concerns and EC competition law in view of the integration principle? What the role for environmental concerns should be is not easy to answer. According to Article 6, this role should amount to an 'integration'. What this concept of integration means is nowhere made clear in the Treaty. Moreover, as the fact that two themes in connection with the integration principle (*i.e.* its legal status and whether it entails a preference for the environment) are still recurring shows, the exact content of Article 6 EC is still far from clear.[5] We have seen above how the ideal situation would be one where the powerful instrument of competition would be used to achieve more environmental protection.

This book consists of three parts. In Part One we will examine how this ideal situation where competition works for the environment can be achieved

5 See, Dhondt 2003 who, at pages 15-183, addresses these questions and identifies a multitude of opinions.

and what the role of the integration principle is in this respect. Article 6, as we have seen above, prescribes an integration of environmental protection requirements and, *inter alia,* EC competition law and policy. What does 'integrate' mean in this context? For example with regard to EC competition policy the question may be asked when, if at all, an environmental agreement that restricts competition should be exempted on environmental grounds. The role of the integration principle in this, as it will be referred to, competition perspective of the relation between competition and environmental protection will be further investigated in Part One. As a result, the concept of integration enshrined in Article 6 EC is given a well-defined meaning in connection with EC competition law in Part One of this book. Moreover, as may be gathered from the last sentence of the preceding paragraph, competition can, under the right circumstances, function as an exceptionally powerful instrument to bring about environmental protection more efficiently. The advent of many of the new instruments of environmental policy must be seen in this light. In this respect, the relation between competition and environmental protection is two-way in that it is not just competition law that needs to take into account environmental considerations but environmental policy similarly needs to incorporate certain competitive aspects. This, as it will be called, environmental perspective of the relation between competition and environmental protection will also be investigated in Part One.

Because the integration principle binds the Community institutions when they define and implement the Community's policies, the meaning of the concept 'integration' and thus Article 6 EC, can be called a model of integration. Ideally, the role awarded to environmental concerns in EC competition law should comply with that prescribed by the model of integration.

As part of the examination of what the role of environmental concerns and EC competition law *is*, we will also investigate in Part Two whether that role is in accordance with the model of integration developed in Part One as far as the competition perspective of the relation between competition and environmental protection is concerned. In order to do this we need to first establish the role that environmental concerns have played in EC competition law. This question is relatively straightforward to answer. All that needs to be done is to closely examine and analyse the EC competition laws and their application in order to determine what role environmental concerns have played. This constitutes the bulk of Part Two. In this Part the whole of EC Competition law, *i.e.* Article 81-87 of the EC Treaty, the Merger Regulation[6] and the so-called useful effect doctrine,[7] is examined to ascertain the role played by environmental concerns.

---

6 Regulation 4064/89, [1990] OJ L 257/14.

7 Also referred to as 'new norm'. It consists of Article 3(1)(g) in connection with Article 10 and 81 of the EC Treaty.

The perceptive reader will have noticed that the environmental perspective of the model of integration ('to what extent is competition used as an instrument to achieve environmental protection most efficiently?') is not addressed in Part Two. The explanation for this is rather simple. EC environmental policy primarily makes use of Directives that need to be implemented by the national legislator. In this context, the EC Directive lays down the instrumental framework but it is up to the national legislature to prescribe the type of instrument that will be actually used. The Directive will generally only lay down the broad framework for the national environmental policy instrument that must make the Directive practically effective. The question to what extent competition is used as an instrument of environmental policy is therefore best answered at the level of member state implementing legislation. This can be seen with regard to the implementation of the Packaging Directive.[8] Whilst the transposition of this Directive has resulted in monopolistic producer responsibility organisations in Germany, France and other member states, the United Kingdom's approach to the implementation resulted in the creation of a market on which several competing producer responsibility organisations are active. Interestingly, the approach adopted by the UK is as much a correct transposition of the Directive as that used by the German or French governments. This striking difference in terms of the market structure resulting from the implementation of one Directive shows that the Directive itself is not the primary factor that determines whether or not and to what extent competition is used to achieve environmental objectives most efficiently.

In Part Three we will look at the findings of Part One and Two from three different perspectives as part of a comparative legal analysis. We will thus compare the relationship between environmental concerns and EC competition law both as it is and how it should be according to the model of integration, with, firstly, the role played by cultural considerations in EC competition, secondly, the role of environmental protection and national competition law and, thirdly, the role of environmental concerns in the internal market rules.

This comparative legal exercise will help us to establish the value of the model of integration as well as the validity of our findings with regard to whether or not the model of integration was applied in practice. On the basis of our findings in both Part One and Two, we will be able to discern three factors relative to the model of integration that are typical and decisive in EC competition law and environmental protection. In Part Three we will address these three factors by looking at the model of integration from the three different perspectives listed in the preceding paragraph. Every perspective addresses one of the factors considered to be critical for the model of integration and can thus be

---

8 The implementation of the Packaging Directive and the resulting market structures in Germany and the United Kingdom will be examined in chapter 10.

used to test the model of integration. In a nutshell, the first of these three factors is the mutually reinforcing relationship between competition and environmental protection in view of the polluter pays principle. It is submitted that a similar role cannot be envisaged for other so-called 'non-economic' considerations and that as a result the role of such considerations in EC competition law should differ from that played by environmental concerns. To test this hypothesis, we will examine the role awarded to cultural considerations within EC competition law. Because this comparison takes place within the framework of EC competition law it will be called the internal perspective. The second factor is not so much unique to or decisive for the model of integration but rather is considered relevant for the Community's competition law in general. It has on many considerations been observed by scholars, practitioners, and the Court alike that the competition rules of the EC not only serve to ensure effective competition but also function in the light of the market integration objective. This market integration objective is, by definition, absent in the competition laws of the member states even though these have in many cases been modelled on EC competition law. The second – external – perspective eliminates this market integration objective as a factor that is relevant for EC competition law but at the same time possibly distorting in view of the model of integration.[9] The third factor relates to what will be called the economisation of environmental benefits. As will be shown, EC competition law (partly) takes environmental aspects into account after they have been 'converted' into economic benefits. Such economisation is explicitly refused by the Court in connection with the internal market rules in the EC Treaty. The interpretation of this area of Community law is purely legal. The third – semi external – perspective therefore excludes the economisation as a factor that could possibly affect the operation of the model of integration in practice.

Moreover, as part of the second perspective, the role of environmental protection requirements and national competition law, we will also address the environmental perspective of the model of integration. To this end we will look at the way in which several Directives that lay down a producer responsibility have been implemented. These directives allow for implementation by means of an environmental agreement as an attempt to introduce more 'market-based' instruments of environmental policy. The harsh reality is, however, that in many cases the resulting producer responsibility organisations are in fact large-scale nationwide monopolists. As part of Part Three we will therefore examine the factors that are responsible for this failure to effectively make competition work for the environment.

9 The distortive effect of the market integration objective can be seen in, for example, the initially (overly) wide scope of Article 81(1) EC. See further, *infra*, paragraph 7.2.

On the basis of the findings in these three parts we will formulate our conclusions and make recommendations. These recommendations should allow us effectively to use the most efficient economic instrument known to man to achieve better environmental protection through bringing about a competition *for* the environment.

PART ONE

*Integration: the act or process of combining two or more things so that they work together*
Oxford Advanced Learners Dictionary

# Competition and Environmental Protection: The Search for a Model of Integration

CHAPTER I

# An Introduction to Integration

## 1 An introduction to integration

At first sight the concepts competition and environmental protection have about as much to do with each other as do the concepts of free market economy and pollution. All four concepts are abstract and hard, if not impossible, to define accurately. For a legal scholar this definitional uncertainty is nothing more than an inconvenience as soon as he is able to retreat into his habitat that is filled with well-defined legal concepts and reasoning. The inconvenience becomes a core question as soon as this habitat is 'polluted' with a legal principle that is less than well defined. An example of such a site that requires rehabilitation is Article 6 EC. This provision contains a so-called integration clause and reads as follows:

*'Environmental protection requirements must be integrated into the definition and implementation of the Community policies and activities [...], in particular with a view to promoting sustainable development.'*

To the relief of the lawyer, the wording of this provision, '*must* be integrated', indicates that it is a legally binding obligation to integrate environmental considerations. Moreover, the judgment in *PreussenElektra* shows that the Court has recourse to this provision in order to be able to interpret Community law in a specific case.[1] Yet another case shows that other environmental principles can be invoked in legal proceedings and are thus certainly not confined confined to the political arena.[2] A further reading of the provision similarly comforts the legal scholar as he can learn from Article 3 of the EC Treaty what exactly are the 'Community policies and activities' mentioned in Article 6 EC.

Interestingly, and this brings us to the main theme of this research, competition policy is one of the Community policies.[3] The institutions responsible for the definition and implementation of the Community's competition policy are thus under an obligation to integrate environmental protection requirements and competition requirements. However, already in the introduction to this book a number of questions arose the answers to which are far from obvious. Simply prohibiting environmental agreements without even mentioning the environmental aspects involved will probably fall foul of the integration principle in Article 6 EC. Similarly, granting the parties unlimited possibilities to restrict competition as soon as some environmental interest is involved is also uncalled for. The answer to the question what role for environmental considerations in EC competition law Article 6 EC exactly requires, is obscure and probably lies

---

1 Case C-379/98, *PreussenElektra* v. *Schleswag* (PreussenElektra), [2001] ECR I-2099, para. 76.

2 Case C-341/95, *Bettati* v. *Safety High Tech* (Bettati), [1998] ECR I-4355, paras. 32-36.

3 Article 3(1)(g) EC.

somewhere between the two extremes mentioned above. The first part of the main question indicated in the introduction asks precisely this question: 'what role should environmental protection requirements play in the EC's competition law and policy?'

Initially, this research took the abovementioned Article 6 EC as a point of departure in order to embark on a purely legal journey. The first part of the main question is, however, impossible to answer within this purely legal framework. According to Article 6 this role should amount to an 'integration'. This only leads to the question what the concept of integration exactly means. Most explanations of this concept verge on the tautological in that they boil down to a statement that the environment must 'be fully taken into account' or 'should be taken into consideration'.[4] The Court's case law refers to the integration principle on a number of occasions concerning the choice of the legal basis for Community action in a certain field. These cases, even though they again show the legal character of the integration principle, do little to clarify the concept of integration itself.[5]

Fortunately, Article 6 itself already contains the beginning of an answer to the riddle of what constitutes integration. Such integration, according to Article 6, should in particular 'promote sustainable development'.[6] This leads us to the question of how sustainable development must be defined. Again in a nutshell, sustainable development means that there is economic development, however, it should be in keeping with, *inter alia*, environmental protection considerations.[7] Sustainable development does not mean a return to the early hominid way of life even though that will undoubtedly mean less environmental degradation. The other extreme, unmitigated economic growth without any consideration for other factors than economic growth and financial profit, certainly also falls outside the scope of sustainable development. Sustainable development is all about finding a *modus vivendi* for economic growth and environmental protection. This balanced relationship cannot be found using legal reasoning alone. As it concerns economic growth, economic reasoning should also form part of the analysis.

In order to define what constitutes sustainable development and, consequently, integration within the meaning of Article 6 EC, the legal scholar must venture into a world where economics and the law are not studied as separate things that exist in a vacuum. He must enter a world where economics and law

4 Krämer 2000, p. 14, 16.

5 See for an overview of this case law: Jans 2000, p. 10, 12 and 44 *et seq.*

6 This objective could also be deducted from Article 2 EC where it is listed as one of the ends of the Community.

7 An example of other considerations taken into account as part of sustainability would be the social and working conditions.

are seen as two methods (instruments) to explain and, to a greater or lesser extent, steer behaviour in a society. In this view, neither law nor economics is seen as absolute and both are recognised to be interrelated (and related to other factors).

Economics and the law have already been tentatively applied to the specific problem of environmental pollution in the introduction. We can see everywhere around us how, if left uncorrected, the free market economy, relying on competition as its foremost allocative mechanism, can lead to environmental degradation.[8] This is not inherent in the free market economy or competition but is the result of the external nature of the environment. A certain amount of environmental degradation will not involve costs for any specific economic actor but for society in general only and even then in many cases only on the longer term. Pollution in many cases does not entail any direct costs for an individual economic actor. This is the external nature of the environment and this is why the individual, guided by economic efficiency considerations, will not consider it necessary to protect the environment or invest in environmental innovations. The existence of externalities has been recognised in economics for a long time.[9] Moreover, the implications of externalities for the free market economy and competition have received considerable attention in economic writing. Basically, economists see externalities as a market failure. Such a market failure is a factor that will generally lead to something being considered, in the economic sense, a public good or bad. According to some economists that is where the government, and with it regulation and lawmaking, enters the market. The answer to the question of what the concept 'integration' means, takes a beginning in the appreciation of the economic relations between competition and the free market economy on the one hand and environmental protection on the other.

This research is thus, in part, such an escape from the legal habitat into the 'real world' where economics and law interrelate and neither is absolute. More precisely, we will first investigate the evolution of competition law and policy and how it relates to the free market economy. This will be called 'a legal and economic analysis of competition' and will take place in chapter 2. In the course of this overview we will also deal with the concept of externalities and its relation with competition as the prime instrument of the free market economy. After the competition-side of the matter has thus been charted, the evolution of environmental law and policy will be investigated in chapter 3 to reveal how competition and environmental policy have slowly become interrelated. In this

8 For example, the success of low-budget air carriers has resulted in (ridiculously) low air fares. Such low fares encourage air travel (one Dutch carrier advertises with a family who decide on Saturday to spend a Sunday in London) which is certainly not beneficial to the environment.

9 It can be traced back British economist Arthur Cecile Pigou's work from the beginning of nineteenth century. Probably, Pigou's thinking on externalities has its roots in the earlier work of Marshall.

chapter environmental law and policy are analysed from a legal as well economic perspective. Since the writer of this book has not been educated as an economist and this book has been prepared as a PhD thesis for a law faculty, the economic reasoning contained in this chapter will be limited and open to refinements. With the help of the insights into this mutually reinforcing relation between competition and the protection of the environment we will define a model for the integration of environmental protection requirements and competition in chapter 4. This model will be used to answer the question of what the role of environmental protection requirements in competition law *should* be.

CHAPTER 2

# A Legal and Economic Analysis of Competition and its Regulation

## 2.1 Introductory remarks

The EC Treaty clearly states that the economic policy of the Community and the member states shall be 'in accordance with the principle of an open market economy with free competition'.[1] This already shows the two major players in this research: law and economics. In essence, both are instruments for explaining and (to a certain extent) steering the behaviour of the actors in a society. These two are interrelated: law, as the EC Treaty shows, can be used to direct economic polices. At the same time certain areas of law are subject to economic reasoning. This interrelation can very clearly be seen with regard to competition. The desired degree or intensity and scope of competition on a market are prescribed by law.[2] At the same time the operation of the laws that concern this intensity of competition is subject to economic analysis. This relation between law, competition and economics is, even for those who haven't read Bork's *The Antitrust Paradox*, at times problematic.[3] The thought of having something as unwieldy and, as it is often argued, inefficient as law govern something that is considered to actually embody efficiency and dynamism may strike one as paradoxical indeed.

The twists and turns of over forty years of EC competition law show that the relation should not so much be characterised as paradoxical but rather as difficult. Since it takes place within a legal framework, the regulation of competition needs a justiciable objective in the light of which the competition laws can be interpreted and applied. The search for such an objective (justiciable or not) as a *leitmotiv* for competition policy has laid the basis for a considerable branch of economics that can be said to have started with Adam Smith. Below we will succinctly sketch the development of economic and legal thinking with regard to competition and its regulation with a view to establishing the *status quo* as EC competition law and policy are regarded. Because this thinking has in many cases been developed as a reaction to earlier doctrines, the treatment will be largely (chrono) logical. The following paragraphs can necessarily only be incomplete as fully charting the theoretical backgrounds to competition and its regulation would mean writing a book in itself.[4] This overview of theories concerning competition only serves to further clarify what competition, and the limits to it, is about. It will show that throughout the history of economic thinking with regard to competition, a major role has been played by the exceptions to the rule that competition will lead to optimal results.

---

1 Article 4(1) EC.

2 According to the European Court of Justice, for example, the EC seeks to attain 'workable competition', *cf.* Case 26/76, *Metro* v. *Commission* (Metro I), [1997] ECR 1875, para. 20.

3 R.H. Bork, *The Anti-trust Paradox – A Policy at War with Itself* (New York, Basic Books 1978)

4 *E.g.* Hildebrand 2002.

## 2.2 Competition as an economic phenomenon

One of the factors that has made man such a successful species is probably that fact that we have organised ourselves in societies with the members of this society opting for specialisation. This specialisation has, however, brought with it the problem of how to coordinate who will produce what commodities in which quantities. In the small informal society this coordination will have worked accordingly informal. As societies grew and wants as well as production not only increased in absolute numbers but also in diversity, this coordination became increasingly difficult. The solution was the introduction of currencies. This in turn created a market. Left to itself, this market would by and large ensure that production met the needs of the society.[5] Problems, however, could arise as the production of certain commodities came into the hands of one or a few parties. These parties could then raise the prices for these goods by, for example, artificially restricting production thereby turning these goods into a scarcity. This problem, that of the monopolist distorting the market, is addressed by the earliest examples of what we now call competition law.

Our experiences as consumers will certainly help in understanding why a monopoly is a less than wholly satisfactory market structure. On the other hand, the opposite market structure – a very large number of suppliers – does not inevitably lead to better results. What exactly competition is and how its intensity should be measured and controlled has been the subject of myriad works. One the recurring themes in these works has been the inevitable exception to the rule that competition is the best method to organise a market. In a sense, this debate can be said to have started with the first description of the competitive process by Adam Smith.

Adam Smith was the man who first described the competitive process and the dangers to it. Smith grew up in a corporatist or mercantilist world and saw inefficiencies everywhere.[6] When examining this theory one of the most important things to keep in mind is the era in which it was conceived. The Wealth of Nations,[7] as it is often called, first appeared in print in 1776, which is before the Industrial revolution. The excesses that came along with the Industrial revolution hadn't occurred and society was still dominantly agrarian. The cities were bristling with trade and here the governments' influence on society was felt the

---

5 For a rather elegant description see Plato's Republic, Book II. A perhaps more scholarly examination may be found in J. M. Diamond's Guns, Germs and Steel – the Fates of Human Societies (London, Cape 1997).

6 In this society the government played a central role in regulating trade. The governments' main objective under this system would be the accumulation of as much gold as possible. This would be accomplished through promoting exports and restricting imports.

7 A. Smith, *An Inquiry into he Nature and Causes of the Wealth of Nations*. Edited by D. Cannan, 1994.

most. The government was quite active on the market and regulated all sorts of economic activities. Trade was conducted only through the great trading companies, large profits were made and the rural country was very much lagging behind in development. Smith calls this organisation of society The Policy of Europe. In this context Smith devises his theory that a liberal organisation of the market results in the greatest allocative efficiency and thus the greatest welfare for all.[8] Any deviation from this liberal organisation, either by individuals or government, was deemed detrimental to welfare. Smith envisaged that a market would function optimally if there was *free competition*.[9] The concept of free competition thus sees to the economic order and is described by the results of that order on the market. More particularly is this situation described as a market where the market price is the natural price. The market price is the price which exists for a good on a real market. This price comes about by the market that brings together the supply for a certain price of a good and the demand, for this price for a good. The natural price is the sum of the production costs and a reasonable or average profit.[10] This natural price will be the price to prevail in the long run on a market that is freely competitive. It is an equilibrium price in that supply and demand are now in balance. In Smith's words the equilibrium is reached through the 'invisible hand' which describes what is now known as the market-mechanism.

Even though they are not necessarily identical, the natural price and the market price are strongly related to each other. Differences in the short term will disappear in the long run when the market price is in fact equal to the natural price. Smith describes this process as a price 'to which the prices of all commodities are continually gravitating'.[11] For the market price to become the natural price there needs to be free competition on a market. Smith nowhere really defines this the circumstances on this market but some basic propositions for this market can be deduced from his work. Stigler distinguishes a total of five more exactly formulated prerequisites for a market to be freely competitive.[12]

- Independent behaviour of competitors.
- A sufficiently large number of competitors so as to eliminate extraordinary profits.
- Economic entities must have sufficient knowledge of the market.
- Freedom from social pressure so that this knowledge can be followed

8 Allocative efficiency is the efficiency with which production factors are used. Inefficient use will increase costs with no extra outcome thus reducing profit.

9 Smith 1994, p. 69.

10 Smith does not define this margin of profit in any more detail but uses these terms to describe this margin, Smith 1994, p. 53.

11 Smith 1994, p. 65.

12 G.J. Stigler 1975, p. 31 *et seq.*

without compromise.
- Sufficient time for production factors to re-allocate.

Despite their more indicative character even these five criteria lack quantitative clearness. Nevertheless, precisely this general character lends Smith's concept much of its charm and beauty. Smith envisaged two reasons which might hinder free competition from fully functioning or existing in the first place. Firstly, the government policy could stand in the way of free competition and, secondly, the behaviour of individuals on the market might keep free competition from truly functioning.

In the days of Smith the government was rather active in regulating trade. It did this through the granting of trade monopolies to the trade companies and secondly many of its regulations prevented the free access to a market. Trading companies, that had been granted the exclusive right to conduct trade, found themselves in a monopoly position. They could effectively control the supply and thus price for a good in which they traded. The natural urge to maximise profits would in fact lead, according to Smith, to the monopoly price being the highest price possibly squeezed out of market.[13] Many of those active in a regulated profession found themselves in a similar position. Government regulations dictated that certain professions, mostly the crafts, could only be exercised by a limited number of people in a city or that only a limited number of people were allowed education in a certain profession. These regulations kept the access to the market closed so that existing craftsmen were effectively monopolists and displayed the accompanying behaviour.

In those areas of the economy where there was free access to a market or where there were competitors, Smith expected problems because of the urge of competitors to work together rather than compete. This leads Smith to one of he most quoted passages of his book concerning the natural urge to conspire to raise prices through reductions of supply. As this constituted a very realistic danger, Smith considered it necessary for the government to prevent such conspiracies. The government's task however would be quite different from that which the authorities fulfil nowadays in enforcing anti-cartel law. Smith thought that it would be useless to actively investigate into these cartels and consequently attack them. He rather thought that the government should just not encourage or facilitate these meetings in the first place. The most potent weapon against these cartels, Smith thought, would be the same urge that drove the competitors to conspire in the first place. The striving for profit maximisation would only have to lead one competitor out of the cartel and prices would come down as this rebel supplied the market to its full demand. Government policy should be

[13] Smith 1994, p. 69.

aimed at discouraging meetings between competitors and thus keep the market open to new competitors.[14]

Furthermore, government policy should refrain from regulation that would result in increased barriers to entry on a market. With this last form of regulation Smith aims at regulations restraining the number of craftsmen in a certain town or regulations restraining access to training in a craft or otherwise barring competition. This sort of regulation was induced by pressure from these groups and only served to protect the monopoly they had.[15]

Apart from these regulations the government could also frustrate the market by artificially oversupplying it or by blocking the efficient allocation in practice. As a nowadays perhaps somewhat incredible example of oversupplying the market Smith mentions the great inflow of religious men into clerical education. The result of this was an excess of clergymen who found no occupation or only for very little reward. The government could also keep the optimum allocative efficiency from being attained by literally prohibiting people and goods from moving or being moved to other places. Another way in which the government could influence economic processes was through *bounties* and *premiums*.[16] What Smith calls bounties resembles present-day subsidies or state aids. Premiums would appear to have more in common with rewards to encourage inventions. Smith comes to the conclusion that bounties cost the society more than they generate through the subsidisation of certain groups. This, again, leads to a rather restrictive view of the role of government in society. The governmental activities on the market are all concerned with externalities in that they either create them (excess clergymen) or seek to offset them (bounties).

With regard to the relationship between monopolies and free competition several observations are possible. Firstly, Smith generally considered the monopoly to be a sub-optimal situation. They brought along undersupply of the market, inefficient management,[17] and higher prices on the market. Secondly, free competition, contrary to monopoly, with its optimum allocative efficiency, resulted in the lowest possible production costs and a correspondingly low market price, thus guaranteeing maximum welfare. Thirdly, a market was either freely competitive or it was a monopoly, any organisations between these two extremes were not thought of.[18] Despite this neglecting of intermediary market structures, Smith did envisage a tendency towards freely competitive markets.

---

14 Smith 1994, p. 148.

15 Smith mentions as an example the prohibition on the import and export of wool, woollen products and sheep induced by pressure from the wool manufacturers. Smith 1994, p. 700.

16 Smith 1994, p. 560.

17 Thus Adam Smith appears to have identified the problem of x-inefficiencies *avant la lettre*.

18 This almost dialectic relation between competition and monopoly was further exacerbated in the theories of complete competition, see para. 2.6.

This tendency is inherent in Smith's conception of competition as a dynamic process. This dynamic view of sees competition as an incessant drive behind suppliers to deliver the best quality products for the lowest price. The same drive exists for the buyers who will want to buy the best quality for the lowest price. Competition as a dynamic process will force the competitor to outperform his fellow competitors. As a result a process of continuing improvement is initiated. This improvement can be to reduce the price of a good but Smith also predicted improvements to quality, service, and conditions of delivery.[19] Furthermore competition was recognised as the best guarantee to good management.[20]

While the simplicity of Smith's theory resulted in its use for a long period, the advent of mathematics, however, had as a consequence that theories of competition needed to become more quantitatively precise rather than merely descriptive.[21] This was accomplished through the introduction of models of competition where the only parameters were output and price. The fact that only two parameters are included show that they are simplifications or abstractions of reality, they offer clear quantitative outcomes on the cost of a certain departure from reality. Adam Smith's contrast between monopolies and free competition was further enhanced by many different concepts of what competition was. In addition, it is in this enhancement that the greater distance from reality, that is inherent in these models, is most obvious. Part of this retreat from a fairly realistic idea of an actual market into the realm of economic and econometric models was perhaps offset by the introduction of the notion of external costs into these models. We will see that this notion, although originally not directly triggered by environmental problems, is of great importance with regard to the relation between competition and environmental protection.

A first attempt to introduce mathematics into theories of competition was undertaken by Cournot.[22] The basic premise is that economically rational behaviour would lead to profit maximisation. Thus examining competition from a mathematical perspective, profit was expressed as the difference between revenues and costs. As revenues are the product of price and output, the question is how output and revenues relate to each other. Cournot proposed that competition involved a situation where, for the single supplying competitor, price and output are fixed. The demand-curve is horizontal and competitors are 'price-takers'. This describes the situation where, because of their small share of the market and the large number of other competitors, no individual competitor has an influence, through his output, on the market price. The optimum

---

19 Cox & Hübner 1981, p. 9 *et seq.*

20 Smith 1994, p. 149, 170.

21 See on this subject: Tolksdorf 1980, p. 787.

22 A French economist who was played a major role in introducing mathematics in economics, Hildebrand 1998, p. 141.

situation for a competitor on such a market is found at the output where his marginal costs equal the market price for that output. Beyond this point the costs of producing an additional unit would no longer be completely covered by price that he would get for the increased output. The monopolist, however, is a 'price maker' and faces a downward sloping demand curve. His market price and therefore revenue fall with increased output. Because of this, the monopolist's optimum, where marginal costs equal marginal revenue, is necessarily at a lower output compared to the situation where a market is competitive.[23]

The great advantage of a perfectly competitive market is that the situation on that market is Pareto-optimal.[24] This describes the situation on a market where any change in the welfare for any individual must necessarily be detrimental to the welfare of another. Welfare is therefore at its maximum and optimally distributed. The situation that is attained in a Pareto optimum enables the deduction of certain preconditions for a system in which this optimum is reached.[25] Competition theories, conceived under the maxim of pareto-efficiency, are therefore aimed at defining these preconditions. As different theories to attain pareto-efficiency were conceived, different preconditions were the result. These preconditions serve to distinguish the three major forms of perfect competition and indicate the 'model-character' of these theories.[26]

One of the major contributions of the theories of perfect competition was the introduction of a static view of competition. This was, irrespective of current valuations of this concept, a very important step in economic thinking. Where Adam Smith's concept of competition described a *process*,[27] competition, according to the theories of complete competition, denotes a *situation*. In this view competition is a certain, static, organisation of a market. As a result, the perspective can be aid to have changed from the process to the end result of that process.[28]

The practical implementation of theories that are so far removed from reality as the theories of perfect competition is not easy. The existence of a very clear goal, namely maximum efficiency through the realisation of competition, is

---

23 For a fuller treatment of this economic reasoning the reader is referred to: Ph. Areeda, *Antitrust Analysis, problems, text, cases*, 1974; R. van der Bergh, *Economische analyse van het mededingingsrecht*, 1993; F.M. Scherer & D. Ross, *Industrial Market Structure and Economic Performance*, 1990.

24 H. Bartling 1980, p. 12; Schmidt 1993, p. 7.

25 Bartling 1980, p. 13 *et seq.*

26 E.H. Chamberlin 1962, p. 7 *et seq.*; Scherer & Ross 1990, p. 17; Bartling 1980, p. 13. Another distinction is found in: Van den Bergh 1993, p. 17. Perfect competition, for example, requires many suppliers with each only minute market shares, a fully transparent market, homogeneity of products, Free access to the market for new competitors, absolute mobility of factors of production and infinite adjustment speed.

27 *Supra*, paragraph 2.5.5.

28 Cox & Hübner 1981, p. 11.

immediately offset by the difficulty of fulfilling prerequisites that are largely unrealistic.

One strand of thinking has made it from theory to practice. This is the competition theory devised by the so-called Ordoliberals of the *Freiburger Schule* that had Walter Eucken as their major proponent.[29] This school of thought introduced perfect competition as a pillar of a complete economic system and competition policy.[30] These ideas were to a large extent implemented in the German competition act, because of the positive effects that full competition would have on welfare particularly when this market-based system is contrasted with centrally governed economies.[31]

Before going into the more substantive aspects of this competition theory, the setting within which competition law and policy were to function will be explored in some detail. One important feature of ordoliberal thinking on competition was the role they envisaged for law. According to the ordoliberals, perfect competition would provide economic as well as non-economic benefits to society but only where this form of competition was maintained by a public policy on the organisation of the market: *Ordnungspolitik*. The task of the government is therefore to establish the necessary structures for competition but not to influence the competitive process itself. The competition laws were to be applied by an autonomous entity that would apply legal standards. The legality of the acts of the competition authority would have to be subject to judicial review.[32] The juridical nature of this procedure involved a major break from the traditional system of administrative application of the competition provisions.

Eucken defined the concept of full competition[33] not only through the prerequisites but also by distinguishing it from what it not entailed. According to him full competition had to be distinguished from *Laissez faire*-policy and the so-called *Monopolkampf*.[34] Full competition entailed a *Leistungswettbewerb*.

---

29 Within the ordoliberal school some other streams of thought can be distinguished. For the purpose of this book the distinction between these schools and their features will not be explored any further. See for further references D.J. Gerber, *Law and Competition in Twentieth Century Europe – Protecting Prometheus*, 1998.

30 German scholar Schmidt argues that within the Ordoliberals there were in fact two schools. One that proposed a statical approach to competition (represented by Eucken) and another that advocated a workability-approach (represented by von Hayek and Lutz). Schmidt 1966, p. 699 *et seq*. Despite the differing opinions on these terminological problems, Walter Eucken will be taken as the proponent of the Ordoliberals as one theory.

31 Kartte 1969, p. 39.

32 Gerber 1998, p. 254.

33 Eucken refers to '*Vollständiger Wettbewerb*' which is essentially a *species* from the *genus* of perfect competition.

34 Eucken 1960, p. 247.

This described the situation where competitors strive to compete not against but alongside each other. In an analogy with the constitutional state, Eucken states that competition law should create a system where the individual freedom of the one is limited and balanced with the freedom of the other. The freedom being, in this context, the freedom to compete.

## 2.3 Concepts of workable competition

As the theories of perfect competition were removing themselves more and more from the practice and models had become increasingly complex and theoretical the search for a more realistic method of understanding competition gained impetus. A first step towards this more realistic approach, even within the theories of perfect competition, was accomplished through the abolition of perfect competition as a maxim. Rather than researching this practically unattainable form of competition, several authors focussed their attention on imperfect competition or monopolistic competition.[35] This shift of focus, however, did not mean a departure from the logic and reasoning inherent in static price theories. This departure took place only in 1940 when Clark published his article on workable competition.[36] This concept entailed a dynamic approach to competition and was taken further by the Harvard School that developed it into their theory of Industrial Organisation. This theory studies the behaviour of entities on a market in relation to the organisation or *structure* of that market. The theories proposed by the Harvard School will be most intensively studied whereas Clark's concept will be treated in lesser detail. German scholars used the concept of workable competition and developed it further into a theory that analyses competition as a *process*. The theories devised by German doctrine will only be examined insofar as they are relevant for the integration of environmental concerns.

### 2.3.1 Workable competition

Clarks' introduction of workable competition in 1940 did not mean a total break with the theories of complete competition. Complete competition is still the ideal but he considered it unattainable.[37] It is only in his *magnum opus*[38] that Clark rejects the idea of complete competition as an ideal

---

35 Robinson 1948 and Chamberlin 1962.

36 Clark 1940, p. 241 *et seq*. Translated as: *Zum Begriff eines funktionfähigen Wettbewerbs*, in: Herdzina 1975, p. 143 *et seq*.

37 Clark, in: Herdzina 1975, p. 143; Cox & Hübner 1981, p. 14; Kartte 1969, p. 40. Otherwise: Van den Bergh 1993, p. 29.

38 J.M. Clark, *Competition as a Dynamic Process*, 1961.

value.[39] Clark's contribution to the development of competition theory can be summed up under two headings: realism and dynamism.

Clark's activities under the first heading involve the basic perception that complete competition can never be attained on a real market. The approach should consequently not consist of attempts at removing imperfections. Such deviations from complete competition are called remedial imperfections and can act as an 'antidote'[40] to neutralise other imperfections. The theory that advocates the use such imperfections to create a workably competitive market is called the theory of second-best. This is done principally on the ground that the prerequisites for a system of perfect competition are cumulative. Where one or ore of the prerequisites for a system have not been fulfilled, the competition remaining on that market does not necessarily constitute a 'second-best' compared to the situation where all prerequisites are found on a market. This is proved by the following example of the introduction of an open price system on an oligopolistic market with homogenous goods.[41] The market is imperfect in that the amount of suppliers is less than would be necessary for a perfectly competitive market. The introduction of an open-price system, where prices are to be reported centrally, was thought to increase competitiveness, under theories of perfect competition, because of the increased transparency.[42] The result on the real market, however, can be quite the opposite in that competitive behaviour might be replaced by parallel behaviour thus reducing competition. Heterogenisation of products, seen by the theories of perfect competition as an imperfection, could lead to increased intensity of competition or workable competition.

The other breakthrough accredited to Clark is the reintroduction of a dynamic perspective to the theory of competition. After Smith, the theories of complete competition turned to a static perception of competition. Clark studied competition as a process; as a result, the factor time was introduced. Competition was now seen as a process of initiative and imitation. The entrepreneur fulfilled a pivotal role in this process because his initiatives functioned as the motor behind competition. This recognition of competition as a process of innovation and imitation was inspired by the views introduced by Schumpeter.[43]

---

39 Clark 1961; Cox & Hübner 1981, p. 15; Kartte 1969, p. 41.

40 Van den Berg calls this *'tegengif'* *cf.* Van den Berg 1993, p. 29; Cox & Hübner use the term *'Gegengift'*, Cox & Hübner 1981, p. 14; Schmidt 1993, p. 9.

41 As it exists on such markets in the UK, USA and Germany.

42 Thus the fullfillment of one extra condition posed by the theories of complete competition, see *supra* paragraph 2.6.2.

43 Schumpeter introduced the innovative and following type of entrepreneur. Together, in a process he described as *'schöpferische Zerstörung'* or creative destruction they kept competition going. J.A. Schumpeter, *Kapitalismus, Sozialismus und Demokratie*, 1950. This concept was taken and elaborated by Ernst Heuss in his book, *Allgemeine Markttheorie*, 1965, where different types of entrepreneurs and markets for products are introduced.

One of the critiques directed at the theories of perfect competition is that they would result in what has been described as '*Schlafmutzenkonkurrenz*'.[44] This is a situation where there is perfect competition but no innovation whatsoever. Not only are the profits so minimal that there will hardly be any budget for research and development, more importantly, there will be no incentive. The absolute transparency and infinite speed of adjustment on the perfectly competitive market would make it useless and, most importantly, unattractive to innovate since there are only costs and no profits. The result is a competition between the sleeping.

For innovation to occur there need to be market imperfections which enable the innovator to enjoy the fruits of his investment. Furthermore innovation mostly occurs in large firms which have the resources to fund research and development. These two preconditions are very hard to reconcile with perfect competition. The result is the so-called *dilemma-thesis*.[45] Only a competitive market can ensure optimum allocation of factors of production, best fulfilment of consumer wishes, lowest prices, and thus optimum welfare. A more monopolistic market will, however, generate more development. This problem was taken further by the Harvard School of Industrial Organisation that intensively studied the relationship between market structures and, ultimately, the results on that market.

### 2.3.2 The Harvard School

Mason laid the foundations for the Harvard School in the 1940's by defining the *structure-behaviour-performance-paradigm*.[46] This describes the core theory of the Harvard School where the structure of a market influences the behaviour of economic entities on that market which, in turn, determines the results of that market. The structure of a market entails factors such as the number of suppliers and consumers, product differentiation, barriers to entry etc.[47] Behaviour on a market consists of pricing behaviour, investments, research and development etc.[48] The results of a market are formed by production, allocative efficiency development and other indicators.[49] Along with these three factors, two other parameters play an important role in this paradigm: the basic conditions and public policy. The basic conditions describe the fundamental properties of a market which consist of, amongst others, avail-

44 Lutz 1956, p. 32.

45 Cox & Hübner 1981, p. 15; Schmidt 1993, p. 34.

46 Van den Berg 1993, p. 31; Scherer & Ross 1990, p. 4.

47 Scherer & Ross 1990, p. 5.

48 Scherer & Ross 1990, p. 5.

49 Scherer & Ross 1990, p. 5.

ability of factors of production, demand side elasticity. Public policy consists of tax regulations, product regulations but also competition policy. The Harvard School owed a great deal of its appeal to the clear policy guidelines it offered and the fact that empirical evidence was available to verify the paradigm. Public policy needed only to be aimed at allowing the market to function so that *good performance* could be expected. This concept of good performance is a multidimensional concept that goes beyond mere economic progress.[50]

Typical for the Harvard School approach to competition policy is the fact that this is placed in a broader context to reach multiple goals.[51] Competition policy is thus seen as a means to achieve certain goals. Bain describes a system in which this instrumental character of competition policy can function optimally.[52]

The highest-ranking goals are of a general nature such as optimum results for the whole economy. Just below this there are the more economically tinted goals such as efficient allocation, stability and progress. To reach these objectives, certain market results are needed: efficient production, absence of chronic excesses or shortages, maintaining resources etc. Departures from the optimum market order can be: to many small enterprises, monopolisation, and unwanted external effects. To cure these deficits it might prove necessary to use public policy and interfere with the market. This mainly is done through competition policy. Depending on the specific nature of the deficit a certain instrument of competition policy may be used. For the purpose of this study it is expedient to concentrate on the policy with regard to unwanted external effects.

According to Bain there are different aspects of performance on a market and these also entail performances in other than directly economic areas. One of these is the so-called *conservation-performance*.[53] This refers to the maintainability of resources which can be subject to external effects.[54] For example, misuse of resources may entail external costs in that the present use or extraction of factors of production is impossible to maintain in the long run and will then result in extra costs. Bain attributes bad conservation performance to four factors:[55]

- A situation of *antagonistic exploitation* may exist where competition in exploitation will result in a contest to exploit the resource before others have.
- Inherent short-sightedness of entrepreneurs.

---

[50] Hildebrand 1998, p. 157 *et seq.*

[51] In fact, Clark appears to have done this already by posing the question 'What do we want competition to do for us?', Clark 1961, p. 63 *et seq.*

[52] Bain 1968, p. 497 *et seq.*

[53] Bain 1968, p. 425 *et seq.* and 489 *et seq.*

[54] See also Gabriel 1971, p. 802 *et seq.*

[55] Bain 1968, p. 426.

- Small margins of profit disabling entrepreneurs to invest in long-term conservation.
- Stupidity.

With regard to the relation between industry structure and conservation performance in general, Bain remains ambiguous. Despite the fact that he expressly notes the problem of antagonistic exploitation, which is a problem due to competition, not to the existence of a monopoly, Bain does not clearly indicate whether monopolies or competitive markets are more prone to bad conservation performance.[56]

In the chapter concerning antagonistic exploitation, Bain offers some policy guidelines with regard to the improvement of the conservation performance. He considers restructuring the industry the most viable option in that the market should be reorganised to a monopoly.[57] In his view, this is preferable above detailed regulation of competitors' behaviour, as this last option would cost society more than one regulated monopolist. This is an example where the intensity of competition is decreased for, mainly, reasons related to externalities. Further clarification of the issue of integration can be found in Bain's reasoning concerning areas exempted from competition in general.

Bain distinguished a number of areas in economy where he considered governmental regulation to lead to a better result than competition or market regulation. These areas coincide with present day public utilities and are called exemption areas. Bain mentions two basic distinguishing features:[58]

1) Companies active in these areas produce commonly used service or products for which no substitutes are available.
2) They are natural monopolies or oligopolies because:
   - The advantages of large scale production would inevitably result in monopolistic competition if it would be attempted to install competition and
   - An attempt to install competition would lead to a reduction of welfare because of the technological nature of the industry concerned.

Areas of the economy that fit this profile are thus eligible for exemption from competition. Many areas of activity in industry with obvious environmental implications fit this profile and would thus, according to Bain, be considered exemption areas. With regard to these exemption areas two questions are asked:

---

56 Bain 1968, p. 494, 495.

57 Gabriel also prefers intervention in the market structure to cure bad performances, Gabriel, 1971, p. 805.

58 Bain 1968, p. 581, 634.

firstly, is the exemption from competition truly necessary and secondly, is the exemption 'workable'?

Whereas the first question is generally answered positively, the second question needs some more attention before it can be answered in the positive. Existing regulation of exemption areas generally shows shortcomings where ensuring adequate market results is concerned. All in all Bain can be considered critical of the workability of these exemption areas and regards them as second-best solutions. This second-best character of exemption areas is balanced by the otherwise negative effects that would arise if competition would be allowed in these areas.

This critical approach to exemption areas is also found in the work of Turner.[59] He recognizes that the problem of external effects and the resulting inappropriate allocation of resources needs to be solved. In this respect he describes the encouragement that some voluntary private cooperative measures have gotten from the government to meet specific social goals. He specifies this in an example of the creation of a joint venture to solve the problem of air pollution.[60] Whereas such a pooling of resources may be the first solution to spring to mind, the question is whether this is the most effective solution. Turner doubts the effectiveness of the cooperation on research not so much because of the elimination of competition as such but more because competition is often considered beneficial to research as well. A reduction or elimination of competition on research may very well result in less productive research, according to Turner. All in all, Turner, as a representative from the Harvard School, can be said to be reluctant to exempt too many areas, because of the externalities present in them, from the competitive regime.

With this conclusion, the study of the Harvard School of Industrial Organisation, as an implementation of the workability concept is completed for this research. German doctrine developed the concept of workable competition as a process rather than structure. The discussion between German scholars is by and large very abstract and specialist and will thus only be treated insofar as is necessary for this research. The development of this doctrine took place in two camps and gave rise to, sometimes heated,[61] discussions between the followers of the *Funktionsfähigkeits* concept and those who attested to the concept of *Wettbewerbsfreiheit*.

---

[59] Turner 1970, p. 67 *et seq.*

[60] Turner 1970, p. 70, 71.

[61] In particular the discussion between Hoppmann and Kantzenbach in the *Jahrbuch für Nationalökonomie und Statistik.*

### 2.3.3 Theories of *Funktionsfähigen Wettbewerb* and *Wettbewerbsfreiheit*

German scholar Erhard Kantzenbach elaborated Clark's idea of workable competition into the concept of *Funktionsfähigen Wettbewerb*.[62] In accordance with Clark's concept, competition is seen as an instrumental concept, a means to an end. Kantzenbach concretises this instrumental character in five economic goals or functions of competition.[63]

- Functional distribution of income on the basis of market results.
- Adjustment of demand and supply.
- Efficient allocation of factors of production.
- Flexible adjustment of production capacity to extra-economic factors.
- Continuing technological progress in products and production methods.

When Lutz' remarks concerning *Schlafmutzenkonkurrenz* are brought to mind, the dilemma-problem, as it was called by Kantzenbach, becomes clearer. For the last two of the goals to be fulfilled, for the existence of progress, there needs to be some deviation from all to severe competition. This is found in the adoption of a particular form or Organisation of the market where there would be an optimum intensity of competition. Kantzenbach considered the wide oligopoly[64] to be the Organisation of the market where an optimum compromise between static and dynamic functions[65] of competition would exist.

Opposed to this view, where competition is put in the perspective of certain goals is the concept of *Wettbewerbsfreiheit*.[66] Central to this concept is the idea that freedom lies at the basis of competition. In this respect it builds upon the work of the Von Hayek who saw competition as a process of discovery and thus placed the freedom to do such discoveries at the core of competition. In this view the freedom to discover, compete, develop and innovate is the driving force behind competition. This, in turn, leads to the requirement that the freedom to compete be central to concepts of competition rather than making competition subject to the attainment of certain goals. After this short introduction to these concepts of competition, the stance these theories take towards the integration of environmental considerations will be studied.

---

62 Kantzenbach, *Die funktionsfähigkeit des Wettbewerbs*, 1966. Kantzenbachs concept will hereafter be called 'functional competition'.

63 Kantzenbach 1966, p. 16 *et seq.*

64 '*Weites Oligopol*', Kantzenbach, 1966, p. 49 and 130; Kantzenbach 1967, p. 235.

65 Of the abovementioned five, the first three are the static functions of competition and the last two are considered to be the dynamic functions of competition, Schmidt 1993, p. 12.

66 Most fervently defended by Hoppmann. He introduced and elaborated this concept in several articles. This concept will hereafter be called 'freedom of competition'. Hoppmann 1966, p. 286 *et seq.*

Both theories regard environmental considerations as extra- or non-economic factors. Kantzenbach starts the introduction of his concept of functional competition with the express remark that such factors are not taken into account this theory.[67] He balances this by recognising that competition has obvious social implications. Nonetheless, he considers the causal relationship between competition and the social implications to be very unclear and furthermore the implications themselves are very hard to value economically. Above all, the integration that would ensue would entail a political judgement in which two normative systems would be valued against the other. This complex and political nature justifies the exclusion of such factors from his economic system. According to him such judgements can always be made later. The deviations from the economic optimum would then constitute the economic costs to society for the attainment of these non- or extra-economic goals.

Kantzenbach devised a relation between the fulfilment of the functions of competition and the form or organisation of that market. In this respect, his perspective on competition doesn't differ that much from the Harvard approach. Where the Chicago School opposed the Harvard paradigm, the concept of functional competition was juxtaposed to that of the freedom of competition. The ensuing discussion enabled the elaboration of both concepts.

Hoppmann starts out by denying the very existence of a dilemma-problem. According to him, competition shows the unity of the concepts of freedom of competition and progress. They are inherent in each other and furthermore presume each other.[68] This denial of other extra-economic goals implies, according to Kantzenbach, either of two opinions on the integration of extra-economic goals. Either other extra-economic goals remain uninfluenced by competition or these other goals are irrelevant. The first view is obviously wrong, the second opinion shows such an extreme preference for one such goal that it is rendered useless.[69] Rather than recognising environmental concerns and declaring them outside the scope of a concept of competition, as Kantzenbach does, Hoppmann appears to deny them altogether. Hoppmann's concept of welfare entails nothing more than the sum of the individual economic advantages. Other concepts, of a more general nature, would only result in extra-economic value judgements being 'smuggled' into the concept of welfare.[70] As regards the question of the integration of environmental concerns, Kantzenbach thus envisages this possibility but declares it a political choice. Hoppmann denies the choice altogether.

With regard to the stance taken towards exemption areas in general, Hoppmann's reasoning is remarkably parallel to that followed by Bain. Only in

---

[67] Kantzenbach, 1966, p. 13 and 16; Kantzenbach 1967, p. 195 *et seq.*

[68] Hoppmann 1966, p. 291 *et seq*; Hoppmann 1967, p. 77 *et seq.*

[69] Kantzenbach 1967/1968, p. 236.

[70] Hoppmann 1967, p. 81.

markets with natural monopolies would competition be impossible because of bad market results and therefore other methods of regulation should apply. The definition of a natural monopoly, as used by Hoppmann, is also largely identical to that of Bain.[71] In thus defining areas of exemption Hoppmann has been accused of creating his own tautologies.[72] Möschel argues that exemption areas are necessarily created through a political process and choice and cannot be deduced by means of a tautological reasoning.[73] In particular with regard to the problem of external effects, where environmental pollution is expressly named, he acknowledges the necessity of political value judgements in order to create exemption areas.[74]

In conclusion, both theories leave, implicitly or explicitly, the decision to declare an area exempt from competition to a political moment. This last brief discussion of German doctrine introduced the strand of theories that leave great room for individual freedom. This concept of freedom of competition has also been developed on the other side of the Atlantic and has resulted in the Chicago School of competition theory. A study of this last concept of competition and the possibilities left for integration conclude this chapter.

## 2.4 The Chicago School

With the meagre results of American firms came the realisation that the Harvard School was not infallible. Interference in the structure of a market proved to be no certain recipe for good results or performance. This realisation, which ate away at much of the empirical foundations of the Harvard School's central paradigm, together with the policy of a new administration[75] resulted in a greater influence for the Chicago School of competition theory. Quite the opposite of the Harvard School, which was characterised by state influence on the market, the pendulum had now swung to the other side. The state had to exercise little or no influence at all on the market. Competition theory embedded a firm believe in the self-healing properties of the market. Inefficient economic entities would be exterminated through a survival of the fittest and Darwinism thus found its way into economics. The self-healing power of the market would even remove imperfections from a market. The instrumental character of competition was brought down to just one goal which

---

71 See page 24 *supra*.

72 This occurred in a discussion between Tolksdorf and Hoppmann in the *Jahrbuch für Nationalökonomie und Statistik* from 1969 on.

73 Möschel 1981, p. 99 *et seq*.

74 Möschel 1981, p. 100.

75 The so-called 'Reaganomics'

was consumer welfare.[76] Other, non-economic goals were denied. With the maximisation of consumer welfare as sole objective, productive and allocative efficiency became the standards by which the market behaviour in individual cases was measured. This was done through the models of price theory. It was not tried to enact these on the real market but they did function as a guide light.[77] Many forms of behaviour were translated into economic terms and all economic behaviour was consequently judged on the basis of the effects it would have on efficiency.[78] This use of efficiency as standard was most obvious with regard to competition law. Bork in particular is very explicit in this respect when he states:[79]

> *'The whole task of antitrust can be summed up as the effort to* IMPROVE ALLOCATIVE EFFICIENCY *without impairing* PRODUCTIVE EFFICIENCY *so greatly as to produce either no gain or a net loss in* CONSUMER WELFARE.*'[Emphasis added]*

The reliance on efficiency, economically rational behaviour coupled to a firm believe in the long term effectiveness of the market resulted in a restrictive stance towards government interference on the market. In general, measures affecting the structure of the market were rejected because the present day situation of the market was considered a reflection of the economic Darwinism.[80] Bork distinguishes two forms of growth: internal and external (trough horizontal mergers), he judged both to be expressions of greater efficiency and thus compatible with competition.[81] With regard to market behaviour Chicago-school advocates a more interventionist approach. Collusion on a market is judged differently depending on whether it is horizontal or vertical.[82] Where horizontal agreements are generally regarded detrimental to competition and consequently

---

76 Bork 1978, p. 81 *et seq.*; Schmidt 1993, p. 19, 24; Schmidt & Rittaler 1989, p. 26 *et seq.*

77 As Bork makes very obvious in his book by comparing the enacting of these theories on a real market to the detonation of several nuclear bombs, Bork 1973, p. 92; *Cf.* Hildebrand 1998, p. 170.

78 Posner, in his book on the economic analysis of law, indicates the economic side of several, diverse, forms of behaviour covered by law. These include family law, sexual regulation, criminal law, employment law, safety and health law and many others. The criteria by which behaviour in these fields is to be judged is whether it increases or decreases efficiency. Posner 1992; *Cf.* Schmidt 1993, p. 19.

79 Bork 1978, p. 91.

80 Survival of the fittest, size was considered to be a reflection of effectiveness, Schmidt & Rittaler 1989, p. XIII.

81 Bork 1978, p. 164, 197 and 198 *et seq.*

82 Horizontal collusion takes place between economic entities operating at the same level of the production or distribution chain (e.g. two manufacturers or two retailers). Vertical collusion involves economic entities that are active at different levels of the distribution chain (e.g. a manufacturer, distributor and a retailer).

prohibited, a more lenient approach is taken towards vertical collusion among competitors.[83] The creation of barriers to entry in a vertical relationship is generally deemed economically irrational and therefore considered not to occur with an exclusionary intention. When such practices occur nonetheless they are thought to increase the efficiency of the competitor.[84]

This restrictive approach to government intervention, believe in the self-healing powers of the market and adherence to consumer welfare as the single goal of competition policy are reflected in the stance taken towards the integration of environmental consideration into competition law.

Defining consumer welfare as the single goal of competition policy has obvious implications for the integration of non-economic objective. When a policy is aimed at achieving such a narrowly defined goal, there is very limited or no room at all to take other consideration into account. Bork expressly excludes 'ethical and sumptual components' from the term consumer welfare as it is used in competition law.[85] The competitive process is seen as distinct from the consumer choice itself, it merely permits consumers to define by their expression of wants in the marketplace what things they regard as wealth.[86] According to Schmidt and Rittaler this neglects the fact that externalities can be seen as inefficiencies and hence decrease consumer welfare.[87] Furthermore Bork expressly excludes the integration of environmental considerations from the competition litigation.[88] Or, as he puts it:[89]

*'Antitrust litigation is not a process for deciding who can be rich or poor, nor can it decide how much wealth should be expended to reduce pollution [...]'*

Bork thus recognises the problem of environmental pollution, but the exclusion of environmental considerations is not even half the solution. Posner does propose some solutions to pollution which can only be qualified as interactive but nowhere as truly integrative.[90] Could it then be argued that the concept of consumer welfare entails non-economic aspects as well? A closer look at the

[83] See, critically with regard to the Chicago school's approach to vertical integration in merger cases: Lofaro & Ridyard 2002, p. 151.

[84] This, of course, greatly underestimates the impact such practices might have on competition as a whole, Schmidt 1993, p.23.

[85] Bork 1978, p. 90.

[86] Bork 1978, p. 90.

[87] Schmidt & Rittaler 1989, p. 50

[88] Bork 1978, p. 115; Schmidt 1993, p. 21.

[89] Bork 1978, p. 90, 91.

[90] These solutions entail the use of market based instruments such as auctions and pollution taxation to internalise external costs. Posner 1992, p. 61 *et seq.*, 367 *et seq.*

treatment of this concept by Bork clarifies the very economic nature of this goal.[91] It is contrasted with meta- or non-economic goals such as the preservation of a number of smaller enterprises. The responsibility for environmental protection is left entirely with the legislator who can chose to follow the regulatory path in trying to influence environmental behaviour or by influencing consumer choice in that their 'wants' should be changed to include 'environmental wants'.

This paragraph can be so short because of the clear and absolute rejection of the integration of environmental concerns into competition law and policy. According to the Chicago School environmental considerations simply do not belong in the framework concerning competition.

## 2.5 A European concept of competition?

Competition authorities in the United States have accepted the Chicago School.[92] Moreover, as the recent row over the diverging decisions in the *GE/Honeywell* merger shows, Europe and the U.S. have different standards by which they judge competition cases.[93] This leads to the question what the European concept of competition is. As far as the theories underlying the application of competition law are concerned, many of the same economic instruments are used on both sides of the Atlantic (e.g. predatory pricing tests, contestability). The divergence can probably be traced back the U.S. authorities' reliance on economic welfare as the ultimate objective of competition policy and the resulting more less stringent approach to larger companies because of the economies of scale that are possible in such enterprises.[94] The European Commission, as will be shown below in Part II, is more concerned with maintaining competition itself thereby ensuring optimal welfare.[95]

## 2.6 Competition and the inevitable exceptions to it

On the basis of this overview of doctrines and schools concerning the concept of competition a number of observations may be made. For one, there does not appear to be one concept of competition that is universally

91 Bork 1978, p. 90.

92 See with regard to Chicago and post-Chicagoans: Hildebrand 2001, p. 152.

93 It should, however, be kept in mind that the divergence in *GE/Honeywell* is more the odd one out than the norm.

94 *Cf.* Schaub in Ehlermann & Laudati 1998, p. 125.

95 See further: Monti 2002, p. 1059 *et seq.*

accepted. Even though it is commonly accepted that competition is not an end in itself but only an instrument to achieve objectives such as allocative and dynamic efficiency, economic welfare or welfare in a more general sense, the choice of these objectives is all but universal.[96] Furthermore, it could also be seen that economists have ever since Adam Smith been trying to define the intensity or degree of competition that would best attain these objectives. At the same time they have tried to identify those areas of the economy where competition does not achieve optimal results. One such notable area concerns the natural monopolies. Another can be seen where there are external effects (positive or negative). Natural monopolies and external effects are likely to occur wherever environmental protection plays an important role. This is why unleashing unmitigated competition in cases where environmental protection is involved is often counter-productive, both in terms of competition as well as environmental protection. Consider, for example, the case where the producers of a certain good agree to cooperate in order to take back and recycle the products that they have marketed once these products have reached their end of life and are thus considered waste by the consumers. Such an initiative will involve setting up a fine-meshed collection network with large sunk costs.[97] In general, such organisations tend have the properties of a natural monopoly.[98] Moreover, if left to the individual parties, the environmental goal would probably not be achieved since the environmental benefit is external. Not all consumers are willing to pay extra for this benefit whilst there are actual costs for the parties who undertake the environmental action. In this situation, all it takes is one free rider to stop the parties from protecting the environment.[99] The obvious solution to this free rider problem would be for the parties to commit themselves to the protection of the environment whilst ensuring the mutual commitment through a controlling mechanism. Applying unadulterated competition law to this situation would mean that there is a restriction of competition since the parties have bounds themselves with regard to what they will do with their waste products. In terms of competition, this means the loss of a potential extra aspect with regard to which competition is possible. Moreover, the controlling mechanism may very well also have some anti-competitive effects. From the environmental perspective, looking at this situation purely from a competition point of view would probably mean the end of the initiative and thus a lower level of environmental protection. Essentially, the fact that environmental protection currently consti-

[96] As is evidenced by the controversy surrounding the diverging decisions on either side of the Atlantic in the *GE/Honeywell* merger.

[97] In this respect we could point to the the advertisement campaings required to change consumer behaviour.

[98] See in general with regard to natural monpolies: Viscusi, Vernon & Harrington 2000, p. 337 *et seq.*

[99] A free rider is an economic actor who benefits from a (collective) good without paying for it.

tutes an externality means that the objective of trying to achieve competition cannot be applied unchecked. For this to be possible, there first needs to an internalisation of environmental costs. This internalisation is one of the objectives of environmental policy.

CHAPTER 3

# The Evolution of Environmental Law and Policy

## 3.1 Introductory remarks

Even though the internalisation of environmental costs is often associated with the recent use of more 'economic' or 'market based' instruments of environmental policy, it can also be seen in many other environmental instruments. If, for example, a company is forced to install an extra filter in order to meet new and more stringent governmental emissions standards, this will involve extra costs for this company. The company will try to incorporate these costs in the price of its products so that, ultimately, the consumers end up paying the costs of protecting the environment. This internalisation has an effect on the competitive situation – the level playing field – on a market. The enterprises that are forced to invest in new and more environmentally friendly processes or filters or to cease certain activities, face extra costs that others may not have to bear. In that sense there has been a connection between *the competitive situation* on the one hand and environmental law and policy on the other ever since environmental regulation has existed.

This relation between competition and environmental protection can lead to a further connection between, on the one hand, *competition law* and policy and, on the other, environmental law and policy. An example of this secondary connection may be the grant of government subsidies to industry in order to compensate the extra costs resulting from environmental regulation. Such subsidisation is likely to fall within the scope of Article 87 EC according to which state aids are prohibited.

Yet another relation between environmental law and policy and competition law and policy has come about as result of the idea that environmental protection requirements should be made an integral part of the economic process rather than simply forced upon private parties. The emergence of this idea coincides with the shift from so-called 'command-and-control' legislation to instruments of environmental policy that require an active participation of the industry. In view of the economies of scale that can be achieved as well as the wish to prevent free riding, the companies have an incentive to cooperate and coordinate their actions with regard to the protection of the environment. As undertakings start to coordinate their environmental activities, Article 81 EC is likely to become relevant. It is this development in the instruments of environmental law and policy in general and the relation with competition as well as competition law and policy that are described in this chapter.

## 3.2 The regulatory approach

The emergence of the 'environmental problem' in the nineteen sixties and seventies together with the then dominant perception of the state and its role in society resulted in the adoption of so-called 'command and control' legislation.[1] This term describes an instrument of environmental policy whereby certain environmental aspects are strictly regulated. An example would be a regulation stating that certain enterprises may emit no more than x kilograms of carbon dioxide per year. This type of environmental regulation has a number of economic consequences.

Firms facing stricter environmental standards are very likely to face accordingly higher costs. Furthermore, environmental regulations may concern specific categories of products and therefore have an effect on the supply-side substitutability of these products. Because of the predominantly national level on which regulation takes place, most effects occur on the level of international competition, *i.e.* competition between enterprises in different countries. Such stricter standards and the costs that arise from the investments needed to meet these standards are often compensated by the public authorities in order to maintain the competitiveness of the industry. This could be in the form of a government subsidy relative to the investment made. Indeed, the policy of the Commission with regard to such investment aids has – albeit subject to certain conditions – consistently allowed for such state aids. In these cases, governments will grant subsidies and the Commission will declare it compatible with the EC prohibition on state aids essentially because the subsidy only serves to compensate a distortion of the level playing field.

Another example of a regulatory type of instrument that has implications for the level playing field as well as competition law is the exclusive right. We have seen how environmental protection can be characterised as an externality. Moreover, the environmental protection will in many cases by a non-value added activity. An example of such an environmental activity is the environmentally friendly treatment or disposal of waste. The benefit (a cleaner environment) will be an external one whereas in many cases the treatment or disposal of the waste will not add any value to the product. Even in cases where the waste is recycled and the secondary raw materials arising there from can be sold on the market, the price for these raw materials may not be sufficient to cover the costs of recycling. In these circumstances, achieving economies of scale may actually tip the balance so that the treatment or recycling does become profitable and therefore a value added activity. Governments may try to achieve such economies through the grant of exclusive rights to certain enterprises. These companies will thus obtain a statutory monopoly. Such monopolies, in turn, effectively rule out competition since entrants wishing to become active on the market are simply not allowed to do this. This may bring the government's granting of the exclusive right within the scope of the competition law provisions of the EC Treaty.

---

1 *Cf.* Bonus 1997, p. 13.

The use of regulatory or 'command and control' instruments may thus have clear implications on the level of the application of competition law. Similarly, command and control instruments may affect the competitive situation on a market. We have seen above how competition can be understood as a situation on a market in which the allocation is optimal as well as a dynamic process where innovation is central. The use of regulatory instruments has important implications for this latter view of competition. One of the disadvantages of regulatory instruments is considered to be the fact that they contain no incentive to go beyond the level of environmental protection prescribed by the regulations. According to this view, a company that meets the prescribed level of protection will not invest in research into pollution abatement technologies that will allow it to go beyond that level. Furthermore, even if the companies do invest in the development of such new technologies, there is nothing to ascertain that these new technologies will also result in a higher level of environmental protection. This argument may meet with the reply that the company could invest in even more innovative and more efficient environmental protection technologies so that it can reach the prescribed level at lower costs. This, however, still does not guarantee that the company will indeed opt for a higher level of protection at the same costs instead of going for costs saving while 'merely' meeting the prescribed levels of protection. Again, because of the external nature of the environment, there is simply no incentive for the company to invest more than it has to in order to meet the prescribed level of environmental protection. The internalisation of the environmental costs mentioned in paragraph 3.1 above, can thus be said to take place only insofar as is prescribed by the regulation.

The mobilisation of the market forces by such regulatory instruments is therefore rather limited. As it is widely recognised that the market mechanism is probably the most efficient allocative instrument, this can certainly be called a missed opportunity. Attempts to make more of the potential that the market mechanism or competition offers, have led to the emergence of new class of instruments of environmental policy.[2]

## 3.3 Towards market-based instruments

In some respects, the shift in environmental policy instruments from command and control to the more market-based instruments can be said to be the result of the wish to more adequately internalise these external costs. Command and control type of regulation focuses on a specific aspect of the environmental deterioration and tries to cure this by imposing certain

[2] See in general about the disadvantages of command and control instruments and the shift to other instruments: Hussen 2000, p. 237 *et seq.*

behaviour on the actors. The result of this type of regulation, from the perspective of the internalisation of environmental costs, is that the taking into account of environmental benefits is still not truly and fully internalised but remains external, prompted by regulation rather than by the competitive process. This is generally considered to make command and control instruments both less effective as well as efficient. The lower effectiveness relates to the fact that the environmental performance of command and control instrumentation is lower than that of instruments that actively involve the private actors. The absence of an incentive to go beyond what has been prescribed by the command and control instrument is just one example of the lower effectiveness. Furthermore, the setting of a specific norm brings with it an opportunity for the individual actor to bargain for a less strict norm.[3] The lower efficiency of command and control instruments refers to the fact that the costs involved in meeting a certain environmental objective are generally considered to be higher when command and control instruments are used. One explanation for this is the fact that the actors involved in market based instruments can generally be considered to know best where they can achieve a given environmental improvement at the lowest costs.[4]

The only way to make environmental considerations truly a part of the competitive decision-making by actors is to allow these actors some freedom in their approach to an environmental problem. In this view, environmental protection should not be forced upon the parties as an exogenous factor that needs to be respected. Rather, it should become an integral part of everyday decision-making. This has resulted in environmental policy instruments that allow for more self-regulation. This can, for example, take the form of legislation that lays down certain specific objectives but at the same time allows industry the freedom to attain these goals by means of an environmental agreement. Furthermore, depending on the organisation and structure of an industry, enterprises may chose to cooperate to address a certain environmental problem in order to pre-empt the enactment of (command and control-type) environmental regulation. In these cases, industry will negotiate an environmental agreement tailored to the strengths and weaknesses of the companies that are parties. The efficiency and effectiveness of these instruments can, however, also be doubted as self-regulation is liable to degenerate into a vehicle by which the industry leader consolidates his leading position or by which the industry is seeking only to postpone regulatory activities. This can essentially be traced back to the fact that what is called *self-regulation* must often be characterised as *reregulation*. As a result, the internalisation of environmental aspects as a result of these instruments is still far from complete.

---

[3] That this is not unlikely to happen is evidenced by what is called the captive regulator problem, *cf.* Esty 1999, p. 1515.

[4] *Cf.* Van der Straaten 1998, p. 71, 72.

Environmental protection requirements must first be made an integral part of everyday decision-making in the industry. For this we need, as it were, a translation of environmental protection requirements into the language of the industry. This language is that of price and costs and, if we pursue the analogy, the dictionary is the polluter pays principle. Quantity based systems (tradable permits), do not rely on the price mechanism but rather entail a direct reduction of the environmental degradation (*e.g.* through a reduction of the number of emmissions permits). Since specific action on the part of competition law with regard to this type of environmental instrument seems unlikely, we will not devote further attention to it.

### 3.3.1 The polluter pays principle from a Coasian perspective

In legal terms, the internalisation of external environmental costs in the competitive process is governed by the polluter pays principle. According to this generally accepted principle, the polluter should bear the costs of his damage to the environment. In theory this principle could lead to a full internalisation of all environmental costs as a result of which greener products would actually be cheaper than their polluting counterparts and thus leading to a more environmentally friendly world. All this would take is to clearly identify all the environmental external costs and assign these to a party. Intuitively, this party should be the polluter or person responsible for the pollution. Conferring the costs of the environmental damage to him then almost gets the character of a punishment that is rightfully deserved for damaging the environment. This brings the so-called Coase theorem into the picture.[5] It is submitted that the Coase theorem can be seen as an attempt to take the internalisation of external costs out of the morally laden world of crime and punishment. According to the Coase theorem, the property rights arising from an internalisation can freely be assigned to anyone ('polluter' or 'victim') involved in the environmental degradation. Bargaining will then result in the level of pollution that is socially optimal. Coase, however, makes his theorem subject to the proviso that transaction costs are zero or negligible. This requires that all the parties involved know each other's costs and the implications of any outcome for their own situation. The problem, of course, is that we do not live in a zero-transaction cost world and that transaction costs are even further from zero for externalities such as the environment.[6]

The Coase theorem is for the purpose of this research understood to be primarily significant for the insight that the property rights arising from the

5 Theorem proposed by Nobel laureate Ronald A. Coase in his seminal article 'The Problem of Social Cost'.

6 As Coase himself acknowledges in section VI of his article.

internalisation of environmental costs should be assigned to the person who can most efficiently cure the environmental damage and thus curb the environmental costs assigned to him even when this person may not be the (sole) polluter. This insight is particularly important in situations where it is difficult, if not impossible, to appoint a specific polluter. Secondly, the Coase theorem is considered to be important for the understanding that the reduction of transaction costs may also contribute to a more efficient internalisation of environmental costs. This second view of the Coase theorem is important in that it leads to the conclusion that in situations where it is difficult to appoint a specific polluter, the environmental costs should be assigned in a way that minimises the transaction costs involved in sharing or redistributing the environmental costs among the polluters.

The following cases illustrate the difficulties involved in assigning the environmental costs. According to the principle of producer responsibility, the producers are responsible for the collection and recycling of the waste that their products become once these have reached their end of life and the consumer would like to dispose them. The producers are thus made to bear the costs involved in collecting and recycling the products. In the terminology of the polluter pays principle, that is often considered to be implemented through the principle of producer responsibility,[7] the producers are considered to be the polluters. A pertinent question, however, would be to ask who ultimately decides on what is produced in which quantities and qualities. Is not the whole idea behind the free market economy guided by competition that consumer preferences (even though they may be influenced by the producers) are what ultimately steers the market? As a result, cannot the absence in certain cases of, for example, so-called 'design for recycling'[8] also be traced back to the fact that consumers are simply not interested in environmentally friendly designed products? Furthermore, we may ask ourselves why environmentally friendly producers need to be subsidised. At first sight, this is necessary because these production methods are often more expensive than the not so environmentally friendly production processes. The real problem, however, is the fact that consumers are generally unwilling to pay more for the green products. Many people will, for example, still buy the cheap industrially produced meat in supermarkets instead of the more expensive ecologically friendly meat. Could it not be said that in these cases the consumers, and not the industrial meat producers, are the actual polluters?

---

7 *Cf.* the Commission's explanatory memorandum to the WEEE Directive, COM (2000) 347 final, OJ 2000 C 365 E/184, paragraph 4.3.

8 Design for recycling or eco-design means that the ease with which products can be recycled is already taken into account at the design stage. Poor eco-design often leads to higher recycling costs thereby reducing the possibilities of recycling.

How can environmental costs be internalised most effectively taking into account the difficulties involved in appointing the polluter? The traditional solution would have been the imposition of a tax on the use of the externality. This corrective mechanism has been proposed by the economist Arthur C. Pigou and is since referred to as a Pigovian tax.[9] Basically, it involves a government-imposed tax on the use of the externality.[10] This could take the form of a tax per unit of pollutant emitted. As a result the polluter will have an incentive to cut back on his emissions right up to the level where the costs of further limiting emissions will no longer offset the costs arising from the tax. This also indicates the great difficulty inherent in the Pigovian tax.[11] In order to effectively limit pollution to the socially optimal level, the tax needs to be set at exactly the right amount. Too much tax will not only reduce pollution but also welfare whereas too little taxes will not result in the desired level of environmental protection. Setting the Pigovian tax at the right level is very likely to involve considerable costs.[12] Moreover, the level of the tax may have to be quite high before it results in any behavioural changes. Finally, the Coase theorem gnaws at the theoretical foundations of the Pigovian approach to the internalisation of externalities.[13] In short, the Pigovian approach, however simple, appealing, and promising it may seem at first sight, starts from shaky theoretical presumptions and must overcome serious hurdles in order to work effectively in practice.

### 3.3.2 Producer responsibility

A more refined form of a Pigovian approach to internalising environmental costs can be seen in the producer responsibility principle. According to this principle, as we have seen above, the producers are responsible for their products 'from the cradle to the grave'. As a result they have to take back and recycle their products once these have outlived their useful life and are thus considered waste by the consumers. As a result, the producers have to bear the costs arising from the collection and recycling and will thus have an incentive to minimise these costs by designing their products with the recycling in mind.[14] This can be characterised a Pigovian approach in that the government imposes these costs on the producers. It is more refined in that it leaves the actual definition of the costs to the market. In a producer responsibility scheme the government does not dictate that, for example, every different type of plastic

---

9 Proposed by Pigou in his *Wealth and Welfare*.

10 Pigovian subsidies are, of course, also possible.

11 See, for a critical approach to Pigovian Taxes: Cornes & Sandler 1996, p. 79 *et seq*.

12 See, for further references: Hussen 2000, p. 248.

13 Coase 1960, in section VIII *et seq*.

14 Commonly referred to as 'eco-design' or 'design for recycling'.

used in the production of a certain good[15] will cost an x amount of tax. Instead, it creates a market in which the price for an extra type of plastic and the resulting reduced recyclability is the result of supply and demand.

If we look at the principle of producer responsibility from a Coasian perspective, a number of questions arise. Firstly, why has the (financial) responsibility for the waste that products become once they reach their end of life, been assigned to the producers and not to the consumers?[16] Taking into account the observations made above in paragraph 3.3.1, the consumers would appear to be the polluters as much as the producers. Secondly, how does the cooperation of producers, in order to fulfil the producer responsibility, relate to the assignment of costs? Such cooperation can generally be expected in the environmental context as a result of the enormous potential for economies of scale. This potential is even larger in the case of producer responsibility schemes as we will see below.

Firstly, the question why the responsibility is allocated solely with the producers. In general the consumers share with the producers the responsibility for the fact that most products are not designed with the recycling in mind. Consumers have, to put it bluntly, not cared for eco-design. The answer to the question why the costs have been assigned to the producers probably follows from efficiency considerations. Firstly, making the consumers responsible would mean that the enforcement costs are probably much higher. This for the simple reason that the number of persons with regard to which the regulation laying down the responsibility would then have to be enforced, increases tremendously. Moreover, this problem would only become more pressing as assigning the responsibility to the consumers would in this case mean that the costs are incurred at the moment when the product reaches the end of its useful life. This, in turn, is likely to result in wild dumping.[17] A further reason is the fact that a price difference of, say, ten Euros reflecting different recyclability of one product compared to another may not influence the consumer's decision while a thousand times ten Euros for an entire production run will probably influence the producers' decision. It is thus submitted that allocating the responsibility for waste products to the producers is primarily the result of the wish to effectively and efficiently internalise environmental costs. It is not so much an inherent consequence of the application of the polluter pays principle to this specific situation. As a result, the fact that the environmental costs arising from the waste-

[15] Assuming that this will lower production costs but reduce the recyclability and thus increase the costs of recycling.

[16] Another way of putting it would be to ask why there is no such thing as a consumer responsibility?

[17] With regard to the the Diftar-system in the Netherlands, according to which consumers have to pay per unit of waste, a study on behalf of the Ministry of Justice concludes that 'it cannot be ruled out that the introduction of tariffs leads to more illegal dumping', report by B & A Groep, to be found on the website of the Ministry: <http://www.minjust.nl/a_beleid/handhaven/bestpractices/bp/milieu/bastortenverbranden.doc>, p. 14, 15.

stage of production and consumption have been *assigned* to the producers does not mean that they have to actually *bear* these costs.

The second question relates to the allocation of the responsibility between the various producers when they cooperate. As we have seen the economies of scale argue very much in favour of cooperation. Moreover, the desire to reduce the incentives for illegal dumping or – to formulate more positively – to increase consumer participation, have resulted in various requirements that try to ascertain that the system involves minimal hassle for consumers. In effect, these requirements mean that waste products have to be picked up close to or even from the home of the consumer.[18] Moreover, the collection will be more successful if it takes place on a non-brand specific basis.[19] Finally, as the current chaos surrounding the deposit and return fee for one way beverage containers in Germany shows, consumers need a clear structure and the existence of parallel (deposit and return) systems will not help the environmental effectiveness.[20] These additional requirements that serve to increase the consumer acceptation of a producer responsibility scheme, involve setting up a considerable network that will involve entire distribution chain and notably the retailers. As a result, the potential for economies of scale is quite significant. These scale advantages may be achieved through a cooperation between the producers that also involves the retailers.

A further reason for a cooperative approach to producer responsibility relates to the problem of the so-called 'historical waste'. Assigning the responsibility to the producers from a certain moment on, introduces an element of what may be called solidarity in such a cooperative system. Most producer responsibility schemes take the form of an obligation to take back and recycle a certain category of products from a certain date onwards. If the period between the entry into force of this obligation and the date on which the producer responsibility obligation becomes effective, is shorter than the lifespan of the product in question, it will effectively mean that the producers are made responsible for products that they have already designed, produced and marketed before the respon-

---

18 An example of this is the old for new rule according to which the producers are responsible for taking back the old product when a consumer buys a comparable new product. If this new product is delivered to the home of the consumer, the producer is obliged to take back the old product from that house.

19 It is not difficult to envisage that the consumer will be more tempted to illegally dump his old product if he has to first locate a collection point that will take back his brand. *Cf.* a similar argument forwarded by the Danish government in the *Danish Bottles* case, Case 302/86, *Commission* v. *Denmark* (Danish Bottles) [1988] ECR 4607, paras. 15, 16.

20 In Germany most of the supermarkets have actually implemented their own deposit and return system. As a result, the deposit will only be returned if the consumer bring the packaging back to the shop where he bought the packaging in the first place. The environmental effectiveness of this system is greatly diminished by the fact that consumers are unwilling to take the empty containers back to the shop where they bought it.

sibility was enacted.[21] With regard to these products, design for recycling in order to minimise the costs of recycling is impossible for the simple reason that the products in question have already been produced and marketed and are thus physically outside the reach of the producer. For the first years following the entry into force, the parties will thus be taking back historical waste. In terms of the producer responsibility principle, these are products with regard to which no differentiation on the basis of the recyclability is possible. This impossibility to differentiate the costs on the basis of the actual recyclability of the specific product involved is further increased by the fact that the take-back will often take place on a non-brand specific basis. The latter requirement will mean that current producers will, for example, be taking back products that were designed, produced and marketed by companies that have since then ceased their activities on the market. Similarly, a successful newcomer with a significant but only recently acquired market share may end up taking back the products of his once-successful competitors. In these and other cases, the parties will all have their incentives to free-ride.[22]

In their cooperation, the parties will want to avoid eventual free rider-problems that are to be expected whenever a collective is internalising external costs. This for the simple reason that free riding is likely to keep the parties from meeting their producer responsibility targets. Moreover, the parties know that free riding will increase the costs of the cooperation to such an extent that less cooperative alternatives become interesting, thus leading to the end of the collective approach and as a result foregoing the economies of scale. The need to control free riding is all the more pressing because the external nature will make keeping a check on whether all parties indeed contribute to the internalisation extra difficult.[23]

---

[21] This is not only probable but an actual problem if we consider that such producer responsibilities have been enacted for durable consumer goods such as cars and electronical and electrical equipment. The life span of these products is measured in years whereas producer responsibilities generally become effective within a year from the entry into force of the regulation. Annual reports of the producer responsibility scheme for end of life vehicles show that the average age of the vehicles recyled at this moment is over ten years and still increasing.

[22] The newcomer may, for example, advise to its retailers to indicate to consumers that only its brand will be taken back by the retailer. It has an incentive to do so because the newcomer will thus minimise the costs arising from the producer responsibility compared to the situation where it also takes back the incumbent's products.

[23] There will, for example, considerable costs involved in checking whether or not and to what extent parties do not actually use the system for more waste products than they have paid for. It would mean that in practice the producer of every single appliance that was collected would have to be identified. While this may be feasible with regard to certain branded goods, it will become more difficult for OEM-products whereas it becomes nigh on impossible for PVC pipes, a product for which there is a producer responsibility scheme in the Netherlands, *infra*, paragraph 10.5.2.

The above paragraphs have dealt with the principle of producer responsibility as a new and promising environmental policy instrument. At the moment, the term 'producer responsibility' is used only with regard to the responsibility for products that have outlived their useful life. It thus only deals with the waste-related environmental impact of a product. It is submitted that producer responsibility can be used to analyse a far wider array of environmentally friendly initiatives by an industry. Furthermore, producer responsibility can also be used as an environmental policy instrument to deal with other environmental aspects of the production process as well as products. These areas include those that are now covered by the environmental agreements that were characterised as essentially *reregulatory* above.[24]

Examples of such producer responsibility agreements in the wider sense are the environmental agreements concerning the energy efficiency of electrical appliances or the agreement concluded by the automobile manufacturing industry according to which they will reduce the carbon dioxide emissions of the cars they produce.[25] Such agreements are often concluded in order to avoid government regulation of the matter.[26] The fact that parties decide to address an environmental problem themselves has as a consequence that the parties will have to find alternative means to enforce the obligations arising from the agreement in order to prevent free riding. The need to prevent free riding will thus result in tightly drafted comprehensive agreements (hence 'reregulatory') that may involve some rather far-going obligations such as the exchange of information.

In sum, the incentive to come to a collective approach, the solidarity that is inherent in this collectivism and the wish to prevent free riders will mean that the parties have to make agreements in order to effectively and efficiently implement producer responsibility. Such agreements are very likely to involve restrictions of competition. This is so because in the end, as we have seen in chapter 2, competition inherently involves a degree of wastefulness. A number of companies may, for example, work independently of each other at a solution to the same environmental problem. The fact that these companies all need to have the laboratories and personnel means that resources are wasted. In particular with regard to the internalisation of an externality that is still far from internalised with the consumers, the companies will want to do everything but waste resources. The more resources are wasted, the worse the competitive position of the companies involved becomes. As a result the chance of actually protecting the environment only becomes slimmer.

---

24 *Supra*, paragraph 3.3

25 This referes to, respectively, the CECED and ACEA agreements. See further, *infra*, paragraph 8.4.2.3.

26 This is evidenced by the fact that regulation is often used as a stick (in the meaning of the stick and carrot) in that such regulation will be enacted should the parties not meet the targets.

CHAPTER 4

# Integration as a Mutually Reinforcing Relation between Competition and Environmental Protection

## 4.1 Introductory remarks

In the preceding two chapters three central issues have been identified. Firstly, the idea that competition is the best instrument to achieve dynamic and allocative efficiency. Secondly, the fact that a full and universal internalisation of all environmental externalities (excluding Pareto-irrelevant externatlities the internalisation of which will not contribute to Pareto-optimality) would, in the presence of effective competition, result in socially optimal levels of environmental protection. Thirdly, the finding that this internalisation is still being undertaken and far from complete. Just as much as the combination of these three factors or central issues leads to the problem of environmental agreements that restrict competition while being environmentally beneficial, these three factors also hold the key to solving the problem. This key is the integration of competition and environmental protection. In this chapter, we will develop the model of integration that will allow us to value the solutions that were adopted in practice in order to solve the competition and environment conundrum.

## 4.2 Competition, internalisation and lacking internalisation

Competition, as economic history shows us, is without doubt the best method to organise a market. Countries that have free market economies have in general fared much better than their opposites the centrally guided economies. This is so because competition ascertains static efficiency (optimal allocation of production factors) as well as dynamic efficiency (innovation; the development of new products). The only disadvantage of competition is its inherent wastefulness. This relates to both the static and dynamic efficiency component of competition. For one, the whole idea behind competition is an economic 'survival of the fittest'. This means that the companies that make the worse mousetrap will be pushed out of the market, thus wasting resources.[1] With regard to the dynamic efficiency component of competition we may point at the fact the innovation consumes considerable resources. Innovation may on the one hand be best served with cooperation and a bundling of the resources of companies that would individually not have been able to innovate at all. On the other hand – to borrow a famous saying – the greatest of all monopoly profits may very well also be not having to invest in research and the development of new products.

Competition and its inherent propensity to waste resources become particularly important in the context of the internalisation of externalities such as the

1 These resources may of course be taken over by the surviving firms.

environment.[2] Because of the fact that environmental protection is to a large extent a non-value added – or, better, an external added value – activity, profit margins are small and the case for a non-multiplication of the costs becomes better. All in all, externalities are, as could be seen in chapter 2, are often found in the company of natural monopolies.

This would be otherwise only if there would be full and universal internalisation of all externalities. The harsh reality, however, is that the internalisation is lacking in more than one respect. For one, competitors may not have internalised certain environmental aspects. The result of one group of companies going ahead of the industry is a deterioration of the competitive position of that group *vis a vis* the rest of the industry. A more important aspect of lacking internalisation is connected to the consumers. The overwhelming majority of the consumers have not yet internalised the environmental externalities in their purchasing decisions and are thus unwilling to pay more for an environmentally friendly product. Even in the absence of full and universal internalisation of all environmental externalities among the producers, a full internalisation among the consumers would have greatly mitigated the deterioration of the competitive situation of the leading group. This for the simple reason that a consumer that has internalised environmental concerns in his purchasing decisions will, provided that he is financially capable, is willing to pay more for the greener product. Consumers in a rich country such as the Netherlands are capable to buy, for example, sustainable generated 'green' electricity instead of 'grey' electricity. In doing so they might end up paying more but preserving a healthy environment for their children. That this switch to environmentally friendly products is not taking place on a massive scale in the rich industrialised nations is a sign of the poorly developed capability of man to envisage and take account of longer-term effects. It is, in short, a sign of lacking internalisation.

Where, then, do we start to internalise environmental costs? In the minds of millions of citizens or in the corporate strategies of a relatively limited number of companies? The principles of the free market economy and competition would dictate that the consumers' preferences need to the point of departure. Consumer preferences and the wants of all individuals combined are what guide the market like an invisible hand. Reasons of effectiveness and efficiency, however, point at the producers as the best point from which to start changing the perceptions of a society and internalising environmental costs.

---

[2] These wastes are of course to a large extent only a transitory problem arising from, for example, the bankruptcy of an inefficient firm. However, insofar as the wastefulness follows from the fact that certain investments are multiplied precisely because of competition (for example, three companies all funding an R & D department) the waste is inherent and non-transitory.

The latter point of departure is, as we have seen above, indeed the one predominantly chosen by environmental law and policy. This was partly given in by reasons related to the efficiency and effectiveness of environmental policy. It can, however, probably also be seen as a recognition of industry's capability to change our preferences. As an example of this power, we may ask ourselves how often we would be in dire need of a means of communication for twenty-four hours per day, ten years ago. The enormous popularity and use of mobile phones today in no way reflects the crowds that must have been standing behind nearly every public phone ten years ago. Perhaps the extra impetus for the internalisation of environmental costs with consumers needs to come from the same people who made us believe that we need mobile telephony and new clothes for every new season. Moreover, these 'masters of marketing' have an incentive to internalise the environment as it gives them yet another means by which they may distinguish and thereby market their products.

It is thus submitted that industry has a major role to play in internalising environmental externalities.[3] This means that industry will have to take the lead in first internalising those costs itself. Industry will only do this if it does not deteriorate or jeopardise its own competitive position. This will in turn result in the industry asking for government induced distortions of competition or restricting competition itself in order to compensate the deterioration. As a result of this, industry and the government will meet with competition law and it at this point that competition and the environment need to be integrated.

## 4.3 A model of integration

It is recognised that sustainable development cannot possibly be understood to require zero economic growth. The other way around sustainability seems to be irreconcilable with unlimited economic growth. Probably the only way forward if humanity wants to enjoy this planet as its home for much longer, is to achieve sustainable development. This requires a full and universal internalisation with producers as well as consumers. During this process of internalising the environmental externalities restrictions of competition are necessary. The model of integration thus requires that the competition rules are applied in the light of the objective of achieving internalisation. It is therefore submitted that during the transitory phase, when the process of internalisation is taking place, restrictions and distortions of competition must be allowed insofar as they are necessary to internalise environmental externalities. After this transitory phase, all environmental costs will have been internalised so that

3 That is to say that placing trust in the government alone as the principal agent to bring about this internalisation is at least equally naïve and probably less efficient.

unrestricted and undistorted competition will actually work for the environment.

The following example will clarify this. Consider a group of companies that wants to internalise the environmental costs arising from emissions from their installations by installing equipment that will reduce these emissions. This group, however, is active on a highly competitive international market. Moreover, their activity together with the competitive nature of the market does not allow them profits of the kind that will pay for the considerable investments needed. Since the companies know that simply installing the emissions reductions equipment is beyond their financial capabilities, they apply for a government subsidy. Such a subsidy will probably constitute a state aid within the meaning of Article 87(1) of the EC Treaty. As such, it is prohibited but may be exempted by the Commission on the basis of Article 87(3) EC. It is submitted that the model of integration requires the Commission to allow this subsidy insofar as it aids the internalisation. In practice this will mean that the investment aid will have to be exempted insofar as it covers the extra costs arising from the environmental investment and insofar as this is necessary to compensate the deterioration of the competitive position. If, for example, the competing companies also start investing in emissions reductions equipment, the investment is no longer necessary.

Suppose that the group of companies does not get the government subsidy. They could then abandon the entire project and could just continue their environmentally unfriendly business as usual. If they want, however, to continue improving their environmental track record, the parties will firstly have to acquire some form of market power by which they can partially offset the deterioration of their competitive position. They will achieve this by cooperating.[4] As they will want to prevent free rider problems and since they are unable to bear the investments themselves, they may decide to collectively pass the costs of the investments on to their consumers. In the absence of this collective approach, members of the group may soon succumb to pressure from their consumers to no longer pass the costs on. This would, in turn, mean that the necessary investments will no longer be done and the free riding begins, leading to the abandonment of the project altogether. This coordination of competitive behaviour by the group will fall within the scope of Article 81(1) EC. Moreover, traditional competition law and policy would seem to indicate that, since it concerns a decision with regard to the price, it is probably prohibited while it is unlikely that it may be able to benefit from an exemption pursuant to Article 81(3) EC. However, according to the model of integration, competition law should facilitate this internalisation of environmental costs by allowing the coordination of competitive behaviour insofar as this is necessary for the internalisation.

---

4 Note that the group may also want to cooperate in order to achieve economies of scale.

In both cases, the state granting aid and the coordination of competitive behaviour by the companies, the withdrawal of competition law should be neither unconditional nor indefinite. This because a complete disapplication of competition law would fully rule out the allocative and dynamic efficiency benefits that competition may bring with it. As a result the mutually reinforcing relation between competition and the environment, that is considered to form the core of the model of integration, is forgone. In the context of the application of EC competition law to the examples above, the subsidy should be considered a state aid and be granted an exemption on the basis of Article 87(3) EC. Such an exemption, as opposed to a solution whereby environmental subsidies would be considered to fall outside the scope of Article 87(1) in the first place, ensures that the Commission is able to keep a check on whether and to what extent the aid is necessary for the internalisation. Similarly, the agreement between the industry should not be taken outside the scope of Article 81(1) altogether[5] but rather be exempted on the basis of Article 81(3). The model of integration therefore does not require an artificial narrowing of the scope of the prohibitions on the grounds related to the protection of the environment or the internalisation of environmental costs. Instead, the model of integration requires that the discretionary powers to disapply the prohibitions or grant exemptions should be exercised in the light of the need to achieve an internalisation.

This will allow the companies to internalise environmental costs without compromising their competitive situation. As the environment becomes more internalised with the producers as well as the consumers, competition can start to play its reinforcing role. An increasingly unmitigated application of competition law to these environmental initiatives will ultimately result in a competition for the environment. In this end-phase, the environment will have become an aspect with regard to which competition is not only possible but also actually occurring. In that phase both the environment and competition are better off. Competition is not only intensified because of the creation of a new factor with regard to which competition is possible, it is also less distorted since the need to offset competitive disadvantages has disappeared.

That, however, takes us into the future. At the moment, the model of integration is still very much occupied with the transitory phase. Environmental considerations are slowly seeping in our everyday actions and becoming part of all the decisions that we make on a day-to-day basis. It is thus in this transitory phase that the authorities applying competition law may need to take a step back in order to advance, at a later time, two steps. Only then may competition law and policy play their part in the internalisation of the environment. Only then do we stand a chance of accomplishing truly sustainable development.

---

5 Unless there is no appreciable restriction in the first place.

CHAPTER 5

# Applicability of the Model of Integration

## 5.1 Introductory remarks

Now that the outlines of the model of integration have been charted, a number of things have become clear. For one, the model of integration, as it was developed above, is not specific to any legal context. Above, we have referred to EC competition law only for the purpose of giving examples. Moreover, the initial reference in the introduction to Article 6 functioned only functioned as a starting point for further investigations. In many respects, it can be called the legal frame of something that is essentially an economic painting. The model of integration developed above is all but endemic to EC competition law. It thus lends itself just as well for an application in the context of the European Community's as well as the member states' competition laws. This observation and the non-legal character of the model of integration does, however, not mean that it is unnecessary to further inquire into the legal framework within which it should be applied.

Particularly from the side of the German competition authority concerns have been voiced as to the appropriateness of any inclusion of non-competition considerations in the competition laws. Similar concerns can be heard in the Netherlands where the prohibition of *détournement de pouvoir*[1] is cited as precluding such practices.[2] Moreover, there is no such thing as an integration clause in, for example, the competition laws of Germany or the Netherlands. The result of the inclusion of non-competition factors in the process of administering the competition laws, according to these criticisms, would be that the objective of these laws is changed so as to include these considerations. The absence of any specific considerations or provisions to this effect in those competition laws, so the argument continues, must mean that the legislator did not intend for this to happen. As a result, purely legal considerations result in the exclusion of any role for environmental concerns and thus completely rule out the applicability of the model of integration. These questions and concerns all deal with the problem of the applicability of the model of integration to a certain legal context.

In the following chapter we will deal with the issues surrounding the applicability of the model of integration to a number of specific legal contexts. We will thus examine the competition laws of the EC, the Netherlands and Germany. These considerations will necessarily have to be of a somewhat more general nature since we will compare these systems of competition law more extensively in Part Three.[3] Below, we will be looking at the place that the

1 This a prohibition, as part of general administrative law, to use a power for other objectives than those for which it was first conferred upon the administrative entity.

2 Van der Meulen 2000, p. 196 *et seq.*

3 *Infra*, chapter 10.

competition laws occupy in these societies and how that influences the structure and administration of these laws. Despite the fact that we will embark upon this exercise, it is useful to bear in mind the conclusion formulated above, that the model of integration is not alien to any specific system of competition law. An integration of environmental and competition considerations in accordance with the model of integration neither means nor requires that the objectives of competition law are changed. Rather, it means that the objective of achieving and maintaining effective competition is temporarily set aside in order to achieve more effective competition on the longer term. It is thus perfectly compatible with a longer-term perspective on the maintenance of competition as the objective of competition law.

## 5.2 European competition policy – the special case of the integration principle

The structure of EC competition law is that of a widely construed prohibition together with an exception or the possibility of an exemption. With regard to, for example, prohibition of cartels the exemption clause in Article 81(3) EC provides proof of the fact that a restriction of competition is not necessarily prohibited but may actually be tolerated because of its benefits to society at large. The very structure of the competition provisions with the omnipresent possibility of exemptions from the basic rules, points at the fact that EC competition law serves other objectives alongside the maintenance of effective competition.[4] Furthermore, as we have seen above, the question whether environmental protection requirements should play a role in European competition policy already seems to have been answered by the Treaty's drafters in the form of Article 6 of the EC Treaty.[5]

In its current form there is relative consensus among scholars that the integration principle represents a legal obligation.[6] Moreover, the judgment of the European Court of Justice in *Bettati*, show that the Court is willing to test – be it marginally – whether Community legislation is in accordance with the environmental principles enshrined in then Article 130 R which at that time, also contained the integration principle.[7] The judgments in PreussenElektra and *Concordia Bus* illustrate that the Court will – be it slightly haphazardly – invoke

4 *Cf.* Monti 2002, p. 1059 *et seq.*

5 *Cf.* Wasmeier 2001.

6 *Cf.* Jans 2000, p. 22, Doherty 1999, p. 381, Dhondt, Uylenburg 2000, p. 127 and Dhondt 2002, p. 154 and Advocate-General Jacobs' opinion in case C-379/98, *PreussenElektra*, [2001] ECR I-2099, para. 231. However, Grimeaud appears to be more reluctant, Grimeaud 2000, p. 215 *et seq.*

7 Case C-341/95, *Bettati*, [1998] ECR, I-4355, para 33 *et seq.*

Article 6 in order to substantiate its decision to uphold an environmental practice of a member state.[8] As the wording of Article 6 shows, 'environmental protection requirements must be integrated into the definition and implementation of *the Community policies and activities* referred to in Article 3' (emphasis added). According to Article 3, first paragraph, sub g, of the Treaty 'the activities of the Community shall include (...) a system ensuring that competition in the internal market is not distorted'. Clearly, therefore, the Community's competition policy is subject to the integration principle.

Moreover, the structure of Article 3 and Article 2 of the EC Treaty lends even further support to this thesis. Furthermore, it may also provide an answer to the question of whether the integration principle could result in environmental protection being one of the objectives of European competition policy even though this would not be necessary for the model of integration. As we understand it, the very structure of the EC Treaty leads to the conclusion that achieving sustainable development and ensuring a high level of environmental protection are among the objectives of EC competition law.[9] This conclusion is based on the reasoning that the policies and activities mentioned in Article 3 EC are means to attain the whole catalogue of objectives formulated in Article 2 of the Treaty, taken together.

It is common ground that the means listed in Article 3 serve the attainment of the Community's goals listed in Article 2.[10] The problem, however, is that according to Article 2 the Community seeks the attainment of a multitude of objectives some of which may perhaps be difficult to reconcile with another. A solution to this problem would be to accept the Community's objectives as one and indivisible. Another view of the relation between Articles 2 and 3 and the objectives listed in Article 2 is that they represent a 'three stage rocket'.[11] This approach holds that Community substantive secondary law (the third stage) follows from Part Three of the Treaty (the second stage), which in turn is based on Articles 2 and 3 (the first stage). A possible implication of this approach could be that the specific means listed in Article 3 are linked only to the corresponding specific objectives in Article 2. This in turn leads to the conclusion that the system ensuring that competition is not distorted does not necessarily have to aim at, *inter alia*, protecting the environment. We would argue against this

---

8 Case C-379/98, *PreussenElektra*, [2001] ECR I-2099, at para. 76 and Case C-513/99, *Concordia Bus Finland* v. *Helsingin Kapunki* (Concordia Bus), [2002] ECR I-7213, para. 57.

9 See further Wasmeier 2001 and Monti 2002, who at p. 1078 considers it possible that the duty to integrate may even bring with it a preference for the protection of the environment over the protection of competition.

10 The very wording of Article 3 EC makes this clear beyond doubt. *Cf.* Kapteyn, VerLoren van Themaat 1998, p. 117.

11 *Cf.* Kapteyn, VerLoren van Themaat 1998, p. 115.

approach to the scheme of the Treaty and the structure of Articles 2 and 3 in particular on the following ground. With regard to some of the means listed in Article 3, no clear link can be established with an objective mentioned in Article 2. Whereas, for example, the Treaty envisages a 'contribution to education and training of quality and to the flowering of the cultures of the Member States'[12], no corresponding objective is to be found in Article 2. If not all means listed in Article 3 serve a corresponding objective in Article 2, the *a contrario* conclusion must be that the means serve the attainment of *all* the objectives of Article 2. The Court's judgment in *Albany* reflects this. On the basis of, *inter alia*, the fact that social protection as well as effective competition is listed in both Article 2 and 3 of the EC Treaty, the Court comes to the conclusion that it needs to opt for 'an interpretation of the provisions of the Treaty as a whole which is both effective and consistent'. In doing so, the Court explicitly recognises that the objectives listed in Article 2 EC cannot be seen separately.

The Community's objectives include 'a (...) sustainable development of economic activities, (...) sustainable (...) growth (...) a high level of protection and improvement of the quality of the environment (...)'. The conclusion must therefore be that environmental protection is certainly one of the objectives of the EC and as a result also an objective of EC competition policy. This conclusion is further substantiated by the fact that Community competition policy is primarily made by the Commission acting which is a collegiate body.[13] Accordingly, all Commissioners, including the Commissioner responsible for the environment, in principle have to agree with a decision and may thus influence decision-making.[14] Once more, we can see how the administration of the Community's competition laws, although it takes place in a strictly legal framework, is essentially a *policy* serving the objectives mentioned in Article 2 EC.[15]

The above legal exercise, even though in principle superfluous because of the nature of the model of integration, was undertaken nonetheless because legal considerations are often invoked are reasons against a role for non-competition considerations as part of competition law. It may be concluded that the structure of the Competition rules and their place within the Treaty clearly show that the model of integration may be applied to EC competition law.

---

[12] Article 3(1), (q).

[13] *Cf.* Goyder 1998, p. 128 *et seq.*

[14] See in general: Bellamy & Child 2001, p. 915 *et seq.* More specifically with regard to the effects that this may have on the decision: Monti 2002, p. 1070.

[15] *Cf.* Monti 2002, p. 1070.

## 5.3 Netherlands competition policy – the special case of the indirect effect of the integration principle?

The structure of the competition provisions in the Netherlands is identical to those of the EC. Therefore, the possibility of an exception or exemption from the prohibition can also be taken as proof of the only relative status of the maintenance of effective competition as the objective of the Dutch competition laws. With regard to the question of whether environmental considerations form an objective together with that of the maintenance of effective competition, matters are not as clear as they are for the competition policy of the EC. This is so because the Netherlands Competition act is a piece of legislation that functions in relative isolation from other laws and policies.[16] It is not part of an overarching system as is the case with the Community competition provisions. Moreover, in the Netherlands no specific legal provision comparable to the integration principle may be found.[17] On the level of environmental policy making, however, external integration is considered as a means to achieve environmental protection.[18] All in all there is little *a priori* certainty as to whether environmental protection can be said to rank among the objectives of the Netherlands competition rules and policy.[19] Matters are further complicated because the Competition act is applied by a separate, semi-independent authority that is incomparable to the collegiate body that the Commission is. The most obvious place to look for an answer to the question of whether environmental protection is one of the objectives of Dutch competition law and policy would seem to be the preparatory work concerning the Competition act.

The explanatory memorandum to the Competition act shows that the primary motive for a new Competition act was the wish to intensify competition policy.[20] Whereas the old competition act[21] was based on the abuse system, the Competition act prohibits cartels, signifying a departure from the partly positive attitude towards cooperation among competitors that formed the basis of the old competition act.[22] Furthermore, the wish to bring national competition law in line with European competition law can be named as a major reason for the Competition act.[23]

---

16 The *Mededingingswet* (Mw.), Stb. 1997, 242.

17 *Cf.* Dhondt, Uylenburg 2000, p. 121.

18 *Nationaal Milieubeleidsplan* (national environmental policy plan) 3, p. 45.

19 Of course, the model of integration would not require this.

20 *Memorie van Toelichting* (explanatory memorandum), TK 1995-1996, 24 707, nr. 3, p. 3 *et seq.*

21 *Wet economische mededinging*, amended and republished, Stb. 1958, 413.

22 *Cf.* Mok 1998, p. 67 *et seq.*

23 *Memorie van Toelichting* (explanatory memorandum), TK II, 24 707, nr. 3, p. 3.

As regards the objectives of the Competition act, the explanatory memorandum states that the basic principle of the Act is that 'competition is good but that certain forms of cooperation between enterprises may lead to benefits to society'.[24] During the parliamentary debates, the Minister explained that the Act aimed at bringing about and protecting 'workable competition'.[25] All in all, the Act appears to have as a primary objective the maintenance of a certain degree or intensity of competition while simultaneously recognising that competition is not an end in itself. In this respect, the situation as regards the objectives of the Competition act is comparable to that of the European competition rules. Furthermore, during the parliamentary debates considerable attention was devoted to the role of so-called non-economic considerations in the Competition act. This attention was caused by a difference of opinion between the Council of State[26] and the Minister as regards the role of non-economic considerations. The Council of State concluded, on the basis of *inter alia* the Commission decision in *Exxon/Shell*, that the exemption clause (Article 81(3) EC) allowed the Commission to weigh non-economic considerations against the correct functioning of the market.[27] The Minister rejected this view and came to the conclusion that the Commission could take these non-economic goals into account in deciding on an exemption. Furthermore, according to him non-economic goals were not weighed against the correct functioning of the market mechanism.[28] The result of this difference of opinion and the opinion of the Minister was an amendment that proposed to add an extra paragraph to the exemption clause in the Competition act according to which the Minister could grant an exemption in cases where non-economic concerns were in play.[29] In the end this amendment was withdrawn when the Minister proposed a different solution to the problem of the role of non-economic concerns.[30] This solution was the introduction of Article 4(2) into the Competition act according to which the Minister can issue general recommendations as regards the way in which the Competition authority should take non-economic concerns into account when applying the exemption clause.

From all this, the conclusion may be drawn that environmental protection is one of the ancillary objectives that the Dutch competition act seeks to attain. If it is firstly recognized that competition is not and end in itself but rather serves

---

[24] Translated by the author, TK II, 24 707, nr. 3, p. 9

[25] TK II, 24 707, nr. 12, p. 24.

[26] The Council of State (*Raad van State*) is a high advisory body to the government.

[27] TK II, 24 707 A, p. 8. 'Hierbij kan worden gedacht aan de afweging van niet-economische belangen, zoals belangen op het gebied van het milieu (...) tegen de belangen van een goede marktwerking'.

[28] TK II, 24 707 A, p. 9

[29] Amendment proposed by De Jong and Van der Ploeg, TK II, 24 707 nr. 29.

[30] We will take a closer look at these events in paragraph 10.5.2 *infra*.

the benefit of society and, secondly, environmental concerns can partly justify an exemption, the conclusion should be that these environmental concerns form an ancillary goal of Dutch competition policy.

The Competition act is primarily applied by the Director-General (*Directeur-Generaal*) of the Dutch Competition authority (*Nederlandse Mededingingsautoriteit* or *NMa*).[31] This holds true in particular with regard to the application of the exemption clause and exceptions to the rule in general. Several general norms such as the central prohibitions may also be invoked in civil procedures and can consequently be applied by a judge. At this moment the Competition authority is hierarchically subject to the Minister of Economic Affairs yet functions autonomously in that it has certain powers which flow from the Competition act.[32] This hybrid construction makes the Competition authority an administrative organ (bestuursorgaan) and therefore subject to the General act on administrative law.[33]

As such, with regard to the possibility for the authority to take environmental concerns into account, it is bound by, *inter alia*, the prohibition of so-called *détournement de pouvoir.* Article 3:3 of the General act on administrative law states that an administrative body shall not use its decision making powers for objectives different from that for which the powers were granted. The first paragraph of Article 3:4 of the General act states that an administrative organ shall weigh all the concerns that are directly involved insofar as this is not limited by a statutory provision or by the nature of the powers that are to be exercised. Whereas it may appear that the concerns thus to be taken into account are fairly broadly defined, a limitation to the diversity of concerns that can be taken into account is imposed by the so-called speciality principle. In many respects, this principle is enshrined in the abovementioned Article 3:3 of the General act.

It is therefore important to have an idea of the objectives for the attainment of which the decision-making powers were granted to the Competition authority. As it has turned out in paragraph 4.2.2.1 the Competition act, and therewith the powers flowing from this act, primarily aim at achieving and maintaining effective or workable competition. This in itself already shows that the degree or intensity of competition is not and end in itself but rather serves the benefit of the society. As a healthy environment also benefits the society, the conclusion would have to be that environmental concerns would have to be taken into account alongside the objectives in the competitive sphere.

---

31 Hereafter it will simply be referred to the (Netherlands) Competition authority even though formally it is the Director-General who applies section 17 and other provisions of the Competition act.

32 There are, however, plans to make the Competition authority into a completely independent body, *cf.* Proposal for an amendment of the Competition act, TK 27 639, nr. 1, 2.

33 *Algemene wet bestuursrecht* (Awb), Stb. 1992, 315, amended since.

As regards the relation between European law and Dutch competition law, it may be interesting to take into account the explicit wish to attune the Competition act to European competition law. As a result of this, the Dutch Competition authority has in many of its decisions explicitly referred to the fact that European competition law functions as a guideline for interpreting the provisions of the Competition act. This intended parallelism was recognized to have its limits as regards certain concepts that were considered unique to the Community setting.[34] The explanatory memorandum shows that, in this respect, the Minister appears to consider primarily those concepts and criteria that depend on the European market with regard to which the European competition rules apply.[35] The exclusion of these, jurisdiction-based, criteria and concepts seems only logical. A different matter, however, is the question whether other specifically European elements that play a role in interpreting European competition law can also play a role in interpreting the analogue provision in the Competition act. It is particularly interesting to consider the integration principle as an example of such a specifically European element.

As its very wording shows, the integration principle does not address the member states or any particular actor for that matter. The principle is defined only in that it requires the integration of environmental concerns into – put shortly – Community law and policy. Moreover, the judgment in *Concordia Bus* shows that the integration principle will allow member states to take into account environmental considerations in their own policies based on European legislation.[36] In that sense, the integration principle stops just short of conferring upon the member state authorities the right or even duty to take environmental concerns into account in their own policies.[37]

However, even though the integration principle does not address the member states (or any other particular actor for that matter) and furthermore does not oblige them to an integration of environmental concerns, the wish to align Netherlands competition law with Community competition law may bring with it an interesting indirect effect the integration principle. If, for example, the integration principle results in a particular interpretation of Community competition law, the explicit wish to achieve and maintain parallelism between the Competition act and Community law could result in a similar interpretation of the Competition act.

---

[34] TK II, 24 707 A, p. 10.

[35] TK II, 24 707, nr. 3, p. 10.

[36] Case C-513/99, *Concordia Bus*, [2002] ECR I-7213. This case concerned a public tender that allegedly contravened the provisions of one of the public procurement directives.

[37] Although a combination of the duty of loyalty to the Community (art. 10 EC) and the integration principle may indeed result in an obligation on the part of the member states to integrate environmental concerns in the other policy areas for which they are responsible. See further: Dhondt 2003, p. 48 *et seq.*

Whether or not this analogous application should or even could take place without the Competition authority sidestepping the mandate conferred upon it by the Competition act and the General administrative law act, essentially depends which one is the stronger: the wish to have parallelism or the *communautaire* character of the integration principle. On the one hand, the legislator explicitly wanted Dutch competition law to be and remain in line with the Community's competition rules as they stood and evolved. On the other hand, if such an evolution takes place with an explicit recourse to Article 6 EC, it must be recognised that Article 6 is unique to the EC Treaty and probably has been included because of the particular nature of the European Community. Moreover, as we have seen above, the duty to integrate is explicitly limited to the Community legal context. In this respect it should also be recalled that the European Community is an entity that has numerous competences with regard to a number of policy areas that do differ in their scope, exclusiveness and the degree to which they can be said to be of a 'Community nature'.[38] It is therefore concluded that the integration principle contained in Article 6 EC is of a *communautaire* nature. As a result, an application or interpretation of the competition rules of the EC that is founded this provision does not lend itself for application outside the context of the EC Treaty and its implementing legislation.

In some respects the use of the integration principle in the application of Community competition law can thus be said to lead to unexpected negative consequences. The same holds true for other interpretations of European competition law that are specific for the legal context in which European competition law functions. An example of such an interpretation is the *Albany* exception *ratione materiae* which the Court has based on the place of the competition provisions in the overarching whole of the EC Treaty.[39] It makes no sense to transpose this holistic interpretation of a Treaty in its entirety to the situation where one national law is interpreted. This, however, has not kept the Competition authority from doing just that.[40]

Again, it should be kept in mind that this should not obstruct the application of the model of integration since it is by no means confined to EC competition law. Moreover, the structure of the provisions in the Competition act, that closely resemble those of the EC, effectively points to the conclusion that was

---

38 Environmental protection, for example, is a Community competence where the member states have the – albeit clausulated – power to apply more stringent measures (Article 176 EC). Other policy areas, however, consist of little more than a coordination of the national policies of the member states coupled to an explicit prohibition for the Community to harmonise the legislation of the member states in that field.

39 ECJ Case C-67/96, *Albany International* v. *Stichting Bedrijfspensioenfonds Textielindustrie* (Albany), [1999] ECR, I-5751, See chapter 3, paragraph 3.2 *infra* on this exception.

40 Case 1012, *Van Eck Havenservice*, para. 36.

reached with regard to the Community's competition rules: competition is not an end in itself but rather serves more general goals among which environmental protection can certainly function.

## 5.4 German competition law – the special case of the fear of *Instrumentalisierung*

Above, we have seen that the Ordoliberal tradition can to a large extent be said to have stood at the cradle of the German Act Against Restrictions of Competition.[41] This fact explains the legal structure of the Act. Section 1 of the Act contains a widely construed prohibition of restrictions of competition that reminds one of the prohibition to be found in Article 81(1) EC. This prohibition is immediately followed by several possibilities for an exemption from the prohibition (Sections 2-8 GWB). The exemption clauses contained in Sections 2-7 are to be applied by the Federal Cartel Office,[42] whereas Section 8 allows for a ministerial exemption when an agreement cannot be exempted on the grounds listed in Sections 2-7. A comparison of the wording of the exemptions clauses with that of Article 81(3) quickly reveals a difference. Whereas Article 81(3) is a general exemption clause that may in principle be used to exempt any practice from the prohibition, Sections 2-7 of the Act are formulated much more restrictively as regards their scope. This is the so-called *Enumerationsprinzip* according to which an exemption can only be granted on the basis of the law and not on the basis of a necessarily uncertain interpretation of a vaguely formulated general exemption clause. Closely connected to this principle is the discussion about the objectives of competition policy. A general exemption clause that uses open wording is liable to being used for political purposes whereas the *Enumerationsprinzip* is seen as a means to prevent such a *politische Instrumentalisierung*, a term used to describe that competition law is made subject to other considerations than just that of maintaining competition.[43] This, of course, reflects the Ordoliberal belief in the juridification of the process of applying the competition laws. This belief, the fear of an *Instrumentalisierung* and the relinquishing of competition as the sole objective of competition law, are still very much core concerns of the Federal Cartel Office.[44] One notable exception to the *Enumerationsprinzip* can be found in Section 7 of the Act. At first sight this provision appears to be a transposition of Article 81(3) to the German Act. A closer look, however, reveals that Section 7 is still drenched with the desire to have only clearly and

41 The *Gesetz gegen Wettbewerbsbeschränkungen*, abbreviated as *GWB*.

42 The *Bundeskartellamt*.

43 See more extensively, Immenga 1976 and Schaub 1998, p. 124.

44 *Cf.* statements by then president of the Federal Cartel Office, Wolf, in Ehlermann & Laudati 1998, p. 24.

conclusively formulated exemption clauses. For one, Section 7 is drafted in more precise language than its European counterpart. For example, Section 7 expressly provides for the possibility to exempt agreements 'which contribute to improving the (...) taking back or disposal of goods or services' and fulfil a number of other criteria. This provision was introduced to allow the exemption of certain cartels on environmental grounds.[45] The opinion of the Monopolies Commission (*Monopolkomission*) provides further proof for this view of these changes effected by the Sixth Act.[46] Similarly, the then President of the Federal Cartel Office, Wolf, has referred to this as a *Systemwechsel* or a complete change of the system.[47]

Thus, with the *Enumerationsprinzip* partly done away with, the Federal Cartel Office must now apply a provision that, unlike any other provision that it has to apply, is couched in vague terminology. As a result, a margin of discretion is conferred upon the Federal Cartel Office and this in turn raises fears over an *Instrumentalisierung* of the competition laws. These fears basically follow from the idea that competition must remain effective and may not be subjected to the possibility of politically induced distortions or restrictions. These fears are aptly embodied by statements by the Federal Cartel Office with regard to the European Commission's decision to exempt the *CECED* agreement on energy efficiency.[48] According to the Federal Cartel Office the exemption was granted on environmental grounds. It then stated that:

> *'The Federal Cartel Office is sceptical of this policy because it introduces non-competition criteria into the appraisal on the basis of competition law in certain cases.'*

In the view of the Federal Cartel Office, competition law is only about achieving and maintaining competition.[49] An argument often heard in this connection is that competition has no lobby and is thus only protected by competition law. This, it is respectfully submitted, does not recognise that even if it is looked

---

45 *Cf.* the explanatory memorandum (*Begründung*) to the Sixth Act, BT Drucksache 13/1920, paragraph 2 (ee).

46 XIIth Main Opinion (*Hauptgutachten*) of the Monopolies Commission. BT Drucksache 13/11291, paragraph 94.

47 Wolf 1997, p. 2.

48 Federal Cartel Office, Activity Report (*Tätigkeitsbericht*) 1999/2000, BT Drucksache 14/6300, p. 66. Translated from: 'Das Bundeskartellamt steht diese Politik skeptisch gegenüber, da sie nicht-wettbewerbliche Kriterien in die Wettbewerbliche Beurteilung von Einzelfällen einführt.'

49 *Cf.* the statement by the then President of the Federal Cartel Office, Wolf, in Ehlermann & Laudati 1998, p. 24.

at from a purely economic welfare-oriented perspective, competition is only a means to an end.

The balancing of competition with non-competition objectives is, again according to the Federal Cartel Office, a political decision that needs thus to be taken at the political level. Thus, before Section 7 was included, the possibility of a ministerial exemption according to Section 8 GWB was considered by academia to be the only way to legalize cooperation on environmental grounds.[50] Even though Section 8 has never actually been used on environmental grounds, the fact that the possibility exists, shows that even prior to the amendments by the Sixth Act certain general concerns were considered to override the so-called *Wettbewerbsprinzip*. It may, however, be doubted to what extent the inclusion of Section 8 has actually detracted from the *Enumerationsprinzip* and indeed provides proof of the fact that the *Instrumentalisierung* was already envisaged by the Act itself. The fact that the Federal Cartel Office explicitly placed the process of weighing these concerns outside the context of the normal application of the Act shows that it was considered more a political than a legal appreciation of a competitive situation.

The fact remains that even in the presence of fears surrounding the *instrumentalisierung*, the application of the model of integration does not involve introducing non-competition considerations into the framework of competition law. As was said above, the model of integration requires only that a longer-term perspective on competition is adopted.

## 5.5 The model of integration and its application

In the preceding paragraphs it was shown that there are no legal objections that stand in the way of an application of the model of integration to the competition laws of the EC, Netherlands and Germany. It was concluded that the application of the model of integration is greatly facilitated if environmental protection is one of the objectives of a system of competition law. An environmental objective is, however, not a prerequisite for the application of the model of integration as was shown by the German Act Against Restrictions of Competition.

As far as the competition policy on the basis of the EC Treaty is concerned, it is recognised that the competition rules are only instrumental to the attainment of the objectives listed in Article 2 EC. In the Netherlands, the place of the competition rules and the function that they serve is quite similar. The fact that the maintenance of competition is not the ultimate objective of these systems of competition law will facilitate the application of the model of integration. With

[50] *Cf.* Paschke 1997, p. 58, Ehle 1996, p. 119 *et seq.*, Friedrich 1977, p. 201 *et seq.*

regard to German competition law, an application of the model of integration should not be impossible either. Even though the exceptions in the GWB are much more restrictively formulated, the fact remains that the Federal Cartel Office can grant exemptions from the prohibition to restrict competition. One such exemption may be granted for specialisation agreements. Of course the whole idea behind a specialisation agreement is that parties are allowed to swap production in order to produce more efficiently and thus increase welfare while at the same time be able to compete more effectively.[51] If such an agreement is allowed despite the obvious restrictions of competition, the application of the model of integration should be unproblematic as well. This for the simple reason that the model of integration requires only a temporary restriction of competition whereas a specialisation agreement could in theory be exempted and legally restrict competition for as long as the companies will keep on manufacturing the product for which they have decided to specialise. Essentially, the model of integration requires little more than the adoption of a longer-term perspective on competition law.

Ultimately, applying the model of integration will only lead to a more level playing field and the introduction of a new factor with regard to which competition is actually occurring. As a result, competition and the environment will both be better off.

---

51 *Cf.* the preamble to the relevant group exemption regulation 2658/2000, OJ 2000 L 304/3.

PART TWO

'Community law provides that environmental considerations must be integrated into all other Community policies. This includes European competition policy.'[1]

# EC Competition Law and Environmental Concerns

CHAPTER 6

# Introductory Remarks

## Introductory remarks

The examination of the relationship between competition law and environmental concerns in the preceding part of this book started in chapter one on an abstract and theoretical level. Gradually the research transformed from this theoretical exercise to the level of the practical implications of this relation. With the help of the model of integration developed around Article 6 EC in Part One, we will now turn to the role of environmental concerns in the practice of EC competition law. First we shall look at EC competition law and policy in general. With regard to the specific areas of law and policy we shall examine if there has been a role for environmental concerns and, if so, what this role has been. This will involve an overview of literature, case law and decision-making practice. Furthermore, we will be paying attention to the question of whether a role for environmental concerns is possible taking into account the model of integration referred to above and legal constraints. In this respect we shall investigate whether certain provisions could be used to let environmental considerations play a role in the application of competition law. Furthermore, this will involve answering the question of whether the role for environmental concerns thus described conforms to the model of integration developed in chapter 4 of Part One. In short, the objective of this second part of the book is to chart the role that environmental considerations currently play in Community competition law and what that role *could* and *should* be.

To do this we shall examine all the instruments of EC competition law. Community competition law exists of a number of different instruments that are all designed to tackle a specific type of restriction or distortion of free competition. Firstly, the Treaty contains a number of rules directed at 'undertakings' or firms. These are Article 81 that concerns co-operative behaviour among firms ('the cartel prohibition') and Article 82 that governs abuse of a dominant position. A later addition to these two was the Merger Regulation that should prevent competition problems from arising due to mergers by firms. Community competition law is also concerned with the influences that member states may have on competition. Essentially, three sets of rules govern member state interference with competition. The first and broadest set of rules was invented by the Court and cannot as such be found in the Treaty. This is the useful effect doctrine according to which member states may do nothing that detracts from the useful effect of the competition rules directed to undertakings. The second set of rules can be found in the Treaty and is strongly linked to the useful effect doctrine but is confined to a special group of companies that shall be referred

---

1 J.-F. Pons, Deputy Director-General DG Competition European Commission in his contribution 'European competition policy for the recycling markets' to the Pro Europe International Congress 'Recycling as Part of Daily Life in Europe', Madrid, 20 September 2001.

to as public undertakings. These rules can be found in Article 86 EC. Finally, member states may distort competition by granting aid to one or more companies. Articles 87 and 88 of the Treaty govern such practices.

With regard to EC competition law one of the first things to spring to mind is the considerable body of law and literature devoted to nearly every nook and cranny of it. Studying the role of environmental concerns in EC competition law is therefore likely to result in yet another rather voluminous addition to an already well-stocked library. Despite this obvious drawback, the best approach would nevertheless seem to first start with a description of the whole of EC competition law as a basis and to consequently focus the attention on those areas where environmental concerns may play their role. Firstly we shall look at the so-called fundamentals of EC competition law. These involve, *inter alia*, the scope of application, some fundamental concepts common to all provisions and the place of the competition provisions in the Treaty. Secondly the specific substantive provisions will be examined (*i.e.* the instruments referred to above). Finally we will come to some interim conclusions.

CHAPTER 7

# The Fundamentals of EC Competition Law

## 7.1 Introductory remarks

The fundamentals of EC competition law involve the role and place of competition law in the Treaty, the sectoral scope of application, and several concepts that the provisions have in common. These will receive further attention below starting with the role of the competition provisions in the system of the Treaty. Inherent in this role is the fact that competition law plays a part in the process of integration. These functions of competition law will also involve an attempt at an answer to the question of what concept of competition EC competition law seeks to attain. Following this, the focus of our attention will shift towards the sectoral scope of the European competition rules. In this respect, the scope of the competition rules *vis a vis* the agricultural, transport and defence sectors is studied. Lastly, the concept of an 'undertaking' will be examined.

## 7.2 The role of competition law in the Treaty

In some respects, thinking about the role of competition in the Community can be said to have been influenced by a German intellectual movement even during the Second World War: the Ordoliberals. Just after the Second World War, the competition laws of the European countries were quite unlike those that can now be found in the EC Treaty and most of the member states. Cartels were not generally perceived to be detrimental and most competition laws could hardly be called *anti*-trust laws. In the words of the Commission: 'Europe missed a competition spirit'.[1] This changed with the American influences during the occupation of Germany. The US had at that time already an extensive anti-trust culture and brought this to Europe. Moreover, a German group of scholars had during the war developed their own system of, *inter alia*, competition law. As occupied Germany was seeking to rebuild its economy, the Ordoliberal perception of economy, economic policy and the role of competition in the economy proved successful. Although only after a fierce debate, many of the Ordoliberal ideas found their way into the GWB, the German Act Against Restrictions of Competition.[2] One characteristic of the Ordoliberal conception of competition policy was that, in essence, this should come down to the application of legal norms by an independent institution as opposed to the exercise of political discretion. This view of competition also found its way into the ECSC Treaty's rules on competition.[3] Despite their relatively limited impact, the inclu-

---

1 Commission, White Paper on the Modernisation of the EC competition rules, OJ 1999 C 132/1.

2 Gesetz gegen Wettbewerbsbeschränkungen.

3 This may, however, be better explained with recourse to the political circumstances than by the general acceptance of the German (Ordoliberal) ideas, *Cf.* Gerber 1998, p. 337, 338.

sion of competition rules in the ECSC Treaty in many respects paved the way for the competition rules in the EEC Treaty.

The Spaak-report, which can be considered to contain the *traveaux préparatoires* for the Rome Treaty, already made clear that competition rules were considered a vital element of the new Community's legal structure.[4] The establishment of the common market hinged not only on the removal of governmental barriers to trade but required just as much the removal of private barriers to trade.[5] In this last respect competition rules were of vital importance. This functional approach to the competition rules, as an instrument to establish the common market,[6] is now laid down in Article 3(1) (g) EC.[7] This provision contains

*'[f]or the purposes set out in Article 2 [...] (g) a system ensuring that competition in the internal market is not distorted'.*

Thus the establishment of the common market[8] and the rules on competition are instrumental to the Community's objectives to be found in Article 2 EC.

The Court has constantly ruled that the Treaty's competition rules have to be interpreted in the light of these two provisions.[9] This brings with it that the ultimate objective of the European competition provisions has both an economic and political aspect. Economic in that competition as the market-order for the common market is supposed to ensure optimal economic efficiency. Political, in the sense that the goal of creating a common market is a political objective in the end. In the *Consten & Grundig* case, the Court stated that the Treaty aims at abolishing the barriers to trade between states and thus 'could not allow

4 Report of the Heads of Delegation of the Governmental Committee set up by the Messina Conference. Cf. the Commission's White Paper on modernisation of the rules implementing Articles 85 and 86 of the EC Treaty, COM (99) 101, OJ 1999 C 132/1, para. 10 *et seq.*

5 Gerber notes in this respect that the inclusion of competition rules in the (then) EEC Treaty seems to have been almost certain from the beginning on, Gerber 1998, p. 343.

6 *Cf.* Faull & Nikpay 1999, p. 81, Gerber 1998, p. 347 *et seq.* and Everling 1990, p. 1000.

7 Before the changes by the Treaty of Amsterdam this was Article 3 (g) and before that a nearly identical provision could be found in Article 3 (f).

8 Although they may not be completely identical, the terms common- and internal market will be treated as synonymous. See further with regard to these concepts: Kapteyn & VerLoren van Themaat (Ed. Gormley) 1998, p. 780.

9 *E.g.* Case 6/72, *Europemballage and Continental Can* v. *Commission* (Continental Can), [1973] ECR 215, paras. 22-26, Case 85/76, *Hoffmann-la Roche* v. *Commission* (Hoffmann-La Roche), [1979] ECR 461, paras. 125, Case 13/77, *GB-INNO-BM* v. *ATAB*, [1977] ECR 2115, para. 29, Joined Cases T-305-307/94, T-313-316/94, T-318/94, T-325/94, T-328, 329/94 and T-335/94, *Limburgse Vinyl Maatschappij et al.* v. *Commission* (PVC), [1999] ECR II-931, para. 150.

undertakings to reconstruct such barriers'.[10] This is not to say that the objective of the competition rules consisted (or consists) solely in the creation of the common market or European integration in general. Nor can it be said that the maintenance of a certain degree or level of competition was an end in itself. Rather, both goals were fused and considered mutually interdependent. This, as was already touched upon above, has had a thorough effect on the concept of competition and system of competition law as it was developed in the EC.[11]

As a result, for example, the Court had to fill the lacunae of European competition law.[12] Contrary to the ECSC-Treaty, the EC Treaty lacked rules on concentrations. In its celebrated *Continental Can* judgment, the Court of Justice decided that in some cases, the acquisition of another firm could qualify as abuse of a dominant position.[13] In the *VCH* case, it was established that a cartel spanning the territory of one member state[14]

*'by its very nature has the effect of reinforcing the compartmentalisation of markets on a national basis, thereby holding up the economic interpenetration which the Treaty is designed to bring about [...]'.*

Another example is the creation of the so-called 'useful effect rule'. Although the Treaty provisions on competition distinguish between those provisions directed at undertakings and those directed at member state authorities, the Commission and Court have created a new, hybrid, rule. In the *GB-Inno-BM* v. *ATAB* case the Court rules that, although Articles 81 and 82 (then Articles 85 and 86) EC were directed at private enterprises, member states are prohibited by Article 10 (then Article 5) EC from introducing legislation or introducing measures that may deprive the competition rules of their effectiveness.[15]

All these judgments, however different their specific content may be, show the teleological method of interpretation according to which the effectiveness of the provisions is what ultimately counts. It is through this method that competition is firmly put in place in the overarching system of the Treaty.

This teleological interpretation, which ensures that the goals of Community competition law are merged with the objective of market integration, can also be seen in the concept of competition itself. Apart from the preamble to the

---

10 Joined Cases 56, 58/64, *Consten & Grundig* v. *Commission* (Consten & Grundig), [1966] ECR 429 at p. 340.

11 See, Monti 2002, p. 1064.

12 It has, however, also resulted in the limiting of the scope of the competition rules in certain cases, see, *infra*, paragaph 8.2 on the Albany exception *ratione materiae*.

13 Case 6/72, *Continental Can*, [1973] ECR 215.

14 Case 8/72, *Vereniging van Cementhandelaren* v. *Commission* (VCH), [1972] ECR 977, paragraph 29.

15 Case 13/77, *GB-Inno-BM* v. *ATAB*, [1977] ECR 2115.

Treaty which states that the Community shall be based on 'free competition', and Article 3 of the Treaty, no reference is to be found to a specific concept of competition that is to function as a guideline for Community competition policy. However, the functional approach to competition that, as has been shown above, pervades Community competition law has also had an influence on the concept of competition itself.

The Commission and Court have thus defined the concept of competition sought after as 'effective' or 'workable' competition.[16] This only reiterates that the competition that the Treaty seeks to enact or protect is not an end in itself. In *Metro I* the court made this very clear when it stated:[17]

*'The requirement that contained in Articles 3 and 85 of the EEC Treaty [Now Articles 3(1)(g) and 81 EC] that competition shall not be distorted implies the existence on the market of* WORKABLE COMPETITION, *that is to say the degree of competition necessary to ensure the observance of the basic requirements and the attainment of the objectives of the Treaty, in particular the creation of a single market achieving conditions similar to those of a domestic market.' [Emphasis added]*

Here, we see the influence of the Treaty context on the concept of competition. In this respect it must be noted that the fact that competition is understood functionally does not mean that the primarily economic objectives of competition have been replaced with political objectives. Rather, and this also follows from the observations mentioned above, the political and economic objectives have been merged into a concept of competition *sui generis*.[18]

It is this concept of competition that functions as a guideline for European competition policy: to maintain effective or workable competition. As a result, the seemingly strict wording of, for example, Article 81, has been interpreted in such a manner that not every restriction of competition is forbidden. Only those agreements that restrict competition to an extent that is more than *de minimis* fall within the scope of Article 81. This practice is referred to as the principle of appreciability and should not be confused with the principle that any restriction of competition must also appreciably affect intra-community trade.[19] Logically,

---

16 *E.g.* Case 6/72, *Continental Can*, [1973] ECR 215, para.24, 25; Case 26/76, *Metro* v. *Commission* (Metro I), [1977] ECR 1875, para. 20.

17 Case 26/76, *Metro I*, [1977] ECR 1875, para. 20.

18 *Cf.* A-G Fenelly's opinion in Case C-214/99, *Neste Markinointi Oy* v. *Yötuuli Ky*, [2000] ECR I-11121., para. 26.

19 *E.g.* Joined Cases C-215 and C-216/96, *Carlo Bagnasco* v. *Banca Popolare di Novara* (Bagnasco), [1999] ECR I-135, See, further with regard to the distinction between the effects on competition and the effect on intra-community trade the 2001 Commission Notice on Agreements of minor imprtance which do not appreciably restrict competition within the meaning of Article 81(1) EC (*De Minimis* Notice) OJ 2001 C 368/13, at para. 3.

the principle of appreciability has only been applied with regard to Article 81 and 87.[20] As such the manifestations of the principle of appreciability will only be investigated within the context of these two provisions.[21]

## 7.3 The scope of the competition rules

### 7.3.1 Introductory remarks

As was shown above, the Community's competition rules seek to preserve or enact workable or effective competition. The Treaty accepts competition as the basic market order for the entire common market. However, the treaty recognises exceptions to this rule of competitive markets at the same time. For certain sectors of the economy, the Community's founders acknowledged that competition could not be allowed as the market order. For the agricultural, transport, defence and coal and steel sectors of industry, an exception was laid down in the Treaty.[22] This resulted in the possibility for a special regime for the application of the competition rules in certain sectors of the economy.[23] These special regimes exist only where the Treaty allows this and, as with any exception to a rule, they are interpreted narrowly.[24]

Below, the application of the Community's competition laws to the agricultural, transport and defence sectors of industry will be studied.[25] Each of these sectoral exceptions will be scrutinised for the role that environmental concerns have played or could play.

Further below, out attention will focus on the scope *ratione personae* of EC competition law. This is defined by the concept of an 'undertaking'. This concept and the role of environmental considerations in this respect will be studied in

---

20 It is inherent in the fact that Article 82 sees only to 'abuse' by undertakings in a 'dominant position' that such abuse necessarily appreciably restrict competition.

21 See with regard to Article 81, *infra*, chapter 8 and with regard to Article 87, *infra* chapter 13.

22 The coal and steel sector is subject to the competition provisions in the ECSC Treay (by virtue of Article 305(1) EC which fall outside the scope of this book and will therefore not be treated in any detail. Suffice it to say that the competition rules of the ECSC Treaty are comparable to those of the EC Treaty.

23 Article 83(2) (c) EC. The fact that these rules concern the application *ratione materiae* of Community competition law distinguishes them from the so-called block exemptions; below paragraph However, as the block exemption for the insurance insurance sector (Commission Regulation 3932/92, OJ 1992 L 398/7) shows, clear, the border between the sectorial regimes and block exemptions may not always be that clear-cut.

24 Case 209-213/84, *Ministère Public* v. *Asjes et al.* (Asjes), [1986] ECR-1425, paragraph 40 *et seq*. Gerven, Gyselen, Maresceau & Stuyck 1997, p. 13, 14

25 *Infra*, parapraph 7.3 *et seq*.

paragraph 2.4. As for the scope *ratione loci* our attention will be limited to the jurisdictional scope referred to by the 'effect on trade between Member States' that is required for the application of the Treaty's competition provisions to any restriction of competition.[26] In this respect, some attention will also be devoted to the extraterritorial application of the Community competition rules and its implications in an environmental context.

### 7.3.2 Agriculture

The agricultural market has traditionally been fraught with problems.[27] This is primarily due to two causes: the fact that supply is to a very large degree dependent on factors other than market forces (climate, biological factors) and the fact that agricultural products and production factors are strongly interrelated. This has lead to intensive governmental interference in the agricultural market. These governmental interferences were continued under the Community rule in the common agricultural policy. The extensive influence of the (public) authorities on the agricultural sector resulted in a special regime for the competition rules in the agricultural sector.

According to Article 36 EC the competition provisions of the EC shall apply to the production of and trade in agricultural products only to the extent determined by the Council taking into account the objectives of the common agricultural policy.[28] The last sentence of Article 36 specifies this with regard to the granting of aids.[29] Apart from governmental interferences such as the granting of aids or the fixing of prices or quota, the economic actors themselves may also wish to act in a manner that is contrary to competition law but necessary for the attainment of the objectives of the common agricultural policy.

Pursuant to Article 36 EC the Council has issued Regulation (EEC) No. 26 of 1962.[30] This Regulation declares Articles 81 to 86 applicable. The Articles governing state-aids are thus excluded from the scope of this Regulation. Article 2 of this Regulation declares Article 81(1) EC inapplicable to certain agreements where these agreements are, *inter alia*, necessary for the attainment of the objectives of the common agricultural policy. On a more general level, the European Court of Justice has recognised the priority of the agricultural policy

---

26 *Infra*, paragraph 7.5.

27 See on this subject and for further references Kapteyn & VerLoren van Themaat (ed. Gormley) 1998, p. 1128 *et seq.*

28 See Article 33 EC for these objectives.

29 According to Van Gerven *et al.* this is where the derogation is most significant: Gerven 1997, p. 34.

30 Council Regulation No. 26 of 1962 applying certain rules of competition to production and trade in agricultural products, OJ 1962 30/993.

over the objectives of the Treaty in the field of competition.[31] It has also ruled that, as an exception to a general rule, it should be interpreted strictly.[32]

Apart from the possibility of an exemption according to Article 81(3) EC, Article 2 of Regulation 26/62 provides for two exceptions from article 81(1). A final possibility for an exception exists for those agreements that follow from a Community measure pursuant to the common agricultural policy. With regard to Regulation 26 an exception is firstly envisaged for agreements that form part of a national market organisation. Secondly agreements that are necessary for the attainment of the objectives of the common agricultural policy are removed from the ambit of Article 81. It may be argued that the second sentence Article 2 of Regulation 26 contains a third possibility for an exception with regard to agricultural cooperatives. However, the wording of the abovementioned Article 2 could be taken to show that it is in fact only a more specific example of the application of the criteria of the first sentence.[33]

Regulation 26 is in fact only one of many instruments that have been based on Article 36 EC. This basis has also been used to issue the Regulations laying down the common market organisations. A fourth exception exists in that practices that restrict competition and were prescribed by such common organisation will fall outside the scope of the competition provisions of the Treaty.

With regard to the first exception, a problem arises because of the absence of a definition of the concept 'national market organisation'. The concept of a 'national market organisation' was defined by the European Court of Justice as the[34]

> *'totality of legal devices placing the Regulation of the market in the products in question under the control of the public authority, with a view to ensuring, by means of an increase in productivity and of optimum utilisation of the factors of production, in particular of manpower, a fair standard of living for producers, the stabilisation of markets the assurance of supplies and reasonable prices to the consumers.'*

The objectives of the national market organisations are thus the same as those of the EC's common agricultural policy as laid down in Article 33.[35] It appears

---

31 Case C-280/93, *Germany* v. *Council*, [1994] ECR I-4973, para. 62 at p. I-5061. Case 139/79, *Maizena* v. *Council*, [1980] ECR 3393, para. 22 *et seq.* at p. 3421 *et seq.*

32 Case C-399/93, *Oude Luttikhuis* v. *Coberco*, [1995] ECR I-415, para. 22, 23.

33 *Cf.* Cockborne 1988, p. 306. However, Ottervanger considers this opinion (which is shared by the Commission) to be incorrect: Ottervanger 1990, p. 218 *et seq.* See also Gerven, Gyselen, Maresceau & Stuyck 1997, p. 39.

34 It did this in Case 48/74, *Charmasson* v. *Ministre de l'Économie et des Finances*, [1974] ECR 1383, para. 26 at p. 1396.

35 *Cf.* Ottervanger 1990, p. 213.

that the conditions for the two exceptions are therefore comparable. The practical importance of this exception is further limited by the fact that such national market organisations have been almost completely replaced by common organisations.[36] Moreover, in the apparently only decision to date in which this provision was applied, the Commission appears to have 'reintroduced' the condition that competition is not reduced below what is considered workable.[37] All these reasons have limited the scope of the first exception and have as a result greatly diminished its importance for the purpose of this research.

The second exception provides that Article 81 EC is inapplicable to agreements that are necessary for the attainment of the goals listed in 33 EC. To our knowledge, this exception has not been applied to exclude an agreement from the scope of Article 81 to this date.[38] For the purpose of applying Regulation 26, the goals listed in Article 33 should be considered indivisible. As a result it is presumed that agreements have to be necessary to attain all the goals of the common agricultural policy for them to fall outside the scope of Article 81.[39] Furthermore, the necessity test applied by the Commission is rather strict.[40]

Irrespective of whether or not the second sentence indeed contains a separate third exception some general remarks will be made. As a result of its perception of this exception,[41] the Commission requires that the conditions of both exception in the first sentence are fulfilled as well as the conditions provided for by the second sentence itself. The exception appears rather limited because it applies only to horizontal agreements between farmers in one state. Furthermore those agreements may only concern the production or sale of agricultural products or the use of certain joint facilities while not involving any restriction of price competition. Interestingly, the burden of proof has been reversed in that it is for the Commission to show that competition is excluded or that the attainment of the objectives of Article 33 is put in peril.

The conclusion with regard to this exception for the agricultural sector should be that it is rather limited. This flows from the fact that it only shields this sector from Article 81 whereas Articles 82 to 86 EC and the Merger Regu-

---

36 See further: Kapteyn & VerLoren van Themaat (ed. Gormley) 1998, p. 1135 and Ottervanger 1990, p. 213, 214.

37 Commission Decision 88/109, *New Potatoes*, OJ 1988 L 59/25, under heading B. II, See further: Cockborne 1988, p. 300, 301

38 *Cf.* Cockborne 1988, p. 303, Ottervanger 1990, p. 216 and Ritter, Braun & Rawlinson 2000, p. 699.

39 E.g. Commission Decision 74/433, Frubo, OJ 1974 L 237/16, Case 71/74, *Frubo* v. *Commission*, [1975] ECR 563, para 25-27 and Joined Cases T-70/92 and T-71/92, *Florimex* v. *Commission*, [1997] ECR II-693, para. 152, 153.

40 Cockborne 1988, p. 303.

41 *Supra*, footnote 37.

lation[42] are still applicable to the agricultural sector.[43] However, with regard to the competition rules on state aid the second sentence of Article 36 EC allows for the Council to authorise the granting of aid for certain goals. The regime on state aid in the agricultural sector is laid down in The so-called Rural Development Regulation and the guidelines for agricultural aid.[44] These instruments will receive closer attention in the paragraph devoted to the rules on state aid.[45]

#### 7.3.2.1 The role of environmental concerns

Environmental concerns have certainly played and continue to play their role in the agricultural law and policy of both the EC and the member states.[46] That, however, is not the subject of this research. As regards the role of environmental concerns in connection with this exception, it was already remarked above that the exception is limited indeed. In fact, Regulation 26 only offers some protection from Article 81. As a consequence, all other restrictions of competition remain subject to the 'standard' competition rules.[47] The application of the exceptions is in itself already rather limited. Again, to the author's knowledge, none of these exceptions has to this date been applied on (partly) environmental grounds.

The question whether these exceptions could function as a vehicle for the integration of environmental concerns and competition law in fact comes down to the question whether they may be used to create an exception, on (partly) environmental grounds, for agreements that would otherwise restrict competition. In this connection the following remarks may be made. Firstly, the short sketch of the exceptions has revealed that by and large the primary requirement for the exception to apply is that this is in accordance with the objectives of the common agricultural policy. Although Article 33(1) EC does not contain any reference to the protection of the environment, the objective listed under (a) can

---

42 The eighth recital to the Merger Regulation (*infra* chapter 10) explicitly states this.

43 Cf. Cockborne 1998, p. 295 who, in footnote 11, cites a minority dissenting opinion with regard to the applicability of Article 82 EC.

44 Respectively, Regulation (EC) No. 1257/99 on support for rural development from the European Agricultural Guidance and Guarantee Fund (EAGGF) and amending and repealing certain Regulations, OJ 1999 L 160/80 and the Community Guidelines for State Aid in the Agriculture Sector, OJ 2000 C 28/2.

45 *Infra*, chapter 13.

46 See, on the integration of environmental concerns into the Common Agricultural Policy, Dhondt 2003, p. 199 *et seq.*

47 *Cf.* Gerven, Gyselen, Maresceau & Stuyck 1997, p. 34 and Waelbroeck & Frignani 1997, p. 53. However, only the rules on state aid seem to be of interest in this respect and it is therefore only to these rules and the role that environmental concerns can play in their application, that some attention will be devoted in chapter 13 below.

probably be interpreted so as to incorporate environmental protection considerations.[48] This is confirmed by the fact that the Rural Development Regulation envisages a clear environmental competence while being based on 36 and 37 EC and aiming at the attainment of the objectives listed in Article 33 EC.[49] It should be kept in mind, however, that the agreement would have to satisfy all the objectives of the common agricultural policy.

Secondly, it has become clear that much of the organisation of the market has taken place on a Community level. As a consequence, the exception for national market organisations has lost much of its importance. Furthermore, common organisations generally involve an exhaustive harmonisation of the sector concerned. As such, member states are precluded from enacting measures in those areas.[50] Insofar as environmental concerns have not been harmonised by the common market organisation, member states are, subject to the rules of the Treaty, still free to enact national measures.[51] This holds true by analogy on the level of private action with regard to agreements with an environmental objective in an agricultural sector governed by a common market organisation. It will, however, be difficult to establish that the agreement is indeed necessary for the attainment of the objectives of Article 33 (*i.e.* the second exception). In the presence of a common organisation, it is generally to be expected that the attainment of these goals has already been adequately secured. Measures going further in this respect will therefore be extremely difficult to uphold.[52] With regard to the relevance of the third (cooperative) exception in connection with environmental considerations, it has to be pointed out that the exception offered is quite limited. It should, however, be possible to take environmental aspects of cooperative agreements into account, as these are very likely to concern the 'production or sale of agricultural products'. As regards the possibility to apply the fourth exception as a vehicle for the integration of environmental concerns, the conclusion must be that it falls outside the scope of this research. Only where the common organisation requires a certain agreement the exception will apply. The initiative to integrate environmental concerns resides therefore with the Community legislature and not with private parties or member states.

---

48 *Cf.* Barents 1994, p. 33.

49 Regulation (EC) No. 1257/99 on support for rural development from the European Agricultural Guidance and Guarantee Fund (EAGGF) and amending and repealing certain Regulations, OJ 1999 L 160/80.

50 Case C-1/96, *The Queen* v. *Minister of Agriculture, Fisheries and Food, ex parte Compassion in World Farming* (Compassion in World Farming), [1998] ECR I-1251, para. 41.

51 *Ibid.*, paras. 56, 64, 65.

52 Ottervanger 1990, p. 216.

### 7.3.3 Transport

Not unlike the agricultural sector, the Transport sector was also one of intensive governmental interference. Within the framework of the Treaty, transport, being one of the pillars of the common market,[53] is also granted a special sectoral regime as regards Community competition policy. Shortly after Regulation 17 granted the Commission wide ranging and exclusive powers to apply Community competition law, Regulation No. 141 of 1962 temporarily suspending the application of the competition rules to the transport sector, was enacted.[54] The preamble to this Regulation already indicates that two sectors can be distinguished within the transport sector. On the one hand transport by rail, road and inland waterway and, on the other hand, transport by sea and air.[55] This bifurcation will be followed in the treatment of the sectors below. Firstly, inland transport will be studied. After that maritime and air transport are examined.

As was envisaged by the Council, rules on the application of the competition provisions to transport by rail, road and inland waterway proved relatively easy to attain. With the enactment of Council Regulation (EEC) No. 1017/68 a regime for this area within the transport sector was put in place.[56] This Regulation governs the application of the competition provisions on concerted practices, abuse of dominant positions and public undertakings in the transport sector. A first thing to be noted when reading the Inland Transport Regulation is that the Council made an effort not to apply the Treaty provisions on competition themselves to the transport sector. Instead, it formulated, with the Treaty provisions as an obvious example, new substantive provisions.[57]

Article 2 of the Regulation prohibits concerted practices in a way that is similar to Article 81(1) EC. Articles 3, 4, and 5 of the Regulation then continue by providing for, respectively, the exception from, exemption from and non-applicability of the prohibition in Article 2 of the Regulation. Article 3 created an exception for agreements and concerted practices the object and effect of which is to apply technical improvements or to achieve technical cooperation.[58] This

---

53 If transportation is insufficient, free movement becomes useless.

54 Council Regulation No. 141 of 1962 exempting transport from the application of council regulation No. 17, OJ English Special Edition Series II, Chapter 1959-1962, p. 291.

55 Seventh recital of the preamble that states that the introduction of rules on competition as regards transport by rail, road and inland waterway are 'possible to envisage within a reasonable period' whereas the introdcution of rules on competition for transport by sea and air 'are impossible to foresee'.

56 Regulation (EEC) No. 1017/68 applying the rules of competition to transport by rail, road and inland waterway (Inland Transport Regulation), OJ 1968 L 175/1, OJ Special Edition 1968 I p. 302.

57 Blanco & Houtte 1996, p. 59 *et seq.*

58 Hereafter referred to as 'technical agreements'. In this respect it is interesting to note that the relevant (eighth) recital in the preamble speaks of the 'exemption' as oposed to 'exception' of agreements that seek technical improvements.

can be through, *inter alia*, standardisation of equipment, transport supplies, vehicles or fixed installations.[59] Such agreements do not fall under the prohibition of Article 2 of the Regulation and in this respect it may be called a 'block negative clearance'.[60] An important thing to note is the fact that the English version of Article 3 does not require the technical improvement to be the *sole* object and effect of the agreement. This is most probably a translation error as other language versions do require the technical improvement to be the agreements' only object and effect.[61] As a consequence Article 3 should be read to include the word 'sole'.[62]

Since the *French Seamen* case it is clear that Article 2 of the Regulation is to be understood as a representation of Article 81(1) EC.[63] In secondary legislation based partly on Article 83 EC, the Council cannot deviate from the substantive provisions of the Treaty when the Treaty itself does not foresee such special rules.[64] It is then submitted that Article 3 of the Regulation is to be understood as providing an exception only for those technical agreements that are unrestrictive of competition. If the prohibition of Article 2 of the Regulation is to be read in the context of, and should be understood as hierarchically lower than Article 81(1) EC, the exception in Article 3 must fulfil the requirements that are necessary for an exception from the Treaty rules. Article 253 EC requires that the reasons on which legislation is based, shall be stated. With regard to Article 3, the Regulation's eighth preamble merely states that the technical agreements are exempted 'since they contribute to improving productivity'. This further reinforces the interpretation of Article 3 as a 'block negative clearance'.[65] Following this interpretation, Article 3 is understood as merely summing up the agreements that are deemed not to restrict competition in the first place.[66]

Article 5 of Regulation 1017/68 provides for non-applicability of the prohibition of Article 2. This provision appears similar to Article 81(3) but there are some differences.[67] These differences are of minor importance, however, now

---

59 Article 3(1)(a). Article 3 lists six other means which are not included because they appear to be of little interest for the purpose of this work. This list of means (a-g) is limitative but Article 3(2) states that it may be reviewed. This, however, hasn't happened since 1968: Blanco & Houtte 1996, p. 70.

60 Ritter, Braun & Rawlinson 2000, p. 704; Blanco & Houtte 1996, p. 74.

61 *Cf.* Blanco & Houtte 1996, p. 71.

62 Which is wat the Commission has done in its decision on the tariff structures: Commission Decision 93/174, *Tariff Structures in the Combined Transport of Goods*, OJ 1993 L 73/38.

63 Case 167/73, *Commission* v. *France* (French Seamen), [1974] ECR 359.

64 Groeben, Thiesing & Ehlermann 1991, p. 1938, 1939.

65 Blanco & Houtte 1996, p. 73, 74, Groeben, Thiesing & Ehlermann 1991, p. 2034. Otherwise Mestmäcker who refers to Article 3 as a *'Legalausnahme'* (legal exception), Mestmäcker 1971, p. 687 *et seq.*

66 Schröter calls this an *'allgemeines Negativattest'* which he compares with Article 4(2)(3) of Regulation 17.: Groeben, Thiesing & Ehlermann 2000, p. 2/1001.

67 Blanco & Houtte 1996, p. 79, Ritter, Braun & Rawlinson 1991, p. 572.

that the Commission has interpreted Article 5 as the equivalent of the third paragraph of Article 81(3) EC.[68] Notwithstanding this, an important difference appears to exist in the fact that 'improving the quality of transport services' is an extra positive requirement compared to Article 81(3) EC.

The requirement in Article 81(3) that the consumers are allowed a fair share is replaced by the requirement that the agreement 'takes fair account of the interests of transport users'. This reformulation has two consequences. First, 'consumers' is replaced by 'interests of transport users'. Schröter holds that this change in wording should be considered as an attempt to take the special character of the transport sector into account. Following the *Consten & Grundig* case, this provision should be interpreted so that there is a general benefit and not just a benefit for the parties only.[69] The fact is that the Commission has interpreted this provision as only including the users of transport and not in a wide sense such as to include consumers in general. Secondly, there is a difference as Article 81(3) requires that consumers are 'allowed' a fair share whereas for the application of Article 5 it suffices when the agreement 'takes fair account' of these interests. Schröter is of the opinion that this part of Article 5 can be interpreted in conformity with the Treaty and thus Article 81(3).[70] Mestmäcker holds that this forms part of the recognition of the interests of the transport sector. As such it constitutes a test that is easier to satisfy than that under Article 81(3).[71] As mentioned above, the Commission has stated that it considers Article 5 to be 'essentially modelled on the rules in Article 81(3)'[72] From this it would seem to follow that the scope for exemptions under the Regulation is probably not much broader than that in Article 81(3) EC.

With regard to the air- and sea transportation sector the regime is somewhat different. As these areas are also governed by international conventions, the room for Community action is limited. The judgment of the Court in *French Seamen*[73] confirmed that the transport sector was subject to, inter alia, the Treaty's competition provisions. This ruling was further clarified by the Courts' ruling in *Asjes*.[74] This has resulted in the, albeit belated, adoption of two Regulations concerning the competition rules in these sectors. For maritime trans-

---

68 Paragraph 20 *et seq.* of Decision 93/174/EEC, *Tariff structures in the combined transport of goods*, OJ 1993 L 73/38.

69 Joined Cases 56, 58/64, *Consten & Grundig*, [1966] ECR 429 at p. 348.

70 Groeben, Thiesing & Ehlermann 2000, p. 2/1004.

71 Mestmäcker 1971, p. 693.

72 Paragraph 19 of Commission Decision 93/174/EEC, *Tariff structures in the combined transport of goods*, OJ 1993 L 73/38.

73 Case 167/73, *French Seamen*, [1974] ECR 359.

74 Joined Cases 209-213/84, *Asjes*, [1986] ECR 1425.

ports, Regulation 4056/86 was enacted.[75] With regard to consortia, the Council enacted Regulation 479/92.[76]

The twenty years that passed between the enactment of the Inland Transport Regulation and these Regulations has had a thorough impact on the structure of these Regulations. For example, the first recital of the Maritime Transport Regulation explicitly recognises the fact that the Treaty's competition rules apply to the maritime transport sector Council, thus ending the debate on the applicability of the competition provisions to the transport sector. With regard to the question of integrating environmental concerns, Articles 2 and 3 of the Maritime Transport Regulation seem to be of most interest. These contain substantive differences from the normal rules applicable to agreements. Article 8 of the Regulation only concerns 'effects incompatible with Article 82 of the Treaty' To that effect, direct reference is made to the substantive provisions of Article 82 EC and no substantial differences exist in this respect between the maritime transport sector and industry in general.

Article 2 of Maritime Transport Regulation contains the 'block negative clearance'[77] for technical agreements similar to that in Article 3 of the Inland Transport Regulation.[78] [79] Whatever substantial differences occur between the two exceptions is due to the nature of the activity covered. The remarks made with regard to Article 3 of the Inland Transport Regulation can thus be repeated for the Maritime Transport Regulation. Article 3 contains the block exemption for liner conferences. Article 7(2) of the Maritime Transport Regulation ensures that such liner conference agreements do not have effects incompatible with Article 81(3). It explicitly lists 'acts of the conference which may prevent technical or economic progress (...)'.[80] Article 12 of the Maritime Transport Regulation provides for an opposition procedure as regards the application of Article 81(3) in this sector. The Consortia Regulation adopts the test of Article 81(3) EC for

75 Council Regulation (EEC) No. 4056/86 laying down detailed rules for the application of Articles 85 and 86 of the Treaty to maritime transport (Maritime Transport Regulation), OJ 1986 L 378/4.

76 Council Regulation (EEC) No. 479/92 on the application of Article 81(3) of the Treaty to certain categories of agreements, decisions and concerted practices between shipping liner companies (Consortia Regulation), OJ 1992 L 55/3.

77 Blanco & Houtte 1996, p. 107.

78 Greaves 1994, p. 109; Rabe & Schütte 1988, p. 701. Waelbroeck & Frignani 1997, p. 64.

79 At least one, probably translational, difference can be found in the German version of the Maritime Transport Regulation which reads that the object or effect of an agreement should be technical. The English version, however, does require both the object and effect to be technical. This appears to have been the intent of the legislator.

80 Article 7(2)(b)(iii) Maritime Transport Regulation.

the exemption of consortia agreements.[81] The same holds for the Commission Regulation adopted pursuant to the Consortia Regulation.[82]

The Air Transport Regulation[83] also allows for an exception for technical agreements. Article 2 of this Regulation creates an exception for technical agreements in a way similar to that in the Inland- and Maritime Transport Regulations.[84] A major difference follows from the fact that the list of technical agreements is not exhaustive.[85] The contents of the list do not differ that much from the lists under the other Regulations. Again, the comments made with regard to the exception for technical agreements under the Inland Transport Regulation can be repeated here.

Finally, it needs to be pointed out that Regulation 1/2003, the new Regulation implementing Articles 81 and 82, envisages a number of extensive changes to, *inter alia*, the Transport Regulations.[86] Articles 36 to 43 of Regulation No. 1/2003 amend and repeal several Regulations that are relevant to the transport sector. Article 43(2) of Regulation No. 1/2003 repeals regulation No. 141 of 1962. The specific procedural rules contained in those Regulations are repealed whereas the substantive rules are left in place.[87] In Article 36 of Regulation No. 1/2003 amends the Inland Transport Regulation in that, most importantly, Articles 2 and 5 to 29 are deleted. Furthermore, Article 3(1) of the Regulation is changed so as to refer directly to Article 81(1) instead of Article 2 of the Regulation. The amendments to the Maritime Transport Regulation by Article 38 of Regulation No. 1/2003 do not entail any consequences for Articles 2 and 3 of the former, that were identified as being relevant in this context. Similarly, the

---

81 Article 1(1) Consortia Regulation.

82 Commission Regulation (EC) No. 870/95 on the application of Article 81(3) of the Treaty to certain categories of agreements, decisions and concerted practices between liner shipping companies (consortia) pursuant to Council Regulation (EEC) No. 479/92, OJ 1995 L 89/7.

83 Council Regulation (EEC) No. 3975/87 laying down the procedure for the application of the rules on competition to undertakings in the air transport sector, OJ 1987 L 374/1. On the same day another Regulation concerning competition in the air transport sector was adopted. This Regulation (Council Regulation (EEC) No. 3976/87 on the application of Article 81(3) of the Treaty to certain categories of agreements and concerted practices in the air transport sector, OJ 1987 L 374/9) enables the Commission to issue block exemptions. None of these are of interest for the purpose of this study. See Bellamy & Child 2001, p. 1081 *et seq.* for the block exemptions that have been issued in the transport sector.

84 Groeben, Thiesing & Ehlermann 2000, p. 2/1000. One difference, again occurring only in the German text, is the reference to the object or effect (*supra* note 78). Again, it is submitted that this is probably a translational error.

85 Article 2(1) last sentence Air Transport Regulation.

86 Council Regulation (EC) No. 1/2003 on the implementation of the rules on competition laid down in Article 81 and 82 of the Treaty, OJ 2003 L 1/1.

87 *Ibid.*, explanatory memorandum with regard to Articles 37-40.

amendments to the Air Transport Regulation by Article 39 of Regulation No. 1/2003 would not seem to be of great importance as these relate only to Articles 3 to 19 of that Regulation thus effectively leaving the provisions that have been identified as relevant in this respect, untouched.

#### 7.3.3.1 The role of environmental concerns

Like the agricultural sector, the Community's and member states' transport policies have recently been concerned with environmental protection which is not surprising taking into account the fact that the transport sector is a major polluter.[88] From a general point of view, two provisions that can be found in all Regulations for the transport sector appear to be of interest for the purpose of this research: firstly, the exception for technical agreement and, secondly, the exemption possibility. As the exemption possibility is insofar as it is different from Article 81(3), is in essence a particular application of the general exemption clause contained in Article 81(3) EC, attention with regard to the role of environmental concerns, will also focus on the differences that have been noted to exist between these exemption clauses and Article 81(3).

Firstly, the exceptions for technical agreements. As was shown above, this exception or block negative clearance can apply only if there is no restriction of competition in the first place. As such it seems impossible to have recourse to this provision in order remove a restriction of competition from the competition provisions' scope on environmental grounds. Notwithstanding this rather limited scope, the exception might still be of interest. The pivotal question is of course in how far environmental considerations can be brought under the heading of technical agreements. Undoubtedly, this is possible. With regard to, for example, the exception for agreements involving the 'standardisation of equipment' it is certainly possible that this exception may also be applied with regard to agreements also involving environmental benefits.[89] Or, in another example, an agreement between undertakings to cooperate and pool their transportation means to achieve environmental benefits, is very likely to profit from the exception for technical agreements.[90] For this is it necessary that the environmental benefits coincide with the technical improvements or technical cooperation. Furthermore, these benefits must be its sole object as well as effect of the agreement.[91] The conclusion therefore would have to be that despite the possibility of

88 See, in general with regard to the integration of environmental considerations in this sector: Dhondt 2003, p. 293 *et seq.*

89 Article 3(1), sub (a) Inland Transport Regulation.

90 Article 2(1), sub (b) Maritime Transport Regulation.

91 Commission Decision 93/174/EEC, *Tariff structures in the combined transport of goods*, OJ 1993 L 73/38, paragraph 43.

using this exception with respect to certain environmental agreements, its scope is very limited.

As regards the role of environmental concerns with regard to the possibility for an exemption under the transport Regulations a first remark concerns the wording used in Article 5 of Regulation 1017/68. The fact that it refers to a fair share for transport users means that the interest of consumers in general are not necessarily or at least not directly taken into account. This could mean that negative environmental effects, that are more likely to affect consumers in general rather than the transport users, are less likely to play a role. Furthermore, two cases appear to be of interest. Firstly, the Trans-Atlantic Conference Agreement or *TACA* case.[92] In the proceedings against them, the TACA members invoked, *inter alia*, environmental benefits with regard to the possibility of an individual exemption for the pilot project of the so-called 'hub-and-spoke' system.[93] This system entailed the creation of so-called inland hubs and spokes between, firstly, the ocean port and the hub; the so-called trunk leg and, secondly, between the hub and the shipper's premises. According to the TACA parties, all container transports between the ocean port and the inland hub (*i.e.* the trunk leg) will take place by rail or inland waterway. As a result of this, the parties claimed that the system would contribute to a reduction in transport by road, thereby reducing congestion and bringing environmental benefits.[94] However, in order to achieve these benefits the parties considered it necessary to collectively fix the prices for their inland transport activities. The Commission, however, did not consider this to be indispensable. Apparently, the parties consider the price-fixing necessary in order to be able to lower the costs so that transportation by rail and inland waterway becomes competitive with road transports.[95] The Commission starts out by stating that it does not address the merits of the hub and spoke system itself nor the necessity of the price-fixing agreements.[96] However, as the parties have provided no evidence at all as to the effectiveness of the system in bringing about the claimed benefits in practice and because the elaboration of the system seems somewhat hypothetical, the Commission considers that an exemption is not warranted. It appears that the Commission might have granted an exemption in this case if the parties had substantiated their claim with (more) evidence. As a result, the possibility for environmental

---

92 Commission Decision 1999/243/EC, *Trans-Atlantic Conference Agreement* (TACA), OJ 1999 L 95/1.

93 *Ibid.*, para. 47 *et seq.* See also the Final report of the multimodal group of November 1997, to be found on the Competition DG's website: http://europa.eu.int/comm/competition/antitrust/others/ (20-02-2001).

94 Commission Decision 1999/243/EC, *TACA*, OJ 1999 L 95/1, para. 54 *et seq.*

95 *Ibid.*, para. 439.

96 *Ibid.*, para. 438.

considerations to play a role in the exemption procedure cannot be ruled out *a priori* on the grounds of this decision.[97]

Further evidence that environmental concerns may play a role in the procedure for an exemption can be found in the second case, concerning the *Hansa-Ferry* agreement.[98] The parties to this agreement had established a new ferry service. In its notice pursuant to Article 12(2) of the Maritime Transport Regulation[99] the Commission cited the following arguments put forward by the parties:

*'[...] The agreement implies that the parties can use their resources more efficiently, rationalising costs and take greater regard to environmental considerations.*

*[...] The improved planning will benefit the population at the coast via a lower environmental impact.'*

This case ended silently with the Commission issuing an unpublished exemption ex. Article 12 of the Maritime Transport Regulation.[100] However, this case and the *TACA* case show that in its application of the exemption possibility under the transport regulations, the Commission appears willing and able to take environmental aspects into account.

As regards the special exemption clause provided for by Article 5 of the Inland Transport Regulation, there is no case law involving environmental concerns. Furthermore, as the wording of Article 5 shows, it closely resembles Article 81(3) EC as a result of which the Commission is of the opinion that Article 5 cannot go beyond what Article 81(3) allows.[101]

### 7.3.4 Defence

Not so much a true sectoral exception, Article 296 EC entails the derogation for matters of 'essential interest of its security which are connected with the production of or trade in arms, munitions and war material'. This derogation, however, is restricted in that it only applies to products that are 'intended for specifically military purposes'. By analogy, it seems that this exception is also limited to, in general, *technology* intended for specifically military purposes. With regard to what are called 'dual use products' (i.e. products that

---

97 However, the Commission does seem to rule out the the necessity of an agreement to fix prices to achieve the (environmental) benefits of another part of the TACA, the EIEIA, *Ibid.*, paragraph 431.

98 Notice pursuant to Article 12(2) of Regulation (EEC) 4056/86 concerning Case IV/MAR/35.488, *Hansa-Ferry*, OJ 1996 C 118/5.

99 Which is comparable with the notice under Article 19(3) of Regulation 17 of 1962, OJ English Special Edition [1962], 87.

100 See: http://europa.eu.int/comm/competition/antitrust/closed/en/1996.html#452 (22 Jan 2001).

101 Commission Decision 94/985/EC, *Far Eastern Freight Conference*, OJ 1994 L 378/17, paragraphs 60-62.

have a civilian as well as military use),[102] the Commission subjects the civilian use of the products to a normal competition scrutiny.[103] It follows from the case *French State/Suralmo*[104] that the Commission is generally sceptical of the 'military' characterisation of dual use products. When a product is not really primarily intended for military use, it should be subjected to the normal competitive regime. As a result the possibility that this derogation is applied on environmental grounds is very limited if not non-existent as military objectives often rule out other, and perhaps in particular environmental, objectives.

## 7.4 The concept of an undertaking

### 7.4.1 Introductory remarks

A core concept of European competition law is that of an 'undertaking'. In fact this concept can be said to define the scope *ratione personae* of the Community competition rules.[105] This is exemplified by the fact that part of the substantive provisions of competition law is directed at undertaking whereas the remainder is not directed at but still concerns undertakings. In short, the concept of an undertaking may be equated with an enterprise or a firm. Below this concept will be examined in greater detail. This will involve, firstly, an appreciation of the definition of this concept. Secondly, it will be seen that inherent in this concept are several exceptions. These exceptions will be examined in general. Thirdly, it will be seen to what extent these exceptions are relevant in an environmental context.

### 7.4.2 A definition of the concept of a undertaking

To anyone familiar with European law it will not come as a surprise that the pivotal concept of an undertaking was left undefined by the Treaty's drafters. As a result, it was up to the Commission and Court to define it. While there was some case law as to the concept of an undertaking as regards the competition rules in the ECSC Treaty,[106] this concept was clarified for the EC

[102] Commission merger decision of 23/09/1996 in Case IV/M.820, *Brittish Aerospace/Lagardère*, OJ 1997 C 22/6.

[103] See in general on dual use goods: Case C-83/94, *Criminal proceeding against P. Leifer et al.* [1995] ECR I-3231.

[104] Commission, IXth. Competition Report (1979), p. 73. This Case concerned systems for diesel engines that were considered not to be specifically (or even mostly) intended for miliatry purposes.

[105] *Cf.* Louri 2002, p. 143.

[106] Joined Cases 17 and 20/61, *Klöckner-Werke AG and Hoesch* v. *High Authority*, [1962], 619.

competition rules only in the *Höfner & Elser* case decided in 1991. In this case the Court gave the following broad and, most importantly, functional interpretation of the concept':[107]

*'[...] the concept of an undertaking encompasses every entity engaged in an economic activity, regardless of the legal status of the entity and the way in which it is financed [...]'*

Thus it is function and not the form that matters in deciding whether or not an entity is an undertaking in the context of European competition law. The decisive criterion in answering the question of whether or not an entity is an undertaking therefore depends on whether or not the activity engaged in by that entity is 'economic'. However broad and functional this concept may be, one exception is inherent in it. Entities engaged in non-economic activities fall outside the scope of the competition provisions. Before going deeper into these exceptions some attention will be devoted to the other emanations of the concept of an undertaking.

Apart from the concept of an undertaking, Article 81 EC also refers to 'associations of undertakings'. These consist of nothing more than the sum of a number of undertakings. Again, therefore, the meaning of the word undertaking is decisive. Another element of EC competition law that, although in itself not directly connected to the concept of an undertaking,[108] would seem to be relevant in this respect is to so-called intra-enterprise doctrine.[109] According to this doctrine, agreements between a parent company and its wholly controlled subsidiaries fall outside the scope of Article 81(1).[110] Instead, the behaviour of the concern, formed by the parent and subsidiaries, may constitute abuse of a dominant position.[111]

It is certainly possible that the intra-enterprise doctrine is applied to an agreement between a parent company and a subsidiary on environmental aspects.[112] However, as the application of this doctrine is limited to Article 81, the implications of such an application will be looked at below in the section devoted to Article 81(1).[113]

[107] Case C-41/90, *Höfner & Elser* v. *Macrotron* (Höfner & Elser), [1991] ECR I-1979, para. 21.

[108] It would rather seem to be connected to the element of Article 81(1) that there be an 'agreement *between* undertakings'.

[109] Ritter, Braun & Rawlinson 2000, p. 42 *et seq.*

[110] *E.g.* Case T-102/92, *Viho Europe BV* v. *Commission*, [1995] ECR II-17, confirmed by Case C-73/95 P, *Viho Europe BV* v. *Commission*, [1996] ECR I-5457.

[111] Case C-73/95 P, *Viho Europe BV* v. *Commission*, [1996] ECR I-5457, para. 17.

[112] For example an instruction by a parent of a subsidiary to take care of the collection and recycling of its products when they reach their end of life.

[113] *Infra*, paragraphs 8.3-8.6.

### 7.4.3 The exception for non-economic activities

#### 7.4.3.1 General remarks

The Court's case law with regard to the concept of an undertaking also involves a slowly but certainly growing body of case law on the – still somewhat undefined – exceptions to this concept. Particularly in the field of (semi) public enterprises have these exceptions been developed. Competition law in this area of the economy is governed mainly by Article 86 EC. This case law has had, essentially, two effects. Firstly, certain market activities by public institutions may fall within the ambit of the competition rules. Secondly, certain activities undertaken by company-like entities are taken outside the scope of the competition rules.[114] For the purpose of this research, the second type of effect is the most interesting and we will therefore concentrate on this effect.

As we have seen, the crucial question is whether an activity can be considered 'economic'. In *AAMS*, the Court already concluded that[115]

*'any activity consisting of offering goods and services on a given market is an economic activity'.*

A further hint that may help us to determine whether or not an activity is economic was given in *Höfner & Elser.* In this case it held that the activity concerned, employment procurement, was indeed economic because[116]

*'Employment procurement has not always been, and is* NOT NECESSARILY, *carried out by public entities.' [Emphasis added]*

This approach forces us to consider *why* certain activities are necessarily carried out by public entities. Economically speaking the distinction between economic and non-economic activities comes down to an appraisal of the results of those activities. Whenever an activity yields general or diffuse (non excludable) as opposed to specific benefits, it is unlikely to be taken on by an entity subject to the laws of the market economy.[117] These diffuse results will be difficult to

---

[114] See, as regards the first type, *e.g.* Case 118/85, *Commission* v. *Italy*, (AAMS), [1987] ECR 2599 and (as an exception to the general rule concerning the first type) Case T-319/99, *Federación Nacional de Empresas de Instrumentación Científica, Médica, Técnica y Dental (FENIN)* v. *Commission* (FENIN), judgment of 4 March 2003, n.y.r. and, as regards the second type, *e.g.*, Case C-343/95, *Diego Calí* v. *Servizi Ecologici Porto di Genova* (Diego Calí), [1997] ECR I-1547.

[115] Case 118/85, *AAMS*, [1987] ECR 2599, para. 7.

[116] Case C-41/90, *Höfner & Elser*, [1991] ECR I-1979, para. 22.

[117] See further with respect to the distinction between diffuse and specific activities: Buendia Sierra 1999, p. 48 *et seq.*

quantify (if they are recognised to exist at all) and as a result the possibility of a remuneration and therewith the possibility of an economic relation between the provider and receiver of this benefit disappears.

This reasoning has been applied by the Court in two different settings.[118] Firstly in those cases that concerned the exercise of a power that is typically one of a public authority. These cases may be summarised as involving a 'state prerogatives test' (the *Diego Calì* and *SAT Fluggesellschaft* cases[119]). Secondly in those cases where an activity involved, essentially, such a high degree of solidarity that it would not be performed by an entity subject to the market economy rules (*Poucet & Pistre, FFSA, Albany* and *Pavlov* cases[120]). Accordingly, this test will be referred to as the 'market economy test'.[121]

How these two tests relate to one another is somewhat uncertain. It appears that the state prerogatives test is used as sort of a short cut in those cases where the Court does not have any doubts as to the non-economic nature of an activity. Where there is no *prima facie* evidence of the non-economic nature, the court appears to use the market economy test.[122] The relationship between these tests is further complicated as a result two further problems. Firstly, the market economy test used by the Court in determining whether or not an entity engaged in a particular activity is an undertaking closely resembles and appears to be connected to the test applied by the Court within the application of Article 86(2) EC. Secondly, connected with this problem, certain scholars opine that

---

[118] *Cf.* Loozen 1999, p. 274-285, at p. 280, who speaks of a 'two track approach' and Louri 2002, who at p. 169 characterises the exception pursuant to the market economy test as a new category that is to be distinguished from the exception that is governed by the state prerogatives test.

[119] Respectively Case C-343/95, *Diego Calí*, [1997] ECR I-1547 and Case C-364/92, *SAT Fluggesellschaft* v. *Eurocontrol* (SAT Fluggesellschaft), [1994] ECR I-43.

[120] Respectively, Joined Cases C-159/91, *Christian Poucet* v. *Assurances Générales de France and Caisse Mutuelle Régionale du Languedoc-Roussillon* and C-160/91, *Daniel Pistre* v. *Caisse Autonome Nationale de Compensation de l' Assurance Vieillesse des Artisans* (Poucet & Pistre ), [1993] ECR I-637, Case C-244/94, *Fédération Française des Sociétés d' Assurance et al.* v. *Ministère de l'Agriculture et de la Pêche* (FFSA), [1995] ECR I-4013, Case C-67/97, *Albany International* v. *Stichting Bedrijfspensioenfonds Textielindustrie* (Albany), [1999] ECR 751 and joined Cases C-180-184/98, *P. Pavlov et al.* v. *Stichting Pensioenfonds Medische Specialisten* (Pavlov), [2000] ECR I-6451.

[121] The reader well versed in the ways of EC competition law and notably the state aid provisions will recognise the similarity to the test used by the Commission and Court in relation to investments. This test is referred to as '(private) market economy investor principle'. *E.g* Joined Cases T-129/95, T-2/96, T-97/96, *Neue Maxhütte Stahlwerke and Lech-Stahlwerke* v. *Commission* (Neue Maxhütte Stahlwerke), [1999] ECR II-17.

[122] The Commission's Communication on Services of general interest in Europe, OJ 2001 C 17/4, appears to classify the market economy test as a subsidiary test in relation to the state prerogatives test, paras. 28 and 29.

the market economy test should not be applied at all in determining the (non) economic nature of an activity.[123]

Below, we will first subject the state prerogatives test to closer scrutiny after which our attention will focus on the market economy test and the problems with regard to this test as they were noticed above.

#### 7.4.3.2 The state prerogatives test

As was mentioned above, the Court appears to use the state prerogatives test in cases where the non-economic nature of an activity is clear at first sight. This approach can be called a short cut because, on a more abstract level, the (more or less implicit) reasoning underlying the state prerogatives test appears to be the diffuse/specific benefits reasoning employed by the Court in the *Höfner & Elser.* Below we will take a closer look at the only two cases in which the Court used the state prerogatives test: the *SAT Fluggesellschaft* and *Diego Calì* case.

The *SAT Fluggesellschaft* case started when Eurocontrol demanded payment by SAT Fluggesellschaft of the so-called 'route charges'.[124] Eurocontrol is an international organisation that was made responsible for, *inter alia*, the control of air traffic over Europe. To finance its activities, Eurocontrol could demand route charges that, according to SAT Fluggesellschaft violated the Community's competition rules. After citing, among others, the *Höfner & Elser* case as authority for the functional concept of an undertaking in Community competition law, the Court comes to the following conclusion:[125]

*'Taken as a whole, Eurocontrol's activities, by their nature, their aim and the rules to which they are subject, are connected with the exercise of powers relating to the control and supervision of air space which are typically those of a public authority. They are not of an economic nature justifying the application of the Treaty rules of competition.'*

The Court reaches this conclusion by first pointing out the sovereignty that states have over the airspace above their territory after which it refers to the Convention establishing Eurocontrol as evidence of the delegation of part of this sovereignty.[126] In this respect the Court appears to attach particular weight to Eurocontrol's tasks and the fact that it may collect charges and has certain rights and 'powers of coercion'. Finally the Court reiterates the fact the Eurocontrol is

---

[123] *Cf.* Buendia Sierra 1999, p. 58 and Gyselen 2000, p. 439.

[124] Case C-364/92, *SAT Fluggesellschaft*, [1994] ECR I-43.

[125] *Ibid.* para. 30.

[126] *Ibid.* paras. 20-24.

financed by the Contracting States.[127] As Buendia Sierra has pointed out, these criteria are not very helpful in determining the reasons for the Court to consider this activity of a non-economic nature.[128] Rather more helpful would appear to be the reference by the Court to the fact that Eurocontrol is to ensure the territorial security of the Contracting States and the fact that Eurocontrol is to provide its services to any aircraft even where the owner has not paid the route charges. This boils down to the Court stating that Eurocontrol's service entails a general, diffuse benefit (air safety) for which adequate remuneration is not always possible and, in a certain sense, required.[129]

The second case in which the Court used the state prerogatives reasoning is the *Diego Calì* case.[130] This case concerned a dispute similar to that in the *SAT Fluggesellschaft* case. Again a company refused to pay charges levied by an entity on grounds that these were incompatible with Community competition law. Interestingly for the purposes of this research, the entity in the *Diego Calì* case, SEPG, was responsible for the protection of the environment in the Port of Genua. The Court's approach seems reminiscent of that in the *SAT Fluggesellschaft* case but is slightly more satisfying in that the Court does a somewhat better job of clarifying the reasoning underlying its state prerogatives 'short cut'.[131]

In paragraphs 19 and 20 the Court states that the dispute concerns the payment of levies for anti-pollution surveillance activities by SEPG without any actual pollution having taken place. The Court moves closer to its conclusion when it refers to the fact that the Order concerning SEPG's activities explicitly distinguishes between, on the one hand, the preventive surveillance at hand and, on the other hand, the intervention in cases where actual pollution had occurred. The Court concludes as follows:[132]

*'The anti-pollution surveillance for which SEPG was responsible in the oil port of Genoa is a task in the public interest which forms part of the essential functions of the state as regards protection of the environment in maritime areas.*

*Such surveillance is connected by its nature, its aim and the rules to which it is subject with the exercise of powers relating to the protection of the environment which are typically those of a public authority. It is not of an economic nature justifying the application of the Treaty rules on competition [...]'*

---

[127] *Ibid.* para. 26. Interestingly, the Court had ruled in *Höfner & Elser* that the legal status and method of financing were irrelevant in determining whether an activity is of an economic nature.

[128] Buendia Sierra 1999, p. 51.

[129] This charge was not related to, for example, the safety record of a specific aircraft.

[130] Case C-343/95, *Diego Calì*, [1997] ECR I-1547.

[131] See, however, Buendia Sierra 1999 who, at p. 52, considers the lack of reasoning 'deplorable'.

[132] Case C-343/95, *Diego Calì*, [1997] ECR I-1547, paras. 22 and 23.

As regards the levying of the charges by SEPG, the Court considers this to be an integral part of its surveillance activities.[133] The Court's reasoning shows, much less implicitly than in the *SAT Fluggesellschaft* case, that the activities concerned (preventive surveillance) involved diffuse benefits only for which no remuneration would be possible. As can be expected, we will come back to this case in the paragraph below when we will examine the role played by environmental concerns in determining the scope of the concept of an undertaking.

#### 7.4.3.3 The market economy test

Where the exercise of state prerogatives is out of the question because, for example, there is competition on the market, the Court appears to use the market economy test. In the *Poucet & Pistre, FFSA, Albany*[134] and *Pavlov* cases this involved a complex appreciation of several criteria resulting in a rather diverse and heterogeneous concept of undertaking.[135] This test has to this date only been applied in the cases involving entities active in the field of social security. Its application is, however, not necessarily confined to this area alone, as closer scrutiny of these cases will show.

All of the cases mentioned above show a remarkable resemblance as to the facts underlying them. In all of them, the dispute started when an individual refused to pay contributions to a social security scheme on the grounds that this entity violated Community competition rules. As the Court's reasoning in the *Albany* and *Pavlov* cases provides us with a good summary of the earlier case law (*i.e.* the *Poucet & Pistre* and *FFSA* cases),[136] our attention will focus on the *Pavlov* case.[137]

The Court started out by summarising its judgment in *Poucet & Pistre* and in particular pointing out the role that solidarity had played in that case. The following factors were considered to be relevant by the Court:

- The benefits were uniform despite the fact that the contributions were proportional to income,
- Pensions were financed by the active workers,

---

[133] *Ibid.* para. 24.

[134] *Albany* is in fact only one of three nearly identical Cases. The other two were joined Cases C-115-117/97, *Brentjens' Handelsonderneming* v. *Stichting Bedrijfspensioenfonds voor de handel in bouwmaterialen*, [1999] ECR I-6025 and Case C-219/97, *Maatschappij Drijvende Bokken* v. *Stichting Pensioenfonds voor de vervoer- en havenbedrijven*, [1999] ECR I-6121.

[135] *Cf.* Berg 2000, p. 172.

[136] Perhaps Advocate General Jacobs did an even better job at providing an overview, Opinion of the A-G, paras. 306-348.

[137] Joined Cases C-180/98 to 184/98, *Pavlov*, [2000] ECR I-6451.

- Pensions were not dependent on the contributions and
- Funds with a surplus helped finance funds with shortages.[138]

It then reiterated its judgment in the *FFSA* case where the degree of solidarity was considered insufficient to remove the entity's activities from the scope of the competition rules on the following grounds:
- Membership to the scheme was optional,
- The scheme functioned according to the capitalisation principle,
- Benefits depended on contributions and the performance of investments by the scheme.

The scheme's social objective, non-profit making nature, limited solidarity requirements and the fact that, in its investment policy, the scheme was subject to certain restrictions were insufficient for this to be otherwise.

The Court's approach in *Pavlov* is quite comparable to that in the *Albany* case. The Court lists the following facts as grounds for considering that the schemes at hand in *Pavlov* and *Albany* were engaged in an economic activity:
- The schemes themselves determined the contributions,
- The scheme functioned according to the capitalisation principle and
- Membership was optional.

In sum, the case law of the Court with regard to solidarity as ground for qualifying an activity as non-economic shows that the bar is high indeed. Any, if not the slightest, presence of market mechanisms (*i.e.* optional membership and operation according to the capitalisation principle) is sufficient for the Court to conclude that activity is at least in principle governed by the competition rules. Apparently, this is otherwise only in those cases where there is unmitigated solidarity. Does this fit in well with the diffuse/specific benefits reasoning that was identified above as underlying the Court's approach? The answer has to be in the negative as these social security schemes do provide a specific benefit. That, in an individual case, this benefit is to a greater of lesser extent unrelated to the specific, individual, contributions cannot detract from this. Only if one were to consider income redistribution (which is, in essence, the result of solidarity) as the benefit of the scheme, would this be different as redistribution is indeed a diffuse benefit.[139] As a result, the solidarity considerations would fit in better in the test of Article 86(2) as the Court explicitly stated in the *Albany* case.[140]

[138] *Ibid.* para. 109.

[139] *Cf.* Gyselen 2000, p. 439 *et seq.*, Berg 2000, p. 172 and Buendia Sierra 1999, p. 58.

[140] Case C-67/97, *Albany*, [1999] ECR I-5751, para. 86. The Court seems to have recognised this already in the *FFSA* Case, C-244/94, *FFSA*, [1995] ECR I-4013, para. 20. See further Case T-319/99, *FENIN*, judgment of 4 March 2003, n.y.r., where at paras. 14 *et seq.* these arguments are repeated.

### 7.4.4 The role of environmental concerns

The overview of the case law on the concept of an undertaking in EC competition law has shown that in essence both exceptions involve similar reasoning. As the *Diego Calì* case has furthermore made clear, an application of this diffuse/specific-benefits reasoning in an environmental context seems fairly obvious. Environmental benefits are, by their very nature, diffuse benefits even when they may occasionally also involve a specific benefit for an individual. The diffuse character is, however, limited to certain environmental activities or services. The *Diego Calì* case has provided us with an example of such a service and may also serve to indicate the limits to the activities that can be considered to yield sufficiently diffuse benefits. In this regard it is important to consider that, in itself, the concept of a benefit already involves a weighing of costs and results.[141] Therefore, the mere fact that (clearly quantifiable) costs are involved (in that, for example a fee is to be paid) does not preclude the existence of a diffuse benefit.[142] Of course, determining exactly how diffuse a benefit should be in order for the provision of this benefit no longer to constitute an economic activity is far from clear. In this respect the borders of this doctrine are uncertain.

The application of the diffuse/specific-benefits reasoning to activities in the social sphere is subject to the same uncertainty. A number of relevant factors can be distilled from the Court's case law. However, the weight to be accorded to these factors is unclear.

On a general level, however, the room for the non-economic activities doctrine appears to be shrinking. The increased internalisation of environmental costs will ultimately result in the conclusion that the environment no longer represents a non-economic sphere of activity. As we have seen above, the Court is generally more reluctant to apply the diffuse benefits reasoning and openly links this reasoning to the possibility of an exception pursuant to Article 86(2) EC.[143] The most important message is therefore be that, notwithstanding the Court's simple and straightforward reasoning with regard to the state prerogatives exception in *Diego Calì*, the border between economic and non-economic activities is on the move. Moreover, it appears to be moving towards a more narrowly defined exception for non-economic activities as the market mechanism is applied to more sectors of the economy.

---

141 In this regard it may actually be better to speak of a *positive net result*.

142 *Cf.* Case C-343/95, *Diego Calì*, [1997] ECR I-1547, para. 24.

143 See, *e.g.* Case C-67/96, *Albany*, [1999] ECR I-5751, para. 86.

### 7.5 Effect on intra-community trade

EC competition law applies only when the distortion or restriction of competition has an effect on trade between the member states.[144] The Court has given this element a very wide meaning in two early cases.[145]

*'In this connexion, what is particularly important is whether the agreement is capable of constituting a threat, either direct or indirect, actual or potential, to freedom of trade between member states in a manner which might harm the attainment of the objectives of a single market between states'*

The broad concept given in these cases seems like a precursor to the so-called *Dassonvile*-formula with regard to the free movement of goods.[146] In a later case the Court ruled that Community competition law applied only where the trade between member states is appreciably affected, thereby effectively introducing a *de minimis* rule.[147] This appreciability-criterion applies to the effect on the intra-Community trade as well as to the restriction of competition. The notion of appreciability in connection with the restriction of competition has received some attention above and will be further dealt with below.[148] The result of a restriction of competition not affecting intra-Community trade is that European competition law doesn't apply but national competition laws may. Accordingly, the criterion that the restriction should have an effect on intra-community trade can be described as a jurisdictional criterion. Put differently, it may be considered to indicate the scope *ratione jurisdictionae.*

The effects of this jurisdictional clause are, in essence, twofold. It may, firstly, serve to allow or to rule out the application of Community competition law to a restriction of competition involving enterprises established in part of the common market. This may be deemed the intraterritorial jurisdictional effect. Secondly, it may determine the extraterritorial application of the Community competition rules to restrictions of competition involving enterprises from outside the common market that nevertheless have an effect within the common market.[149] Similarly, it may also rule out the application of the Community

---

[144] Joined Cases 56, 58/64, *Consten & Grundig*, [1966] ECR 429. *Cf.* Ritter, Braun & Rawlinson 2000, p. 46.

[145] Most importantly joined Cases 56, 58/64, *Consten & Grundig*, [1966] ECR 429 and Case 56/65, *La Technique Minière* v. *Maschinenbau Ulm* (LTM v. MBU), [1966] ECR 235.

[146] Case 8/74, *Procureur du Roi* v. *Benoît and Gustave Dassonville* (Dassonville), [1974] ECR 837.

[147] ECJ, joined Cases C-215 and C-216/96, *Bagnasco*, [1999] ECR I-135, para. 47 *et seq.*

[148] *Infra*, paragraph 8.4 of this chapter.

[149] This is referred to as the 'effects doctrine' or 'implementation doctrine'. It is considered to have been accepted by the European Court of Justice in the *Woodpulp* case, Joined Cases 89, 104, 114, 116, 117 and 125 to 129/85, *A. Ahlström Osakeyhtiö and others* v. *Commission* [1988] ECR 5193, *cf.* Ritter, Braun & Rawlinson 2000, p. 61, Bellamy & Child 2001, p. 142.

competition rules to restrictions of competition involving European firms yet having an effect on the competition in a non-Community market. With regard to the extraterritorial effect it needs to be noted that this criterion hinges not only on the effect on intra-community trade but also on the effect on 'competition within the common market'. Below, the role and influence of environmental concerns on these two jurisdictional effects will be examined.

### 7.5.1 Environmental concerns and the jurisdictional clause

Two jurisdictional effects have been identified above. Firstly, it may rule out the application of Community competition law to restrictions that take place within the Community. Secondly, it may enable the extraterritorial application of Community competition law. With regard to the first, intraterritorial, effect the most interesting situation is that where the application of Community competition law is ruled out because of the lack of effect on intra-community trade. In general this could occur in two situations. Firstly, there may be a transboundary restriction of competition (*i.e.* involving entities in two member states) that is, however, of minor importance. Secondly, the restriction of competition could have no transboundary element at all (*i.e.* taking place within one member state) whilst having no or only a very remote connection to intra-community trade.

Moreover, and also on a general level, the test applied by the Commission and Court in determining whether or not intra-community trade is appreciably affected has both a quantitative and a qualitative aspect. The Commission has adopted a primarily quantitative approach to this appreciability criterion. In its notice on agreements of minor importance, the Commission primarily relies on the parties' market shares.[150] The Court refers, apart from the market share, in general to the need to take into account the economic reality of a case.[151] In practice, this means that the Court will take into account the nature of the restriction of competition. In this respect, there could be an opening for environmental concerns. An environmentally inspired restriction of competition involving a transboundary element may be considered not to appreciably affect intra-community trade because the environmental aspects concerned are themselves of limited importance. A possible example of such a situation could

[150] Commission Notice on agreements of minor importance which do not fall within the meaning of Article 85(1) of the Treaty establishing the European Community Commission Notice on agreements of minor importance which do not fall within the meaning of Article 85(1) (*De Minimis* Notice), OJ 2000 C 368/13.

[151] Case C-306/96, *Javico* v. *Yves Saint Laurent Parfurms*, [1998] ECR I-1983, para. 17 and Case 73/74, *Groupement des Fabricants de papiers peints de Belgique et al.* v. *Commission* (Belgian Wallpaper), [1975] ECR 1491, para. 27.

be an agreement between firms in different member states to reduce certain emissions. Provided that such an agreement remains confined to these environmental aspects, no effect on intra-community trade is likely.

As regards the situation where the restriction of competition has no transboundary element, the Courts' case law clearly indicates the application of Community competition law is not ruled out merely because the restriction of competition involves only parties in one member state.[152] However, in such cases there will need to be a connection between the restriction of competition and intra-community trade.[153] This connection can be present because the restriction directly concerns intra-community trade (*e.g.* discrimination of imports)[154] or because the restriction covers the entire territory of a member state and thus 'by its very nature has the effect of reinforcing the compartmentalisation of markets on a national basis'[155] Again, a role for environmental concerns seems possible. An agreement between firms in one member state on environmental matters may very well lack any influence on intra-community trade. This appears to have happened in the *Stibat* case.[156] In this case, an agreement on the take back and recycling of waste batteries involving over 90 per cent of the industry in the Netherlands was considered by the Commission not to affect intra-community trade. The Commission thus issued a comfort letter in which it indicated that intra-community trade was not affected.[157] Apparently, the fact that the market for batteries is in fact Community-wide (a large percentage of batteries is imported from other member states) together with the fact that this agreement involved some far-going restrictions of competition, did not stand in the way of a finding that intra-community trade was not affected. This approach may be contrasted with the stance taken by the Commission in the *VOTOB* case.[158] *VOTOB* concerned an environmental agreement between the independent[159] Dutch firms active on the market for the storage of chemicals. The agreement

[152] Case 8/72, *VCH*, [1972] ECR 977, para 26 *et seq.*

[153] Ritter, Braun and Rawlinson refer to a 'nexus' in this respect, Ritter, Braun & Rawlinson 2000, p. 53 *et seq.*

[154] Commission Decision 82/371, *NAVEWA-ANSEAU*, OJ 1982 L 167/39, upheld by the ECJ in joined Cases 96-102, 104, 105, 108 and 110/82, *IAZ*, [1983] ECR 3369.

[155] Case 8/72, *VCH*, [1972] ECR 977, para 29.

[156] *NMa* decision of 18 December 1998 in Case 51, *Stibat* and decision of 31 May 1999 on administrative appeal in Case 51, *Stibat*. See further, *infra* paragraph 16.5.2

[157] In the original decision of the *NMa*, thus was not entirely clear. In the decision on administrative appeal, however, it became clear that the Commission had based the negative clearance (which is a decision stating that Article 81(1) is not applicable) on the absence of an effect on intra-community trade, *NMa* decision of 31 May 1999 in Case 51, *Stibat*, para. 51.

[158] Commission XXIInd. Competition Report (1992), paras. 177-186. See further, *infra* paragraph 8.7.4.2.

[159] *I.e.* unconnected to any chemical company.

and the purely national scope of the *VOTOB* case are in many respects comparable to those in the *Stibat* case. The change on the part of the Commission in this respect can probably be attributed to the fact that at the time of the *Stibat* case, the Netherlands had an active competition authority whereas the competition laws in place during the *VOTOB* case were applied at best only infrequently, if at all.[160] This signals the only marginal role for environmental (or any other) concerns in this respect. Even if environmental concerns result in the exclusion of a certain restriction from the scope of the Community competition rules, national competition laws may still apply.

This is equally true for the extraterritorial effect of the jurisdictional clause. As was mentioned above, the extraterritorial effect depends not only on whether or not intra-community trade is affected but also on whether or not competition within the common market is restricted. An agreement between non-Community enterprises having an effect on competition within the common market will fall within the scope of the Community's competition rules. This may be called the positive extraterritorial effect. *Vice versa*, the negative extraterritorial effect occurs where Community competition law will not govern restrictions between firms based in the Community having an effect outside the common market. However, such restrictions may very well fall within the ambit of the competition laws of the country where the agreement has its effect.

The positive extraterritorial effect of the Community competition laws is based purely on the *effect* on *competition* of a certain restriction. As such, a role for environmental concerns is certainly conceivable. It may, for example, be considered that an environmental agreement between foreign car manufacturers involving vehicles destined for, *inter alia*, Europe has a very small or no effect on competition on the common market because of the inappreciability of the effects on competition.[161]

The negative effect is based on the absence of an effect on competition within the common market but is limited by the requirement that there may be no effect on intra-community trade.[162] In this respect, the same observations that have been made above with regard to the intraterritorial effects may be repeated.

---

[160] See further *infra* paragraph 8.7.4.2

[161] See, for such an environmental agreement the agreement on the reduction of carbondioxde emissions from cars by the Japanese Auto Manufacturers Association (JAMA) and the Korean Auto Manufacturers Association (KAMA), press release IP/00/381.

[162] Case 174/84, *Bulk Oil* v. *Sun*, [1986] ECR 559, para. 44 and Case C-306/96, *Javico* v. *Yves Saint Laurent Parfurms*, [1998] ECR I-1983, para. 29.

## 7.6 Environmental concerns and the scope of the competition rules

The above paragraphs show that the scope of the Community's competition rules can be characterised as rather wide. At the same time, it is inherently limited to the economic arena thus excluding many areas that are considered to be non-economic. Moreover, environmental considerations have been used and probably could be used to take certain entities and activities outside the scope of the competition provisions. However, on the basis of the research conducted above, it is also fair to assume that the mere presence of environmental aspects does not suffice in this respect. This begs the question what the role of environmental concerns in this respect should be. Should, for example, the presence of environmental concerns lead to the inapplicability of the competition rules? Moreover, could the integration principle, when applied according to the model of integration, lead to this result?

From the perspective of the model of integration developed in Part One, the answer must be in the negative. It was seen that competition and environmental protection could operate in a mutually reinforcing relation. It is precisely this relation that will with the greatest certainty lead to both better environmental protection and economic growth, in short: sustainable development. As we have seen, Article 6 is geared toward achieving sustainable development and since the creation of an exception for environmental concerns is unlikely to lead to such sustainable development – in fact it may very well be counterproductive in this respect – Article 6 cannot have this effect.

Simply placing all environmental restrictions or distortions of competition outside the scope of competition law cannot therefore be the result of Article 6 EC when it is applied in accordance with the model of integration.

The fact that certain areas of the economy and certain activities, including environmental ones – see *Diego Calì* –, have been placed outside the scope of the competition provisions is therefore not welcomed. Provided, however, that it is recognised that the boundaries of these exceptions may vary with time and place, the harm done in terms of the bypassing of chances to achieve a competition for the environment is limited. The Court's stout, straightforward and slightly legalistic reasoning in *Diego Calì* should not be taken as written in stone in this respect. In this connection it may be interesting to note that the Court appears to have become more reluctant to declare certain activities outside the scope of the competition provisions altogether.[163] Rather, the Court addresses

---

[163] *Cf.* Case 309/99, *Wouters*, [2002] ECR I-1577, where the Court declined to exclude a decision from an association representing the members of the bar from the scope of the concept 'decision by associations of undertakings' within the meaning of Article 81 EC (paras. 45-71). See also Case C-475/99, *Ambulanz Glöckner* v. *Landkreis Südwestpfalz* (Ambulanz Glöckner), [2001] ECR I-8089 where medical aid organisations offering emergency and patient transport services were considered to be 'undertakings', paras. 19-22.

the tensions that arise from the unmitigated application of the competition rules in these situations with the help of much more fine-tuned instruments such as Article 86(2) EC.[164]

[164] *Cf.* Case C-67/96, *Albany*, [1999] ECR I-5751, para. 86.

CHAPTER 8

# Article 81

## 8.1 Introduction

Article 81 has been the subject of more decisions and judgments than any other substantive competition provision. This should not come as a surprise given the extremely wide-ranging wording of the provision. In many respects it can be called the mainstay of Community competition law. Article 81 reads as follows:

1) The following shall be prohibited as incompatible with the common market: all agreements between undertakings, decisions by associations of undertakings and concerted practices which may affect trade between Member States and which have as their object or effect the prevention, restriction or distortion of competition with in the common market, and in particular those which:
   a) directly or indirectly fix purchase or selling prices or any other trading conditions;
   b) limit or control production, markets, technical development or investment;
   c) share markets or sources of supply;
   d) apply dissimilar conditions to equivalent transactions with other trading parties, thereby placing them at a competitive disadvantage;
   e) make the conclusion of contracts subject to acceptance by the other parties of supplementary obligations which, by their nature or according to commercial usage, have no connection with the subject of such contracts.
2) Any agreements or decisions prohibited pursuant to this Article shall be automatically void.
3) The provisions of paragraph 1 may, however, be declared inapplicable in the case of:
   - any agreement or category of agreements between undertakings;
   - any decision or category of decisions by associations of undertakings;
   - any concerted practice or category of concerted practices,

   which contributes to improving the production or distribution of goods or to promoting technical or economic progress, while allowing consumers a fair share of the resulting benefit, and which does not:
   a) impose on the undertakings concerned restrictions which are not indispensable to the attainment of these objectives;
   b) afford such undertakings the possibility of eliminating competition in respect of a substantial part of the products in question.

As a professor of competition law once said: 'Article 81 (and 82) should be treated as if they are provisions of criminal law; all elements must be proved before anyone can be found guilty of infringing them'. In this paragraph we will therefore examine closely all the elements that Article 81 is made up off and see what role environmental concerns may play. Article 81 quickly reveals its essentially bifurcated structure: it consists of a broadly formulated prohibition of agreements that restrict competition whereas an exemption may be granted from such a prohibition. This structure has resulted in a number of interesting points with regard to this provision. For one, the direct effect of the prohibition together with the Commission's exclusive right to grant exemptions has had an extensive influence on Article 81's application. The recently adopted Regulation No. 1/2003, which provides for the direct applicability of Article 81(3) EC, will change this to a large extent.[1]

## 8.2 The Albany exception ratione materiae

### 8.2.1 Introduction

In a number of recent cases, the Court of Justice has created a special exception to the scope of Article 81 for collectively negotiated social agreements. Because this exception exists only with regard to Article 81, it has not been treated as a general limit to the scope of the competition provisions. For the moment, this exception exists only in the social context. However, as the application of comparable reasoning outside the context of social relations cannot be ruled out, we will have a more detailed look at this exception. Below, we will first analyse the *Albany* exception. After that, the possibilities for the application of the exception in an environmental context will be examined.

### 8.2.2 An analysis of the *Albany* exception

In the *Albany* case the Court was asked to rule on the compatibility with the useful effect rule (Article 3(1) (g) in connection with Article 10 in connection with Article 81 EC) of the decision declaring collectively bargained agreements concerning a sectoral pension scheme generally binding.[2] For such a decision declaring an agreement generally binding to be contrary to Community competition law, it needs first to be established that the 'underlying' collective agreement itself violates Article 81. It was through this 'detour' that the Court thus had to consider whether Article 81 precluded collectively negotiated agreements in the social sphere.

---

[1] See, for further information on the possible effects of Regulation 1/2003, *infra* paragraph 8.9.

[2] Case C-67/96, *Albany*, [1999] ECR I-5751, joined Cases C-115/97, C-116/97 and C-117/97, *Brentjens' Handelsonderneming* v. *Stichting Bedrijfspensioenfonds voor de handel in bouwmaterialen*, [1999] ECR I-6025 and Case C-219/97, *Maatschappij Drijvende Bokken* v. *Stichting Pensioenfonds voor de Vervoer- en Havenbedrijven*, [1999] ECR I-6121. As the judgments of the Court in these three Cases are nearly identical we will only refer to the *Albany* Case.

The Court started out by analysing the Treaty provisions with regard to such agreements. Thus, it cited Article 81(1).[3] Next, it turned its attention to the Community's policies and objectives. In this connection, it observed that the Community has not only a policy to ensure that competition in the internal market is not distorted (Article 3(1)(g) EC) but also a 'policy in the social sphere' (Article 3(1)(l) EC).[4] Moreover, the Court cited the Community's tasks as including the promotion of 'a harmonious and balanced development of economic activities' and 'a high level of employment and of social protection' (Article 2 EC). Furthermore, the Court observed the more precise tasks of the Community and Commission in encouraging collective bargaining (Articles 136-145 EC and the Agreement on social policy[5]).

On the basis of this sketch of the Treaty context, the Court used the following reasoning to justify its exception:[6]

*'It is beyond question that certain restrictions of competition are inherent in collective agreements between organisations representing employers and workers. However, the social policy objectives pursued by such agreements would be seriously undermined if management and labour were subject to Article 85(1) [now Article 81(1)] of the Treaty when seeking jointly to adopt measures to improve conditions of work and employment.*

*It therefore follows from an interpretation of the provisions of the Treaty as a whole which is both effective and consistent that agreements concluded in the context of collective negotiations between management and labour in pursuit of such objectives must, by virtue of their nature and purpose, be regarded as falling outside the scope of Article 85(1) [now Article 81(1)] of the Treaty.'*

The conflict between the two sets of Treaty principles is solved with the help of contextual, systematic interpretation of the Treaty as a whole.[7] This approach shows resemblance with the '*praktischer Konkordanz*' principle employed in German (constitutional) law for solving conflicts.[8] However, the Court's approach has also been classified as being 'teleological'.[9] It is submitted that the qualification of this solution as teleological ignores the fact that it does not seek to attain some sort of useful effect that is in accordance with a given objective.[10]

---

3 Case C-67/96, *Albany*, [1999] ECR I-5751, para. 53.

4 *Ibid.*, para. 54.

5 OJ 1992 C 191/91.

6 Case C-67/96, *Albany*, [1999] ECR I-5751, paras 59, 60.

7 *Cf.* The opinion of Advocate General Jacobs in Case C-67/96, *Albany*, [1999] ECR I-5751, para. 177. See also: Bredimas 1978, p. 73.

8 Hesse 1984, p. 27.

9 Loozen 1999, p. 278, Berg 2000, p. 171, Koenig & Sander 2000, p. 979.

10 *Cf.* Schermers & Waelbroeck 1992, p. 18 *et seq.*,

On the contrary, the solution employed by the Court in the *Albany* case follows from the recognition that there is not one objective but rather that there are two potentially colliding objectives in the Treaty.

In any case, the Court formulated a double test that needs to be satisfied for the exception to apply: both the nature and purpose of the agreement should warrant an exception. The Court then went on to consider whether the nature and purpose of the agreement justified the application of this exception in this particular instance. In determining whether the nature of the agreement justified the application of the exception, the Court concentrated on the form and the formal modalities of the agreement. It observed that it was concluded in the form of a collective agreement and as the result of collective bargaining. As regards the purpose, the Court concluded that the agreement contributed directly to the improvement of one of the working conditions. Consequently, the Court considered this agreement to fall outside the scope of Article 81(1). In doing so, the Court largely followed Advocate General Jacobs' opinion. However, the Court applied a slightly different test from that advocated by Jacobs. Apart from the necessity of defining the nature and purpose, the advocate general considered that, as a third test, the exception should also be limited to the core subjects of collective bargaining and conditional on the fact that third parties or markets are not directly affected.[11] The second part of this third criterion can be described as requiring a minimum distance from the market.[12] Whereas the first part of this extra test (limitation to the core subjects) can be said to be inherent or implicit in the Court's test as regards the purpose of the agreement, the 'market proximity test' has, at least not explicitly, been applied by the Court.

Following *Albany*, the precise extent of the exception was still rather uncertain.[13] In this respect, the status of the third test proposed by the advocate general is only one uncertainty. Two further cases have since then shed some light on the scope of the *Albany* exception. In the *Pavlov* case, the Court was asked whether an agreement concerning an occupational pension scheme could qualify for an '*Albany* exception'.[14] Although comparable to a sectoral pension fund as regards, *inter alia*, its social objectives and the fact that it was concluded following collective bargaining, an occupational pension fund is slightly different. In fact, it was sufficiently different for the Court to conclude that the *Albany* exception did not apply. The Court repeated its *Albany* case law to conclude that both the nature and the purpose of the agreement would have to justify the application of the exception.[15] The outcome was that, even though the

---

11 Opinion in Case C-67/96, *Albany*, [1999] ECR I-5751, para. 193.

12 *Cf.* Loozen 1999, p. 278

13 See further: Van den Bergh & Camesasca 2000, p. 501.

14 Joined Cases C-180/98 to 184/98, *Pavlov*, [2000] ECR I-6451.

15 *Ibid.*, para. 67.

purpose of the agreement was to improve an element of the working conditions, the agreement was not concluded in the context of collective bargaining.[16] The Court reiterated the importance of the 'nature-test' by recalling the provisions on which it had in the first place (partly) based the *Albany* exception.[17] These contain no provisions encouraging the conclusion of collective agreements by members of the liberal professions. This lends support to the thesis that the *Albany* exception is of a 'constitutional' as opposed to 'competition law' nature. With this it is meant that the exception created by the Court is not inherent in competition law *in se* but rather follows, as we have also argued above, from the constitutional and holistic interpretation of the Treaty. The *Albany* exception could only be justified on the ground that the Treaty encourages the conclusion of collective agreements while at the same time it also contained rules that may very well preclude the conclusion of such agreements.

Another case shedding further light on the nature and extent of the *Albany* exception was the *Van der Woude* case.[18] The collective agreement at issue in this case concerned a health care insurance scheme. This, according to the Court, means that the purpose of the agreement is to improve working conditions thus bringing it within the scope of the *Albany* exception.[19] Furthermore, Van der Woude argued that the *Albany* exception could not apply by virtue of the fact that the agreement directly influenced third parties.[20] This, of course, reminds us of the third criterion (the market proximity test) proposed by Advocate General Jacobs in the *Albany* case. The Court pays no explicit attention to the market proximity test. Rather, it appears to consider this issue implicitly when it states that the mere fact that the health insurance scheme was subcontracted cannot exclude the application of the exception.[21] It would thus seem possible that a collective social agreement in which the market aspects are more pertinent than the social aspects would fall outside the scope of the *Albany* exception by virtue of its non-social purpose. With the limits of the *Albany* exception somewhat clearer, it is now time to turn to the possibilities that the *Albany* exception leaves for environmental agreements.

### 8.2.3 Environmental concerns and the *Albany* exception

As has been shown in the introduction, the *Albany* exception is considered to be of interest in the environmental sphere as well.[22] In this

---

16 *Ibid.*, para. 68.

17 *Ibid.*, para. 69.

18 Case C-222/98, *H. Van der Woude / Stichting Beatrixoord* (Van der Woude), [2000] ECR I-7111.

19 *Ibid.*, para. 25.

20 *Ibid.*, para. 20.

21 *Ibid.*, para. 26. However, see Loozen 2000, p. 303, who appears to argue that the Court doesn't apply the market proximity criterion at all.

22 *Supra*, paragraph 8.2.

paragraph we will consider whether a widening of the scope of the *Albany* exception to include collective environmental agreements, is possible. In this respect two possibilities can be examined. Firstly, the possibility of applying the *Albany* exception to the situation where a collective agreement in the social sphere also contains clauses pertaining to environmental protection (paragraph 8.2.3.1).[23] Secondly, the possibility of applying the *Albany* exception outside the social sphere to environmental agreements (paragraph 8.2.3.2). These two possibilities differ in their conceptual relation to the *Albany* exception. The first option essentially concerns the conditions for the applicability of the exception (*i.e.* the social nature and purpose of the agreement) whereas the second option involves the constitutional foundations of the *Albany* exception.

#### 8.2.3.1 Collective social agreements concerning environmental aspects

As we have seen the scope of the *Albany* exception is limited to those agreements that have both a 'social' nature as well as purpose. As such one may wonder whether collective agreements in the social sphere that also concern some environmental aspects could benefit from the *Albany* exception. It is at this time that Advocate General Jacobs' third requirement, that the agreement be sufficiently far removed from the market and only concern the core subjects of collective negotiation, gains importance. The Court can be said to have taken the first part of this test on board in deciding that the purpose of the agreement is, together with its nature, decisive for the applicability of the *Albany* exception. Furthermore, with regard to determining the purpose of an agreement, *Van der Woude* shows us that the Court will consider the requirement concerning the purpose of an agreement to be fulfilled whenever the agreement contributes to the improvement of the working conditions. Taking into account the fact that, being an exception to a rule, the *Albany* exception is to be construed narrowly, it would appear improbable that environmental objectives are considered to contribute to the improvement of the working conditions. This would only be otherwise for that category of environmental concerns that directly concern the working conditions (*e.g.* a provision prescribing a reduction in the emissions of certain substances in industrial plants).[24] If a collective social agreement would include such provisions, then these provisions could probably benefit from the *Albany* exception. Environmental provisions in collectively negotiated social agreements that are further removed from the 'working floor' (such as *e.g.* a provision stating that only sustainably logged wood may

---

[23] See, to this effect, Franssen *et al.* 2000, p. 331.

[24] *Cf.* the reference in Article 95(4) and (5) EC to the 'working environment' as opposed to the 'environment' in general.

be used for new plant buildings[25]) would probably fall outside the scope of the *Albany* exception.

#### 8.2.3.2 Collective environmental agreements outside the social sphere

The second possible role for environmental concerns in connection with the *Albany* exception would be the creation of an exception by analogy, outside the sphere of social agreements, for collective environmental agreements.[26] To see whether such an exception alongside the *Albany* exception is possible, the constitutional foundations of the *Albany* exception need first to be further analysed. After that has been done it will be examined whether an exception for environmental agreements can thus be founded.

We have seen above that the *Albany* exception is of a constitutional nature. Its foundations lie in the fact that the EC Treaty contains two colliding sets of norms. When analysed, it becomes clear that this collision actually consists of two separate moments. Firstly, the Treaty dictates both social as well as competitive objectives and policies for the Community. Secondly, the Treaty prescribes that the Community actively encourages certain actions that may at the same time violate another Community policy. From the constitutional status or nature of the exception it may be deduced that both moments of collision need to be present within the Treaty itself. A conflict between two sets of norms of which only one has Treaty status would be resolved by means of the general rule that the Treaty has primacy over lower (secondary) Community legislation.[27] In such cases there simply is no conflict at all.

When we apply this analysis of the constitutional foundations of the *Albany* exception to the environmental context, the following picture emerges. The Community's objectives are enshrined in Article 2 EC. Reading this provision, it is very clear that the Community has a strong environmental objective as well. Article 2 prescribes that the Community's objectives shall, *inter alia*, include:

*'The community shall have as its task, by establishing a common market and an economic and monetary union and by implementing common policies or activities referred to in Articles 3 and 4, to promote throughout the Community a harmonious balanced and* SUSTAINABLE DEVELOPMENT *of economic activities, a high level of employment and of social protection, equality between men and women, sustainable and non-inflationary growth, a high degree of competitiveness and convergence*

---

[25] An example gleaned from Franssen *et al.* 2000.

[26] An example of such an agreement would be an environmental agreement between a very large part of the industry and the public authorities.

[27] Article 230, second paragraph, EC.

*of economic performance,* A HIGH LEVEL OF PROTECTION AND IMPROVEMENT OF THE QUALITY OF THE ENVIRONMENT, *the raising of the standard of living and quality of life, and economic and social cohesion and solidarity among Member States'. [Emphasis added]*

Furthermore, according to Article 3(1) (l) EC, the Community shall have 'a policy in the sphere of the environment'. The conclusion must therefore be that the Community has both a task as well as the means with regard to the protection of the environment. From the *Albany* case we know that the Community also has an objective as well as a policy with regard to the maintenance of competition. Whether the two sets of objectives and policies thus identified in Article 2 and 3 with regard to competition and environmental protection will collide, depends on the absence of a hierarchy between the two sets. It is presumed that there is no hierarchy between the various Community objectives and policies.[28] The text of Articles 2 and 3 does not indicate that such a hierarchical relation exists. Moreover, the *Albany* exception itself clearly shows that even if there is a hierarchical relation between the objectives and policies of the Treaty, there is no general primacy for the market integration objectives of the Community. In fact, the text of Article 2 may even point at a preference for environmental protection goals over competition objectives. Article 2 clearly lists environmental protection as one of the Community's objectives whereas one searches Article 2 in vain for a passage indicating that the maintenance of a certain degree of competition is a Community objective. On the contrary, Article 2 contains a number of objectives that are generally presumed to be best attained through effective competition.[29] Whatever may be of this, the conclusion must be that, for environmental agreements, the first moment leading to the collision is fulfilled.[30]

However, with regard to second moment, the case for an environmental exception *ratione materiae* for collectively negotiated environmental agreements appears less clear-cut. In *Albany* the Court bases the creation of the exception on a number of provisions in the EC Treaty and the Agreement on social policy. According to the Court these provisions instruct the Community and notably the Commission to actively encourage collective bargaining in the social field. The Treaty, or, for that matter, any protocol to it, contains no provisions that could be construed so as to encourage collective bargaining in the environmental sphere in a way that is comparable to the clauses that the Court referred to when it created the *Albany* exception. The best thing in this respect, with regard to environmental agreements, can be found in a number of pieces of second-

28 *Cf.* Bogdandy 2000, p. 15, rn. 64. However, Basedow argues in favor of the primacy of 'market integration goals' ('*Ziel der marktintegration*'), Basedow 1995, p. 56 *et seq.*

29 See, with regard to some of these objectives, Goyder 1998, p. 10.

30 *Cf.* Vedder 2001, p. 42 *et seq.*

ary legislation and some other instruments. Firstly, some directives explicitly provide for implementation through so-called environmental or voluntary agreements.[31] These, however, cannot be considered to actively encourage the conclusion of such agreements. Secondly, the Commission, Council and European Parliament have all stated in various documents that they recommend the use of environmental agreements. In, for example, the decision on the review of the Fifth Environmental Action Programme, the European Parliament and Council both agreed on encouraging voluntary agreements as an instrument of environmental policy.[32] This has returned in the Commission's proposal for the Sixth Environmental Action Programme.[33] Moreover, the Commission has issued a recommendation[34] on the use of environmental agreements whereas the Council has adopted a resolution[35] in this respect. However, for the purpose of this research two remarks should be made. Firstly, all of these instruments encourage environmental agreements but only insofar as they are in accordance with the Treaty, notably the competition rules therein. This brings us to the second remark, one that has already been made earlier, being that these instruments should, without exception, be characterised as lower (secondary) Community legislation. As such they cannot depart from the Treaty and therefore no collision is possible in the first place. The conditions for the second moment of the collision would thus not seem to be fulfilled. However, the following may be added to this. A close scrutiny of the provisions that the Court relies on to come to the *Albany* exception, reveals that not all of these provisions actually encourage the conclusion of collectively bargained social agreements on the national level. In the *Albany* case the Court bases its exception, *inter alia*, on the fact that Article 118 and 118b of the Treaty and the Agreement on social policy encourage the conclusion of collective social agreements.[36]

---

31 *E.g.* Directive 94/62 on packaging and packaging waste, OJ 1994 L 365/10, Articles 3(12) and 7 and Article 8 of Directive 2002/96 on waste electrical and electronical equipment (WEEE), OJ 2003 L 37/24.

32 European Parliament and Council, decision 2179/98 on the review of the European Community programme of policy and action in relation to the environment and sustainable development 'Towards sustainability', OJ 1998 L 275/1, Article 3, (1), (f).

33 COM (2001)29 final of 24 January 2001, Article 3, (4) of the proposal for a decision of the European Parliament and of the Council laying down the Community Environment Action Programme 2001-2010.

34 Commission, Recommendation 96/733 concerning the use of environmental agreements implementing Community directives, OJ 1996 L 333/59.

35 Council, Resolution of 7 October 1997 on environmental agreements, OJ 1997 C 321/6.

36 Case C-67/96, *Albany*, [1999] ECR I-5751, paras. 55-58.

The reference to Article 118 which, as the Court cites it, 'provides that the Commission is to promote close cooperation between Member States in the social field, particularly in matters relating to the right of association and collective bargaining between employers and workers' relates only very indirectly to the actual conclusion of collective social agreements. Interestingly, the Court, in reciting Article 118,[37] omitted the fact that this provision applies, 'without prejudice to the other provisions of this Treaty and in conformity with its general objectives'.

As second pillar under its reasoning, the Court lists Article 118b according to which the Commission is to endeavour to develop the dialogue between management and labour at European level which could, if the two sides consider it desirable, lead to relations based on agreement.[38] This provision, again, concerns only indirectly to the conclusion of the collective social agreements such as those that were at stake in the *Albany* case. In this respect it may be pointed out that Article 118b concerns collective bargaining at the European level. Moreover, the Commission is only to encourage the dialogue and not the conclusion of agreements, although such agreements would seem to be the logical consequence of negotiations.

Finally, the Court refers to the Agreement on social policy. In particular it refers to Articles 1, 4(1) and 4(2) of that Agreement. Article 1 sets out the general objectives of the Agreement. Article 4 represents little more than a repetition of Article 118b with the exception that the role of the Commission in encouraging collective bargaining is not to be found in Article 4 but in Article 3 of the Agreement. With regard to Article 4 it must be noted that this provision is again only indirectly related to the conclusion of collective social agreements as it concerns, like Article 188b, negotiations and agreements on the Community level. Moreover, the preamble to the agreement explicitly states that it is 'without prejudice to the provisions of th[e] Treaty, particularly those relating to social policy [...]'.

In sum, the provisions named by the Court as leading to the collision and thus forming the very foundations of the exception, are not entirely convincing. Whether this flawed reasoning could be construed to also provide an opening for an exception *ratione materiae* for environmental agreements is uncertain. On the one hand, it could be argued that the use of these rather weak arguments by the Court in construing the *Albany* exception show that this exception is primarily 'politically' inspired and not so much the result of sound legal reasoning. In that respect, provided that the political will exists, similar reasoning could be applied with regard to environmental agreements. On the other hand, the Court has been clear about the fact that the *Albany* exception constitutes an

37 This provision has moved in essentially unchanged form to Article 140 EC as a result of the amendments to the EC Treaty by the Treaty of Amsterdam.

38 This provision appears to have been split and can forthwith be found in Articles 138 and 139 EC.

exception to the rule and, as such, has to be construed narrowly. In our opinion, this last view probably has more weight. The mere fact that an exception is based on weak arguments cannot lead to the conclusion that even weaker grounds may be used to create similar exceptions. In this respect, it has to be taken into account that the weaknesses in the Court's reasoning as regards the *Albany* exception do not involve the hierarchical relation between the provisions leading to the collision inasmuch as it would if an analogue exception for environmental agreements were contemplated. After all, the fact remains that the provisions leading to the collision – *quod non* – resulting in the *Albany* exception were on the Treaty level whereas the closest thing to lead to a comparable collision in the environmental sphere can only be found in a non-binding document. Moreover, it can be doubted whether Article 6 could lead to a collision since it necessitates nothing more than an integration of environmental concerns and cannot of itself be construed so as to directly encourage the conclusion of environmental agreements.

## 8.3 Agreements and concerted practices between undertakings and decisions of associations of undertakings

The prohibition of Article 81 applies to 'agreements between undertakings, decisions by associations of undertakings and concerted practices'. For a detailed analysis of the concept of undertakings in EC competition law, the reader is referred to paragraph 7.4 of above. Article 81 EC concerns cooperative behaviour of undertakings. Purely unilateral measures are thus excluded from the scope of Article 81 but may nonetheless fall under Article 82 EC.[39] In defining any behaviour as an 'agreement, decision or concerted practice' it should always be kept in mind that in European competition law, such concepts are interpreted functionally and thus substance, and not form, matters.[40] Furthermore, the dividing line between these concepts is very hard to draw and may very well not exist. In any case, the functional approach to these concepts by the Court has made the precise characterisation of lesser importance.[41] With regard to environmental concerns it may be noted that the very mechanism encouraging the conclusion of environmental agreements will also ensure that restrictions involved are very likely to be legally binding agreements or decisions of associations of undertakings. As we have seen a major driving force behind the conclusion of such agreements is the exclusion of free riders, a task than

39 See, on the dividing line between unilateral and cooperative behaviour, Case T-41/96, *Bayer* v. *Commission*, [2000] II-3383, para 66 *et seq.*

40 *Cf.* Ritter, Braun & Rawlinson 2000, p. 80.

41 *Cf.* Case C-49/92 P, *Commission* v. *Anic Participazioni* (Polypropylene), [1999], I-4125, para. 106 *et seq.*

can be much better achieved when using legally binding instruments. In this respect, Community competition law is very unlikely to present many possibilities or problems with regard to environmental agreements.

## 8.4 Which have as their object or effect the prevention, restriction or distortion of competition

Apart from the fact that agreements, in order to fall within the scope of Article 81(1), need to affect trade between member states[42] they must also have 'as their object or effect the prevention restriction or distortion of competition within the common market'. A number of interesting issues arise in connection with this element. Firstly, the distinction between the object and effect of an agreement. Secondly, the concept of competition and, following from this, the concept of a 'prevention, restriction or distortion' of competition. Thirdly, the connection between the object or effect on the one hand and the restriction[43] of competition on the other hand. These three issues and some ancillary notions will be examined in this paragraph.

### 8.4.1 The object or effect

As the text of Article 81(1) clearly shows, the object and effect of an agreement are listed as alternatives.[44] In this respect, the alternative nature of both conditions must primarily be understood to increase the reach of Article 81.[45] As a consequence, not only the agreements that aim to restrict competition but also those that have the (unintended) effect of restricting competition while having no such objective fall within the scope of Article 81. The alternativity also works the other way around in that the Court considers it unnecessary to establish an actual effect on competition once it has been ascertained that the object of an agreement is to restrict competition.[46] In the environmental context, this distinction and the consequences that have been attached to it by the Court, can lead to essentially two results. Firstly, an environmental agreement having an effect on competition will fall within Article 81's ambit irrespective of its environmental object. Secondly, the parties to an environmental agreement that has the object of restricting competition (*i.e.* a 'disguised cartel'[47]) will plead its envi-

---

[42] See, *supra*, paragraph 7.5.

[43] Hereafter, we will refer to the 'restriction' of competition in general.

[44] *E.g.*, Case 56/65, *LTM* v. *MBU*, [1966] ECR 235.

[45] Joined Cases 56, 58/64, *Consten & Grundig*, [1966] ECR 429, Case 56/65, *LTM* v. *MBU*, [1966] ECR 235. *Cf.* Ritter, Braun & Rawlinson 2000, p. 77.

[46] *E.g.*, Joined Cases 56, 58/64, *Consten & Grundig*, [1966] ECR 299, at p. 342.

[47] *See* Commission, Guidelines on the application of Article 81 to horizontal agreements, OJ 2001 C 3/2, para. 25.

ronmental object or its only minimal effects on competition in vain. The fact that an agreement having effect on competition falls within the scope of Article 81 despite its environmental objectives cannot be considered very surprising. As we have seen above, the alternative nature of the object and effect test in Article 81 can only be understood as widening its scope.

The fact that environmental agreements that are deemed to have as their object the restriction of competition fall under the prohibition irrespective of the (purely) environmental objectives of the parties or the negligible effects on competition is less obvious. This follows from, one the one hand, the fact that the concept of the 'object of restricting competition' is an objective one and, on the other hand the alternativity of the object and effect. As the alternativity of object and effect has already received some attention, we will now focus on the objective nature of the term 'object' in Article 81(1) EC.

This objective nature is of interest for the purpose of this investigation for two reasons. Firstly, if object is indeed an objective notion, the parties' intent becomes irrelevant. This, in turn, would completely remove the possibility of excluding environmental agreements from the scope of Article 81 precisely because of the lack of subjective intent to restrict competition. Secondly, the case law of the Court is not entirely clear on this point and may leave some room for the interpretation of object as subjective intention.[48]

Ever since the *Miller Schallplatten* case[49] but probably already in the *Consten & Grundig* case,[50] *communis opinio* has been that the object of an agreement is an objective concept flowing from the *nature* of an agreement and not from the parties intentions.[51] In the context of agreements that are claimed to be (partly) environmental, the *IAZ* case is interesting.[52] This case is the appeal against the Commission decision in the *NAVEWA-ANSEAU* case.[53] In this decision the Commission prohibited an agreement establishing a system of conformity checks for washing machines. The claimed purpose of the agreement was the protection of the water quality through ensuring the conformity of washing machines with the norms pertaining to water quality. However, closer scrutiny revealed that the agreement also had the object of hindering parallel imports. Before the Court the parties to the agreement argued that the Commission had not established that the agreement's purpose was to restrict competition. According to the Court 'the agreement clearly expresses the intention of treating

---

48 *Cf.* Odudu 2001A.

49 Case 19/77, *Miller Schallplatten* v. *Commission*, [1978] ECR 131, para. 7.

50 Joined Cases 56, 58/64, *Consten & Grundig*, [1966] ECR 299, at p. 343.

51 *Cf.* Bellamy & Child 1993, para. 2-100 at p. 93, Ritter, Braun & Rawlinson 2000, p. 93 and Faull & Nikpay 1999, para. 2.61 at p. 82.

52 Joined Cases 96-102, 104, 105, 108 and 110/82, *IAZ*, [1983] ECR 3369.

53 Commission Decision 82/371, *NAVEWA-ANSEAU*, OJ 1982 L 167/39.

parallel imports less favourably'.[54] To come to this conclusion the Court took into account the content, origin and circumstances of the implementation of the agreement.

This case effectively shows that the absence of a subjective intent to restrict competition does not rule out the possibility of the agreement being considered restrictive of competition by object. This will have as an effect that the (partly) environmental objective of the parties to the agreement will not suffice to keep certain agreements from being deemed to restrict competition by their object.

### 8.4.2 The concept of a restriction of competition

Article 81 prohibits the 'prevention, restriction or distortion' of competition. As the borders between the concepts 'prevention', 'restriction' and 'distortion' are considered to be fluid and these concepts are used interchangeably,[55] we will hereafter only refer to the general concept of a restriction of competition. Taken literally, Article 81(1) applies to every restriction of competition irrespective of the impact of the agreement on competition. From this perspective, it could be argued that a restriction of competition is inherent in every contract. Such an interpretation of Article 81(1) would clearly be disproportionate and lead to an unworkable situation.

It is for this reason probably that the Court has restricted the scope of Article 81(1) to encompass only *appreciable* restrictions of competition. This is referred to in doctrine as the requirement of appreciability. Furthermore, the restriction of competition on one level following from an agreement may also be compensated for by increases of competition on other levels. The result of this could be that there is no appreciable restriction of competition as a *net result*. This is often referred to as the 'rule of reason' in competition law.[56] In general both concepts are closely related and can both be called examples of an economically realistic application of Article 81(1). With regard to the concept of the rule of reason two remarks need to be made. Firstly, there is a considerable amount of semantics involved in the scholarly discussions surrounding this concept. To a large degree these discussions also involve the difference between the concept of appreciability and the rule of reason. We will not attempt to give the final answer to these questions but rather limit ourselves to a description and appreciation insofar as this is necessary for the purpose of this research. Secondly, European law with regard to the free movement of goods also knows a rule of reason. It is very important to clearly distinguish these two rules. Below we will first look at the appreciability requirement and after that the rule of reason will be scrutinised.

---

54 Joined Cases 96-102, 104, 105, 108 and 110/82, *IAZ*, [1983] ECR 3369, para. 23.

55 *Cf.* Faull & Nikpay 1999, p. 81.

56 *Cf.* Jones & Suffrin 2001, p. 142.

### 8.4.2.1 An introduction to appreciability

The concept of appreciability found its way in European competition law at an early stage. Already in 1965, in the *Völk* v. *Vervaecke* case, the Court decided that only those agreements that have more than insignificant effects on the market fall within the scope of Article 81(1).[57] This case involved an agreement conferring absolute territorial protection between two rather insignificant parties. The parties' market share was less than 1 per cent. It is interesting to note that in this judgment the Court appears to have introduced an appreciability criterion with regard to both the requirement of an effect on intra-community trade as well as the need for there to a restriction of competition if Article 81(1) is to apply.[58]

The Commission has laid down its view of this appreciability criterion in the Notice on agreements of minor importance.[59] In this notice the Commission distinguishes essentially three types of agreements and corresponding levels of appreciability. With regard to vertical agreements (*i.e.* agreements between firms on different levels of trade which are not actual or potential competitors) the Commission considers that a combined market share on the relevant market of less than 15 per cent will generally render the agreement *de minimis*, causing it to fall outside the scope of the prohibition. With regard to horizontal agreements (*i.e.* those between firms on the same level of trade who are actual or potential competitors on the markets concerned) the bar is put at a market share of 10 per cent. Certain types of restrictions are considered to appreciably restrict competition irrespective of the market share of the parties. These restrictions concern, *inter alia*, the fixing of prices, market sharing and are often referred to as 'hard core' or 'per se' restrictions.[60] In general therefore, two types of appreciability criterion may be discerned. On the one hand there is a quantitative notion of appreciability that depends on the market share of the parties and on the other hand there is a qualitative concept of appreciability that hinges on the nature of the restriction involved. As we saw above, the nature of restrictions of price competition results in them being considered to be, *qualitate qua*, appreciably restrictive of competition. Another way to describe them would be to consider them to be *per se* quantitatively restrictive of competition. On the other hand, there may be subjects of agreements that will be deemed not to appreciably restrict competition no matter what the parties' market share is. Particu-

---

57 Case 5/69, *Völk* v. *Vervaecke*, [1969] ECR 295, para 5/7.

58 See, with regard to the requirement of an effect on trade, *supra* paragraph 7.5.

59 Commission Notice on agreements of minor importance which do not fall within the meaning of Article 81(1) (*De Minimis* Notice), OJ 2001 C 368/13. This notice replaces the 1997 *De Minimis* Notice that placed the bar at 10 and 5 per cent for vertical and horizontal agreements.

60 Ritter, Braun & Rawlinson 2000, p. 102, Faull & Nikpay 1999, p. 82.

larly with regard to this second, qualitative, concept of appreciability and the rule of reason, there appears to be considerable disagreement and confusion among scholars.[61] Below we will pay further attention to both concepts or notions of appreciability and their importance in the environmental sphere. In the context of the quantitative concept of appreciability we will also try to demarcate the borders between this concept and the rule of reason.

#### 8.4.2.2 The quantitative concept of appreciability and environmental protection

As we have seen above the quantitative concept of appreciability revolves around the parties' market share. Moreover, it is the earliest recognised concept of appreciability originating in the 1965 judgment in the *Völk v. Vervaecke* case. As such it is relatively well established. For one, the Commission has laid down, in the *De minimis* notice, precise levels of market share in this respect. In the environmental context the recent Commission Guidelines on the applicability of Article 81 of the EC Treaty to horizontal cooperation agreements are of great interest.[62] In chapter 7 of these guidelines the Commission indicates its policy with regard to environmental agreements. In doing so, it distinguishes, as regards the assessment of environmental agreements under Article 81(1), between three types of agreements. In section 7.3.1.3 the Commission addresses the third type of agreement that 'may fall under Article 81(1)'. The central criterion used by the Commission in order to determine whether such agreements actually fall under the scope of the prohibition appears to be the parties' market share.[63] In these Guidelines, the Commission does not provide us with a clearly quantified market share cap but rather limits itself to indicating that 'significant market shares' will cause Article 81(1) to apply.[64] Moreover, the Commission appears to have applied the quantitative concept of appreciability in a number of environmental cases. However, these instances were only to the effect that such agreements were considered to appreciably restrict competition. In the case involving an agreement between the importers and producers of washing machines in Europe (*CECED*), the Commission considered that Article 81(1) applied because the parties represented more than 95 per cent of the market.[65] Similarly, in the case involving an agreement by European association of manufacturers of consumer electronics (*EACEM*) to reduce

[61] See, for an overview of the debate: Odudu 2001B.

[62] Commission, Notice Guidelines on the applicability of Article 81 of the EC Treaty to horizontal cooperation agreements (Guidelines on horizontal agreements), OJ 2001 C 3/2.

[63] *Ibid.*, p. 27.

[64] In any event, the thresholds of the *De Minimis* Notice apply.

[65] Commission Decision 2000/475, *CECED*, OJ 2000 L 187/47, para. 42.

energy consumption, the Commission granted an informal exemption.[66] This implies that the agreement was considered to fall under Article 81(1) in the first place because the parties held a market share in excess of 64 per cent.[67] This indicates the likely scenario with regard to the application of the appreciability criterion to environmental agreements. As we have noted above, a major driving force behind the conclusion of environmental agreements is the achievement of economies of scale. This in turn will generally result in a large percentage of the market joining an environmental agreement thus effectively ruling out the possibility of an environmental agreement being considered to not to appreciably restrict competition from a quantitative perspective.

### 8.4.2.3 The qualitative concept of appreciability and environmental protection

A much more recent addition to the appreciability tree is the qualitative concept of appreciability. In this concept whether or not an appreciable restriction of competition exists depends on the nature or quality of the restriction. A good example of the application of this concept of appreciability can be found in the Commission decision in the *APB* case.[68] This case concerned the agreement by the Belgian association of pharmacists to set up a quality label. The Commission granted a negative clearance for the system setting up this quality label because other quality labels could freely be created and because 'the quality of pharmaceuticals was *only one means of competition among others*' (emphasis added).[69]

In the *Servicemaster* case, the Commission considered the prohibition in a franchise agreement for the franchisee not to obtain a more than 5 per cent interest in a competing firm not to appreciably restrict competition on the following grounds.[70]

*'Although the prohibition against acquiring non-controlling financial interest in the capital of a competing publicly-quoted company can be a restriction of competition falling within Article 85(1) [Now Article 81(1)], in this particular case it is not*

---

66 Commission notice pursuant to Article 19(3) of Council Regulation 17, *EACEM*, OJ 1998 C 12/2. The 'exemption comfort letter' in this Case was not formally published. However, from the Commission's annual competition report in 1998, it becomes clear that the decision substantively entailed an exemption, 1998 Competition Report, p. 152.

67 Commission notice pursuant to Article 19(3) of Council Regulation 17, *EACEM*, OJ 1998 C 12/2, paras. 3, 4.

68 Commission Decision 90/33, *APB*, OJ 1990 L 18/35.

69 *Ibid.* paras. 41, 42; Commission, 1989 Competition Report, p. 62, 63.

70 Commission Decision 88/604, *Servicemaster*, OJ 1988 L 332/38, para. 10.

*considered to be an appreciable restriction because the franchisees are generally small undertakings for which the prohibition against acquiring more than 5 per cent of a publicly-quoted company does not normally constitute a real hindrance in the development of their own activities. Furthermore, the franchisees are completely free in the acquisition of financial interests in non-competing companies.'*

In both cases the Commission bases its judgment on the appreciability of the restriction on the nature or content of the obligation in question and analyses this in its factual and legal context.

The abovementioned Guidelines on horizontal cooperation also contain examples of the qualitative concept of appreciability in the environmental sphere. The Commission seems to be referring to what has been deemed *per se* qualitative appreciability when it speaks of agreements that will almost always come under Article 81(1).[71] More interesting is the fact that the Commission also seems to recognise instances where an agreement is considered not to appreciably restrict competition from a qualitative perspective. In section 7.3.1.1 the Commission is concerned with agreements that do not fall under Article 81(1) irrespective of the parties' market share. According to the Commission this may occur where there is no precise individual obligation for the parties because, for example, more than one means are available to attain the goals of the agreement.[72] Another example given by the Commission concerns agreements on the environmental performance of products or processes. Insofar as these performance standards do not appreciably influence product or production diversity or only marginally influence purchasing decisions, the agreement will be considered not to appreciably restrict competition. When an agreement results in the phasing out of certain products, the ensuing restriction will be considered unappreciable if these phased out products represent only a minor proportion of the market.[73]

The Commission appears to have used this line of reasoning in a number of cases. In the *ACEA* case the Commission considered that an agreement among the members of the European association of manufacturers of automobiles to reduce carbon dioxide emissions from cars by the members of that association did not appreciably restrict competition.[74] The reason for this was firstly the fact that they had agreed only on a sector-wide emissions reduction objective. Thus the agreement did not result in a specific obligation for individual members. Furthermore, the technical means by which the parties are to attain this objective were left completely free. The Commission has also granted negative clear-

71 Commission, Guidelines on horizontal agreements, OJ 2001 C 3/2, section 7.3.1.2.

72 *Ibid.*, para. 185.

73 *Ibid.*, para. 186.

74 Commission press release IP/98/865, see also Commission Competition Report 1998, para. 131.

ance to an agreement to improve the energy efficiency of electric motors on the basis of similar reasoning.[75]

In the *CECED* case the Commission applied the reasoning set out above to come to the conclusion that the restriction was in fact appreciable.[76] The CECED agreement concerned the phasing out of energy inefficient washing machines. As we have seen above the parties held more than 95 per cent of the market and from the quantitative perspective the agreement was considered to appreciably restrict competition. This did not keep the Commission from investigating whether or not the agreement entailed qualitatively appreciable effects on competition and trade between Member States. Firstly the Commission stated that 'energy consumption is not negligible as a purchase criterion'.[77] This reference to the environmental performance not being 'negligible' as a purchase criterion appears to be going further than the requirement that the Commission has formulated the Guidelines on horizontal agreements, of it being 'marginal' as a purchase criterion. Something that is marginal clearly does not need to be negligible. Furthermore, an interesting nexus between this criterion and the final condition for an exemption may be noted. We shall pay more attention to this nexus in the paragraph devoted to the final condition for exemption.[78]

Outside the environmental context, qualitative appreciability reasoning has also been applied in the Commission's decision in *Irish Banks' Standing Committee*.[79] Among others, the agreement harmonised the banks' opening hours. According to the Commission opening hours are an aspect of competition. The Commission goes on to state that, however, only some of the banking services are actually affected and moreover competition between the parties with regard to the affected services is not otherwise impinged upon. As a result the Commission considers that competition is not appreciably restricted.[80]

The European Court of Justice appears also to be applying a qualitative notion of appreciability. In the abovementioned *Pavlov* case, the pension scheme set up by medical specialists was considered not to be able to benefit from the *Albany* exception.[81] However, the Court ruled that Article 81(1) did not apply because the agreement was not contrary to Article 81(1). The Court starts its reasoning in this respect by observing that for the application of Article 81(1) it is necessary to take into account the relevant economic and factual circumstances in which the agreement operates.[82] The Court then sets out to analyse

---

75 Commission press release IP/00/508, see also Martínez-López 2000, p. 24, 25.

76 Commission Decision 2000/475, *CECED*, OJ 2000 L 187/47.

77 *Ibid.*, para. 42.

78 *Infra* para. 8.7.5.

79 Commission Decision 86/507, *Irish Banks' Standing Committee*, OJ 1986 L 295/28.

80 *Ibid.*, para. 17.

81 Joined Cases C-180/98 to 184/98, *Pavlov*, [2000] ECR-6451.

82 *Ibid.*, para. 91.

the effects of the agreement and comes to the conclusion that these restrict competition with regard to one cost factor, namely that connected with pension insurance.[83] It follows the opinion of Advocate General Jacobs in that it observes that those restrictive effects are limited because they concern only one cost factor that is insignificant in comparison with the total amount of costs faced by medical specialists.[84]

Precisely because the Court follows the opinion of the Advocate General in this respect, it is interesting to take a closer look at this opinion. The Advocate General starts his observations in this respect by observing that only in special sectors or with regard to special categories of agreements the factual and economic circumstances need to be taken into account.[85] He continues by listing four arguments to substantiate his conclusion that competition is not appreciably restricted.[86] Firstly, only a cost factor and not a price factor is harmonised. Secondly, this cost factor is of relatively minor importance in comparison with other factors. The third reason listed by the Advocate General appears in fact only to repeat the second argument. Fourthly, the Advocate General considers that medical specialists vigorously compete on other factors such as the quality of their services.

Accordingly, both the Court and the Advocate General reach the conclusion that competition is not appreciably restricted by the agreement to set up a collective pension fund.[87] The reasoning applied by both the Court and the Advocate General can only be characterised as an application of a qualitative appreciability test whereby they look at the actual content of the agreement and not at the market share held by the parties to determine the impact on competition. In actual fact, the Commission appears to have taken this ruling into account in drawing up the abovementioned Guidelines on horizontal agreements.[88]

As the Commission's Guidelines show, the qualitative concept of appreciability may very well result in an environmental agreement being considered to fall outside the scope of Article 81(1) simply because competition is not appreciably restricted. From the Guidelines and Commission and Court practice a number of instances where this might take place, can be discerned.

Firstly, the case where an environmental agreement contains only general and sector wide targets and leaves parties considerable room as regards the means by which they can attain that target. Secondly, an agreement on envi-

83 *Ibid.*, para. 92, 93.

84 *Ibid.*, para 94, 95.

85 *Ibid.*, para 137 of the opinion.

86 *Ibid.*, paras 139-142 of the opinion.

87 It must be noted that the Court also appear to use the rule of reason in coming to the conclusion that competition is not appreciably restricted.

88 Commission, Guidelines on horizontal agreements, OJ 2001 C 3/2, para. 23.

ronmental aspects may very well only marginally affect production or products. Despite the fact that energy efficiency was considered by the Commission as not being negligible as a purchase criterion, it is certainly possible to argue that an agreement on energy efficiency has no significant effect on product or production diversity. This will hold true all the more when multiple means to attain these energy efficiency goals are available. Where, as a third example, an environmental agreement entails the phasing out of certain products, Article 81(1) will not be concerned whenever the market share of the products that are removed from the market is minor. This example is somewhat paradoxical from an environmental perspective in that the fact that only a minor portion is phased out also limits the amount of environmental gain to come from such a phasing out. This example may, however, be very interesting in connection with the Court's application of the appreciability criterion in the *Pavlov* case. In this case the Court considered an agreement harmonising only a minor percentage of the parties' costs not to appreciably restrict competition. When this is taken a bit further, the following reasoning could result. An agreement having a harmonising effect on costs will invariably also have a harmonising effect on the prices, as these are a necessary consequence of the costs. Current Commission competition policy prescribes that any agreement on prices, no matter what percentage of the price is concerned, invariably results in an appreciable restriction of competition. This is so because agreements restricting price competition are deemed to be *per se* restrictions of competition. However, agreements limiting outputs are also considered to constitute *per se* restrictions.[89] If the Commission is willing to consider the percentage of products phased out into account in determining whether or not a restriction is appreciable, a similar reasoning could be applied with regard to the percentage of the price affected by an environmental agreement. This could prove to be particularly important with regard to environmental agreements involving an environmental surcharge or a removal fee. Such agreements have occurred in the Netherlands and have met with resistance from the Netherlands Competition authority.[90] We shall pay closer attention to the possibilities that this reasoning offers in chapter 16.

#### 8.4.2.4 The rule of reason and environmental protection

The rule of reason originates in U.S. antitrust law where section one of the Sherman act prohibits 'every contract [...] in restraint of trade' without offering the possibility of an exception to that prohibition.[91] Primarily as a reaction to the application of Article 81(1), that was perceived to be overly wide

---

89 *E.g. ibid*, paras. 18 and 188.

90 The *Stibat* and *Wit en Bruingoed* Cases, see *infra*, paragraph 16.5.

91 *Cf.* Joliet 1967, p. 20 *et seq.*

and legalistic, some scholars have argued for the creation of a comparable rule in European competition law.[92]

Whether or not a rule of reason actually exists in the competition rules of the European Community is uncertain for a number of reasons. For one, the concept of the rule of reason is subject to a considerable amount of semantics. Whilst it is often equated with the balancing of pro- and anti-competitive effects in order to establish whether or not there is a (net) restriction of competition within the meaning of Article 81(1), it is also perceived as entailing a *'bilan economique'* in which a restriction of competition is balanced with offsetting economic benefits. Moreover, it should be said that the existence of a rule of reason in European competition law has neither been formally acknowledged nor rejected by the Courts.[93] At the same time, the Commission, in its White Paper on the modernisation of the rules implementing Articles 81 and 82 EC, has explicitly admitted that it has had recourse to the rule of reason.[94] Matters are further complicated by the fact that the rule of reason is considered by a number of scholars to have actually been applied by the Commission and the Community Courts.[95]

The uncertainty and semantics[96] surrounding the debate about the existence of a rule of reason in European competition law are reflected in *Métropole II*.[97] In this case the Court of First Instance held that a number of judgments that are often considered to be the result of the rule of reason, could not be 'interpreted as establishing the existence of a rule of reason in Community competition law'. In the view of the Court of First Instance, the pro- and anti-competitive effects need to be balanced within the framework of Article 81(3) EC because this provision would otherwise 'lose much of its effectiveness'.[98] The judgments brought forward by the parties as evidence of the existence of a rule of reason were considered by the Court of First instance to be

*'part of a broader trend in the case-law according to which it is not necessary to hold, wholly abstractly and without drawing any distinction, that any agreement*

92 See for further references Jones & Sufrin 2001, p. 138 *et seq.*

93 *E.g.* Case T-14/89, *Montedipe* v. *Commission*, [1992] ECR II-1155, para. 265. See, however, *Métropole II*, discussed *infra* in this paragraph.

94 Commission, White Paper on the Modernisation of the Rules Implementing Articles 85 and 86 of the EC Treaty, OJ 1999 C 132/1, paras. 56, 57.

95 *E.g.* Gerven 1997, p. 185-188.

96 See, *e.g.* Monti 2002, who, at p. 1086, introduces an European rule of reason alongside an US rule of reason.

97 Case T-112/99, *Métropole télévision (M6), Suez-Lyonnaise des eaux, France Télécom and Télévision française 1 SA (TF1)* v. *Commission* (Métropole II) , [2001] ECR II-2459, para. 76.

98 *Ibid.*, para. 74.

*restricting the freedom of action of one or more of the parties is necessarily caught by the prohibition laid down in Article 85(1) [now Article 81(1)] of the Treaty. In assessing the applicability of Article 85(1) [now Article 81(1)] to an agreement, account should be taken of the actual conditions in which it functions, in particular the economic context in which the undertakings operate, the products or services covered by the agreement and the actual structure of the market concerned.'*

The Court of First instance's basic argument to reject the rule of reason is the fact that this interpretation of Article 81(1) would be 'difficult to reconcile with the rule prescribed by that provision'.[99] In *Métropole II* we can see how the parties considered that the pro- and anti-competitive effects needed to be balanced. The Court then considers that this is incompatible with the general scheme of Article 81 as a whole. According to the Court this balancing act should take place as part of the application of the third paragraph of that provision. It is submitted that this reading of Article 81 disregards the actual wording of Article 81 EC. For the applicability of the first paragraph of this provision a 'prevention, restriction or distortion of competition' is necessary. The cases referred to by the parties because they are considered to contain an application of the rule of reason show that the Court is actually establishing whether or not there is a *net restriction* of competition. A limitation of the intra brand competition, for example, is considered to be compensated for by an increase of the inter brand competition. Where a net restriction of competition has been established,[100] there may be benefits that are not related to the degree of competition that offset the restriction of competition. These non-competition benefits find their place in Article 81(3) EC. Essentially, the rule of reason involves a *bilan concurrentiel* whereas Article 81(3) is submitted to be a *bilan economique*. This interpretation of Article 81(1) is by no means incompatible with the wording of that provision and does not deprive Article 81(3) of its effectiveness.[101] In this respect, and because the European Court of Justice has not explicitly rejected the rule of reason and can even be considered to have applied it recently,[102] it is still interesting to further examine the rule of reason in European competition law.

Typically, an application of the rule of reason by the Court is preceded by the statement that[103]

99 *Ibid.*, para. 73.

100 Because, for example, the restriction of intra brand competition goes beyond what is necessary to ensure the functioning of an agreement in such a manner that ascertains an increased inter brand competition.

101 *Cf.* Wesseling 2000, p. 106.

102 *Cf.* Monti 2002, who, at p. 1086, introduces a European rule of reason that, contrary to the US rule of reason, is not about balancing pro- and anti-competitive effects but instead incorporates the rule of reason from the free movement provisions into Community competition law. See further on this incorporation of legal concepts from the free movement provisions: Mortelmans 2001.

103 *E.g.* Joined Cases C-180/98 to 184/98, *Pavlov*, [2000] ECR-6451, para. 91.

*'account should be taken of the economic context in which undertakings operate, the products and services covered by the decisions of those undertakings, the structure of the market concerned and the actual conditions in which it functions'.*

A good recent example of what may be called an application of the rule of reason can be found in the *Pavlov* case. As we have seen above, the Court in this case came to the conclusion that the agreement to set up a collective pension scheme did not fall under Article 81(1) because it did not appreciably restrict competition. It reached this conclusion on the basis of two types of reasoning. Firstly, as we have seen above, the Court applied a qualitative appreciability test. Secondly, the Court had recourse to the rule of reason. In this respect the Court observed that the decision to set up a collective scheme enabled the medical specialists 'to share the risks insured against while achieving economies of scale'.[104] From the wording used, it can be inferred that this consideration was to large extent inspired by the Advocate-General's opinion.[105] The Advocate-General, on the basis of this reasoning, comes to the following conclusion:[106]

*'Accordingly, the pro-competitive effects of the institutionalised management cooperation are much stronger than any (theoretical) anti-competitive effects. The setting-up of the Fund, like the setting-up of an agricultural cooperative association, improves efficiency. As such it is not caught by Article 85(1) [now Article 81(1)]'*

This weighing of pro-competitive and anti-competitive effects, as we have seen above, is precisely what the rule of reason is all about. The result is that only net restrictions of competition end up needing an exemption under Article 81(3).

With regard to the rule of reason and environmental protection the following remarks may be made. The rule of reason as it was identified above is inherently limited to the balancing of pro- and anti-competitive effects. Other positive or negative effects, such as an improvement or deterioration of the environment, cannot be taken into account within the rule of reason as that would run counter to the very essence of the rule of reason.[107]

The European rule of reason that Monti identifies in, *inter alia*, the Court's judgment in *Wouters*, is a completely different matter. The European rule of reason can be compared to what Vogelaar and Mortelmans have called the 'inherent restriction-approach.[108] According to this approach certain restrictions of competition are considered by the Court to be inherent in the regulation

[104] *Ibid.*, para. 96.

[105] The Advocate-General uses allmost identical wording in his opinion, *ibid.*, para 146 of the opinion.

[106] *Ibid.*, para. 148 of the opinion.

[107] *Cf.* Ehle 1996 who at, p. 115, gives further references.

[108] Vogelaar 2000, Mortelmans 2001, p. 628

of a certain activity.[109] As a result, they should be accepted under Article 81(1) provided that the aim of the regulation is acceptable and the restriction does not go beyond what is necessary.

The European rule of reason is in fact a transplantation of a doctrine that was developed as part of the Treaty provisions on free movement (Articles 28, 39, 43, 49 and 56 EC). According to this Court-developed exception, national rules that apply without distinction do not fall foul of the prohibitions on restrictions of the free movement, if they are necessary to protect a mandatory requirement.[110] As such, it can in principle accommodate any mandatory requirement (the proper practice of the legal profession in *Wouters*) including the protection of the environment,[111] provided that the restriction of competition is necessary to protect the mandatory requirement. However appealing this European rule of reason may seem at first sight, it is submitted that such an interpretation of Article 81(1) does indeed entail the risk, that the Court of First Instance feared in *Métropole II*, of rendering Article 81(3) superfluous.

Nevertheless, even if we understand the rule of reason as only encompassing a balance between pro- and anticompetitive effects, this in no way precludes the application of the rule of reason to an environmental agreement. Particularly in the environmental sphere efficiency gains from cooperation are obvious. Furthermore, agreements on certain environmental aspects of production or products may very well add a new (environmental) dimension on which competition is possible. Even more importantly, the environmental agreement may result in the creation of an entirely new market. The Commission recognises this in its Guidelines on horizontal agreements. According to the Commission, agreements that lead to genuine market creation will not be considered to restrict competition insofar as the parties are unable to organise the activity independently and alternatives and/or competitors are not present.[112] This rationale possibly underlies the Commission's positive appreciation of the *Eco-Emballages* scheme.[113] This case concerned a collective take back and recycling scheme that, not unlike DSD, was set up following legislation laying down a producer responsibility for packaging waste. To a large extent the institutional and operational layout of Eco-Emballages is similar to that of DSD.[114] Eco-

[109] See Case C-309/99, *Wouters*, [2002] ECR I-1577, para. 97.

[110] *E.g.* Case C-55/94, *Reinhard Gebhard* v. *Consiglio dell'ordine Deglo Avvocatie Procuratori di Milano* (Gebhard), [1995] ECR I-4165, para. 37 and Case C-3/95, *Reisebüro Broede* v. *Gerd Sanker* (Reisebüro Broede), [1996] ECR I-6511, para. 28. Further on this: Mortelmans 2001, p. 617 *et seq.*

[111] Recognised as a mandatory requirement in Case 203/86, *Commission* v. *Denmark* (Danish Bottles), [1988] ECR 4607.

[112] Commission, Guidelines on horizontal agreements OJ 2001 C 3/2, para. 187.

[113] Commission, Notice pursuant to Article 19(3) of Regulation 17, OJ 2000 C 227/6, Decision 2001/663, *Eco-Emballages*, OJ 2001 L 233/37.

[114] As the Commission recognised in its press release in this Case; IP/01/850.

Emballages is the company that administrates the take back system for which it concludes contracts with the producers that use packaging. This contractual relation revolves around the licensed right for the producer to print a 'green dot' on the packaging and the licence fee that has to be paid for this. These license fees constitute Eco-Emballages' income with which it funds the take back and recycling. Secondly, Eco-Emballages has acquired the right to sub-licence the green dot from the Europe-wide licence holder 'Pro Europe'. Thirdly, Eco-Emballages has concluded contracts with the local (municipal) authorities. These authorities are under the statutory obligation to ensure the environmentally sound treatment of household waste on their territory. By concluding a contract with Eco-Emballages they receive financial support for this from Eco-Emballages in return for which the municipalities will have to either hand over the collected waste to the take-back company designated by Eco-Emballages ('designated take back firms') or to a take-back company chosen by the municipality itself. Fourthly and finally, Eco-Emballages has a contractual relation (so-called sectoral and operational take-back contracts) with the take-back firms. The latter are responsible for the taking back and recycling of the household waste. At the moment there are five so-called sectors (steel, aluminium, paper, plastic and glass) and Eco-Emballages will conclude a sectoral contact with only one firm per sector. These firms are then free to contract the designated take-back firms who will then take care and organise the actual taking back and recycling.

The decision with regard to the Article 81 aspects involved in DSD show that the Commission is willing to go quite far in applying a rule of reason type of approach to cases involving the creation of a new market. Among the types of packaging waste collected through the DSD system are plastic sales packaging and composite packaging containing plastics. The producer responsibility for these materials was included in the relevant German legislation only at a later stage.[115] The Commission sees this as the creation of a new 'area for business activity'.[116] With regard to plastics and composite packaging containing plastics, DSD has maintained the obligation for the collectors to pass these on free of charge (the so-called zero interface or *Schnittstelle Null*).[117] The fact that the Commission – 'in view of the exceptional circumstances and conditions surrounding the establishment of a new, functioning market'[118] – considered that competition was not appreciably restricted by this rather controversial clause shows that the Commission is willing to take to rule of reason approach to considerable lengths. The Commission indicated that the fact that these

[115] For paper, glass, board, tinplate and aluminium packaging waste, a producer responsibility existed from the very beginning.

[116] Commission Decision 2001/837, *DSD* (Article 81) OJ 2001 L 319/1, para. 112.

[117] *Ibid.*, para. 113.

[118] *Ibid.*, para. 114.

contracts would be put out to tender facilitated this conclusion. This indicates that relatively little weight must be attached to the consideration by the Commission that the zero interface addressed the problem that in the past this type of waste was directed into cheaper (and probably less environmentally friendly) disposal channels. Therefore the Commission's generous application of the rule of reason can probably be traced back to a purely competitive appraisal where environmental considerations have played a relatively unimportant and indirect role.

This short sketch of the Eco-Emballages and DSD systems reveals that DSD's and Eco-Emballages' role can be characterised as that of the 'spider in the web'. The primary competition concerns therefore relate to the upstream and downstream effects of exclusivities granted by or to Eco-Emballages or DSD in any of its four contractual relations. The competition problems posed by these exclusivities will be address in the following paragraph.

### 8.4.2.5 Exclusivities as restrictions of competition

Environmental protection is a relatively new area of economic activity. As such it is characterised by the presence of certain risks[119] as well as the need to make considerable investments in order to establish the necessary infrastructure. Often, the parties concerned will want to minimise these risks by, for example, agreeing upon certain exclusivities and thereby possibly preventing free rider type of problems. This can be seen in the cases dealing with large scale take back and recycling systems set up pursuant to producer responsibility obligations such as *DSD* and *Eco-Emballages*. The competitive appraisal in these cases predominantly concerns the exclusionary effects that follow from the relatively strong market position of these organisations.[120] This is confirmed by the decision reached by the Commission in *Eco-Emballages* according to which the agreements setting up the organisation with that name do not infringe Article 81(1). The Commission's appreciation of the Eco-Emballages system focuses primarily on the exclusivity clauses and exclusionary effects that may flow from the system.[121] This approach could also be expected from the Commission's Guidelines on horizontal agreements. In the relevant paragraph the Commission attaches great weight to the exclusivity resulting from a collective system.[122] Finally, the Commission's decision in the Article 81-case

---

[119] An example of such a risk can be seen in the financial crisis that DSD experienced in 1993, see Bastians 2002, p. 60

[120] See, with regard to this market position the Commission decision in *DSD* (Article 82), Decision 2001/463, OJ 2001 L 166/1, *infra*, chapter 9.

[121] Commission Decision 2001/663, *Eco-Emballages*, OJ 2001 L 233/37, paras. 72-85.

[122] Commission, Guidelines on horizontal agreements, OJ 2001 C 3/2, para. 191.

involving DSD is also primarily concerned with the exclusivities that result from the collection and recycling network set up by DSD.[123] Many of the competitive problems could be avoided by the fact that DSD had agreed to amend certain contracts so as to limit the exclusionary effects arising from them.[124] Indeed, the only appreciable restriction of competition in the DSD case could be traced back to the exclusionary effects of the contracts concluded between DSD and the local collectors and sorters.[125] In these contracts DSD agrees to employ only one company to collect and sort the waste in a given region. This self-limitation of DSD together with the fact that DSD is Germany's leading purchaser of such services brings the Commission to conclude that competition is appreciably restricted. In this respect the Commission considers it important that the exclusivity is an 'unusually long lasting one'.[126] Anyone interested in exactly why the duration was considered excessive will have to content himself with the rather general conclusion that, on the basis of a detailed analysis of 24 out of more than 500 so-called service agreements, the duration was considered not indispensable to ensure that the investments actually carried out would be recouped.[127] Ultimately, the Commission granted an exemption for this restriction. We shall examine this exemption below.

### 8.4.3 The connection between the object or effect and the restriction of competition

A problem in connection with the both appreciability tests and the rule of reason is that they are often considered superfluous in cases involving a per se restriction or a restriction by object. This problem follows from the fact that the appreciability and rule of reason tests are considered to be inherent in and limited to the establishment of an effect on competition. The alternative nature of the object and effect of a restriction of competition within the meaning of Article 81(1), as it was interpreted by the Court in *Consten & Grundig*, then leads to the conclusion that it is unnecessary to prove an appreciable restriction of competition in a case involving a *per se* or hard core restriction.[128] However, already the *Völk* v. *Vervaecke* case shows us that even in the case of hard-core restrictions it is necessary to ascertain whether the object of the agreement

[123] Commission Decision 2001/837, *DSD* (Article 81) OJ 2001 L 319/1.

[124] *Ibid.*, para. 55.

[125] *Ibid.*, section 2.4.

[126] *Ibid.*, para. 130.

[127] *Ibid.*, para. 55. In this respect, the Court's reasoning with regard to a similar issue on the basis of Article 86(2) in *Sydhavnens* is more elucidating, see *infra*, paragraph 12.6.

[128] See, for example, the decision of 18 December 1998 of the Netherlands Competition authority in Case 51, *Stibat*, para. 52.

is to appreciably restrict competition.[129] Furthermore, the Commission has on a number of occasions considered it necessary to prove that competition was restricted to an appreciable extent even when hard-core restrictions were involved.[130] In the Guidelines on horizontal agreements the Commission considers that agreements involving hard-core restrictions will '*almost* always fall under Article 81(1) (emphasis added)'.[131] It reaches this conclusion because it 'presumes' that such agreements have negative market effects. This presumption, it is submitted, may never stand in the way of an economically realistic market analysis as to whether or not competition has been appreciably restricted.

With regard to the rule of reason, the Court of First Instance appears be following a slightly different course in this respect. In a number of cases involving hard-core restrictions the Court of First Instance has held that recourse to the rule of reason is precluded.[132] In the more recent *Métropole II* case, the Court of First Instance explicitly rejected the rule of reason.[133] This approach, it is submitted, cannot be reconciled with that followed by the hierarchically higher placed European Court of Justice. The fact the obvious or *per se* restrictions are involved may very well lead to the conclusion that the pro-competitive effects are insufficient to off-set the restrictive effects but it can never obviate the need for a comprehensive market analysis to establish that competition has (as a net result) been appreciably restricted. It is furthermore submitted that the qualitative and quantitative appreciability test and the rule of reason test are cumulative tests in that all three need to be fulfilled before a restriction can be considered appreciable. This means that, for example, even in cases involving the absolute majority of an industry (therefore quantitatively appreciable) regard must be had to both the qualitative concept of appreciability and the rule of reason. This holds true just as much as that, the other way around, quantitative appreciability needs to be shown even in cases where there are no or insufficient pro-competitive effects and where the restriction is considered to be qualitatively appreciable as the Court held in the *Völk* v. *Vervaecke* case.[134]

---

129 Case 5/69, *Völk* v. *Vervaecke*, [1969] ECR 295, paras. 5/6.

130 Commission Decision 1999/210, *British Sugar et al.*, OJ 1999 L 76/1, para. 77 with regard to price fixing and decision 98/273, *VW*, OJ 1998 L 124/60, para. 147 with regard to a restriction on parallel imports. Also the Commission's *De Minimis* notice allows for the possibility of agreements not having as their object an appreciable restriction of competition falling outside the scope of Article 81(1), OJ 1997 C 372/13, para 2.

131 Guidelines on horizontal agreements, OJ 2001 C 3/2, para. 25.

132 Case T-148/89, *Tréfilunion* v. *Commission*, [1995] ECR II-1063, para 109, Joined Cases T-374/94, T-375/94, T-384/94 and T-388/94, *European Night Services* v. *Commission*, [1998] ECR II-3141, para. 136.

133 Case T-112/99, *Métropole II*, [2001] ECR II-2459.

134 Case 5/69, *Völk* v. *Vervaecke*, [1969] ECR 295.

## 8.5 The concept of the compulsory cartel and environmental concerns

### 8.5.1 Introductory remarks

As was shown in the above paragraphs, the restriction of competition presupposes the presence of competition. If parties had no freedom to conclude an agreement, then no restriction of competition can be said to have taken place. Even though the term is not used in English language writing on competition law,[135] this doctrine can be called that of the 'mandatory' or 'compulsory cartel' in accordance with the German concept of the '*Zwangskartell*'. In the environmental context this doctrine is of particular importance as the overwhelming majority of environmental agreements show considerable government involvement. Below, we will first take a closer look at the concept of the compulsory cartel in European competition law. After that we will shift our attention to the role that this concept may play in connection with environmental agreements.

### 8.5.2 The concept of the compulsory cartel

The concept of the compulsory cartel has played a role in Community competition law primarily in connection with the notoriously over-regulated agricultural sector. However, a very useful definition of what constitutes such a compulsory cartel can be found in a one of the judgments in the *Ladbroke* saga:[136]

> *'Articles 85 and 86 [now 81 and 82] of the Treaty apply only to anti-competitive conduct engaged in by undertakings on their own initiative [...]. If anti-competitive conduct is required of undertakings by national* LEGISLATION *or if the latter creates a* LEGAL FRAMEWORK *which itself eliminates any possibility of competitive activity on their part, Articles 85 and 86 do not apply. In such a situation, the restriction of competition is not attributable, as those provisions implicitly require, to the autonomous conduct of the undertakings [...]'. [Emphasis added]*

This definition relies predominantly on the presence of a legislative framework eliminating all possibilities for competition. Therefore this, as it will be called, Ladbroke test can be classified as rather strict. As such it may be contrasted with

---

[135] See, however, Bellamy & Child 2001 who, at p. 113 *et seq.* devote an entire paragraph to 'State authorisation or compulsion'.

[136] Joined Cases C-359/95 P and C-379/95 P, *Commission and France* v. *Ladbroke*, [1997] ECR I-6265, para. 33.

the apparently wider test applied by the Court of First Instance in the *Asia Motor France III* case:[137]

> *'In the absence of any binding regulatory provision imposing the conduct at issue, the Court considers that the Commission is entitled to reject the complaints for want of autonomy on the part of the undertakings in question only if it appears on the basis of objective, relevant and consistent evidence that that conduct was unilaterally imposed upon them by the national authorities through the exercise of irresistible pressures, such as, for example, the threat to adopt State measures likely to cause them to sustain substantial losses.'*

The Court of First instance, in accordance with the approach adopted by the Court, requires unilateral conduct on the part of the government authorities. However, the requirement that this conduct have a purely legislative origin is dropped and replaced by a criterion that seems to also accommodate 'economic pressure' as a factor leading to a compulsory cartel. This could be called the 'economically compulsory cartel' approach. Given the fact that the Ladbroke case was decided later and by a hierarchically higher court, the Ladbroke test can be assumed to currently stand as the law. It has to be pointed out that in the appeal against the *Asia Motor France III* case, the European Court of Justice upheld the judgment of the Court of First instance without, however, having to rule explicitly on the criterion itself. Moreover, in the *Irish Sugar* case, the Court of First Instance applied the European Court of Justice's Ladbroke test.[138]

### 8.5.3 The compulsory cartel and environmental concerns

The concept of the compulsory cartel in itself leaves no room to take environmental concerns into account. Moreover, this would not make sense, as an agreement does not become any more or less compulsory upon parties when there are some environmental aspects involved. However, as was already alluded to above, many environmental agreements are characterised by some form of government involvement. For example, the ACEA agreement was not only concluded between the Commission and the European automobile manufacturers association, the former has also stated that it will consider legislation, which can be presumed to be more costly for the manufacturers than the agreement, if the agreement fails to deliver. Furthermore, the Eco-Emballages and DSD agreements, although concluded between private parties, both are a reaction to obligations imposed by national legislation adopted pursuant to the Packaging directive.[139]

---

[137] Case T-387/94, *Asia Motor France et al.* v. *Commission*, [1996] ECR II-961, para. 65.

[138] Case T-228/97, *Irish Sugar* v. *Commission*, [1999] ECR II-2969, para. 130.

[139] Commission Notice pursuant to Article 19(3) of Council Regulation 17, OJ 1997 C 100/4 and OJ 2000 C 227/6.

Although the legal framework in these cases generally falls short of the legislative measures that 'eliminates any possibility of competitive activity' within the meaning of the Ladbroke test, the reactions of industry can hardly be called surprising when this framework is scrutinised. If we take the legislation implementing the packaging directive as an example, it will become clear that cooperation on as large a scale possible is the only economically rational outcome from industry's point of view. Generally, this legislation lays down a 'producer responsibility' according to which the producer is responsible for the waste generated once his products reach their end of life. Thus there is a nexus between the producer and 'his' waste. To fulfil the producer responsibility producers are offered two options. They may decide to collect and recycle their waste individually, which of course is horribly inefficient and prohibitively expensive in most cases. For this reason, such legislation generally offers the second option of fulfilling the producer responsibility by joining a collective scheme. Economies of scale almost inevitably result in the largest possible scale of collection and recycling activities in these schemes.[140]

As was said above, such legislation most probably cannot be considered to exclude any competitive activity within the meaning of the Ladbroke test. However, the test adopted by the Court of First Instance in the *Asia Motor France* case seems to be capable of being fulfilled in these cases. Certainly, legislation leaving the choice between expensive individual solutions and much less expensive collective solutions can be considered to exert 'irresistible pressures' on industry to cooperate.[141] Such reasoning of course only takes the cooperation itself outside the scope of Article 81(1). It would still have to be established whether the further restrictions of competition are also the result of the government's pressure.

## 8.6 An increased role for environmental concerns in Article 81(1)?

As we have seen the role of environmental concerns in terms of an integration of environmental concerns is limited to the role that environmental concerns have in the economic process. To be fair, this role is still rather minor. In this respect, all that is called for is an economically rational application of competition law. There is, for example, no reason to completely do away

140 *Cf.* Lehman 2000, paragraph 6. Moreover, as the current chaos with regard to the deposit and return system for one way beverage containers in Germany shows, the environmental benefits of cooperation are also significant, FAZ 25 July 2003 'Entsorger sagen weiteren Streit um Dosenpfand voraus'.

141 See, with regard to dominant position held by the collective system that may thus the result, paragraph 9.6.

with the appreciability test in cases involving a hard-core restriction. Furthermore, in these (and other) cases recourse should be had to the quantitative as well as the qualitative appreciability test.

In this connection, the *VOTOB* case may be mentioned as an interesting example.[142] The VOTOB agreement was concluded between the six independent firms offering tank storage capacity for chemicals in the Netherlands.[143] These firms had signed an agreement with the local government to bring down emissions from their installations. The necessary investments in this respect exceeded the financial capacities of the individual firms but could be partly subsidised on the basis of a general investment scheme.[144] When after concluding the agreement with the government, suddenly, the Dutch government withdrew this investment scheme altogether, the firms were faced with a budget deficit. The firms decided to finance their investments by laying a uniform 'environmental surcharge' on the price of their services. This surcharge varied per product to be stored (depending on the polluting potential) and had to be passed on completely to consumers and moreover, had to be mentioned separately on the invoice. The Commission considered the agreement to pass a fixed charge on to consumers to be horizontal price fixing and therefore prohibited. In doing so the Commission apparently took no account of the fact that this charge amounted to less than 5 per cent of the total costs.[145] The Commission thus clearly refused to take into account the economic (and ecologic) background of the case

It may, however, be wondered whether, on a somewhat more general level it can be argued that an environmental agreement falls outside the scope of Article 81(1) because of its environmental objective and the presence of the integration principle? In other words, can the presence of an environmental aspect lead to a new or a wider exception to the scope of Article 81(1)? As far as the scope of the competition rules in general is concerned, we have seen the answer to this question to be negative. With regard to the particular requirements of Article 81 – the presence of an appreciable restriction of competition – much the same holds true. The objective of achieving sustainable development requires that some competitive pressure remains with regard to the environmental aspects. This demands that some sort of check on the restriction of competition involved remains. This is best achieved through the exemption clause, which of course

---

[142] Unfortunately, this case, allthough often being considered a 'landmark case' never resulted in a formal decision and has had to contend itself with a mere mentioning in the Annual Competition Report, Commission, XXIInd Competition report 1992, paras. 177-186.

[143] They were independent in that they were not connected to up- or downstream (chemical) companies.

[144] This remains unclear in the Commission's account of the case but can be found in the article by Vogelaar describing the case, Vogelaar 1995, p. 550 *et seq.*

[145] *Ibid.* , p. 551.

presupposes that Article 81(1) is applicable in the first place. On the basis of this reasoning, Article 6 EC – the integration principle – cannot be relied upon to take environmental agreements *a priori* outside the scope of Article 81(1). Similarly, the broader 'European rule of reason' identified by Monti should also not be used to restrict the scope of Article 81(1). An agreement that restricts competition cannot be taken outside the scope of Article 81(1) simply because it is necessary to protect a mandatory requirement. As the wording of Article 81 clearly shows, restrictions – that can be the result of the anti-competitive impact that outweighs the pro-competitive effect – of competition are prohibited by Article 81(1) without any room in that provision for an exception or justification. This exception (or, at the moment, exemption) can be found in Article 81(3) EC.

A slightly different question is whether negative environmental effects may result in an agreement being considered to fall within the scope of Article 81(1) by virtue of these environmental effects alone. Take, for example, a research and development joint venture that set up to develop a new, but very energy inefficient product. Furthermore, because of the parties' market shares (well below 5 per cent), this agreement would normally be considered *de minimis* and therefore fall outside the scope of Article 81(1). Could it be argued that, on the basis of the integration principle, such an agreement would fall within the scope of the prohibition just because of the negative environmental impact of the agreement? This becomes all the more interesting once we notice that there is currently no European legislation prescribing minimum energy efficiency criteria.

We would argue against this for a number of interrelated reasons. Firstly, the (negative) implications of any activity are or should be governed by environmental legislation. In the context of the example above this would mean that the agreement setting up the joint venture is subject to competition scrutiny. The actual activities and the products developed on the basis of the agreement should conform to environmental regulations. The absence of environmental legislation (which is the case with, for example, energy efficiency) cannot be an excuse to pursue environmental policy through the application of competition law. It has to be observed that environmental legislation is a matter of the Council (i.e. the member states) acting together with the Parliament. Either way, if the Commission were to use competition policy as a *de facto* environmental instrument to act in the absence of European legislation, it would bypass the Council and Parliament. Secondly, legal certainty and the connected principle of equality stand in the way of this. In this connection it must be observed that there is no obligation, except for when the parties want to obtain legal certainty, to apply for a negative clearance. The result of taking negative environmental effects into account within Article 81(1) could therefore be that those who voluntarily apply for a negative clearance are worse off than the parties that do not apply for such clearance. A third reason that would seem to argue against taking environmental degradation into account in interpreting Article 81(1) is the integration principle itself. As we have seen above, the integration principle applies only to the activities and policies listed in Article 3 EC. These policies and activities all presuppose some positive action involving the exercise of discretion. Within Article 81, this discretion is exercised in applying the third paragraph whereas the interpretation of the prohibition in the first paragraph is a matter of interpreting the law.[146] This is evidenced by the Court's attitude when it checks the legality of a Commission decision. In this respect only a manifest error of appraisal by the Commission will infringe 81(3) whereas the Court will stick closely to the wording of the first paragraph in judging whether the Commission has applied Article 81(1) correctly. The conclusion must therefore be that only the application of the exemption clause contains a policy element that justifies the application of the integration principle.

## 8.7 Article 81(3) – the possibility of an exemption

### 8.7.1. Introductory remarks

If a restriction of competition is appreciable and all the other requirements of Article 81(1) are fulfilled, the second paragraph of Article 81 declares an agreement to be automatically null. The only way to have an enforceable agreement even though Article 81(1) is violated is to qualify for an exemption. The starting point for an exemption must be Article 81(3) that provides that Article 81(1) may be declared inapplicable if four requirements are satisfied.

Firstly, the agreement must contribute to improving the production or distribution of goods or to promoting technical or economic progress. In short, the agreement has to result in a benefit. Hereafter we will refer to this as the requirement of technical or economic progress. Secondly, the consumers must receive a fair share of this benefit. Thirdly, the restrictions must no go beyond what is necessary to attain the benefits. This is often referred to as the proportionality requirement. Fourthly, the agreement may not allow the firms the possibility to restrict competition in respect of a substantial part of the products in question. This requirement seeks to ascertain that sufficient residual competition remains despite the agreement. Currently only the Commission can apply Article 81(3) in what is called an individual exemption.[147] When the Commission has gained enough experience with a particular type of agreement, it may lay down this experience in a so-called group exemption. With regard to these exemptions the Court has held that the application of Article 81(3) involves an

[146] *Cf.* Schröter 1999, p. 2/29, rn. 25.

[147] This will change from 1 May 2004 onwards when Article 81(3) becomes directly applicable by virtue of Regulation 1/2003. See further, *infra*, paragraph 8.9

assessment of complex economic facts so that judicial review is limited to cases involving a manifest error of assessment.[148] The result of this limitation of the judicial review is that we will have to concentrate on the Commission's decision practice in this respect. Nevertheless, the following considerations of the European Court of Justice are of some interest.[149]

> *'As the court pointed out in its judgment in Metro I, the powers conferred upon the Commission under Article 85(3), [Now Article 81(3)] show that the requirements for the maintenance of workable competition may be reconciled with the safeguarding of objectives of a different nature and that to this end certain restrictions on competition are permissible, provided that they are essential to the attainment of those objectives and that they do not result in the elimination of competition for a substantial part of the common market.'*

This shows that the third paragraph of Article 81 is all about balancing the restriction of competition on the one hand with the non-competition advantage of the agreement on the other hand. The Court of First Instance's judgment in *Métropole I* echoes this view of Article 81(3) where it states that:[150]

> *'Admittedly, in the context of an overall assessment, the Commission is entitled to base itself on* CONSIDERATIONS CONNECTED WITH THE PURSUIT OF THE PUBLIC INTEREST *in order to grant exemption under Article 85(3) [Now 81(3)] of the Treaty.' [Emphasis added]*

For the reasons indicated above, we will concentrate on the Commission's practice with regard to Article 81(3). Moreover, we will first study the application of Article 81(3) in individual cases. After that the group exemptions will be looked at in more detail. In both cases we shall pay particular attention to the possible implications of the integration principle. Essentially, the integration principle can have two different effects. Firstly, it may play its role with regard to environmental agreements in that it could result in an exemption in cases that could not be exempted on pure competition considerations. This effect will be referred to as the positive effect of integration in that it result in a positive act namely the adoption of an exemption decision. Secondly, the integration principle could play its role in the appreciation of agreements that have no particular environmental objective. In this connection the integration principle could be interpreted so as to preclude an exemption of an agreement that has a negative environmental impact. This will be called the negative effect of integration since the result will

---

[148] E.g. Case T-17/93, *Matra Hachette* v. *Commission* (Matra), [1994] ECR II-595, para. 104.

[149] Case 75/84, *Metro* v. *Commission* (Metro II), [1986] ECR 3021, para. 20.

[150] Joined Cases T-529/93, T-543/93 & T-546/93, *Métropole et al* v. *Commission* (Métropole I), [1996] ECR II-649, para. 118.

be the refusal of an exemption decision. In both cases the Commission will be prone to criticism that it abuses competition law to conduct environmental policy. As will be shown, this criticism is unjustified in that it departs from the false premise that the Community has a number of completely separate policies that do not interrelate. Moreover, it fails to recognise the integrative framework provided by the Treaty. Below, we will first look at the first type of situation, *i.e.* the positive effect of the integration principle with regard to the competitive assessment of environmental agreements. This will take place individually for the four specific requirements to be found in Article 81(3). After that we shall concentrate on the negative effect of the integration principle with regard to Article 81(3) as a whole. Finally, the effects of the direct applicability that Regulation 1/2003 will bestow upon Article 81(3) will be examined.

### 8.7.2 The requirement of technical or economic progress and the protection of the environment

Taken literally, Article 81(3) would never allow for an exemption on environmental grounds. The first requirement refers only to economic benefits. Not unlike the Court, which created an environmental exception to the free movement provisions when the Treaty was silent on this matter, this silence has not kept the Commission from taking the environment into account in applying this requirement. However, before we move on to this core issue, it is useful to first indicate the general concepts involved in establishing economic and technical progress. In one of the very first competition cases to come to it, the *Consten & Grundig* case, the Court gave the following consideration with regard to this requirement:[151]

*'The question whether there is an improvement in the production of distribution of the goods in question, which is required for the grant of exemption, is to be answered in accordance with the spirit of Article 85 [Now Article 81]. First, this improvement cannot be identified with all the advantages that the parties to the agreement obtain from it in their production or distribution activities. These advantages are generally indisputable and show the agreement as in all respects indispensable to an improvement as understood in this sense. This subjective method, which makes the content of the concept of 'improvement' depend upon the special features of the contractual relationships in question, is not consistent with the aims of Article 85 [Now Article 81]. Furthermore, the very fact that the Treaty provides that the restriction of competition must be 'indispensable' to the improvement in question clearly indicates the importance which the latter must have. This improvement must in particular show* APPRECIABLE OBJECTIVE ADVANTAGES *of such a character as to compensate for the disadvantages which they cause in the field of competition.' [Emphasis added]*

[151] Joined Cases 56, 58/64, *Consten & Grundig*, [1966] ECR 429, at p. 348.

This paragraph confirms the objective nature of the benefits required to satisfy the first part of the exemption clause. In general the following remark in a Commission exemption decision may shed some light on the Commission's perception of the function of this criterion.[152]

*'For the agreements to contribute to the improvement of production or distribution, or to promote technical or economic progress, they must objectively constitute an improvement on the situation that would otherwise exist. The fundamental principle in this respect, established at the time the common market was formed, lays down that fair and undistorted competition is the best guarantee of regular supply on the best terms. Thus the question of a contribution to economic progress within the meaning of Article 85(3) [Now Article 81(3)] can only arise in those exceptional cases where the free play of competition is unable to produce the best result economically speaking.'*

Furthermore, in the *Matra* case already referred to above, the Commission made the following statements concerning the first requirement for an exemption.[153]

*'Finally, according to the Commission, it is possible to take into account, as regards the contribution to economic and technical progress, factors other than those expressly mentioned in those provisions. They include, for example, the maintenance of employment [...]. Accordingly, regional policy concerns may be taken into consideration, for the purposes of Article 85(3) [Now Article 81(3)] of the Treaty, in conformity with the requirements of Article 130A [Now Article 158] of the EC Treaty. That certainly does not mean that the restrictions of competition deriving from the agreement were declared valid solely because of the geographical location of the joint venture. As is apparent from paragraph 36 of the Decision, it is based primarily on the intrinsic merits of the project.'*

This, we think, very clearly sets out the Commission's approach with regard to the possibility to take other factors than those listed in Article 81(3) into account. The Commission certainly considers it possible to do so and will do so. However, such factors can of themselves never warrant an exemption. This idea resurfaces in a number of early exemption decisions in the environmental context. In its 1974 decision concerning the selective distribution system set up by *BMW*, the commission, in granting an exemption, took account of the fact that cars need regular maintenance to prevent them from, *inter alia*, 'having a harmful effect

[152] Commission Decision 76/172, *Bayer/Gist-Brocades*, OJ 1976 L 30/13. Repeated in Commission Decision 72/474, *Cimbel*, OJ 1972 L 303/24, para. 24.

[153] Case T-17/93, *Matra*, [1994] ECR II-595, para. 96.

on the environment'.[154] Similarly, in the decision on the *Carbon Gas Technologie* joint venture the Commission took into account the fact that the new process of coal gasification would lead to environmental benefits.[155] This approach was repeated in the *BBC Brown Boveri* case which concerned a joint venture set up to develop new high power batteries. According to the Commission the agreement could be exempted because the development of such batteries would facilitate the introduction of electrically powered cars that are environmentally friendly in that they do not emit noise or exhaust gases.[156] In the decision in the *Assurpol* case, the Commission exempted an agreement to set up an economic interest grouping for the co-reinsurance of environmental damage risks. In doing so the Commission considered that the cooperation enabled better assessment of the environmental risks and thus the development of industrial processes that are less hazardous for the environment.[157] In the decision on the *Ford Volkswagen* joint venture to develop a new MPV, the Commission considered, in granting an exemption, that the MPV being developed will be improved with respect to environmental requirements. With regard to these improvements the Commission points out that the use of hazardous materials will be brought down and the recyclability will be increased while the new MPV should lead the pack in terms of low emissions and fuel consumption.[158] Similarly, when considering the *Exxon Shell* joint venture for the production of polyethylene, the fact that the agreement would obviate the need to transport raw materials and thus avoids health and environmental risks involved in such transports was taken into account by the Commission. Furthermore, the new process used in the joint venture plant would result in a reduction of the amount of raw materials used by customers and therewith reduce the volume of plastic waste.[159] As a final example we would refer to the *Philips Osram* joint venture decision in which the Commission granted an exemption on partly environmental grounds.[160]

In none of these cases the exemption was granted on environmental grounds alone.[161] Rather, these were just taken into account and were clearly subordinate to the economic benefits. This can be deduced from the decisions themselves and becomes even clearer when the Commission's competition report is read with regard to these decisions. Not a single word on the environmental

---

[154] Commission Decision 75/73, *BMW,* OJ 1974 L 29/1, para. 24.

[155] Commission Decision 83/669, *Carbon Gas Technologie,* OJ 1983 L 376/17.

[156] Commission Decision 88/541, *BBC Brown Boveri,* OJ 1988 L 301/68, para 23.

[157] Commission Decision 92/96, *Assurpol,* OJ 1992 L 37/16, para. 38.

[158] Commission Decision 93/49, *Ford/ Volkswagen,* OJ 1993 L 20/14 paras. 25, 26.

[159] Commission Decision 94/322, *Exxon/ Shell,* OJ 1994 L 144/20, paras. 67, 68.

[160] Commission Decision 94/986, *Philips/Osram,* OJ 1994 L 378/37, para. 25.

[161] *Cf.* Mortelmans 2000, p. 25, Vogelaar 1995, p. 547.

aspects and their role in granting the exemption is to be found.[162] However, on other occasions the Commission has stated in its competition reports that it takes environmental considerations into account as a factor contributing to the improvement of production or distribution and technical and economic progress.[163]

All these decisions show that the discussion on whether environmental protection considerations are taken into account by the Commission in granting an exemption can be closed. The more interesting question in this respect is whether environmental considerations can of themselves and provided that the other three requirements are fulfilled, justify an exemption. Furthermore, it is with regard to this question that the positive effects of the integration principle as implemented through the model of integration should come into play.

To answer this question, we need to look at current Commission practice with regard to 'purely environmental' agreements. The joint ventures that we looked at above simply did not require any role for the environmental concerns other than to just 'green' the Commission's decision-making practice. It is only with regard those agreements that serve primarily or even only have an environmental objective that the true importance of environmental concerns becomes clear.

Under the heading of 'economic benefits' the Commission considers such agreements in its Guidelines on horizontal agreements.[164] Because of their importance these considerations merit quotation in full.

*'193. Environmental agreements caught by Article 81(1) may attain economic benefits which, either at individual or aggregate consumer level, outweigh their negative effects on competition. To fulfil this condition, there must be net benefits in terms of reduced environmental pressure resulting from the agreement, as compared to a baseline where no action is taken. In other words, the expected economic benefits must outweigh the costs (55).*

*194. Such costs include the effects of lessened competition along with compliance costs for economic operators and/or effects on third parties. The benefits might be assessed in two stages. Where consumers individually have a positive rate of return from the agreement under reasonable payback periods, there is no need for the aggregate environmental benefits to be objectively established. Otherwise, a cost-benefit*

---

[162] *Cf. Eg.* Commission, XIIth. competition report 1983, para. 116 (*Carbon Gas Technologie*), XVIIIth. competition report 1988, para. 64 (*BBC Brown Boveri*), XXIInd. competition report 1992, para. 140 (*Assurpol*), XXIIIrd. competition report 1993, para. 139 (*Ford/Volkswagen*) and XXIVth. competition report 1994, p. 426 (*Exxon/Shell*).

[163] *E.g* Commission, XXVIIIth. Competition report 1998, para. 129.

[164] Commission, Guidelines on horizontal agreements, OJ 2001 C 3/2, chapter 7, p. 26 *et seq.*

*analysis may be necessary to assess whether net benefits for consumers in general are likely under reasonable assumptions.'*

We can immediately notice that the Commission refers only to the 'economic benefits'. However, a further point that springs to mind is the fact that the Commission is referring to, in the context of establishing such economic benefits, 'net benefits in terms of reduced environmental pressure'. This seems to suggest that the Commission was thinking of purely environmental benefits in this respect. Furthermore, these economic benefits can exist on two levels: the individual and the aggregate consumer level. The reference to 'net' environmental benefits could be taken to refer to the possibility of certain environmental improvements actually resulting in an environmental degradation.[165] It is, for example, possible that increases in efficiency and thus lower running costs of appliances will also lead more intensive use of these appliances, thereby impinging on the environmental improvement. However, the final sentence of paragraph 193 where the Commission appears to be summarising its previous remarks again points at a purely economic approach to the environmental benefits.[166] Moreover, the fact that the Commission speaks of economic benefits outweighing the costs (in terms of reduced competition) points at the introduction of an extra proportionality criterion within the first requirement for an exemption. It can be doubted whether Article 81(3) allows for such an extra proportionality test apart from the necessity test that forms the third requirement of Article 81(3). A final remark concerns the second requirement, that consumers receive a fair share in the benefit. The Commission appears to take this requirement together with the first in its Guidelines. We will have a closer look at this requirement below but at this stage it can be said that this taking together does little for the clarity of the Guidelines in this respect.

The Commission's decision in the *CECED* case may be helpful in this respect.[167] In this decision the Commission is again taking the existence of the benefit and the fair share for the consumers together. The Commission considered that the CECED agreement entailed benefits that would allow it to be exempted. According to the Commission, the agreement is designed to reduce the energy consumption by at least 20 per cent.[168] Furthermore, the reduced energy consumption will result in less pollution resulting from the generation of electricity.[169] The Commission appears to be referring to the contribution of the

165 *Cf.* Commission Decision 2000/475, *CECED*, OJ 2000 L 187/47, para. 49 and footnote 8.

166 Vedder 2001, p. 89 *et seq.*

167 Commission Decision 2000/475, *CECED*, OJ 2000 L 187/47. This decision shows a remarkable resemblance to the fictional case given at the end of Chapter 7 of the Guidelines on horizontal agreements.

168 *Ibid.*, para. 47.

169 *Ibid.*, paras 48 and 51.

agreement to technical progress where it considers that washing machines that are more energy efficient while other factors remain constant can be considered 'objectively more technically efficient'.[170] Finally the Commission into account the fact that the agreement could encourage innovation resulting in energy efficiency levels even beyond what is currently possible.[171] This part of the Commission's reasoning seems to fit in rather well with the traditional division of Article 81(3) into four different requirements. When the Commission goes on to establish individual economic benefits and collective environmental benefits it appears to take the first and second test together. According to the Commission, the CECED agreement entails individual *economic* benefits because the initial increase in purchasing costs will be recouped by the individual consumer in 6 to 40 months because of the lower running costs.[172] Furthermore, the Commission appears to take into account the somewhat speculative effect that the restriction of competition with regard to energy efficiency will trigger increased price competition thereby actually lowering the prices of the more efficient machines.[173] As regards the collective environmental benefits the Commission first quantifies the avoided damages resulting from the reduced emissions. The Commission estimates these to be seven times greater than the increased purchase costs of the more efficient washing machines.[174]

On the basis of all of this the Commission comes to the following conclusion:[175]

*'The expected contribution to furthering energy efficiency both within the current technological limits of categories A to C and beyond the limits of category A, the cost-benefit ratio of the standard and the return on investment for individual users point to the conclusion that the agreement is likely to contribute significantly to technical and economic progress whilst allowing users a fair share of the benefits.'*

All in all the Guidelines and the *CECED* decision leave the impression that the Commission has not made up its mind entirely with regard to the first requirement for an exemption in connection with environmental agreements. A number of reasons can be given to substantiate this conclusion. Firstly, the Guidelines and *CECED* seem to be not entirely consistent. For one, the Guidelines expressly state that it is unnecessary to show collective benefits once individual benefits have been shown.[176] This may be contrasted with the fact that the

---

170 *Ibid.*, para 48.

171 *Ibid.*, para. 50.

172 *Ibid.*, para. 52.

173 *Ibid.*, para. 53.

174 *Ibid.*, para. 56.

175 *Ibid.*, para. 57.

176 Commission, Guidelines on horizontal agreements, OJ 2001 C 3/2, para. 194.

*CECED* decision shows that there are collective benefits even when it has already been established that the agreement entails individual benefits. Furthermore, the Commission appears to equate the increased purchase costs of washing machines with the costs of the agreement.[177] This seems far from obvious as the costs of the agreement, as the Commission rightly puts in the Guidelines, include, among others, the effects of lessened competition and compliance costs for economic operators. Secondly, and more importantly, the role of environmental benefits as factors justifying an exemption of themselves can at best be called uncertain. In the Guidelines, the Commission only takes environmental improvements into account as economic benefits. In the *CECED* decision, the Commission takes the benefits of the agreement into account as individual economic benefits and as collective environmental benefits. With regard to the latter, the Commission is in actual fact referring to economic benefits despite the heading of the paragraph.[178] At best, the Guidelines and the *CECED* decision can be taken to show that the Commission will no longer just 'take account of' the environmental improvements in granting an exemption but that these improvements are placed on equal footing with the economic benefits.[179]

The *DSD* case concerning Article 81 EC confirms this uncertainty as to what exactly is the role played by environmental concerns. It may be recalled that this case dealt with the nationwide collection and recycling system set up and operated by DSD pursuant to the German Packaging Ordinance. The Commission considered that the exclusivity clause in the so-called service agreements (between DSD and the local collectors/sorters) restricted competition within the meaning of Article 81(1) EC. Accordingly, an exemption pursuant to Article 81(3) EC was the only way to save DSD in this respect. In checking whether the conditions for an exemption were fulfilled the Commission's very first consideration is perhaps telling.[180]

> 'ANY POSITIVE EFFECTS *brought about by the exclusivity clause [...] must be weighed against the restrictive effects of the agreements.' [Emphasis added]*

The Commission starts out its considerations by stating that DSD was set up in order to meet the obligations of the German Packaging Order and the Packaging Directive, both of which are examples of environmental legislation and thus 'providing a high level of environmental protection'.[181] The Commission

---

[177] Compare para. 56 of the *CECED* decision (Commission Decision 2000/475, *CECED*, OJ 2000 L 187/47) with para. 194 of the Guidelines, *ibid.*

[178] *Cf.* Monti 2002, p. 1074. For a critical appraisal of the economic reasoning in *CECED* see: Maks 2002, p. 35.

[179] *Cf.* Van de Gronden 2001, p. 162, Monti 2002, p. 1075, 1091.

[180] Commission Decision 2001/837, *DSD* (Article 81), OJ 2001 L 319/1, para. 142.

[181] *Ibid.*, para. 143.

then moves on to observe that the service agreements are necessary to make the system work and as a result give 'direct practical effect to environmental objectives'.[182] Only at the very last stage does the Commission revert to its old habit of bringing some purely economic reasoning into the decision in the form of a recognition of the efficiencies that flow from the organisation.[183] On the basis of *DSD* is could possibly be argued that environmental considerations have been the primary justification for this exemption. In this connection it should however be recalled that the Commission is explicitly referring to environmental legislation – by the Community and a member state – that stood at the cradle of DSD. This could be taken as in – albeit implicit – recognition of the sovereignty involved as an other reason for the exemption. The effect of not granting an exemption to DSD with regard to this clause would in effect boil down to greatly impeding the smooth functioning of DSD and thus frustrate its ability to meet the objectives prescribed by the European and German environmental legislator. Following *DSD*, the role for environmental concerns can therefore certainly be said to have become greater whilst the certainty has not been improved to the same extent.

As to the question of what the role of environmental concerns could and should be in this regard we need to return to the Guidelines and the *CECED* and *DSD* decisions once more. In these documents, the Commission extensively refers to many of the Community's environmental principles. Strikingly absent, however, is the integration principle. Article 6 of the EC Treaty requires that environmental protection requirements *must* be *integrated* into the definition and implementation of the Community policies. The word 'must' clearly indicates the obligatory nature of this provision.[184] Furthermore, the concept of 'environmental protection requirements' is of a more general and abstract nature than the concept of the environmental benefits resulting from an agreement. Article 6 refers *in abstracto* to the process of integrating environmental concerns in Community policy in general. It would therefore be overly simplistic to say that Article 6 amounts to nothing more than an obligation to interpret 'economic and technical progress' so as to also encompass environmental benefits. The outcome of this process of integration should amount to sustainable development. Sustainable development, as we have seen in chapter two, in the context of the application of Article 81 requires the right mix of cooperation and competition between firms. Whether this mix is right and therefore conducive to sustainability, depends ultimately on the proportionality or necessity of the restrictions of competition. Article 6 can therefore, at the very least be said not to oppose an increased role for environmental concerns in the context of the first requirement for an exemption.

---

[182] *Ibid.*, para. 144.

[183] *Ibid.*, para. 145.

[184] *Cf.* Opinion of A-G Jacobs in Case C-379/98, *PreussenElektra*, [2001] ECR I-2099.

Taken further, the positive effects of the integration principle could, ultimately, result in an exemption being granted on environmental grounds alone. As was said above, this makes the Commission liable to be criticised of pursuing environmental policy through competition law. In the terminology of administrative law: the Commission could be considered to commit *détournement de pouvoir.* German scholars have voiced such allegations of 'Instrumentalisierung' most fervently.[185] We have already indicated a number of reasons why such criticism is unjustified. Firstly, this criticism simply ignores the presence and purpose of the integration principle the very essence of which is to ensure that environmental considerations play a role in the Community's other policies. Secondly, it fails to recognise that competition law is not an isolated area administered solely by the responsible commissioner together with the directorate-general for competition. The Commission takes decisions on competition matters as a collegial body. Moreover, competition law and policy exist by virtue of and thus functions within the framework of the EC Treaty. The framework thus provided is integrative in that it lays down one common goal for all activities of the Community in Article 2. As Article 2 contains a clear and unambiguous environmental objective for the Community, all Community policies should contribute to attaining these objectives by virtue of Article 3 EC. Criticism that, by taking environmental considerations into account, the Commission is conducting environmental policy with competition law cannot therefore be upheld because it disregards the constitutional and integrative nature provided by the EC Treaty.

The Commission's 'economisation' of the environmental concerns can be taken to mean two things. Firstly, the Commission could only be economising the environmental benefits and still consider them sufficient to justify an exemption of themselves. Secondly, the Commission could be economising the environmental benefits and still be requiring a 'truly economic' (efficiency) benefit alongside. Both interpretations seem compatible with the Commission's decision in the *CECED* case. The Commission's considerations under the heading of the 'collective environmental benefits' seem to fit in well with the first interpretation. There, the Commission quantifies the environmental benefits resulting from the agreement in monetary terms and considers that[186]

*'such environmental results for society would adequately allow consumers a fair share of the benefits even if no [economic] benefits accrued to individual purchasers.'*

The decision as a whole points at the second interpretation. In this respect it has to be noted that the Commission has explicitly proved that there are 'individual

[185] *E.g.* Immenga 1976 and Möschel 1995 at p. 183, *supra* paragraph 5.4.

[186] Commission Decision 2000/475, *CECED*, OJ 2000 L 187/47, para. 56.

economic benefits' and that these benefits together with the possible technological progress and the collective environmental benefits warrant an exemption.[187]

However, from the perspective of our question what the role for environmental concerns should be, this economisation is of limited value. Converting environmental benefits into economic benefits will invariably lead to the outcome that the pursuit of a worthwhile environmental improvement will always coincide with an economic improvement.[188] The costs of environmental degradation are enormous and become exponentially greater as time passes and the degradation dissipates and spreads throughout the environment. Acting now and possibly even in a preventive manner will therefore invariably result in economic benefits. Furthermore the cooperation between firms that brings conduct within the scope of Article 81 will generally bring efficiency gains with it. These efficiency gains will again be considered as economic benefits. This is of course not to say that the whole process of integrating environmental protection requirements into competition law wouldn't become much easier if these were able to justify an exemption *per se*.

### 8.7.3 The requirement of a fair share for consumers and environmental protection

Not only will the agreement have to bring about certain benefits, a fair share in these benefits also has to accrue to consumers. The rationale of this requirement is fairly self-evident. Almost any agreement voluntarily entered into between two or more profit maximising firms will result in a benefit for these firms. Otherwise, they would not have agreed at all.[189] The purpose of Article 81(3), on the contrary, is to allow an exemption for agreements that have some redeeming qualities for society as a whole. With regard to environmental agreements this requirement should not prove to be a stumbling block as environmental benefits inherently accrue to society in general. This is because the environment is a collective good by its very nature. This approach will be referred to as the collective approach.

In the environmental context the 1991 exemption for the joint venture set up by *KSB/Goulds/Lowara/ITT* is interesting. This joint venture concerned the development of new type of pump. In the course of establishing the benefits for consumers the Commission made the following statements:[190]

---

[187] *Ibid.*, paras. 52-54 and 57.

[188] As the *NMa* in a slightly over-generalised manner recognises in its decisions in the *Stibat* and *Wit- en Bruingoed* Cases, *infra* paragraph 16.5.

[189] See, with regard to environmental agreements, Maks 2002, p. 33.

[190] Commission Decision 91/38, *KSB/Goulds/Lowara/ITT*, OJ 1991 19/25, para. 27.

*'The advantages arising from the cooperation benefit consumers at the very least through the improvement in the quality of water pumps. Moreover, two aspects of the new pumps, i.e. energy conservation and the fact that the fluids handled by the pump are not polluted, are environmentally beneficial. This effect is reinforced by the higher performance capacity of the pumps. This constitutes an improvement in operating characteristics. At least at present, a further advantage is that these pumps are offered to consumers at the same price as cast-iron pumps.'*

This seems to indicate that the Commission is willing to consider environmental benefits arising from agreements to inherently entail a fair share for consumers. This view is substantiated to a certain extent by the Commission's Guidelines on horizontal agreements and the *CECED* decision. In the Guidelines the Commission distinguishes between an individual and a collective share in the benefit for consumers. According to the Commission there is no need to investigate whether an agreements results in 'aggregate environmental benefits' if it has been shown that the individual consumer will have a 'positive rate of return'.[191] This confirms the line of reasoning of the Commission in the *KSB/Goulds/Lowara/ITT* decision in that aggregate environmental benefits could be sufficient to satisfy the second requirement.[192] On the other hand, such benefits seem to be considered as secondary grounds and need only to be established once it has been impossible to show a positive rate of return. This last, 'individual', approach to the requirement of a fair share for consumers seems more restrictive than the collective approach. For one, environmental improvements will be costly and, as a consequence, the (partly) passing on these environmental costs to consumers will generally render a positive rate of return impossible. One case where the Commission has accepted a positive rate of return is the *CECED* case that has already been mentioned several times above. According to the Commission the increase in purchase price of washing machines as a result of the phasing out would be recouped by the average consumer within 40 months because of the lower running costs.[193] In this case the collective environmental and individual economic benefits coincide and thus yield a positive rate of return. There are, however, a number of cases where the collective environmental benefit does not result in or coincide with such a direct individual economic benefit. These will notably be the cases where environmental costs are actually internalised and (partly) passed on to consumers. In these cases the consumer, will never have a positive rate of return because he will invariably be economically off worse than before the internalisation. The mere fact that the environment as a whole benefits does nothing for the individuals'

[191] Commission, Guidelines on horizontal agreements, OJ 2001 C 3/2, para. 194.

[192] *Cf.* Monti 2002, p. 1076.

[193] Commission Decision 2000/475, *CECED*, OJ 2000 L 187/47, para. 52.

rate of return as defined by the Commission. This would be otherwise only if it is accepted that the cooperation reduces the amount of internalised costs and that this reduction in itself constitutes a benefit in which there is a fair share for consumers. However, to arrive at that conclusion it would have to be accepted that having to pay less constitutes a 'positive rate of return' To date there have been no cases involving this type of agreement that have concerned this point.[194] However, the Netherlands Competition authority has dealt with a number of such schemes and as such we will pay closer attention to this issue in the relevant chapter.[195]

In the *CECED* decision the Commission has also – and, if judged by its Guidelines, superfluously – established the collective environmental benefits. In doing so the Commission relied on the fact that the estimated saved (avoided) external costs (the benefits) exceeded the increase in purchase costs of washing machines (the costs) by about seven times.[196] The Commission goes on to state that 'such environmental results for society would adequately allow consumers a fair share of the benefits even if no benefits accrued to individual purchasers of machines'[197] This decision, however, still leaves room for quite some uncertainty with regard to the lower border of the magnitude of the benefits compared to the costs. In this respect, the Guidelines provide no extra certainty whatsoever.

This collective line of reasoning, even though it is adopted as a secondary line of reasoning, shows that purely environmental benefits, even when they do not coincide with individual economic benefits can still result in a fair share for consumers. This last line of reasoning, in our opinion, is the one to be followed primarily whereby the existence of individual economic benefits would constitute a 'nice extra'. The weight currently attached by the Commission to the individual approach, as has been shown above, fits in rather badly with the collective nature of the goods protected by an environmental agreement.

Ideally, a distinction would have to be made between the economic and the environmental benefits arising from an environmental agreement. This distinction would then serve to identify the environmental benefits as such and, as a result, clarify the weight that has been attached to them in the decision. At the same time the environmental benefits would have to be integrated into the elements of Article 81(3) EC. With regard to the environmental benefits, the collective approach to determining a fair share for consumers should be followed because that would be in accordance with and recognise the diffuse

---

194 Unfortunately, the Commission chose to deal with *VOTOB* in an informal way. As a result, nothing is known about the Commission's appraisal of such cases with regard to Article 81(3) apart from the general statement that an exemption is unlikely.

195 *Infra*, paragraph 16.5

196 Commission, Guidelines on horizontal agreements, OJ 2001 C 3/2, para. 56.

197 *Ibid.*

nature of this type of benefit. Only with regard to the economic benefits of an agreement, arising, for example, from the economies of scale of cooperation, is closer scrutiny in the form of the determination of an individual fair share called for. This is inherent in the purpose of the requirement of establishing a fair share for consumers, which, as has been said above, is to ascertain that only advantages that not only benefit the parties themselves are exempted. Environmental benefits, by their very nature, cannot be kept for oneself. Economic benefits, on the contrary, may very well not be passed on to consumers. In this regard the Commission's reasoning is not entirely consistent with its previous practice where it relied, in proving a fair share for consumers, on the presence of some competitive pressure.[198] The reasoning behind this is that the presence of competitive pressure will force the firms to pass the (economic) benefits on to consumers. In the Guidelines and the *CECED* decision, no reference to this reasoning is to be found. Instead the Commission seems to consider only the case where the economic and environmental benefit coincide naturally and therefore the presence of competition is not required to ensure the passing on of the advantages at all. With regard to the passing on of the economic benefits arising from an environmental agreement (for example in the form of lower prices for waste collection services because of cooperation), the ideal situation would rely on the presence of competitive pressure and not so much on the coincidence of economic and environmental benefits that the Commission has found.

Again, the more recent *DSD* decision appears to entail a certain evolution. With regard to the fair share for consumers, the Commission follows a bifurcated approach. It starts out its appraisal by observing somewhat generally that the operation of the DSD system is consumer friendly.[199] Then the Commission observes that DSD's structure and operation will allow for scale and scope advantages and thus efficiencies. According to the Commission, it can be accepted that these cost savings will be passed on the consumers. This observation is formulaic in two respects. Firstly because it is the standard approach to this requirement for an exemption. Secondly, because it cannot be called anything more than a mere statement: the Commission fails to indicate why the savings will be passed on.

The other observation by the Commission is of much more interest for the purpose of this research. Again, it merits quotation in full:[200]

*'[...] consumers will likewise benefit as a result of the improvement in environmental quality sought, essentially the reduction in the volume of packaging'.*

---

[198] Ritter, Braun & Rawlinson 2000, p. 125, Faull & Nikpay 1999, p. 110 *et seq.*

[199] Commission Decision 2001/837, *DSD* (Article 81), OJ 2001 L 319/1, para. 147.

[200] *Ibid.*, para. 148.

With this statement the Commission is coming dangerously close to the reasoning whereby environmental benefits, precisely because of their open and diffuse nature, inherently accrue to an open group and thus always entail a fair share for the consumer. Thus, this aspect of *DSD* confirms what has already been said above with regard to the treatment of the first requirement for an exemption. By and large the role for environmental concerns appears to have increased. Nevertheless, the presence of an – albeit unsubstantiated – economic argument in this connection does little to really clarify the role actually played by the environmental considerations.

The same obscure clarity can be seen in the recent judgment of the European Court of Justice on the German solidarity fund for illegally transported waste.[201] This case consists of a Treaty infringement procedure (Article 226 EC) against Germany. According to the Commission, the mandatory payments by companies that are active in the waste shipments sector into a fund that would be used to cover the costs of the retrieval of illegally transported waste, amounted to a charge of equivalent effect within the meaning of Articles 23 and 25 EC. According to the German government, the payments were not prohibited by Articles 23 and 25 even though they closely resembled a charge having equivalent effect. One of the arguments brought forward by the German government was the fact that the waste exporting companies would actually benefit from this fund so that the payment could be seen as a remuneration for a service actually provided that.[202] The European Court Justice rejected this argument using, among others, the following reasoning.[203]

*'In those circumstances, compliance by the Federal Republic of Germany with an obligation which Community law imposes on all the Member States in pursuit of a general interest, namely protection of health and the environment, does not confer on exporters of waste established in its territory any specific or definite benefit'.*

Here we see the Court qualifying the ultimate goal of the German measure as one that serves 'the general interest, namely the protection of health and the environment'. Subsequently, the Court is of the opinion that this objective does not confer any 'specific or definite benefit'. It is submitted that this absence of a specific or definite benefit can be explained by the fact that the Court sees environmental protection as a diffuse benefit that inherently benefits an open group.

---

[201] Case C-389/00, *Commission* v. *Germany*, judgment of 27 February 2003, n.y.r.

[202] *Ibid.*, para. 29.

[203] *Ibid.*, para. 35.

### 8.7.4 The proportionality requirement and environmental protection

#### 8.7.4.1 Introductory remarks

Even if the benefits arising from an agreement are passed on to consumers, it will have to be shown that the restriction of competition does not go any further than is necessary to attain those benefits. The basic idea behind this test can be said to be that the advantages of the agreement must outweigh the disadvantages arising from the restriction of competition. It is therefore a balancing act of two different objectives. On the one hand the objective of maintenance of effective competition and, on the other hand, the objective of the agreement, which, for the purpose of this research will generally be the protection of the environment. In general, the rule would seem to be that the greater the disadvantages resulting from the restriction of competition, the more important the advantages will have to be. For a start, reference may be made to the judgment of the Court of First Instance in the *Matra* case where it held that in principle there is no restriction that is *a priori* unexemptable.[204] This obvious statement defines the absolute minimum of what can be said about the proportionality requirement. For more specific information on the application of the proportionality test we need to look at the Commission's decision-making practice and the Courts' case law. In this respect, it may be useful to first set out the different sub-tests identified by doctrine in the proportionality test.

Within the proportionality test, essentially four different sub-tests can be discerned.[205] Firstly, a test determining whether the actual aim of the measure is justified. The purpose of this test can be said to sort the wheat from the chaff in order to uncover what the Commission calls 'disguised cartels'.[206] Secondly, it will have to be shown that the measure is effective. In other words: the question is asked whether the measure is actually likely to contribute to the attainment of the objective. This could also be called a causality test. Thirdly, it will have to be established that the objective cannot be attained with less restrictive means. This test is commonly referred to as the necessity test.[207] In this test the objective of the agreement, and, more precisely in the context of environmental agreements, the level of protection sought, is accepted. Only the means chosen by the agreement are subject to scrutiny in this test. Fourthly and finally, the two objectives must be in balance with each other. In the context of an environmental agreement: the environmental benefit must be proportionate to the restriction of

---

[204] Case T-17/93, *Matra*, [1994] ECR II-595, para. 85.

[205] Gerven 1991, p. 77.

[206] Commission, Guidelines on horizontal agreements, OJ 2001 C 3/2, para. 188.

[207] *Ibid.*

competition. Contrary to the necessity test, the, as it will be called, true proportionality test will call into question the actual environmental objective (the level of protection) itself. It has to be pointed out that this distinction is of scholarly origin and is not applied rigorously by the Court or the Commission.

#### 8.7.4.2 The application of the proportionality test to environmental agreements

The wording of the proportionality test in Article 81(3) – the agreement may not 'impose on the undertakings concerned restrictions which are not indispensable to the attainment of these objectives' – clearly points at a necessity test.[208] The objectives ('these objectives' in the wording of Article 81(3)) of the agreement are to be accepted and only the means chosen (i.e. the restrictions of competition) are subject to scrutiny as to whether or not they are necessary or indispensable to attain these objectives. This interpretation is confirmed by the judgment of the Court of First Instance in the *Matra* case.[209] The applicant in this case challenged the legality of the Commission's decision to approve the *Ford Volkswagen* joint venture to develop and produce a multipurpose vehicle.[210] The Commission granted an exemption in this case because the joint venture would produce a, then new and innovative, type of vehicle. Furthermore, as regards to indispensability, the Commission considered that the Ford and Volkswagen alone could not developed this new product as fast and efficient as the joint venture would allow them to. Among others, the legality of this reasoning was challenged before the Court. Even though the Court first appeared to be embarking on a true proportionality type of reasoning,[211] it ended up confining itself to checking whether there was an alternative to the joint venture (*i.e.* no joint venture but the parties acting independently) which would also lead to the result.[212]

In other cases, the Commission also limits itself to checking whether other, less restrictive, alternatives are available. In, for example, the case involving the *Philips Osram* joint venture, the Commission limited itself to ascertaining whether or not alternative means were available.[213] Moreover, the Commission has consolidated this approach to the proportionality requirement to a certain extent in its Guidelines in which it made the following statement:[214]

---

[208] *Cf.* Faull & Nikpay 1999, p. 112, 113.

[209] Case T-17/93, *Matra*, [1994] ECR II-595, para. 135 *et seq.*

[210] Commission Decision 93/49, *Ford/Volkswagen*, OJ 1993 L 20/14.

[211] *Ibid.*, para. 135.

[212] *Ibid.*, para. 138.

[213] Commission Decision 94/986, *Philips/Osram*, OJ 1994 L 378/37, para. 28.

[214] Commission, Guidelines on horizontal agreements, OJ 2001 C 3/2, para. 35.

*'If there are* LESS RESTRICTIVE MEANS *to achieve similar benefits, the claimed efficiencies cannot be used to justify the restrictions of competition.' [Emphasis added]*

The reluctance in acknowledging that the Commission in the above statement indeed adopted a necessity test follows from the fact that the Commission refers to 'similar benefits' instead of the benefits as identified in the first criterion for an exemption. This could be taken to mean that the Commission will opt for a lower level of protection than envisaged by the parties if the means necessary to achieve the original level prove disproportionate in the sense of the true proportionality test. However, in the chapter devoted to environmental agreements in the Guidelines, the Commission is referring to a necessity test.[215]

This is confirmed by the Commission decision in the *CECED* case. The agreement to phase out the energy inefficient washing machines was considered by the Commission to be indispensable because there are no 'less restrictive alternatives that would be able of delivering similar reductions based on other approaches'.[216] In this respect the Commission investigates whether an industry-wide target, information campaigns or an eco-labelling scheme could lead to the same result. The Commission ultimately reached the conclusion that these alternatives would either not lead to the same results or would do so only at higher costs or while being more restrictive.[217]

In exceptional cases the Commission does not get beyond the first or second sub-test identified in the proportionality test. In, for example, the *NAVEWA-ANSEAU* case, the Commission considered that the actual objective of the agreement was to create a barrier to entry for the Belgian market for washing machines and dishwashers.[218] Similarly, in *Ansac* the Commission simply considered that the agreement did not contribute to the alleged benefits.[219] This case concerned the agreement between the US producers of natural soda ash (an ingredient used to make glass) to set up a joint export company pursuant to the Webb-Pomerene Act. According to the parties, natural soda ash (which is produced primarily in the US) has environmental advantages over synthetic soda ash. Therefore, the U.S. producers argued, the agreement to jointly export this product to the EC would, at least, qualify for an exemption under Article 81(3). The Commission denied the exemption on the grounds that, while it did not dispute the environmental benefits of natural soda ash, the agreement concerned only the setting up of the joint sales agency and was therefore uncon-

215 *Ibid.*, para. 196.

216 Commission Decision 2000/475, *CECED*, OJ 2000 L 187/47, para. 59.

217 *Ibid.*, paras 60-63. See, for a critical but not very convincingly substantiated appraisal : Maks 2002, p. 35.

218 Commission Decision 82/371, *NAVEWA-ANSEAU*, OJ 1982 L 167/39, para. 63.

219 Commission Decision 91/301, *Ansac*, OJ 1991 L 152/54.

nected with the environmental benefit.[220] This can be considered an application of the second sub-test, the causality test.

Finally, the case concerning the *VOTOB* agreement lays down the principles of the Commission's approach to environmental agreements that also concern the costs of environmental protection.[221] In this case the Commission examined an agreement between the six Dutch firms offering tank storage capacity. These firms had agreed to limit the emissions from their installations and to this end they had concluded a covenant with the local authorities. On the basis of this covenant the parties had to make significant investments in pollution abatement technology. While the project was eligible for subsidisation, the parties had to pay for the investments themselves when the subsidy scheme was withdrawn altogether. The VOTOB members apparently were aware of the risk of future financing problems and decided to recoup the costs associated with the investments from the chemical industry in the form of an environmental surcharge. This charge was uniform and varied according to the polluting potential of the product stored. Furthermore, the charge had to be passed on entirely to the consumer (i.e. the chemical companies seeking storage capacity) and moreover the charge had to be invoiced as a separate item. The Commission identified three restrictions of competition. Firstly, the uniform nature of the charge disregarded the fact that the parties faced different investments and thus different costs in order to meet the environmental obligations. Secondly, the fact that the charge was fixed (i.e. the obligation to pass the charge on to consumers entirely) effectively meant a fixed price increase. Thirdly, the Commission objected to the obligation to invoice the charge as a separate item because this would leave the impression that the charge was government imposed like, for example, the VAT, and thus would reinforce the price-fixing effect. The Commission rejected the exemption on proportionality grounds.[222] In doing so it considered that a system whereby the total price was invoiced while it was stated that this price included the environmental costs, would have been acceptable. Fixing the uniform surcharge, requiring it to be passed on and separately invoiced went, according to the Commission, beyond what was necessary to attain the environmental objectives.[223] In the Guidelines on Horizontal agreements, the Commission considers that an agreement involving a uniform fee irrespective of the parties' individual actual costs could in principle be indispensable. This, however, still rules out the possibility of the passing through and separate billing being considered indispensable. We will have a closer look at cases involving environmental charges in the chapter devoted to case studies in the Netherlands.[224]

---

[220] *Ibid.*, para 23.

[221] Commission, XXIInd. Competition Report (1992), paras. 117-186, p. *106 et seq.*

[222] *Ibid.*, para. 177.

[223] *Ibid.*, para. 185.

[224] *Infra*, paragraph 16.5.4.

One final area where the proportionality criterion is of interest is that of environmental agreements concerning the collection and processing of waste. Environmental agreements in this field have become quite numerous as a result of the producer responsibility introduced by the Packaging and Packaging Waste Directive.[225] The law implementing this directive may leave the industry two options to comply with the producer responsibility. In principle, they have an individual responsibility to collect and recycle their packaging waste. However, they can also become party to a collective collection and recycling scheme and thereby avoid the (relatively expensive) individual obligation. This has lead to the emergence of several nationwide private packaging collection and recovery systems.[226] The collection and recycling of waste needs to involve large volumes for it to be profitable and therefore allows for significant economies of scale. Moreover, free rider problems are to be expected[227] and therefore most systems will involve some sort of exclusivity coupled with control mechanisms. It is this exclusivity that results in competition problems as the collective system will opt for the greatest degree of both 'upstream' (*i.e.* the firms responsible for the waste) and 'downstream' (*i.e.* the firms actually collecting and recycling the waste) exclusivity.[228] The competition authority, however, will want to keep the degree of exclusivity to an absolute minimum. In one of the first of this type of cases to come before the Commission, the *IFCO* case, the exclusivity was indeed the core issue.[229] The International Fruit Container Organisation (IFCO) is as system for reusable plastic fruit containers set up by a number of German food retailers. Initially, it looked like these founding fathers would consider the IFCO system to be exclusive in that they would only accept fruit in IFCO containers. This was thought necessary to start the system up and get a minimum amount of containers in circulation. The Commission objected to, *inter alia*, this exclusivity. When this was dropped and some other amendments were made to the

---

[225] Directive 94/62 on Packaging and Packaging Waste, OJ 1994 L 365/10. Moreover, the entry into force of the so-called WEEE Directive (Directive 2002/96, OJ 2003 L 37/24) is likely to lead to an increase in the number of agreements establishing producer responsibility organisations.

[226] See, in general on the issue of packaging waste management systems: Commission 2001.

[227] Because of the sheer number of companies involved as well as the relative difficulty of identifying the producer of the packaging once it has become waste

[228] There is an incentive for upstream exclusivity (i.e. longer duration of contacts by which the producers are bound to the collective system) because that will increase the continuity of the system in view of the considerable investments that need to be done. Similarly, as the actual collection and recycling of waste involves putting into place a considerable fine meshed network, the downstream companies will demand certainty that they will be able to recoup their investments.

[229] Information on the *IFCO* Case is fragmented and can be found in: Commission, press release IP/93/430, XXIIIrd. Competition Report (1993), para 165, p. 102, XXVIIIth. Competition Report (1998), p. 165 and notice pursuant to Article 19(3) of Council Regulation 17, OJ 1997 C 48/4.

system, it was considered no longer to violate Article 81(1) in the first place.[230] In *Valpak*, the case concerning the largest British packaging recovery scheme, the Commission was again concerned with the exclusivity involved.[231] Under the Valpak scheme, the parties wanting to join had to use the Valpak scheme for all of their packaging (the 'all or nothing approach'). Thereby, competition was effectively excluded. Nevertheless, the Commission considered that this 'all or nothing approach' was justified in order to create sufficient momentum. Accordingly, the Commission granted an informal exemption while at the same time reserving itself the right to re-examine the case after three years.

Again, the exclusivity of the scheme featured prominently in *DSD*. The long duration of the exclusivity granted to collection and sorting companies in the service agreements meant that they restricted competition within the meaning of Article 81(1) but did not keep the Commission from granting an exemption. Above, we have already looked at the way in which the Commission dealt with the first two requirements for an exemption. The outcome above was that in general the Commission appears to have awarded greater weight to environmental considerations whilst at the same time it has not clarified exactly how much importance has been attached to the environmental protection requirements. In determining whether the exclusivity is indispensable the uncertainty as to what role the environmental concerns have played has increased. For one, the Commission writes not a word about the indispensability (or not) of the exclusivity in view of the environmental benefits that were identified pursuant to the first requirement.[232] On the contrary, the Commission is solely addressing the economic and legal backgrounds of the decision to invest considerable sums at significant risk and to what extent these factors necessitated the exclusivities. This approach is not unsatisfactory from the perspective of the model of integration because essentially the Commission is checking to see whether the restriction of competition is necessary in order to allow for the erection of an infrastructure that will as a consequence enable the internalisation of external costs. However, this aspect of the decision does indicate that *DSD* cannot be said to be a purely environmentally motivated decision.[233]

In general, the interpretation of the third requirement for an exemption as a necessity test is satisfactory from the perspective of the integration of environmental concerns and competition law. The criterion of necessity accepts the level of protection chosen and only checks on whether or not the means chosen are indispensable. This will preclude the Commission from substituting its own

---

230 Commission, XXVIIIth. Competition Report (1998), p. 165.

231 *Ibid.*, p. 152-153.

232 Commission Decision 2001/837, *DSD* (Article 81), OJ 2001 L 319/1. Indeed, the word 'environment' is not to be found in paragraphs 150-157 that are devoted to the indispensability.

233 See for an equally cautious approach in this respect: Monti 2002, p. 1074.

vision of a sufficient level of environmental protection for that of the parties in cases where the means necessary to attain the latter are more restrictive of competition than those necessary to attain the level that the Commission would consider sufficient. In general, therefore, this test involves a greater 'respect' for the environment than a true proportionality test would.[234] Moreover, the purpose of Article 6 and the model of integration, the attainment of sustainable development, also require the presence of some competitive pressure. In this respect, the proportionality requirement fulfils an essential role.

### 8.7.5 The requirement of sufficient residual competition and environmental protection

#### 8.7.5.1 Introductory remarks

The fourth and final requirement for an exemption can be said the represent the outer limits of what Article 81 can take. Whatever the compensating benefits may be, the cooperation between the parties may never completely annihilate competition. Basically, there are two ways of looking at whether or not there is sufficient residual competition. Firstly, the amount or intensity of competition between the parties to the agreement (internal competition) may be ascertained. Secondly, one may look at the amount of competition between the parties on the one hand and the third parties (external competition) on the other hand. These two ways of looking at the remaining competition can be described as communicating vessels in that internal competition needs to be more intensive when external competition is diminished to a larger extent and *vice versa*. Furthermore, the requirement of sufficient residual competition has already played an important role in the second requirement for an exemption; establishing a fair share for consumers. This connection with the second requirement partly explains the limited attention that the Commission generally devotes to this requirement.[235] This short outline of the test applied with regard to the fourth requirement also signals the parallelism between the appreciability test within the scope of Article 81(1) and the residual competition test. After these introductory comments we shall now look at the Commission's decision-making practice and the Court's judgments with regard to this criterion.

---

[234] See, for a true proportionality test and the effects that the application of this test has on the level of protection, Case C-302/86, *Commission* v. *Denmark* (Danish Bottles), [1988] ECR 4607.

[235] *Cf.* Faull & Nikpay 1999, p. 114.

#### 8.7.5.2 The application of the residual competition test to environmental agreements

The two views on determining sufficient residual competition involve two different tests. When the internal competition between the parties to an agreement is concerned, the test applied shows a great resemblance to the qualitative appreciability test described above. On the other hand, the external residual competition test relies primarily on the market share of the parties to the agreement (i.e. the quantitative appreciability) and the general conditions of competition on the market. Practice with regard to this test reveals no particular order or preference for either one of the views on residual competition.

As regards the external residual competition the basic criterion is that of market power of the parties involved in the agreement. It can be said that this requirement also functions to some extent as a nexus between Article 81 and Article 82. Given this function, the Commission's practice in this regard becomes easier to understand. Basically, the purpose of the requirement of sufficient residual competition is to rule out any agreements that will reinforce a dominant position or that will lead to such a position coming about.[236] From the case law on dominance the following rules of thumb can be inferred. Market shares below 30 to 40 per cent will generally not confer a position of dominance.[237] On the other hand market shares over 75 per cent are very likely considered to bring dominance with it.[238] Whether anything in between these two extremes will be considered to confer a dominant position will rely strongly on the actual situation of the market.

From these rules of thumb it may be concluded that an aggregate market share below 30 to 40 per cent will generally not be a problem from the point of view of ensuring sufficient external competition. However, in the *United Reprocessors* case[239] the Commission has allowed an agreement between parties that had very significant market share well exceeding 40 per cent.[240] United Reprocessors was a joint company established by the major European reprocessing firms with a view to coordinating the parties' reprocessing capacity.[241] As can be guessed the initial investments involved in this type of operation are quite high. As a result such facilities require a high degree of efficient utilisation (load factor) for them to be profitable.

---

[236] Commission, Guidelines on horizontal agreements, OJ 2001 C 3/2, para. 36.

[237] Commission Decision 85/404, Grundig, OJ 1985 L 233/1.

[238] Case 85/76, *Hoffman-La Roche* v. *Commission* (Hoffmann-La Roche), [1979] ECR 461, para. 41 and Case T-30/89, *Hilti* v. *Commission*, [1992] ECR II-1439, paras. 89-94.

[239] Commission Decision 76/248, *United Reprocessors*, OJ 1976 L 51/7.

[240] According to Portwood the market share was in excess of 90 per cent, Portwood 1994, p. 156.

[241] Reprocessing is an operation whereby the useable fissile materials are recovered from spent nuclear fuels.

On the basis of the exceptional nature of the market involved the Commission came to the conclusion that the fourth requirement would also be fulfilled despite the very high market share of the parties. In this respect the Commission took into account the fact that the parties would have to compete after a certain transitional period had passed. Moreover, the Commission expected sufficient pressure from the electricity generating companies, the consumers of the joint company, was considerable. In its competition report the Commission made an extra effort at ensuring that *United Reprocessors* could not be construed as setting a precedent in this connection.[242]

Environmental concerns may play a particular role with regard to the market share test employed in this respect. It is not entirely unconceivable that environmental considerations may actually prompt a narrower market definition than otherwise would have been the case. This, in turn, will result in a higher market share for the parties involved on the market for environmentally friendly products and thereby an increased likeliness that residual competition is found to be insufficient.[243]

Generally speaking the market share approach itself adopted by the Commission is a fairly technical exercise that leaves little or no room for an increased role for environmental concerns. However, an indirect role is possible that involves taking the environmental backgrounds of the case into account not so much in establishing but rather in judging the market share. In this connection the concept of the economically compulsory cartel could come into play.[244] As a reminder, according to this hypothesis, a cartel agreement could also be considered compulsory by government act if the conclusion of the cartel is the only economically rational approach to a government-imposed obligation. Short of accepting that such economic pressure keeps these agreements wholly outside the scope of Article 81(1), the inherent incentive to achieve economies of scale could nevertheless lead to larger market shares still being considered acceptable. It has to be taken into account that determining whether or not there is sufficient residual competition is task that cannot take place in abstract terms but, on the contrary, should take into account the actual economic situation on the markets. If this situation is such as to inherently lead to large scale operations with the accordingly large market share, the test whether or not sufficient residual competition remains should take this fact into account. Moreover, as the Commission's practice shows, it can and will take such special features of markets into account.[245]

---

[242] Commission, Vth. Competition Report (1975), para. 45.

[243] We will return to and have a closer look at the influence of environmental concerns on market definition issues in the paragraph concerning Article 82, *infra*, paragraph 9.2.3.

[244] *Supra*, paragraph 8.5.

[245] Commission Decision 76/248, *United Reprocessors*, OJ 1976 L 51/7.

With regard to the second view on determining sufficient residual competition the following can be said. Intuitively, and on the basis of the parallel with the appreciability test it may be concluded that agreements on environmental aspects are very likely to leave internal competition intact to a sufficient degree. This is evidenced by the Commission's decision in the *CECED* case. The Commission's basic approach in this case recognises that coordination with regard to environmental concerns leaves many other (more important) factors on which competition is possible, untouched.[246] Moreover, the Commission took into account that the technical means by which parties are to achieve the sector-wide energy efficiency target were left open.[247] It did this in a manner that is very much reminiscent of the reasoning adopted in the Guidelines on Horizontal Agreements in connection with agreements that do not fall under Article 81(1).[248] Finally, the Commission relied on the fact that, although the machines to be phased out represent 'account for a significant volume of final sales', parties are free with regard to 90 per cent of the market.[249]

The Guidelines on Horizontal Agreements, unfortunately, address a different point in this respect. The Commission starts by setting out the basic purpose of this requirement. It then moves on by giving the example of the exclusive rights granted to an operator providing down stream services (such as collection and recycling). According to the Commission the duration of this exclusivity should take into account the possibility of new competitors entering the market. Of course this type of restriction involves a vertical relation. Moreover, this type of reasoning concerning the duration of exclusive rights seems more appropriate in connection with the proportionality test.[250] In general there is a clear incentive for the upstream parties (in the Commission's example, the producer responsibility organisation) to keep the duration of the exclusivity limited. Moreover, the contracts could be awarded on the basis of public tender. As with the qualitative notion of appreciability, the integration principle requires little more than an economically sound appraisal. As the *CECED* case shows, there are generally few problems to be expected in this regard. This is confirmed by the decision in the *DSD* case. With regard to the exclusivity in the service agreements the Commission firstly observes that the collectors excluded by DSD remain free.[251] Secondly, the Commission addresses the real problem

[246] Commission Decision 2000/475, *CECED*, OJ 2000 L 187/47, para. 64.

[247] *Ibid.*, para. 65.

[248] Commission, Guidelines on horizontal agreements, OJ 2001 C 3/2, para. 185, *supra* para. 3.4.2.3.

[249] Commission Decision 2000/475, *CECED*, OJ 2000 L 187/47, para. 66.

[250] Commission, Guidelines on vertical agreements, OJ 2000 C 291/1, para. 141.

[251] Commission Decision 2001/837, *DSD* (Article 81), OJ 2001 L 319/1, para. 159. This, of course, cannot be the measure by which the existance of sufficient remaining competition is judged as – one would hope at least – firms that have no contractual relation are not impeded in their freedom by a contract to which they are no party.

that concerns the 'free and unimpeded access to the collection infrastructure set up by collectors contracted to DSD.'[252] Since the Commission has managed to ascertain this access, competition is not eliminated and thus the fourth and final requirement for an exemption satisfied. Accordingly, the Commission is able to grant an exemption to DSD.[253]

In sum, the fourth requirement for an exemption is unlikely to stand in the way of most environmental agreements. Even if the parties to the agreement have a high aggregate market share, the characteristics of the market could well be taken into account and thus make the restriction palatable from a competition perspective. However, as DSD shows, ensuring sufficient remaining competition may sometimes involve imposing rather far-going obligations upon the parties.[254]

### 8.7.6 Negative effects of the integration principle

#### 8.7.6.1 Introductory remarks

In the paragraphs above we have looked at the positive effects that the model of integration may have on the application of the exemption clause. Furthermore, we have already noted that there is no negative role for the model of integration with regard to the interpretation of the third paragraph of Article 81. In this paragraph we shall look at the negative effects of the model of integration. Essentially this comes down to the question to what extent negative environmental effects stand in the way of an exemption.[255] Using the example of the joint venture for the research and development of the new but energy inefficient product, what would happen if Article 81(1) was to apply and from a competition point of view the agreement would qualify for an exemption? With regard to taking negative environmental effects into account, three different sub-questions can be discerned. Firstly, can negative environmental effects be taken into account in the first place? Secondly, if so, how do we take them into account? This is a more technical matter and involves determining exactly with regard to which of the four criteria of the exemption clause these effects can play their role. Thirdly, the effects of taking the negative environmental impact into account need to be determined.

---

[252] *Ibid.*, para. 162.

[253] The Commission has attached obligations in this respect in order to further ensure the free access, *ibid.*, para. 182, 183.

[254] *Ibid.*, para 165 *et seq.* where the Commission addresses the objections that DSD has formulated against the obligations. See further with regard to the possible competition and tendering problems arising: Lotze & Pape 2003.

[255] This paragraph is written on the basis of the current system where the Commission has the sole power of exemption. The effects of the direct applicability of Article 81(3) will be examined *infra* in paragraph 8.9.

### 8.7.6.2 Is there a role for environmental degradation in Article 81(3)?

The question whether there is a role for negative environmental effects in the application of the exemption clause is the mirror image of the question asked above with regard to the positive effects of the integration principle in connection with the exemption clause. As a result, it would be expected that the outcome of the question is identical, yet mirrored. These effects should be taken into account however, instead of increasing the possibilities of obtaining an exemption, negative effects should lessen or preclude this chance. Essentially the same arguments that were put forward in that respect can also apply here.[256] However as we have seen there are a number of reasons that plead against taking negative environmental effects into account in interpreting Article 81(1). It can therefore be asked whether these reasons apply analogously to the application of the exemption clause.

To start with the last argument that was brought forward above: the nature of the model of integration and the integration principle. As we have seen, the application of the integration principle presupposes the existence of some discretionary power, *i.e.* the power to engage in a policy of some sort. Moreover, we have also seen that such discretion is inherent in the application of Article 81(3).[257] Secondly, the problems of legal certainty and equal treatment are not insurmountable in that the exemption clause can only be applied upon notification. Of course the policy chance that follows from taking negative environmental effects into account will have to comply with the constitutional demands imposed by the Treaty.[258] If these requirements are satisfied, the fact that an agreement has to be notified to obtain an exemption effectively precludes problems such as the ones identified above. This leaves us with only one reason pleading against taking negative environmental effects into account: the fact that doing this will lead to competition policy becoming an environmental instrument. Essentially, two opposing arguments can thus be identified. On the one hand, the constitutional argument that competition policy cannot function as an environmental policy instrument. On the other hand, the obligation for the Commission, as an institution conducting a policy that is subject to Article 6 EC, to integrate environmental considerations in all its policy areas. We would argue that on the whole the constitutional problems that follow from the Commission pursuing an environmental policy that has not been attributed to it and thus bypassing the Council and Parliament, would in general stand in the

[256] *Supra*, para. 8.7.1 and 8.7.2.

[257] The implications of the direct applicability of Article 81(3) after the entry into force of Regulation 1/2003 will be discussed *infra* in paragraph 8.9.

[258] *E.g.* it will have to be made public and retroactivity is in principle not allowed.

way of taking negative environmental effects into account. How this would work in an actual case, however, relies strongly on the form in which the Commission takes these negative environmental effects into account. Accordingly, in our opinion, as will be shown below, this problem can be overcome if the Commission *identifies* environmental degradation as an *explicit* and *external factor* but at the same time *integrates* it into one of the four conditions for an exemption. Consider, for example, an agreement that may lead to economic progress within the traditional meaning of Article 81(3) as well as environmental degradation. This agreement may very well be considered not to fulfil one of the criteria of Article 81(3) in the first place. This leads us to the second question.

#### 8.7.6.3 Where does environmental degradation enter into the picture?

Now that it has been established that negative environmental effects should play a role in the application of the exemption clause just as positive environmental effects have to be taken into account, the question arises *how* these effects should play their role. In this respect a number of solutions have been put forward. Jacobs has argued that the integration principle should lead to the addition of an extra, fifth, criterion to the four requirements listed in Article 81(3).[259] Geradin proposes to take negative environmental effects into account in analysing the proportionality of the measure.[260]

In our opinion, the most appropriate place within Article 81(3) to take negative environmental effects into account would seem to be the first requirement: establishing economic and technical progress.[261] Interpreting Article 81(3) so as to introduce an extra, fifth, criterion would run counter to the clear and – in this respect – unambiguous wording of Article 81(3) which contains only four requirements for an exemption. Furthermore, the explicit addition of an extra criterion is very likely to lead to the constitutional problems described in the above paragraph. With regard to the solution proposed by Geradin the following remarks may be made. Within the four criteria for an exemption the proportionality test is only about balancing, on the one hand, the advantages with, on the other hand, the restrictions of competition. It can therefore be called a *bilan economique*. This balance should only include the (environmental) advantages of the cooperation and the detrimental effects on competition.

The most logical alternative is thus to interpret the first requirement; the presence of 'economic and technical progress' so as to include only '*net* economic and technical progress'.[262] In the words of Advocate-General VerLoren

---

[259] Jacobs 1993, p. 58.

[260] Geradin 2001, p. 123 *et seq.*

[261] See also Vedder 2000, p. 374.

[262] *Cf.* Schröter 1999, p. 2/309, rn. 298.

van Themaat in the *Book prices* cases: the *'bilan économique'* should take place within the first requirement.[263] Commission decisions reveal that it will require objective (net) benefits to arise from the agreement in order for the first requirement to be fulfilled.[264] The result of negative ecological effects in combination with positive economic effects could be that the Commission would have to make an, admittedly difficult, balancing act the outcome of which could be that there are simply no net benefits to warrant an exemption. In the context of the example of a joint venture to develop a new but energy inefficient product it can thus be argued that the new product is simply not an improved product let alone that it involves technical *progress*.

If at this point we look back at the previous paragraph we are faced with the question whether this runs counter to the constitutional lay out of the Treaty. In our opinion that does not necessarily have to be the case. If the Commission is explicitly prescribing a certain level of environmental protection below which the compensating (economic) benefits will not be considered to lead to a net benefit, the constitutional problem could be said to arise. In the context of the joint venture for the development of the energy inefficient product, the Commission will probably not be allowed to state that there is no technical or economic progress because the energy efficiency of the product to be developed is below a certain value. Such a finding would amount to the Commission effectively imposing (in this case) a minimum level of energy efficiency level. On the other hand it could probably consider that, in the specific case at hand, the benefits inherent in the development of a new product are compensated by the negative fact that the new product is energy inefficient. The result of this finding would be that this agreement is considered not to bring with it any advantages. The difference between the two approaches is that in the first the Commission is laying down a general rule whereas in the second approach it merely applies (a part of) the exemption clause to the broader (because the environment is included as well) facts of the case. This leaves us with the third question identified above: what are the effects of it all?

#### 8.7.6.4 What are the effects of taking environmental degradation into account?

The possible effects manifest themselves on three levels that correspond to the three stages of the process of applying Article 81. Firstly, the notification form A/B. Currently, agreements have to be notified to the Com-

[263] Opinion of A-G VerLoren van Themaat in joined Cases 43 and 63/82, *VBVB and VBBB* v. *Commission*, (Book prices) [1984] ECR 19 at p. 88.

[264] Commission Decision 78/156, *Video cassette recorders*, OJ 1978 L 47/42, para. 29, Decision 83/672, *Saba*, OJ 1983 L 376/41, para. II.B.1.

mission in order to be eligible for an exemption. Such notifications must use the so-called form A/B.[265] The Commission could include in the form A/B a section on the environmental impacts of the agreement. The impact of this could range from a simple question whether any negative environmental impacts are expected to an obligation for the notifying parties to attach as an annex a complete environmental impact assessment. The second stage is the notification itself. Depending on what the Commission requires in its form A/B, the parties could suffice with a simple statement that the agreement is expected not to have any negative effects or they may be under an obligation to submit a full-blown environmental impact assessment. The third stage is that where the Commission actually checks to see whether or not an exemption can be granted. It is at this point that the Commission will actually have to balance the (economic) advantages with the negative environmental effects to see whether there is economic and technical progress. If there is no such progress then one of the four conditions for an exemption is not fulfilled. Because these conditions are cumulative, no exemption can be granted.

## 8.8 Group exemptions

### 8.8.1 Introductory remarks

Once the Commission has gained sufficient experience with a specific type of agreement it can decide to adopt a so-called group- or block exemption. These take the form of Commission Regulations. At the moment there is one general Regulation for vertical agreements whereas there are two block exemptions concerning horizontal restrictions. The vertical block exemption Regulation basically consists of what is called a 'safe haven' market share of 30 per cent below which the exemption applies except for when certain hard-core restrictions are present.[266] For horizontal agreements there are two Regulations that also adopt the 'safe haven approach' combined with a 'black list' consisting of hard-core restrictions that will preclude the applicability of the block exemption. These Regulations cover specialisation agreements and research and development agreements.[267] These Regulations confer an advantage on those agreements that fall within their scope because they are exempted from Article 81(1) without any need for an individual exemption and the corresponding need to notify the agreement. With regard to environmental agreements a simple look

[265] Commission Regulation 3385/94, OJ 1994 L 337/28.

[266] Commission Regulation 2790/1999, OJ 1999 L 336/21.

[267] Respectively, Commission Regulation 2658/2000, OJ 2000 L 304/3, and Regulation 2659/2000, OJ 2000 L 203/7.

at the legislation confirms that there is no group exemption for environmental agreements as such. Therefore our research can concentrate on the effects of the integration principle on the group exemptions. In this connection we shall first look at the positive effects of the integration principle. In this regard two questions may be asked. Firstly, does the integration principle lead to the applicability of the group exemption to an agreement that would otherwise not qualify for such an exemption? Secondly, is it possible to adopt a group exemption for environmental agreements? With regard to the negative effects of the integration principle it may be asked whether negative environmental effects can lead to the refusal or withdrawal of block exemption benefits.

### 8.8.2 Group exemption benefits and environmental protection

A clause extending the block exemption benefit to agreements that would, if it were not for their environmental beneficial impact, fall outside the scope of the group exemption, is firstly expected to be found in the Regulations themselves. However, close scrutiny of these Regulations reveals that no such clauses are present. Moreover, past Commission practice reveals that it is unwilling to enlarge the scope of then applicable block exemption Regulations in cases where it did acknowledge the environmental advantages in granting an individual exemption. In the *BBC Brown Boveri* case[268] the Commission denied the applicability of the old research and development group exemption Regulation[269] because one of the parties was not allowed to market the new products after the expiry of the five-year limit laid down in the Regulation.[270] In the later *KSB/Goulds/Lowara/ITT* case the Commission again ruled out the applicability of old research and development Regulation this time on the ground that the market share cap (which at that time was put at 20 per cent) may be exceeded.[271] In both cases the fact that the Commission did take the environmental advantages into account in granting an individual exemption apparently kept it from extending the block exemption benefit.

It may then be asked whether it is sensible and possible to argue that, on the basis of the integration principle and the model of integration, block exemption benefits may be extended even when the Regulation itself, does not provide for this possibility. We would argue that this is neither possible nor sensible. The impossibility follows already from the text of Article 6 EC itself. This refers to the integration of environmental protection requirements into the definition and implementation of the Community *policies and activities*. In the case of

---

268 Commission Decision 88/541, *BBC Brown Boveri*, OJ 1988 L 301/68, para. 21.

269 Commission Regulation 418/85, OJ 1985 L 53/5.

270 *Ibid.* Article 4(1)(f).

271 Commission Decision 91/38, *KSB/Goulds/Lowara/ITT*, OJ 1991 L 19/25, para. 24.

block exemptions the block exemption Regulations themselves are the Commission's policy. Therefore the model of integration can at the most – and in our opinion does – result in the requirement on the part of the Commission to consider, when it is drafting the Regulation, the possibility of introducing into it a mechanism extending automatically the block exemption benefit to environmental agreements that would normally fall outside its scope. Of course, certain limits (for example, a second, higher market share cap) may be imposed in this respect. Requiring the Commission, as the author of the block exemption Regulation, to do anything else than taking environmental protection requirements into account in drafting the Regulation would not make any sense. Arguing that Article 6 and the model of integration have any effect *vis a vis* the Commission at a later stage than the drafting stage could only mean that the Commission is under an obligation to extend the group exemption benefit upon application. This would greatly reduce the block exemption benefit because parties are again burdened with administrative necessities. As a result, the whole idea behind the block exemption would be negated.

Would it then be possible to argue before a national court (and, ultimately, the European Court of Justice) that the block exemption benefit has to be extended to an agreement that would normally fall outside the scope? Consider the following case involving the *KSB/Goulds/Lowara/ITT* research and development. This agreement was considered to fall outside the scope of the Regulation because of the parties' market share. Suppose that the parties, because they exceeded the market share cap only marginally and because of the environmental objective of their agreement, decided not to notify the agreement in order to obtain an individual exemption. Suppose, furthermore, that before a national court someone invokes the nullity of the agreement because it violates Article 81(1). In that case it could be argued that, since the Regulation itself is Commission policy and Article 6 EC contains an unconditional obligation ('*must* be integrated') concerning Commission policy, a national court is under an obligation to extend the group exemption benefit to the agreement in question. It is submitted that this would fail primarily because Article 6 is insufficiently clear in that it contains vague concepts such as for example 'environmental protection requirements'.[272] Apart from the fact that Article 6 can probably not be invoked before a national court,[273] this would also fail on the basis of the Court's judgment in *Delimitis* where it held that national courts could only apply the group exemption regulations, not modify their scope.[274]

---

[272] Case C-9/99, *Echirolles Distribution SA* v. *Association du Dauphiné* (Échirolles), [2000] ECR I-8207, paras. 15-26.

[273] This is not to say that a national court cannot consider itself to be an addressee of the integration principle and as a result under an obligation to integrate environmental protection requirements in his application of Community legislation, see *infra* paragraph 8.9.

[274] Case C-234/89, *Stergios Delimitis* v. *Henninger Bräu* (Delimitis), [1991] ECR I-935, para. 46.

Since there is no group exemption regulation for environmental agreements and the scope of the existing Regulations cannot be extended to encompass such agreements the question remains whether it is possible to adopt such a Regulation for environmental agreements. This would certainly seem possible. The general rules laid down by the Commission in the Guidelines on horizontal agreements could very well be elaborated to the effect that they become sufficiently clear to warrant legal certainty. The horizontal, sector-wide nature of environmental protection does not have to stand in the way of such a Regulation as the currently existing safe-haven block exemptions exemplify. What could stand in the way of the practicability of such an exercise is the diffuse nature of the restrictions involved. These, as we have seen, range from vertical to horizontal, research and development to exclusivities, phasing in and phasing out of products. This diversity in restrictions and clauses will greatly hamper such efforts.

As to the negative effects that the integration of environmental concerns may have, thoughts centre around the possibility of withdrawing the group exemption benefit in cases where the environmental disadvantages outweigh the benefits. Much of what was said in connection with the individual exemption also applies here. Interestingly, the current block exemption Regulations all contain a mechanism by which block exemption benefits may be withdrawn.[275] As these read, none of them explicitly offers the possibility of withdrawing the benefits on environmental grounds. However, this reading will reveal that essentially, the Commission or, in the case of the Vertical Block exemption Regulation the national authority, can withdraw the benefit when the conditions of Article 81(3) EC are no longer fulfilled.[276] This, in turn, means that environmental protection requirements may play the same role here as they play within the scope of the application of Article 81(3) in individual cases.[277]

## 8.9 The effects of the direct applicability of Article 81(3) EC

On 1 May 2004, Regulation 1/2003 will enter into force.[278] On the basis of Article 1 of this Regulation, the third paragraph of Article 81 will become directly applicable. This means that national courts may apply Article

---

275 Article 6 and 7 of Commission Regulation 2790/1999, OJ 1999 L 336/21, Article 7 of Commission Regulation 2658/2000, OJ 2000 L 304/3, and Article 7 of Regulation 2659/2000, OJ 2000 L 203/7

276 As has happened in, *inter alia*, Case T-7/93, *Langnese-Iglo* v. *Commission*, [1995] ECR II-1533, paras. 173 *et seq.*

277 *Supra*, paragraph 8.7.

278 Regulation (EC) No. 1/2003 on the implementation of the rules on competition laid down in Articles 81 and 82 of the EC Treaty (hereafter Regulation 1/2003), OJ 2003 L 1/1.

81 in its entirety.[279] As a result, they may declare an agreement that falls within the scope of Article 81(1) not to be prohibited, if they consider the requirements of Article 81(3) to be fulfilled. A necessary corollary to this is the relinquishing of the exclusive right to grant an exemption by the Commission. After the entry into force of Regulation 1/2003, the Commission can only issue group exemption regulations[280] and issue, in the Community public interest, decisions in which Article 81(1) is stated not to apply or decisions in which the requirements of Article 81(3) are considered to be fulfilled for a certain agreement or decision.[281] As a result, Article 81(3) will no longer be an exemption but rather an exception. This new setting does not necessarily have to affect the integration of environmental concerns to a large extent.

We have seen above how the model of integration is based on a number of foundations that are not specific to any particular system of competition law and policy. The mutually reinforcing relationship between competition and environmental protection that the model of integration seeks to attain can by definition be applied to any system of competition law hat allows for a disapplication of the prohibition of cartels. As a result, the change of character that Article 81(3) undergoes by reason of Regulation 1/2003 should not be such as to completely rule out the possibility of an integration of environmental concerns.

What will change is the legal framework in which Article 81(3) is be applied. If the Commission applies it in so-called landmark cases,[282] it will as a Community institution enacting a Community policy, be bound by Article 6 EC. Moreover, the Commission will have to take into account the fact that Article 81 is part of the EC Treaty and must therefore, even without any particular reference to Article 6 EC, be interpreted with the objectives of Article 2 EC in mind. This is of interest because the in the White Paper preceding Regulation 1/2003, the Commission stated that Article 81(3) could not allow 'the competition rules to be set aside because of political considerations'.[283] This appears to signal that the Commission is opting for an interpretation of Article 81(3) that will restrict the role that non-competition (*e.g.* environmental) considerations can play in that provision.[284] Such a changed interpretation of Article 81(3) is submitted to

---

[279] Note that the wording of Article 6 of Regulation 1/2003 suggests a choice for national courts whether of not to apply Article 81(3), *cf.* Vogelaar 2002, p. 23.

[280] The Commission can continue to do this on the basis of the Regulations that currently empower it to do so.

[281] Regulation 1/2003, Article 10.

[282] These are the decisions that the Commission can take in the Community public interest pursuant to Article 10 of Regulation 1/2003.

[283] White Paper on Modernisation of the Rules implementing Articles 81 and 82 of the EC Treaty, OJ 1999, C 132/1, para. 49.

[284] *Cf.* Wesseling 2000, p. 105, 107.

be contrary to the integration principle as well as the fact that Article 81, as any Treaty provision, is to be interpreted in the light of the objectives listed in Article 2 EC. Moreover, as we have seen in this chapter, it would mean a departure from the Commission's current practice pursuant to Article 81(3).[285]

Finally, another important reason for a continued role for environmental considerations in Article 81(3) relates to the legal character of these 'landmark cases'. The Commission has been enabled to act in these cases in order to clarify the law and to ensure a consistent application and development of the law throughout the Community particularly in cases that have not been dealt with.[286] These decisions then bind the national courts and authorities in that they cannot take decisions that run counter to decisions already taken by the Commission.[287] Moreover, the national authorities must avoid giving decisions that would conflict with decisions that the Commission is 'contemplating'.[288] Furthermore, the member states are under an obligation to ensure that decisions and judgments of their national authorities in which Article 81 is applied, are sent to the Commission.[289] The decentralisation of the application of Article 81(3) is thus to a large extent subject to the Commission's guidance. Implicit in this is the fact that national authorities are not completely free to interpret Article 81(3) as they like. In doing so, these national authorities will have to follow the guidance provided by the Commission. This in turn means that the Commission is, much more than in the current situation, under an obligation to give this guidance. Guidelines, such as the Guidelines on horizontal agreements that were examined above and well-reasoned and published decisions are necessary in this respect. It is submitted that the current Guidelines and decisions are insufficient in this respect. As was shown above, the Commission's practice cannot be said to be consistent or overly clear.

A second change relates to the disappearance of the notification procedure. As a result of this, the integration of environmental considerations can no longer take the form of an 'environmental impact statement' that needs to accompany the notification. However, this procedural change does not mean that, substantively, the Commission is no longer able to refuse an exemption if the negative environmental impact outweighs the (economic) advantages of an agreement.

The position of national authorities and courts that apply Article 81(3) is more complicated. If they apply Article 81(3), it is uncertain whether and to what extent they will be bound by Article 6 EC or the fact that this provision is part

---

285 Cf. Wesseling 2000, p. 107 and Monti 2002, p. 1090 *et seq.*

286 Regulation 1/2003, 14th recital of the preamble.

287 *Ibid.*, Article 16.

288 Interestingly, it remains uncertain exactly how the national authority or a national court is going to find out *that* the Commission is contemplating a certain decision and *what* this decision is going to be.

289 *Ibid.*, Article 11(3) and (4) and Article 15(2).

of the EC Treaty and thus subject to Article 2 EC. The most interesting situation for the purpose of this book would be one where the Commission would refuse to integrate environmental protection requirements whereas a national authority or judge is willing to do so. We could, for example, think of a 'green dot' system in the Netherlands that is comparable but not identical to the DSD system. As has been shown above, the latter has already been the subject of a Commission decision. The question is whether the duty pursuant to Article 16 of Regulation 1/2003 not to decide in conflict with a Commission decision applies only to a Court before which there is a specific case involving the actual DSD system and the same restriction or, more generally, to cases before national courts that involve 'DSD-like' parties and restrictions? Regulation 1/2003 provides that in this situation, the decision of the national body may not run counter to a Commission decision.[290] Depending on the answer to the question formulated above, the Dutch court that has to rule on the applicability of Article 81 to the Dutch green dot system is either free to apply Article 81 or bound by the Commission decision in, *inter alia*, the *DSD*-case.

It is uncertain what the effect is pursuant to Article 16 of Regulation 1/2003 of Commission (landmark) decisions. The text of Article 249 EC makes it clear beyond doubt that a decision is only binding upon its addressees. Since national courts are not the addressees of Commission decisions (whether or not of the landmark type), they are not bound by them. This is also evidenced by the fact that Commission decisions are authentic only in the language of the proceedings and the parties. Finally, a binding effect upon all national courts that deal with comparable cases would endow the decisions of the Commission with effects that are normally reserved for Regulations. It is submitted that such an effect would render the distinction that Article 249 EC makes between decisions and regulations useless.[291] These considerations all plead in favour of a relatively narrow binding effect for Commission decisions.[292] On the other hand, the logic behind the landmark decision is to ensure a Community-wide uniform interpretation of the law. This would be jeopardised if any national court could simply ignore a Commission decision with regard to a case that is comparable to the one before that court. Furthermore, the wording of Article 16 that does not refer to a particular case, parties and restriction as the subject of the Commission decision but instead uses the more abstract wording 'agreements, decisions or practices', also hints at a more general binding effect.

Moreover, if the binding effect of the Commissions decisions under Article 16 of Regulation 1/2003 is more general, the interesting situation could arise

[290] *Ibid.*, Article 16.

[291] See, for regulations and directives: Case C-91/92, *Facini Dori* v. *Recreb*, [1994] ECR I-3325.

[292] *I.e.* limited only to cases before national courts that involve the addressees of a Commission decision and the same restriction of competition that was also subject of the Commission decision.

in which the Dutch court that has to judge on Dutch green dot system considers itself obliged by the integration principle to award a more important role to environmental concerns than the Commission had done in *DSD*.

As we have seen, Article 6 EC is not limited with regard to its addressees. As a result, it could be said that any national court that is applying Community law, such as Article 81 EC, is under an obligation to integrate.[293] Further *a contrario* evidence for the fact that Article 6 can be invoked by a national court in the application of Community law can be found in the fact that other 'integration clauses' do explicitly refer to Community institutions as their addressees.[294]

The question that then arises is to what extent a national court that departs from a previous Commission decision is thus actually deciding on the legality of this decision and thus comes within the realm of *Foto Frost*.[295] Since the decision is not addressed to the national court, that court is not bound by the decision. As a result, the court would not be putting it aside or ruling on the validity of that Community act thus keeping out of *Foto Frost*'s way. Moreover, any decision involving Article 81(3) necessarily involves a complex appraisal of factors that are very much specific to the case at hand. As such, it should not be difficult to distinguish the situation before the national court from that on which the Commission has decided. Depending on the degree of integration adopted by the Commission and the willingness of the national court to actually integrate environmental concerns to a greater extent, the result of the direct applicability for the integration of environmental concerns may actually benefit. The Commission's suggestion that it wants to narrow the scope of Article 81(3) so as to exclude political considerations is expected to only increase the incentive for national courts to go further in this respect. These national courts, even though they may not be obliged on the basis of *Foto Frost*, may well want to make a preliminary reference in this respect.

Moreover, there is something to be said for also allowing such a departure from the Commission's interpretation of Community law in cases where that interpretation is in the form of a block exemption regulation. Above, we have seen that the Court held in *Delimitis* that national courts could only apply such regulations; not extend their scope.[296] This limitation of the national courts' powers with regard to a block exemption regulation was based on the fact that:[297]

*'Any such extension, whatever its scope, would affect the manner in which the Commission exercises its legislative competence'.*

---

[293] *Supra*, paragraph 5.3.

[294] *E.g.* Article 151(4), 153(2) and 157(3) EC.

[295] Case 314/85, *Foto Frost* v. *Hauptzollamt* (Foto-Frost), [1987] ECR 4199.

[296] Case C-234/89, *Delimitis*, [1991] I-935, para. 46.

[297] *Ibid.*

This legislative competence was, as the Court explained in that case, in turn the result of the exclusive competence of the Commission to adopt decisions that implement Article 81(3).[298] After the entry into force of Regulation 1/2003, the Commission will no longer possess the exclusive competence to apply Article 81(3). On the contrary, the Commission will share this competence with; *inter alia*, the national courts. As a result of this, the rationale behind the Court's reasoning in *Delimitis* disappears. The national authorities should thus be able to actually interpret the provisions of a block exemption regulation in order to achieve an integration of environmental concerns. They should do this in a manner analogous to the way in which the national courts are required to interpret national legislation in conformity with directives.[299] This would ensure sufficient respect for legal certainty. Since most of the provisions of the currently existing block exemption regulations have been formulated in such a way that the room for interpretation is very limited indeed, national courts would in practice thus only be left with the option of setting the group exemption regulation aside. This, of course, is not allowed by the principle that Community legislation must be interpreted uniformly throughout the Community as established by the Court in *Foto Frost*.[300] In these cases, the national courts are obliged to make a preliminary reference. For national competition authorities, which are also addressees of Article 6 EC if they apply Community legislation, making preliminary references to the European Court of Justice is impossible. They are left only with the possibility under Article 11(5) to consult the Commission. Interestingly, the Commission does not appear to be under any particular duty of cooperation aside from the general statement that it 'shall apply the Community competition rules in close cooperation' with the national authorities.[301]

The dangers to the consistency and uniformity of the interpretation of Article 81 throughout the Community that result from this interpretation of Article 6 in connection with the direct applicability of Article 81(3), is a problem that must firstly be resolved by the Commission and not by a rule precluding 'dissenting opinions' by member state authorities. The obvious solution is of course for the Commission, in providing guidance, to correctly integrate environmental concerns. If this does not happen, the result is very likely to be yet another increase in the number of preliminary references to the already overburdened European Court.[302] The fact is that Article 81(3) is and remains

---

298 *Ibid.*, para. 44.

299 Case C-106/89, *Marleasing* v. *Comercial Internacional de Alimentacion*, [1990] ECR I-4135.

300 Case 314/85, *Foto Frost*, [1987] ECR 4199.

301 Article 11(1) of Regulation 1/2003.

302 *Cf.* Vogelaar 2002, p. 27. Of course, the Commission, as *amicus curiae* pursuant to Article 15(3) of Regulation 1/2003 and institution that is going to receive a copy of every judgment from a court in the Community that involves Article 81 or 82 EC (Article 15(2) Regulation 1/2003), can also expect to be kept busy.

an open-worded provision that allows for a certain degree of political discretion in its application.[303] As a result, declaring it to be directly applicable is inevitably going to lead to different interpretations across the Community. The risk of these divergent interpretations can at the most be restricted to purely economic reasons if Article 81(3) is interpreted narrowly but it can never be completely ruled out.[304] It is submitted that a narrow interpretation of Article 81(3) (thus excluding environmental benefits) is not the solution to the problem.[305] It deserves repetition that such an interpretation of Article 81(3) would run counter to the current interpretation of Article 81(3) that does take environmental considerations into account. More importantly it would also be contrary to the integration principle Article 6 EC and the model of integration. As such the possibility to bring about sustainable development through Article 81(3) is foregone.

---

303 *Cf.* Odudu 2002, p. 20 et seq., Wesseling 2000, Monti 2002, p. 1092.

304 Whish suggests a narrowing of Article 81(3) to purely economic benefits, Whish 2001, p. 128.

305 See Monti 2002, p. 1096 *et seq.* for an interesting solution.

CHAPTER 9

# Article 82

## 9.1 Introductory remarks

Where Article 81 is concerned with restrictions of competition that are the result of cooperation between two or more competitors, Article 82 is primarily, though not uniquely, concerned with the repercussions on competition of actions by one undertaking. This undertaking is required, for Article 82 to apply, to be in a *dominant position*. Moreover, the undertaking in question must *abuse* this dominant position. These are the two major elements of Article 82. Many more interesting points can further be identified. The dominant position, for example, does not exist in a vacuum but involves an actual market that has to be defined as both a geographically identifiable area and a product market. With regard to the abuse, Article 82 contains an indicative list of abusive behaviour. Doctrine, Commission decisions and judgments have served to further elaborate this list. In short, it can be said that there is no justification clause, such as Article 81(3), with regard to abuse. Abuse is prohibited and cannot be justified. There are, however, situations where abuse simply does not exist in the first place because the behaviour that is alleged to be abusive is objectively justified.

Environmental requirements may come into play at a number of stages. Firstly in defining the relevant product market and the geographical market. It may, for example, be possible that environmentally friendly products (*e.g.* hybrid cars) are considered not to compete with their environmentally unfriendly counterparts (normal cars with an internal combustion engine). In that case, the environmentally friendly car is in a league of its own and may constitute a separate product market. The result of this will be that the undertaking producing these cars will be much more likely to be in a dominant position. Also with regard to the geographical market environmental considerations may very well reduce the size of the market because nationally differing environmental standards may separate one member states' market from another. As was mentioned above, this relation between competition law and the environment will not be considered as 'integration' as defined in the model of integration.[1] However, we will pay close attention to these interactions between environmental considerations and competition law precisely because many environmental innovations actually place the products in a 'league of their own' and thus problems involving dominance are likely to occur. Moreover, market definition and the influence of environmental concerns in this respect, also play an important role in the application of Article 81. If the market has been defined, the question of establishing dominance arises. In most cases this is a fairly technical exercise that relies primarily on the market share of the firms on the market. However, in the arena of environmental protection the dust has not yet settled and new

1 *Supra*, chapter 4.

entrants are eager to enter a developing market. As we have seen with regard to agreements concerning waste recycling, such schemes in many cases actually create markets. Therefore, environmental concerns may introduce new dynamics in this exercise as well. Again, the role of environmental concerns in this respect will be a result of the technical exercise involved and therefore it can be characterised as an interaction rather than integration. The final question arising because of the application of Article 82 to environmental situations involves establishing abuse. In this connection, one can think about the possibility of relying on the environmental aspects as an objective justification. This final question is the only one that could actually involve some integration, as opposed to interaction, of environmental concerns and competition law.

## 9.2 Market definition

As we have seen in the above paragraph, applying Article 82 starts with defining the relevant market involved.[2] Moreover, environmental concerns may play an – interactive – role in this respect. Below we will differentiate between the definition of the relevant product market and the geographical market. With regard to both, the role of environmental concerns will be investigated.

### 9.2.1 The relevant product market

Defining the relevant product market involves designing those products that compete with each other. Products may compete with one another from two perspectives: the supply and demand side perspective. From the demand side, the product market is defined by asking the question what products consumers see as substitutes for each other. This can be determined by the 'SSNIP' or 'Small but Significant Non-transitory Increase in Price'-test.[3] In this test the price of the product in question is raised by a small but significant amount for a longer period and those products to which consumers shift are considered to fall in the same product market. From the supply side it is, essentially, asked to what products producers can reasonably adapt their product lines. Such products are deemed to be supply substitutes.

How does this relate to environmental considerations? An obvious example would be an environmentally friendly version of a product (a zero emissions car) that does not compete with the normal (environmentally unfriendly version of a)

---

2 Case 27/76, *United Brands* v. *Commission* (United Brands), [1978] ECR 207, para. 10.

3 See Commission Notice on the definition of the relevant market for the purpose of Community competition law, OJ 1997 C 372/5.

product and therefore may fall in a separate product market. Whether environmental considerations warrant designating certain products as a product market of their own is unclear. In essence, this depends on demand side substitutability, or how much the consumer is willing to pay for the environmentally friendly version of a product. If the price difference between the 'green' and the 'grey' car is less than the difference in manufacturing costs, the environmentally friendly and the environmentally unfriendly version of the product are in the same product market. Only if what the consumer is willing to pay for the environmentally friendly version equals or exceeds the extra production costs of that environmentally friendly version compared to the environmentally unfriendly version, can there be a separate product market. This is so because only in these cases is there, from the perspective of the consumer, an added value from the fact that a product is environmentally friendly. In the situation where the consumer is unwilling to pay at least the extra production costs involved in making the green product, the conclusion must be that the environmentally friendliness of the product does not, from the viewpoint of the consumer, distinguish it from the not so green product.

Apart from the demand side, there is also supply side substitutability. Also with regard to this perspective on product markets environmental considerations can play a role in defining separate product markets. Producing an environmentally friendly version a product may in fact require such a completely different method of production that switching becomes increasingly difficult. Take, for example, a farmer who wants to shift from standard to organic cattle rearing. Even though the meat may in many respects be identical, the farmer will have to change his production methods completely (it is for example conceivable that he has to use new cattle because, for example, his old livestock was vaccinated).

The Commission's perspective on supply side substitutability can be found in the Notice on the definition of the relevant market. Basically, the Commission ascertains whether it is possible to switch production in the short term and whether the producer incurs significant risks or costs offset only by a small change in prices.

Apart from the economic reasons underlying a separate product market for an environmentally friendly product, the impact of environmental regulation must also not be underestimated. For example, different processing requirements for different types of waste may very well result in there being separate product markets for the treatment of those types of waste.[4]

---

4 *Cf.* Case C-209/98, *Entreprenørforeningens Affalds/Miljøsektion (FFAD)* v. *Københavns Kommune* (Sydhavnens Sten & Grus), [2000] ECR I-3743.

### 9.2.2 The relevant geographical market

In addition to the relevant product market, the relevant geographical market should also be defined. This, according to the Court, is the area in which the conditions of competition are sufficiently homogeneous for there to be effective competition.[5] Again consumer preferences with regard to the environmentally friendliness and environmental regulation may play a role. Where consumers in one country or region generally attach more weight to environmental considerations than those in other regions a separate geographical market may be the result. Furthermore, differing environmental standards may be very effective in separating geographical markets.[6]

### 9.2.3 The influence of environmental considerations on market definition

The greater the influence of environmental concerns, the more likely that the environmentally friendly products are in a market of their own. This has consequences for the application of competition law. With regard to Article 82 this means that a dominant position is more likely to occur. Furthermore, in connection with Article 81, restrictions of competition may very well be more significant. All of this means that the scope that the competition rules provide for the environmentally friendly behaviour of enterprises is likely, with respect to market shares, to become narrower.

## 9.3 The dominant position in a substantial part of the common market

Dominance is, in the first place, the result of the market share. Therefore, market shares are a good indication of whether or not dominance may be said to exist. The Court has held that market shares exceeding 50 per cent normally confer a dominant position on an undertaking.[7] Whether dominance exists for any other market share or in certain exceptional circumstances, is a question of several other factors. Among these are, the market shares of direct competitors, potential competition, structure of the undertakings (high degree of vertical integration). As can be seen from this short outline, establishing dominance, including market definition, is a technical matter that provides

[5] Case 27/76, *United Brands*, [1978] ECR 207, para. 11. Commission Notice on the definition of the relevant market for the purpose of Community competition law, OJ 1997 C 372/5, at no. 8.

[6] Commission Decision 2001/463, *DSD* (Article 82), OJ 2001 L 166/1

[7] Case C-62/86, *AKZO* v. *Commission* (AKZO), [1991] ECR, I-3439, para. 60.

for rather limited discretion and therefore leaves very little or no room at all for the integration of environmental concerns.

Moreover, the dominant position must have its effect in a substantial part of the common market. This element of Article 82 is the corollary to the 'effect on trade between member states' requirement within Article 81. The Court has held this jurisdictional criterion to be fulfilled where the market of one member state was involved.[8] The farthest going application of this criterion took place in the cases that concerned the Port of Genoa. In these cases the Court held that the port of Genoa constituted a substantial part of the common market.[9] In the more recent *Sydhavnens* case, the Court appeared to consider it possible that the market for processing building and construction waste in the area of the municipality of Copenhagen was a substantial part of the common market.[10]

Looking at dominance in an environmental context, the following general remarks may be made. Despite harmonisation, disparities in national (environmental) regulations are still likely to lead to, for example with regard to waste processing, geographical markets being defined on a national basis.[11] The remarks of the Court in the *Dusseldorp* and *Sydhavnens Sten & Grus* cases, where it held that the free movement of waste destined for recovery could not be obstructed on the basis of the proximity principle and source principle, provide only a beginning of a European market for waste.[12] En the end, many waste processing systems are still set up on a national basis.[13] This includes the so-called green dot systems that, although used in more countries, are still set up for the territory of one member state only.

Moreover, the relevant product market is also likely to be narrowly defined. Again, with regard to waste processing, the technical characteristics of this market will often result in a narrowly defined market. In the *Dusseldorp* case, the market concerned was that for the processing of waste oil and products contaminated with waste oil. Dutch legislation prescribed that one undertaking, AVR, could only process this waste. Moreover, export of this waste was only

---

8 *E.g.* Case C-203/96, *Chemische Afvalstoffen Dusseldorp* v. *Minister van Volkshuisvesting, Ruimtelijke Ordening en Milieubeheer* (Dusseldorp), [1998] ECR, I-4075

9 Similarly, large airports may also constitute a substantial part of the common market, see, e.g. Commission Decision 98/190, *Flughafen Frankfurt/Main*, OJ 1998, L 72/30, paras 57 and 58.

10 Case C-209/98, *Sydhavnens*, [2000] ECR, I-3743, para. 64.

11 See, *e.g.* Commission decision pursuant to the Merger Regulation in case Case No IV/M.1160 – *GKN/Brambles/SKP*, OJ 1998 C 117/14, para. 13.

12 *Ibid.*, para. 48 and Case C-203/96, *Dusseldorp*, [1999] ECR, I-4075.

13 The so-called Basle Regulation, Reg. 259/93, that governs the supervision and control of shipments of waste does not aim to bring about a European waste market. Rather, as the recitals show, the member states must set up waste management installations that will allow the Community as a whole to become self-sufficient.

allowed if AVR's capacity was exceeded and it could be shown that the processing abroad was of at least an equal quality to that offered by AVR. On the basis of this the Court rightly held that AVR occupied a statutory monopoly. From this the Court inferred the existence of a dominant position in a substantial part of the common market for AVR. In the *Sydhavnens Sten & Grus* case the Court appeared more reticent in this respect. In this case there was another statutory monopoly granted to three undertakings for the collection and recycling of building waste emanating from the municipality of Copenhagen. Instead of simply applying the Dusseldorp reasoning *mutatis mutandis*,[14] the ECJ stressed the need of a fully-fledged market definition.[15] In defining this market, the regulatory framework can certainly play a role.

In the *DSD* case, for example, the Commission relied strongly on the regulatory framework applicable. The German Packaging Ordinance, made the producers of packaging responsible for the collection and recycling of waste packaging. Producers were left a choice, by the Ordinance, between, on the one hand, setting up an individual or collective system (so called '*Selbstentsorgerlösung*' or self-management system or, on the other hand, joining a so-called '*Befreiungssystem*' or exemption system. Such exemption systems may be set up on the basis of Section 6(3) of the Packaging Ordinance. This latter option has been included as a result of pressure by the German industry and has been used by it to create DSD. Because such an exemption system has to cover the entire area of at least one Bundesland and because rather high collection and recycling quota have to be met, the Commission concluded that such systems would be difficult to set up. At least they would be more difficult to set up than the other (collective) option offered by the Packaging Ordinance. As a result the Commission came to the conclusion that there was a separate relevant product market for exemption systems from the Packaging Ordinance.[16] Because DSD is the only undertaking offering such a system in Germany, this resulted in a 100 per cent market share. Moreover, DSD collects and recycles over 80 per cent of the packaging waste in Germany and therefore the Commission held that DSD was also in a dominant position from a turnover-perspective.

## 9.4 Abuse of the dominant position

Mere dominance will not bring an undertaking in violation of Article 82. Only *abuse* of the dominant position will result in a violation of

[14] As A-G Léger apparently suggested, cf. his opinion in Case C-209/98, *Sydhavnens*, [2000] ECR, I-3743, paras. 70 and 73.

[15] *Ibid.*, para. 57, *cf.* Vedder 2001, p. 112.

[16] Commission Decision 2001/463, *DSD* (Article 82), OJ 2001 L 166/1, para. 80.

Article 82. The concept of abuse is an objective one. Whether or not the intention of the enterprise in question was to abuse its dominant position is therefore not relevant for determining if the abuse that Article 82 prohibits, has taken place. Furthermore, the company in a dominant position should be aware of this position on the market and the accompanying special responsibility not to distort competition.[17] In *Hoffmann-La Roche* the ECJ gave its definition of what constitutes abuse:[18]

*'The concept of abuse is an objective concept relating to the behaviour of an undertaking in a dominant position which is such as to influence the structure of a market where, as a result of the very presence of the undertaking in question, the degree of competition is weakened and which, through recourse to methods different from those which condition normal competition in products or services on the basis of the transactions of commercial operators, has the effect of hindering the maintenance of the degree of competition still existing in the market or the growth of that competition.'*

Essentially two different types of abuse exist. Obstructive or exclusionary abuse relates to abuse that seeks to affect the market structure whereas exploitative abuse concerns the abuse that not so much aims to affect market structure but rather wants to exploit the dominant position.[19] An example of the first type of abuse would be the activities of an undertaking in a dominant position in order to keep other competing companies from challenging its position. Exploitative behaviour is not necessarily addressed at competing enterprises but seeks to reap the monopoly benefits by, for example, charging excessive prices. Both types of abuse may occur in an environmental context as the *DSD* case shows.

The very concept of abuse rules out the possibility of an exemption. However, the absence of an exemption clause like Article 81(3) and the objective nature of abuse do not stand in the way of certain behaviour, though *prima facie* seeming abusive, being considered not to constitute abuse within the meaning of Article 82. This brings us in the realm of the 'objective justification'. Behaviour that can be objectively justified will not constitute abuse even when it resembles the practices listed in Article 82.

Below we will look at some types of abuse identified by Commission practice and Court rulings. In doing so we will also consider the possibility of an objective justification on (partly) environmental grounds.

---

17 Case 322/81, *Michelin* v. *Commission*, [1983] ECR, 3461, para. 57.

18 Case 85/76 *Hoffmann-La Roche*, [1979] ECR, 461, para. 91.

19 *Cf.* Bellamy & Child 2001, p. 720, Ritter, Braun & Rawlinson 2000, p. 351.

### 9.4.1 Unfair prices

The indicative list of abuses in Article 82 is headed off by abuse consisting of charging 'unfair prices'. Prices may be unfair in three respects. Firstly, a company in a dominant position may ask unfairly high prices. A second, seemingly more far-fetched example of an unfair price occurs where the dominant enterprise charges excessively low prices in order to push a competitor out of the market.[20] The third form of an unfair price is the discriminatory price.[21] The landmark case with regard to excessive pricing is *United Brands.*[22] In this case the Commission sought to rely on earlier Court case law that stated that price are unfair whenever they are excessive in relation to the economic value of the product. The Commission then presumed that United Brands made a profit on the Irish market. Therefore, the Commission continued, United Brands charged excessive prices on all markets where prices were even higher than on the Irish market. The Court did not accept this reasoning. The result of this is that establishing excessively high prices is no longer a question of straightforward mathematics. The reticence of the Commission in this respect[23] appears to have disappeared with its recent decision in the *DSD* case.

In this case, the Commission held, *inter alia*, that DSD abused its dominant position by charging excessive prices whenever it would demand a so-called license fee because a producer had placed a 'green dot' on his packaging whereas this producer would not actually use the DSD system to retrieve and recycle its packaging.[24] The DSD system, already referred to above in general, is funded by license fees paid by producers that have joined the system in order to be exempted from their obligations under the Packaging Ordinance. The contact between DSD and these companies requires the latter to place the 'green dot' sign on their packaging so as to make clear to consumers that this packaging is to separately collected outside the normal system for household waste (hence *dual* system Germany). Because DSD holds the trademark for the green dot, producers have to pay a license fee whenever they want to make use of the DSD

---

[20] So-called predatory pricing. The landmark case in this respect is the *AKZO* case (Case C-62/86, [1991] ECR, I-3439). Since establishing predatory pricing is a technical exercise (according to the ECJ predatory exist where prices are below average variable costs and, if there is intention to predate, when prices are above average variable costs) that leaves no room for environmental considerations we will not pay any further attention to it. Since the intention of the company that uses predatory pricing is to push a competitor out of the market, it can also be seen as an example of obstructive abuse.

[21] As a discriminatory pricing policy is primarily prohibited because of its discriminatory nature and not so much because it will result in unfair prices we shall look at this form of abuse *infra*, paragraph 9.4.1.

[22] Case 27/76, *United Brands*, [1978] ECR 207, para. 235 *et seq.*

[23] *Cf.* Bellamy & Child 2001, p. 723.

[24] Commission Decision 2001/463, *DSD* (Article 82), OJ 2001 L 166/1, para. 111.

system. The license fees are calculated according to the actual costs incurred in collecting and recycling a particular type of packaging material. Therefore the fees collected for a type of packaging material should represent the costs incurred for this material.

According to the Commission, DSD charges excessively high prices whenever it charges the license fee from companies for products that were not actually collected and recycled through the DSD system. This may occur when a company does not use the DSD system for its packaging in Germany but nonetheless participates in a green dot system set up in another member state and wants to use uniform packaging for the German market and the other market. It may also occur where a company wants to make use of the DSD system for only part of its products for the German market.[25] In both cases, the companies are obliged to pay for the placing of the license fee on the packaging and not so much for the fact that the packaging waste has actually been collected and recycled through the DSD system. Furthermore, the factual situation will make it nigh impossible for these companies to mark only that part of their products with the green dot with which they would actually want to participate in the DSD system. Similarly, it is also impossible and, moreover, it would run counter the very idea of the common market, if these firms would want to ascertain that products using a green dot system in another member state are not exported to Germany.[26] According to the Commission, DSD thus charges excessive prices because the price charged is clearly disproportionate to the costs incurred by DSD.[27]

With regard to this reasoning the following remarks may be made. DSD's cost structure, with very limited cross-subsidisation between the different packaging materials, would seem to warrant the conclusion that DSD faces only minimal costs when it does not actually collect the packaging waste. Therefore disproportionality can be said to exist. However, this would mean that it would actually have to be shown that certain packaging is collected and recycled through alternative systems so that DSD indeed does not incur any costs. This will be very difficult to show in practice as the recycling quota for both self-management and exemption systems are below 100 per cent.[28] This could mean that a system that competes with DSD could very well achieve its quota under the Packaging Ordinance whereas DSD would actually collect and recycle a nearly unchanged amount of packaging waste and hence faces only slightly lower costs. This is likely to occur precisely because DSD is the well established and by far the largest recycling system to which consumers have gotten used

25 *Ibid.*, para. 101.

26 This would mean that those companies would have to prevent parallel imports from occurring.

27 *Ibid.*, para. 111.

28 *Ibid.*, para. 18.

for nearly a decade. In practice, therefore, meeting the Commission's objections to DSD's financing structure would boil down to obliging DSD to subsidise the entrant.

### 9.4.2 Limiting production, markets or technological development

A number of practices fall under this category. With regard to technological development it should be noted that, in the section devoted to Article 81(3), environmental improvements were considered 'technological development'. In a number of cases, the Commission has held that Article 82 was infringed because production and technological development were limited. In *British Telecom* the refusal by BT to participate in a telex forwarding system limited technological progress.[29] Similarly, the refusal by Irish broadcasters to give *Magill* access to their programme schedule prevented Magill from marketing a new product (programme guide) and therefore technological progress was limited.[30]

These examples show that behaviour by a dominant undertaking that keeps an environmentally friendly product from being marketed could possibly constitute abuse. An example of such behaviour could be the case where a dominant producer responsibility organisation (e.g. DSD or Eco-Emballages) refuses to use new and more environmentally friendly recycling methods offered to it by a down-stream company.

In an environmental context the Court has considered 'outlets' to have been restricted in the *Dusseldorp* case. In this case Dutch environmental law prescribed that all dangerous waste (in this case oil filters) had to be processed by one company, AVR. Exportation of this waste was only allowed if there is insufficient capacity in the Netherlands and if it could be shown that the processing abroad would be of an at least equally high quality. These rules, according to the Court, resulted in waste being treated by AVR that was destined for another party. This was deemed a 'restriction of outlets in a manner contrary to Article 90(1) (Now 86(1), HV) in conjunction with Article 86(Now 82, HV) of the Treaty'.[31] Firstly, it should be noted that the Court probably meant that,

---

29 Commission Decision 82/861, British Telecommunications, OJ 1982 L 360/36, para. 35. Upheld in Case 41/83, *Italy* v. *Commission*, [1985] ECR 873. The Court, however, did not address specifically the question whether there was a limitation of technological progress in this Case.

30 Commission Decision 89/205, *Magill TV Guide* v. *ITP, BBC and RTE* (Magill), OJ 1989 L 78/43, para. 23. Upheld in Joined Cases C-241/91P and C-242/91 P, *Radio Telefis Eireann (RTE) and Independent Television Publications Ltd (ITP)* v. *Commission* (Magilll), [1995] ECR I-0743.

31 Case C-203/96, *Dusseldorp*, [1999] ECR, I-4075, para. 63.

within the meaning of Article 82 (b) EC, 'markets' were limited to the prejudice of consumers.[32]

Secondly, it has to be taken into account that this reasoning occurred in an Article 86 case with AVR holding exclusive rights. It is most unlikely that any enterprise, however dominant, will be able to keep someone from going to a competitor.[33] The Court's approach to abuse, dominance, legislation and the connection between the three is specific to the provision on public undertakings and will therefore be considered separately.[34]

### 9.4.3 Discriminatory or unfair conditions

In a general manner all unfair or discriminating trading conditions are prohibited as an abuse of a dominant position. With the price being one of the – if not the – most important trading condition discriminatory pricing is likely to constitute abuse. In the *United Brands* case, the Commission argued that United Brands' pricing policy was discriminatory. Generally, discrimination exists where like cases are treated dissimilar and where unlike cases are treated alike. In the *United Brands* case the Court considered United Brands' pricing policy to be discriminatory contrary to Article 82.[35] However, it should be taken into account that the policy of United Brands discriminated on grounds of nationality and therefore ran directly counter to the very essence of the common market.[36]

A company in a dominant position may want to encourage environmentally friendly products or production processes in upstream or downstream firms. In this case the dominant undertaking may further decide to use its pricing policy as instrument. In other words: it may start to charge higher prices to downstream firms that are environmentally unfriendly. Similarly, it may decide to pay lower prices to upstream firms that supply relatively environmentally unfriendly products. Such a development is not unlikely since the environmental tack record is considered increasingly important by all sorts of firms.[37]

Such upstream and downstream companies may argue that unfair conditions are imposed or that they are discriminated. As regards the discrimination, an obvious counter-argument is of course that the environmentally unfriendly

---

32 The language used by the Court in the Dutch, French en German versions of the judgment (resp. *'afzet'*, *'débouchés'* and *'absatzmarkt'*) seems to indicate this.

33 Although the dominant company could try to tie other companies to his undertaking, *infra*, para. 9.4.4.

34 *Infra*, paragraph 12.5 (concerning Article 86 EC).

35 Case 27/76, *United Brands*, [1978] ECR 207, para. 214.

36 *Ibid.*, paras. 232-234.

37 *Cf.* the extensive advertising campaigns by Shell and BP as well as the fact that the three P's (planet, people and profit) play an increasingly important role in the management of firms.

firms are dissimilar to their environmentally friendly counterparts. In that case, the dominant firm would do nothing more than treating unlike cases in an unlike manner which does not constitute discrimination. The central question therefore is whether and to what extent the environmental friendliness can justify different treatment. We shall look closer at this question in the paragraph concerning the objective justification. Similarly, an unfair condition exists only when it is not justified or disproportionate to the interest that it serves.[38] In the *DSD* case the Commission, relying on *United Brands*, appears to consider the principle of proportionality as a general standard by which all conduct of the dominant undertaking is measured.[39] Again, reference is made to paragraph 9.5 concerning the objective justification for a fuller account.

### 9.4.4 Tying

The dominant undertaking may want to consolidate its market share by ensuring that its customers are tied to it. This is a good example of exclusionary or obstructive abuse. Such tying, binding or bundling occurs in two forms: *de jure* or *de facto*. *De jure* tying is fairly obvious and will mostly require a factual condition. *De facto* tying, however, is all the more interesting. In its decision in *Van den Bergh Foods*, the Commission came to the conclusion that Van den Bergh Foods had *de facto* tied ice cream retailers to it through so-called freezer exclusivity.[40] This freezer exclusivity comes down to the following. Van den Bergh Food supplies ice cream sellers with free freezer cabinets subject to the widely used condition that only Van den Bergh ice will be sold from those cabinets. Despite the fact that the contract left these retailers were completely free to place another freezer cabinet in their shop or to replace the Van den Bergh cabinet with another one, the Commission considered that it was unlikely that retailers would actually do this. Because of factual constraints (lack of space in the retail shops, extra costs etc.) they were *de facto* tied to Van den Bergh.[41]

The Commission has used the same sort of *de facto*-tying reasoning in the *DSD* case. The DSD scheme, as we have seen above, is financed through the license fee for placement of the green dot on packaging. The scheme as it currently functions forces producers wishing to join the DSD scheme with only a part of their total amount of packaging to place the green dot on only that part of their total packaging. Furthermore, connected to this need to set up separate packaging lines, the producers would be forced to set up separate distribution channels in order to ascertain that the non-green dotted products do not end

---

38 Case 27/76, *United Brands*, [1978] ECR 207, paras 158-159.

39 Commission Decision 2001/463, *DSD* (Article 82), OJ 2001 L 166/1, para. 112.

40 Commission Decision 98/531, *Van den Bergh Foods Limited* OJ 1998 L 246/1.

41 *Ibid.*, paras. 158-184, 264.

up in the DSD collection system.[42] The extra costs involved with this option, as the only alternative to joining both the DSD and another system for the total amount of packaging, according to the Commission result in a *de facto* tie to the DSD system.[43]

Though not particular to the environmental context of the case, the Commission's reasoning in *DSD* is nonetheless interesting because similar packaging waste collection systems that use the green dot and license fees exist throughout Europe.

### 9.4.5 Access to essential facilities

Increasingly, environmental requirements are imposed on companies wishing to bring products on the market. The concept of (extended) producer responsibility has played and continues to play a key role in this respect. In the overwhelming majority of cases, the imposition of a producer responsibility in fact comes down to a product responsibility as was shown above. In such cases the only effective and efficient solution for the companies is to cooperate. Such cooperation, as the *DSD* case shows, may very well result in the emergence of a dominant organisation the membership of which is necessary in order to gain access to that market.

In this situation a company that is refused membership of such an organisation will be tempted to plea that the dominant firm refuses to grant it access to an essential facility. This appears to have happened in the *Spa Monopole* v. *GDB* case.[44] In this case, Belgian mineral water producer Spa was refused access to the pool of reusable glass bottles and crates set up by the Association of German Sources, (*Genossenschaft Deutsche Brunnen* (GDB)). Initially the Commission rejected the complaint by Spa because it was still allowed and feasible to import mineral water into Germany using other bottles. However, following the entry into force of new German legislation Spa's alternatives were narrowed down to either setting up an alternative pool for reusable bottles of its own (or together with other parties) or ensuring the recycling of its one way bottles. Neither option proved economically viable or practicable due to the costs involved and the unwillingness of retailers to participate in multiple systems. Therefore, the Commission considered that access to the GDB pool was 'essential in order to compete effectively in the mineral water market'.[45]

---

42 Commission Decision 2001/463, *DSD* (Article 82), OJ 2001 L 166/1, para. 112.

43 *Ibid.*, paras. 114, 115.

44 Unfortunately this Case never got beyond a mentioning in the Commission's annual competition resport, Commission, Competition Report 1993, para. 240.

45 *Ibid.*, at p. 159.

Whether a sequel to *Spa Monopole* v. *GDB* has become more likely due to the proliferation of collective producer responsibility systems depends on a multitude of factors. For one, the producer responsibility systems currently set up are structured in such a manner as to make the abuse of the system as a barrier to entry increasingly unlikely. The institutional structure of, for example, DSD, renders it nigh impossible for German producers to use the voting rights arising from their membership as a vehicle to keep foreign manufacturers from the market.[46] Furthermore, *communis opinio* has it that the essential facilities doctrine has become more difficult to invoke as a result of the Court's *Bronner* judgment.[47]

## 9.5 The objective justification

Seemingly abusive behaviour that can be objectively justified will not violate Article 82. In some of the paragraphs above, we have already seen some examples of seemingly abusive behaviour that may be objectively justified and will therefore not constitute abuse. The doctrine of the objective justification can be seen as the result of the fine line between, on the one hand, contractual freedom and, on the other, the need to protect competition, that has to be tread when applying Article 82. We have already seen that the dominant company has a special responsibility. However, we may wonder whether this special responsibility should keep the firm in a dominant position from acting in accordance with its commercial interests. In *Télémarketing*, the Court had to rule on the question whether a dominant undertaking that keeps a neighbouring market to itself and in doing so keeps a competitor from becoming active on that market, has abused its position.[48] According to the Court this refusal to supply constituted abuse unless there was an 'objective necessity'. Certainly, a company in a dominant position cannot be required to bring itself to ruin and should therefore be allowed to act if this is objectively justified. The dominant firm that requires environmentally friendly behaviour of other companies will consider that its behaviour is objectively justified by the interest of protecting the environment. The Commission has addressed the issue of whether the behaviour by a dominant undertaking was objectively justified in a number of cases.[49]

---

[46] See, further to DSD's institutional structure Lehmann 2000 en Velte 1999, p. 100 *et seq.*

[47] Case C-7/97, *Bronner* v. *Mediaprint* (Bronner), [1998] ECR I-7791, *cf.* Ritter, Braun & Rawlinson 2000, p. 381, Jones & Sufrin 2001, p. 395 *et seq.*

[48] Case 311/84, *Centre Belge d'Etudes de Marché Télémarketing* v. *Compagnie Luxembourgeoise de Télédiffusion* (Télémarketing), [1985] ECR 3261, para. 26.

[49] See, e.g., Commission Decision in Case 2000/12, *Comité Français d'Organisation de la Coupe du Monde de Football 1998* (French Organising Committee of the 1998 World Cup,CFO) OJ 2000 L 5/55, para. 105 *et seq.*

However, in all of these cases the Commission came to the conclusion that the behaviour was not objectively justified. Similarly, the Commission looked at the arguments put forward by DSD only to come to the conclusion that they did not constitute an objective justification.

DSD brought a number of reasons forward in this respect. Firstly, it sought to rely on the German Packaging Ordinance since that Ordinance would stand in the way of using the green dot for anything less than the total amount of packaging brought on the market for which responsibility is accepted through the DSD system.[50] In the light of the principle of supremacy of Community law this first argument may seem awkward. However, it probably has to be understood as a plea by DSD that it was compelled by the Ordinance to act as it did. If this were the case, DSD would have had no freedom to in this respect and therefore its behaviour would not be governed by the competition laws.[51] According to DSD the marking is necessary to ensure the transparency of the system and was for that reason included in the Packaging Ordinance. The mark should indicate to the consumer that she can take the packaging home and dispose of it near home. Non-marked packaging (*i.e.* packaging not covered by an exemption system) should be brought back to or left at the shops for further collection and recycling. If the green dot mark were affixed to quantities of packaging that were not actually collected through the DSD system, the consumer, according to DSD would be misled.

The Commission did not share DSD's interpretation of the Packaging Ordinance in that consumers had no freedom to choose where to leave packaging (near the shops or near home).[52] The transparency required by the Ordinance only served to make clear to the consumer whether he should leave the packaging near the shop or take it home and dispose of it there. Therefore, the Packaging Ordinance did not compel DSD to abuse its dominant position.

Secondly, DSD relied on trademark law. According to DSD the green dot trade mark would lose its meaning if packaging that was not part of the DSD system and therefore had to be collected otherwise would nonetheless be marked with the green dot.[53] Ultimately, this would render the green dot meaningless and would lead to less packaging flowing into the DSD system and thus bring about DSD's demise.

The Commission applied the Court's standard case law with regard to exclusive rights.[54] This means that the exercise of an exclusive right could constitute abuse. This is only not so where the exercise of the exclusive right is necessary

---

50 Commission Decision 2001/463, *DSD* (Article 82), OJ 2001 L 166/1, para. 136.

51 By analogy to the '*Zwangskartell*' hypothesis this could be deemed '*Zwangsmißbrauch*', *supra*, para. 3.5

52 Commission Decision 2001/463, *DSD* (Article 82), OJ 2001 L 166/1, para. 138.

53 *Ibid.*, para. 143.

54 *Ibid.*, para. 144.

to fulfil the essential function of the exclusive right. The pivotal question is therefore what constitutes the 'essential function' of the green dot trademark. In line with what the Commission considered above with regard to the Packaging Ordinance, the Commission considered that the essential function of the green dot was to inform consumers that they have a *choice* to dispose of the packaging waste through the DSD system.[55] Therefore, the essential function of the green dot is not jeopardised when the total amount of packaging has the green dot on it whereas the producer participates in the DSD system with only a partial amount. Similarly, the Commission rejects DSD's argument that the option whereby the green dot is placed on all packaging including the portion for which the producer does not participate in DSD may lead to misuse.[56] DSD brought forward that is very likely that consumers will make use of the DSD system for larger quantities than that which the producers have contracted with DSD. This is indeed likely to happen as consumers have gotten used to using the DSD system for nearly 10 years. Therefore, DSD considers that obliging it to grant partial licenses effectively imposes on DSD an obligation to finance costs in advance and all the risks that go with that obligation. The Commission counters this by pointing to the fact that competing exemption systems as well as self-management solutions will have to comply with the same collection and recycling quota as DSD. Should one of these systems therefore fail to achieve these quotas, it would have to join the DSD system for the remaining quantity. The Commission proposes a system whereby at the end of the year the amounts of collected and recycled waste for each system are compared to the quota. If the quotas have not been met by a competing exemption system or self-management system, compensation should take place.[57]

As part of its plea based on trade mark considerations, DSD advances the argument that it cannot be obliged to provide a service that it has not provided before (i.e. the granting of isolated licenses to use the trade mark) since the difficulties that Commission classifies as abuse are not caused by DSD but by the organisation and activities of the producers.[58] The Commission simply refers to the fact that it has already established that it is DSD financing structure that is at the root of the problems. Moreover, the producers could avoid such problems only at disproportionate costs.[59]

Finally, the Commission puts aside DSD's contention that the balance between license fee income and costs of collectors and recyclers would be

---

55 *Ibid.*, para. 145.

56 *Ibid.*, para. 147.

57 *Ibid.*, para. 148.

58 *Ibid.*, para. 149.

59 See also Case C-7/97, *Bronner*, [1998] ECR I-7791, where, at para. 28, Mediaprint seems to be forwarding a similar argument that appears to have been accepted by the Court.

disturbed.[60] The Commission simply points at the fact that the companies that do the actual collecting and recycling on behalf of DSD will also do less collecting and recycling. Accordingly, DSD will have to pay a lower fee to the recycling and collection companies.

On the basis of the abovementioned arguments, the Commission reaches the conclusion that there is no objective justification for DSD's behaviour. As a result, the Commission is of the opinion that DSD abuses its dominant position.[61]

It is submitted that DSD's financing structure could very well be objectively justified on environmental and efficiency grounds. Producer responsibility places the responsibility on the producers' shoulders. However, it should not be forgotten that it is the consumer who in the end is expected to hand in and to some degree sort the packaging waste. Moreover, the consumer is often considered to be the weakest link. The emergence of multiple systems (marked with, for example, green, red and pink dots) is likely to confuse the consumer and may even lead to 'recycling fatigue'.[62] Furthermore, the Commission's proposal for a compensation system can hardly be expected to increase the efficiency of the system. It will, for example, be interesting to see how the compensation will work if there are multiple (self-management and exemption) systems that do not reach their quota.[63] Another interesting difficulty is the result of the fact that the collection and recycling quota are currently at around 75 per cent. This makes it perfectly possible that one system actually meets the quota whereas DSD also meets its goals. In that case, DSD will not be able to ask for compensation (since the other systems have met their quotas) while it will have to pay for the total amount of packaging collected for which it, in turn, it will not receive the full amount of license fees since some of the producers may have joined competing systems. Taking into account that DSD is the well-established player, it is likely that consumers will keep on using the DSD system relatively more than other systems. All in all, the Commission's decision may have some unpleasant side effects for DSD. The question what we should do with such monopolistic systems from a competition point of view is addressed in the following paragraph.

---

60 *Ibid.*, para. 151.

61 *Ibid.*, para. 153.

62 Empirical evidence can be found in the chaos that currently exists with regard to the *dosenpfand* (deposit and return for one way beverage packaging), see www.pfandpflicht.info.

63 Furthermore, DSD will, for example, probably have to reserve funds for the advance financing-risks.

## 9.6 Producer responsibility organisations as natural monopolies or universal service providers

Even though the Commission has characterised the behaviour of DSD also as a form of exploitative abuse (excessive prices),[64] it in fact did little more than recycling the reasoning that underlies the exclusionary abuse. Thus, in the end the Commission only reproaches DSD for keeping an effective competitor from entering the market. In this respect the Commission recognises that it is highly unlikely that a viable competitor for DSD will emerge from one moment to another. Therefore the Commission argues that the market for a regional exemption system or a self-management solution could act as a springboard for the market for exemption systems. Certainly, DSD's yearly turnover of DEM 4.2 billion may make it quite tempting to want to jump on the recycling bandwagon but it must be kept in mind that turnover is not profit. If we take into account that DSD calculates the license fees so that they only cover the costs, the sheer magnitude of the costs involved becomes clear.

Moreover, the requirements imposed by the Packaging Ordinance on exemption systems would also seem to inhibit the chances of a viable competitor for DSD entering the market for exemption systems. According to this Ordinance, an exemption system must cover at least one *Bundesland*. In this area the system must guarantee so-called *haushaltsnahe* collection or collection in the vicinity of the consumers' house. All in all these requirements will require setting up an extensive and costly infrastructure. This is true to a much lesser extent for regional exemption systems of self-management solutions. The only actual potential competitor that the Commission mentions in its decision is the system for professional hair-care products.[65] This is set up to take back and recycle the packaging waste from hairdressers (empty shampoo bottles). The fact in itself that such as system is set up by economically rational undertakings shows that it is possible to put in place a take back and recycling system for a niche market at lower costs than those involved in joining the DSD system. However, it must surely be recognised that organising the collection and recycling of one relatively homogeneous sort of packaging waste from a limited number of hairdressers is something quite different from the system run by DSD. The difference in the number of collection points (*i.e.* hairdressers v. households) alone is enormous. This appears to have been recognised by the Commission in its decision on the basis of Article 81 EC concerning DSD when it considers that:[66]

---

64 Commission Decision 2001/463, *DSD* (Article 82), OJ 2001 L 166/1, paragraph 2.2.1.

65 Set up by the *Industrieverband Friseurbedarf* (Hairdressing Supplies Industrial Association) and disposal contractor *Vfw, ibid.*, para. 6.

66 Commission Decision 2001/337, *DSD* (Article 81), OJ 2001 L 319/1 para. 160.

*'[T]here are considerations of spatial economics, collection logistics and traditions of waste collection established among consumers which make it economically difficult in many cases to duplicate the arrangements for collection from households.'*

More generally, the parameters set by the Packaging Ordinance have been identified as impediments to effective competition.[67] Firstly, it can probably be said that under the requirements imposed by the Ordinance, the choice between and individual solution or a collective approach should not be that difficult to make. Setting up or joining one collective system is in fact the only economically rational reaction to producer responsibility in these circumstances.[68] Secondly, the demands placed on such collective systems are such to effectively lead to one collective system for the overwhelming majority of packaging waste.

In the course of looking at the *DSD* case, we have already hinted at the possibility of characterising the DSD system as a natural monopoly. Could it not be argued that the demands in the Ordinance have created a market that can bear only one company?[69] The notion of *Zwangsmißbrauch* or compulsory abuse mentioned above is in certain respects closely connected to the concept of a natural monopoly.[70] It can be said that a firm that has a natural monopoly cannot avoid committing exclusionary abuse. By its very nature the firm in such a position will always act contrary to the interest of potential competitors as the market simply can bear only one company. Moreover, the exploitative abuse that the Commission reproaches DSD for actually consists of nothing more than the behaviour by a natural monopolist that sees itself unable to cater to the needs of 'cherry-pickers'.

Taking the 'cherry-picking reasoning' a bit further, the emerging picture of the legal obligations with which an exemption system must comply, shows some resemblance to the definition of a service of general economic interest given by the Court in *Corbeau*.[71] This brings the concept of the universal service or, in the terminology of Article 86(2) EC, the service of general economic interest into the picture. If this exception applies, Article 82 is no longer applicable. We shall be looking closer at this provision below. However, as we will see, the obvious difference with *Corbeau* is that the 'natural monopolist' in that case had in fact a statutory monopoly. For Article 86(2) to apply there will need to be, as the law

---

67 *Cf.* Benzler *et al.* p. 33, 60.

68 *Cf.* in this respect the remarks by the Dutch environment minister with regard to the producer responsibility for waste electrical and electronical equipment in the Netherlands, Vedder 2002, p. 86.

69 *Cf.* Bonus 1997, p. 31. Furthermore, this option was also considered by the Swiss Competition commission in relation to take back and recycling systems, *cf.* Wettbewerbskommission und Preisüberwacher 1996, p. 56. See also: Commission 2003, p. 32.

70 *Supra*, p. 35 and 39.

71 Case C-320/91, *Criminal proceedings against Paul Corbeau* (Corbeau), [1993] ECR I-2533, para. 15.

stands today, some sort of regulatory instrument that confers the monopoly position. With regard to DSD, however, it seems unlikely that the legal framework created by the Packaging Ordinance will be considered as *entrusting* DSD with a task of general economic interest within the meaning of Article 86(2) EC.

Staying in the realm of the universal service obligation, a parallel with the 'standard' utilities may be drawn. These were also once considered to be natural monopolies. This, however, changed when, after liberalisation, 'the market' showed that separate markets existed on which vigorous competition was possible.[72] All of this requires the presence of some sort of regulator or government authority to not only monitor competition but also to take into account the requirements flowing from the universal service character of the sector concerned. In many cases, liberalisation will effectively come down to the government shaking the tree so that picking the cherries will become easier to pick for entrants to the market. However, to use the other common analogy in this field, you need the cream to make the rest of the cake taste good.

The more general point underlying the observations made above with regard to the character of a natural monopoly or universal service is actually threefold. Firstly, unleashing standard competition law as opposed to market liberalisation laws may not be the best method to tackle the competition problems that are perceived to take place. Undoubtedly, other players may occupy niche markets but whether these markets can actually function as springboards is far from clear and nowhere substantiated by the Commission.[73] Furthermore, taking the example of the system set up for professional hair-care products, what is going to happen to the license fee for shampoo bottles not destined for professional hairdressers but the normal consumer? It seems likely that this license fee would actually increase and, as other niche markets are discovered, license fees in general may go up. This is the standard problem encountered in liberalising utilities markets. Such liberalisation takes place on the basis of the standard competition laws but simultaneously takes into account the fact that it is liberalisation and not (yet) competition that we are talking about.

Secondly, and this relates to the fact that we speak of 'perceived' competition problems, authorities could better concentrate on upstream and downstream effects of DSD's dominant position rather than trying to create competition. The emergence of a viable competitor to DSD for the entire territory of Germany is not only unlikely it may also very well be inefficient (effectively doubling the investments in infrastructure and thus increasing costs). Efficiency gains and more effective competition are more likely if competition authorities would concentrate on the effects of DSD's behaviour on upstream and downstream

---

72 *Cf.*, with regard to the telecommunication market: Nihoul.

73 Moreover, the environmental effectiveness of a situation where multiple systems function alongside eachother may be doubted.

markets. Through, for example, keeping exclusivities granted to upstream companies (i.e. companies that provide the actual collection and recycling services) to a minimum and ensuring that such contacts are concluded following public tenders, efficiency losses are likely to be minimised. With regard to downstream markets (i.e. the producers that want to place the green dot on their packaging) it has to be ascertained that the license fee does not exceed the costs. To a large degree both issues can be efficiently addressed by means of DSD's institutional structure. Moreover, evolutions in DSD's institutional structure have indeed solved this problem to a large extent.[74] These evolutions mean that at the moment both upstream as well as downstream industries are represented in DSD's board. Moreover, both industries' presence can be called atomistic.[75] The fact that upstream as well as downstream industries are represented effectively rules abuse of DSD as vehicle to either increase license fees (to the detriment of consumers) or to lower license fees (to the detriment of the collection and recycling companies). Moreover, the atomistic representation makes it impossible for members of upstream or downstream industry to use the license fee as an instrument to put certain types of packaging at a disadvantage.[76]

The third observation is that the emergence of DSD as a monopolistic system as well as the emergence of similarly monopolistic systems almost throughout Europe as a result of the imposition of producer responsibility may very well be the direct result of the environmental laws prescribing producer responsibility. With the exception of the UK, producer responsibility for packaging waste has led to the setting up monopolistic systems. Moreover, the producer responsibilities introduced in the Netherlands for batteries and accumulators and waste electronical and electrical equipment have also resulted in nationwide monopolists.[77] The Directive laying down a producer responsibility for waste electrical and electronical products[78] is very likely to lead to a proliferation of monopolistic systems such as the one that emerged in the Netherlands.[79] With regard to the Packaging Ordinance we have identified the individual product responsibility as opposed to producer responsibility as a factor leading to the creation a large-scale exemption systems. Furthermore, the requirement of blanket coverage

---

74 *Cf.* Lehmann 2000.

75 Currently, about 400 parties hold shares in DSD.

76 One could imagine a case where, for example, part of the dairy food industry (that mainly uses carton aseptic packs) wants to increase the license fee for plastic bottles because these are used by a competitor. The idea behind this would be to increase the competitor's costs and thereby push him out of the market.

77 See, further, Vedder 2002, p. 169 *et seq.*

78 Directive 2002/96 on waste electrical and electronic equipment (hereafter the WEEE Directive), OJ 2002 L 37/24.

79 See, further, Vedder 2002, p. 3.

of at least one Bundesland, together with the obligation to ensure collection in the vicinity of households, can be identified as factors hindering the emergence of anything else than one monopolistic system in which all the parties cooperate. In the proposed WEEE directive, the so-called 'old-for-new obligation' can be identified as a factor likely to lead to the creation of large scale, monopolistic producer responsibility organisations.[80] Furthermore, the discussion in Europe on whether or not a visible fee should be introduced in the Directive shows that environmental regulation takes into account competition concerns and, moreover, actively interferes with competition on a market. The visible fee effectively rules out any competition with regard to the passing through of the environmental costs.[81] In many respects, the plans to allow for a visible fee for ten years following the entry into force of the Directive can be seen as a transitional measure that is necessary in the liberalisation process.

The old-for-new obligation takes into account the fact that the producer responsibility extends to the so-called historical waste. This is the waste that will be generated when the products that are already on the market before the entry into force of the directive, will be discarded. Consumers are likely to want to get rid of their old products when they buy the replacement product. This has led to the old-for-new obligation whereby retailers (and ultimately producers and importers) must accept, irrespective of the brand, the old product free of charge when the consumer buys a similar new appliance. It is generally accepted that the old-for-new obligation can lead to a distortion of competition particularly for those producers that have a rather high market share at the moment but were not present on the market a few years ago. For this reason, the producers have always advocated a visible fee. This is a fee that should be passed on through the retail chain to the consumer and be mentioned separately on the invoice. The fee should cover the costs for the recycling of a particular type of product. Such a visible fee, it is submitted, is akin to a transitory arrangement in a liberalisation measure.[82]

Particularly if we take into account the fact that waste management was – and in many respect still is – a government task, the liberalisation nature becomes even clearer.

It is submitted that the Community's and member states' current environmental policy should take more account of competition considerations in draw-

---

80 Proposal for the WEEE Directive COM (2001) 314 final, Article 4(2). See further, Commission 2003 where, at p. 32, it is recognised that 'the implementation of the ELV (end of life vehicles, HV) and WEEE directives may give rise to further cases (involving producer responsibility schemes and Article 82 EC, HV)'.

81 See further, *supra*. Paragraph 16.5.4.

82 A parallel may be drawn with the postal dues that were levied in the *TNT Traco* case for the universal service, Case C-340/99, *TNT Traco* v. *Poste Italiane* (TNT Traco), [2001] ECR I-4109.

ing up environmental legislation laying down producer responsibilities. Furthermore, the Commission's competition policy with regard to large-scale producer responsibility organisations should focus on the upstream and downstream effects of these organisations rather than try to create competition. All in all, the circus surrounding DSD reminds one of the exclamations of Dr. Frankenstein: 'Abhorred monster! (...) come on, then, that I may extinguish the spark which I so negligently bestowed.'

This ends our observations with regard to Article 82 and its application in an environmental context. It is now time to turn our attention to the Merger Regulation.

CHAPTER 10

# Merger Control

## 10.1 Introductory remarks

Contrary to the ECSC Treaty the EC Treaty did not envisage a Community competence to control mergers. Only with the *Continental Can* case was some sort of make shift concentration control regime acknowledged by the Court.[1] However, it took the EC and primarily the Commission, until 1990 to put in place an effective *ex ante* merger control regime. This happened with the entry into force of the Merger Regulation.[2] Since then Regulation 1310/97 has amended it.[3] Below we shall address the rather technical details of this Regulation only very briefly. Suffice it, at this point, to say that the Merger Control Regulation was from the very outset on indented to be a pure competition-orientated instrument.[4] However, a number of features may indicate a role for non-competition issues nonetheless. Below, we shall first provide a general outline of the Merger Regulation after which we will turn our attention to the features that suggest some role for considerations other than competition.

## 10.2 An outline of the Merger Regulation and its application

Essentially the part of the Merger Regulation that is not concerned with notifications, time-limits and other procedural issues can be divided into a number of jurisdictional and a number of substantive provisions. The jurisdictional clauses concern the question whether an operation is to be notified to the Commission. Basically this hinges on the concept of a concentration and certain turnover thresholds that determine whether or not the transaction is of a 'Community dimension'.

Under the Merger Regulation companies are to notify to the Commission any plans for concentrations with a Community dimension before these effectuated. The concept of a concentration encompasses mergers *strictu sensu* (Article 3(1)(a) and the situation where one or more firms acquire control over one or more other firms (Article 3(1)(b). In order to have a Community dimension the undertakings concerned must pass a number of turnover thresholds (Article 1(2) and (3)).

---

1 Case 6/72, *Europemballage Corporation and Continental Can Inc* v. *Commission* (Continental Can), [1973] ECR 215, paras. 18-27.

2 Regulation No. 4064/89 On the Control of Concentrations Between Undertakings, OJ 1989 L 395/1.

3 Regulation No. 1310/97 Amending Regulation 4064/89 On the Control of Concentrations Between Undertakings, OJ 1997 L 180/1. The Commission is currently engaged in the so-called Merger Review operation that will further change the concentration control in the EU. The Commission's proposal for a new Regulation to replace Regulation 4064/89 as well as 1310/97 can be found in OJ 2003 C 20/4.

4 *Cf.* Pijnacker-Hordijk 1999, p. 119, Whish 2001, p. 781.

If the operation constitutes a concentration and is of Community dimension, the Commission will appraise it on the basis of the Merger Regulation. This is the actual substantive part of the Merger Regulation. The test in this respect is provided in Article 2 and hinges on whether the concentration is 'compatible with the common market'. This again pivots on whether or not a dominant position is created or strengthened as a result of which effective competition in the common market would be significantly impeded (Article 2(2) and (3)). The concept of dominance referred to here is identical to that within the meaning of Article 82 EC.[5] As we have seen above, establishing dominance is a fairly technical exercise where theoretically no discretion exists for the Commission. At best, environmental considerations can play a role in the market definition leading up to the appraisal of dominance.

This has happened in a number of cases concerning the market for waste recycling.[6] In *Rhône Poulenc Chimie/SITA* the envisaged joint venture should become active on the market for the recycling of special (toxic) industrial waste.[7] In assessing the markets concerned, the Commission took account of the special nature of the waste and environmental regulations in place. Similarly, in *Suez Lyonnaise des Eaux/BFI*, the Commission distinguished between the market for the treatment of normal waste and that for the treatment of special industrial waste.[8] Environmental considerations have played a role in market definition also outside the recycling context. In *Orkla/Volvo*, the Commission considered Norway to be a separate geographical market because of, *inter alia*, an environmental taxation scheme with regard to packaging.[9]

Pursuant to Article 2(4), joint ventures that fall within the scope of the Merger Regulation while leading to a coordination of the competitive behaviour of the parents will be screened in the light of Article 81(1) and 81(3). This effectively bestows upon the Merger Regulation the same possibilities for an integration of environmental concerns as exist with regard to Article 81 EC. Again, the reader is referred to the relevant paragraphs in this chapter.

This short sketch of the main features of the Merger Regulation confirms the statement made above that it is a pure competition oriented instrument that, unlike for example Article 81, does not allow for a restriction of competition to be balanced by a benefit of some sort. However, as was noticed above, there are a number of provisions in the Merger Regulation that may qualify this statement.

---

5 *Cf.* Whish 2001, p. 770.

6 *E.g.* Cases IV/M.1260, *EDON/ROVA/REKO*, CELEX No. 398M1260, IV/M.868, *GKN/Brambles/Mabeg*, CELEX No. 396M868, IV/M.283, *Waste Management International/SAE*, CELEX No. 392M283, IV/M.168, *Flachglas/VEGLA*, CELEX No. 392M168.

7 Case No. IV/M.266, CELEX No. 392M0266.

8 Case No. IV/M.1059, CELEX no. 397M1059.

9 Commission Decision 96/204, *Orkla/Volvo*, OJ 1996 L 66/4, para. 49.

## 10.3 Possibilities to take non-competition factors into account

In the introductory paragraph we have already indicated that the possibilities to take non-competition factors into account are small as it is considered to be an instrument geared only to maintaining competition. This, however, does not mean that non-competition considerations were from the outset on out of the picture nor does it mean that such factors have no role to play in the current form of the Regulation.

Merger control in the United States, for example, allows for a so-called 'efficiency defence'. Under this line of reasoning a merger that restricts competition can be allowed because of overriding efficiency gains. The result of this is of course that non-competition considerations enter the equation. It should, therefore, not come as a surprise that, despite the fact that the systems for merger control then functioning in EC member states did not allow for such a defence, that initial proposals for the Merger Regulation expressly provided for a balancing act. The 1988 and 1989 drafts both contained a provision explicitly allowing the Commission to authorise mergers if these 'contribute to the attainment of the basic objectives of the Treaty in such a way that, on balance, their economic benefits prevail over the danger they cause to competition'.[10] The scope of this provision would indeed probably even be wider than that of Article 81(3).

This provision, as the current version of the Merger Regulation shows, did not make it to the final version. Moreover, the then Commissioner responsible for competition, Sir Leon Brittan, has made it clear beyond doubt that the Merger Regulation would be concerned with maintaining competition and nothing else.[11] Nevertheless, the Regulation still contains some ambiguities in this respect. The first of these is the thirteenth recital of the preamble to the Regulation in which it is stated that:

*'Whereas it is necessary to establish whether concentrations [...] are compatible or not with the common market from the point of view of the need to maintain and develop effective competition; whereas, in doing so, the Commission must place its appraisal within the general framework of the achievement of the objectives referred to in Article 2 of the Treaty, including that of strengthening the Community's economic and social cohesion, referred to in Article 130A [now Article 158]'*

It should be noted that this recital is not reflected in the operative part of the Regulation. From a legal perspective its value therefore seems limited. However, the operative part of the Merger Regulation is not completely silent with regard

---

10 Jones & González-Diaz 1992, p. 156, Article 2(4) of the 1988 draft, OJ 1988 C 130/4, Article 2 of the 1989 draft, OJ 1989 C 22/14.

11 Cited by Jones & González-Diaz 1992, p. 156.

to non-competition factors and the role they play in the Commissions application of the Regulation. According to Article 2(1)(b) of the Merger Regulation the Commission, in assessing a concentration, shall take into account

*'the development of technical and economic progress provided that it is to the consumers' advantage and does not form an obstacle to competition'.*

Thus, the thirteenth recital taken together with Article 2(1)(b) could be taken to mean that it is still possible for the Commission to take non-competition factors into account in giving the go-ahead for a merger that restricts competition.

However, we should immediately note that Article 2(1)(b) is not directly implementing the thirteenth recital. The obvious differences in wording between the two provisions already indicate this. Textually, Article 2(1)(b) looks more like an 'amputated' version of Article 81(3) of the Treaty than the thirteenth recital. Moreover, as regards the non-competition objectives that may play a role, Article 2(1)(b) nowhere refers to the 'the objectives referred to in Article 2 of the Treaty' but instead refers to technical and economic progress. These difficulties surrounding the legal status of the thirteenth recital (in connection with Article 2(1)(b)) has not kept the Court of First Instance from giving it an unusual, perhaps unexpected, role in the *Nestlé/Perrier* case.[12]

This case started when the Commission approved the takeover by Nestlé of Perrier subject to conditions.[13] Two worker representation organisations brought actions for annulment of the Commission decision approving the takeover because of fears of job losses. The Commission was of the opinion that the organisations' action was inadmissible because it considered that they did not have an interest in the procedure.[14] This, in turn, was considered by the Commission to be the result of the fact that the primary purpose of the Merger Regulation was to maintain competition and not to take into account the social implications. Therefore, the Commission considered that it was not under any obligation to perform a detailed analysis of the employment concerns of each concentration. Only if the organisations are able to show *prima facie* that the concentration authorised by the Commission clearly runs counter to the objectives of Article 2 EC, would they be admissible.

The Court took a slightly different route. It considered that, pursuant to Article 2(1)(b) of the Regulation, the Commission was under an obligation to draw up 'an economic balance' that may 'entail considerations of a social nature'.[15] Furthermore, the Court, while confirming the 'primacy given to the

---

[12] Case T-12/93, *Comité Central d'Entreprise de la Societé Anonyme Vittel and others* v. *Commission* (Nestlé/Perrier), [1995] ECR II-1253.

[13] Commission Decision 92/554, *Nestlé/Perrier*, OJ 1992 L 356/1.

[14] Case T-12/93, *Nestlé/Perrier*, [1995] ECR II-1253, para. 14.

[15] *Ibid.*, para. 39.

establishment of a system of free competition', appeared to hold the Commission under an obligation to 'ascertain whether the concentration is liable to have consequences, even if only indirectly, for the position of the employees'.[16] Matters, therefore, are not as simple as the Commission may have wanted them to be. There would appear to be an obligation on the part of the Commission to at least investigate the possibility of effects on employment.[17] If this is taken a bit further, the conclusion could be that the Commission would be under a similar obligation with regard to environmental considerations. Environmental concerns feature just as prominently in Article 2 EC as do social considerations. Moreover, with regard to the environment, the integration principle enshrined in Article 6 EC would seem to put the Commission under an obligation to at least take such considerations into account.

Whatever may be of this interesting interpretation of the thirteenth recital, it must still be taken into account that the operative part of the Merger Regulation must, as far as the possibility of taking non competition factors into account, content itself with Article 2(1)(b). Even though it looks like Article 81(3), we should not be tempted to think that this provision, like Article 81(3), allows the Commission balance a restraint of competition under the Merger Regulation with certain other (not necessarily competition-related) benefits. As always the sting is in the tail. The wording of Article (2)(1)(b) and in particular the fact that it speaks of insofar as it 'does not form an obstacle to competition' seems to indicate that technical and economic benefits are irrelevant as soon as there is a obstacle to competition.[18] This is in accordance with the statement made above, that the Merger Regulation is an instrument of pure competition policy.

Commission practice reaffirms this view of the Merger Regulation. In *Danish Crown/Vestjyske Slagterier*, the parties argued that the concentration would lead to increased efficiencies. The Commission pointed to the text of Article 2(1)(b) only to come to the conclusion that 'the creation of a dominant position (...) therefore, means that the efficiencies argument put forward by the parties cannot be taken into account in the assessment of the present merger'.[19] In *MSG Media Service*, the Commission objected to the creation of a joint venture. Again, the parties' arguments concerning technical and economic progress were simply put aside as irrelevant since the operation was likely to lead to form an obstacle to competition.[20]

---

16 *Ibid.*, para. 38.

17 Cf. Arnull 1996, p. 331.

18 *Cf.* Whish 2001, p. 128, 778 and 779.

19 Commission Decision 2000/42, *Danish Crown/Vestjykse Slagterier*, OJ 2000 L 20/1, para. 198.

20 Commission Decision 94/922, *MSG Media Service*, OJ 1994 L 364/1, para. 100. Furthermore, the competition problems caused the Commission to be sceptical about the achievement in the first place of the technical developments, para. 101. Much the same happened in Commission Decision 96/177, *Nordic Satellite Distribution*, OJ 1996 L 53/20, paras. 145-152.

Finally, social considerations and the thirteenth recital have played a role in the *Kali + Salz* saga. In this case the Commission applied the 'failing company theory' and in doing so referred to the structural problems in former Eastern Germany.[21] Advocate-General Tesauro was the only one to pay any attention to this issue. On the basis of the *Nestlé/Perrier* case he came to the conclusion that the Commission was right to take social considerations into account provided that these were subsidiary to the competition concerns involved.[22]

Therefore, with regard to the possibility to take non-competition issues into account, Article 2(1)(b) is limited to those cases where there are no competition concerns in the first place. It may therefore be wondered what the use of this provision is in the first place.

A final interesting provision is to be found in Article 21(3) of the Merger Regulation. Pursuant to this provision 'Member States may take appropriate measures to protect legitimate interests other than those taken into consideration by this Regulation and compatible with the general principles and other provisions of Community law.' The Regulation explicitly recognises 'public security, plurality of the media and prudential rules' as such legitimate interests. That this is an indicative list is made clear by the third paragraph of Article 21(3), which contains a procedure for the recognition by the Commission of other legitimate interest than those mentioned expressly. Such interests are to be communicated by the member state to the Commission. The Commission shall assess the compatibility of these interests with the general principles and other provisions of Community law.

This provision brings with it a number of interesting legal issues. Firstly, the question of what exactly the purpose of Article 21(3) is. Can it only be used to block concentrations that do not represent a problem on competition grounds or can it also be used to approve mergers? The wording of Article 21(3) appears to leave this point open. However, it is submitted that Article 21(3) can only be used negatively, *i.e.* to scrutinise and eventually prohibit a merger on grounds of legitimate interests while it has been authorised by the Commission.[23] This follows from the system of the Merger Regulation whereby the Commission is the only authority to apply the Merger Regulation to operations falling within its sphere.[24] The fact that Article 21(3) can only be used negatively makes it of limited interest for this research.

---

[21] Commission Decision 94/449, *Kali-Salz/MdK/Treuhand* (Kali + Salz), OJ 1994 L 186/38, paras. 77 and 95.

[22] Opinion of the A-G in joined Cases C-68/94 and C-30/95, *French Republic and Société Commerciale des Potasses et de l'Azote (SCPA) and Entreprise Minière et Chimique (EMC)* v. *Commission* (Kali + Salz), [1998] ECR I-1375, paras. 50-57.

[23] *Cf.* Commission Notes on Notes on Council Regulation (EEC) 4064/89, re Article 21(3). Published in 'Merger control law in the European Union', European Commission, Brussels-Luxembourg, 1998.

[24] Article 21(1) and (2) of the Merger Regulation.

The list of legitimate interests recognised in Article 21(3) is only indicative and does not contain any reference to environmental considerations. The final paragraph of Article 21(3) entails a procedure to have other interests recognised. In this regard a second interesting point to notice is the fact that this provision speaks of 'interests other than those taken into consideration by this Regulation'. This seems to indicate that the technical and economic benefits of Article 2(1)(b) cannot play a role for a second time within the confines of Article 21(3).[25] This, however, does not rule out a role for environmental considerations as it may very well be that such considerations have not been taken into account pursuant to Article 2(1)(b).

All in all, practice with regard to Article 21(3) is scant. In *Newspaper Publishing* the Commission took account of the fact that, on the basis of the Fair Trading Act, the Secretary of State had to grant formal consent because issues such as the accurate presentation of news and freedom of expression were involved.[26] In the *Thomson-CSF/RACAL* case the Commission's press release indicated that it had taken account of the fact that the UK authorities intended to scrutinise the public security aspects involved. In *Banco Santander Central Hispanico/A. Champalimaud* the Portuguese Finance Minister blocked a concentration that fell within the scope of the Merger Regulation.[27] As an exception to the general rule, the Commission interpreted Article 21(3) narrowly. It held that interests not listed in Article 21(3) itself had to be notified to the Commission in accordance with the procedure in the final paragraph of that provision. Since the interests on which Portugal sought to rely had not been notified, Article 21(3) did not apply. Furthermore, the protection of strategic and national interests was rejected as a legitimate interest within the meaning of Article 21(3) since it was in fact an example of discrimination on grounds of nationality.

Though it is very difficult to conceive such a situation, we shall now investigate whether national authorities can use Article 21(3) on environmental grounds. The Commission's interpretation of Article 21(3) in the *BSCH/A. Champalimaud* case does not seem to rule out the possibility of national authorities having another look from an environmental perspective at a concentration already authorised by the Commission. Environmental considerations do not feature among the interests recognised in the Regulation itself. Member states will therefore have to follow the procedure provided for in the final paragraph of Article 21(3). Essentially this requires that the member states communicate the interest to the Commission who will then assess the compatibility with the general principles and other provisions of Community law. As protection of the

---

[25] *Cf.* Commission Notes on Council Regulation (EEC) 4064/89, re Article 21(3).

[26] Commission Decision in Case IV/M.423, *Newspaper Publishing*, para. 22.

[27] Commission Decision in Case IV/M.1616, *Banco Santander Central Hispanico/A. Champalimaud* (BSCH/A. Champalimaud).

environment is a recognised interest in Community law, this should not need to be the stumbling block. From the *Lyonnaise des Eaux/Northumbrian Water* and *BSCH/A. Champalimaud* cases we learn that the Commission will positively assess compatibility with Community law when the basic rules of Community law as well as the principle of proportionality have been observed. In making this assessment, the Commission is likely to look at existing Community (secondary) law for guidance as to what constitutes a legitimate interest.[28] Again, this does not have to make recourse to Article 21(3) impossible when environmental interests are involved.

In sum, the role for environmental considerations in the application of the Merger Regulation is, as was indicated at the beginning of this paragraph, weak to say the least. Such considerations play a role in the definition of the market. Furthermore, they could play a role of secondary importance under Article 2(1)(b) as technical or economic progress. The role that environmental considerations play in this respect is secondary at best and does not amount to an integration of environmental concerns. It is submitted that the Commission is under an obligation to integrate environmental concerns also in its application of the Merger Regulation. It is, however, also submitted that this should not be irreconcilable with the very limited role for environmental concerns in the Merger Regulation. It may be recalled that the primary test under the Merger Regulation is whether a dominant position is created or strengthened as a result of which competition is restricted. In this respect it should be pointed out that it is rather difficult to conceive a situation where the creation or strengthening of a dominant position would actually benefit the environment. The protection of the environment as well as the internalisation of external costs is probably best served in open and competitive market.

28 *Ibid.*, para. 34-37.

CHAPTER II

# The Useful Effect Doctrine

## II.1 Introduction

In the previous chapters we have been looking at the rules that govern restrictions of competition by undertakings. Competition may, however, also be restricted or distorted by the member states acting in their public authority. Such government-induced restrictions and distortions are also within the ambit of Community competition law. The first instrument within this group of competition law that we will look at is the so-called useful effect rule.[1]

As we will be seen in the following paragraph, the useful effect rule was a later, Court-made, addition to the Community's lists of competition instruments. Despite the fact that the existence of the useful effect rule was thus acknowledged at a later stage, is can be seen, as will also be shown below,[2] as a *lex generalis* with regard to Article 86 EC. Acknowledging this *lex generalis* character is a very helpful tool to understand the useful effect doctrine and relate its application to that of Article 86.

In this chapter we shall first have a look at the useful effect doctrine in general and secondly we will investigate the possibilities to take environmental considerations into account.

## II.2 A general outline of the useful effect doctrine

As we have seen the EC Treaty contains rules directed at both firms as well the member states. However, the latter set of rules (Articles 86 and 87-88 EC) contained a loophole in that certain forms of public-private cooperation were not covered by any particular competition rule. This loophole is of particular interest to, *inter alia*, the Netherlands where, for example, the Environmental Management Act provides for a possibility to declare an agreement between the majority of the members of an industry on a removal fee to be generally binding on the entire sector.[3] Such removal fees show some

---

1 Because this rule was a later addition to the body of EC competition law it has also been called the 'new norm' (see, e.g., Mortelmans 2001, p. 619). Since this rule, at the moment, exists for over twenty years already and it can therefore hardly be called new, we will refer to it as the useful effect rule or doctrine. Cf. Buendia Sierra who refers in this respect to the 'effet utile principle', Buendia Sierra 1999, p. 263 et seq. Furthermore, by analogy to the U.S. doctrine, it also referred to as the 'state action doctrine' cf. Hoffman 1990, p. 12 and opinion of A-G Jacobs in Case C-198/01, *C.I.F. Consorzio Industrie Fiammiferi* v. *Autorità Garante della Concorrenza e del Mercato*, opinion of 30 January 2003, n.y.r., to be found on www.curia.eu.int.

2 *Infra*, paragraph 12.1.

3 Section 15.10 of the Environmental Management Act (*Wet milieubeheer*), Most recently amended by Stb. 1999, 208. See further on this possibility Vedder 2002, p. 33. Thus, the fact that, as Ritter, Braun &

resemblance to the privately agreed environmental surcharge that was under consideration in the *VOTOB* case and therefore, it cannot be ruled out that the agreement between the industry in itself is contrary to Article 81. However, in this scenario the government act does not fall within the scope of Article 86 or 87 since it involves neither the granting of a special or exclusive right nor the transfer of any public funds. Furthermore, the underlying agreement is no longer just an agreement between undertakings but has been taken out of the private sphere, soaked in public law and thus removed from the scope of Article 81. The Court subsequently plugged this loophole when it came up with the useful effect doctrine in the *GB-Inno-BM* v. *ATAB* case.[4] In this case, the Court held that, although, Articles 81 and 82 are directed at undertakings, member state authorities are under an obligation not to detract from the useful effect of these provisions. This follows from Article 10 in connection with Article 81. Following this judgment, the most important question was what exactly was the scope of this obligation. Later case law has clarified this to some extent and has provided us with the following definition of the useful effect rule.[5]

*Although Article 85 [Now Article 81] of the Treaty is, in itself, concerned solely with the conduct of undertakings and not with measures adopted by Member States by law or regulation, the fact nevertheless remains that Article 85 of the Treaty, in conjunction with Article 5 [Now Article 10] requires the Member States not to introduce or maintain in force measures, even of a legislative nature, which may render ineffective the competition rules applicable to undertakings.*

*Such would be the case if a Member State were to require or favour the adoption of agreements, decisions or concerted practices contrary to Article 85 or to reinforce their effects, or to deprive its own rules of the character of legislation by delegating to private economic operators responsibility for taking decisions affecting the economic sphere.*

The test thus laid down is threefold. Firstly, member states may not require or favour the adoption of agreements that are contrary to Article 81. Secondly, member states may not reinforce the effects of such agreements and, thirdly, member states may not delegate to economic operators the responsibility for decisions affecting the economic sphere. With regard to these three tests, essentially two branches can thus be discerned: on the one hand the requir-

Rawlinson rightly remark, the possibility to declare an agreement generally binding has disappeared with the new Netherlands Competition Act, does not rule out similar acts on the basis of the Environmental Management Act, Ritter, Braun & Rawlinson 1998, p. 785.

4 Case 13/77, *GB-INNO-BM* v. *ATAB*, [1977] ECR 2155.

5 Case 267/86, *Van Eycke* v. *ASPA*, [1988] 4769, later confirmed in Case C-35/96, *Commission* v. *Italy* (CNSD), [1998] ECR I-3851, paras. 53 and 54.

ing, favouring and reinforcing of an agreement and, on the other hand, the delegation of powers.[6] However, wide-ranging these three tests may seem, the applicability of the first branch – *i.e.* requiring or favouring the adoption of an agreement or reinforcing its effects – of the test still requires an 'underlying' agreement that is contrary to Article 81. This two-tier approach can be seen in the Dutch pension funds cases where the court ruled out the applicability of the useful effect doctrine to the member state action precisely because the underlying agreement was not prohibited by Article 81.[7] With regard to the third test – delegating to economic operators the responsibility for decisions affecting the economic sphere – there is no link with Article 81. The Court's case law appears to indicate that such a delegation can be said to exist in situations where a regulation allows a private actor to take certain decisions without taking considerations other than those of the industry concerned, into account. In *Reiff*, the Court addressed this issue and considered whether a procedure whereby road haulage tariffs were agreed by a committee consisting of, mostly, representatives of the transport industry. In doing so it took into account the following factors. Firstly, it looked at the objectives of the national laws in place and came to the conclusion that these were not intended to serve the interests of the industry but rather served the general interest.[8] After that the Court looked at the way the system operated in practice. The Court appeared to attach great weight to the fact that the minister could participate in the discussions leading up to the conclusion of the tariffs. Furthermore, the minister could replace a decision by the committee with his own decision if the decision by the committee took insufficient account of the general interests.[9] As a result, it can be said that a member state does not delegate its powers if it retains a decisive influence by which it can ascertain that interests other than those of the industry concerned are observed.

As may be expected, the Court's useful effect doctrine was not been given an equally warm welcome by everyone. The combined application of Article 10 and 81 has led to the addition of a new instrument to the EC's arsenal of competition law. Moreover, this instrument deeply encroaches upon the member state's sovereignty to regulate (together with the industry) everyday life on markets. It has therefore been argued that the useful effect doctrine is an undue extension of the EC's competition laws into the daily life of the modern corporatist state.[10]

6 *Cf.* Gyselen 2000, p. 432, 436.

7 Case C-67/96, *Albany*, [1999] ECR I-5751, para. 66 and joined Cases C-180/98 to 184/98, *Pavlov*, [2000] ECR-6451, para. 58.

8 Case C-185/91, *Bundesanstallt für den Güterfernverkehr* v. *Reiff* (Reiff), [1993] ECR I-5801, para. 21.

9 *Ibid.*, para. 22. See also Case C-153/91, *Germany* v. *Delta Schiffahrts und Speditionsgesellschaft* (Delta), [1994] ECR I-2517, paras. 20-22.

10 See, more extensively, Neergaard 1998.

These criticisms boil down to a subsidiarity type of reasoning whereby it is argued that member states should retain some powers to shape the day-to-day economic operation on their territories. It is submitted that such reasoning is flawed to some extent. To demonstrate this, the two branches of the useful effect doctrine should be separately looked at. For a member state to act in contravention of the first branch of the useful effect doctrine, the underlying cartel must of itself violate Article 81. Is widely accepted that the mere fact that an agreement is contrary to Article 81 is in itself sufficient for the Community to be able to oppose this agreement. The Community's free market economy is inherently opposed to restrictions of competition and for this very reason agreements that are restrictive of competition are either prohibited or exempted by the Commission. If this is common ground, then why should the fact that an agreement is taken outside the private sphere and given some public law status suffice to bring it completely outside the scope of Community law? It is more than likely that conferring this public law status upon the agreement actually increases the restrictive effects of the agreement. Moreover, as the alternative 'object' and 'effect' tests in Article 81 already show, Community competition law will not content itself with legal formalism but also looks at the actual effects on competition. If we recognise this effects-based approach, should the useful effect doctrine then come as a surprise? The Treaty itself already provides evidence of an effects-based approach by not only governing more or less specific types of state action (*e.g.* the free movement provisions) but also by laying down a more general duty of loyalty to the Community in Article 10. Therefore, it is submitted that with regard to the first branch of the useful effect rule, criticisms that the EC is unduly extending the scope of its powers to govern also state actions, are flawed.

With regard to the second branch of the useful effect rule the criticisms appear to be well founded. In these cases there is no underlying cartel that violates a Treaty provision. It may therefore be asked whether the effects-based approach has not been taken too far in this context. The rationale behind the delegation of certain decision-making powers to representations of industry is often one that hinges on the need to make use of the industry's expertise. In the environmental context this is explicitly recognised by the Community and national policies with regard to environmental agreements and so-called 'flexible regulation' as opposed to so-called 'command and control' type of instruments.[11] It is often considered that such agreements are more efficient means to attain certain environmental goals since industry knows much better than the government how to attain these goals at minimum costs. Taking into account these legitimate reasons for cooperation between the state and industry, an unmitigated application of the useful effect doctrine seems unnecessary and

---

11 Commission Communication on Environmental Agreements, COM (96)561, OJ 1996 L 333/69.

indeed an undue extension of the Community's competences to review acts of the member states. However, the test adopted under the second branch reflects these concerns in that a delegation of powers is allowed insofar as this is in the public interest and the state ensures compliance with this public interest. It will be seen below that the Court takes these considerations into account in its recent case law on the useful effect doctrine.

In sum, the two branches of the useful effect doctrine still allow the national authorities considerable room. The first branch requires an underlying agreement contrary to Article 81. As *Albany* and *Pavlov* have shown, instances can certainly be conceived where the underlying agreement is simply not contrary to Article 81. In chapter 3 we have seen a number of possibilities for an agreement to either fall outside the scope of Article 81(1) in the first place or to be justified by an exemption. In either case the agreement will not be contrary to Article 81 so that any government action with regard to this agreement will escape the useful effect rule. The second branch essentially requires that member states retain some power to ascertain that the general interest is indeed taken into account.[12]

## 11.3 Exceptions to the useful effect doctrine

In the light of what has been said in the preceding paragraph, the two branches of the useful effect doctrine seem to allow member states a sufficient margin to conduct national policy. This begs the question of whether and to what extent these exceptions can function in an environmental setting. In other words: can environmental concerns be integrated into the application of the useful effect doctrine? In this respect it must be said that, as far as we are aware, there are no decisions or judgments on the application of the useful effect doctrine in an environmental context.[13]

With regard to the first branch of the useful effect rule, the interpretation of Article 81 in itself allows for sufficient room to integrate environmental concerns as was shown above. Many environmental agreements may, for example, be considered to restrict competition only to an extent that is non appreciable. Similarly, an agreement that benefits from an exemption will not, for the duration of the exemption, be contrary to Article 81. At the moment, this effectively means that such agreements have to be notified with the Commission in order to obtain an exemption before a member state can, for example, declare

12 Case C-38/97, *Autotrasporti Librandi* v. *Cuttica spedizioni e servizi internationali* (Librandi), [1998] ECR I-5955, para. 45.

13 The Commission, however, has hinted at the possibility of applying this rule to environmental regulations on a few occasions, Commission, XXIInd. Competition Report (1992), para. 77.

such an agreement generally binding without violating the useful effect rule. As there is no block exemption for environmental agreements and the existing block exemptions do not apply, any agreement that falls within the scope of Article 81(1) can only not be contrary to Article 81 if it benefits from an individual exemption. Irrespective of the practical difficulties involved in obtaining an exemption, this should not prove to be a stumbling block.

However, with regard to the need to obtain an exemption the following can be said. In the introductory paragraph we have already noted the fact that the useful effect rule can be seen a *lex generalis* with regard to Article 86. With regard to this provision, Article 86(2) allows member states to justify possible incursions on Article 86(1). Although it is not entirely certain, there are reasons to assume that the applicability of Article 86(2) may also make it unnecessary to obtain an exemption.[14] It is submitted that insofar as the possibility to justify actions that fall within the scope of Article 86 on the basis of Article 86(2) may obviate the necessity of an exemption pursuant to Article 81(3), that a similar possibility should exist with regard to useful effect doctrine.

After the entry into force of Regulation 1/2003, Article 81(3) will have become directly applicable. As a result, the notification procedure as well as the Commission's monopoly to grant exemptions will also cease to exist. With regard to the useful effect doctrine this will not lead to any particular difficulties. A (national) court before which the useful effect doctrine is invoked can simply rule on the applicability of Article 81 as a whole. If it considers Article 81 not to apply to the underlying agreement (either because Article 81(1) does not apply or because the conditions of Article 81(3) are fulfilled), the useful effect doctrine will not apply to the government's action with regard to that agreement.

Similarly, the second branch of the useful effect rule will not necessarily prove to be an insurmountable obstacle to government action. Essentially, it only requires that the public authorities possess and actively use their supervisory powers to ascertain that an agreement indeed serves the objective of the protection of the environment. In the context of the example of the possibility to declare an agreement on removal fees generally binding, the Environment minister should actively supervise the amount of the removal fee in order to ascertain that it does not exceed the costs incurred in the collection and treatment of the products concerned.

Interestingly, the recent case law of the Court pursuant to the useful effect doctrine appears to allow for the possibility to justify member state actions that fall within the scope of the useful effect doctrine. This justification seems to find its origin in the opinion of A-G Jacobs in the *Pavlov* case. In his opinion the Advocate-General argued that the link between, on the one hand, the fact that the underlying agreement must be contrary to Article 81 and, on the other hand,

---

14 *Infra*, paragraph 12.5.

the government act is unsatisfactory.[15] He considers this because the underlying decision in *Pavlov* was of itself not restrictive enough and therefore falls outside Article 81 whereas the government intervention, which increases the restrictive effects, also falls outside the scope of the useful effect doctrine precisely because of the insufficiently restrictive effects of the underlying agreement.[16] Instead he proposes to opt for a presumption of illegality that can be justified on public interest grounds.[17] More precisely, he proposes an alternative test whereby state measures that are taken in pursuit of a legitimate and clearly defined public interest objective are allowed when the member state also actively supervises the underlying concertation even if this state measure reinforces the restrictive effects. The Court appears to have adopted this test to some extent in paragraphs 98 and 100 of its ruling.[18]

*'As for the request, made to the public authorities by an organisation representing the members of a profession, to make membership of the occupational pension fund it has set up compulsory, it is made under a scheme identical to those existing under the national law of a number of countries concerning the exercise of regulatory authority in the social domain. Such regimes* ARE DESIGNED TO PROMOTE THE CREATION OF SUPPLEMENTARY PENSIONS OF THE SECOND TYPE *and* INCLUDE A NUMBER OF SAFEGUARDS WHOSE OBSERVANCE THE COMPETENT MINISTER MUST ENSURE, *so that a request by the members of a profession for membership to be made compulsory cannot constitute an infringement of Article 85(1) [Now Article 81(1)] of the Treaty.*

*[...]*

*Thus, for the same reasons, a decision by the Member State in question to make membership of such a fund compulsory for all members of the profession is not contrary to Articles 5 [Now Article 10] and 85 of the Treaty either.' [Emphasis added]*

The Court, in short, comes to the conclusion that the member state action in this case is designed to provide, put simply, social protection (*i.c.* pensions) and it is for the Minister to ascertain that the underlying agreement only serves that social purpose. This apparently takes the government action outside the scope of the useful effect doctrine. The exception thus created shows a striking resemblance to the test adopted by the Court under the second branch of the useful effect doctrine. This is also apparent in the opinion of Advocate General Léger

---

15 Buendia Sierra is a bit more outspoken and considers that it 'is bordering on the infantile in its formalism', Buendia Sierra 1999, p. 265.

16 Opinion of A-G Jacobs in joined Cases C-180/98 to C-184/98, *Pavlov*, [2000] ECR I-6451, para. 161. For similar reasons, A-G Léger concurs with Jacobs in his opinion in *Wouters*, Case C-309/99, *Wouters*, [2002] ECR, I-1577.

17 *Ibid.*, para. 163, Jacobs speaks of '*prima facie* infringement' in his opinion.

18 *Cf.* Loozen 2000, p. 305 and Mortelmans 2001, p. 643 *et seq.*

in the *Wouters* case.[19] In its judgment in *Wouters*, the Court also appears to have adopted this test to the extent that it considers the restrictive regulation by the Bar of the Netherlands, to fall outside Article 81(1) because it was necessary for the proper practice of the legal profession.[20] Although the test adopted by him is quite the same as the one adopted by the Court in *Pavlov* the idea underlying both exceptions appears to be identical and has, with regard to the professions, been brought to the fore by Advocate-General Jacobs in *Pavlov.*[21] Basically, the idea is that on the one hand the increased efficiency of self-regulation compared to command-and-control government regulation must be balanced with, on the other hand, the need to maintain control in order to ensure that the self-regulation does not turn into self-enrichment. The main elements are therefore the need to ascertain that the general interest is and will remain the prime objective. Below we shall refer to the exception thus created as the general interest exception. The addition, by the Court, of a possibility for a general interest exception with regard to the useful effect doctrine should not come as a surprise. As will be seen below, the relation between the useful effect rule and Article 86 is one of *lex generalis* and *lex specialis*. With regard to a more or less defined area of application, the two rules address the same point: member states may not restrict or distort competition by using private firms. This relation between Article 86 and the useful effect doctrine has a number of consequences. Firstly, the substantive legality standards (*i.e.* in how far is a member state allowed to cooperate with industry and restrict competition to attain general interest objectives?) must be identical. Secondly, the essential procedural aspects (most importantly the burden of proof) should also be identical under both provisions.

With regard to the first consequence, it cannot be accepted that the substantive legality standards under the useful effect rule and Article 86 diverge. In other words, it should not matter whether a member state grants exclusive rights (a practice governed by Article 86) or whether it opts for self-regulation to attain the objectives of general interest. It is therefore submitted that, essentially, the legality standards as far as the *prohibitions* in both norms is concerned, Article 86(1) and the useful effect doctrine are comparable. However, as we will see below, Article 86(2) provides for a potentially wide-ranging possibility to justify actions that may fall within the scope of Article 86(1). The standards of legality under the useful effect doctrine and Article 86 as a whole would diverge if the useful effect rule would not allow for a justification or an exception similar to Article 86(2). It is submitted that in *Pavlov* the Court acknowledged this

[19] Opinion of A-G Léger in Case C-309/99, *Wouters*, [2002] ECR, I-1577, paras. 207, 212-228.

[20] Case C-309/99, *Wouters*, [2002] ECR, I-1577, para. 109. Note that this relates to Article 81(1) not read in conjunction with Article 10 EC. See further, *supra*, paragraph 8.4.2.4 with regard to the the European Rule of Reason.

[21] *Ibid.*, para. 209.

discrepancy and addressed it by providing for the exception possibility with regard to actions that fall within the scope of the useful effect doctrine. As regards the remarks made above with regard to the need to obtain an exemption if a member state wants to avoid breaching the first branch of the useful effect doctrine, it is submitted that, insofar as Article 86(2) obviates the need for an exemption, the applicability of the general interest exception should also make an exemption superfluous.

With regard to the second consequence, the existence of a general interest exception to the useful effect doctrine restricts the scope of application of this doctrine as a tool to maintain or bring about effective competition. The dilemma is therefore identical to that existing with regard to Article 86(2) which also balances the need to maintain undistorted competition with the legitimate interest that member states may have in 'steering the economy' through distortions of competition. With regard to Article 86(2) the burden of proof lies primarily with the member state or the firm that benefits from the exclusive right.[22] By analogy, it should be for the parties to the underlying agreement and the member state to establish, firstly, that the agreement indeed serves the general interest and, secondly, that there is active supervision to ensure that this is indeed the prime objective for the general interest exception to apply.

Let us now consider the question of whether or not the general interest exception could apply in an environmental context. *Prima facie* there is nothing to prevent the reasoning underlying the general interest exception from applying with regard to environmental agreements. In fact, A-G Jacobs explicitly refers to the possibility that member states may want to extend the effects in the environmental sphere to more actors than just the parties to the underlying agreement. If the new escape route from the useful effect doctrine is to be seen as an indication that the Court is more reluctant to apply the doctrine without any reservations, then this refining of the doctrine addresses the concerns mentioned above.[23] In that case, the fact that the Court's reluctance to apply the useful effect doctrine can be explained by reasons of subsidiarity, should also not stand in the way of applying this reasoning to government measures in the environmental context. If the general interest exception, as is submitted, is all about striking the right balance between the freedom that member states should have to efficiently organise their economies and the need to maintain competition, then this should also not keep it from applying to environmental agreements. Particularly, in a highly technical area of law such as environmental law, self-regulation is considered to bring with it clear efficiency gains. It is precisely through the general interest exception that such efficiencies should be taken

[22] Buendia Sierra 1999, p. 354, Case C-159/94, *Commission* v. *France* (French Electricity and Gas), [1997] ECR I-5815, para. 94 and Case C-203/96, *Dusseldorp*, [1999] ECR, I-4075, para. 67.

[23] As would seem to be the rationale, *cf.* Neergaard 1998.

into account in creating an exception for government action with regard to self-regulation provided that the authorities ascertain (supervise) that environmental protection remains the prime objective.

As a final means to escape from the useful effect doctrine, it is possible that the parties to an agreement that is subject to government involvement may benefit from the exception offered by Article 86(2) EC. We shall be looking closer at this provision and its application in the context of environmental protection below.[24]

[24] *Infra* chapter 12.

CHAPTER 12

# Article 86

## 12.1 Introduction

The place of Article 86 in the Treaty, tucked away somewhere between the competition provisions, belies its great importance. For one, a quick look at the second paragraph of Article 86 already reveals the fact that it makes it possible to trump all other rules in the Treaty. However, Article 16 of the EC Treaty has brought the pervasive influence of the second paragraph of Article 86 to the fore. A further general aspect that has already been noted with regard to Article 86 is that it can be seen as a *lex specialis* of the useful effect doctrine in that, contrary to the latter, Article 86 is limited to a closed set of government actions.[1] Article 86 only concerns companies that have been granted 'special or exclusive rights'. With regard to these companies the general rule of the useful effect doctrine that member states must act loyally to the Community applies.

From a competition law perspective this brings with it the same problems that were also identified in relation to the useful effect doctrine. By simultaneously regulating both member state as well as private party actions that have an impact on competition difficult questions of causality as well as doctrinal problems arise. To what extent, for example, can there be said to be freedom to compete and hence a possibility to restrict competition in the first place if a company has been given a statutory monopoly? Furthermore, who is responsible?

These problems are considered by some to be reflected in the text of Article 86 itself. Article 86 has been noted for its 'clear obscurity' as opposed to the 'obscure clarity' of Article 31 EC.[2] This is in turn reflected in the case law and legal writing on Article 86 that is complex to say the least. Basically, Article 86 reflects the layout of any Community provision. In its first paragraph it contains a wide-ranging prohibition whereas the second paragraph allows for a derogation. Below we shall first look at Article 86(1) after which we will turn our attention to Article 86(2). As a reading of Article 86 already shows, it is a so-called *renvoi* provision, which means that in itself it contains no substantive legality standard. For this Article 86 relies on other Treaty provisions. Below, we shall be considering the application of Article 86(1) in connection with Article 82 simply because the vast majority of the case law on Article 86 concerns these two provisions. With regard to the derogation we will consider the application of Article 86(2) with both Article 82 and 81 EC. The latter has been included because of the parallel with the useful effect doctrine. In looking at these provisions we will also address the possibilities for an integration of environmental concerns.

---

1 *Cf.* Opinion of A-G Jacobs in Case C-67/97, *Albany*, [1999] ECR I-5751, para. 371.

2 Opinion of A-G Tesauro in Case C-202/88, *France* v. *Commission*, [1991] ECR I-1223, para. 11.

## 12.2 Article 86(1)

According to the first paragraph of Article 86 member states shall not enact or maintain any rule contrary to the Treaty with regard to public undertakings and firms that have been granted special or exclusive rights. With regard to the first paragraph of Article 86 a number of things may be noted. For one, it addresses the member states and not firms. In this respect, Article 86(1) prohibits any state measure with regard to an 'undertaking'. This means that the entity with regard to which the state measure is taken must exercise an economic activity.[3] This undertaking can be a 'public undertaking' or an undertaking to which Member states have granted 'special or exclusive rights'. The Commission has defined the concept of the public undertaking in the Transparency Directive as[4]

*'any undertaking over which the public authorities may exercise directly or indirectly a dominant influence by virtue of their ownership of it, their financial participation therein, or the rules which govern it'.*

What matters, therefore, is *control* by the public authorities over the public undertaking. A second category of undertakings is those firms that have been granted 'special or exclusive rights'. It is submitted that exclusive and special rights are two different concepts.[5] An exclusive right must by definition be limited to one beneficiary only. Special rights have been defined by the Commission as those rights that are granted to a limited number of firms by a discretionary decision on the part of the public authorities.[6] According to A-G Jacobs, the Court, in *British Telecoms*, adopted this definition.[7] On the basis of this ruling he considers that a special or exclusive right must fulfil four essential requirements. The rights in question must

- be granted by the authorities of a Member State,
- be granted to one undertaking or to a limited number of undertakings,
- substantially affect the ability of other undertakings to exercise the economic activity in question in the same geographical area under

3 See, *supra*, paragraph 7.4.

4 Article 2 of Commission Directive 80/723 (Transparency), OJ 1980 L 195/35. See, on this concept, Case 118/85, *Commission* v. *Italy*, [1987] ECR 2599. The new Transparency Directive 2000/52 has not changed this definition, OJ 2000 L 193/75, Article 2(b).

5 Case C-202/88, *France* v. *Commission*, [1991] ECR I-1223, paras. 44-46, acknowledged by the Commission in, *inter alia*, the Transparency Directive, Directive 200/52, OJ 2000 L 193/75, Article 2 (f) and (g).

6 Article 1(b) of Directive 94/46 (Satellite communication), OJ 1994 L 268/15.

7 Opinion of A-G Jacobs in case C-475/99, *Ambulanz Glöckner* v. *Landkreis Südwestpfalz* (Ambulanz Glöckner), [2001] ECR 8089, para. 86.

substantially equivalent conditions, and
- be granted otherwise than according to objective, proportional and non-discriminatory criteria.[8]

In *Ambulanz Glöckner*, the Court appears to have, *grosso modo*, adopted this test.[9] It may be remarked that the Court often takes the concepts of an exclusive and a special right together without really distinguishing between the two.[10] Furthermore, the *Sydhavnens Sten & Grus* case shows the remarkable ease with which the Court disregards the distinction between an exclusive and a special right. In this case the fact that a right was given to three companies did not keep the Court from classifying it as an exclusive right.[11]

If we look at the text of Article 86(1), it would seem that the government measure with regard to the public or privileged undertakings should be a different measure from the act whereby the exclusive or special right is granted. In other words an undertaking is first granted a special or exclusive right and only after that will state measures with regard to that company fall within the scope of Article 86(1). However, later case law has shown that the Court considers it possible that the act whereby an exclusive or special right is granted and the state measure within the meaning of Article 86(1) are actually identical.[12] This means that the act itself whereby the exclusive or special right is granted may be 'contrary to the rules contained in this Treaty'

A final point to be noted is that Article 86(1) of itself contains no substantive legality standard but rather refers to the other provisions of the Treaty in this respect. This is why Article 86 is always applied in connection with another provision of the Treaty. As special or exclusive rights correspond roughly with the notions of, respectively, a monopoly and a legal oligopoly, it will not come as a surprise that Article 86(1) has to this date primarily been used in connection with Article 82.[13] However, as the wording of Article 86(1) already shows, it is a *renvoi* provision with regard to all the Treaty rules and particularly the non-discrimination and competition rules. Below, we shall concentrate on the application of Article 86(1) together with Article 81 and 82.

---

8 *Ibid.*, para. 87.

9 Case C-475/99, *Ambulanz Glöckner*, [2001] 8089, para. 24. The Court did not explicitly repeat the first and fourth requirement identified by the Advocate-General although it did address these in paragraph 23 of its judgment.

10 For this reason we shall, in the footsteps of Temple Lang, be referring to the companies benefiting from such exclusive or special rights as privileged companies without distinguishing between the two.

11 Case C-209/98, *Sydhavnens Sten & Grus*, [2000] ECR I-3743, paras. 53, 54. *Cf.* Whish 2001, p. 192.

12 *Cf.* Faull & Nikpay 1999, p. 287, Akyürek-Kievits 1998, p. 25 *et seq.*

13 *Cf.* Faull & Nikpay 1999, p. 282.

## 12.3 Article 86(1) in connection with Article 82

Because by far most experience has been gathered with regard to the combined application of Article 86 and 82 we shall start by looking at this area of he case law. This combined application is fraught with difficulties as it governs simultaneously member state actions as well as the abusive behaviour of the firm. The difficult part consists of establishing a causal connection between the grant of the special or exclusive right and the abuse. However, the Court's approach to establishing dominance is also not without difficulties.

In a number of cases the fact that an exclusive or a special right existed was equated with the existence of a dominant position on that market.[14] However, in the more recent *Sydhavnens Sten & Grus* case the Court fortunately appears to have abandoned the automatism in this respect. The Court stressed the need to define the relevant product and geographical market in order to determine whether the privileged undertaking was in a dominant position.[15] However, in *Deutsche Post* the Court reverted to its old habit of equating special or exclusive rights with the existence of a dominant position for the privileged undertaking.[16]

Whatever may be of this, with regard to the application of Article 86 in connection with 82, the nettle is in establishing abuse. Essentially, this boils down to whether or not there is a causal connection between the grant of the exclusive or special right on the one hand and the abuse on the other. The Court almost invariably starts its considerations in this respect by referring to the *Sacchi* case in which it held that[17]

> *'Merely creating a dominant position by the grant of special or exclusive rights within the meaning of Article 90(1) [Now Article 86(1)] of the Treaty is not in itself incompatible with Article 86 [Now Article 82] of the Treaty'.*

The rationale behind this is that Article 82 itself does not prohibit the existence of a dominant position so that the Treaty cannot prohibit member states from doing something that private parties can freely do. This reasoning, it is submitted, is flawed for the simple reason that, ever since the entry into force of the Merger Regulation, private parties cannot create a dominant position. If firms are not allowed to concentrate if the result would be an undertaking

---

14 *E.g.* Case C-203/96, *Dusseldorp*, [1998] ECR I-4075, paras. 58 and 60. See for a critical view in this respect: Buendia Sierra 1999, p. 153 *et seq.* en Vedder 2001A, p. 112 *et seq.*

15 Case C-209/98, *Sydhavnens Sten & Grus*, [2000] ECR I-3743, paras. 57-65.

16 ECJ joined cases C-147/97 and C-148/97, *Deutsche Post* v. *Gesellschaft für Zahlungssysteme and Citicorp Kartenservice* (Deutsche Post), [2000] ECR I-825, para. 38.

17 Case 155/73, *Sacchi*, [1974] ECR 409, para. 14.

in a dominant position, then why should member states be allowed to create dominant positions? In fact, despite the steadfast reference to the rule given in *Sacchi*, the Court's case law may be seen as calling into question the creation of the dominant position (*i.e.* the grant itself of the exclusive or special right) as an action contrary to Article 82 in connection with 86(1). To explain this, we must look at the second part of the Court's constantly recurring considerations in this respect:[18]

> *'A member state is in breach of the prohibitions contained in those two provisions [Articles 86(1) and 82] only if the undertaking in question, merely by exercising the exclusive rights granted to it, is led to abuse its dominant position or when such rights are liable to create a situation in which that undertaking is led to commit such abuses'.*

The Court's case law in this respect is not entirely consistent. However, a number of different doctrines can probably be discerned.[19] In *Höfner & Elser,* the Court laid down the basis of the 'Fallow Field' doctrine.[20] This case concerned German legislation that reserved the right to act as an intermediary with regard to employment services to the Federal Employment Office. This Office, however, was not quite up to this task and as a result numerous agencies, such as that of Höfner and Elser, were set up and tolerated. According to the Court Articles 82 and 86(1) are infringed where a member state upholds an exclusive right with regard to a company that is 'manifestly not in a position to satisfy demand'.[21] A second line of cases concerns the conflict of interests. These cases concern the situation where, for example, the privileged undertaking has both commercial activities as well as regulatory capacities with regard to the same market. In *RTT* v. *GB-Inno-BM*, the Belgian authorities had given RTT, the public undertaking the power to lay down the technical specifications for telephone equipment as well as the powers to supervise compliance by other companies with these regulations while RTT itself sold telephone equipment.[22] According to the Court this was[23]

---

18 *E.g.* Case C-209/98, *Sydhavnens Sten & Grus*, [2000] ECR I-3743, para. 66.

19 Whish 2001, p. 198 *et seq.*, Fall & Nikpay 1999, p. 292 *et seq.*

20 Case C-41/90, *Höfner & Elser,* [1991] ECR I-1979. This name was coined by Ritter, Braun & Rawlinson 2000, p. 764, See also: Whish who speaks of 'manifest inability to meet demand' and Buendia Sierra who refers to 'the demand limitation doctrine', Whish 2001, p. 199, Buendia Sierra 1999, p. 163.

21 Case C-41/90, *Höfner & Elser,* [1991] ECR I-1979, para. 31.

22 Case C-18/88, *Régie des Télégraphes et des Téléphones* v. *GB-Inno-BM* (RTT v. GB-Inno-BM), [1991] ECR I-5941.

23 *Ibid.*, para. 25.

> *'tantamount to conferring upon it the power to determine at will which terminal equipment may be connected to the public network, and thereby placing that undertaking at an obvious advantage over its competitors'.*

The Court held that such regulatory powers had to be carried out by an entity that was independent from the company that was active on the market. Similarly, in *ERT,* the Greek public broadcasting company produced its own programs but was also the only company that could retransmit foreign programs.[24] As such there was a conflict of interests whereby ERT might be tempted to discriminate in favour of its own productions and to the detriment of the programs originating from abroad.

Connected to the conflict of interests doctrine is the so-called 'extension of dominant position-doctrine.[25] According to this doctrine a privileged company with a dominant on one market may not extent its monopoly position to a neighbouring but separate market.[26] This doctrine was already known from the case law on Article 82.[27] The Court applied the extension of dominance test in an Article 86-setting for the first time in *RTT* v. *GB-Inno-BM*. In this case it held that[28]

> *'[...] the fact that an undertaking holding a monopoly in the market for the establishment and operation of the network, without any objective necessity, reserves to itself a neighbouring but separate market, in this case the market for the importation, marketing, connection, commissioning and maintenance of equipment for connection to the said network, thereby eliminating all competition from other undertakings, constitutes an infringement of Article 86 [Now Article 82] of the Treaty.'*
>
> *[...]*
>
> *Accordingly, where the extension of the dominant position of a public undertaking or undertaking to which the State has granted special or exclusive rights results from a State measure, such a measure constitutes an infringement of Article 90 [Now Article 86] in conjunction with Article 86 of the Treaty.'*

A further interesting point in *RTT* v. *GB-Inno-BM* is the Court's statement that for an infringement of Article 86 in connection with 82 to have taken place it is not necessary for there to have been actual abuse.[29] In one of the many

---

24 Case C-260/98, *Elliniki Radiophonia Tiléorassi AE and Panellinia Omospondia Syllogon Prossopikou* v. *Dimotiki et al.* (ERT), [1991] ECR I-2925, para. 37.

25 Whish 2001, p. 200, Buendia Sierra 1999, p. 169.

26 Case C-18/88, *RTT* v. *GB-Inno-BM*, [1991] ECR I-5941, para. 18.

27 Case 311/84, *Télémarketing*, [1985] ECR 3261, para. 26.

28 Case C-18/88, *RTT* v. *GB-Inno-BM*, [1991] ECR I-5941, paras. 19 and 21.

29 *Ibid.*, paras. 23 and 24.

cases concerning the – at least among competition jurists – famous Port of Genua, *Merci convenzionali* v. *Siderurgica Gabrielli*, the Court developed the case law with regard Article 86 and 82 even further.[30] In this case it held that the privileged firm had committed several abuses.[31] Interestingly, this case had none of the features that had led the Court to apply Articles 86 and 82 in earlier cases. Thus, it has been concluded that the sheer number of and types of abuse committed in this case could only have been the result of the dominant position conferred upon the privileged company in question.[32] This ever-stricter case law reached its apogee in *Corbeau* where the Court seemed to have come to the conclusion that the grant of an exclusive right of itself was contrary to Article 86(1) in connection with Article 82.[33] In this case, the Court did not pause at establishing whether or not abuse has taken place or even could take place but rather went straight on to the possibility of justifying the grant of the exclusive right on the basis of Article 86(2). Implicitly, the Court therefore seemed to have come to the conclusion that insofar as Article 86(2) could not justify the statutory monopoly, the monopoly itself was contrary to Articles 86(1) and 82.[34] This had been called the automatic abuse doctrine.[35] In later cases, however, the Court has retreated from this automatic abuse doctrine and will require that the grant of exclusive rights lead the privileged undertaking to abuse its position.[36] Having thus set out the basic doctrines that have been distinguished in the Court's case law, we shall now turn our attention to the application of Articles 82 and 86(1) in an environmental setting.

## 12.4 The application of Article 86(1) and 82 in an environmental context

Essentially, there are two quite similar cases in this respect: *Dusseldorp*[37] and *Sydhavnens Sten & Grus*.[38] Both cases came before the Court as a result of a preliminary reference. In both cases, national authorities considered

[30] Case C-179/90, *Merci convenzionali porto di Genova SpA* v. *Siderurgica Gabrielli SpA* (Merci convenzionali), [1991] ECR I-5889.

[31] *Ibid.*, para. 18.

[32] Faull & Nikpay 1999, p. 295.

[33] Case C-320/91, *Corbeau*, [1993] ECR I-2533, paras. 13-16.

[34] Whish 2001, p. 200, 201.

[35] Buendia Sierra 1999, p. 173.

[36] *Ibid.*, p. 176, or, as the author puts it in Faull & Nikpay: 'The pendulum swings back', Faull & Nikpay 1999, p. 298.

[37] Case C-203/96, *Dusseldorp*, [1998] ECR I-4075.

[38] Case C-209/98, *Sydhavnens Sten & Grus*, [2000] ECR I-3743.

that granting an exclusive right to treat a certain type of waste would be only way to guarantee a sufficient inflow of waste into an installation so as to ensure its profitability. In *Dusseldorp* the installation operated by the privileged undertaking AVR featured a high tech rotary furnace that required a specific mixture of different types of waste to operate optimally. To ensure that this inflow was sufficient, the Dutch authorities granted AVR the exclusive right to treat certain categories of dangerous waste. This exclusive right was complemented by a prohibition to export those wastes without a permit granted by the Environment Minister. Such a permit would only be granted if there was insufficient capacity in the Netherlands and where the treatment abroad was at least an equally high standard as that offered by AVR. When the Dutch company Dusseldorp wanted to export waste oil filters for treatment by the German company Factron, a permit was refused because there was no shortage of capacity with AVR. Dusseldorp appealed against this refusal to grant it a permit and pleaded that, *inter alia*, it was contrary to Article 86 in connection with Article 82 EC.

In the *Sydhavnens Sten & Grus* case, there was a comparable situation. Under Danish environmental law, local authorities are competent to issue regulations on the collection and treatment of waste. This is why the Municipality of Copenhagen issued in 1992 a regulation concerning, *inter alia*, the collection and treatment of non-hazardous building waste with a view to the recovery of that waste (1992 Regulation). The 1992 Regulation was issued following a regional plan, which, in turn, was the direct result of a 1988 study that indicated that only a very small percentage of the waste emanating from the Copenhagen region was recovered. This was considered a serious problem because this region produced one third of all building waste, which amounted to 20 per cent of all waste produced in Denmark.

To solve this problem, the Municipality considered it necessary to create a large-scale recovery plant capable of recycling the large amounts of waste. This resulted in the creation of the Grøften recovery plant, operated by a company called RGS. In addition, the 1992 Regulation allowed Copenhagen to conclude contracts for the collection and recovery of building waste with only a limited number of business undertakings. In the end only RGS and two other firms were awarded such contracts. This limit on the number of firms allowed to collect and recover the waste was deemed necessary to ensure that the Grøften plant and the other two firms received sufficiently large amounts of waste for them to be profitable. In 1998 a new regulation replaced the 1992 Regulation. The new Regulation differs from the 1992 Regulation in that the export and import of building waste falls outside the scope of the Regulation and therefore seems to be free.

The result of the system put in place by these Regulations was that the claimant in the national procedure, Sydhavnens, which has all necessary permits and already processes building waste from other regions than Copenhagen, is excluded from collecting and processing waste originating in Copenhagen because the Municipality was unwilling to award it a contract. Sydhavnens appealed against this refusal. In its appeal, Sydhavnens pleaded that the Regulations contravened, *inter alia*, Article 82 in connection with Article 86 EC because the Regulations kept it from offering its services on the market.[39]

With regard to establishing whether or not the privileged undertaking occupied a dominant position in a substantial part of the common market the Court's approach already differs between the two cases. In the *Dusseldorp* case, the Court took the short route to come to the conclusion that the privileged undertaking AVR occupied a dominant position. According to the Court[40]

*'the grant of exclusive rights for the incineration of dangerous waste on the territory of a Member State as a whole must be regarded as conferring on the undertaking concerned a dominant position in a substantial part of the common market.'*

This may be contrasted with the approach the Court took in *Sydhavnens Sten & Grus*. In that case the Court left the decision on whether or not there was dominant position to the national judge but not without making clear that this was no clear-cut matter. Firstly, the Court provided guidance as to how the relevant product market and geographical market should be defined. In particular with regard to the latter aspect of market definition, the Court hinted at the possible influence of the national rules on the definition of the market.[41] With regard to the thus defined market the Court reminded the national judge of the necessity to establish that this area constitutes a substantial part of the common market.[42]

It is submitted that the test adopted in *Sydhavnens Sten & Grus* is the correct, economically sound, one whereas the *Dusseldorp*-approach can be characterised as legalistic. Moreover, the Court, by reiterating the need to correctly define the market, explicitly refused to follow the Advocate-General. Advocate-General Léger merely applied the *Dusseldorp* type of reasoning only to come to the conclusion that it need only be established that the area over which the exclusive right extended was a substantial part of the common market.[43]

A dominant position, or any restriction of competition for that matter, can only take place on a market. If no such market has been defined, all statements concerning a restriction of competition can at best be called speculative. Despite this step in the right direction with regard to market definition, the Court in

---

39 Sydhavnens also wanted to recycle building and construction waste, for which it had obtained the necessary permits from the municipal government.

40 Case C-203/96, *Dusseldorp*, [1998] ECR I-4075, para. 60.

41 Case C-209/98, *Sydhavnens Sten & Grus*, [2000] ECR I-3743, paras. 62 and 63.

42 *Ibid.*, para. 64.

43 *Ibid.*, opinion A-G Léger, para. 71.

*Sydhavnens Sten & Grus* did not think it necessary to provide the referring judge with any guidance as to the existence of a dominant position. Certainly, this question should not pose that many difficulties in a situation where one firm has been granted an exclusive right. However, in the *Sydhavnens Sten & Grus* case not one but *three* companies had been granted an 'exclusive' right. Moreover, what should we think of the fact that the exclusive right 'should be reconsidered upon expiry of the normal writing-off period of its plant at the Grøften centre' when considering dominance?

Having addressed the question of dominance, the Court moved on to consider whether the privileged undertakings had led to abuse their dominant position or whether the exclusive rights were liable to create a situation which the privileged undertakings are led to commit such abuses. Again the two cases diverge. In *Dusseldorp* the claimant wanted to export its waste to a German company but was kept from doing so by the Dutch regulations. According to the Court this[44]

> *'[...] has the effect of favouring the national undertaking [AVR] by enabling it to process waste intended for processing by a third undertaking. It therefore results in a restriction of outlets contrary to Article 90(1) [Now Article 86(1)] in conjunction with Article 86 [Now Article 82] of the Treaty.'*

This reasoning appears to be an application of the fallow field doctrine. However, as Whish rightly points out, the Court seems to have gone a bit further than it had in *Höfner & Elser* or any other case applying this doctrine.[45] From the facts stated in the Court's judgment, it does not appear that the privileged undertaking in the *Dusseldorp* case, AVR, did indeed fail to satisfy the demand for its services. A strict application of the fallow field doctrine in this case would have meant that for the doctrine to apply, the Dutch regulations, for example, would have to preclude exports even in cases where AVR was unable to meet demand. Indeed, in *Dusseldorp,* the privileged undertaking in question does not appear to have committed any abuses (*e.g.* its prices were not excessive and the quality of the treatment offered by it was at least equal to that offered by the German company Factron). The only action that infringed Articles 82 and 86(1) was the fact that the Dutch government applied the Dutch regulations, an action in which the privileged undertaking had no part. It is therefore submitted that the Court applied the automatic abuse doctrine in *Dusseldorp* in the form of a so-called 'extended fallow field doctrine'.[46] According to this extended fallow

44 Case C-203/96, *Dusseldorp,* [1998] ECR I-4075, para. 63.

45 Whish 2001, p. 198.

46 This name indicates that the reasoning behind it is similar to that underlying the fallow field doctrine (*i.e.* the privileged undertaking precludes potential competitors from becoming active on the market for which the privileged undertaking has been granted an exclusive right) whereas it also recognises the fact that in *Dusseldorp* the Court has clearly gone beyond its ruling in *Höfner & Elser.*

field doctrine, the mere fact that third undertakings are kept from offering competing services due to the exclusive right, is already contrary to Article 86(1) in conjunction with 82. Furthermore, the Court seems to have been aware of this broadening of the fallow field doctrine and immediately provided for the possibility of an objective justification by analogy to the doctrine of the extension of a dominant position. In the paragraph 68 of *Dusseldorp* the Court holds that Article 86 in conjunction with Article 82

*'[...] precludes rules [that] require [...] undertakings to deliver their waste [...] to a national undertaking on which it has conferred the exclusive right to incinerate dangerous waste unless the processing of their waste in another Member State is of a higher quality than that performed by that undertaking if,* WITHOUT ANY OBJECTIVE JUSTIFICATION *[...] those rules have the effect of favouring the national undertaking and increasing its dominant position.'[Emphasis added]*

This consideration is mysterious for several reasons. Firstly, the possibility of an objective justification appears to add another escape route to Article 86 in conjunction with 82 alongside the possibility of a justification contained in Article 86(2). It is far from certain how the two relate to one another. Secondly, the objective justification appears like a *deus ex machina* right at the end of the Court's considerations without having been mentioned at all in any of the preceding paragraphs. Thirdly, with regard to the fact that the Court speaks of rules that have 'the effect of favouring the national undertaking and increasing its dominant position' one may wonder how the dominant position in *Dusseldorp* can be increased. In this respect it may be recalled that the privileged undertaking AVR enjoyed an exclusive right and thus found itself in a position of absolute dominance. It would seem more correct to say that those rules have the effect of ascertaining that the privileged national undertaking processes all waste and thereby *establish* its dominant position. That this in itself may be contrary to Article 86(1) in conjunction with Article 82, as it would be under the extended fallow field doctrine, is confirmed by the *Sydhavnens Sten & Grus* case. In this case the Court considers that[47]

*'In that regard, it should be pointed out, first, that the grant of an exclusive right over part of the national territory for environmental purposes, such as establishing the capacity necessary for the recycling of building waste,* DOES NOT IN ITSELF CONSTITUTE AN ABUSE OF A DOMINANT POSITION.*' [Emphasis added]*

This consideration is important for two reasons. Firstly, it proves that the Court considers it possible that the grant of an exclusive right does indeed of itself

[47] Case C-209/98, *Sydhavnens Sten & Grus*, [2000] ECR I-3743, para. 68.

constitute abuse of a dominant position. Interpreting this consideration as a mere repetition of the Court's standard reference to the rule given in *Sacchi* does not make any sense because this consideration (as the words 'In that regard' show) is actually the implementation of the preceding paragraph. In that preceding paragraph the Court summarised its case law according to which member states may grant exclusive rights provided that the privileged firms do not abuse their dominant position or are not led to necessarily commit an abuse. Secondly, the consideration that the grant *for environmental purposes* of an exclusive right does not in itself constitute an abuse, seems to mirror the general interest exception that exists with regard to the useful effect doctrine. The precise extent and impact of this consideration remain, however, still rather uncertain.

The Court's ruling in *Dusseldorp* may be contrasted with that in the *Sydhavnens Sten & Grus* case, where the claimant apparently relied on the Court's reasoning in *Dusseldorp* to establish that abuse had taken place.[48]

As will be recalled, in *Dusseldorp*, the undertaking that gave its name to the case wanted to export its waste to have it processed by the German company Factron but was kept from doing so by the same rules that gave AVR its exclusive right. Essentially, Dusseldorp is therefore arguing that the exclusive rights keep Factron, or any other company for that matter, from becoming active on the market for the treatment of waste oil filters. This is reflected in the Court's conclusions with regard to Article 86(1) and 82.[49]

In *Sydhavnens*, the claimant itself wants to become active on the market for which the Danish authorities had granted an exclusive right. The Court initially appears to leave the question of whether or not abuse had taken place or was likely to take place as a result of the exclusive rights unanswered by immediately moving on to Article 86(2) EC. However, at a later stage, and, since it had already concluded that Article 86(2) applied, as an *obiter dictum*, the Court nevertheless considered that there was nothing in the documents before the Court to suggest that the exclusive right would necessarily lead the privileged undertakings to abuse their dominant position.[50]

However, the Court's refusal in *Sydhavnens Sten & Grus* to apply the extended fallow field doctrine that it had just developed in *Dusseldorp* cannot be satisfactorily explained by the fact that in *Sydhavnens Sten & Grus* the claimant was a potential competitor whereas Dusseldorp was itself a customer of the privileged undertaking. Indeed, the (extended) fallow field doctrine presupposes that and inherently departs from the possibility for competing firms to become active on the market for which the privileged undertaking holds an exclusive right.

---

48 *Ibid.*, para. 72, the wording of which ('limiting outlets' and 'favouring the Grøften centre to the detriment of competitors') closely follows that of paragraph 63 of the *Dusseldorp* case.

49 Case C-203/96, *Dusseldorp*, [1998] ECR I-4075, paras. 62 and 63.

50 *Ibid.*, para. 82.

Moreover, as we have seen above, the logic that appears to underlie the Court's ruling in *Dusseldorp* can apply also in the setting that occurred in *Sydhavnens Sten & Grus.*

It is, however, submitted that the change in the Court's approach between *Dusseldorp* and *Sydhavnens Sten & Grus* can be explained by the facts of the cases. With regard to establishing the existence of a dominant position, it must be taken into account that the exact scope of the exclusive rights in *Sydhavnens Sten & Grus* was far from certain. For one, Sydhavnens and the Municipal government could not agree on whether or not export of the wastes was allowed. Secondly, the fact that three companies had been granted an exclusive right seems to make answering the question whether there was dominant position even less straightforward.

Similarly, the outcome of the two cases as regards the abuse can probably also be explained on the basis of the facts underlying the case even though this does not become clear from the Court's judgments themselves. Basically, Dusseldorp wanted to export the waste oil filters to Germany. The processing there by Factron was obviously at least just as expensive but probably cheaper than that offered by AVR. Furthermore, the processing offered by Factron was considered by the Netherlands authorities to be of at least an equally high quality as that offered by AVR. However, to our (admittedly layman's) mind, the process employed by Factron (separating the metal, plastic and paper parts, cleaning these parts and reprocessing the waste oil) seems a bit more environmentally friendly than that offered by AVR (incineration, or as it is also known euphemistically: burning with energy recuperation). These facts, though unmentioned in the judgment, are likely to have influenced the outcome of the Court's decision in *Dusseldorp.* On the contrary, no such facts appear to be present in the *Sydhavnens Sten & Grus* case. So, even though the Court fails to mention this in its judgment, the lower quality of the services offered by the privileged undertaking could probably be taken to also underlie the extended fallow field doctrine.

## 12.5 Article 86(2) in connection with Article 82 and 81

As was already said in the introduction, a quick look at the second paragraph of Article 86 reveals that it can be used to set aside all other provisions in the Treaty. Therefore, even if an undertaking is led to abuse its dominant position by the grant of exclusive right, all is not lost. According to Article 86(2), the Treaty rules, and in particular the competition rules, apply only insofar as this does not obstruct the performance, in law or in fact, of the particular task assigned to an undertaking entrusted with the operation of services of general economic interest.[51] The final sentence of Article 86(2) adds the proviso that the development of trade must not be affected to such an extent as would be contrary to the interests of the Community. The relatively recent case law of the Court has put this provision from its obscure place between the competition provisions right at the forefront of European law.[52] Up till *Corbeau*, Article 86(2)'s importance was considered to be minor but widening the scope of the prohibition in that case (Article 86(1) in connection with 82) had to be accompanied by a corresponding widening of the derogation. Thus, the Court held that[53]

> *'That provision [Article 86(1)] must be read in conjunction with Article [86(2)]'*.

Furthermore, the new Article 16, though of limited legal value, certainly has focussed political attention on the issue of the application of the Treaty rules on companies that provide services of general economic interest. Moreover, the Charter of Fundamental Rights of the European Union solemnly reaffirms the Union's respect for access to services of general economic interest.[54] As we have stated above, both provisions' legal importance may be doubted. For one, both Article 16 EC and Article 36 of the Charter apply without prejudice to Article 86. Furthermore, the Charter's status as a 'solemn declaration' is uncertain to say the least. It is therefore submitted that the importance of Article 16 resides primarily in its character of a political declaration.[55] Finally, the Commission has issued a number of Notices concerning services of general importance.[56]

Essentially, Article 86(2) contains four elements. Firstly, there must be a 'service of general economic interest'. Secondly, a company needs to have been 'entrusted' with the operation of this service of general economic interest. Thirdly, the rules in the Treaty shall not apply to this undertaking but only 'insofar as this does not obstruct the performance of the particular task assigned to this undertaking'. Fourthly, Article 86(2) demands that 'The development of trade must not be affected to such an extent as would be contrary to the interests of the Community'. Before we pay closer attention to these four core elements, two preliminary remarks need to be made. From the short outline of

---

51 Below, we shall not be considering the second category of undertakings to which Article 86(2) refers, 'undertakings [...] having the character of a revenue producing monopoly' since these are of rather limited interest for the purpose of this study. See further on this concept: Buendia Sierra 1999, p. 286 *et seq.*

52 See further Buendia Sierra 1999, p. 273 *et seq.*

53 Case C-320/91, *Corbeau*, [1993] ECR I-2533, para. 13.

54 Article 36 of the Charter of Fundamental Rights of the European Union, OJ 2000 C 362/1.

55 See further with regard to Article 16: Ross 2000.

56 OJ 1996 C 281/4, OJ 2001 C 17/4.

Article 86(2) it will be seen that it concerns undertakings only. Therefore, the same remarks that were made with regard to the concept of an undertaking in general also apply here. Interestingly, the Court, in *Albany*, explicitly recognised the connection between the concept of an undertaking and the applicability of Article 86(2).[57] The Court considered that although certain obligations would render the services performed by the pension fund less competitive compared with private pension insurers, those obligations were insufficient to justify the conclusion that the activities of the funds were non-economic. Nevertheless, these same obligations could very play a role in the applicability of Article 86(2). In our opinion, explicitly recognising this nexus between, on the one hand, exceptions to the concept of an undertaking and, on the other, Article 86(2) represents the first step in a process whereby the exceptions to the concept of an undertaking are interpreted ever more narrowly.[58] A second preliminary remark is of a more general nature. As a derogation from the general rule, Article 86(2) is subject to the same rule that applies to all Treaty provisions; it must be interpreted narrowly. Particularly with regard to Article 86(2) the width of which, as was noted above, is clearly related to the scope of Article 86(1), it should be kept in mind that the Court will always treat Article 86(2) as a derogation from the general rule.

The concept of a service of general economic interest is a Community concept. Notwithstanding this, the Court has always seemed receptive of national ideas of what should constitute such a service. The precise content of this concept is unclear and should probably remain so in that it is a dynamic concept that should be flexible enough to accommodate developments in society. To understand its application of Article 86(2), the Court's considerations in the Electricity cases may be of interest.[59] In, for example, the *Dutch Electricity* case the Court considered that[60]

> *'[...] in allowing derogations to be made from the general rules of the Treaty in certain circumstances, Article 90(2) [Now Article 86(2)] seeks to reconcile the Member States' interest in using certain undertakings, in particular in the public sector, as an instrument of economic or fiscal policy with the Community's interest in ensuring compliance with the rules on competition and the preservation of the unity of the common market.'*

---

57 Case C-67/96, *Albany*, [1999] ECR I-5751, para. 86.

58 See further, *supra*, paragraph 7.4.

59 Case C-157/94, *Commission* v. *Netherlands* (Dutch Electricity), [1997] ECR I-5699, C-158/94, *Commission* v. *Italy* (Italian Electricity), [1997] ECR I-5789, C-159/94, *Commission* v. *France* (French Electricity and Gas), [1997] ECR I-5815 and C-160/94, *Commission* v. *Spain* (Spanish Electricity), [1997] ECR I-5851. Hereafter we shall refer to these cases as the 'Gas and Electricity Cases'.

60 Case C-157/94, *Dutch Electricity*, [1997] ECR I-5699, para. 39.

This consideration confirms the fact that essentially Article 86(2) EC is about competences. Thus it seeks a balance between, on the one hand, member state competence to regulate markets in order to reach certain policy goals and, on the other hand, Community competence to establish a common market with undistorted competition. If this is the rationale behind this provision, the concept of a service of general economic interest must necessarily be an open one. Despite this open character, the outer limits of the concept may certainly be charted.

The word 'service' is to be understood as a wider concept than that in Article 50 EC. Indeed the provision of certain goods has also been considered as a service of general economic interest.[61] Furthermore, the inclusion of the word 'economic' is of great interest for the purpose of this research because environmental protection requirements are often considered to be of a non-economic nature. Is it therefore safe to conclude that environmental objectives will necessarily fall outside the scope of Article 86(2) EC? Quite the contrary is submitted to be true. Indeed, the Court has frequently omitted the word 'economic' in many judgments concerning this provision.[62] Buendia Sierra has interpreted the Court's and the Commission's practice in this regard as follows. In his opinion, Article 86(2) EC is intended to accommodate economic means to attain certain non-economic goals.[63] Indeed, in its 1996 Communication on this subject, the Commission distinguishes between 'services of general interest' and 'services of general economic interest'.[64] The Commission has maintained this in its 2000 Communication on Services of General Economic Interest[65] and in its Report to the Laeken European Council.[66] Essentially, the Commission appears to see the concept of 'services of general interest' as an overarching concept that encompasses both market and non-market services which are considered of general interest and subject to specific public service obligations. The notion of 'services of general economic interest', corresponds to this definition but applies only to 'market services'. Therefore, the Commission appears to base the distinction between, on the one hand, services of general interest and, on the other, services of general economic interest not on the objectives that are served with that fact that something is of general interest but rather on the nature of the activity with regard to which the general interest-exception is invoked.[67] The distinction

---

61 *E.g.* the provision of electricity and gas (in case C-393/92, *Gemeente Almelo et al.* v. *IJsselmij* (Almelo), [1994] ECR I-1477, para 28, the Court considered electricity to be a good within the meaning of Article 28 EC), *cf.* Case C-159/94, *French Electricity and Gas*, [1997] ECR I-5815.

62 *E.g.* Case C-320/91, *Corbeau*, [1993] ECR I-2568, para. 16.

63 Buendia Sierra 1999, p. 278.

64 Commission Communication on Services of General Interest in Europe, OJ 1996 C 281/4, para. 20, 21.

65 Commission Communication on Services of General Interest in Europe, OJ 2000 C 17/4, Annex II.

66 Commission, Report to the Laeken European Council, COM (2001) 598 final, Annex.

67 *Cf.* Buendia Sierra 1999, p. 278.

between market and non-market services would therefore, in the opinion of the Commission, seem to coincide with the concept of an undertaking.[68]

As has already been mentioned, the concept of a service of general economic interest is a Community concept. Effectively, this means that it leaves member states free to define what constitutes such a service whilst at the same time ensuring that the Court remains the ultimate arbiter of whether or not a member state was right to do so.

As forthcoming as the Court may be with regard to the question whether or not a service is of general economic interest, when deciding if an undertaking has been *entrusted* with the operation of this service, the Court's approach tends to be formalistic to say the least. In general, the Court will require an act in the exercise of the public function by a public authority of a member state.[69] Furthermore, this act has to be specific with regard to the privileged undertaking. The result of this act must be that the privileged undertaking is under certain obligations with regard to the service of general economic interest.[70] In *Corbeau* the Court stated that postal delivery was a service of general economic interest

> *'[...] consisting in the* OBLIGATION *to collect, carry and distribute mail on behalf of all users throughout the territory of the Member State concerned, at uniform tariffs and on similar quality conditions, irrespective of the specific situations or the degree of economic profitability of each individual obligation.'*[71] *[Emphasis added]*

In the *French Electricity and Gas* case, the Court clearly indicated the necessity of a link between the obligation for the privileged undertaking and the public act with regard to that undertaking.[72] General requirements that must be fulfilled by all entities that are active on a certain market will not result in an undertaking being entrusted with observing that these requirements are observed.[73] Therefore, the Court considered that the obligations regarding environmental protection and regional policy could only be taken into account in this respect 'if those obligations are specific to those undertakings and to their business'.[74]

As regards the specificity of the obligations that must concern the undertaking for it to have been entrusted with the performance of a service of general economic interest, the *GVL* case is also of interest.[75] In this case, GVL, which is

68 Commission Communication on Services of General Interest in Europe, OJ 2000 C 17/4, para. 28.

69 Case C-159/94, *French Electricity and Gas*, [1997] ECR I-5815, para. 65.

70 *Cf.* Whish 2001, p. 203.

71 Case C-320/91, *Corbeau*, [1993] ECR I-2568, para. 15.

72 Case C-159/94, *French Electricity and Gas*, [1997] ECR I-5815, para. 66.

73 *Ibid.* paras. 68, 69.

74 *Ibid.* para. 69.

75 Case 7/82, *Gesellschaft zur Verwertung von Leistungsschutzrechten* v. *Commission* (GVL), [1983] ECR 483.

the only copyright management company in Germany, sought to rely on Article 86(2). In this respect it relied on the German Copyright and Related Rights Management Act.[76] According to this Act, copyright management companies must, *inter alia*, be officially authorised, are subject to monitoring by the German Patent Office and are obliged to conclude certain management agreements. Despite these obligations imposed on GVL by the Act, the Court considered that: [77]

*'[...] the German legislation does not confer the management of copyright and related rights on specific undertakings but defines in a general manner the rules applying to the activities of companies which intend to undertake the collective exploitation of such rights.*

*Even if it is true that the monitoring of the activities of such companies as provided for by that law goes further than the public supervision of many other undertakings, that is however not sufficient for those companies to be included in the category of undertakings referred to in Article 90(2) [Now Article 86(2)] of the Treaty.'*

The conclusion must therefore be that the mere fact that legislation imposes extra strict requirements on a company because that undertaking exercises a particular activity is insufficient for this company to be entrusted within the meaning of Article 86(2).

The third core element of Article 86(2) essentially involves a proportionality test. It declares the rules in the Treaty applicable only in so far as this does not obstruct the performance of the special task. The words 'in so far' indicate that the attention now turns to the question of whether or not is *necessary* to exempt a certain company from the application of the Treaty rules. A very considerable amount of literature and case law has been produced on the subject of proportionality.[78] We will therefore have to confine ourselves to just indicating the basic outlines of the principle's application within Article 86(2).

In *Corbeau*, the Court considered that:[79]

*'The question which falls to be considered is therefore the extent to which a restriction on competition or even the exclusion of all competition [...] is necessary in order to allow the holder of the exclusive right to perform its task of general interest and in particular to have the benefit of economically acceptable conditions'.*

---

76 Gesetz über die Wahrnehmung von Urheberrechten und verwandten Schutzrechten.

77 Case 7/82, *GVL*, [1983] ECR 483, paras. 31, 32.

78 See, also for further references, Buendia Sierra 1999, pp. 300-341.

79 Case C-320/91, *Corbeau*, [1993] ECR I-2568, para. 16.

The Court then went on to state that an analysis of proportionality should start from the premise that the privileged firm should be able to compensate the loss generated in non-profitable sectors with the profits made in other sectors. In short, the Court considered that such companies should be able to cross-subsidise and that, in turn, would require keeping out the cherry pickers.[80]

In the later *French Electricity and Gas* case, the Court was able to further develop its case law with regard to the question of what constitutes 'economically acceptable conditions'. In that case the Commission argued that Article 86(2) could apply only when 'the economic viability of the undertaking itself would be threatened'.[81] The Court agreed with the Commission that, being a derogation, Article 86(2) was to be interpreted narrowly. However, the Court did not put the bar as high as the Commission had done. According to the Court, it would be sufficient if the applicability of the Treaty rules would 'obstruct the performance, in law or in fact, of the special obligations incumbent upon that undertaking'. In this respect the Court explicitly pointed out that it would not be necessary for the viability of the undertaking to by jeopardised.[82] Moreover, recent case law of the Court suggests that the Court is applying a proportionality test that leaves more room for the national authorities to restrict competition if this is necessary to ensure the fulfilment of the task of general economic interest.[83]

The fourth and final element of Article 86(2) only adds to obscurity of the already enigmatic Article 86. Buendia Sierra extensively charts the (early) discussions among scholars with regard to the meaning of the second sentence of Article 86(2).[84] A first questions that had to be answered was whether the second sentence contained a norm that was independent from that in the first paragraph. This could have important consequences as it was accepted that the defence of the Community's interests is clearly a task for the Commission. Interpreting the first and second sentence as a whole, would therefore effectively rule any direct effect for Article 86(2).

The Court, it is submitted, has not done much to clarify the meaning of this last sentence. Most probably it is little more than a clarification of the proportionality test contained in the first sentence and therefore devoid of any legal meaning independent of the first sentence.[85] In the *French Electricity and Gas* case the Court considered whether or not this final criterion was fulfilled so that Article 86(2) could apply. In this case the Commission had argued that relinquishing the exclusive import and export rights of the French Gas and Electri-

---

80 *Ibid.*, paras. 17, 18

81 Case C-159/94, *French Electricity and Gas*, [1997] ECR I-5815, para. 52.

82 *Ibid.*, para. 59.

83 *Cf.* Jones & Sufrin 2001, p. 445.

84 Buendia Sierra 1999, p. 341 *et seq.*

85 Buendia Sierra 1999, p. 351, 352 and Blum & Logue 1998, p. 35, 36.

city monopolists would make it possible and foster the development of trade in the interest of the Community.[86] According to the Court, merely stating this was insufficient in order to prove that the French government had failed to fulfil its obligations under the Treaty.

Whatever, may be of this, the fact remains that since the *Gas and Electricity* cases, the Court has consistently omitted any reference to this element of Article 86(2). As we shall see below, the Court has, in a number of recent preliminary rulings where it acknowledged the applicability of Article 86(2), not addressed this fourth element at all. With regard to the fourth element the following concluding remarks may be made. As the law stands at the moment, the Court does not attach any particular weight to the last sentence. Rather it appears to, as some have argued, consider it to be nothing more than a repetition of the proportionality criterion in the first sentence specially designed for those occasions where the Commission wants to use Article 86 to liberalise certain sectors of the industry. In these cases, where the Commission acts pursuant to Article 86(3) or, as happened in the *Gas and Electricity* cases, Article 226 in conjunction with Article 86, the Commission is under an obligation to show that it is defending the Community's interests. This would explain why the Court has not referred to this element on a single occasion in a case that came to it through a preliminary reference.

Now that the basic requirements for the applicability of Article 86(2) have been outlined, let us now look at the consequences that arise from the application of Article 86(2) to an undertaking. In this respect, we must first conclude that Article 86(2) is directly effective.[87] As a result, national courts may decide on whether or not it applies. If it considers that Article 86(2) is applicable, the result is, as the wording of this provision shows, that the firm in question is no longer 'subject to the rules contained in this Treaty, in particular the rules on competition'. With regard to the combined application of Article 82 and 86, this means that even if the privileged undertaking abuses its dominant position, Article 82 will not be of any help to end these abuses in so far as the exclusive rights are necessary for the fulfilment of the task of general economic importance. Article 82 will simply not apply.

It is submitted that much the same holds true with regard to Article 81. As we have seen above, Article 81(1) may only be declared inapplicable by the Commission. Regulation 17 has conferred this exclusive competence upon it.[88] As a Treaty exception, Article 86(2) is hierarchically higher than the rule laid

---

[86] Case C-159/94, *French Electricity and Gas*, [1997] ECR I-5815, para. 111.

[87] Case 66/86, *Ahmed Saeed Flugreisen et al.* v. *Zentrale zur Bekämpfung Unlauteren Wettbewerbs* (Ahmed Saeed), [1989] ECR 853, para. 53.

[88] Article 7(1) of Regulation 17 of 1962. Note that this competence will disappear as a result of the direct applicability of Article 81(3) after the entry into force of Regulation 1/2003, see, *supra*, pargraph 8.9.

down in Regulation 17. As such the mere fact that Article 81 applies should not stand in the way of a national judge or the Court declaring Article 81 as a whole inapplicable by virtue of the fact that Article 86(2) applies. Therefore, the applicability of Article 86(2) removes the need to notify an agreement in order to obtain an exemption. The Court appears to have confirmed this in *Almelo*.[89]

This is an important observation with regard to useful effect doctrine. In Chapter 11 and the introduction to this chapter above, we have noted that Article 86 can be seen as the *lex specialis* compared to the *lex generalis* of the useful effect doctrine. In this regard we have further observed that an exception or justification with regard to Article 86 should have a counterpart in the useful effect doctrine.[90] Moreover, these exceptions should be comparable both substantively as well as procedurally. From a substantive perspective, the general interest exception appears to fit in nicely with Article 86(2). From a procedural point of view, the main procedural aspects of the general interest exception to the useful effect doctrine should mirror those of Article 86(2). In this respect, the effects of the applicability of the general interest exception and Article 86(2) should be identical. Therefore, since the applicability of Article 86(2) renders it unnecessary to notify the underlying agreement for an exemption, it is submitted that the applicability of the general interest exception should have the same consequences. Having thus set out the basic elements of Article 86(2), we may now turn our attention to the application of this provision in an environmental context.

## 12.6 The application of Article 86(2) in an environmental context

As already became clear in Part One of this book, environmental costs often represent so-called external costs. Therefore, many 'environmental services' (such as the environmentally friendly treatment of waste) will be difficult to perform under market circumstances. This, in connection with the fact that the authorities will often consider it very important to ascertain a high level of environmental services, has led many authorities to create 'environmental monopolies'. Below, we shall look at a number of such environmental monopolies and in particular the application of Article 86(2) to these monopolies. Furthermore, we shall also be addressing the effects on Article 86(2) of 'environmentally unfriendly monopolies'.

---

89 Case C-393/92, *Almelo*, [1994] ECR I-1477, para. 50. *Cf.* Blum & Logue 1998, p. 94. However, Buendia Sierra appears reticent in this respect, Buendia Sierra 1999, p. 360.

90 *Supra*, paragraph 11.3.

The first reference to Article 86(2) in a case that involved environmental protection requirements, is to be found in the *Inter-Huiles* case.[91] This case concerned the legality of a French scheme for the collection and treatment of waste oils according to which waste oils would have to be collected and treated by a limited number of designated undertakings within a certain territory. One of those designated undertakings was the Syndicat. The Syndicat started proceeding against Inter-Huiles for having violated its collection and treatment monopoly. In these proceedings, Inter-Huiles challenged the compatibility of this scheme with the EC Treaty. Since the Syndicat essentially was in a monopoly position, both parties invoked Article 86.

In this case Article 86(2) did not make it beyond the Advocate-General's opinion. In her opinion, Rozés considered that it that the firm in question, the Syndicat, could probably be taken to have been entrusted with the performance of a task of general economic interest. However, she considered the French scheme in question was not necessary to ensure the fulfilment of this task.[92] The Court did not address any of the substantive issues of Article 86 but confined itself to stating that Article 86(2) could not create individual rights that the national courts must protect.[93]

Article 86 played a similarly minor role in the *Vanacker* case.[94] This case concerned the same French scheme that gave rise to the *Inter-Huiles* case. This time, two Belgians, Vanacker and Lesage were accused of having collected and transported waste oils within the meaning of the French legislation, however without having obtained the necessary permits. Again, only the Advocate-General considered whether Article 86 could apply. According to Advocate-General Lenz, Article 86(2) was irrelevant since the measure at hand, the creation of regional collection and treatment monopolies by the state, was unconnected with any behaviour by an undertaking.[95] This time the Court does not address Article 86 at all.

This silence with regard to Article 86(2) changed with the *Almelo* case.[96] This case concerned, *inter alia*, the applicability of Article 86(2) to a scheme that prohibits a local electricity distributor from importing electricity. In this case the regional electricity distributor, IJsselmij, had prohibited the local distributor, the municipality of Almelo, from importing electricity. With regard to IJsselmij, the Court observed that it had been entrusted with the performance of a task of

---

[91] Case 172/82, *Syndicat National des Fabricants Raffineurs d'Huile de Graissage et al.* v. *Groupement d'Intérêt Économique 'Inter-Huiles' et al.* (Inter-Huiles), [1983] ECR 555.

[92] *Ibid.*, opinion of A-G Rozés, at p. 581.

[93] *Ibid.*, para. 15.

[94] Case C-37/92, *Criminal proceedings against José Vanacker et al.* (Vanacker), [1993] ECR I-4947.

[95] *Ibid.*, opinion of A-G Lenz, para. 40 and 41.

[96] Case C-393/92, *Almelo*, [1994] ECR I-1477.

general economic interest (the supply of energy in sufficient quantities to meet demand at any given time, at uniform tariff rates and on terms which may not vary save in accordance with objective criteria applicable to all customers). As a result, the Court held that[97]

> *'Restrictions on competition from other economic operators must be allowed in so far as they are necessary in order to enable the undertaking entrusted with such a task of general interest to perform it. In that regard, it is necessary to take into consideration the economic conditions in which the undertaking operates, in particular the costs which it has to bear and the legislation,* PARTICULARLY CONCERNING THE ENVIRONMENT, *to which it is subject.' [Emphasis added]*

Even though *Almelo* does not concern an environmental monopoly; it is very significant for the purpose of this study because the Court here explicitly takes into account environmental considerations as part of the proportionality test under Article 86(2). If, in deciding whether an electricity distribution company can rely on Article 86(2), environmental requirements play a role, then, it is submitted, such requirements should be of even greater importance in determining the proportionality in connection with an environmental monopoly. This, of course, subject to the proviso that such an environmental monopoly is considered to constitute a task of general economic importance.

Whether or not environmental services could constitute services of general economic importance within the meaning of Article 86(2) was considered in the *Dusseldorp* case. As was set out above, the Court considered that the Dutch government had acted contrary to Article 82 in connection with Article 86(1) by conferring the exclusive right to process certain types of waste on AVR. The Court then went on to consider whether Article 86(2) could be relied upon.[98] The Dutch government had pleaded that the exclusive right was necessary to ensure a sufficiently large flow of waste to AVR. This was considered important because the rotary furnace that AVR uses to treat the dangerous wastes apparently needs a rather specific blend of waste in order to operate effectively. Should, therefore, the amount of waste oil filters be insufficient, then AVR would have to buy a replacement fuel, which would increase its operating costs and thus jeopardise its profitability.[99]

The Advocate-General in the *Dusseldorp* case, Jacobs, considered it unnecessary to address the applicability of Article 86 in great detail.[100] As such he

97 *Ibid.*, para. 49.

98 Case C-203/96, *Dusseldorp*, [1998] ECR I-4075, para. 64.

99 *Ibid.*, para. 66, from the report of the hearing it appears that the Netherlands government considered this issue to be unimportant as well, para. 77.

100 *Ibid.*, opinion of A-G Jacobs, para. 98.

confined himself to indicating that in his opinion 'a waste management function might well be said to constitute a service of general economic interest'.[101] Furthermore, he also considered it likely that AVR was actually 'entrusted' with the performance of this service of general economic interest. Since he considered them to be questions of a factual nature, he left the final word on this to the national judge.

Similarly, Jacobs restricts himself to indicating the basic tenor of the Court's judgments with regard to the proportionality test.[102] Having repeated the Netherlands government's economic profitability argument, he concludes that it is for the government to show to the satisfaction of the national judge that there are no alternative means by which the objective cannot be achieved equally well.[103]

The Court was even less forthcoming with regard to Article 86(2) when it considered that[104]

*'Even if AVR's task could constitute a task of general economic interest, however, it is for the Netherlands Government [...] to show to the satisfaction of the national court that that objective cannot be achieved equally well by other means.'*

The Court hardly conceals its scepticism in this respect. Firstly, it doubts whether, as Jacobs called it, the waste management function could qualify as a task of general economic interest. Secondly, the Court does not leave the impression of being completely convinced by the economic profitability reasoning brought forward by the Netherlands. Apparently, the Court's scepticism was also apparent to the national judge, the *Raad van State* (Council of State). In a short and straightforward judgment, the Council did little more than repeating the Court's considerations in this respect only to come to the conclusion that the government had not convinced it of the necessity of the measure.[105]

*Quelle surprise*, when the Court pronounced its judgment in the *Sydhavnens Sten & Grus* case. As we have seen, the differences in the Court's approach with regard to Article 86(1) and 82 can probably be explained on the basis of the different facts of the two cases.[106] Probably much the same holds true with regard to the differences in the Court's approach to Article 86(2) in both cases. However, again, these differences in the facts are nowhere mentioned in the judgments themselves.

---

[101] *Ibid.*, opinion of A-G Jacobs, para. 103.

[102] *Ibid.*, opinion of A-G Jacobs, para. 106-108.

[103] *Ibid.*, opinion of A-G Jacobs, para. 108.

[104] *Ibid.*, para. 67.

[105] *Afdeling Bestuursrechtspraak Raad van State* 28 January 1999 in Case No. E03.95.0106-A, AB 1999, 154.

[106] And the fact that the representative of the Netherlands government apparently thought the issues concerning Article 86(2) EC of little importance.

*Sydhavnens Sten & Grus*' first surprise is to be found in paragraph 75 of the judgment, a consideration that merits quotation in full.

*'The management of particular waste may properly be considered to be capable of forming the subject of a service of general economic interest, particularly where the service is designed to deal with an environmental problem.'*

Gone is the reticence that pervades the *Dusseldorp* case. The Advocate-General in the *Sydhavnens Sten & Grus* case did not get beyond repeating the Court's considerations in the *Dusseldorp* case[107] whilst, admittedly, adding a few critical remarks.[108] The full Court (as opposed to the sixth chamber in *Dusseldorp*) made a 180-degree turn compared to *Dusseldorp*. The statement by the Court, even though it is couched in cautious terminology, is clear and straightforward: environmental management services constitute services of general economic interest. The last part of the above consideration seems somewhat nonsensical in that it is very difficult to imagine a waste management function that is not 'designed to deal with an environmental problem'. It is therefore submitted that the Court seems to have wanted to make it clear beyond doubt that it were the environmental protection requirements in this case that led the Court to this conclusion.

*Sydhavnens Sten & Grus* holds a second surprise when it comes to the proportionality test adopted by the Court. The exclusive rights in the *Sydhavnens Sten & Grus* case were granted for much the same reason as those in the *Dusseldorp* case: to ensure profitability or economic viability. Admittedly, the reasoning of the Danish authorities was a bit more straightforward than that employed by the Netherlands government. In *Sydhavnens Sten & Grus* it was simply argued that a high-capacity centre needed to be set up to ensure sufficient recycling capacity and thus a high degree of recycling. Logically, a high-capacity centre needs a large flow of waste to operate profitably.[109] The Danish authorities thus avoided the somewhat strenuous reasoning employed by the Dutch government. The reasoning employed by the Netherlands government hinged on the need to buy more expensive replacement fuels. Thereby an extra element is added to establish the causal connection between the profitability on the one hand and need to ensure sufficient inflow of waste on the other hand. Thus the profitability argument of the Dutch authorities was less direct. However, the mere fact that the profitability-type of reasoning in the *Dusseldorp* was less direct, does not detract from the underlying logic which is that to ensure profitability it is sometimes necessary to ensure a large flow by means of an exclusive right. Indeed, the

---

[107] Case C-209/98, *Sydhavnens Sten & Grus*, [2000] ECR I-3743, opinion of A-G Léger paras. 105 and 106.

[108] *Ibid.*, opinion of A-G Léger, para. 104.

[109] *Ibid.*, para. 78.

Court in the Sydhavnens Sten & Grus case accepted precisely this argument.[110] However, as will be shown below, the profitability reasoning used in *Dusseldorp* has quite a different environmental impact from that used in *Sydhavnens Sten & Grus.*

In any case should it be noted that the Court does not accept the profitability reasoning unqualifiedly. The Court clearly indicates in *Sydhavnens Sten & Grus* that it also considered it important that the exclusive right was granted only for the duration of the amortisation period of the installations.[111]

How, then, are we to explain the 180 degree turn in the Court's case law that occurred in Sydhavnens Sten & Grus? Again, it is submitted that the environmental facts of the case have been, though implicitly, decisive. In her case note on the *Dusseldorp* case, Denys concludes by stating that[112]

> *'[...] whether it is right to state that* Dusseldorp *has surrendered the environment to the merciless commercial logic of the internal market ultimately depends on the final word of the Raad van State [...]'*

As was said above, the case was already decided when the Court gave its sceptical considerations on the applicability of Article 86(2). The Raad van State merely 'got the hints'. We may, however, wonder whether the 'merciless commercial logic' that Denys fears so in her case note is actually such a bad thing. The fact is that the processing by Factron was of at least an equally high quality and at a lower cost. In *Dusseldorp*, the merciless commercial logic would rather appear to actually work in favour of environmental protection. In *Sydhavnens Sten & Grus,* the Court rightly recognised that in order to *create* a market, temporary exclusive rights may be necessary. After such a market is established, the commercial logic will force the market participants to make their best effort at providing environmental services at the lowest possible price.[113]

Furthermore, the different treatment of the profitability arguments brought forward in *Dusseldorp* and *Sydhavnens* can probably also be explained on the basis of the environmental impact.[114] In *Dusseldorp* the Dutch government effectively sought to attain a cross subsidisation between waste that is difficult to incinerate and waste that is highly flammable. The highly flammable oil filters that Dusseldorp wanted to export were needed in order to make the

[110] *Ibid.*, para. 80. See, however, for a critical view of the necessity of the exclusive rights: Van Rossem & Vedder 2000, p. 216.

[111] *Ibid.*, para. 79.

[112] Denys 1999, p. 30.

[113] Naturally, a minimum level of environmental protection has to be ascertained but exclusive rights are not the way to do this.

[114] See also Vedder 2003.

rotary furnace of AVR operate most effectively because other wastes incinerated would not burn as well thus leading to more and more dangerous incineration residues. Moreover, the oil filters were also necessary in order to ensure the profitably because primary fuels would have to be bought in the absence of oil filters for the other, less flammable wastes, to be incinerated anyway. This type of profitability reasoning can thus be called a 'cross subsidisation profitability' in that, essentially the relatively low costs of incineration of one type of waste (e.g. oil filters) are used to cross subsidise the relatively high costs of incineration of another type of waste (e.g. the no so flammable waste).

We may contrast this with the profitability that the Copenhagen municipal government sought to achieve in *Sydhavnens Sten & Grus*. In the case of the Grøften recycling centre, the profitability was the result of the high capacity. The sheer volume of building and construction waste handled in that centre, reduced the costs to such an extent that the initial investments could be recouped. This type of profitability argument can be characterised as an 'economies of scale profitability'.

If we compare both types of profitability reasoning from an environmental perspective it becomes clear that the cross subsidisation profitability actually leads to a distortion of the waste treatment costs to the detriment of waste that is relatively cheap to treat. In *Dusseldorp*, the oil filters were used to cross subsidise the incineration of dangerous wastes that were less flammable. This cross-subsidisation directly runs counter to the polluter pays principle and is for that reason already environmentally objectionable. If a given type of waste is so dangerous that incineration is the only acceptable method of disposal and this is difficult because the waste is inflammable, the disposal costs should be so high as to constitute an effective incentive to reduce the production of this type of waste. The economies of scale profitability that lay at the foundations of *Sydhavnens Sten & Grus* has no such environmentally unfriendly distorting effects.

Finally, in both the *Dusseldorp* and *Sydhavnens Sten & Grus* case the Court does not address the fourth element of Article 86(2) that trade must not be affected to an extent that is contrary to the Community's interests. The importance of this criterion, in general and in an environmental context, therefore remains uncertain.

In sum, Article 86(2) can now save the day for environmental monopolies. Since its effect is to basically remove such a monopoly from the scope of the Treaty provisions altogether, such companies and the governments granting them special or exclusive rights need not worry about, among others, Article 81, 82 and 87 EC. The other way around, it may be wondered what the effect on the application of Article 86(2) is if the public undertaking is environmentally unfriendly. In this respect two different cases must be discerned. The easier of the two is the case where the authorities or the public undertaking itself rely on Article 86(2) because of the environmental task of the public undertaking.

If such an 'environmental monopoly' turns out to be not so environmentally friendly, then we are likely to see a repetition of the (Court's proportionality reasoning in) the *Dusseldorp* case. The Court will simply not consider the disapplication of the Treaty rules to be necessary in order to ensure the environmental task. The other case is slightly more difficult and involves the situation where a public undertaking has a non-environmental task the exercise of which leads to damage to the environment. An example of such a situation would be an authority that refuses to allow a new electricity generator using a new environmentally friendly production process to become active on the market because it has granted an exclusive right to an existing producer that uses an environmentally unfriendly production method. The proportionality reasoning in the *Dusseldorp* case is not likely to apply simply because the privileged undertaking was not awarded that position because of environmental objectives. However, the *Almelo* case may be of relevance. In that case, the Court took into account, among others, the environmental obligations that an electricity-producing firm was under in assessing the proportionality of the exclusive rights. However, in cases where the privileged undertaking is not even indirectly under any environmental obligations, the situation becomes more difficult. In these cases, the wording of Article 86(2) together with the fact that it is directly effective and therefore not the sole dominion of the Commission would probably rule out a negative role for environmental concerns. If the task assigned to the privileged firm in no way encompasses any environmental aspects, than these remain outside the Article 86(2) equation altogether as the only test laid down in Article 86(2) is whether the disapplication of the Treaty rules is necessary for the fulfilment of 'the particular tasks assigned to them'. This would only be different if the (national) court, in applying Article 86(2) would consider itself to be under an obligation to integrate environmental protection requirements. Since Article 6 EC has no specific addressee and is only limited with regard to legal context, this should be possible.

# CHAPTER 13

# Article 87

## 13.1 Introduction

The last stone in the fortress that should protect the common market from distortions of competition is the prohibition on state aids. Technically speaking, Article 87(1), by contrast with Articles 81 and 82, does not *prohibit* anything but confines itself to stating that the aid shall be incompatible with the common market. Nevertheless we shall be speaking of the prohibition on state aids.[1] This prohibition is to be found in Article 87 EC. The structure of Article 87 closely resembles that of the other Treaty competition provisions: a broadly formulated prohibition in the first paragraph together with a number of exempt and exemptible forms of state aid in the second and third paragraphs. Below, we will first look at the scope of the prohibition. After that we shall turn our attention to the various means by which state aids may nonetheless be legalised. In the Course of this we shall look at the application of Article 87 and the various exemptions in an environmental context. No particular attention will be paid to the procedural issues involved in Article 87 and 88 EC.

Since the Community is becoming increasingly active as an institution that grants subsidies and distributes large funds, we shall also be addressing the issue of state aid control and Community subsidies and aids. Finally, much of the Commission's policy with regard to state aids in the environmental field has been codified in the form of so-called guidelines. Most recently such Guidelines in the field of environmental protection have been published in 2001. Below, we will look at the 2001 Environmental aid Guidelines as well as its predecessors in considerable detail.

## 13.2 Article 87(1) – the prohibition of state aids

The first paragraph of Article 87 prohibits any aid granted by a member state or through state resources in any form whatsoever which distorts or threatens to distort competition by favouring certain undertakings or the production of certain goods insofar as trade between the member states is affected. Essentially five elements can be identified in this definition. Firstly, there needs to be aid in any form whatsoever. Secondly, it must be granted by a member state or through state resources. Thirdly, it is necessary that such aid threatens to distort or actually distorts competition by, and this is the fourth element, favouring certain firms or the production of certain goods. According to the fifth element, trade between member states must be affected. Below, we shall address these five elements.

1 Case C-143/99, *Adria-Wien Pipeline GmbH and Wietersdorfer & Peggauer Zementwerke GmbH* v. *Finanzlandesdirektion für Kärnten* (Adria-Wien), [2001] ECR I-8365, para. 30.

### 13.2.1 The Concept of an 'Aid'

With regard to the first element it should be noted that the EC Treaty nowhere defines the concept of an 'aid'. Completely in line with this, the Court has consistently refused to define the concept of an aid and has adopted an effects-based approach in the light of the objective of Article 87. This is nothing more than the application within Article 87(1) of the functional approach that we have identified as characteristic for the entire body of EC competition law. Effect, and not form, is what counts, as the Court states in the *Deufil* case[2]

*'Article 92 [Now Article 87] does not therefore distinguish between the measures of state intervention concerned by reference to their causes or their aims but defines them in relation to their effects [...]'.*

The objective of Article 87 is to attain and maintain a level playing field throughout the common market. This effects-based approach together with this objective has constantly been the Court's starting point for the analysis of state measures under Article 87(1). As, however, an unmitigated effects-based approach would bring nearly every state measure within the scope of the state aid rules, the Court has identified the latter four of the five criteria mentioned above to consequently limit the scope of the concept of an aid. Therefore, the exercise undertaken by the Court appears to start from the premise that the effects bring a state measure within the scope of Article 87(1) whereas any of the last four elements can be used to distinguish state measures outside the scope of Article 87 from 'state aids'. Examples of the different types of state measure that have been held by the Commission or Court to constitute state aids can be found in the literature.[3] The most obvious example of a state aid is the subsidy. It should, however, be remembered that the concept of state aid encompasses that of and is much wider than the concept of a subsidy.[4] In accordance with the effects-based approach, the Court has consistently held that[5]

*'In determining whether a State measure constitutes aid, it is necessary, according to settled case-law, to establish whether the recipient undertaking receives an economic advantage which it would not have obtained under normal market conditions'.*

---

2 Case 310/85, *Deufil* v. *Commission* (Deufil), [1987] ECR 901, para. 8.

3 D'Sa 1998, p. 56, 57 and Hancher, Ottervanger & Slot 1999, p. 42-52.

4 With regard to the ECSC Treaty (that mentions both subsidies and aids in Article 4(c)): Case 30/59, *Gezamenlijke Steenkolenmijnen in Limburg* v. *High Authority*, [1961] ECR 1, at p. 19. Case C-53/00, *Ferring* v. *Agence Centrale des Organismes de Sécurité Soci*ale (Ferring), [2001] ECR I-9067 para. 15.

5 Case T-270/97, *EPAC – Empresa para a Agroalimentação e Cereais* v. *Commission*, [2000] ECR II-2267, para. 66.

Basically, the effects based approach to state aids encompasses all measures whereby member states give resources or procure advantages for firms to further the attainment of the objectives of the state.[6] Taken to its limits, this effects-based approach would include, for example, government provided education since that will benefit the firms established in that member state because they can rely on a well-trained workforce for the education of which they did not have to pay. Clearly, the unconditional effects-based approach is not appropriate and this is where the last four criteria of the five identified above come into play. Furthermore, we should point out that the advantage must be granted to an undertaking. The remarks that were made above with regard to the concept of an undertaking therefore also apply within the context of Article 87. Thus Article 87 applies to all entities performing an economic activity irrespective of whether they are private undertakings or public undertakings within the meaning of Article 86 EC.[7] *Vice versa*, Article 87 does not apply to advantages granted to entities that do not qualify as undertakings.

### 13.2.2 Aid granted through state resources

As regards the second element: 'aid granted by a member state or through state resources in any form whatsoever'. This element is striking because of its wide scope. A first question to arise from this wide scope concerned the alternative character of, on the one hand, 'aid granted by a member state (hereafter referred to as the first branch)' and, on the other, 'through state resources in any form whatsoever (hereafter referred to as the second branch)'. The alternative character could be taken to mean that the first branch concerned the state measures whereby funds would actually be transferred from the state to other parties whereas the second branch could practically concern any measure whereby the state exerts its influence to confer an advantage on other parties without a transfer of public funds being necessary. This view of the alternativity of the branches would greatly extend Article 87(1)'s scope. However, the Court, in *PreussenElektra*, chose interpret the alternativity contained in Article 87(1) in a different manner.

The *PreussenElektra* case concerned the German *Stromeinspeisungsgesetz* according to which regional electricity distribution companies were required to buy and feed into their grid all the renewable electricity produced in the region for which they were responsible.[8] Not only were these regional distribution companies obliged to purchase the green electricity, they also had to pay

6 *Cf.* Case 61/79, *Amministrazione delle Finanzo Stato* v. *Denkavit Italiana* (Denkavit), [1980] ECR 1205, para. 31.

7 Case 78/76, *Steinike & Weinlig* v. *Germany* (Steinike & Weinlig), [1977] ECR 595, paras. 16-18.

8 Case C-379/98, *PreussenElektra* v. *Schleswag* (PreussenElektra), [2001] ECR 2099.

the generators a minimum price that was higher than the economic value of the electricity. As the German legislator envisaged that the purchase obligation together with the minimum price requirement could bring certain regional distribution companies into financial trouble, the so-called 'hardship clause' was introduced. According to this hardship clause, the upstream network operator must compensate the extra costs resulting from the purchase obligation and the minimum price to be paid if the total amount of green electricity purchased by the regional distributor exceeds 5 per cent of the total output of this regional distributor. A closer look at the full name of the case will immediately reveal to anyone who has ever been to the northern part of Germany why this case came to the Court. The regional distributor, Schleswag, operates in the *Bundesland* of *Schleswig-Holstein* an area of Germany that is known for the fact that it is rather windy. As a result of this, Schleswag reached the 5 per cent threshold in April 1998 and requested compensation pursuant to the hardship clause from its upstream network operator PreussenElektra. The compatibility of the *Stromeinspeisungsgesetz* with Article 87 has been uncertain from its very inception onwards.[9] This was so because the obligation to purchase all renewable electricity at a fixed minimum price that is higher than the economic value obviously confers an advantage on the producers of the renewable electricity. In the national proceedings between Schleswag and PreussenElektra with regard to the compensation, the latter therefore called into question the compatibility of the *Stromeinspeisungsgesetz* with Article 87.

The Court, after concluding that the preliminary questions were admissible, immediately recognised that the obligation to purchase renewable electricity at a fixed minimum price flowing from the *Stromeinspreisungsgesetz* undeniably conferred upon the producers of renewable electricity an economic advantage,[10] addressed the alternativity issue identified above and quickly resolved it in accordance with its own well-established case law.[11] According to the Court the

---

9 *Ibid.*, opinion of A-G Jacobs, para. 16, 17.

10 *Ibid.*, para. 54.

11 However, Baquero Cruz & Castillo de la Torre consider that the Court was concerned with defining the concept of 'State resources' rather than with the requirement of financing from public funds: Baquero Cruz & Castillo de la Torre 2001, p. 492. It is submitted that this distinction between the concept of state resources (as an element of Article 87(1)) and the requirement of a transfer of public funds, is flawed. Public funds or 'State resources' necessarily involve a transfer of private funds to the public authorities (through taxation). What distinguishes private from public funds is therefore the presence of government control over these funds. In principle a state can exercise influence over all (private and public) funds in a member state (and this is what the German government in *PreussenElektra* had done on a very limited basis through the *Stromeinspeisungsgesetz*). The Court therefore appears to implicitly recognise that government control over funds is a useless criterion that will take it down a blind alley (just as accepting the reasoning that a deterioration in economic results will lead to a decrease in tax

alternative nature of the two branches serves only to bring within the meaning of Article 87(1) those measures whereby the state grants aid directly as well as those schemes whereby the member states grant aid through private institutions. In either case, it is required that there is a direct or indirect transfer of funds from the state to the undertakings.[12] Since the advantage to the renewable electricity producers was paid by the electricity distribution companies and the network operators (through the compensation mechanism), no public funds were transferred and, as a consequence, the measure falls outside the scope of Article 87(1).[13] It is worthwhile to point at the fact that the Court explicitly recalled the fact that the electricity companies concerned were both completely privately owned.[14]

Furthermore, the Court refused to enlarge the scope of Article 87 in light of the fact that the purchase obligation in connection with the minimum price will most probably result in a deterioration of the economic results of the undertakings that are under the purchase obligation and therefore reduce government income from taxes.[15] Normally, reductions or exemptions from taxation schemes will constitute state aid. In this case, however, the Court held that the reduction of tax income was inherent in the *Stromeinspeisungsgesetz* and could not constitute a means to transfer public funds to firms. Finally, the Court rejected a proposal by the Commission to establish a useful effect rule (see chapter 11 above) for state aids. The Court's reasoning in this respect is submitted to be far from convincing but the fact remains that as the law stands a transfer of public funds is necessary for a measure to come within Article 87's ambit.[16]

Despite this narrow reading of the element that aid must be granted through state resources, the Court's judgment in *PreussenElektra* should not be taken to mean that Article 87(1) now has its wings clipped. Basically, the focus has been shifted away from the question whether or not a transfer of public funds is necessary to the question of what constitute 'public funds'. This concept coincides to a large degree with that of the 'state'. The concept of the state is very broad and encompasses lower authorities as well. Furthermore, all bodies,

income and therefore a transfer of public funds, would have, para. 62 of the judgment). Instead, the Court adresses the formalistic (and therefore usable) criterion of whether or not there was a transfer of public funds. We should, however, note that the Court has accepted the control-criterion with regard to the entity responsible for distributing the aid: Case C-482/99, *France* v. *Commission* (Stardust Marine), [2002] ECR I-4397.

12 *Ibid.*, para. 58.

13 *Ibid.*, paras. 59, 60.

14 Case C-379/98, *PreussenElektra*, [2001] ECR 2099, para. 55.

15 *Ibid.*, para 62.

16 See for a critical analysis of the Court's reasoning with regard to the usefull effect rule for state aids: Vedder 2001B, p. 152-153 and Baquero Cruz & Castillo de la Torre 2001, p. 495.

whether public or private, that are under the control of the state also fall within the ambit of Article 87(1).[17] In *Van der Kooy*, for example, the Court considered that preferential tariffs for gas charged by the private company Gasunie constituted aid. The fact that the Netherlands authorities held 50 per cent of the shares (the other half was held by private parties) and had a 50 per cent representation in the supervisory board together with the possibility for the authorities to veto tariff decisions, was sufficient for the Court.[18] Furthermore, this wide concept of the state is also helpful in understanding the Court's case law with regard to so-called parafiscal charges. These are charges that are paid by private parties to a private institution that has been appointed by an act of a public authority.[19] The fact that such funds are fed with charges levied from private parties (mostly the undertakings that benefit from the fund) does not detract from these funds being considered state resources.[20] What matters is the fact that such funds, though administered by private entities, are set up by the public authorities and are under control by these authorities. The interesting question is of course what amount of control is required for the funds administered by such a private entity to constitute state resources? In the *Italian Textiles* case, the Court has addressed this issue and held that[21]

*'The argument that the contested reduction is not a 'state aid', because the loss of revenue resulting from it is made good through funds accruing from contributions paid to the unemployment insurance fund, cannot be accepted.*

*'As the funds in question are financed through compulsory contributions imposed by state legislation and as, as this case shows, they are managed and apportioned in accordance with the provisions of that legislation, they must be regarded as state resources within the meaning of article 92 [Now Article 87], even if they are administered by institutions distinct from the public authorities.'*

From this essentially two requirements may be distilled.[22] Firstly, the entity must be funded by compulsory contributions imposed by legislation. Secondly, the management by the entity of the funds must take place in accordance with the provisions of the legislation. The later *Commission* v. *France* case added the

---

[17] See, with regard to the concept 'state resources' and the imputability to the state of grants by companies that are a subsidiary of a state controlled undertaking, Case C-482/99, *Stardust Marine*, [2002] ECR I-4397.

[18] Case 67/85, *Kwekerij Gebroeders Van der Kooy et al.* v. *Commission* (Van der Kooy), [1985] ECR 1315., paras. 33-37.

[19] See, *e.g.* Case 47/69, *France* v. *Commission*, [1970] ECR 487.

[20] Case 78/76, *Steinike & Weinlig*, [1977] ECR 595, para. 22.

[21] Case 173/73, *Italy* v. *Commission* (Italian textiles), [1974] ECR 709, para. 16.

[22] Schina, however, identifies four requirements: Schina 1987, p. 21.

requirement, that albeit implicitly could perhaps already be found in *Italian Textiles*, the grant of the funds must be subject to approval by the public authorities.[23] From these cases it may be concluded that purely private funds can constitute state resources even if they are not actually collected by the state but where such funds remain in the private sphere (*i.e.* administered by a private entity) if the three requirements mentioned above are fulfilled. This has important consequences for the Dutch practice of declaring removal fees to be generally binding. Such removal fees are paid by the producers and, ultimately, the consumers into a private fund set up by the industry. The government is as such not involved in the setting up of this fund. However, industry may ask the Environment Minister to declare such a removal fee generally binding.[24] The question may then be asked whether there is an element of state aid involved. Prior to the act declaring the removal fee to be generally binding no state aid is involved simply because there is no government involvement in either the collection of the removal fees or the distribution of the funds. After the removal fee has been declared generally binding, it could be said that there now is a pervasive government influence on the collection of the fees. However, the fund itself still decides on the way in which the funds are spent. In our opinion, the environmental regulations in place do not contain the precise conditions for the management and apportioning of the funds. Furthermore, specific decisions on the grant of the funds are not subject to government approval. Thus the last two requirements are not satisfied and therefore these funds do not constitute state resources the administration of which must take place in accordance with Article 87. This has been confirmed in the *Dutch Car Wrecks* case.[25] This case concerned the scheme that was voluntarily set up by the industry in order to ensure the environmentally friendly disposal of car wrecks and afterwards declared generally binding by the Environment Minister. The system is financed through a € 45 levy that has to be paid into a fund for every new car that is registered. The fund is managed by a private entity set up as part of the voluntary agreement. From this fund, so-called recycling premiums are paid to the dismantling companies. According to the Commission, the fund, even after the scheme had been declared generally binding, does not involve state resources.[26]

Yet another element of the concept of state resources concerns taxation. Money that is owed to the state or has come under the control of the state will

---

23 Case 290/83, *Commission* v. *France*, [1985] ECR 439, para. 15.

24 See further: Vedder 2002, p. 33 *et seq.*

25 This case was mentioned in a press release: IP/01/1518 and in the Commission's Competition Policy Newsletter 2002, Nr. 2, p. 87 *et seq.*

26 Strangely enough the Commission appears to consider that 'the levy has a voluntary or at least an optional character'. This would appear to contradict the fact that the scheme has been declared generally binding.

constitute state resources. As a result, not collecting certain taxes may very well be state aid. Similarly, granting exemptions or rebates from taxes is also likely to fall within the scope of Article 87(1). This, of course, is of great importance with regard to the member states' energy taxation schemes. Almost invariably the putting into place of such schemes goes hand in hand with the granting of exemptions for the energy intensive industries with a view to maintaining competitiveness. Such reductions and exemptions are likely to constitute state aids. Whether this is the case will depend on, *inter alia*, the selectivity of the reductions or exemptions granted. We shall come back to this when looking closer at the fourth requirement. Finally, it is submitted that state resources will also include Community resources if the member state can decide freely on the use of such funds. If, however, the state merely passes Community funds through to the actual beneficiaries without any real discretion on the part of the state, the funds will constitute Community funds and, as a consequence, their distribution will not constitute the granting of aid.[27]

This brings us to the question of to what extent the Community is bound by Article 87? Firstly, can the funds distributed by the Commission be seen as state aids within the meaning of Article 87(1)? In our opinion, Community funds do not fall under Article 87(1) *sec*. The wording of Article 87(1) is simply too clear to be interpreted in such a way as to include 'Community aid'. However, it is submitted that the principle of loyalty to the Community, enshrined in Article 10 EC, may come to the rescue here. Article 10 has been applied by the Court with regard to a Community institution (the Commission) in the *Zwartveld* case.[28] The Court held that Community institutions must also be loyal to their Treaty obligations. Through Article 2 in connection with Article 3(1)(g) of the Treaty, the Community, and thus, *inter alia*, the Commission, is obliged not to distort competition. Even though there is no Court ruling that has ever confirmed this reasoning, the Commission and Council do seem to consider themselves under an obligation not to distort competition. Thus the Community funds that can be used for environmental purposes all contain clauses designed to ensure that competition is not distorted as a result of the Community funds.[29] Furthermore, in the group exemption Regulation for aid to small and medium-sized enterprises, the Commission expressly recognises that Community funds may also have an impact on competition and intra-Community trade so that such funds must also be taken into account when determining if an aid is

[27] Joined Cases 213/81-215/81, *Norddeutsches Vieh- und Fleischkontor Herbert Will et al.* v. *Bundesanstallt für Landwirtschaftliche Marktordnung* (BALM), [1982] ECR 3582, Opinion of A-G VerLoren van Themaat, para. 5 at p. 3617.

[28] Case C-2/88 Imm, *J. J. Zwartveld et al.* (Zwartveld) [1990] ECR I-3365, paras. 15-17.

[29] See further: Jans, Sevenster & Vedder 2000, p. 400, 401 and 633 *et seq.*

compatible with the common market or not.[30] In practice, the Commission will now check whether European subsidies give rise to a distortion of competition.[31]

### 13.2.3 Distortion of competition

The third element requires that such aid threatens to distort or actually distorts competition. It could be said that any aid will necessarily distort competition since it places one firm or a group of firms at a competitive advantage compared to the other firms that do not receive such aid. Initially, the Commission appeared to take this stance.[32] The Court has, however, on later occasions demanded some analysis of the market to show that competition is distorted or, in the case of aid that has not yet been granted, likely to be distorted.[33] This market analysis does not have to be as detailed as that pursuant to Article 81, 82 and the Merger Regulation.[34]

Now that we have set out the extent to which a distortion of competition needs to be investigated and demonstrated let us turn our attention to the substantive test that is used to determine whether there is a distortion of competition. The Court has set out its approach in this respect in the *Italian Textiles* case.[35] In this case the Court proposed to look at the competitive situation before and after the state measure and compare the two:[36]

*'[...] the point of departure must necessarily be the competitive position existing within the common market before the adoption of the measure in issue. This position is the result of numerous factors having varying effects on production costs in the different member states [...] unilateral modification of a particular factor of the cost of*

30 Commission Regulation 70/2001 on the application of Articles 87 and 88 of the EC Treaty to State aid to small and medium-sized enterprises (SME aid Regulation), OJ 2000 L 10/33, Article 8.

31 *Cf.* the answer given by Mr. Monti, Commissioner for Competition Policy, on written question E-1680/99 by MEP Von Wogau, OJ 2000 C 170 E/73.

32 Hancher, Ottervanger & Slot 1999, p. 36.

33 Joined Cases 296/82 and 381/82, *Netherlands and Leeuwarder Papierfabriek* v. *Commission* (Leeuwarder Papierfabriek), [1985] ECR 815, paras. 22-26.

34 *Cf.* Commission Notice on the definition of the relevant market for the purposes of Community competition law, OJ 1997 C 372/5, footnote 1, where the Commission indicates that the approach to market definition set out in the Notice is not of primary interest in state aid cases. *Cf. e.g.* Case T-55/99, *Confederación Española de Transporte de Mercancías* v. *Commission* (Plan Renove Industrial), [2000] ECR II-3207, paras. 102-105.

35 See further: Case C-6/97, *Italy* v. *Commission*, [1999] ECR I-2981, opinion of A-G Ruiz-Jarabo Colomer para. 34.

36 Case 173/73, *Italian textiles*, [1974] ECR 709, para. 17. This test resembles that with regard to Article 81(1) in Case 56/65, *LTM* v. *MBU*, [1966] ECR 235.

*production in a given sector of the economy of a member state may have the effect of disturbing the existing equilibrium'.*

The wording of the test thus proposed by the Court leaves no room for a *de minimis* rule according to which the 'existing equilibrium' will not be appreciably distorted by an aid that is *de minimis*.[37] However, a number of questions are still left unanswered by this test. For one, could it be argued that a government measure that merely compensates for the deterioration of the competitive position of the nation industry as a result of new (environmental) standards does not distort competition and therefore falls outside the scope of Article 87(1)? Tempting as it may seem to argue the opposite, the answer should nevertheless be in the negative. The Court has consistently held that, as far as Community law is concerned, member states are, put bluntly, free to allow the competitive position of their national industry to deteriorate.[38] Furthermore, the Court has also held that a distortion of competition in one member state does not compensate a distortion in another. Member states are therefore not free to grant state aid simply because another member state does the same.[39] Similarly, the mere fact that a measure only serves to bring certain costs in one member state in line with the (lower) costs in other member states will not keep it from constituting state aid.[40] On the other hand, an investment by a public authority that could also have been done by a private investor acting according to the principles of a market economy will not constitute a state aid.[41] According to the Court, it is necessary to determine whether[42]

*'in similar circumstances, a private investor of a dimension comparable to that of the bodies managing the public sector could have been prevailed upon to make capital contributions of the same size [...], having regard in particular to the information available and foreseeable developments at the date of those contributions.'*

This test is based is based on the premise that any investment made under market conditions, whether by a public authority or by a private investor, does not constitute state aid. The further assumption is that any private investor will

37 We shall look closer at the concept of *de minimis* in connection with Article 87(1) in paragraph 13.2.5 *infra*.

38 Case C-11/92, *The Queen* v. *Secretary of State for Health, ex parte Gallaher Ltd et al.* (Gallaher), [1993] ECR I-3545, paras. 18-22.

39 Case 78/76, *Steinike & Weinlig*, [1977] ECR 595, para. 24.

40 Joined Cases 6/69 & 11/69, *Commission* v. *France*, [1969] ECR 523, paras. 20 & 21.

41 This is the so-called Market Economy Investor principle. See, for a case in which this principle is applied: Case C-482/99, *Stardust Marine*, [2002] ECR II-4397, paras. 68 *et seq.*

42 *Ibid.*, para. 70.

act economically rational in deciding whether or not to invest whereas public authorities are considered to also base their decision on non-economic (political) factors.[43] It is submitted that in today's market, where sustainable banking is becoming more important, the market economy investor principle should not rely purely on the economic rationality but also take into account factors related to the sustainable development. In the current market where the 'three P's'[44] play an increasingly important role in corporate governance and sustainable investments in the Netherlands have increased by € 760 million to well over € 6 billion, environmental protection requirements can no longer be juxtaposed to economically rational behaviour.

Moreover, in the recent *Adria-Wien* case, the Court has held that Austrian legislation pursuant to which rebates were granted from an eco-taxation scheme to firms manufacturing goods, constituted a state aid precisely because it sought 'to preserve the competitiveness of the manufacturing sector, in particular within the Community'.[45]

What, then, should we think of governments that pay damages for unlawful acts by those governments or the situation where a government pays for a service provided to it? With regard to the former, the Court has held in *Asteris* that damages that governments must pay to compensate for damage caused by the governments to individuals do not constitute state aid.[46] As regards the latter, in *ADBHU*, the Court addressed the question of indemnities for services provided by waste oil collection and disposal companies.[47] In that case it was argued that the provisions of the Waste oils directive that provide for the possibility of paying indemnities to such companies were contrary to Article 87. The Court held that:[48]

*'In that respect the Commission and the Council, in their observations, rightly argue that the indemnities do not constitute aid within the meaning of articles [87]* et seq. *of the [EC] Treaty, but rather consideration for the services performed by the collection or disposal undertakings.*

*It is also important to note that according to the second paragraph of article 13 of the Directive 'the amount of these indemnities must be such as not to cause any significant distortion of competition or to give rise to artificial patterns of trade in the products'.'*

---

43 *Ibid.*, para. 71.

44 This refers to 'Planet, people and profit'as the new management maxim.

45 Case C-143/99, *Adria-Wien*, [2001] ECR I-8365, para. 54.

46 Joined Cases 106/87-120/87, *Asteris et al.* v. *Greece* (Asteris), [1988] ECR 5515, paras.22-24.

47 Case 240/83, *Procureur de la République* v. *Association de Défense des Brûleurs d'Huiles Usagées* (ADBHU), [1985] ECR 531, paras. 16 *et seq.*

48 *Ibid.*, paras. 18 & 19.

Therefore, payment for services rendered will not constitute state aid as long as there is no overcompensation. This reasoning seems to have been behind the Commission's decision in the *Danish Waste Tyres* case as well.[49] This case concerned a levy imposed on all new or rerubbered tyres that were manufactured in or imported to Denmark. The proceeds of this tax will be used to compensate the collection companies' extra costs incurred in collecting the waste tyres and transporting them to a rubber-powder plant. The Commission was of the opinion that the tax only constituted remuneration for a service delivered by the collection companies and therefore did not constitute state aid. Similarly, the Commission concluded that compensation paid by the Danish government to waste oils collection companies as part of the implementation of the Waste oils Directive was only a remuneration for services.[50]

The Court has addressed this issue most recently in the *Ferring* case.[51] This case involved a preliminary reference on the compatibility of a French system a taxation whereby only wholesale sales from 'laboratories' were taxed whereas similar sales from wholesale pharmacists were not taxed. The idea behind the tax was apparently to compensate the extra costs that such pharmacists faced compared to the laboratories because of the special obligations upon them to always keep a minimum stock. According to the Court such a tax did not constitute a state aid simply because laboratories were treated differently from wholesale pharmacists if this difference in treatment was 'objectively justified by reasons related to the logic of the system'.[52] The Court then repeated the objective of the French legislation, which was to compensate the extra costs.[53] After that the Court reiterated and applied its standard case law with regard to Article 87(1) only to come to the conclusion that the tax exemption constituted state aid leaving aside the obligation to keep a minimum stock.[54] Then, the Court shifted its attention to the minimum stock requirement resting upon the wholesale pharmacists. The Court concluded, while referring to the *ADBHU* case, that insofar as the tax advantage only compensates the extra costs resulting from the service that they provide to the public, it did not constitute state aid. Moreover, the Court reiterated that, provided that the tax exemption does not exceed the costs resulting from the minimum stock obligation, no real advantage would be conferred upon the wholesale pharmacists because the only effect of the tax is to put the laboratories and the pharmacists on an equal competitive footing.[55]

---

49 Commission XXIVth Competition Report (1994), para. 388 (p. 193) and Annex II section 2.14 (p. 532 & 533)

50 Commission XXXIrd. Competition Report (1993), para. 421 (p. 262).

51 Case C-53/00, *Ferring*, [2001] ECR I-9067.

52 *Ibid.*, para. 17.

53 *Ibid.*, para. 19

54 *Ibid.*, para. 22.

55 *Ibid.*, para. 27.

A related though slightly different question is whether compensation for lawful acts by the government qualifies as aid.[56] In the Netherlands and in many other member states it is commonly accepted that disproportionate costs arising from government actions with regard to a company or a sector of the industry can be compensated. Sections 15.20 and 15.21 of the Environmental management act (*Wet milieubeheer*) provide for the possibility of a compensation of costs that 'cannot reasonably remain the permit holder's sole responsibility'.[57] The local authorities that are responsible for the permit give such compensation. However, the Environment Minister can in turn compensate these local authorities. The rather general criterion of 'costs that cannot reasonably be borne by the permit holder' is elaborated in a circular letter by the Environment Minister.[58] Whether the hands and feet sufficiently limits the amount of discretion for the selectivity requirement to no longer be met, will be examined in general below in paragraph 13.2.4.

Could it be said that in cases where companies' extra costs resulting from stricter environmental legislation are compensated, that compensation is actually a remuneration for a service provided in the form of a higher level of environmental protection? It is submitted that in such cases there is no service as there was in *ADBHU* or *Danish Waste Tyres*. For this to be successfully argued, it would have to be established that achieving a high level of environmental protection is solely the government's task. Only then could it possibly be said that a service is performed for the government for which remuneration should take place. However, in accordance with the polluter pays principle, (financial) responsibility for the environment rests with the polluter. Therefore, as a rule, compensation for costs resulting from environmental requirements imposed by the member states will not fall outside the scope of Article 87(1) as remuneration.

The only exception to this rule can also be traced back to the polluter pays principle. In cases where the polluter no longer exists or cannot be held responsible, compensation of the costs by the government will not constitute state aid. It could be said that in such cases the government is indeed the only party that can be considered responsible for the environment. This occurs primarily with regard to soil pollution. With regard to the rehabilitation of industrial sites the

---

56 See with regard to this issue: Jans 2000, p. 298. He appears to consider that the issue turns on the degree of discretion that the authorities have in their decision to grant compensation. The degree of discretion, however, appears rather to relate to the selectivity requirement and will as such be addressed in paragraph 13.2.4 *infra*.

57 The Dutch tetxt speaks of '[..] kosten die redelijkerwijze niet of niet geheel voor rekening van de vergunninghouder behoren te blijven'.

58 *Circulaire Schadevergoeding* (Circular letter) of December 1997, State Gazette 1997, nr. 246, p. 32 *et seq.* as supplemented by the circular letter of 13 July 1998, State Gazette 1998, nr. 168, p. 9.

Commission has stated in general that compensation for such costs in cases where the polluter cannot be identified or cannot be called to account, will not constitute state aid.[59] In the *Kiener Deponie Bachmanning* case the Commission recognised that the contribution by the Austrian government to the rehabilitation of an old landfill site did not constitute state aid with regard to the firm that was responsible for the pollution. The polluter, Kieba, had gone into insolvency and was being liquidated. As such, it could neither be held responsible nor receive an advantage.[60]

### 13.2.4 Selectivity

The fourth element demands that the measure must favour certain firms or the production of certain goods. This is often referred to as the selectivity requirement.[61] This element is closely connected to the third element, that competition be distorted, and is helpful to distinguish general measures from state aids. If, for example, a member state decides to lower corporate tax rates across the board then such a measure will not benefit a select group of undertakings and will therefore fall outside the scope of Article 87.[62] Should, however, the effect of such a seemingly general measure of economic policy be that there is a benefit to one group of firms, the measure will constitute (sectoral) aid.[63]

The distinction between general measures and general aid schemes hinges on the criteria that are used and the discretion that the authorities have in their decisions with regard to the actual grant of the aid. If such criteria are general and not related to a specific branch of industry or a specific company the measure is likely to fall outside Article 87.[64] Similarly, if there is no discretion in the administration of the scheme (*i.e.* the application of the criteria), the measure will not constitute an aid. The Court has addressed the issue of selectivity in the *DMT* case.[65]

*'It follows from the wording of Article 92(1) [Now Article 87(1)] of the Treaty that general measures which do not favour only certain undertakings or the production of only certain goods do not fall within that provision. By contrast, where the body*

59 Commission XXIVth. Competition Report (1994), para. 389 (p. 193).

60 Commission Decision 1999/272, *Kiener Deponie Bachmanning*, 1999 OJ L 109/51.

61 D'Sa 1998, p. 82 *et seq.*, Hancher, Ottervanger & Slot 1999, p. 29 *et seq.*

62 Case 57/86, *Greece* v. *Commission*, [1988] ECR 2855, para.7-10. With regard to monetary decisions by a member state.

63 Case 173/73, *Italian textiles*, [1974] ECR 709, para. 15.

64 *Ibid.*, see notably the opinion A-G Warner at p. 603.

65 Case C-256/97, *Déménagements-Manutention Transport SA* (DMT), [1999] ECR I-3913, para. 27.

*granting financial assistance enjoys* A DEGREE OF LATITUDE WHICH ENABLES IT TO CHOOSE *the beneficiaries or the conditions under which the financial assistance is provided, that assistance cannot be considered to be general in nature'. [Emphasis added]*

Therefore, discretion on the part of the authorities that grant the aid, can be seen as a major factor leading to selectivity. However, as the *Adria-Wien* case shows, even seemingly general systems of taxation that confer no discretion with regard to exemptions may be considered to fulfil the selectivity criterion.[66] *Adria-Wien* concerned the compatibility with Article 87 of an Austrian eco-taxation scheme whereby electricity and natural gas consumption were taxed. Interestingly, the tax law envisaged, upon application, a rebate for firms 'whose activity can be shown to consist primarily in the production of goods'. The question of selectivity did not prove to be straightforward to answer in this case as is evidenced by the fact that the opinion and judgment diverge in this regard. With regard to the national judge's second question of whether an ecology tax that allows for a rebate for all undertakings concerned constitutes state aid, the Advocate-General and Court agree on the answer to be given. Both come to the conclusion that such a measure does not fulfil the selectivity requirement and therefore does not constitute aid within the meaning of Article 87.[67]

The first question asked by the national judge concerns the situation where the tax rebate is granted only to undertakings that are primarily involved in the manufacture of goods. Whether or not the selectivity requirement was met here, was the subject of a diverging opinion by the Advocate-General and Court. According to the Advocate-General the main question in this regard was whether the rebate amounted to a derogation from the standard application of the system. The Commission, having set out the Court's standard case law with regard to rebates from taxation and social security schemes, considered this to be the case. Advocate-General Mischo, however, did not consider there to be a derogation from the general rule. Citing the Danish and Austrian governments, he contends that the Austrian scheme amounts to a new general ecology tax which, from its outset on, followed the principle that the primary and secondary sectors of the economy should not be disproportionately taxed.[68] Mischo considers that the Austrian eco-tax is based on objective criteria and does not leave any discretion to the administration as regards the rebate. Therefore, he concludes that the scheme in its totality, rebates and all, constitutes the normal legal situation so that there cannot be said to be a derogation. The Commission relies

---

[66] Case C-143/99, *Adria-Wien*, [2001] ECR I-8365. The UK government argued along the same lines in the case concerning the UK Climate change levy, C 18/2001, OJ 2001 C 185/22, at p. 23.

[67] *Ibid.*, para. 33-36, Opinion of A-G Mischo, paras. 27-31.

[68] *Ibid.*, Opinion of A-G Mischo, para. 42.

on the Court's judgment in *Maribel bis/ter*[69] to come to the conclusion that the mere fact that a scheme applies to a large number of diverse industries does not make it a general scheme.[70] The Advocate-General recognises the Commission's point in this respect but goes on to hold that, in his mind, the rebates still do not constitute a derogation from the normal rules. He does this by pointing to the proposed directive for the taxation of energy products. According to Mischo, the Commission's involvement in this proposal shows that the Commission accepts that not all undertakings should be taxed an equal amount under an eco-taxation scheme.[71] However, he immediately recognises that the criterion adopted by the Commission in its proposal does not distinguish between different sectors of industry but rather turns on the energy consumption of an individual firm. Nevertheless, the Advocate-General is of the opinion that the criterion for a rebate adopted in the Austrian taxation scheme is valid and does not constitute a derogation.[72] In this respect, and not so much in connection with the selectivity requirement, the Advocate-General goes on to consider that a distortion of competition or an effect on intra-community trade do no seem very likely in view of the fact that the tax amounts to only 0.35per cent of the net production value.[73]

The Court, however, did consider the tax rebate for firms that primarily produce goods as a derogation. To come to this conclusion the Court first repeated its standard case law according to which any advantage provided by the state can constitute a state aid.[74] After that the Court focuses the attention on the issue of selectivity and repeats the arguments brought forward by the Danish and Austrian authorities.[75] The Court first repeats its reasoning from the *Maribel bis/ter* case. Secondly, the Court notes the fact that a justification for the difference in treatment for firms that are primarily active in the production of goods is nowhere to be found in the Austrian legislation. The Court concludes by stating that[76]

*'[...] the ecological considerations underlying the national legislation at issue do not justify treating the consumption of natural gas or electricity by undertakings supplying services differently than the consumption of such energy by undertakings manufacturing goods. Energy consumption by each of those sectors is equally damaging to the environment.*

---

69 Case C-75/97, *Belgium* v. *Commission* (Maribel bis/ter), [1999] ECR I-3671.

70 Case C-143/99, *Adria-Wien*, [2001] ECR I-8365, Opinion of A-G Mischo, paras. 45-47.

71 *Ibid.*, Opinion of A-G Mischo, paras. 53-56.

72 *Ibid.*, Opinion of A-G Mischo, para. 61.

73 *Ibid.*, Opinion of A-G Mischo, paras. 65-80.

74 *Ibid.*, paras. 38-41.

75 *Ibid.*, paras. 43-47.

76 *Ibid.*, paras. 52 & 53.

*It follows from the foregoing considerations that, although objective, the criterion applied by the national legislation at issue is not justified by the nature or general scheme of that legislation, so that it cannot save the measure at issue from being in the nature of State aid.'*

The conclusion must therefore be that objective criteria for a rebates or exemptions, even when they do not leave any discretionary room for authorities, will not suffice to take such rebates or exemptions ousted the scope of Article 87(1). For this to occur such criteria must be justified by the nature or general scheme of the legislation.

However, the ill fate that thus befell the Austrian eco-taxation scheme should not have to bleaken the prospects for tax differentiation in other eco-taxation schemes. Indeed, the Court's *obiter dictum* shows that it considers that the rebates were actually intended to preserve the competitiveness of the Austrian *vis a vis* its European competitors.[77] If the Court has identified this as the rationale, then its reluctance to allow this measure to fall outside the scope of Article 87 is perfectly understandable. As was mentioned above, this ruling does not rule out tax differentiation in eco-taxation schemes completely.

Consider, for example, an eco-taxation scheme that taxes energy use but where a rebate is granted for gas appliances that emit less carbon dioxide. It is submitted that such a tax would be justified, in the Courts words, 'by the nature of the legislation'. Even though an advantage would be granted, it would follow from the general nature of the system, which is to encourage environmental protection and therefore not constitute state aid. The Court's case law therefore starts to remind one of the 'inherent restrictions-approach' that can be identified in other areas of Community law as well.[78]

### 13.2.5 Affecting intra-community trade

Pursuant to the fifth element, trade between member states must be affected. Above, we have seen that the court will demand some market analysis from the Commission in order to show that competition was or is likely to be distorted. With regard to the connected requirement of an effect on intra-community trade, the Court has adopted an approach the logic of which seems reminiscent of that in the *VCH* case. According to the Court state aid will readily affect intra-community trade because:[79]

---

77 *Ibid.*, para. 54.

78 Joined Cases C-51/96 and C-191/97, *Christelle Deliège* v. *Ligue Francophone de Judo et Disciplines Associées ASBL et al.* (Deliège) [200] ECR I-2549, para. 69. See further, *supra*, paragraph 8.4.2.4.

79 Case 730/79, *Phillip Morris* v. *Commission*, [1980] ECR 2671, para. 11.

*'When state aid strengthens the position of an undertaking compared with other undertakings competing in intra-community trade the latter must be regarded as affected by that aid.'*

This type of per *se* reasoning by the Court seems can still be seen in the Court's case law. In the *Adria-Wien* case, the Advocate-General explicitly doubted whether the measure in question, given that it amounted to 0.35 per cent of the net value only, could possibly distort competition or affect trade between member states. The Court did not address the issue but simply came to the conclusion that the measure constituted a state aid within the meaning of Article 87(1). This ruling shows that the Court still has not adopted a *de minimis* rule with regard to Article 87.[80]

What then, are we to think of the fact that the Commission has a long-standing policy in this field and, moreover, the fact that the Commission has recently issued a *de minimis* Regulation?[81] The *De minimis* Regulation was adopted pursuant to Article 2 of the so-called Enabling Regulation[82] that was itself adopted on the basis of Article 89 EC. According to Article 89, the Council may lay down appropriate regulations for the application of Articles 87 and 88 EC. Therefore, it can now be said the *De minimis* Regulation now has a clear legal basis.

If all the five requirements of Article 87(1) are fulfilled, a measure will constitute state aid and be considered 'incompatible with the common market'. However, as with any prohibition in the Treaty, there are also exceptions to the incompatibility with the common market prescribed in Article 87(1). These are to be found in the second and third paragraph of Article 87.

## 13.3 Exempted and exemptible aid – Article 87(2) and (3)

Even if a measure constitutes an aid within the meaning of Article 87 all is not lost since Article 87(2) and (3) contain a number of types of aid that are compatible or may be considered to be compatible with the common market. The difference between compatibility in the second paragraph and the fact that the third paragraph speaks of 'may be considered to be compatible' denotes an important difference with regard to the discretion that the Commission has in applying the two paragraphs. With regard to the second paragraph, the Commission can, basically, only decide whether or not a state measure falls within the wording of one three types of state aid mentioned there. If this is the

80 *Cf.* Hancher, Ottervanger & Slot 1999, p. 38.

81 Commission Regulation 69/2001, *De Minimis*, OJ 2000 L 10/30.

82 Regulation 6994/98 On the Application of Articles 92 and 93 of the Treaty Establishing the European Community to Certain Categories of Horizontal State Aid, OJ 1998 L 142/1.

case, the measure shall be compatible with no room for discretion on the part of the Commission. With regard to the third paragraph things are different in that the Commission has a wide margin of discretion in deciding whether or not one of the four exemptions listed there indeed applies to a state aid scheme.[83] Below, we shall look closer at the exemption for aid having a social character (Article 87(2)(a)) and aid granted to compensate the damage caused by natural disasters (Article 87(2)(b)) because these may be applicable in an environmental context. With regard to the second paragraph, we will not consider the exemption for aid granted to certain areas of Germany affected by the division of the Country (Article 87(2)(c) for the simple reason that, following the reunification of Germany, this provision has lost much of its meaning.[84] For similar reasons we shall only be addressing the 'European interest exemption' (Article 87(3)(b)) and sectoral aid exemption (Article 87(3)(c)) of the four types of exemption listed in the third paragraph. Pursuant to Article 87(3)(e), the Council may exempt other forms of aid. As this provision has seen only very limited use to this day and it is not foreseeable that it will be used in an environmental context, we will not look at this provision.[85]

### 13.3.1 Aid having a social character – Article 87(2)(a)

With regard to Article 87(2)(a) there is precious little case law.[86] To our knowledge this provision has, to this date, been invoked only once in a case before the Court. In that case, *Benedetti* v. *Munari*, the Court was unable to address the issue in great depth because the referring judge had neglected to provide the necessary details.[87] Similarly, Advocate-General Reischl made only a few fairly general comments on the issue in that case. It has been considered on the basis of *Benedetti* v. *Munari* that Article 87(2)(a) requires that the aid must benefit the consumers and not the firms that supply the consumers.[88] It is submitted that this already follows from the clear wording of Article 87(2)(a) whereas the judgment is not particularly conducive in this respect.

Pivotal to this provision is the concept of 'aid having a social character'. We would submit that the word 'social' relates only to the fact that the aid must be granted to individual consumers and does not serve to indicate or limit the scope

83 Case T-55/99, *Plan Renove Industrial*, [2000] ECR II-3207, paras. 109 & 110.

84 *Cf.* Hancher, Ottervanger & Slot 1999, p. 70-72. See Case C-159/98, *Germany* v. *Commission*, [2000] ECR I-6857, paras. 46-57.

85 See, with regard to Article 87(3)(e): Hancher, Ottervanger & Slot 1999, p. 80.

86 As is evidenced by the fact that Hancher, Ottervanger & Slot devote less than a page to it, Hancher, Ottervanger & Slot 1999, p. 70. In similar vain D'sa takes one page to address this provision, D'Sa 1998, p. 129.

87 Case 52/76, *Luigi Benedetti* v. *Munari Filli* (Benedetti v. Munari), [1977] ECR 163, para. 19.

88 Hancher, Ottervanger & Slot 1999, p. 70.

of the objectives of the aid measures. Thus, it relates more to the means than to objectives of the national measures. Environmental goals will therefore not take a state aid outside the scope of this provision as is evidenced by the Commission's practice with regard to this provision.

The only proviso with regard to Article 87(2)(a) is that such must be granted without discrimination as to origin of the products concerned. The Commission has applied this proviso in two early decisions concerning a Dutch and a German scheme designed to lower the costs of flour.[89] According to the Commission, the schemes at hand were aimed at increasing the consumption of nationally produced flour and therefore fell foul of Article 87(2)(a).

However, despite its relative obscurity in the Court's case law, the Commission has used Article 87(2)(a) in a number of environmental cases. In the German *Catalytic converter* case, the scheme at hand gave a tax exemption to consumers that bought cars with catalytic converters. This tax reduction was aimed to make purchase of such a car more attractive and thereby encourage environmental protection. The Commission was of the opinion that this measure qualified under Article 87(2)(a) provided that it did not result in discrimination contrary to Article 28 EC.[90]

In its XXIVth Competition Report the Commission paid closer attention to the concept of discrimination. The Commission comes to the conclusion that is should be taken to mean that there may be no discrimination as to the origin of the supplier rather than that there should not be any distinction between the product for which the aid is given and competing products.[91]

In such a case it may be wondered whether there is a state aid in the first place. If the term 'individual consumers' is taken to exclude individuals that perform an economic activity (*i.e.* one-man undertakings), then it is hard to see any advantage being granted to a specific firm. This would appear to be the stance taken by the Commission in its 1994 Guidelines on State Aid for Environmental Protection (1994 Guidelines).[92] In paragraph 3.5 of these Guidelines the Commission states that measures that encourage the purchase of environmentally friendly products will not constitute aid in the first place because they do not confer a 'tangible financial benefit' upon one or more undertakings.

89 Commission Decision 67/217, OJ 1967, 1275 and Decision 67/218, OJ 1967, 1277.

90 Hancher, Ottervanger & Slot 1999, p. 70.

91 Commission XXIVth. Competition Report (1994), para. 354 (p. 170).

92 Commission Community guidelines on State aid for environmental protection (1994 Guidelines), OJ 1994 C 72/3.

### 13.3.2 Aid to compensate damage caused by natural disasters – Article 87(2)(b)

It may be doubted whether Article 87(2)(b) can in the first place be used to grant environmental aid. It is submitted that as such this is not the case. The wording of this provision makes it clear beyond doubt that only the aid to make good the damage caused by natural disasters or exceptional circumstances can fall within Article 87(2)(b).[93] All aid that serves another objective, such as to further develop a region after it has been struck by a natural disaster will fall outside its scope. Similarly, aid to prevent the (re) occurrence of a natural disaster will probably fall outside the scope of Article 87(2)(b).

Therefore, the importance of the exemption for natural disasters for the environmental context is limited at best. Environmental considerations may even play a negative role in this respect. Consider, for example, flooding as a natural disaster.[94] It is common ground that many floods are at least partly the result of extensive alterations of the environment in the upstream regions of rivers. Excessive logging and the development of entire mountain ranges into ski slopes, for example, will greatly reduce the capacity of these mountainsides to absorb water and hence increase the risk of floods in downstream areas. A correct application of the polluter pays principle would mean that the costs resulting from floods should, save faults by the downstream authorities, be borne by the persons responsible for the alteration of the upstream environment. It is recognised that this approach is not devoid of practical problems. However, the Water Framework Directive with its river basin management approach may be helpful in this respect.[95]

### 13.3.3 Aid for important projects of common European interest – Article 87(3)(b)

Of the two objectives for aid schemes mentioned in Article 87(3)(b), we will only be paying attention to aid that is granted 'to promote the execution of an important project of common European interest'. Certainly, answering the question whether a project is important or not involves great deal of discretion and therefore we will leave this issue as it is.

A second question is what constitutes a project of 'common European interest'. The fact that a project needs to be of *common European* interest indi-

---

93 See for a list of examples of such disasters: Community Guidelines for State aid in the agriculture sector, OJ 2000 C 28/2, section 11.2.2 at p. 14.

94 See Commission decision of 7-5-1999 in case N 28/99 concerning a Belgian scheme to make good the damage caused by flooding in September 1998.

95 Directive 2000/60 Establishing a framework for Community action in the field of water policy, OJ 2000 L327/1.

cates that it has to be transnational in nature. This can be so because several member states are involved in it or because the project addresses a transnational problem. Of course, this is where environmental protection enters the picture since the environment and its protection are typically transboundary affairs.

This view has been confirmed in the *Glaverbel* case.[96] This case concerned a Belgian scheme according to which investment aid would be granted to a Belgian glass producer, Glaverbel, for the improvement of a production line. As a result of these improvements, energy use and working condition would be ameliorated. This case arose from an action for annulment of the Commission's decision prohibiting the implementation of the aid scheme. The applicants based their case in part in the fact that the aid would promote an important project of common European interest since Glaverbel participated in an ESPRIT project concerning the design of thin-layer photovoltaic cells.[97] The Commission considered in its decision that[98]

*'A project may not be described as being of common European interest for the purposes of Article [87(3)(b)] unless it forms part of a transnational European programme supported jointly by a number of governments of the member states, or arises from concerted action by a number of member states to combat a common threat such as environmental pollution'.*

The Court was of the opinion that the Commission had not committed a manifest error of assessment in adopting this policy. How, then are we to understand the Commission's refusal to allow aid to be granted to Glaverbel who participated in a joint European project that was meant to combat a common threat? To answer this question we will probably have to look at the facts of the case. The Advocate-General qualifies the reasoning employed by Glaverbel to show that it could qualify for the common European interest exemption, as terse.[99] Indeed, the connection between the aid and the improvement of the environmental situation through a transnational action does not, to say the least, immediately become clear. Moreover, as far as the Court was concerned, the only result of the Belgian aid measure would be to enable the use of a new production method, which in itself was insufficient for the measure to fulfil the criteria for an exemption pursuant to Article 87(3)(b). The Court considered this to be all the more so if, as was the case, the products would have to be sold on a saturated market.[100]

---

96 Joined Cases 62/87 & 72/87, *Exécutif Régional Wallon and SA Glaverbel* v. *Commission* (Glaverbel), [1988] ECR 1573.

97 *Ibid.*, para. 20.

98 *Ibid.*, para. 22.

99 *Ibid.*, Opinion of A-G Lenz, para. 34.

100 *Ibid.*, para. 25.

## 13.4 The Guidelines on state aid for environmental protection

When, in the 1970's, the Commission was faced with the increasing use of environmental subsidies, the Commission considered it necessary to provide some guidance as to its position on the role of environmental concerns in the rules on state aid.[101] The Commission appears to have always done this from the twofold perspective of the polluter pays principle and the need to ensure undistorted competition.[102] In Part I of this research we have already addressed the general issues arising from the trilateral relation between the polluter pays principle, distortions of competition and environmental protection. With regard to state aids the following can be said. As the Commission saw it and still sees it, the end-situation should be one where the polluter pays principle is fully applied and all environmental costs are completely internalised. State aids run directly counter to this internalisation by transferring part of the environmental costs. The Commission thus recognised the importance of regulating environmental aids from both an environmental and a competition point of view.

This recognition resulted in nine paragraphs in the Fourth Annual Competition Report (1974) in which the Commission set out its stance with regard to environmental subsidies.[103] Back then, the Commission optimistically considered a transitional period of six years, *i.e.* until 31 December 1980, sufficient to ensure the full implementation of the polluter pays principle while at the same time recognising the enormous changes that would have to take place throughout society.[104] The Commission thus distinguished between, on the one hand, its stance towards environmental aid during the transitional period and, on the other hand, its policy with regard to such aid granted after the transitional period or during the transitional period but not fulfilling the requirements (the so-called general principles). According to the Commission, during the transitional period, state aid would qualify for an exemption under Article 87(3)(b) EC as aid necessary for the execution of 'important projects of common European interest' provided that three requirements were fulfilled.[105] Firstly, the aid would have to be necessitated by new major obligations relating to environmental protection. Secondly, the aid would have to be granted for the financing of additional investments in plants already in operation. Thirdly, the Commission specified a degressive maximum aid percentage (45 per cent in the years 1975-1976, 30 per cent in the years 1977-1978 and 15 per cent in the years 1979-1980).

---

101 This section is based on an Article that appeared in the (2001) *ECLR* 365-373.

102 Commission, IVth. Competition Report (1974), para. 176.

103 *Ibid.*, paras. 176-183.

104 *Ibid.*, paras 178 & 181.

105 *Ibid.*, para. 181.

Interestingly, the Commission has thus only specified a framework for the assessment of environmental investment aid. Operating aid granted because of environmental considerations is therefore outside the scope of these guidelines.

For environmental aid exceeding the limits set out above, the Commission provided the Member States with principles of general application.[106] Again, the Commission only addresses the issue of investment aid. The basic tenor of these general principles is one according to which environmental aid exceeding the limits of the guidelines is to be granted even more sparsely. Basically, such aid is only to be granted in cases where sudden major changes in environmental obligations are of such a magnitude that going concerns are faced with difficulties that would threaten the equilibrium in a certain region or industry. Importantly, these general principles allow for an exception to this strict rule in situations where international competition was such as seriously to handicap the firms that would have to abide to the new environmental standards.[107] Such aid would qualify for an exemption pursuant to Article 87(3)(a) or (c).[108]

In 1980 the Commission's assertion that a six-year transitional period should suffice to implement the polluter pays principle was indeed proven to have been overly optimistic. The economic recession that had set in just after 1974 and the fact that harmonisation of environmental legislation on a European level proceeded not as fast as had been hoped, forced the Commission into an additional transitional period.[109] Accordingly, environmental aids would be allowed for another six-year transitional period this time until 31 December 1986. Such aids were exempted under Article 87(3)(b) provided that they were for investments aimed at the implementation of new environmental standards, did not exceed 15 per cent and were granted only for the adaptation of plants already in operation for two years before the entry into force of the new standards.[110] Furthermore, the Commission specified a reporting obligation. The Guidelines remained silent with regard to environmental operating aids.

Finally, in 1986 the Commission realised that its transitional approach was no longer warranted.[111] The need to protect the environment as well as the need to avoid distortions of competition was there to stay. The criteria set out in the 1980 Guidelines were to be applied for the period of the Fourth Environmental Action Programme until 1992. However, the Commission reserved the right to alter its stance with regard to environmental aids on the basis of the outcomes of a review of the application of the polluter pays principle. Following two temporary prolongations of the 1980 Guidelines, 1994 saw the publication of a new set of guidelines.

---

[106] *Ibid.*, para. 182.

[107] *Ibid.* at p. 105.

[108] The Commission stated this only in the Xth. Competition Report (1980), para. 223.

[109] Commission, Xth. Competition Report (1980), para. 224.

[110] *Ibid.*, para. 226.

[111] Commission, XVIth. Competition Report (1986), para. 259.

A first striking feature when comparing the 1994 Guidelines with the previous guidelines is the much more comprehensive character of the former.[112] For the first time, the Commission gave its opinion not only on investment aids but also on environmental operating aids and horizontal measures. All in all, the rules governing environmental aids appeared to have become much more precise which should not come as a surprise since the Commission has gained quite a lot more experience in the mean time. Generally, the 1994 Guidelines allowed for 15 per cent investment aid for adaptation to new standards for all existing firms. Firms undertaking environmental protection in the absence of Community measures or going beyond what is required could be granted 30 per cent investment aid. With regard to operating aid, the Guidelines did not provide much guidance other than indicating the Commission's general stance that such aids will not easily be exempted. More specifically no rate or period over which aid could be granted, was indicated. The legal basis for the exemptions was changed from Article 87(3)(b) into 87(3)(c) as the Commission considered environmental aid as 'aid to facilitate the development of certain activities [...] where such aid does not adversely affect trading conditions to an extent contrary to the common interest'.[113] However, the Commission explicitly allowed for the possibility of exempting state aid schemes at higher rates that contribute to important projects of common European interest.[114]

The 1994 Guidelines were to be reviewed in 1996. This review has not resulted in any changes. According to paragraph 4.3 the Guidelines were to expire on 31 December 1999. On 22 December 1999 their validity was extended until 30 June 2000. This half-year, however, proved insufficient and on 28 June 2000 a further extension was granted until 31 December 2000.

In the meantime, the Environment Council provided an interesting insight into the dynamics involved in drafting such Guidelines. The conclusions of the 2278th. and 2295th. meeting of the environment council both contained a paragraph basically stating that the Commission had to take more account of (national) environmental considerations.[115] Interestingly, the Commission at one point considered 1 January 2001 a feasible date for the new Guidelines to enter into force[116] whereas later on the date of 1 July 2001 was named.[117]

---

[112] Commission, Community guidelines on State aid for environmental protection (1994 Guidelines), OJ 1994 C 72/1.

[113] *Ibid.*, para. 3.6.

[114] *Ibid.*, para. 3.7.

[115] To be found on the internet: < http://ue.eu.int/newsroom/>.

[116] Conclusions of the 2278th. Environment Council meeting, to be found on the internet: < http: //ue.eu.int/newsroom/>.

[117] Answer by Monti to written question P-0441/00 by Breyer, OJ 2000 C 303E/194.

Moreover, in 1998 the Council adopted Regulation 994/98 enabling the Commission to adopt group exemption regulations in the field of state aids.[118] Interestingly, Article 1(1) sub (a) under (iii) explicitly allowed for a Commission group exemption regulation for state aids in the field of environmental protection. Particularly in the light of this explicit reference in the enabling Regulation it could be wondered whether the delays were caused by difficulties encountered in drafting such a regulation.[119] February 2001, however, saw the publication of Guidelines instead of a group exemption regulation. Why the Commission's (extensive) experience with environmental aids did not result in the adoption of a group exemption regulation[120] is somewhat obscure. A good guess would seem to be the dynamic nature of the matter involved. The environment, and as a result, environmental protection has not stopped providing us with new challenges. The 2001 Environmental aid Guidelines, for example, devote considerable attention to carbon dioxide reductions in the wake of the Kyoto Protocol.[121] Climate change as an environmental problem was still largely unknown in 1994. In this respect it can be doubted whether a group exemption will ever be the right tool.

## 13.5 The 2001 Environmental aid Guidelines

When looking at the 2001 Environmental aid Guidelines themselves, a first impression is that they have become even more precise and encompassing than the 1994 Guidelines. In a total of 11 chapters (numbered A-K) and 12 pages and one annex the Commission gives guidance with regard to environmental state aids. Below, we will analyse the 2001 Environmental aid Guidelines chapter by chapter.

### 13.5.1 Introductory chapters

In an introduction (chapter A) the two main principles vis a vis environmental aids are set out. On the one hand, the integration principle laid down in Article 6 EC according to which environmental considerations must be

---

[118] Regulation No. 994/98 on the application of Articles 92 and 93 of the Treaty establishing the European Community to certain categories of horizontal state aid, OJ 1998 L 142/1.

[119] See: Jans, Sevenster & Vedder 2000, p. 416 *et seq.*

[120] when such regulations have in the meantime been enacted for Training aid (Regulation 68/2001, OJ 2001 L 10/20), *De Minimis* aid (Regulation 69/2001, OJ 2001 L 10/30) and SME aid (Regulation 70/2001, OJ 2001 L 10/33).

[121] Communication from the Commission on EU policies and measures to reduce greenhouse gas emissions: Towards a European Climate Change Programme (ECCP), COM (2000)88.

integrated into the Commissions policy on state aids, and, on the other hand, the polluter pays principle. On the basis of these two principles the Commission comes to the conclusion that environmental aids may only be allowed where they are necessary to bring about environmental protection and sustainable development without having disproportionate effects on competition and economic growth.[122] This last addition, that the aid should not have a disproportionate effect on economic growth, is somewhat odd and appears to be new when compared with the 1994 Guidelines.

In the third chapter (C), this general policy brief is further substantiated. Again the integration and polluter pays principles are abundantly (and, it might be added, not always that clearly) referred to. The bottom line, however, is that whereas the granting of state aids is at odds with the polluter pays principle, such aid may nonetheless be justified in two instances. Firstly, where not all costs can be internalised and the aid is therefore to be seen as a temporary second-best solution on the ground that it provides an incentive for firms to adapt to standards. Secondly, aids may be used as incentive for firms to protect the environment either in the absence of standards, or to go beyond what is required by standards. However, since 1994 much has changed and the Commission no longer considers that the granting of aid can be justified by the absence of internalisation. In practice, this comes down to a prohibition of aids granted for investments that merely aim at facilitating firms to comply with new or existing standards (with an exception for SMEs). Aids encouraging firms to go further than Community standards may of course still be granted. With regard to the energy sector the Commission sets out its approach in a special paragraph. In this paragraph some attention is devoted to the problem of reductions or exemptions in eco-taxation schemes. Such reductions constitute operating aid but may be considered necessary for the acceptability and thus adoption or continuation of eco-taxation schemes. Subject to certain conditions exemptions or reductions in eco-taxation schemes may be allowed for a period of 10 years.[123] Furthermore, the Commission reiterates its positive stance with regard to measures to promote renewable energy and the combined production of heat and energy.[124]

The second chapter (B) contains the definitions and sets out the scope of the Guidelines. The definitions generally sound familiar in their wide-ranging wording. An interesting example of a 'dynamic reference' may be found in the definition of renewable energy sources. This definition is linked to that in a Commission proposal for a directive.[125] As regards the scope, there are a number

---

[122] 2001 Environmental aid Guidelines, OJ 2001 C 37/3, para. 5.

[123] *Ibid.*, para. 23.

[124] *Ibid.*, para. 24.

[125] *Ibid.*, footnote 7.

of changes compared with the 1994 Guidelines. Whereas aid for environmental training fell within the scope of the 1994 Guidelines, the 2001 Environmental aid Guidelines do not apply to such aid.[126] The 1994 Guidelines still apply to the steel industry. This is the result of the reference in Article 3 of Decision 2496/96/ECSC (the Sixth Steel Aid Code). Paradoxically, the Sixth Steel Aid Code was intended to bring the regime for the steel sector more into line with that for the other sectors of the economy.[127] For the moment, however, the result appears to be exactly the opposite. It is expected that the 2001 Environmental aid Guidelines will apply from the expiry of the ECSC Treaty (on 22 July 2002) onwards.

Chapter E contains the general conditions for authorising environmental aid. Reminiscent of the 1994 Guidelines, the Commission has divided its policy in three areas: investment aid, aid for horizontal measures and operating aid.

### 13.5.2 Investment aid

With regard to investment aids (paragraph E.1), the notion of 'eligible costs' is particularly important as the aid intensity for investment aid is described as a percentage of these costs.[128] Eligible costs, according to paragraph 37 of the Guidelines, need to be strictly confined to the extra investment costs necessary to reach the environmental goals. This is particularly important in those cases where the investment will result not only in improved environmental protection but also in an increase in production. In that case, the benefits that result from the increase in production capacity, cost savings during five years following the investment and additional ancillary production will have to be detracted from the eligible costs. With regard to the use of renewable energy, eligible costs are those extra costs compared to the situation where it would have used conventionally produced energy. Logically, eligible costs for investments going beyond Community standards will not include the costs for complying with these standards. Moreover, such investments must lead to actual improvements in the environmental performance and not just constitute general investments that any responsible company should do. In, for example, the *Hoffmann-La Roche (Orlistat)* case the Austrian government argued that aid for pharmaceutical giant Hoffmann-La Roche was in conformity with the 1994 Guidelines.[129] This aid was granted for, firstly, measures aiming to reduce the risk of accidents and the effects of such accidents and, secondly, measures aiming to reduce emissions to the air and water.[130] The Commission, however,

[126] *Ibid.*, para. 7.

[127] *Cf.* Hancher, Ottervanger & Slot 1999, p. 189.

[128] *E.g.*, under the 1994 Guidelines, Commission Decision 2000/17, *Nerefco*, OJ 2000 L 6/46, paras. 33-40.

[129] Commission Decision 98/251, *Hoffmann-La Roche* (Orlistat), OJ 1998 L 103/28.

[130] *Ibid.*, on p. 33.

only considered the aid for measures to combat water and air pollution to be justified on the basis of the Guidelines. The aid that was granted with a view to reducing the risk of a serious accident was considered to be general investment.[131]

| **Type of aid** | **Basic rate** | **Bonus** | **Special remarks** |
|---|---|---|---|
| Adaptation of SMEs to new standards | 15 % | | Only for three years following adoption of new standards |
| - Improve on Community standards<br>- Investments in absence of Community standards<br>- Investments to comply with national standards going beyond Community standards | 30 % | +10 % for SMEs | |
| Energy saving measures | 40 % | + 10 % for SMEs | |
| Combined production of heat and electricity | 40 % | + 10 % for SMEs | |
| Promotion of renewable sources of energy | 40 % | +10 % when they serve the needs of an entire Community<br>+ 10 % for SMEs | Up to 100 % can allowed in which case no further aid may be granted |
| Land rehabilitation | 100 %, plus 15 % of the cost of the work | | If identifiable and able to bear the costs, the polluter should pay and no aid may be granted |
| Relocation of firms | 30 % | +10 % for SMEs | - Only when relocating from an urban area or Natura 2000 where the activity was lawfully carried out,<br>- the relocation was ordered by a public authority on environmental grounds, and the strictest standards apply in the new location |

131 *Ibid.*, pp. 34 & 35.

On top of the aid intensities shown in the table above, an extra bonus for assisted regions is allowed. In these regions the maximum aid intensity is either the rate (including bonuses identified above) following from the table plus an extra 5 per cent for 'Article 87(3)(c)-regions' or an extra 10 per cent for 'Article 87(3)(a)-regions' or, if this is higher, the regional aid rate plus 10 per cent.

A number of interesting things may be noted with regard to the framework set out above. Firstly, with regard to the possibility of granting aid to SMEs for the adaptation to new Community standards it may be interesting to note that reference is made to the date of adoption of new Community standards. Taking into account the fact that the overwhelming majority of European environmental standards is laid down in the form of directives, use of the date of adoption as reference date would appear problematic. The date of adoption invariably is earlier than the date of publication and, *a fortiori*, the date of entry into force. Moreover, the deadline for implementation of Directives is likely to be even later. As a result, SMEs may receive aid for the adaptation to standards that have not been transposed in national law or that may not even have entered into force.[132] Furthermore, the result of this would seem to be that SMEs have to pay even greater attention to the activities of 'Brussels', a task for which they would generally seem to be ill-equipped. Secondly, the Kyoto Protocol has certainly resulted in a very favourable position of the Commission with regard to energy related investments. However, only renewable energy installations that serve the need of an entire community qualify for an extra 10 per cent bonus. Installations for the combined production of power and heat, on the contrary, seem unable to qualify for such a bonus. Irrespective of this, all the bonuses can add up quite nicely and, interestingly, it may be wondered what the maximum aid intensity would be for an SME running an installation for the combined production of heat and power using renewable sources of energy while serving the needs of an entire community in an assisted region (an altogether no so improbable combination). Thirdly, the Guidelines provide clear and (relatively) unambiguous guidance in cases concerning land rehabilitation and plant relocation. This is most certainly a step forward compared with the Commission's essentially case-by-case approach in this respect under the 1994 Guidelines. Above, we have noted that in cases where the person responsible for the pollution cannot be identified or held responsible, government funding for the rehabilitation may not constitute aid in the first place. In the 2001 Environmental aid Guidelines, the Commission appears to have taken another approach and considers that such funding will constitute state aid. However, as the Commission allows 100 per cent of the eligible costs plus 15 per cent of the costs of the work to be funded, the diffe-

[132] See, for example, Article 6 of the proposal for a directive on waste electronical and electrical equipment, OJ 2000 C 365E/184 which lists 31 December 2005 as the date by which certain recovery targets must have been met by producers.

rence is primarily a procedural one. The aid will be allowed just as it would be in cases where the polluter could not be held responsible, but the authorities will have to notify the aid. Of particular practical importance is the fact that the Commission leaves the decision on whether or not persons are responsible for the pollution, to the national legislature and judiciary.[133] Thus, the Guidelines leave ample scope for serious distortions of competition through differences in regimes according to which polluters can be held responsible.[134]

With regard to energy related investments (energy saving, combined production and renewable energy) the Commission's policy has also become clearer. Investment aid in these areas is now subject to clear rules whereas under the 1994 Guidelines such aid was treated under the category of investments exceeding standards or where no standards exist.[135] Finally, under the 2001 Environmental aid Guidelines only SMEs can qualify for investment aid for adapting to compulsory standards whereas under the 1994 Guidelines large firms could qualify as well.

### 13.5.3 Aid for horizontal measures

The chapter on aid for horizontal measures (paragraph E.2) has become substantially more concise compared to the 1994 Guidelines. The basic approach in the 1994 Guidelines, however, was that such measures do not constitute aid in the first place. Despite this considerable narrowing of the chapter on aid for horizontal measures, SMEs are still in for a treat. According to the Commission 'advisory/consultancy services play an important part in helping SMEs to make progress in environmental protection'.[136] On this ground, aid may be granted in accordance with Regulation 70/2001.[137] All European SMEs are therefore well advised to get some consultancy service in order to stay up to date with the environmental developments in Europe.[138]

---

[133] 2001 Environmental aid Guidelines, OJ 2001 C 37/3, para. 38, where it is stated that 'By 'person responsible for the pollution' is meant the person liable under the law applicable in each Member State [...]'.

[134] See further: Wilt 2002, p. 31 *et seq.* and Commission proposal for a Directive on environmental liability with regard to the prevention and remedying of environmental damage, COM (2002) 17 final.

[135] See. For example, Commission Decision in case N 114/2000, *France – Régime d'aides `a la gestion des énergies renouvables*, to be found in the State Aid Register, <http://europa.eu.int/comm/competition/state_aid/register/>

[136] 2001 Environmental aid Guidelines, OJ 2001 C 37/3, para. 41.

[137] Reg. 70/2001 on the application of Articles 87 and 88 of the EC Treaty to state aid for small and medium-sized enterprises, OJ 2001 L 10/33.

[138] See above, with regard to investment aid for SMEs.

### 13.5.4 Operating aid

Operating aid (paragraph E.3) represents in many respects the most interesting category of aid because of its almost *per se* prohibited nature.[139] Since the adoption of the 1994 Guidelines, the Commission has been confronted with a number of eco-taxation schemes where operating aid was granted through reductions or exemptions from eco-taxes. Furthermore, numerous schemes granting operating aid for renewable energy sources have come along since then. The experience gathered with these cases is now laid down in the Guidelines.

The Commission deals firstly with operating aid for waste management and energy saving.[140] Operating aid is allowed only where it is shown to be absolutely necessary. Moreover, it should be limited to the extra production costs when compared to market prices. Finally the aid should be temporary and, in principle, degressive. Operating aid for the management of industrial waste may only be granted where the national standards abided by are more stringent than Community standards or where no Community standards exist so that the competitive position is jeopardised. Apparently, operating aid may not be granted for firms voluntarily going beyond what is required by national or Community standards. The fact that the majority of the more detailed rules in this paragraph concern aid for waste management whereas aid for energy saving is left in the dark, perhaps signals a conceptual difficulty encountered by this reader. Energy saving would, generally, seem to involve measures targeting the loss of energy during a process (by adding extra insulation) or measures aimed at making the whole process more energy efficient (by, for example, lowering the temperature at which process takes place). Such measures would seem to 'pay themselves back' because of the lower energy consumption. In this respect, investment aid for the extra investments in the form of extra insulation seems perfectly understandable. Operating aid, however, is different story altogether. If a new, more energy efficient, installation indeed involves higher operating costs, then it may be wondered what these costs are made up of? If these involve, for example, more or different raw materials or more personnel, shouldn't the environmental impact of these factors be taken into account in determining the net environmental benefit? The Commission could certainly have provided a bit more guidance on this point. In any case, the bottom line is that operating aid may be granted for five years only and in a 'degressive' and a 'non-degressive' manner. In the case of degressive aid, the intensity should drop from 100 per cent to zero in a linear fashion over five years whereas the non-degressive variant allows for a 50 per cent aid throughout the five-year period.[141]

---

[139] Case C-288/96, *Germany* v. *Commission*, 2000 [ECR] I-8237, paras. 77 & 78

[140] 2001 Environmental aid Guidelines, OJ 2001 C 37/3, para. 42.

[141] *Ibid.*, paras. 45 and 46.

With regard to reductions or exemptions[142] from eco-taxation schemes, the Commission considers it appropriate to distinguish between national taxation schemes and those taxation schemes that have a Community origin.[143] In the case of purely national taxation schemes, temporary reductions may be allowed. In cases involving taxation schemes having a Community origin, a distinction is made between two cases.[144] Firstly, where the national taxation scheme involves rates higher than the minimum Community rates and the reduction results in a rate that is at least equal to the minimum Community rate, the temporary reduction may be allowed. Secondly, in cases where the national reduction brings the tax rate below the minimum Community rate two things may happen. Firstly, if the rate below the minimum rate prescribed by the Community taxation scheme, is not allowed by the Community scheme, the reduction will be deemed to constitute prohibited aid. Secondly, if this lower rate is allowed by the Community measure, the reduction may be considered compatible with Article 87 on strict grounds. This seems to be the aftermath of the Court's judgment in the *French Biofuels* case.[145]

On a general level, the Commission wants to ascertain that the reductions do not undermine the scheme's objectives. To this end it has formulated a number of criteria that need to be satisfied before such operating aid may be allowed. For new taxation schemes, non-degressive reductions lasting for ten years may be allowed in either of two cases. In the first case the tax reductions must be conditional on the conclusion of agreements between firms and the public authorities or voluntary agreements between firms laying down environmental protection objectives.[146] In the second case, no agreements or commitments are necessary provided that (for taxes having a Community origin) the tax level after reduction is higher than the Community minimum or (for purely national taxation schemes) the tax level results in the firms still paying 'a significant proportion of the national tax'.[147] With regard to the voluntary agreements referred to above, it may be noted that such agreements may fall within the scope of Article 81 EC.[148] Accordingly, both the tax reduction and the voluntary agreement may have to be notified to the Commission. The provisions for reductions from new taxes apply by analogy to significant increases in existing tax schemes. For existing taxation schemes, a non-degressive ten-year reduction can be allowed only when

142 Hereafter only the term 'reduction' will be used.

143 2001 Environmental aid Guidelines, OJ 2001 C 37/3, para. 47.

144 *Ibid.*, para. 49.

145 Case T-184/97, *BP Chemical* v. *Commission* (French Biofuels), [2000] ECR II-3145, paras. 62-80. See also the recent invitation to submits comments the case underlying this dispute, OJ 2001 C 60/4.

146 2001 Environmental aid Guidelines, OJ 2001 C 37/3, para. 51.1, (a).

147 *Ibid.*, para. 51.1, (b).

148 Community guidelines on horizontal agreements, OJ 2001 C 3/2, paras 185 and 189.

the scheme had an appreciable positive environmental impact and the reduction was already decided on at the time of the adoption of the tax or has since then become necessary as a result of 'a significant change in economic conditions'.[149] In relation to the latter situation, the Commission stipulates that the reduction may not exceed the increase in costs resulting from the change in economic conditions.[150] Operating aid in the form of tax reductions may also be given to installations that use conventional (*i.e.* non-renewable) energy sources to create electric power when their efficiency is 'very much higher' than that of conventional processes. Provided, of course, that there is an environmental benefit, a five-year non-degressive reduction may be granted. A ten-year reduction needs to satisfy the tests identified above in general.

Paragraph 53 of the English language version is somewhat mysterious. It concerns tax reductions in cases where the tax has *not* been harmonised in which case it of course makes no sense to stipulate that express authorisation be obtained from the Commission. However, the Dutch, French and German versions all concern the situation of a tax reduction concerning a tax that has indeed been harmonised at Community level. In that case long-term reductions resulting in a level that is equal to or lower than the Community minimum are not justified. In any case the derogation from the Community minimum needs to be expressly authorised.

These fairly complex rules have in the meantime been applied by the Commission in the case concerning the *UK Climate change levy*.[151] In that case the Commission considered the compatibility with the 2001 Environmental aid Guidelines of a number of exemptions from this levy on energy carriers (Gas, Electricity, Coal and Liquefied petroleum gas). With regard to the exemption for dual use fuels (which covers cases where the energy carrier is not used as a fuel) the Commission considered that the aid might be incompatible with the 2001 Environmental aid Guidelines. In this respect the Commission points out that the exemption benefits certain processes that give rise to considerable $CO_2$ emissions whilst the exemption is not temporary nor made conditional on the conclusion of an agreement. Finally, the Commission considered that the UK authorities had not shown that the exempted firms must nevertheless pay a significant proportion of the levy.[152]

---

149 2001 Environmental aid Guidelines, OJ 2001 C 37/3, para. 51.2.

150 Furthermore, the Commission considers that 'once there is no longer any increase in costs, the reduction must no longer apply'. Taken literally, this would seem to mean that the reduction is no longer allowed when the costs are not increasing irrespective of the fact that they may still be higher.

151 Invitation to submit comments concerning case C 18/2001, *UK Climate change levy*, OJ 2001 C 185/22. See also, with regard to the sectors governed by the ECSC Treaty: case C 19/2001, OJ 2001 C 191/3, where the Commission applied the 1991 Guidelines which continue to apply with regard to the Steel Aid Code.

152 *Ibid.*, at p. 40.

For the production of renewable energy, operating aid is allowed to cover the difference between the market price for energy and the costs for producing energy from renewable sources.[153] The Commission distinguishes four options or instruments for granting operating aid for renewable energy production.

The first option recognises that renewable energy generally requires large investments. Under the first option aid may be granted for plant depreciation to compensate the difference between the production costs of renewable energy and the market price of the power concerned. If this option is used, no aid may be granted for further energy produced but a fair return on capital is allowed.

Because of the generally smaller investments but higher running costs, biomass installations may even receive operating aid exceeding the investments provided that the total costs after depreciation are still above the market price. No limit for the duration of this type of aid is given.

Option two concerns the use of market mechanisms such as, for example, the so-called 'green certificates'. In this case, the producers of renewable energy benefit from, firstly, a guaranteed demand and, secondly, a price higher than the market price.[154] Such aid may only be granted for a period of ten years when it is necessary to ensure the viability of the production, does not result in overcompensation and does not remove the incentive for renewable energy producers to become more competitive.

Under the third option aid may be granted on the basis of the 'external costs avoided' compared to the situation where the same amount of energy was produced conventionally. The external costs avoided consist of the difference between, on the one hand, the external costs produced but not paid by the producers of renewable energy and, on the other hand, the external costs produced and not paid by conventional producers. The aid calculated according to this method may not surpass the ceiling of 5 Eurocents per kilowatt-hour. Any aid granted according to this option and exceeding the amount that could be granted following the first option must be reinvested in the production of renewable energy. Furthermore, aid granted according to the third option must result in the increase of the production of renewable energy and not just a transfer of the market shares between the different methods of producing renewable energy. This probably reflects the increasing concern with regard to wind energy. This is at the moment the cheapest and therefore most profitable method of producing renewable energy.[155] The system whereby aids are granted should therefore not result in the increased production of wind energy to the detriment of, for example, biomass installations. In this respect the scheme

[153] See also on state aid for renewable energy: Delvaux 2003, p. 108 *et seq.*

[154] 2001 Environmental aid Guidelines, OJ 2001 C 37/3, para. 61.

[155] *Cf.* the concerns voiced by the Commission in its invitation to submit comments concerning Case C-63/99 *Stromeinspeisungsgesetz*, OJ 1999 C 306/19.

whereby the aid is granted must treat the firms producing renewable energy on the same footing while there may be no discrimination between firms producing the same form of renewable energy. Finally, the scheme must be re-examined every five years.

Option four allows Member States to grant aid in accordance with the standard rules on operating aid (i.e. for five years and degressive from 100 per cent to nil or 50 per cent in a non-degressive manner).

Following the judgment of the Court in the *PreussenElektra* case, Member States may very well prefer the fifth option that was applied by the German government.[156] As may be recalled, in the German system, electricity supply firms were obliged to purchase all the renewable energy produced in their region and to pay a compensation fee for this. According to the Court, this scheme, although it very obviously confers a benefit on the producers of renewable energy, does not constitute state aid in the meaning of Article 87.

Installations for the combined production of heat and energy for civilian use may be granted operating aid using the four options identified above provided that the installations produce an environmental benefit because of their high efficiency.[157] Such operating aid may only be granted when the costs for the production of electricity or heat are higher than the market price. For the combined production of heat and energy destined for industrial use aid may be granted only when the costs of production for one unit of energy are higher than the market price for one unit of energy. A normal return on capital may be included in the unit costs of production but gains resulting in the use of the produced heat must be deducted from these costs. It is taken that the term 'energy' (in the unit costs) is used to encompass both electricity and heat. That, however, would seem to be hard to reconcile with the fact that only the profit resulting from the internal use of heat must be deducted from the costs as the electrical energy produced may equally well be used internally.

### 13.5.5 Miscellaneous aspects

As has been seen, the Kyoto Protocol has played an important role throughout the Guidelines. In Chapter F, the Commission indicates that certain measures adopted to reach the reductions in CO2 emissions may constitute aid. The Commission leaves it at this and provides no guidance with regard to the competition policy vis a vis these Kyoto-measures.

Just as under the 1994 Guidelines, the legal basis for the exemption is Article 87(3)(c) whereas aid may be granted at higher rates for important projects of common European interest as foreseen in Article 87(3)(b).[158] The maximum aid

156 *Supra*, paragraph 13.2.2.

157 2001 Environmental aid Guidelines, OJ 2001 C 37/3, para. 66.

158 *Ibid.*, para. 72 and 73.

intensities identified above apply for overlapping aid from different sources.[159] Chapter I contains the 'appropriate measures' within the meaning of Article 88(1) EC. Accordingly, Member States are to notify state aid schemes where the eligible costs exceed 25 million Euros and where the aid exceeds 5 million Euros.

According to chapter J the Guidelines apply from the date of their publication on and will be withdrawn on 31 December 2007. Instead of a fixed date for a review, the Commission has now chosen to opt for a more flexible system whereby it can amend the Guidelines at any time following consultation of the Member States. The Commission will apply the new Guidelines to notified aid from the moment of the publication of the Guidelines on. With regard to non-notified aid, the Commission will apply the Guidelines in force on the moment that the aid was granted.

Chapter K concerns the application of the integration principle by the Commission with regard to state aids. The Commission will consider how it can best take environmental considerations into account in other Guidelines or frameworks. Moreover, the Commission considers the possibility of asking Member States to provide an environmental impact assessment with the notification of certain aid schemes. Below we will be looking more closely at Commission practice in this area.

## 13.6 The role of environmental considerations in other sectors and Guidelines

As was mentioned above, the Commission has stated in the final chapter of the 2001 Environmental aid Guidelines that it considers itself under an obligation to integrate environmental considerations into the other Guidelines and frameworks as well.[160] Indeed, it has done this even before the 2001 Environmental aid Guidelines were published. In the Community Guidelines for State aid in the agriculture sector, dating from 2000, the Commission has devoted an entire chapter to environmental aid in this sector.[161] However, as far as we have been able to ascertain, the Agricultural aid Guidelines are, as far as the detail is concerned, unique in this respect. In the Community Guidelines on State aid in the maritime sector, for example, the Commission has limited itself to referring to the Environmental aid Guidelines[162] and making one general remark in the chapter concerning investments.[163] In the mean time,

---

159 *Ibid.*, para. 74.

160 See further on the integration of environmental concerns in other policy areas of the EC: Dhondt 2003.

161 Community Guidelines on State aid in the agriculture sector (Agricultural aid Guidelines), OJ 2000 C 28/2.

162 Community Guidelines on State aid to the maritime sector, OJ 1997 C 205/5, chapter 7.

163 *Ibid.*, chapter 5.

however, the 2001 Environmental aid Guidelines have replaced many of the old sectoral frameworks.[164] This is, as far as, for example, aid to the maritime sector is concerned evidenced by the *Italian oil tanker* case.[165] This case concerned an Italian aid scheme designed to speed up the replacement of old single hull tankers with newer single hull or double hull tankers. The Commission considered the compatibility of this scheme with its 2001 Environmental aid Guidelines and expressed its doubts in this regard. Other sectoral regimes governing at activities that will also have a very large environmental impact, such as the fisheries sector, only address the issue of environmental aids rather succinctly.[166] Indeed, the 1997 Guidelines on aid to the fisheries sector explicitly allow for aid for an activity of which the environmental impact can hardly be called positive. In section 2.1.3.1 these Guidelines state that aid for

> *'advertising media to invite consumers to buy a given product, may be regarded as being compatible with the common market provided that it relates to one or more of the following schemes:*
> *(c) generic advertising for fish in general or publicity:*
> *- for species which have rarely or never been used for human consumption, which are not subject to quantitative catch restrictions and catches of which could be increased'.*

It may be wondered whether it is such a good idea to move on to new species now that the traditional species' stocks have been depleted. Moreover, it may be doubted whether the provisos that these species should not be subject to catch restrictions and that catches could be increased, would be sufficient to ensure that not yet another species of fish is wiped out. Fortunately, this provision has been scrapped from the 2001 version of these Guidelines.[167] Furthermore, these Guidelines dedicate slightly more attention to the environmental aspects involved in fishing.[168]

As was already mentioned, the Agricultural aid Guidelines contain by far the most elaborate rules on environmental state aid in that sector. Chapter 5 of the Agricultural aid Guidelines follows the same lines that the 2001 Environmental aid Guidelines do. The Commission distinguishes between a number of aid methods and objectives. With regard to investment aid, the Commission states that it is unnecessary to provide further rules since the particularities

---

[164] 2001 Environmental aid Guidelines, OJ 2001 C 37/3, para. 7.

[165] Invitation to submit comments concerning case C 97/2001, *Scrapping and renewal of the Italian oil tanker fleet* (Italian oil tanker), OJ 2002 C 50/7.

[166] Community Guidelines for the examination of State aid to fisheries and aquaculture, OJ 1997 C 100/12.

[167] Community Guidelines for the examiantion of State aid to fisheries and aquaculture, OJ 2001 C 19/7.

[168] *Ibid.*, para. 1.2 at p. 8, paras. 2.1.2.1 and 2.1.3.2 at p. 9 and para. 2.5 at p. 11.

of environmental investment aids have already been taken into account in the general chapter on agricultural investment aids.[169] Section 5.3 contains rules on state aids for so-called agri-environmental commitments. Such commitments are governed by Articles 22 – 24 of the Rural Development Regulation and aim to protect the environment and maintain the countryside.[170] Farmers who have entered into such commitments may receive support. According to section 5.4 aid may be granted to farmers in areas that are subject to environmental restrictions arising from the implementation of Community environmental law. Such aid may cover the costs incurred and income foregone insofar as there is no over-compensation. With regard to operating aids, the Commission repeats its strict stance according to which such aids will only exceptionally be allowed.[171] The rules in this respect show as great resemblance to those laid down in the 2001 Environmental aid Guidelines in that such operating aid must be temporary and degressive.[172]

We have started this chapter with the observation that the Commission, in the 2001 Environmental aid Guidelines, considers itself under an obligation to integrate environmental concerns into its state aids policy in every sector. Indeed, the Commission did not express this thought for the first time in the 2001 Environmental aid Guidelines. Interestingly, the Agricultural aid Guidelines contain a similar 'integration-provision' to that to be found in chapter K of the 2001 Environmental aid Guidelines.[173] In section 3.9 the Commission cites article 6 EC to come to the conclusion that it covers both the competition as well as the agricultural policy of the Community. On the basis of this the Commission states that particular attention must be given to environmental issues even in cases even in cases where the aid schemes are not specifically concerned with environmental issues. In this respect the Commission states that it will be necessary to show that the effects of certain aid schemes do not run counter to Community environmental protection legislation or otherwise cause environmental damage. Just as in the 2001 Environmental aid Guidelines, the Commission states that notifications 'should in the future contain an assessment of the expected environmental impact of the activity aided'. This brings us to a more general question in how far environmental considerations may play a negative role in the process of the application of the state aid rules.

---

169 Agricultural aid Guidelines OJ 2000 C 28/2, para 5.2 at p. 9.

170 Council Regulation 1257/1999 on support for rural development from the European Agricultural Guidance and Guarantee Fund (Rural Development Regulation), OJ 1999 L 160/80.

171 Agricultural aid Guidelines, OJ 2000 C 28/2, para 5.5.1.

172 *Ibid.*, para. 5.5.2. Note, however, that the Commission does not require aids to offset the extra costs for certain more environmentally friendly products to be degressive, *ibid.*, para. 5.5.3

173 *Supra*, para. 13.5.5.

In other words: to what extent can a negative environmental impact assessment, like the ones mentioned above, actually allow or even oblige the Commission to declare the aid incompatible with the common market even though from a competition perspective there are no objections? The wording of Article 87 appears at first sight not to allow for such a negative role. Above, we have also concluded that much the same holds true with regard to nearly all the other Treaty provisions in the field of competition law. However, as we have also seen, Article 6's influence is far-going in that it puts the Commission under an obligation to at least consider the environmental impact of the decisions it takes. The criterion that state aid is *incompatible with the common market* may function as a useful starting point for our question. The fact that aid is declared incompatible with the common market already indicates the objective of Article 87, which is to bring about and maintain the common market. The common market, as was also shown above, exists not only of an area where there is free movement but is itself also the subject of a number of well-defined environmental objectives as can be seen in Articles 2 and 3 EC. Indeed, this reasoning may have underlined the Commission's potentially far-going statements in the Agricultural aid Guidelines where it held that:[174]

*'All environmental aid schemes in the agricultural sector should be compatible with the objectives of Community environmental policy. In particular, aid schemes which fail to give sufficient priority to the elimination of pollution at source, or to the correct application of the polluter pays principle cannot be considered compatible with the common interest, and therefore cannot be authorised by the Commission.'*

Immediately, we should note that this statement is largely qualified by the fact that it applies to environmental aid schemes only. However, the closing statement, and in particular the fact that it refers to the common interest, seems potentially powerful. This reasoning is clearly capable of being applied outside the agricultural sector and with regard to all other aids. Unfortunately, a similar statement, even with the limited scope (applying to environmental aid only) it has in the Agricultural aid Guidelines, did not make it into the 2001 Environmental aid Guidelines. It is submitted that the Commission has the possibility to refuse authorisation of aid schemes that run counter to Community environmental law or environmental protection requirements in general just as it considers itself under an obligation to not fund environmentally damaging projects with Community funds.

[174] Agricultural aid Guidelines, OJ 2000 C 28/2, para. 5.1.3.

CHAPTER 14

# The Integration of Environmental Considerations in EC Competition Law: an Interim Conclusion

## Interim Conclusion

As we have seen environmental considerations have played a more or less modest role with regard to nearly every provision of Community competition law. Even within areas of competition law where no such practical examples of a role for environmental considerations could be found, we could at least consider the possibility. Thus, for example, practice pursuant to the Merger Regulation was, as far as we have been able to establish, an affair aimed solely at competition objectives. Nevertheless, we were also able to identify some aspects of the Merger Regulation that could possibly allow for a role for environmental concerns.

Did this more or less modest role for environmental considerations also amount to an integration of environmental concerns? In Part I of this study we have concluded that an integration of environmental and competition considerations requires that they can function in a mutually reinforcing relation. This in turn requires not so much that environmental considerations take precedence over competition considerations but rather that they are treated on equal footing with this objective of a mutually reinforcing relation in mind. If, for example, competition considerations can never be set aside for environmental reasons, then no integration can take place. The relation between competition and environmental considerations can in such cases at best be qualified as an interactive one. If we look at the provisions of EC competition law and the practical application of these provisions by the Commission and Court with this model of integration in mind the following picture emerges.

With regard to the competitive appraisal on the basis of Article 81(1), environmental considerations can play an interactive role at best. Article 81(1) is about establishing whether or not there is an appreciable restriction of competition and this, of course, does not allow for weighing of environmental with competitive concerns in the first place. However, environmental concerns can play a role in that agreements on certain environmental aspects may be considered not to appreciably restrict competition. With regard to agreements that involve decisions on 'the environmental price' (*i.e.* environmental surcharges, removal fees), the Commission has taken a strict approach. Such agreements are considered to amount to price fixing and therefore qualify as hard-core restrictions since they restrict the freedom for the consumer to shop around for the lowest environmental price.[1] It is submitted that the Commission's approach in this respect is not entirely consistent. As may be recalled, in the area of state aids, the Commission has allowed schemes whereby environmental costs had to be passed on to consumers in their totality.[2] Allowing the state to make such

[1] *Supra*, paragraph 8.4.

[2] *Supra*, chapter 13.

a decision while completely refusing identical schemes set up by private parties cannot be economically explained. In such cases form (issued by the state or by private parties) would seem to go over function (both amount to price fixing). Moreover, reasoning according to which environmental costs must be borne by the industry because they are the polluters is also submitted not to be valid. It was shown that in many cases the polluter (consumer or producer) could not be appointed. The lacking environmental friendliness of production can most probably be traced back to both consumers and producers. As a result of this, agreements that involve the passing through of environmental fees that arise from a producer responsibility to consumers, should not be qualified as price fixing if this characterisation is accompanied by statements that an exemption will be nearly impossible.

In the sphere of Article 81(3) environmental considerations could be integrated. For this to take place, it would be necessary for the Commission (and Court) to recognise that environmental benefits can, of themselves, constitute 'technical or economic progress' within the meaning of Article 81(3). However, as we have seen, the Commission will not use that provision to directly balance a restriction of competition with an environmental benefit. At best, environmental considerations play a subservient role whereby they may be taken into account as '*a factor which contributes to* improving production or distribution or to promoting economic and technical progress'.[3] [emphasis added, HV] The more recent *DSD* case shows that the weight attached to environmental concerns appears to be increasing. At the same time, however, the uncertainty as to exactly how much weight is attached, remains. Moreover, it is uncertain to what extent the role played by environmental protection requirements in Article 81(3) can actually be said to comply with the model of integration.

It is submitted that particularly in the light of the upcoming decentralisation of the application of Article 81(3) more and clearer guidance from the Commission is needed. Moreover, this guidance will need to be in line with the model of integration. If these preconditions have not been met, the result is very likely to be a diverging application of Article 81(3) throughout Europe as some Courts chose to interpret Article 81(3) in the light of the integration principle whereas others will not integrate environmental protection requirements and Article 81(3).

As to the application of Article 82, decision-making practice is scant at the moment. The *DSD* case, however, conveys a very powerful message: the Commission will not take environmental considerations into account in considering whether or not abuse of a dominant position took place. In fact: the word 'environmental protection' was barely mentioned in the decision. Even more disturbing is the background to the *DSD* case where member states implement

3 Commission XXVth. Competition Report (1995), para. 85 (p. 40).

Community law in such a way as to lead to large monopolistic systems and – together with the Commission – consequently insist on creating competition where it is not *a priori* clear as to how this should work. The conclusion with regard to Article 82 must therefore be that integration could take place if environmental considerations could function as an objective justification. At the moment, however, the role that such considerations play is uncertain to say the least. Most probably, the environmental aspects have played a very limited role in the *DSD* case if they have played a role at all. Integration has therefore not taken place in practice.

Practice pursuant to the Merger Regulation is, as was mentioned above, purely aimed at the competition objectives. The Merger Regulation does allow for a role for environmental considerations if they are taken to constitute 'technical or economic progress' within the meaning of Article 2(1)(b) of the Regulation. Even then the wording of the Merger Regulation is clear beyond doubt in that such benefits can never compensate for a creation or strengthening of a dominant position. The role for environmental considerations could therefore, at best, be interactive.

With regard to the useful effect doctrine much is still uncertain. If the Court indeed adopted the general interest exception, then there may actually be an integration of environmental concerns in this respect. However, the Court's case law is still far from well established. The parallel between the useful effect doctrine and Article 86(2) would, however, seem to point in the direction of the existence of this exception. Furthermore, the parallel between Article 86(2) and the general interest exception within the useful effect doctrine should also have the same effects in that the Treaty rules cease to applicable with regard to agreements and government actions that fall within the scope of the general interest exception.

Since the *Sydhavnens Sten & Grus* case, Article 86(2) allows for a direct balancing of environmental goals with the need to apply the Treaty rules. Insofar as this is necessary for the fulfilment of the special environmental task, the Treaty rules are not applicable. This is nothing short of a true integration of environmental considerations within this area of competition law. Since Article 86(2) applies with regard to all Treaty rules, the impact of this is very significant. It must not, however, be forgotten that Article 86(2) is limited to cases where privileged undertakings have been entrusted with the performance of a special (environmental) task. As the law stands, the 'being entrusted with' is interpreted rather narrowly. The negative role for environmental requirements is limited to cases where the privileged undertaking is directly or indirectly under environmental obligations.

Finally, environmental protection requirements have also been fully integrated in the rules on state aid. The Commission's long-standing policy in this field, as laid down in the Guidelines, shows that environmental objectives may certainly justify the granting of aid if this is necessary to attain the environmental goals and in accordance with the polluter pays principle. The negative role that environmental concerns may play is somewhat more uncertain and probably limited.

PART THREE

'Es gibt *nur* ein perspektivisches Sehen, *nur* ein perspektivisches 'Erkennen'; und *je mehr* Affekte wir über eine Sache zu Worte kommen lassen, *je mehr* Augen, verschiedne Augen wir uns für dieselbe Sache einzusetzen wissen, um so vollständiger wird unser 'Begriff' dieser Sache, unsre 'Objektivität' sein?'[1]

# A Comparison

## Introduction

This part of the book contains comparative legal research with regard to the integration of environmental concerns and competition law. Without going too deeply into the merits and rationales of comparative legal research, it may be stated that the purpose of comparative research can only be to identify and consequently analyse differences between systems of law so as to better understand the reaction of one system of law (*i.c.* EC competition law) to a particular problem (*i.c.* the integration of environmental concerns). To use the words of Nietzsche: it is a recognition that there are more perspectives and an attempt to view a matter from other perspectives in order to better understand this matter. These perspectives from which the reaction of that one system of law are thus examined need to be sufficiently different from that one system of law but must at the same time remain comparable.[2] It would, for example, not appear to make much sense to compare the role of environmental concerns and EC competition law with the reaction of Mexican law in Zinacantan to changes in political leadership.[3] Therefore, the person conducting the comparative legal research must be aware of those differences and almost prejudiced with regard to these differences, as he must select the perspectives from which to conduct the research with these differences in mind. In order to be helpful, the selected perspectives must either include or exclude one of the factors that the researcher considers to be relevant (sufficient difference) while remaining comparable.

From the overview in Part Two, essentially three relevant factors can be distilled. The first factor relates to the *integration* of environmental concerns and competition law as it was developed in part one and seen put into practice to a certain extent in Part Two. We have seen that the model of integration requires that the application of competition law take account of the mutually beneficial role that competition and environmental protection may ultimately play. In Part Two we have also seen this idea being put into practice to a certain extent notably in the area of environmental state aids.

The second factor is one that is typical for EC competition law. This is the market integration objective. It is submitted that all systems of competition law in Europe (possibly the world) share the basic objective of maintaining effective competition. However, of the competition laws of Europe, only EC competition law also has the objective of bringing about and furthering market integration.[4] It has on several occasions been observed that this market integration objective

1 F. Nietzsche, *Zur Genealogie der Moral*, Third Essay (*Was bedeuten asketische Ideale?*), paragraph 12.

2 See, with regard to 'functionality', Zweigert & Kötz 1998, p. 34.

3 See, regarding political leadership and legal change in Zinacantan, Collier 1996.

4 Joined Cases 56/64 & 58/64, *Consten & Grundig*, [1966] ECR 449.

may actually 'pollute' the cadre for the appreciation of restrictions of competition.[5]

A third factor emerging from the examination in Part Two is the economisation of the environmental benefits. Notably with regard to Article 81 EC, the Commission appears to first convert the environmental benefits into more or less clearly defined and quantified economic benefits and only then awards them a role as part of the first requirement for an exemption. Environmental considerations are not of themselves taken into account. This is considered to be the result of the economic nature of the Community's competition rules directed at undertakings.

After having examined the role of environmental concerns in EC competition law in Part Two we will now be looking at the role of environmental concerns in EC competition law thus examined from what may be called an internal, external and semi-internal perspective. These three perspectives refer to three different exercises in comparative legal research and relate to three factors outlined above.

With regard to the internal perspective the following can be said. Environmental concerns, as we have seen in Part One, are not the only non-competition concerns that can play a role in EC competition law. Considerations of a cultural nature may also play a role in the application of the Community's competition laws. We will therefore, be looking at the role played by these cultural considerations and compare that with the role played by environmental considerations. This is called the internal perspective since it also departs from the viewpoint of EC competition law. It concerns the first relevant factor outlined above in that the mutually reinforcing role that was considered to form the basis of the integration of environmental concerns and competition law is submitted to be impossible for culture and competition.

As regards the external comparative perspective, we will study the role that environmental protection requirements play in other systems of competition law. For this, we will study British, German, and Netherlands competition law in their relations to environmental considerations. This is referred to as the external perspective since the point of departure is formed by the different systems of competition law of the member states. In certain respects, this may, however, also be called a semi-external perspective as many of the systems of competition law in the member states have in fact been adapted to mirror EC competition law. Nevertheless, this perspective will serve to eliminate the role that the market integration objective may have played in the application of EC competition law with regard to environmental protection. It therefore addresses the second (market integration) factor identified above.

---

5 See, for a discussion, Jones & Sufrin 2001, p. 138 *et seq.* See also: Monti 2002.

Moreover, as part of the external perspective we will also examine how and to what extent competition considerations have been taken into account in drawing up environmental legislation. As we have seen in the introductory chapter of Part One, competition is generally considered to be a very efficient economic ordering mechanism. Furthermore, we have observed that environmental policy has sought to apply competition as instrument to bring about environmental protection more effectively and efficiently. In this regard the implementation of, for example, the Packaging Directive and German Packaging Ordinance cannot be called a complete success as they can, as we have in seen in chapter 6 above, be said to have resulted in the emergence of large-scale and monopolistic producer responsibility organisations. The presence of such organisations can hardly be said to be conducive to the creation of a market where the competitive forces assure effective and efficient environmental protection. We will, therefore, scrutinise the environmental policies and legislation of a number of member states in order to see whether they have resulted in the emergence of similar organisations, why these monopolistic systems have come about and what can be done to ascertain a greater chance of an effective competition for the environment coming about.

Because it is recognised that EC competition law as well as environmental concerns are subject to different dynamics as regards their interrelation compared to, respectively, other systems of competition law (external perspective) and other non-competition concerns (internal perspective), a third perspective has been introduced. This is the semi-internal – or, for that matter, semi-external[6] – perspective. According to this perspective we will study the role that environmental considerations play in a part of EC law that is closely connected to the competition rules, namely the 'internal market' rules (Articles 23 to 30, 90, 95 and 176 of the EC Treaty). This perspective includes the market integration objective but excludes the (economic) competition related objectives of systems of competition law and replaces that with a purely legal framework for the appreciation of the role of environmental concerns. It thus addresses the third factor identified above.

With the help of a comparison from these three perspectives, we should be able to better value the role that environmental concerns have played and could play in EC competition law and other systems of competition law. Moreover, we can determine whether the model of integration developed in Part One as it was seen implemented to a certain extent in EC competition law in Part Two lends itself for application to other systems of competition law.

This part will consist of three chapters, all of which basically be structured along the same lines: firstly a section setting out the relevance of that area or

6 The term 'semi-external' will, however, not be used so as to avoid confusion with the second perspective identified above.

system of law for the research. In other words: the comparability of that area or system with the integration of environmental concerns and competition law. Secondly, a section giving a basic outline of the area of law and, thirdly, a section devoted to the study whether or not integration has taken place and how that outcome relates to the relevance or comparability.

CHAPTER 15

# The Internal Perspective

## A Study of the Role of Cultural Policy Considerations in EC Competition Law

## 15.1 Introductory remarks

Cultural considerations have always been a sensitive area in the process of integration. Indeed, the topicality of the cultural considerations and competition law already became clear at the very inception of EC competition. The Dutch system of fixed book prices, for example, was notified to the Commission back in 1962.[7] The Single European Act and Maastricht and Amsterdam Treaties have resulted in the insertion into the EC Treaty of a number of cultural clauses none of which, however, have been conducive to solving the riddle of cultural considerations and competition law. Below we will first address the issue of comparability. For that we will need to analyse what exactly cultural policy is about and the relation between cultural policy and competition law. Moreover, we will need to examine how these findings relate to the mutually reinforcing relation that we have seen to exist between competition and environmental protection. In the second part we will look at the European cases that concern the role of cultural considerations and competition law. For reasons of practicability, we will concentrate on Article 81, 86 and 87 EC. There are essentially three reasons for this. Firstly, the overwhelming majority of the competition case law involving environmental concerns concerns these provisions. Secondly, other areas of competition law (notably Merger Control) have been shown to be of limited interest as regards the integration of environmental and competition concerns in that little or no case law exists.[8] Below, we will therefore concentrate on three areas where cultural considerations have played a role in EC competition law. These are: book price fixing (Article 81 EC), state aids for cultural purposes (Article 87 EC) and exclusive rights for cultural reasons (Article 86 EC).

## 15.2 Relevance

The protection of culture, just as the protection of the environment, is a diffuse interest and as a concept 'culture' is difficult if not impossible to define accurately. The EC Treaty, for example, does not define the concept of culture or cultural policy. If cultural policy is taken to consist of the maintenance and furthering of culture, the definitional uncertainty surrounding the term culture will immediately result in definitional uncertainties surrounding the concept of cultural policy. However, this uncertainty should not stand in the way of this research as it in no way contradicts the existence of culture or cul-

---

7 Case C-39/96, *Koninklijke Vereeniging ter Bevordering van de Belangen des Boekhandels* v. *Free Record Shop*, [1997] ECR I-2303, para. 5.

8 See, however, case IV/M.423, *Newspaper Publishing, supra* chapter 5.3, that lead to a so-called Article 21(3) case under the Merger Regulation.

tural policy and the fact that cultural considerations may conflict with competition law objectives.[9]

What, then, appears to be the basic idea underlying cultural policy? In general it can be said that is about maintaining or developing a *certain* culture. As culture is closely connected with identity, the culture that is the object of cultural policy will vary with the different identities that certain groups of people have identified for themselves. The general theme throughout all these different cultural policies, if we focus on the effects that they have or seek to have on the market, is that cultural policy aims to increase the supply of cultural services or goods. Be it through ensuring sufficient income for the artists, ascertaining attractive prices, direct subsidisation or facilitating cross-subsidisation, the result of cultural policies is supply-oriented in that it aims to have, for example, more books being published, more bookstores that carry a wider range of books, more theatre companies or more newspapers with independent editorial boards. Cultural policy does not aim so much at an increase of supply as such but also wants to increase diversity of supply. In short, the aim of cultural policy is to increase or maintain availability and pluriformity on the supply side of culture.[10] In terms of competition, this effectively means that *competitors* are protected, rather than *competition*. Unmitigated competition on the market for cultural goods or services would undoubtedly result in less operas being broadcasted whereas soap operas would probably be televised just as much for the simple reason that operas are a relatively unattractive product for a large group of consumers. So the aim of maintaining pluriformity can actually be said to be primarily directed at what may be called 'high culture': poetry, experimental dance, and classic music. These are the classic merit goods that the market would not bring about by itself.

The relation *vis a vis* competition is therefore fundamentally different for cultural and environmental policy. Whereas environmental policy may in the short-term conflict with competition, both are ultimately mutually reinforcing according to the model of integration. By contrast, cultural policy will, always have to keep the supply and diversity of producers of high culture at a level that would not come about if the market forces were released.[11] Ultimately, competition and culture are antagonistic. How does this relate to the comparability of cultural considerations and competition policy with environmental considerations and competition? A first argument in favour of comparability or relevance is the fact that cultural and competition policies are ultimately irreconcilable.

---

9 *Cf.* Albers 1999, p. 13.

10 This is reflected in the text of the cultural integration provision Article 151(4), infra. See furthermore, fourth consideration of the Council Resolution on the application of national fixed book-price systems, OJ 2001 C 73/5.

11 Unless, of course, a larger group of consumers would develop a liking for high culture or the concept of high culture would be abandoned.

Article 81 prohibits and will always stand in the way of certain agreements that are considered necessary from a cultural perspective. Similarly, certain broadcasters may be unable to survive and are therefore aided by the state for cultural reasons whereas Article 87 actually prohibits such aids. The relation between cultural considerations and competition law should therefore be fundamentally different from that between competition and environmental protection.

A second argument in favour of the relevance of cultural policy for this research is the fact that the EC Treaty also contains an integration clause with regard to cultural policy. According to Article 151(4) EC

> *'The Community shall take cultural aspects into account in its action under other provisions of this Treaty, in particular in order to respect and to promote the diversity of its cultures'.*

Does this, however, immediately render cultural policy and its relation with competition of interest for the purpose of this research? The answer must be: to a certain extent. In our opinion, the relation between environmental concerns and competition law is unique because of the polluter pays principle. Through this principle, as was shown in chapter four, the competition mechanism and environmental protection requirements can stand in a mutually reinforcing relation. Such a relation is not easily conceivable for cultural policy and competition as both are, as we have seen above, ultimately contradictory with regard to their objectives.

Contrary to this, environmental policy does in the end not have to be incompatible with competition policy, as was shown in Part One. Conflicts between competition and environmental policy are likely to arise only during the transitory phase during which the polluter pays principle is being implemented. Once it is fully implemented, distortions of competition no longer necessarily follow from environmental law and offsetting restrictions may very well even be counterproductive precisely because of this polluter pays principle. No such principle easily springs to mind for cultural policy. With regard to cultural policy one could only just begin to imagine a 'culture-barbarian-pays-principle' according to which, for example, those who love soap operas should pay whereas the *aficionados* of operas do not have to pay. To take the example even further, imagine a scheme whereby TV broadcasters have privately set up a fund in which they collect 'soap opera fees' from the consumers[12] which they then distribute over opera houses. However far-fetched and improbable, this is at least possible. The trick is of course in distinguishing high from low culture; the barbarians from the *aficionados*.

[12] Technically, this should not be impossible with pay per view technology.

With these remarks in mind we must come to the conclusion that the role of cultural policy considerations in EC competition is of relevance for the purpose of this research because we can compare the way in which competition law deals with conflicting objectives in cultural cases with the way in which it deals with conflicts between environmental and competition policy. The lack of a principle that functions analogously to the polluter-pays-principle should, however, lead to a different stance on the part of the authorities in charge of competition policy. Precisely because of the absence of such a principle and the fact that in the end competition policy and cultural and industrial policy collide with one another there should be no integration at all. In other words, cultural policy considerations cannot be integrated and can only either take precedence over competition law or be considered of secondary importance to competition considerations. Let us now turn our attention to a study of the Commission decision-making practice and Court case law with regard to cultural policy considerations in EC competition law.

## 15.3 The role of cultural policy considerations in EC competition law

As has been mentioned in paragraph 9.1 above, there have been conflicts between competition law and cultural policy primarily with regard to Articles 81, 86 and 87 of the EC Treaty. In particular, these cases have concerned fixed book prices (relevant with regard to Article 81 EC) and the funding of public television and books (relevant with regard to Articles 86 and 87 EC).

Below, we shall be investigating the role that cultural policy considerations have played in Commission practice and case law in these areas of competition law with regard to the broad areas outlined above. As an intermezzo we shall also be looking shortly at the decisions taken pursuant to the Netherlands competition act with regard to cultural cartels and the system for book price fixing in Germany. Because much has already been said on the general principles underlying EC competition law in Part Two, we shall not be paying any attention to these general principles in this chapter and concentrate on the conflicts.

### 15.3.1 Fixed book prices

In the introduction to this chapter we have seen that fixed book prices have presented a problem for European competition law from its inception onwards. Essentially two systems of book price fixing can be discerned: those set up privately and those set up by the state. With regard to the latter type, the French system of regulatory prescribed fixed prices has been challenged several times but the Court has consistently held that as Community law stand now, it does not oppose such legislation.[13] With regard to private systems, there have been three major cases involving the Dutch,[14] German[15] and English[16] book price fixing schemes. Despite differences in the specificities of the price fixing (individual or collective vertical price fixing) all schemes have in common that they allow a publisher to fix a price that must then be observed in all sales to final consumers, this in order to prevent 'ruinous competition'.[17] Furthermore, the basic cultural rationale behind this appears to be twofold: to ensure pluriformity and availability of books.[18] Moreover, the application of EC competition law has been limited to the cross-border effects of such systems. The Commission therefore does not deal with the purely national implications of fixed book price systems. This may be deemed an application of the integration principle in connection with the subsidiarity principle.[19] It is submitted that this territorial demarcation flows from the system of EC competition law and is, if at all, the result of only the subsidiarity principle in that the Commission effectively leaves the appraisal of such national schemes to national competition authorities.

In the cases where a cross-border element was present, the agreement had effects in one language area that covered several member states. The agreements thus scrutinised all served to make the national systems 'watertight' in that they sought to prevent 'U-turns'[20] or established collective exclusive dealing systems.

The first such case to be examined by the Commission was the *VBBB/VBVB* case that concerned the agreement between the Belgian and Netherlands association of booksellers.[21] This agreement set up a collective exclusive dealing

---

13 Case 229/83, *Leclerc* v. *Au Blé Vert*, [1985] ECR 1 and Case C-9/99, *Echirolles* v. *Association du Dauphiné*, [2000] ECR I-8207.

14 The VBBB/VBVB system that had lead to decision 82/123, *VBBB/VBVB*, OJ 1982 L 54/36, upheld in joined cases 43/82 and 63/82, *VBVB and VBBB* v. *Commission*, [1984] ECR 19.

15 The *Sammelrevers* and *Einzelrevers*-system, notice pursuant to Article 19(3) of Reg. 17, OJ 2000 C 162/25 and Commission press releases IP/01/1035 and IP/02/461.

16 The 'Net book system'; decision 89/44, *Publishers Association – Net Book Agreements*, OJ 1989 L 22/12, upheld by CFI in case T-55/89, *Publishers Association* v. *Commission*, [1992] ECR II-1995, appeal upheld in case C-360/92 P, *Publishers Association* v. *Commission*, [1995] ECR I-23.

17 *Cf.* opinion of A-G Darmon in Case 229/83, *Leclerc* v. *Au Blé Vert*, [1985] ECR 1, para 2 at p. 3.

18 CPB/SCP 2002, p. 25 *et seq.*

19 De Vries 2001, p. 102.

20 A U-turn situation exists where something, for example a book, is exported solely for the purpose of avoiding the effects of national laws or, in the case of the fixed book prices, collective price fixing schemes.

21 Decision 82/123, *VBBB/VBVB*, OJ 1982 L 54/36.

system between the two associations and obliged both associations to respect the prices fixed by the other. The associations had argued before the Commission that the agreement was necessary for the working of the internal system of vertically fixed prices. Furthermore, the fixed prices were considered by the parties to lead to better production and distribution because they would allow the publisher to cross-subsidise the less popular titles with the more popular ones. The Commission refused to accept this reasoning holding that collective vertical price fixing was not necessary to ensure cross-subsidisation so that the proportionality test under Article 81(3) was not satisfied. Moreover, the Commission considered that consumers would not receive a benefit from the agreement in that the fixed price in no way contributes to lower prices while consumers are made to pay (in part) for unpopular books. The Commission's critical attitude towards the cultural objectives of these private agreements can probably best be seen where it holds that:[22]

> *'[I]t is not for undertakings or associations of undertakings to conclude agreements on cultural questions, which are principally a matter for government (although the Commission recognizes that undertakings can also play a valuable part in the dissemination of culture)'* .

This consideration as part of the Commissions appraisal of the indispensability criterion for an exemption could be taken to mean that it will never consider a private agreement to be necessary for the attainment of cultural goals for the simple reason that these matters belong to the *imperium*. The Court of Justice, after having indicated that it concerns the cross-border aspects only, upheld this decision by stating that the Commission had not manifestly exceeded the boundaries of its discretion.[23]

The later *Net Books* and *Sammelrevers* cases confirm this approach by the Commission. It must, however, be taken into account that those cases were also confined to the cross-border effects of those systems and did not address the validity of the pluriformity/availability arguments directly. The Publishers Association applied for annulment of the Commission's decision in the *Net Books* case to deny an exemption. The Publishers Association argued, *inter alia*, that the Commission had failed to take account of a ruling by the British Restrictive Trade Practices Court in which the Net Book system was considered not to be contrary to the public interest and the existence of an English-Irish single language area.[24] The Court of First Instance rejected the application for annul-

---

[22] *Ibid.*, para. 60.

[23] Joined cases 43/82 and 63/82, *VBVB and VBBB* v. *Commission*, [1984] ECR 19.

[24] Case T-55/89, *Publishers Association* v. *Commission*, [1992] ECR II-1995, respectively paras. 77 *et seq.* and paras. 88 *et seq.*

ment but the Court of Justice set this aside. The rejection by the Court of First Instance of the arguments regarding the failure to take account of the ruling of the Restrictive Trade Practices Court was set aside primarily because of procedural reasons. However, the failure to take account of the single Irish-English language area[25] has been taken to be a start of an application of the cultural integration clause.[26]

The *VBBB/VBVB*, *Net Books* and, to a lesser extent, *Leclerc* cases have resulted in a number of public political statements by the Council and European Parliament with regard to the application of Community competition law to national systems of book price fixing. In 1997 the Council adopted a Decision where it recalled that fact that Article 151(4) (then Article 128(4) EC) had been included in the Treaty and asked the Commission to examine whether and to what extent that provision may alter the compatibility with competition of fixed book prices.[27] In a 1999 Resolution that Council called upon the Commission to take account of the integration provision and the special cultural consideration surrounding books while applying EC competition law.[28] Furthermore, the European Parliament adopted a Resolution that follows much the same lines in 1998.[29] Most recently, in its 2001 Resolution on the application of national fixed book-price systems, the Council notes the existence of (now) Article 151 EC and calls upon the Commission to take account of the dual nature of books as both tradable goods as well as carriers of cultural identities.[30]

What we see happening here is the Community legislator becoming active in a way that falls short of actual legislative action. Now that the Commission has been granted the sole power to grant exemptions pursuant to Article 81(3), the Council has only two methods left if it wants to ascertain a larger role for cultural considerations. First, it may issue legislation prescribing such a larger role. Second, it may choose to exert political pressure on the Commission to take cultural considerations into account to a larger extent. As we will see below, the Community legislature has used its legislative powers to increase the role of cultural considerations with regard to state aid law. Differences of opinion as to the usefulness and necessity of book prices fixing as a means of cultural policy have probably kept it from acting in the same manner with regard to Article 81. We will see these differences when we examine the situation with regard to book price fixing in a number of member states.

---

25 Case C-360/92 P, *Publishers Association* v. *Commission*, [1995] ECR I-23, paras.28, 29.

26 *Cf.* Everling 1997, p. 86.

27 Council Decision of 22 September 1997 on cross-border fixed book prices in European linguistic areas, OJ 1997 C 305/2.

28 Resolution of 8 February 1999 on fixed book prices in homogeneous cross-border linguistic areas, OJ 1999 C 42/3.

29 Resolution on common book price-fixing across borders, OJ 1998 C 379/391.

30 Resolution of 12 February 2001 on the application of national fixed book-price systems, OJ 2001 C 73/5.

Since the Commission does not consider itself empowered to examine national systems of book price fixing, it will be interesting to look at the practices in a number of member states. In this respect there are some notable differences. Germany, for one, explicitly allows vertical fixing of book prices ('*Verlagserzeugnise*', published products) in Section 15 of its *Gesetz gegen Wettbewerbsbeschränkungen* (Act Against Restrictions of Competition, hereafter referred to as GWB). Moreover, several German Courts have upheld the legality of these price fixing agreements.[31] The German Parliament is currently preparing legislation that may prescribe book price fixing for Germany.[32]

As we have seen above when we looked at the *Leclerc* cases, the French government actually prescribes book price fixing in its legislation.[33] In the UK, the Net Book System has been abolished in 1995 partly as a result of the advent of large book retailing chains that breached the Net Book Agreements by granting rebates. Currently, book prices are completely free. This, it has been observed, did not lead to decreased pluriformity (number of published titles) or large decreases in availability (number of bookstores) but did result in higher prices.[34] Similarly, Sweden abolished its book price fixing system in 1970 with further liberalisation in 1992. The resulting free market has led to such a decrease in the availability of books (number of bookstores) that the Dutch secretary of state for culture has indicated that he would like to first examine the Swedish experiences before deciding on the fate of book price fixing in the Netherlands.[35]

In the Netherlands the KVB system for Dutch language books has been granted immunity from the *Mededingingswet* (Netherlands Competition Act) through an exemption granted by the government.[36] The reasons for this exemption appear to have been primarily procedural and not primarily related to any cultural objectives.[37] An evaluation of the system concludes that the KVB system is not the best instrument to achieve the cultural objectives sought. Nevertheless, the conclusion is that some correction of the market mechanism (subsi-

---

31 The *Bundesverfassungsgericht* (Consitutional Court) has confirmed the constitutionality of Section 15 GWB, BverfG, decision of 26 Novermber 1986, NJW 1987, p. 1397, see further: Everling 1997, p. 77.

32 *Bundestag* (Parliament), *Drucksache* 14/8854, *Entwurf eines Gesetzes zur Regelung der Preisbindung bei Verlagserzeugnissen* (proposal for an act regulating fixed book prices).

33 The so-called 'Loi Lang' after Minister Jack Lang who introduced this law just two years after book price fixing had been prohibited in 1979.

34 See EIM 2001, p. 22 *et seq*. Report containing an international quick scan prepared for the CPB/SCP report (CBP/SCP 2002).

35 NRC Handelsblad, Thursday 25 April 2002, p. 12.

36 Beslissing inzake verzoek KVB om ontheffing van het verbod op verticale prijsbinding, Stcrt. 1997, nr. 52, p. 8.

37 *Cf.* CPB/SCP 2002, p. 27.

disation) is needed to attain the cultural objectives. With regard to non-Dutch (imported) books, the *Nederlandse Mededingingsautoriteit* (*NMa*; Netherlands Competition Authority) has held that the price fixing does violate the cartel prohibition of the Netherlands Competition Act and, moreover, has refused to grant an exemption.[38] The reasons for this refusal correspond largely to the Commission's findings and the conclusions of the CPB/SCP evaluation report. More specifically, the *NMa* considers that book price fixing for imported books does not lead to the maintenance of a fine meshed distribution systems for books.[39] Moreover, retail price maintenance means that prices are at a level that is higher than would come about under market conditions so that there is no fair share for consumers.[40] Similarly, retail price maintenance makes the advent of more efficient forms of book distribution more difficult resulting, again, in the absence of a fair share for consumers.[41] Finally, the *NMa* considers that the vertical price fixing is not indispensable to achieve the cultural objectives of ensuring availability.[42]

As an interim conclusion with regard to book price fixing it may be said that the role that cultural considerations have played in European competition policy is in conformity with the model of integration developed in Part One as well as the remarks with regard to the relevance made above in paragraph 9.2. The mutually irreconcilable nature of cultural policy and competition law are reflected in the case law of the Commission, Court and national competition authorities in that there are no attempts to achieve integration within the meaning of the model of integration. The role of cultural considerations in the application of competition laws is confined to the standard application of exemption clauses or legislative action by the governments of the member states that serves to remove book price fixing from the scope of the competition laws. The competition laws cannot and are not simply applied or interpreted in such a way as to allow for an integration of cultural concerns. As regards the exemption clause the following may be said. Better availability and more pluriformity of books mean better distribution and production, which means that the first requirement for an exemption is fulfilled. At first sight, this would also seem to

---

38 *NMa* Decision in Case 227, *Nilsson & Lamm*. In the decision of 16 December 1998, the *NMa* considered that the prohibition on cartels was applicable and that no exemption could de granted. In a decision of 22 August 2000 the *NMa* rejected the administrative appeal (*bezwaar*) against the original decision. The Nilsson & Lamm case contains references to similar systems of price fixing for foreign books (para. 3).

39 *NMa* Decision of 16 December 1998, paras. 37-44.

40 *Ibid.*, paras. 46-48.

41 *Ibid.*, para. 49.

42 *Ibid.*, para. 50. Because none of the first three cumulative requirements for an exemption have been fulfilled, the *NMa* does not address the fourth requirement (sufficient residual competition).

mean that there is a fair share for consumers in this benefit. On the other hand, the Commission's reasoning in the *VBBB/VBVB* case in this respect also has something to be said for it: essentially fixed book prices and cross-subsidisation mean that everyone is paying for the 'high culture' pleasures of some. It must, however, also be pointed out that this does not mean that the second requirement for an exemption is impossible to be met for book price fixing schemes. In Part Two it has been shown that the purpose of this requirement is only to exclude the exemption of those agreements that confer an advantage on the parties to the agreement only.[43] Even though a fixed book price does indeed primarily benefit the publishers and booksellers, it still benefits a group of consumers as well. The bottleneck, however, is the indispensability of the fixed book prices to bring about the increased availability and pluriformity. Without wanting to pass judgment on the necessity of fixed book prices as an instrument to ensure pluriformity and availability it can be said that the evidence in this respect is inconclusive. The CPB/SCP, for example, have noted in their evaluation of the fixed book price in the Netherlands that this has not kept the availability as well as pluriformity from decreasing.

All in all, practice with regard to fixed book prices and competition law shows that an *a priori* exception or exemption as part of the application or interpretation of EC competition law by the Commission or Court is out of the question. The role of cultural considerations within Article 81 is thus – and, it is submitted, rightly so – left up to the legislator. As will be seen in the next paragraph, the legislator has indeed provided for a role for cultural considerations with regard to Article 87 EC.

### 15.3.2 State funding of books, films and public television

Funding can be provided though a private scheme (such as the fixed book prices) or by the government. In the latter case, the prohibition on state aids, Article 87 EC, may very well apply. Prior to the amendments made to the EC Treaty by the Treaty on European Union ('Maastricht'), it was uncertain whether and on what legal ground cultural subsidies could be exempted.[44] The Treaty on European Union changed all this by including letter (d) in Article 87(3) EC according to which:

*'(3) The following may be considered compatible with the common market:*
*[...]*
*(d) aid to promote culture and heritage conservation where such aid does not affect trading conditions and competition in the Community to an extent that is contrary to the common interest'.*

---

43 *Supra*, paragraph 3.7.3.

44 *Cf.* Albers 1999, p. 276 *et seq.*

The application of this provision in practice can be seen in the *CELF* saga.[45] This line of cases can in many ways be said to have been started by the consideration that literature must not only be read to further culture in the homeland but it needs also to be read abroad. For this reason, the French government has decided to fund the *Coopérative d'Exportation du Livre Français* (Centre for the exportation of French books, *CELF*).[46] The CELF received an export subsidy for small orders by foreign booksellers. This was allowed because it served a cultural purpose in that it improved the availability abroad of French literature. Furthermore, CELF administered three aid schemes for exports to non-member states. Whilst recognising that books 'are an exceptional product in competition terms' the Commission could not rule out the possibility of a distortion of competition and an effect on trade because of the export aid granted through CELF.[47] In order to determine whether such effects were likely, the Commission wanted to know whether only publishers established in France could join CELF and whether the aid was granted for the export of all French language books or only for books of a certain cultural value. Apparently, the answer by the French government that CELF was open to any French-language publisher wherever it is established while the aid was granted irrespective of the cultural value satisfied the Commission. The Commission thus exempted the aid on the basis of Article 87(3)(c) EC. Because the decision dates from 18 May 1993 and the amendments to the EC Treaty by the Treaty on European Union entered into force on 1 November 1993, the Commission was unable to apply the cultural exemption to be found in Article 87(3)(d). In case T-49/93, the applicant, SIDE, argued that the Commission should have opened the Article 88(2) procedure and could not restrict itself to the preliminary procedure laid down in Article 88(3). Thus, the Court needed to examine whether the Commission could have come to the conclusion that the aid was compatible with the common market so that the Article 88(2) procedure needed not to be opened. In particular, the Court considered whether, firstly, the Commission could conclude that CELF's objective was cultural and, secondly, conditions of competition could indeed be said not to have been affected to an extent contrary to the public interest.[48]

As to the cultural objective, the Court holds that[49]

---

[45] The CELF saga starts with a Commission Decision of 18 May 1993 (OJ 1993 C 174/6) that was annulled in case T-49/93, *Société Internationale de Diffusion et d'Edition (SIDE)* v. *Commission*, [1995] ECR II-2501. The new Decision 1999/133 (OJ 1999 L 44/37), was anulled in a second case brought by the same organisation in case T-155/98, *SIDE* v. *Commission*, [2002] ECR II-1179. The application for annulment by the French government was unsuccesfull, Case C-332/98, *France* v. *Commission*, [2000] ECR I-4833.

[46] Decision 1999/133, *CELF*, OJ 1999 L 44/37.

[47] Case T-49/33, *SIDE* v. *Commission*, [1995] ECR II-2501, para. 13.

[48] *Ibid.*, para. 61.

[49] *Ibid.*, para. 62.

*'it is common ground that the aim of the French government is the spread of the French language and French literature [...] Accordingly, the Court must conclude that determining the aim of the aids at issue did not pose any particular difficulties for the Commission [...].'*

With regard to the requirement that the effect on competition and intra-community trade must not be such as to be contrary to the public interest, the Court came to the conclusion that the Commission could not have come to a positive outcome. In particular, the weight attached by the Commission to the fact that all French language publishers could join CELF and the corresponding failure to take into account the effects on the market for the export of books (on which SIDE is active together with CELF) showed that the Commission's decision not to open the Article 88(2) procedure was not warranted by the facts.[50]

The decision thus annulled was replaced with Decision 1999/133. In this decision the Commission sets out exactly what it meant with the statement that books are 'an exceptional product in competition terms'. The Commission recognises that competition with regard to books is limited by language and culture but this does not completely rule out the existence of competition.[51] Whilst acknowledging that the aid may also benefit the publishers and consumers of books, the Commission is of the opinion that CELF itself is the main beneficiary. After having ruled out the applicability of the exemptions listed in Article 87(2) and those mentioned in Article 87(3)(a), (b) and (c), the Commission is thus left with the cultural exemption listed in Article 87(3)(d) EC. With regard to this exemption the Commission first sets out to analyse the market and comes to the conclusion that the reference market must be that for the export of French language books in general.[52] Furthermore, the Commission considers the scheme to be proportionate in that the aid is limited to cover only the extra costs and not exclusively reserved to CELF.[53] As regards the cultural justification, the Commission refers to the Court's judgment in the first *SIDE* case. Moreover, the Commission gives two further reasons to show that the measure indeed serves a cultural objective. Firstly, the scheme only applies to books published in the French language so that only that language is promoted. Secondly, CELF only subsides small orders that, according to the Commission, can be for specialised works of literature again exemplifying the cultural nature of the scheme. *Ex abundantia* the Commission adds that textbooks for educational purposes are ordered in large quantities and therefore fall outside the scheme. Finally, the Commission addresses the question of whether competition and intra-commu-

50 *Ibid.*, paras. 74 & 75.

51 Decision 1999/133, *CELF*, OJ 1999 L 44/37, chapter IX.

52 *Ibid.*, chapter X.

53 *Ibid.*, chapter XI.

nity trade are affected to such an extent as would be contrary to the common interest. Because of CELF's small share on the market for the export of French language books, the Commission considers that the effects are not such as to be contrary to the common interest.

As was already indicated above, there was a second *SIDE* case in which the second *CELF* decision was also annulled.[54] Basically, the Commission was considered by the Court to have committed a manifest error of assessment as regards the market definition. SIDE had argued that the effects of the aid scheme needed to be investigated not on the market for the export of French books in general but on the sub market of export agencies.[55] It was on this sub-market that CELF competed with, among others, SIDE. The Court agreed with SIDE that the Commission should have examined the effects of the aid measure on competition and trade between other companies that are active on the market for the export of small orders of French books.[56]

What, then, is the lesson to be learned from the *CELF* saga? Apparently, establishing the cultural objective of an aid scheme does not present any particular difficulties for the Commission or Court. The bottleneck has rather proven to be the final criterion pursuant to which the cultural objective is balanced with the common interest in having an undistorted market. In particular, the *CELF* decisions appear to be hampered by the Commission's wish to exempt the French aid scheme even when this may not have been appropriate from a competition perspective. Even though a role for cultural concerns has been ascertained by the legislator through the addition of Article 87(3)(d), the Commission wanted to further increase this role. In doing so, it stretched the limits of its discretion under Article 87 more than was allowed by that provision.

*CELF* involved the dissemination of literature. Even though the governments may prefer the general public to read literature, it has also recognised that watching television and films are far more popular than reading books as a means of consuming culture. As a means to ensure that television broadcasts are 'sufficiently cultural', media content has been regulated to a large extent. Furthermore, this state intervention in the market for the provision of television services has been cleared by the Court as a mandatory requirement with regard to Article 49 EC.[57] Moreover, governments have subsidised the production of cultural as opposed to mainstream ('Hollywood') films. With regard to state aid to the film sector, the Commission has had to make a distinction between state aid for cultural purposes and state aid for the furthering of the industry. According to the Commission state aid for film production may serve a cultural objective and can thus be exempted under Article 87(3)(c). However, such aid

---

54 Case T-155/98, *SIDE* v. *Commission*, [2002] ECR II-1179.

55 *Ibid.*, para. 46.

56 *Ibid.*, para. 71.

57 Case C-353/89, *Commission* v. *Netherlands* (Mediawet), [1991] ECR I-40, para. 30.

schemes may never violate the basic prohibitions enshrined in the Treaty such as the prohibition on discrimination on the basis of nationality.[58] This reasoning has kept the Commission from declaring compatible with the common market a Greek aid scheme that subsided only films that are, *inter alia*, produced by Greeks, with a Greek director and with three-quarters of the personnel having Greek nationality.[59] This direct discrimination on the basis of nationality prevented an exemption. In other cases, the Commission similarly prevented other member states from confusing the nationality of the film crew with the cultural identity.[60] Currently, the Commission allows for a 50% subsidy for films that have a 'cultural impact' (*i.e.* excluding commercial productions) subject to the requirement that the producer must be free to spend at least 20% of the budget in other member states. For 'esoteric low budget movies' a higher aid intensity is allowed.[61]

On average, Europeans went to the cinema 2.03 times in the year 2001.[62] Of the same Europeans 97.6 % watch television.[63] Although, of course, it does not follow from these statistics, they do indicate that there is a good chance that, on average, Europeans will watch television more frequently than they go to the cinema. This was and continues to be recognised by both member state governments as well as the Community institutions. This has resulted in, among others, a protocol on the system of public broadcasting in the Member States annexed to the EC Treaty by the Treaty of Amsterdam. Furthermore, the liberalisation of the broadcasting industry has resulted in a number of commercial entrants on the market. These private companies have complained with the Commission about distortions of competition arising from the funding of public broadcasters.

Among others, this has resulted in the *RTP* (*Radiotelevisão Portuguesa*) case concerning the funding of the Portuguese public broadcaster.[64] In its decision, the Commission concluded on the basis of the findings in the preliminary Article 88(3) investigation that there was no state aid since the funding was provided in a transparent manner and did not exceed the extra costs arising from the public service obligation. Accordingly, the Commission considered that there was no advantage conferred on RTP so that it was not necessary to open the Arti-

58 XXVth. Competition Report (1995), para. 199.

59 Decision 89/441, *Greek Films*, OJ 1989 L 208/38.

60 *E.g.* the French and German schemes mentioned in the XXIInd. Competition Report (1992), paras. 442-444.

61 See answer by Monti to written question E-1568/00, OJ 2001 C 113E/27. See for an application of these rules: Decision 380/00/COL of the EFTA Surveillance Authority with regard to a film subsidisation scheme in Iceland, OJ 2001 L 89/37.

62 Eurostat, Eurobarometer 'Europeans' participation in cultural activities', April 2001, p. 9.

63 *Ibid.*, p. 2.

64 Case T-46/97, *Sociedade Independente de Comunicação (SIC)* v. *Commission*, [2000] ECR II-2125.

cle 88(2) full investigation procedure.[65] Commercial Television Company SIC applied for annulment of this decision with the Court of First Instance on the grounds that the Commission should have opened the Article 88(2)-investigation procedure. Just as in the *CELF* case, the Court set out to ascertain whether the facts indeed warranted the decision by the Commission that there was no *prima facie* state aid.[66] The Court considered that[67]

*'In order to determine whether a state measure constitutes aid, [...] it is necessary to establish whether the recipient undertaking receives an economic advantage which it would not have obtained under normal market conditions.*

*[...] the grants paid [...] by way of compensation have the result of giving that undertaking a financial advantage.*

*The fact that [...] the grants were merely intended to offset the additional cost of the public service tasks [...] cannot prevent them from being classified as aid within the meaning of Article [87] of the Treaty.'*

According to the Court of First Instance such compensatory grants must, contrary to the Commission's appraisal, be considered state aid. The fact that they merely compensate the extra costs arising from the public service obligation can only be taken into account under Article 86(2).[68] This leads us to the interesting question to what extent a public service obligation can remove a certain activity from the scope of Article 87 altogether.

In his recent opinion in the *GEMO* case, Advocate-General Jacobs has set out the discussion with regard to this question in discerning two basic approaches which he calls the state aid and the compensation approach.[69] Under the state aid approach any government funding will constitute state aid and only Article 86(2) or one of the exemptions listed in Article 87(2) or (3) can save such grants from the prohibition of Article 87(1). However, the compensation approach means that only overcompensation of the public service costs will constitute state aid. It may be recalled that the Court's case law in this respect has not been entirely consistent[70] but that in the recent *Ferring* case the Court clearly adopted the compensation approach.[71] If this case law is upheld,[72] the Commission may

65 *Ibid.*, paras. 22-24.

66 *Ibid.*, paras. 70 *et seq.*

67 *Ibid.*, paras. 78, 79 and 82.

68 *Ibid.*, para. 84.

69 Case C-126/01, *Ministre de l'économie, des finances et de l'industrie* v. *GEMO*, n.y.r., paras. 93-95.

70 *Cf. ibid.* para. 96.

71 *Supra*, chapter 8.2.3.

72 Whether the Court will continue to apply the compensation approach can probably be seen in the *GEMO* case referred to in footnote 68 *supra* and in case C-280/00, *Altmark Trans* v. *Nahverkehrsgesellschaft Altmark* both of which have not been decided by the Court at the time of writing.

have to change the approach it adopted in the Communication on the application of State aid rules to public service broadcasting.[73] In this document the Commission considers that government funding constitutes state aid (irrespective of whether it is compensatory or not) and can be exempted pursuant to Article 87(3)(d) or justified on the basis of Article 86(2) EC. As far as the adoption of the state aid approach is concerned, the commission will then have to change its approach.[74] This would in turn mean that Article 87(3)(d) and 86(2) have lost much of their significance as well. This is so because it will be nigh impossible to argue that *over*compensation is necessary to achieve a cultural objective or to ensure the fulfilment of a task of general economic interest.[75]

This uncertainty does not detract from the fact that it is still interesting to examine the general demarcation between Article 87(3)(d) on the one hand and Article 86(2), on the other, proposed by the Commission.[76] This demarcation follows, firstly, from the fact that, as an exemption from the general rule, Article 87(3)(d) is to be interpreted narrowly. Since that provision refers only to aid to promote *culture*, other considerations such as to provide education to ensure democracy are considered to be distinct. In this respect the Commission refers to the Protocol that distinguishes between the democratic, social and cultural needs of a society.[77] On this basis the Commission comes to the conclusion that Article 87(3)(d) is applicable only when the aid is separately granted for cultural purposes. Aid that is granted to public broadcasters without differentiation between the three objectives mentioned in the Protocol can nevertheless be justified with recourse to Article 86(2) EC. The Commission appears to have applied this reasoning *avant le lettre* in the *BBC News 24* decision.[78] That case involved state aid for a dedicated 24-hour advertising-free news channel. Apparently, the UK authorities had not invoked Article 87(3)(d) whilst the Commission did not appear to consider that exemption applicable either As a result, the Commission used the Article 86(2) justification for public undertakings to consider the aid compatible with the common market. It is at the application of Article 86(1) and (2) in the cultural sector that we will be looking in the next paragraph.

---

73 OJ 2001 C 320/5.

74 Indeed, in its report of 30 May 2002 to the Seville European Council the Commission addresses this point and signals the change in the Court's approach and indicates that it considers it advisable to wait for the judgments in *GEMO* and *Altmark Trans* cases, referred to in footnote 71 *supra*, before coming to a final position.

75 *Cf.* Case C-53/00, *Ferring* v. *Agence centrale des organismes de sécurité sociale*, [2001] ECR I-9067, paras. 32 and 33.

76 Commission Communication on the application of State aid rules to public service broadcasting, OJ 2001 C 320/5, paras. 26, 27.

77 Interpretative protocol on the system of public service broadcasting, referrred to *ibid*, at para. 15.

78 Decision of 14 December 1999 in case NN 88/98, para. 36.

However, before we move on to this issue, the interim conclusion with regard to the application of the state aid rules in the cultural sector must be that there is no integration of cultural and competition that corresponds with the model of integration. This is best shown by the cases that involve direct state funding of daily running costs. These aids must be characterised as operating aids, yet the conditions for compatibility with the common market differ markedly from those imposed on environmental operating aids. It may be recalled that the Commission requires environmental operating aids to be of a limited duration and possibly degressive. The rationale behind this, as we saw above in paragraph 8.5.4 is identical to the basic idea underlying the model of integration – in the end subsidisation of environmentally friendly products and production methods should no longer be necessary. With regard to cultural operating aids the implicit idea appears to be that such aids will always remain necessary precisely because an internalisation of cultural costs is impossible.

### 15.3.3 Public broadcasters as public undertakings

On the basis of what has been said above it can be concluded that Article 86(2) is available to save public broadcasters from the wrath of the market. This conclusion, however, should not make us forget that in the first instance Article 86(1) EC applies. An interesting case concerning the grant of a culturally motivated exclusive right is the *VTM* case. Again, the story starts with a decision by the Commission. In this decision the Commission considers the statutory monopoly for the broadcasting of television advertising given to VTM to infringe Community law, in particular Articles 86(1) in conjunction with Article 43 EC.[79] The Flemish legislation at issue in this case moreover demanded that the beneficiary of this exclusive right must be a private company of which at least 51% of the shares must be held by Dutch language newspapers and magazines established in Flanders. This latter requirement, imposing a link between the broadcaster and written media, was the result of cultural considerations. Apparently, the Flemish government noticed the popularity of TV and the accompanying fact that advertising revenue was transferred from the written media to the television broadcasters. To ensure sufficient income for the written media and thus to ensure their survival and the maintenance of pluralism in the press, the exclusive right was granted in this form so as to ascertain that part of the advertising income would be transferred back to the written media.[80] The underlying idea was therefore one of cross-subsidisation between television advertising income and written media.

---

79 Decision 97/606, *Exclusive right to broadcast television advertising in Flanders* (VTM), OJ 1997 L 244/18.

80 *Ibid.*, para. 2.

The Commission qualifies VTM's monopoly over television advertising as applying without distinction but 'incontestably protectionist'.[81] The Commission then states that a restriction on the freedom of establishment would have to be accepted if it was shown to be necessary in the light of an imperative requirements in the public interest. Indeed, the Commission states that the Flemish government initially invoked a cultural justification of the monopoly. However, in the light of developments in the media sector, the Flemish government no longer relied on this argument during the further proceedings. The monopolist itself, VTM, did seek to invoke cultural objectives and the need to ensure pluralism as imperative requirements. According to the Commission, cultural policy and pluralism are indeed imperative requirements. However, in this case they do not justify setting Article 43 EC aside as that would deprive that provision of any effect whatsoever. Moreover, the Commission considers that there is no necessary relationship between the statutory monopoly and the cultural objectives and the preservation of pluralism.[82] It then sets out to substantiate this conclusion with the following reasons. Firstly, there is no guarantee that all members of the written media in Flanders can become shareholders in VTM and thus receive a share in the advertising profits. Secondly, the Commission notes that there is no guarantee that the shareholders will actually use the advertising revenue to overcome the financial difficulties and thus actually preserve pluralism. Finally, the Commission points out that the 51% share may very well end up being held by one company thus having no effect on pluralism at all. This reasoning is in fact quite similar to that employed with regard to book price fixing where the Commission – and, in the Dutch cases, the Netherlands Competition Authority – have held that increasing income does not necessarily result in cross-subsidisation and consequently, pluralism.

The Commission considers that Article 86(2) cannot be relied upon in this case because, firstly, VTM does not appear to have been *entrusted* within the meaning of that provision. Secondly, the Commission considers that the exclusive rights for VTM are disproportionate.[83] The Court of First Instance upheld the decision in the *VTM* case.[84]

Whilst the Commission ruled out the application of Article 86(2) in *VTM*, this provision, as we have seen above, has played a major role in the Commission's practice with regard to the funding of public broadcasting. In the *BBC News 24* case,[85] the Commission applied the test that it would codify in the Communication on the application of State aid rules to pubic service broad-

---

81 *Ibid.*, para. 12.

82 *Ibid.*, para. 13.

83 *Ibid.*, para. 14.

84 Case T-266/97, *Vlaamse Televisie Maatschappij* v. *Commission*, [1999] ECR II-2329.

85 Decision of 14 December 1999 in case NN 88/98, para. 38.

casting.[86] According to this test the member state must first define the public service remit. Secondly the member state must entrust the performance of the special task to an undertaking. Finally, the application of the rules in the Treaty (*i.c.* notably Article 87) may not obstruct the performance of the special task (proportionality).[87] This application of Article 86(2) to cultural considerations is in fact identical to the application of Article 86(2) in general.

## 15.4 Interim conclusion with regard to the internal perspective

This chapter has shown that the role of cultural considerations and (EC) competition law does not amount to integration in the meaning of the model of integration developed in the first part. With regard to Article 81, the experiences gathered in applying that provision to book price fixing schemes show that it is impossible to integrate cultural concerns for the simple reason that the cultural objectives and the objectives of competition law are and remain ultimately antagonistic. The role for cultural considerations is therefore limited to legislative action. Similarly, the application of Article 87 to cultural aid schemes shows that the role for cultural considerations in particular only came about after the Treaty had been amended. The mere fact that cultural considerations are explicitly mentioned as a ground for an exemption from Article 87(1) and the fact that provision (Article 87(3)(d) EC) entails a similar balancing exercise as the provision used to allow environmental state aids, does not mean that an integration has in fact taken place.

This is exemplified by a comparison of the regime in place with regard to operating aid. With regard to environmental operating aid, the Commission is right to state that such aid must be of limited duration and degressive precisely to bring about an integration of environmental concerns and competition law through an internalisation of environmental costs. This approach is completely in line with the model of integration developed in Part One. To cultural operating aid no such logic applies. The production of 'high culture' books, films and television will always require funding in order to compete with commercial productions. The Commission, therefore, imposes no time limits or degressivity requirements on the member states when they grant aids for cultural purposes.

---

86 Commission Communication on the application of State aid rules to public service broadcasting, OJ 2001 C 320/5.

87 *Ibid.*, para. 29.

CHAPTER 16

# The External Perspective

## A Study of Environmental Protection and Competition in Germany, the United Kingdom and the Netherlands

## 16.1 Introductory remarks

Environmental policy, the search for new instruments of environmental policy and the lacking implementation of the polluter-pays-principle are not unique to the EC. Many if not all of the member states are themselves in some way also caught in the competition and environment conundrum. Furthermore, much of the environmental policy of the member states actually consists of the implementation of environmental Directives. Interestingly a number of these Directives explicitly allow for their implementation through environmental agreements. We have seen in chapter 9.6 above how the Packaging Directive and the German Packaging Ordinance can in many ways be said to have resulted in the DSD system. Moreover, the DSD system has not only been challenged by the Commission on Community competition law grounds, it has also been criticised on the basis of the German competition rules. A comparable situation can be seen in many other member states where the principle of producer responsibility has been put to practice as a guiding principle of environmental policy with regard to waste. DSD can therefore be seen as a competition law problem that was (partly) caused by environmental law. The question thus arising is actually twofold. Firstly, how should competition law react to such environmentally induced restrictions of competition? Secondly, how can environmental policy be changed in order to prevent such competition problems from arising in the first place? This last question is of particular interest because at the foundation of these competition problems lies not so much a legal issue but rather a missed opportunity to make use of what is probably the most efficient allocative mechanism that exists: competition.

We will thus scrutinise with the help of, primarily, the Packaging Directive and the WEEE Directive and the relevant implementing legislation of the member states, the relation between competition and environmental protection from both the environmental and the competition point of view that were identified in the introductory chapter of Part One.

Below, we will study the role that environmental considerations have played in British, German and Netherlands competition law. In particular we will first look at the regimes in place in those states as regards competition and environmental protection. Certainly, this book does not lend itself for an extensive study of the environmental and competition laws of these member states and therefore, we shall restrict ourselves to providing a succinct overview only of the relevant law and concentrating on the areas of law where competition and environmental protection meet. The stage having thus been set, we shall then investigate the relation between these two on the legislative level as well as the case law level.

The choice for these three particular jurisdictions can be explained on practical grounds and because of the purpose of this research.[1] With regard to the practicalities of conducting comparative legal research, language is of course a major limiting factor. Furthermore, time and the pages in this book are not infinitely available. These have been the primary negative factors, *i.e.* factors used to exclude certain jurisdictions. On the positive side, these jurisdictions have been chosen because of their particular value for the research. In short, the British system will be studied because of the close links between the producer responsibility regime and competition law and policy. Netherlands and German competition law will be studied because they are to a varying extent based on European Community competition law, yet lack the market integration objective and an integration principle. Moreover, quite a lot of experience with the role of environmental concerns and, notably, the cartel prohibition has already been gathered in the Netherlands. Germany and the Netherlands have also been chosen because of the experiences gathered in those jurisdictions with regard to dealing with large-scale producer responsibility organisations such as those that gave rise to the *DSD* and *Eco-Emballages* cases.

## 16.2 Relevance

Again, we must first address the issue of comparability. As was mentioned in the introductory paragraph, the systems of competition law that will be studied in this chapter have been chosen because of their experiences in dealing with environmental concerns in cases involving large scale producer responsibility organisations. This in itself already makes them a valid choice for conducting comparative legal research with regard to both perspectives identified above, for the simple reason that there is something to compare. The comparison, however, is limited as regards both perspectives. The comparability of the national laws as far as the environmental perspective ('to what extent have environmental legislators and decision makers taken competition into account?') is concerned, is limited to producer responsibility legislation for the reason that this is an instrument of environmental law with regard to which the competitive mechanism is most explicitly considered to play its environmentally friendly role.[2] In the EC the following examples of producer responsibility legislation exist: the Packaging Directive,[3] the End-of-life-vehicles Directive (ELV Directive)[4] and the Waste of electrical and electronical equipment Directive (WEEE

[1] Further comparative research on this subject can be found in Vedder 2002, p. 163 *et seq.*

[2] Another example is emissions trading.

[3] Directive 94/62 on packaging and packaging waste, OJ 1994 L 365/10.

[4] Directive 2000/53 on end-of-life-vehicles, OJ 2000 L 269/34, hereafter the ELV Directive.

Directive).[5] In general, these three are set up much along the same lines. They oblige member states to put into place a producer responsibility upon producers and importers of a certain type of good. The Directives then explicitly allow the member states make it possible for the producers to accept the responsibility either individually or collectively. With regard to this collective option member states are left more or less freedom to regulate the practicalities (terms of access to the system, financing etc.) themselves. In the more recent Directives (notably the WEEE Directive) the fact that these collective solutions may be at odds with the use of the competition mechanism as a means to ensure more efficient environmental protection appears to be recognised more explicitly. Indeed, as was shown in the first part, competition, through the system of producer responsibility, may prove to be a very beneficial means to ensure that environmental protection is achieved at minimum costs. At first sight it would seem that co-operation between those made responsible renders this mechanism much less effective. We will therefore closely look at the implementation of these Directives in the member states mentioned above to see if and to what extent this tension between competition and co-operation has been taken into account.

With regard to the competition perspective ('are environmental considerations taken into account in competition law?'), comparability is limited. This is so because not every instrument of EC competition law has a counterpart on the national level. Provisions such as Article 87 EC and the useful effect rule lack national equivalents simply because they are addressed to the member states. On the other hand, a provision analogous to the second paragraph of Article 86 EC can, for example, be found in the competition law of the Netherlands. Apart from these limitations account should also be taken of the different legal settings and background in which the competition laws function. In chapter 2 of Part Two we have seen that the market integration goals that underlie the EC Treaty have played and continue to play a major role in the interpretation of Community competition law. This objective is irrelevant to the national systems of competition law. Furthermore, the fact that EC competition law has resulted in a spontaneous harmonisation of the national competition laws of the member states introduces an interesting extra dynamic in these national systems. In this respect it may, for example, be wondered to what extent certain European competition law doctrines such as the *Albany* exception *ratione materiae* should or even can be applied in a national context? On the one hand it could be argued that such doctrines should be applied by analogy precisely because the aim of the legislator was to establish and maintain parallelism between Community and national systems of competition law. On the other hand it could also be argued that since, essentially, the *Albany* exception is the result of and contin-

[5] Directive 2002/96 on waste of electrical and electronical equipment, OJ 2002 L 37/24, hereafter the WEEE Directive.

gent upon the interrelated facts that Community competition law is just one of a number of non-hierarchical policies in the Treaty and that there is a conflict between the objectives of these policies, the application by analogy of that exception in national competition laws is not called for because simply because national competition laws do not function in this non-hierarchical system. Furthermore, conflicts between the objectives of national policies and national competition laws can be resolved by other means than the *praktischer konkordanz* type of reasoning that is considered to lie at the basis of the *Albany* exception. In essence, therefore, the question is in how far European doctrines are *communautaire* and therefore unique to European law thus making them impossible to transpose to national laws even if these laws were intended to become and remain mirror-images of Community law? This question has one quite fundamental implication for the purpose of this research that basically comes down to the question to what extent the presence of the integration principle in the EC Treaty renders the integration of environmental concerns and competition law a uniquely *communautaire* thing?

It is submitted that a number of doctrines, such as the *Albany* exception are indeed unique to the setting of Community competition law in the EC Treaty. Insofar it is of a *communautaire* character and therefore transposition of this doctrine to the national context should not be impossible but still be subject to a thorough motivation. The integration of environmental concerns and competition law, on the contrary, is submitted to be all but unique to Community competition law. As was shown in chapter 1 of Part One, the integration principle in the EC Treaty is of itself of rather limited value because of the undefinedness of the concept of integration. Indeed, the concept of integration could only be given a usable content with the help of the polluter pays principle and the internalisation of environmental costs and the price mechanism. These are everything but limited to Community law and can validly be applied with regard to any situation where competition laws and environmental protection requirements meet.

In sum, the relevance of the role of environmental concerns in national competition laws is limited only to the extent that certain doctrines and certain areas of Community competition law do not exist in or hardly lend themselves to transposition into national competition laws.

With the help of this background we will now turn our attention the experiences gathered in Germany, the United Kingdom and the Netherlands with regard to competition and environmental protection.

## 16.3 Competition and the environment in Germany

Collective agreements either among entire branches of industry (*Selbstverpflichtungen*) or between such branches and the government (*Verträge*) have existed for a long time in Germany.[6] Moreover, several of these agreements have been concluded with regard to some environmental protection objective. Examples are the agreements for the taking back and recycling of car-wrecks, used batteries and accumulators, the reduction of carbon-dioxide emissions from cars and the taking back and recycling of packaging waste. The latter has become particularly well known and perhaps even notorious under the name DSD. Below, we will study German practice with regard to competition and the environment from the perspective of the Packaging Ordinance and the concept of product responsibility on a more abstract level. After that we will examine German competition law and its application in cases involving environmental protection.

### 16.3.1 The Packaging Ordinance and DSD

DSD can be said to be the direct result of the German Packaging Ordinance (*Verpackungsverordnung*). According to this Ordinance producers and importers of packaging are responsible for their packaging once this reaches the waste stage.[7] The Ordinance allows for two options with regard to the actual implementation of this responsibility: setting up a so-called self-management solution and joining a collective exemption system.

The basic obligation is laid down in Section 6(1) of the Ordinance according to which:[8]

*'Retailers are under an obligation to take back free of charge from the consumer used and emptied sales packaging at the point of sales or in the direct vicinity. The sales packaging must be forwarded for recycling. The retailer must alert the consumer to this take-back possibility. The take-back obligation is limited to sales packaging of the type, form and size that the retailer has in his assortment. Retailers that have less than 200 square meters only have to take back packaging of the brand that they carry.'*

---

6 *Cf.* Engel 1998, p. 7.

7 The Ordinance distinguishes between: transport, secondary and sales packaging. (section 3(1)). Because the competition problems have arisen primarily with regard to the collective systems set up for the take back and recovery of sales packaging, we will not address the issues surrounding secondary and transport packaging any further.

8 Translation by the author.

The individual systems set up pursuant to this provision are referred to as: self-management systems (*Selbstentsorgerlösungen*). Thus, sales packaging must be taken back, free of charge, in the direct vicinity of the sales point by the retailer.[9] The producers/importers have a similar take-back obligation *vis a vis* the retailer pursuant to the second paragraph of section 6 of the Ordinance. This effectively turns the basic obligation into one where the producer, distributor and retailer must take back and recover the waste packaging that was marketed by them or similar to the packaging marketed by them from every retailer or consumer.[10] It will not take a great amount of imagination that such an obligation upon producers to take back packaging waste from every household in Germany through self-management solutions involves setting up a highly developed infrastructure and thus prohibitively high costs.

In this respect, it must be recalled that the weakest link in any take-back and recovery system is the consumer who needs to do the initial separation and the actual taking back to the shop. Whether the recovery-quota are actually met, thus depends to a large extent on the consumer. The German legislator was therefore completely right in recognising the fundamental importance of centring the system around the consumer. This only serves to reiterate the importance of a clearly communicated and uniform take-back scheme. Needless to say, a multitude of self-management solutions will most probably result in a large part of the packaging waste ending up with the household waste anyway. Additional problems arise on the side of the retailers/producers. For one, the Ordinance has implemented the consumer-friendliness in a way that can be characterised as bottom-up. The starting point is the take back obligation at the outlets. The required further infrastructure is actually the opposite (centralising to a limited number of recyclers) of that with which producers have experience (decentralising from a distribution centre to shops), therefore only increasing costs of setting up this infrastructure. Furthermore, reasons connected to hygiene strongly plead against the storing of empty sales packaging in the stores or at least mean investments in separate facilities to store this waste without any danger to new products. All of these factors result in considerable extra costs for retailers and producers.[11]

Moreover, the bottom up nature of the system presupposes a certain degree of 'solidarity' among retailers and producers/importers as the retailers are under an obligation to take back packaging of the size, type and sort that he carries in his own assortment. This may very well mean that the retailer actually takes back packaging of another brand than the one he sells. This in turn means

9 In the terminology of the Ordinance these are called distributors (*Vertreiber*, Section 3(8) Packaging Ordinance)

10 *Cf.*, with further references, Bastians 2002, p. 46.

11 See, for further references in this respect, Velte 1999, p. 79 and 94.

that the producers/importers may similarly take back packaging waste that was never actually marketed by them. This may be particularly problematic in the case of producers that have ceased to be active on the market (leading to so-called orphaned waste) but a number of other situations involving extra costs for certain producers could also be envisaged. The only way to prevent an undue allocation of these costs is through a mechanism ensuring that a producer will indeed take back and recycle the waste that was marketed by himself. Any producer not taking back and recycling sufficient amounts of waste would then have to purchase additional amounts from other producers. This, however, will require an exchange of information. Moreover, this works only if there is an obligation to take back all the waste that was marketed.[12] All in all, the bottom up approach and resulting high costs and solidarity requirements are all arguments in favour of a collective approach to meeting the product responsibility.

This was also realised during the preparation of the Ordinance and has resulted in the possibility to be exempted[13] from the individual product responsibility obligation by joining a collective 'exemption scheme' (*Freistellungssystem*).[14] According to Section 6(3)

> *'The take-back and recovery obligation does not apply to producers and retailers participating in an extensive system that covers the territory of one* Land *and which guarantees that throughout the retailers' sales area that waste sales packaging is regularly collected from the consumer or in the vicinity of the final consumer.'*

Collective exemption schemes have to meet the same recovery quota as the self-management solutions. Furthermore, collective exemption schemes must be recognised by the authorities of the *länder.* Finally, producers and retailers are under an obligation to make known their participation in a collective scheme. All the above factors, together with the fact that to this date only the DSD collective exemption scheme has been approved, has led to approximately 70% of all sales packaging being marked with a 'green dot'.[15]

This explains the apparent success of the DSD scheme. What, then, explains the structure of the Ordinance that can be said to have contributed to the success of DSD? In this respect, models developed as part of the neo institu-

[12] If, for example, 70% of the materials marketed needs to be recycled it is very well possible that a company will meet the 70% target while other companies are actually taking back more than they are actually obliged to.

[13] This exemption-nature of joining a collective scheme can also be seen in the fact that self-managers who fail to meet the take-back and recycling quota have to join a collective system for the part of their obligation that they have not met, Section 6(3) Packaging Ordinance.

[14] These exemption schemes must not be confused with the possibility, ex Section 11 of the Ordinance, of contracting out the actual take-back and recovery obligations.

[15] Decision 2001/463, *DSD* (Article 82), OJ 2001 L 166/1, para. 95.

tional economics and political sciences may be of assistance. With regard to the interaction between two actors, essentially two behavioural options can be identified: exit and voice.[16] Applied to the situation at hand, the two actors are on the one hand the German legislator and on the other industry. In exercising the exit option, industry members simply move to another jurisdiction in order to avoid the effects of the legislation imposed upon them. The voice-option entails an effort to influence the action by, *inter alia*, submitting comments during the preparatory stages of the legislative process. For economic entities, exercising this exit option generally involves less cost than it would for natural persons. However, with respect to the Packaging Ordinance, exercising the exit option is no realistic option for the industry because of the market structure and the legislation itself. As we have seen, the basic obligation is imposed upon the retailers and exercising the exit option in a large country such as Germany would involve an increase of the distance for consumers to such an extent that consumers would simply stop coming. The constituents are thus only left with the voice option. In accordance with their own (economic) interests, the German industry sought to minimise the costs arising from the producer responsibility while at the same time remaining conscious of the importance of having a 'green image'. The dynamics of the ensuing negotiations between the government and industry reflect this point of departure for industry as well as government awareness of the fact that forcing product responsibility legislation would probably mean greatly increased enforcement costs. The result of these factors was the creation, even before the entry into force of the Packaging Ordinance, of DSD.[17]

### 16.3.2 The Act Against Restrictions of Competition and environmental agreements

Above we have seen how the DSD-system was considered by the Commission to violate Article 81 EC and fell within the scope of Article 81 EC.[18] However, apart from these encounters with European competition law, DSD has also been scrutinised on the basis of German competition law. This was done by the German Federal Competition Authority, the *Bundeskartellamt*, pursuant to the Act Against Restrictions of Competition (*Gesetz gegen Wettbewerbsbeschränkungen*; hereafter referred to as the Act or GWB). Section 1 of the Act prohibits cartels in a way that is reminiscent of Article 81(1) EC.[19] Sections

16 Hirschman 1970, introduces a third concept (loyalty). However, as the status of this third concept is rather controversial, *cf.* Dowding *et al.* 2000, p. 476, and it is of limited use for this study we shall not pay any further attention to it.

17 *Cf.* Becker-Schwarze 1997, p. 90 *et seq.*

18 *Supra*, chapter 3 and 4.

19 It may be noted, however, that Section 1 applies only to horizontal restrictions of competition.

2 through to 7 contain exemptions from this prohibition. At the time when the Federal Competition Authority examined DSD, there was no applicable exemption clause. As a result *DSD* could therefore only be tolerated (*geduldet*) on the basis of the Act concerning minor administrative offences (*Ordnungwidrigkeitengesetz*).[20] Partly with a view to addressing this problem, the GWB was amended in 1998. The changes introduced by this amendment, commonly referred to as the *Sechste Novelle* (sixth amendment) encompassed, inter alia, the introduction of a new Section 7 that was in part introduced precisely to address the problem of large-scale product responsibility organisations.[21] This provision was very much modelled on Article 81(3) of the EC Treaty and the experiences gathered in applying this provision. The result was the introduction of a general exemption clause that was hitherto absent in enumeration-system that lies at the foundations of the GWB. According to the enumeration system the grounds for an exemption from Section 1 GWB are listed exhaustively in the Act itself. Thus, up till the sixth amendment, the Act contained no general exemption clause along the lines of Article 81(3) EC and only a Ministerial Exemption (*Ministererlaubnis*) on the basis of Section 8 could be used to exempt an agreement that fell within the scope of Section 1 and did not qualify for an exemption pursuant to Sections 2-7 of the GWB. By introducing a general exemption clause, the sixth amendment has to some extent changed the entire system of the GWB. Section 7(1) GWB provides:[22]

> *'Agreements and decisions which contribute to improving the development, production, distribution, procurement,* TAKING BACK OR DISPOSAL OF GOODS *or services while allowing consumers a fair share of the resulting benefit, may be exempted from the prohibition under Section 1 provided the improvement cannot be achieved otherwise by the participating undertakings and is of sufficient importance when compared with the restraint of competition connected with it and the restraint of competition does not result in the creation or strengthening of a dominant position.'[Emphasis added]*

---

[20] Pursuant to Section 47 of this Act. *Cf. Bundeskartellamt, Tätigkeitsbericht 1991/1992*, Bundestag Drucksache 13/1660, p. IV, 133.

[21] Bundestag Drucksache 13/9720, BGBl I 2 September 1998, p. 2521.

[22] Translated from the German in Heidenhain, Satzky & Stadler 1999. The German text is: 'Vereinbarungen und Beschlüsse, die unter angemessener Beteiligung der Verbraucher an dem enstehenden Gewinn zu einer Verbesserung der Entwicklung, Erzeugung, Verteilung, Beschaffung, Rücknahme oder Entsorgung von Waren oder Dienstleistungen beitragen können vom Verbot des § 1 freigestellt werden, wenn die Verbesserung von den beteiligten Unternehmen auf andere Weise nicht erreicht werden kann, in einem angemessenen Verhältnis zu den damit verbundenen Wettbewerbsbeschänkung steht und die Wettbewerbsbeschänkung nicht zur entstehung oder Verstärkung einer Marktbeherschenden Stellung führt.'

The introduction of Section 7, being a major departure from the initial logic of the GWB, received considerable attention in the statement of reasons (*Gesetzesbegründung*). Indeed, introducing a general exemption clause constitutes a significant departure from the enumeration system that was followed up till then and has been critically referred to as a *Systembruch*[23] by the German Monopolies Commission (*Monopolkommission*).[24] The importance of this change of the GWB can hardly be overstated as it fact constitutes a departure from an approach to competition law that dates back to the nineteen twenties.[25] Furthermore, the introduction of Section 7 effectively boils down to an introduction of non-competition concerns in competition law, something that has always been regarded very critical by German competition scholars and practitioners alike.[26] These factors were probably at the roots of a number of important differences between Article 81(3) EC and Section 7 of the GWB.

For one, the environmental advantages are explicitly mentioned and not considered to constitute 'technical or economic progress' through an interpretation of Article 81(3).[27] This explicitness is only one side of the coin that is the result of the enumeration system. The other side is the fact that the environmental benefits thus referred to are construed rather narrowly and relate only to take-back and recycling systems. This reference to 'taking back or disposal of goods' must, according to this statement, be taken to refer to exemption systems set up pursuant to producer responsibility legislation.[28] This brings with it an extra difficulty that follows from Section 7's rather awkward place in the enumeration system. According to the subsidiarity clause contained in the second paragraph of Section 7, an exemption pursuant to Section 7(1) can only be granted if Sections 2 – 6 are inapplicable. Moreover, section 7 may not be used to widen the scope of Sections 2 – 6.[29] Thus, Section 7 must be understood to allow only for an exemption of producer responsibility organisations in cases where none of the other exemption possibilities are applicable. Moreover, even within Section 7 there are potential demarcation problems. In this respect, we refer to what has been said in Part three with regard to environmental considerations and Article 81(3) EC according to which environmental improvements may also be considered to constitute technical or economic progress.[30] In this respect

---

23 *Monopolkommission*, XII. *Hauptgutachten* (1996-1997), Bundestag Drucksache 13/11291, p. 60.

24 The Monopolkommission is an advisory board to the government in competition matters set up on the basis of Sections 44-47 of the GWB.

25 *Cf.* Immenga 2001, p. 308.

26 *Monopolkommission*, XII. *Hauptgutachten* (1996-1997), Bundestag Drucksache 13/11291, p. 60., *Bundeskartellamt, Tätigkeitsbericht* 1999/2000, Bundestag Drucksache 14/6300, p. 66.

27 Commission XXVIIIth. Competition Report (1998), para. 129.

28 Bundestag Drucksache 13/9720., *Begründung, 3. Teil under ee.*

29 *Ibid.*

30 *Supra*, chapter 3.7.2.

it may further be recalled that Section 7 also refers to the improvement of the production or development of goods. Accordingly, environmental improvements related to the production of goods will have to be exempted on the basis of this part of Section 7 rather than under the heading of agreements contributing to the improvement of the taking back or disposal of goods. However, even then certain environmental agreements will fall outside the scope of Section 7. It is doubtful whether, for example, an agreement to reduce the energy consumption of products could qualify for an exemption pursuant to this provision.[31]

Secondly, the partial application of the enumeration principle approach in Section 7 brings with it another interesting problem. The requirement that there must be a fair share for consumers in Section 7 corresponds literally to that in Article 81(3) EC. With regard to that requirement within the scope of Article 81(3), we have seen that it is possible to distinguish between the environmental and economic benefits that environmental co-operation may have over individual approaches to environmental problems. Moreover, we have come to the conclusion that problems *vis a vis* the possibility of an exemption ex. Article 81(3) EC are unlikely because of the collective nature of environmental benefits.[32] This reasoning is unlikely to apply to the corresponding phrase of Section 7 precisely because of the collective nature of the environmental benefits in combination with the underlying enumeration principle. In this respect it must be pointed out that Section 8(1) of the GWB allows for an exemption by the Minister for Economic Affairs on grounds of 'prevailing reasons concerning the economy as a whole and the public interest'.[33] The collective nature of the environmental benefits together with the fact that the enumeration principle is considered to dictate that the collective nature of environmental benefits effectively restricts their role to Section 8.[34] This will of course not hold true for the economic benefits that will follow from the environmental improvement. Such benefits can very well be passed on to individual consumers in the form of lower costs for the take back and recycling.

A further difference compared to Article 81(3) is the inclusion of a true proportionality test (as opposed to the necessity test enshrined in Article 81(3) EC) according to which the (environmental) benefits must be directly balanced

---

[31] *Cf.* Schumacher 2002, p. 126

[32] *Supra*, chapter 3.7.3.

[33] Translated from the German in Heidenhain, Satzky & Stadler 1999. The full German text of Section 8 is: 'If the conditions of Sections 2 to 7 are not satisfied, the Federal Minister of Economics may exempt agreements and decisions from the prohibition under Section 1 if, exceptionally, the restraint of comptition is necessary for prevailing reasons of the economy as a whole and the public interest.' The relevant exerpt from the German text reads as follows: 'überwiegenden Gründen der Gesamtwirtschaft und des Gemeinwohls'.

[34] *Cf.* Bender & Rinne 1998, p. 444 *et seq.*

with the restrictions of competition.[35] This true proportionality test is introduced alongside the necessity test that, although using differing wording, must be considered to be transposition of the necessity test included in Article 81(3) EC.[36]

Finally, the last part of Section 7(1) appears to transpose the residual competition test in Article 81(3).[37] However, despite statements to the contrary by the German government, this test is widely considered among scholars to be much more restrictive than the residual competition test contained in Article 81(3).[38] Furthermore, although it is nowhere explicitly stated in the statement of reasons, this more restrictive condition appears to be directed specifically at DSD and other large-scale producer responsibility schemes. For these schemes an exemption on the basis of this provision seems to be out of the question, as they will often entail 'the creation or strengthening of a dominant position'.

One further interesting feature of Section 7 concerns the fact that the German government partially based the inclusion of a reference to 'the taking back or disposal of goods' on Article 6 EC.[39] This reference nicely illustrates the problem of the *communautaire* character of certain principles that was already identified in paragraph 10.2. The reference to Article 6 EC as part of the motivation of the inclusion of a provision that mimics European law shows that principles such as the integration and polluter pays principle, even though having a European origin, can certainly play a role in the national context. They are, as was argued above, therefore not of an exclusively *communautaire* nature.

As far as German practice with regard to the application of the GWB to large-scale producer responsibility organisations is concerned, the *DSD* case is very much at the heart of the matter. Indeed, *DSD* more or less stood at the cradle of at least three Ph.D. theses and numerous articles.[40] Alongside DSD, there exist large-scale product responsibility organisations for car wrecks and for old batteries while similar organisations are expected to come about for other products as well.[41]

The mother of all product responsibility organisations, *DSD*, was considered by the Federal Cartel Office to violate Section 1 GWB. However, as we have seen

---

35 Schumacher 2002, p. 130.

36 *Cf. Bundeskartellamt*, Decision B 6 – 22131 – M – 49/99, *Stellenmarkt Deutschland*, p. 21.

37 *Ibid.*, p. 130.

38 *Ibid.*, p. 130. With further references.

39 Bundestag Drucksache 13/9720, *Begründung, 3. Teil under ee.*

40 Ehle 1996, Velte 1999 and Bastians 2002 have all taken the competition problems resulting from DSD as a point of departure for their studies. These three books contain extensive references to – primarily German – articles concerning the same issue.

41 Known as, respectively, *Arge Altauto* and *Gemeinsames Rücknahme System* (GRS). Following the entry into force of the Altelektronik Verordnung (Ordinance concerning waste electronics) implementing the WEEE Directive another product responsibility organisation is expected to be erected.

above, it ended up being tolerated on the basis of the *Ordnungswidrigkeitengesetz*. This is far from a satisfactory solution because legal certainty and transparency are the clear losers in this approach. Moreover, it seems uncertain whether DSD would be able to profit from the inclusion of Section 7 as was shown above.[42] Scholars have argued that a Ministerial exemption pursuant to Section 8 of the GWB is probably the only possibility for a legalisation of *DSD*.[43] However, no such exemption has ever come about. Moreover, it is far from certain whether such an exemption will ever materialise as Section 8 involves a balancing of the restriction of competition on the one hand with the prevailing reasons concerning the economy as a whole and the public interest on the other. Velte, however, has convincingly argued that there are no less restrictive alternatives to DSD so that an exemption seems apt.[44]

In terms of political involvement in the process of applying and interpreting competition law, the amendment of Section 7 so as to allow for an exemption on environmental grounds, can in many ways be said to run parallel to a Ministerial exemption. For one, both solutions follow from the fact that a solution within the framework of the competition-related justifications (i.e. an application of Sections 2 – 6 before the sixth amendment) proved impossible. Secondly, both solutions require to some extent the involvement of the legislature instead of the specially appointed and independent institution, the *Bundeskartellamt*. Thirdly, neither option allows for a complete and unqualified exception from the prohibition in Section 1. On the basis of Section 10, paragraph 4, of the GWB requires either exemption to be limited in time and, generally, not exceeding five years. What ever may be of this parallelism, the fact remains that DSD is at the moment only tolerated as far as the prohibition on cartels is concerned. Moreover, the Federal Cartel Office has now shifted its attention to applying the provisions on abuse of a dominant position (Sections 19 and 20 of the GWB) to DSD.[45] Even before this statement, attempts by DSD to expand into other areas of the packaging recycling business, through the so-called *DEGI-konzept*, have been stopped because objections voiced by the *Bundeskartellamt*.[46] This DEGI-system would have entailed a collection and recycling scheme for transport and non-retail sales packaging set up along the lines of the DSD system.

However, is DSD actually such a disaster for competition? If we look at the external competition (*i.e.* third parties that would like to access the market),

---

42 Moreover, in the one case in which Section 7 has been applied to this date, *Stellenmarkt Deutschland*, (Decision B 6 – 22131 – M – 49/99), the *Bundeskartellamt* has adopted a restrictive approach in applying a strict necessity and proportionality test.

43 See, with further references, Velte 1999, p. 215 *et seq.*, Ehle 1996, p. 119 *et seq.*

44 Velte 1999, p. 222-257.

45 *Bundeskartellamt, Tätigkeitsbericht 1999/2000*, Bundestag Drucksache 14/6300, p. 178.

46 Decision of 24 June 1993 in case B10-762400-A-82/93, published in *WuW* under WuW/E BkartA 2561.

the situation created by the Packaging Ordinance and DSD is indeed less than totally satisfactory. However, competition is determined by more factors than the number of parties present on a market and the possibility of potential competition. Internally, are a number of factors that assure that competition is not distorted by DSD in the upstream or downstream market. This is assured by the fact that both these industries are represented in DSD's governing board so as to prevent either of them from using DSD as vehicle for any rent-seeking behaviour.[47] Such rent seeking could come from the upstream (collection and recycling industry) side in the form of excessive prices for or low quality of their services. Rent seeking by the downstream (the producers made responsible) side could take the form of unduly low prices for collection and recovery services. In either case, the wishes of one side would be antagonistic to those of the other side and thus could not be realised through DSD. As a result, DSD is unlikely to behave in a manner that will be to the detriment of consumers or the recycling market in general.

As product responsibility has also been enacted with regard to other types of waste than packaging waste, product responsibility organisations have also come about. With regard to spent batteries and accumulators, the industry concerned has set up the *GRS, Gemeinsame Rücknahmesystem Batterien* (Common Take back system for batteries).[48] This system functions within the framework of the Battery Ordinance[49] that implements the Directive on batteries and accumulators.[50] Pursuant to this Ordinance, producers and importers of batteries can only market their products when they provide for a possibility for the consumer to return spent batteries in accordance with the Ordinance.[51] As could be expected, the Ordinance provides for a collective as well as an individual solution for the take back and recycling obligation. Interestingly, the basic obligation is one to either set up or join a collective recycling and take-back scheme on the basis of Section 4(2) of the Ordinance whereas Section 4(3) allows for an individual system (*Selbstentsorgung*, Selfdisposal) as an alternative method of meeting the take back and recycling obligation.[52] Manufacturers opting for the selfdisposal method may contract third parties to do the actual taking back and recycling.

47 *Cf.* Lehman 2000.

48 See website for further information: http://www.grs-batterien.de.

49 *Verordnung über die Rücknahme und Entsorgung gebrauchter Batterien und Akkumulatoren* (Ordinance on the take back and disposal of used batteries and accumulators), BGBl. I 2001, p. 1486.

50 Directive 91/157 on Batteries and accumulators, OJ 1991 L 78/38.

51 Section 3 of the Battery Ordinance.

52 The wording of Section 4(3) indicates this alternative character: 'Paragraph 2 (*i.e.* the obligation to set up or join a collectieve system, HV) does not apply insofar as the producer is able to show that he has set up his own take back system for the batteries marketed by him'. Translated from 'Absatz 2 Satz 1 gilt nicht, sofern ein Hersteller (...) nachweist, dass er ein eigenes Rucknahmesystem für die von ihm in Verkehr gebachten Batterien eingerichtet hat.'

This legal framework has led to the foundation of the GRS whose members represent approximately 80% of the batteries imported into or manufactured in Germany. The remaining 20% are taken back through an individual system. Concerning the report of the Federal Cartel Office over 1999/2000, the German government has expressed its contentment over the fact that the Battery Ordinance has resulted in a certain degree of competition on the market for the take back and recycling of waste accumulators. In this respect, it considered the possibility of selfdisposal (carried out by third parties) to be of considerable importance.[53] However, the framework of the Battery Ordinance is also considered to distort competition in that a number of these selfdisposers are in actual fact taking back, through a third party, spent batteries that were taken back by way of the municipal waste collection system. In that way they do not face the extra costs of setting up and running their own collective take back and recycling system and thus are able to achieve returnquota that are 2.5 times higher at nearly identical costs to that of the GRS.[54] Apparently, the Environment Ministry has sought to amend the Battery Ordinance in order to neutralise this distortion of competition. However, these attempts met with objections from the *Bundeskartellamt*. Moreover, the Bundeskartellamt noted in its report over 1999/2000 that GRS had approached a number of private and municipal companies and implicitly required them to hand over any collected batteries to it because handing them over to a third party would be illegal.[55]

With regard to electronics waste, the WEEE Directive must be implemented in Germany as well. As will be seen below, when we examine the experiences in the Netherlands with regard to product responsibility for WEEE, it is likely that a collective product responsibility organisation will be the result. [56] Moreover, as part of what can probably be called a pre-emptive strike, the Federal Cartel Office has already prohibited DSD from becoming active on the market for the take back and recycling of WEEE.[57]

Finally, the End-of-life-vehicles Directive[58] has been implemented in Germany through the *Altfahrzeug-Gesetz* that amends the *Altauto-Verordnung* and renames it to *Altfahrzeug-Verordnung*.[59] Under this Ordinance, importers and producers are under an obligation to take back, free of charge, the end-of-life vehicles of their own brand only.[60] This take-back obligation is further substanti-

---

53 *Bundeskartellamt, Tätigkeitsbericht 1999/2000*, Bundestag Drucksache 14/6300, p. V.

54 *Bundesministerium für Umwelt, Naturschutz und Reaktorsicherheit* 2001, p. 2.

55 *Bundeskartellamt, Tätigkeitsbericht 1999/2000*, Bundestag Drucksache 14/6300, p. 178.

56 *Infra*, para. 10.5.1.

57 *Ibid*, p. 178.

58 Directive 2000/53 on end-of life vehicles, OJ 2000 L 269/34.

59 *Gesetz über die Entsorgung von Altfahrzeugen*, BGBl. I 2002, p. 2199.

60 *Altfahrzeug-Verordnung* (as amended by the *Altfahrzeug-Gesetz*), Section 3(1).

ated in Section 3(3) of the Ordinance where producers are obliged to collectively or individually set up a take back infrastructure. Moreover, they may decide to conclude contracts with third parties to meet these obligations. Whatever solution is adopted, the distance between the place of residence and the take back location may not be more than 50 kilometres. The result of this product responsibility has been the creation of Arge-Altauto. This organisation was set up by the industry through a so-called voluntary pledge (*Freiwillige Sebstverpflichtung*) and represents the overwhelming majority of the industry.[61] Much attention has been devoted to the financing of this product responsibility. In this respect, it must be pointed out that the product responsibility also covers the historical waste. However, since the product responsibility and thus the financial responsibility relates only to the producers own brand, solidarity related problems are not to be expected. Indeed, collective fund solutions – which are quite common in the Netherlands[62] – have not been adopted in Germany.[63] In the end, the *Bundeskartellamt* has exempted the voluntary pledge, albeit after some amendments to the agreement, on the basis of Section 2 of the GWB.[64] Section 2 allows for an exemption of so-called conditions-cartels that prescribe uniform conditions of trade provided that they do not concern prices.[65]

All in all, the competition controversy surrounding the collective solutions set up pursuant to the Battery and Packaging Ordinances seems to boil down to a cherry-picking problem in that, with regard to spent Batteries, the co-operating selfdisposers are skimming the cream of the cake after which GRS is left with the uninteresting bits.[66] DSD's competition problems can similarly be said to be the result of its wish to prevent cherry picking as well as free riding. These two problems, cherry picking and free riding, are symptomatic of the situation that results from the introduction of competition in sectors that were up till then considered to be the domain of public undertakings such as waste collection and disposal.

---

61 *Cf.* website of Arge-Altauto: http://www.arge-altauto.de/.

62 *Cf.* Onida 2000, p. 283 *et seq.*, who considers the Netherlands – as he calls it – 'scrap fee'-model as a viable financing method throughout Europe.

63 *Ibid.*, under 'forum' (30-7-2002). See, furthemore, the statement of reasons (*Begründung*) by the German government with regard to the *Altfahrzeug-Gesetz* (can be downloaded from the website of the German Federal Ministry for the Environment: http://www.bmu.de), p. 14.

64 *Bundeskartellamt, Tätigkeitsbericht 1997/1998*, Bundestag Drucksache 14/1139, p. 43, 116.

65 See further: Immenga & Mestmäcker 2001, p. 220 *et seq.*

66 *Cf. Bundesministerium für Umwelt, Naturschutz und Reaktorsicherheit* 2001, p. 2 where this is referred to as '*Rosinenpickerei*'.

## 16.4 Competition and the environment in the United Kingdom

In the UK the principle of producer responsibility has been implemented or is considered for a number of sectors. One of the most interesting applications of the producer responsibility has taken place with regard to packaging waste. In the United Kingdom, the Packaging Directive was implemented through the Producer Responsibility Obligations (Packaging Waste) Regulations 1997.[67] These Regulations have been adopted by the Secretary of State for the Environment pursuant to the Environment Act 1995.[68] As the name already indicates, these Regulations enact a producer responsibility for packaging waste. The Regulations apply only to businesses that handle more than 50.000 kilograms of packaging materials and have a turnover of more than GBP 1.000.000. These undertakings are referred to as so-called obligated companies. The actual producer responsibility takes the form of percentages of the amount of packaging material handled in the preceding year that must be recovered and recycled. These percentages depend on the involvement in the packaging industry (raw material manufacturing 6%, converting raw materials into packaging 9 %, filling/packing 37% and selling 48%). Because of this it is also referred to as a shared responsibility.

The obligated companies have two options through which they can fulfil the producer responsibility. They can chose an individual solution or they may choose to join a collective compliance scheme. Just as in other cases where a producer responsibility has been enacted, joining a collective scheme has proven to be the most popular method of meeting the producer responsibility. However, where the choice between the individual and collective solution has in other member states resulted in the creation of large-scale monopolistic systems, it has resulted in the coming about of a flourishing market in the UK. Indeed, there exist 19 such collective schemes at the moment. These vary from nationwide multi sectoral schemes[69] to regional[70] and single sector schemes.[71] Interestingly, such collective schemes have to meet a 'competition scrutiny' on the basis of the Regulations.

From a competition-and-the-environment-perspective essentially two interesting points may be discerned. Firstly, there is the question why the market for recovery and recycling of packaging in the UK can be described as

---

67 SI 1997, 648, amended since. Hereafter referred to as 'the Regulations'.

68 Section 93(1) of the Environment Act 1995.

69 Such as, for example, Valpak and Wastepak that operate through the UK and cover all sorts of packaging material.

70 Such as Pennine Pack that operates in areas of Calderdale and Kirklees in West Yorkshire.

71 An example of this category is the Difpak scheme set up by the dairy industry and will cover only the packaging used by that industry.

flourishing and competitive whereas other producer responsibility laws have resulted in monopolistic systems. Secondly, there is the 'competition scrutiny' according to which there is an *ex ante* appreciation of the competitive impact of a collective scheme. Both points will be further investigated below.

### 16.4.1 The creation of a market for the recovery and recycling of packaging waste

What exactly lies at the basis of this stunning difference between producer responsibility regimes on the continent and the one implemented with regard to packaging waste in the UK? In a nutshell it all boils down to the difference between, on the one hand, a product responsibility and, on the other, a true producer responsibility.[72] It can be said that the German Packaging Ordinance establishes something that must actually be characterised as a *product* responsibility rather than a producer responsibility. As could be seen above, the basic obligation is primarily attached to the products marketed and not so much to any entity that is made responsible. This was characterised as the bottom up approach as the point where the consumer feeds the waste into the system functions as point of departure. The products thus fed into the system must be taken back and be recycled.

The Regulations, however, impose upon the producers an obligation to take back a portion of waste expressed as a percentage of the amount of that substance handled by a company during the preceding year. Furthermore, the take-back obligation is not material-specific (e.g. an obligated producer using glass packaging can fulfil the take-back obligation by taking back paper) whereas the recycling obligation is material specific. Proof of having met these obligations can take either of two forms: firstly, by providing 'documentary evidence' or, secondly, with the help of so-called Packaging Recovery Notes or – in short – PRNs. These PRNs are certificates that are sold by the companies that perform the actual recycling and represent a certain amount of packaging waste that has been recycled. Although the normal situation will be that the PRNs are handed over to the company supplying the waste, there is no obligation to do so, leaving the PRNs freely tradable. As the documentary evidence option involves considerable costs,[73] most companies have embraced the PRN option. Indeed, the existence of these PRNs, can be said to have greatly aided the creation of the market for take-back and recycling services by turning these services into a tradable commodity.[74] The obligated companies can thus freely purchase whatever recycling services they need in order to meet the targets imposed by the Regula-

[72] *Cf.* Bastians 2002, p. 154.

[73] *Cf.* Bastians 2002, p. 112, 113.

[74] It may be added that there is actually an on-line exchange for these PRNs.

tions. All in all the Regulations lay down a true producer responsibility or, in other words, have taken a top down approach to producer responsibility. In this approach the point of departure is the producer who has to meet certain goals as he sees fit. In market terms this means that demand was created for the (new) collection and recycling services. This demand was met by a number of parties offering such services thus creating a market. This is not to say that there were never or are no longer any fears surrounding competition in the British market for packaging waste recycling services.[75]

### 16.4.2 Competition scrutiny

As could already be seen in Part Two, many collective producer responsibility schemes actually operate as a 'spider in the web', bringing together the producers that have been made responsible, transporters, collectors and companies offering recovery and recycling services. As a result, competition concerns relate primarily to foreclosure effects stemming from the vertical relations and the need to prevent the coming about of large-scale organisations. The approach to such competition concerns is, as we have seen above, to a large extent *ex post* in that competition problems first have to actually arise before the competition authorities enter into the picture. The Commission's Article 82 EC case against DSD is in many respects symptomatic for this *ex post* approach.

This situation may be contrasted with that in the UK following the Regulations. During the preparatory phase of the Regulations it was envisaged that all sorts of contacts concluded as part of the operation of a collective scheme could be subject to the Restrictive Trade Practices Act 1976.[76] The resulting essentially *ex post* control was considered inappropriate and inefficient replaced by an *ex ante* review of the competition effects pursuant to Regulation 31. This Regulation, insofar as relevant, reads as follows:

*'[T]he requirements of competition scrutiny in relation to a scheme are that (a) the scheme does not have, and is not likely to have, the effect of restricting, distorting or preventing competition or, where it appears to the Secretary of State that the scheme has or is likely to have any such effect, the effect is or is likely to be no greater than is necessary for achieving the environmental or economic benefits mentioned in section 93(6) of the Act; and*

*(b) the scheme does not lead, and is not likely to lead, to an abuse of market power.'*

---

75 Moreover, and more importantly, this does not include any judgment on the environmental effectivess of the British solution.

76 Now replaced by the Competition Act 1998, 1998 chapter 41.

In practice, a scheme must apply to the Director General of Fair Trading who gives advice to the Secretary of State for the Environment with regard to the competition scrutiny. In the end, the Secretary of State decides on the basis of the Director General's advice. To this day the Director General has conducted a competition scrutiny in relation to 19 schemes. Of these 19 schemes, only one scheme, *Glaspak*, was considered not to meet the requirements of the competition scrutiny.[77] *Glaspak* was set up by the British glass container industry and centres around Glasmo, a company set up to function as a 'spider in the web', and five glass reprocessing companies that represent approximately 95% of the market for reprocessing glass. As part of the Glaspak scheme, these five companies will pass on all the PRNs that they generate on to Glasmo free of charge. Glasmo will, in turn, sell the PRNs, at a fixed price, to third parties. These third parties will primarily be those parties that need glass-recycling PRNs so that only the remaining PRNs will be sold as non-specific recovery PRNs.

As could be expected, *Glaspak* met with concerns pursuant to Regulation 31(1)(b).[78] Firstly, the five reprocessing companies would form a buyer's cartel on the market for the purchase of glass cullet (glass that has already been recovered but still needs to recycled). The market position of this buyer's cartel will certainly enable abuse of the collective dominant position. Secondly, the obligation on the five reprocessing companies to pass all their PRNs on to Glasmo will confer upon the latter a dominant position on the market for the sale of glass PRNs. As the wording of Regulation 31(1)(b) already shows there is no possibility to justify an abuse of a dominant position. However, *ex abundantia cautela*, the Director General addresses the arguments forwarded by Glaspak with respect to the environmental and economic benefits of the scheme within the meaning of Regulation 31(1)(a).[79] In this respect, the Director General considers that only one of the five arguments brought forward by Glaspak cuts ice. This argument addresses the weakest link of any producer responsibility scheme, namely consumer participation. According to the parties, consumers need to be educated in order to ascertain that larger amounts of glass are returned to bottle banks. In this regard, Glaspak argues that free-rider problems will effectively prevent this education from coming about.[80] Assuming that increasing the amount of collected glass from the public can be done most effectively through public bottle banks, the Director General accepts that a co-ordinated effort with regard to publicity and education will increase the environmental as well as economic benefits of the scheme. However, as the wording of Regulation 31(1)(a) shows, it must be shown that the restrictions of competition do not go beyond

77 Report of May 1998, OFT 223.

78 *Ibid.*, para. 6.5 *et seq.*

79 *Ibid.*, para. 6.26 *et seq.*

80 *Ibid.*, para. 6.49 *et seq.*

what is necessary to bring about these benefits. In this respect, the Director General is of the opinion that the co-ordinated approach to publicity and education could just as well be achieved without the restrictions of competition that were identified on the market for the purchase of cullet and that for the sale of PRNs.[81] Again, we see that foreclosure-type problems are at the heart of the matter.

On a more general level, two interesting observations may be made with regard to the competition scrutiny mechanism. Firstly, the fact environmental legislation encompasses such a test that can result in the non-application of the competition rules. This is proof of a much more conscious attitude towards producer responsibility than the one adopted on the continent that essentially comes down to a 'wait and see'-approach.[82] Secondly, there is the content of the competition scrutiny. The first paragraph, under (a), of Regulation 31 explicitly recognises the possibility to offset restrictions of competition with environmental and economic benefits in the case of environmental agreements. No such mechanism is present with regard to an abuse of a dominant position (Regulation 31(1)(b)) as it is impossible to justify an abuse.

The direct balancing of environmental with competition concerns as part of the Regulations may be compared with the appraisal on the basis of Section 7 of the German GWB.[83] A first similarity stems from the fact that both are according to their wording and context specifically geared to the competition problems arising in connection with producer responsibility organisations. Furthermore, both envisage an explicit balancing of environmental (and economic) benefits on the one hand with the restriction of competition on the other. However, Section 7 and Regulation 31 are different with regard to the type of balancing act that is to be conducted. In the case of the competition scrutiny pursuant to Regulation 31, the restriction of competition must be necessary for the attainment of the environmental and economic benefits. Thus competition and environmental protection are placed on the same level when they are weighed. Section 7 of the GWB, on the contrary, encompasses both a necessity test where the restriction of competition is balanced with the economic and environmental benefits that flow from taking back and disposing goods as well as a true proportionality test. In the latter test, the level of environmental protection sought is also subject to scrutiny on the basis of its impact on competition. The inclusion of a proportionality test effectively places the maintenance of competition above the environmental and economic benefits arising from collective take-back and recycling schemes.

---

81 *Ibid.*, para. 6.55 *et seq.*

82 Allthough, as will be seen below, the Netherlands have introduced a sort of *ex ante* competition review mechanism.

83 *Supra*, paragraph 10.3.2.

## 16.5 Competition and the environment in the Netherlands

Producer responsibility has been a mainstay of Netherlands environmental law with regard to waste for a long time. On the basis of the Environmental Management Act (*Wet milieubeheer*), which functions as the framework Act for environmental protection legislation, secondary legislation may be adopted in the interest of waste reduction.[84] Pursuant to this Act a number of Orders in Council (*Algemene maatregel van bestuur*) have been adopted.[85] These may lay down producer responsibilities for certain categories of products. Interestingly, no such legislation exists for a number of areas because the relevant industry has been able to prevent the enactment of such legislation by accepting producer responsibility 'voluntarily'. However, the degree of voluntarity in such producer responsibility schemes can be doubted given that they are in many cases actually the result of the threat of legislative activity.[86] Below, we will start with a short description of producer responsibility in the Netherlands. After that we will look at the relation between environmental protection and competition law in general. Finally, we concentrate on an aspect of the Dutch approach to producer responsibility that is rather controversial from a competition point of view: the removal or disposal fee (*verwijderingsbijdrage*) or – as it is now called – waste management fee (*afvalbeheersbijdrage*).[87] We will first describe this removal fee in general and after that move on to the competition aspects of this fee.

### 16.5.1 Producer responsibility in the Netherlands

Interestingly, producer responsibility, whether imposed or accepted voluntarily, has without exception resulted in large-scale producer responsibility organisations. With regard to packaging waste, the industry concerned has concluded an environmental agreement, the Environmental Agreement on Packaging II (*Convenant verpakkingen II*).[88] With regard to, for example, car wrecks,[89] batteries and accumulators,[90] PVC pipes[91] and waste electrical and

---

[84] Section 10.4 of the Environmental Management Act, Stb. 1992, 551.

[85] See, for an overview: Vedder 2002, p. 22.

[86] See, with further references: Engel 1998, p. 3.

[87] Chapter 15, Title 10 of the Environmental Management Act, Stb. 1992, 551 as amended by the Act of 21 June 2001 (structure for the management of waste) Stb. 2001, 346.

[88] State Gazette (*Staatscourant*) Stcrt. 1997, 247, p. 38 *et seq.*

[89] The industry concerned has set up the so-called ARN system (*Autorecycling Nederland*), hereafter referred to as ARN.

[90] Following the Batteries Order, the industry has set up the Batteries Foundation (*Stichting Batterijen* abbreviated with Stibat), hereafter referred to as Stibat.

[91] This industry scheme is set up by the Association of manufacturers of plastic pipe systems (*Federatie van fabrikanten van Kunststofleidingsystemen*), hereafter referred to as FKS.

electronical equipment,[92] the industry have similarly accepted producer responsibility collectively.

If we take the interim conclusion reached above in paragraph 10.4.1 then this should not come as a surprise since the legislation in fact establishes a product responsibility rather than a true producer responsibility. Pursuant to, for example, the Disposal of Batteries Order (*Besluit verwijdering batterijen*) or the White and Brown Goods Order (*Besluit verwijdering wit- en bruingoed*) producers are basically responsible for collecting and recycling the products that they have brought on the market.[93] The actual collection takes place as follows. If we take the example of the White and Brown Goods Order, retailers are under an obligation to take back at least free of charge all waste products from consumers that buy a replacement new product ('old for new') irrespective of the brand. The retailers can then pass the products on upstream to the producers or importers. The economies of scale that can be achieved by co-operating again effectively rule out recourse to an individual system. Moreover, the old for new-rule introduces an element of solidarity into the system that only reinforces the incentives to collectively accept producer responsibility. Indeed, with regard to the White and Brown Goods Order, the Minister for the Environment has stated in letter to the Parliament 'co-operation cannot be prescribed by law but the Order contains many incentives for a collective approach'.[94]

Thus, as could be expected, the overwhelming majority of the industry concerned decided to accept the product responsibility collectively. Essentially, the Orders allow for two different ways in which producer responsibility can be collectively accepted. Firstly, producers may collectively notify their system and secondly, they may decide to conclude an environmental covenant. Because the collective notification is subject to less procedural requirements than the covenant,[95] the White and Brown Goods Order and Batteries Order have both resulted in a collective notification.[96] The Minister for the Environment must

---

92 Two organisations: the *Stichting Witgoed* (White goods foundation) and *Stichting Bruingoed* (Brown goods foundation), hereafter the Foundations, have been set up. The scheme is managed by the *Nederlandse Vereniging Verwijdering Metalektro Produkten* (NVMP), and will hereafter be referred to as *Wit- en Bruingoed*.

93 Section 5 of the Batteries Order, Stb. 1995, 45, and section 5, 7 of the Disposal of White and Brown Goods Order, Stb. 1998, 238.

94 Translated from '[..] samenwerking kan niet wettelijk worden voorgeschreven, maar in het besluit zijn veel prikkels voor een collectieve aanpak ingebouwd.', Report of a meeting, TK 1997-1998, 25 6000 XI, nr. 39, at p. 6.

95 The collective acceptance through a covenant is explicitly made subject to extra constraints because of extra competition implications, see further: Guidelines for the White and Brown Goods Order (Environment Ministry, 14 July 1998) Chapter 2, p. 5.

96 With regard to electronic and electrical waste the White and Brown Goods Foundations were set up whereas the Stibat organisation administers the collective scheme set up pursuant to the Disposal of Batteries Order.

then approve such a notification before the underlying individual responsibility disappears.

The fact that industry has responded collectively to producer responsibility is in itself not that surprising or interesting and merely confirms the interim conclusion that a product rather than producer responsibility will result in a collective acceptance of the responsibility. What is interesting and of particular relevance to this research is the fact that these collective notifications envisage that the collection and recovery costs are financed through a so-called removal fee. This removal fee would thus have to compensate the so-called chain deficit. This chain deficit consists of the income from the recycling activities with the costs for collection and recycling deducted. Put differently, the removal fee quantifies and internalises[97] the environmental costs associated with the waste stage of production and consumption. In many of the cases involving collective product responsibility organisations that have been scrutinised on the grounds of Netherlands competition law, the removal fee has played a pivotal role. This is so because the whole idea behind the removal fee, as will be shown below, is to make the environmental costs arising from the product responsibility more transparent. From a competition point of view this increased transparency with regard to costs, together with the horizontal character of the product responsibility organisation, comes dangerously close to horizontal price fixing.

### 16.5.2 Environmental concerns and competition law in the Netherlands

As may be inferred from the above outline of environmental agreements and collective notifications, the authority responsible for the enforcement of competition law in the Netherlands, The Netherlands Competition authority (*Nederlandse Mededingingsautoriteit, NMa*) has been quite busy applying competition law to cases that involve environmental concerns. To this date, it has ruled on seven such collective schemes.[98]

However, before we move on to examine these decisions we shall first look at Netherlands competition law in general and notably the provisions that

97 There can be said to be an internalisation because the costs are as a consequence being paid by an anctor in the production and consumption process.

98 *NMa* Decision of 23 July 1999 in Case 12, *FKS*, Decision of 18 December 1998 and 31 May 1999 in Case 51, *Stibat* (Decision in first instance as well as Decision following administrative appeal), Decision of 5 April 2000 in Case 115, *ARN*, Decision of 30 September 1998 in Case 139, *SPRN* (*Stichting Papier Recycling Nederland*, Foundation Paper Recycling Netherlands), Decision of 18 April 2001 in Case 1153, *Wit- en Bruingoed*, Decision in Case 1982 *VKG* (*Stichting Recycling VKG*, Foundation Recycling Plastic Façade Cladding) (has not been officially published) and Decision of 22 October 2001 in Case 2026, *ARN II*.

concern the role of environmental protection requirements in it. Firstly, it may be observed that the Competition Act (*Mededingingswet*) is fairly recent and very much based on European Community competition law.[99] Perhaps as a result of its predecessor, the Act on Economic Competition (*Wet economische mededinging*), which was generally considered to be much more corporatist, a number of concerns were voiced during the parliamentary debates with regard to the Competition Act. Most of these concerned the fear that 'non-economic' objectives would be – to put it dramatically – completely overrun once unrestrained competition would be unleashed in the Netherlands. These concerns were voiced most fervently in connection with the services of general interest and the cartel prohibition. As the rule enshrined in Article 86(2) EC was transposed into the Competition Act by analogy,[100] concerns centred primarily on the implications of the cartel prohibition for all sorts of agreements that were concluded for the furtherance of so-called non-economic objectives. Environmental agreements featured prominently in these fears.[101] Such agreements, if they restrict competition, fall within the scope of Section 6 of the Competition act. This provision closely mirrors Article 81(1) EC. Apart from the possibility of the agreement being considered *de minimis*[102] or the applicability of Sections 11 or 16, the only option is an exemption pursuant to Section 17 of the Competition Act. Section 11 of the Competition Act transposes Article 86(2) EC by analogy in the specific context of agreements.[103] Section 16 of the Competition act provides for a non-applicability of the Competition Act to agreements that are subject to supervision on the basis of other legislation. This provision thus applies only in cases of a conflict of supervision between the *NMa* on the one hand and another authority on the other hand. We will address both provisions in greater detail further below.

Section 17 reflects Article 81(3) EC and contains broadly the same four criteria for an exemption subject to a notification requirement. With regard to the so-called non-economic considerations, the Minister of Economic Affairs stated that since such considerations played a role in the Commission's exemptions, such considerations would play a similar role in the practice pursuant to the new Section 17.[104] However, as parliament feared that the role of environmental concerns in the exemption clause in Section 17 of the Act might prove to be

---

99 The Competition Act was published in Stb. 1997, 242, entered into force on 1 January 1998.

100 In the form of Sections 11 and 25 of the Competition Act.

101 *Cf.* The Advice of the Council of State (*Advies van de Raad van State*) and the reaction by the Minister, TK 1995-1996, 24 707 A, p. 8, 9. Cultural considerations (fixed book prices) were a good runner-up.

102 Either on the basis of Section 7 of the Competition act, that contains an explicit quantitative appreciability criterion, or on the basis of the interpretation of Section 6 by the *NMa*.

103 See: Stuyck *et al.* 2000, p. 177.

104 Explanatory memorandum (*Memorie van toelichting*), TK 1995-1996, 24 707 nr. 3, p. 24.

insufficient, it proposed an amendment. According to this amendment environmental concerns would be explicitly mentioned in Section 17 as a ground that could justify an exemption instead of 'just taking them into account' in granting such an exemption.[105] This was considered to be too grave a departure from the European roots of the Competition Act and therefore unacceptable for the government. Instead, the government proposed to introduce the possibility for the Minister of Economic Affairs to give directions (aanwijzingen) to the authority responsible for the application of the Competition act. This proved acceptable for the MP's that tabled the amendment and thus the amendment was withdrawn and the Section 4 of the Competition Act was changed to read as follows:

1) *Our Minister shall lay down in policy rules general instructions issued to the director general, regarding the performance of the tasks assigned to the director general by this Act*
2) *General instructions within the meaning of the first paragraph may relate to how the director general should take into account non-economic considerations in his decisions pursuant to Section 17 of this Act.*

Section 4, however, has remained unused. Indeed, already during the parliamentary debates, the Minister indicated that Section 4 should and would be used only with the utmost reluctance.[106] Effectively, therefore, the role that non-economic considerations have played and continue to play in Netherlands competition law is up the Netherlands competition authority. The authority, as was mentioned above, has taken a number of decisions with regard to collective product responsibility organisations and thus created a consistent policy with regard to the role of environmental concerns and competition law. Essentially two types of environmental agreements can be discerned: those that involve a co-ordination of the behaviour of the parties with regard to the costs of the environmental protection in the form of an agreement involving removal fees and those that do not involve such co-ordination.

With regard to the latter, the concerns from the competition perspective are identical to those that we have already identified with regard to EC competition law in Part Two. For example, the *ADMES* case concerned an agreement between a number of companies (members)[107] that produce waste by which they set up ADMES to advise them with regard to waste collection and treatment. The *NMa* characterised ADMES as a joint purchasing agreement for waste collection

[105] Amendment nr. 29 (proposed by De Jong and Van der Ploeg), TK 1995-1996, 24 707 nr. 29.

[106] TK 1995-1996, 24 707 nr. 6, p. 81.

[107] These companies are active in markets such as retail (supermarkets, shoes, clothing), shopping centres and wholesale trade.

and treatment services.[108] In accordance with the well-established practice of the Commission the *NMa* first investigated whether competition problems could be expected on the markets on which the members are active as sellers. This was considered unlikely because of the only minimal overlap between the members' markets, the minor importance of ADMES' activities compared to the members' main activities. Secondly, the *NMa* checked for restrictions on the market on which ADMES itself (i.e. the market for the purchase of waste collection and treatment services) is active. Because ADMES' market share was only minute (0,3%) and its members were free to buy their waste management services from other parties than ADMES, competition problems were considered improbable on this market as well.

Another case concerned the requirements imposed upon packaging by the Association of Flower Auctions in the Netherlands (*Vereniging van Bloemenveilingen in Nederland, VBN*).[109] Most of these requirements were considered not to restrict competition in the first place and therefore fell outside Section 6 of the Act, as they were inherent in the logistics of the auctioning process. However, the requirement that the packaging be compatible with the waste policy of the VBN was clearly not inherent in the logistics and therefore did restrict competition within the meaning of Section 6. However, the *NMa* granted an exemption pursuant to Section 17. More precisely, the *NMa* considered that the requirement[110]

*'improved technical progress because it encouraged the reuse of packaging material and reduces the environmental impact'.*

Furthermore, the authority concluded that on the longer term cost reductions could be achieved. With regard to the second requirement for an exemption, the *NMa* considered that consumers would receive a fair share because of two reasons. On the one hand because a more sustainable economic development is promoted; on the other hand because consumers will profit from the long-term cost-reductions.[111] The Authority considered the necessity requirement fulfilled because several suppliers would otherwise need to take into account differing requirements in this respect imposed by the individual auctions to which they deliver their goods.[112] Finally, the *NMa* held that competition was not eliminated

[108] Decision of 21 September 2001 in Case 197, *ADMES* (*Coöperatieve vereniging van ontdoeners van afvalstoffen ADMES U.A.*).

[109] Decision of 9 July 1999 in Case 492, *VBN.*

[110] *Ibid.*, para. 71.

[111] Ibid., para. 72.

[112] *Ibid.*, para. 73. This application of the necessity test adresses only the question of the necessity of the action at the VBN level, not the necessity, in view of the environmental objectives, of the action (imposing environmental requirements upon the packaging) itself.

because 'packaging suppliers can take the requirements into account in choosing the materials'.[113]

Apart from the minor criticisms made above, the outcome of the *VBN* case is to be applauded because it shows that an exemption on primarily environmental grounds is possible. The wording used by the *NMa* – 'Certainly on the longer term cost reductions are also possible because of [the increased reuse]'[114] – clearly indicates that this exemption was first and foremost the result of the environmental benefits of the co-operation.[115] In its decision upon administrative appeal in the *VBN* case, the *NMa* appeared to be backtracking from this initial pro-environmental stance. Possibly as an *obiter dictum*, the *NMa* considered that VBN had demonstrated that the backgrounds of the requirements with regard to the waste policy were of a primarily economic nature.[116] In another case, the *NMa* explicitly stated that[117]

> *'Environmental improvements do not in any case constitute of themselves advantages within the meaning of Section 17 that can warrant an exemption'.*

It must be pointed out that the environmental benefits that were brought to the fore in this case can hardly be called convincing. Nevertheless, the firmness of the wording used by the *NMa* together with the fact that this consideration has been repeated in other cases[118] appears to indicate that environmental improvements can only justify an exemption together with economic advantages.

A further case that deserves mention in this paragraph is *FKS*.[119] This case involved the notification of an agreement between the six major manufacturers

---

[113] *Ibid.*, para. 73. This rather cryptic consideration appears to ignore the fact that the requirements will have a pervasive influence on the market for packaging for flowers destined for auctioning in the Netherlands because over 80% of the production enters the market through VBN-members. Moreover, the VBN has in practice implemented this requirement with regard to one way packaging so that only one type of material can be used, see Decision of 18 September 2000 upon administrative appeal in Case 492, *VBN*, paras. 22, 32.

[114] Translated from 'Zeker op de langere termijn kunnen daardoor [de bevordering van hergebruik] *ook* kostenbesparingen worden gerealiseerd [emphasis added]'.

[115] See, however, Van der Meulen 2000, at p. 198, who considers that the wording of the decision does not allow for this conclusion.

[116] Decision of 18 September 2000 upon administrative appeal in Case 492, para. 54.

[117] Translated from: 'Milieuvoordelen zijn in elk geval als zodanig geen voordelen in de zin van artikel 17 Mw, die een ontheffing kunnen legitimeren', Decision of 23 February 2000 upon administrative appeal in Case 228, *VEBIDAK*, para. 47.

[118] *Ibid.*, footnote 3. However, the *NMa*, contrary to what footnote 3 in the decision suggests, did not consider this in *Stibat* (*infra*, paragraph 10.5.2).

[119] Decision of 23 July 1999 in Case 12, *FKS*.

of plastic pipes in the Netherlands laying down a voluntary[120] product responsibility for plastic pipes. Such pipes are primarily made of PVC and thus constitute a serious environmental hazard when incinerated. Waste of such pipes is generated during the construction or demolition of buildings. Particularly in the latter case it is nearly impossible to discern the producer.[121] To increase the collection and recycling quota, it was decided to make the system as user friendly as possible. This resulted in two collection routes. Firstly, the demolition firms or contractors may bring the waste to any of the FKS-collection points. These collection points – the branch offices of the FKS-members – are under an obligation to take back all plastic pipe waste free of charge. Secondly, the demolition firms and contractors may rent – at their own expense – a dedicated container to put on the building or demolition site. In this case, they receive an encouragement premium of € 0,0454 per kilogram as an incentive to encourage collection. The collected waste, though taken back irrespective of the brand, is divided among the FKS members in accordance with their market shares in 1989.[122] The plastic pipe waste thus collected and divided must then be reprocessed by the FKS members. The waste is first regranulated (ground) and then made into new plastic pipes using so-called three-layer co-extrusion technique of the regranulated waste.

The Competition authority thus identified three restrictions of competition. Firstly, the FKS members have divided among themselves the collected plastic pipe waste. Secondly, the FKS members effectively fixed the price that they charge for the use of their system.[123] Thirdly, the FKS members have limited the reprocessing methods of the waste pipes to the three-layer co-extrusion method to make new pipes.

Since the FKS system falls within the scope of Section 6 of the Competition Act, the *NMa* went on to consider whether an exemption could be granted on the basis of Section 17. According to the *NMa* the first requirement was met because using the regranulated waste to make pipes means that less virgin material is used. Additionally, the *NMa* continued, the environmental effects of the incineration of plastic pipe waste are reduced because less pipes are incinerated while at the same time there are cost savings because there is less dangerous waste that would otherwise result from the incineration.[124] Furthermore, the Authority considered that the common collection system and ensuing division brought

[120] In this case, the manufacturers sought to avoid legislative action, *cf. ibid.*, para. 15.

[121] Such pipes may have been encased in the building for over 20 years or so and will not be removed unscathed.

[122] These market shares have been established in a confidential manner.

[123] In the form of a zero-price (in case of delivery of the waste to the FKS collection points) or a negative price (the premium per kilogram of collected waste in case a container is used).

[124] Decision of 23 July 1999 in Case 12, *FKS*, para. 50.

with it efficiency gains because the alternative (first identifying the producer who should then take back his own waste) would be much more cumbersome if not impossible.[125] In paragraph 52 the *NMa* considers that the take back free of charge and the encouragement premium in connection with the container promotes the separate collection of waste. In paragraph 53 the Authority appears to partially repeat itself when it states that the FKS system contributes to the reuse of waste through the development of new technologies such as the three-layer co-extrusion method. This, in turn, the *NMa* notes, has lead to the creation of a new product. Finally, the *NMa* considers that limiting the reprocessing methods also contributes to improving production or distribution or to promoting technical or economic progress because it achieves high-grade reuse. This, according to the *NMa*, is in line with the Netherlands' government's policy with regard to waste.

With regard to the second requirement for an exemption (fair share for consumers), the *NMa* sees no problems because the FKS system allows the contractors and demolition firms to dispose themselves of their waste on a more advantageous (*voordeligere*) and environmentally friendly manner. It is assumed that the advantageousness relates to the lower costs of handing in waste through the FKS system compared to alternative methods of disposal (incineration). Furthermore, the *NMa* considers the 'contractors and demolition firms have, because of the FKS system, the possibility to reduce the amount of incinerated waste and thus improve the quality of the environment.'[126]

Neither does the third (proportionality) requirement prove to be an insurmountable hurdle. The *NMa* starts out by stating that, firstly, the reuse of plastic pipe waste is, at the moment, unprofitable and, secondly, the efficiency gains that flow from the FKS system can only be attained through co-operation. Therefore, the *NMa* concludes, sharing the collected waste according to the market shares is necessary to ensure the continuity of the system and a fair division of the costs associated with the system. Moreover, sharing the amount of collected waste in accordance with the market shares also fits in best with the principle of product responsibility.[127] Furthermore, the *NMa* considers that the fixing of the take back prices is inherent in this system. If these prices were not fixed, the FKS members could use these prices as an instrument to reduce the amount of waste that is taken back by raising them and thereby reducing the incentive for

---

[125] *Ibid.*, para. 51. This consideration appears to overlap partly with the test involved in the proportionality requirement.

[126] *Ibid.*, para. 56. Translated from: 'De aanbieder van kunststofleidingsystemen wordt door middel van het inzamelsysteem op vrijwillige basis in staat gesteld een bijdrage te leveren aan de verkleining van de hoeveelheid te verbranden afval van kunststofleidingsystemen en daarmee aan verbetering van de kwaliteit van het milieu'

[127] *Ibid.*, para. 57.

contractors and demolition firms to collect and hand over the waste. In view of the fact that the reuse is at the moment loss making and the free-rider problem, this reasoning appears to make sense. As regards the necessity of the limitation of the number of reprocessing methods, the *NMa* considers that abolishing this limitation would mean that no experience is gained with the high-tech co-extrusion technology. Moreover, this limitation prevents the regranulate from being used in low-tech applications that the *NMa* considers to be 'less desirable from an environmental perspective'[128]

Finally, the *NMa* addresses the requirement that competition may not be eliminated. In this respect it considers with regard to the external residual competition that third parties may set up similar recycling systems and that incineration is still possible. As far the internal residual competition is concerned, the *NMa* considers that the FKS members can still compete with regard to the costs of the regranulation and the costs of the reuse of the regranulate.[129]

The end result for the FKS is a five-year exemption for their take back and recycling system. In general, the *FKS* decision brings with it quite a bit more interesting consequences. Firstly, the *NMa* reconfirms its stance according to which environmental considerations can, together with economic or efficiency considerations warrant an exemption. The fact that environmental considerations need to be accompanied by economic gains is, as we have seen above, unproblematic from the perspective of an integration of environmental and competition concerns. This for the simple reason that such advantages, as the *NMa* demonstrates in *FKS*, are simply inherent in the co-operation. What is slightly disappointing, however, is the fact that the *NMa* appears to be a bit uncertain of its case and thus tries to 'economise' the environmental benefits. When, for example, it states that there are savings with regard to virgin materials,[130] it appears to have identified an economic benefit. However, in reality this is a primarily ecological benefit because the use of secondary (i.e. regranulated waste) raw materials is still more expensive than the use of virgin material[131] thus effectively ruling out any short-term economic benefits. On the upside of things, the consideration that there is a fair share for consumers because the contractors and demolition firms can reduce the amount of incinerated waste and thus improve environmental quality[132] appears to come rather close to the reasoning according to which environmental benefits by their very nature involve a fair share for consumers.[133] The considerations with regard

[128] *Ibid.*, para. 60.

[129] *Ibid.*, para. 62.

[130] *Ibid.*, para. 50, first sentence.

[131] *Ibid.*, para. 25.

[132] *Ibid.*, para. 56.

[133] *Supra*, paragraph 3.7.3

to the necessity-requirement are equally interesting because they show how two hard-core restrictions (market-sharing and price fixing) can be exempted within the context of a producer responsibility scheme. Indeed, not allocating market shares would greatly reduce the efficiency of the system and similarly, not fixing prices could lead to their being used as part of a free-riding strategy. The acceptance of these restrictions in *FKS* may however be contrasted with the consistent refusal to accept certain aspects of agreements involving a removal fee.[134] Finally, the considerations with regard to the internal residual competition are a bit puzzling. Apparently, the *NMa* considers it possible that there is still competition possible concerning the costs of the reprocessing technology. The reader, however, could be lead to believe that the reprocessing method was limited to three layer co-extrusion following regranulation. Even, if is still possible to compete with regard to the costs of the regranulation, it would then have to be shown that these costs represent a significant part of the total costs of reprocessing.[135] A more fundamental observation with regard to the limitation of the number of reprocessing methods is the fact that such a restriction effectively stifles innovation. While it prevents the reuse of the regranulate in low-tech applications, it similarly reduces the incentive to search for new reprocessing methods that are even more high-tech and possibly more profitable than the three-layer co-extrusion technology. As we have seen above, innovation is of the utmost importance with regard to the integration of environmental concerns and competition. Moreover, the environmental less-desirability of the use of the regranulate in low-tech applications is, at least to this layman author, not entirely clear. Even in a low-tech application, using secondary raw materials constitutes recycling and is therefore to be preferred over the use of virgin material.

Finally, there is the decision in *VVAV* that we will address here only with regard to the application of Section 11 of the Competition Act.[136] This case concerned a crisis-cartel set up by operators of landfill installations for the restructuring of the landfill industry in the Netherlands. Among others, the parties to the agreement had fixed minimum tariffs that they would charge for certain types of waste. These minimum tariffs were characterised as restrictions of price competition and as such were considered to violate Section 6 of the Competition Act. Interestingly, the VVAV relied, *inter alia*, on Section 11. The *NMa* interpreted Section 11 in a way that is arguably more restrictive than the ECJ's application of Article 86(2) EC.[137] For one, the *NMa* appeared rather sceptical with regard to the question whether or not waste management could

134 *Infra*, paragraph 10.5.2.

135 These costs and their relative importance are, for a layman at least, not specified in the decision.

136 Decision of 19 December 2000 in Case 294, *Verening van Exploitanten van Afvalverwerkingsinrichtingen in Nederland* (*VVAV*).

137 See further Vedder 2002, p. 108 *et seq.*

constitute a service of general economic interest.[138] As we have seen above, the judgment in the *Sydhavnens Sten & Grus* case (rendered before the *NMa* decided in *VVAV*) shows that the Court has no problems in this respect.[139]

Concluding, the decisions in *ADMES*, *VBN*, *VVAV* and *FKS* show that the *NMa* certainly does award a – varying – role to environmental improvements in granting an exemption. This praiseworthy fact is, however, slightly tarnished by the methodological uncertainties that at times surface in the form of considerations that show that the *NMa* is still not at ease with these 'non-economic' considerations.

After this overview of the case law concerning environmental agreements that do not involve a removal fee, we will now turn our attention to the more controversial cases that involve environmental considerations. These concern the product responsibility organisations that are funded through a removal fee.

### 16.5.3 The removal fee, producer responsibility and the polluter pays principle

As something of an intermezzo, we will now have a look at some of the backgrounds of the removal fee before we turn our attention to the *NMa*'s practice with regard to the removal fee.[140] The removal fee is of particular interest for the purpose of this research because it very adequately highlights the tensions and discrepancies between the concept of producer or product responsibility, the polluter pays principle and the free rider problem. Moreover, the removal fee is of great interest from a competition point of view because of the way in which it is often regulated by the parties. Firstly, it is fixed by the parties (manufacturers and importers) to the agreement (*i.e.* horizontally) per product category. Secondly, the removal fee must be passed on to the consumers in its entirety. Thirdly, the removal fee is to be mentioned separately on the invoice. This 'externalisation' of the removal fee (i.e. passing it on through the distribution chain and not integrating it into the price of the products) brings the whole system dangerously close to a horizontal price fixing scheme that, of course, ensures the undivided attention of the competition authorities.

With regard to the backgrounds of the cases involving removal fee-funded take back and recycling schemes, the following remarks can be made in general. The removal fee or waste management fee has its origins in the Environmental Management Act. Basically, it was introduced to reduce free rider problems in collective product responsibility organisations.[141] To further reduce free riding

---

[138] *Ibid.*, paras. 61 and 71.

[139] *Supra*, paragraph 7.6.

[140] New legislation has resulted in the name Environmental management fee (*milieubeheersbijdrage*). For the purpose of this book we shall refer to the term 'removal fee'.

[141] Explanatory memorandum (*Memorie van toelichting*), TK 1992-1993 23 256, nr. 3, p. 1.

by ascertaining that all members of an industry contribute to the funding of the implementation of the product responsibility an environmental agreement containing a waste management fee can be declared generally binding upon the industry.[142] The Environmental Management Act requires that an 'important majority' of the industry has acceded to the agreement.[143] In cases where the fee is actually declared generally binding, the underlying agreement is replaced with the Ministerial decision. In that respect, the agreement falls outside the scope of Section 6 of the Competition Act. However, because competition as well as macro-economic implications can be envisaged, the Environmental Management Act requires consultation of the Minister of Economic Affairs before the agreement can be declared generally binding.[144] This consultation of the Minister of Economic Affairs has now effectively been replaced with a consultation of the *NMa*.[145] Moreover, in cases of collective notifications of schemes funded by means of a removal fee, the Environment Minister will make the approval subject to authorisation by the Competition authority. In principle, the Environment Minister is not obliged to do this as the Environmental Management Act only requires him to consult the Minister of Economic Affairs and thus neither requires him to consult the *NMa* nor does it require prior authorisation by the *NMa*. Section 16 confirms this on a more general level by sidelining the Competition Act in cases where an agreement was already subject to review or approval on the basis of another act.[146] The removal fee is therefore stuck between environmental and competition law. However, even from an environmental perspective, the status of the removal fee is not beyond debate.[147] We will therefore start out examination of the removal fee with an overview of the environmental backgrounds of the removal fee.

What, then, is the relation between producer responsibility, the removal fee and the polluter pays principle? Firstly, we may ask, how this passing on of the removal fee to consumers fit in with the polluter pays principle? Intuitively, one could be tempted to say that that the removal fee must be paid and borne by the producers according to the polluter pays principle. Indeed, the principle of

---

[142] Section 15.36 Environmental Management Act.

[143] In the Explanatory memorandum, 75% of the turnover in the industry is given as an indication of what constitutes an important majority, TK 1992-1993, 23 256, nr. 3, p. 2

[144] Section 15.36(1) Environmental Management Act.

[145] Published in the State Gazette, *Protocol VROM-NMa*, Stcrt. 2000, 274, p. 95.

[146] The *NMa* has used Section 16 in connection with an environmental agreement only twice to this date in its Decision of 30 September 1998 in Case 139, *SPRN* and in its Decision of 5 April 2000 in Case 115, *ARN*. Both cases concerned agreements involving a removal fee that had been declared generally binding.

[147] See, for example, the discussion between Van Ophem and Dresden in *Milieu en Recht*, 1995 April issue p. 77-80 and May issue p. 103-104.

producer responsibility and the polluter pays principle are often casually associated with each other.[148] This, however, would be injudicious as will be shown below.

Let us start by establishing exactly what the removal fee encompasses. Basically, it covers the costs of the environmentally friendly collection and treatment of waste products. It does not cover the costs of transport of the waste products from the consumers to the collection point.[149] Furthermore, as we have seen above, the removal fee includes some costs associated with the organisation of the product responsibility scheme. In short, it covers the environmental costs arising from the waste stage of production and consumption.

Now, let us consider the question of who is the polluter. Again, intuitively the producer would appear to be the polluter. However, we must consider that in a competition driven free market economy, theory at least, prescribes that consumers dictate what is produced in what quantity and, more importantly in this respect, what quality. Certainly, putting the blame solely on producers for having manufactured hard to recycle products that use large amounts of virgin and environmentally dangerous materials fails to recognise the fact that consumers were quite happy to buy these products. The term polluter must in many cases implementing the polluter pays principle not be thought of as concerning any one identifiable person but rather as a method of allocating responsibility. With regard to the environmental impact of production and consumption after the end of life of the product, producers and consumers must probably share the responsibility.

Why then, a further question asks, does producer responsibility put responsibility solely with the producers and, furthermore, why do the producers decide to defer the costs flowing from the product responsibility and pass it on to the consumers? As regards the first sub-question, assigning the environmental responsibility to the producers, rather than sharing it with consumers or putting it completely with the consumers is simply more efficient and effective. For one, the costs flowing from this responsibility are much higher for producers than they are for the individual consumer so that they constitute a much more effective incentive to actually change the design and production of their products. Furthermore, allocating the environmental responsibility for the waste stage with the consumers is likely to involve greater enforcement costs, presuming identical propensities for evasion of the law, for the simple reason that there are

[148] See, *e.g.*, the explanatory memorandum to the proposal for the WEEE Directive, COM (2000) 347 provisional (13-6-2000), at p. 11.

[149] Consumers can leave their old appliance with the retailer when they buy a replacement or they can require him to take back the old appliance when delivering the new product. Similarly, they can take it to the municipal waste collection centre. In all these cases, either the consumer or the retailer bears the costs of the transport.

far more consumers than producers. Producer responsibility can therefore be characterised as a partial implementation of the polluter pays principle guided by efficiency and effectiveness considerations.

This leaves us with the question why the producers have chosen to pass the costs arising from this responsibility on to the consumers. In the three instances mentioned above, the need to opt for financing through a uniform removal fee that has to be passed on to consumers, was explained by the parties by reference to the fact that initially they would be dealing with so-called 'historical waste' only. Producer responsibility for durable consumption goods effectively means that at the moment of entry into force of the responsibility, the producers are actually collecting and recycling goods that they have already, designed, produced and marketed some time ago. For example, the average age of the cars that are treated by the ARN system is currently 14,3 years and still increasing.[150] If the idea behind producer responsibility is to protect the environment by integrating environmental considerations in the design and production stages, then a producer responsibility for historical waste makes little sense since there is nothing that can be done about the environmental impact of these products. Moreover, a portion of the historical waste can be further classified as 'orphaned waste' because the producer or importer can no longer be identified. The fact that the producers would initially only be taking back and recycling historical waste, together with fact that a *product* rather than *producer* responsibility has been imposed,[151] has lead to a collective solution in which all competition with regard to the removal fee was considered impossible and objectionable. To explain this we need to look at the backgrounds to and the legal framework concerning the product responsibility as well as the structure of the industry. Firstly, retailers and ultimately the manufacturers and importers are under an obligation to take back the old products irrespective of the brand (this is referred to as the 'old for new' rule). Secondly, the retailers must take back the products at least free of charge. Thirdly, the industries concerned can be characterised as quite competitive and dynamic. Fourthly, taking back and recycling waste products costs money. Finally, the practice of the removal fee needs to be set out in a bit more detail. The fee is first fixed per product category on the basis of the average costs involved in taking back ad recycling the products. The fee thus includes, *inter alia*, transport costs, recycling costs and costs flowing from the administration of the system. The manufacturers and importers are under an obligation to pay the fee into a fund for every product that they market. Moreover, they are obligated to pass the fee on in its entirety to the next link in the distribution chain so that ultimately the consumer pays the same fee that was paid by the producer. The result is that no one in the production and distribution chain bears the costs of the removal fee.

---

[150] See http://www.arn.nl/resultaten/f_resultaten_wrak.html (26 March 2002).

[151] *Supra*, paragraph 9.6.

Making the removal fee subject to competition could have a number of effects. However, it is most likely that competitive pressure from the demand side will cause a link in the distribution chain to no longer pass the fee on completely. Such competitive pressure is most likely at the retail level where large retail chains may very well be able to exercise considerable buyer power while they have at the same time the possibility to achieve significant savings.[152] The producer/distributor that is thus confronted with buyer power will have to bear the costs of the removal fee himself. This will deteriorate his competitive position *vis a vis* other producers/distributors thus increasing the incentive to seek for alternative, cheaper methods of meeting the product responsibility. A manufacturer with a small market share who sells his products through a relatively exclusive selective distribution system[153] will thus be encouraged to set up his own take back and recycling system. Once this process has been set in motion, the 'good risks' will all soon disappear, leaving the collective system to the 'bad risks', i.e. those manufacturers with a large amount of historical waste and a large current market share. In other words, the product responsibility for historical waste presupposes a large degree of solidarity among the members of the system. Such solidarity in turn requires that the price of the take back and recycling system is not subjected to competition. This is exactly what has been accepted in *FKS* but what the *NMa* has, as we will see below, consistently refused in the removal fee cases.

### 16.5.4 The removal fee and competition law

As was mentioned above, the agreements surrounding the removal fee come dangerously close to horizontal price fixing. Indeed, the *NMa* has qualified this approach to the removal fee as such in a number of cases concerning Dutch product responsibility schemes. These are *Stibat* (spent batteries), *ARN* (car wrecks) and *Wit- en Bruingoed* (WEEE).[154] Because these three cases are quite similar and the decisions by the Netherlands Competition authority are also comparable, we will examine these three cases together.

A number of interesting observations can be made concerning the competitive appraisal of the removal fee. Firstly, with regard to Section 6 of the Competition Act, it was argued in all three cases that the removal fee did not constitute an appreciable restriction of competition. The primary arguments used in

[152] The amount of the removal fee (€ 17,- for a fridge, for example) will probably not be sufficiently interesting for the majority of the consumers to bargain about.

[153] No alltogether inconcievable in the automobile or electronics market.

[154] Respectively, Decision of 18 December 1998 and Decision of 31 May 1999 upon appeal in Case 51, *Stibat*, Decision of 5 April 2000 in Case 115, *ARN*, Decision of 18 April 2001 in Case 1153, *Wit- en Bruingoed* and Decision upon administrative appeal of 19 June 2003 in Case 2495, *Wit- en Bruingoed*.

this respect related to the relative insignificance of the removal fee compared with the price of the product.[155] With regard to these arguments basically two approaches can be discerned in the decisions of the *NMa*. Firstly, there is the hard-core approach according to which appreciability forms part of the effects-test to which it is unnecessary to look once it has been established that there is a hard-core restriction (restriction by object).[156] The second approach involves the quantitative concept of appreciability according to which the market shares of the parties are the only relevant factor in determining appreciability.[157] The *NMa* appears to have relinquished its initial hard-core approach, a step that is to be applauded.[158] Nevertheless, agreements concerning a removal fee are considered to appreciably restrict competition and therefore prohibited.[159] This could be otherwise if the *NMa* were to apply a qualitative concept of appreciability. In that case the Authority would have to investigate the relative importance of the removal fee in the context of all other factors with regard to which competition is possible. Particularly in connection with the removal fee for cars, there is lot to be said for the conclusion that a decision to fix, pass through and separately mention a fee is inappreciable. For one, the fee constitutes an insignificant part of the consumer price. Secondly, the price, as the Court has already stated in the *Metro I* case, constitutes only one, albeit important, of many forms of competition.[160] With regard to automobiles, price is certainly not the only and maybe even not the most important form of competition as brand image, mechanics, colours and after sales service play a major role in consumer decisions.

Indeed in the *ARN II* case, concerning the renewed ARN system, the *NMa* has come to the conclusion that the agreement, even though it is funded by a uniform removal fee, did not appreciably restrict competition.[161] It must be pointed out that this case concerned a uniform fixed removal fee without the obligation to pass the fee on to the consumers or the obligation to mention it separately on the invoice.[162] ARN had in its notification of the agreement explicitly addressed the – in its view – inappreciability of the fee, partly on the

---

155 For example, the removal fee for a car (€ 45,-) constituted less than 0,5% of the average retail price of a car. Typical removal fees for electrical and electronical equipment are € 17,- for a fridge, € 8,- for a television and € 5,- for a washing machine, source: www.nvmp.nl.

156 The *NMa* used this approach in *Stibat*, Decision of 18 December 1998 in Case 51, para. 52.

157 This approach can be seen in the Decision upon administrative appeal in *Stibat*, Decision of 31 May 1999 in Case 51, para. 47.

158 *Cf.* De Pree 1999, p. 310.

159 Decision of 5 April 2000 in Case 115, *ARN*, para. 43 and Decision of 18 April 2001 in Case 1153, *Wit- en Bruingoed*, para. 73.

160 Case 26/76, *Metro I*, [1977] ECR 1875, para. 21.

161 Decision of 22 October 2001 in Case 2026, *ARN II*.

162 *Ibid.*, para. 9.

basis of the ruling in *Pavlov.*[163] The *NMa* first reiterated that the competitive appraisal in this case related solely to the fixing of a uniform removal fee. Then the Authority referred to the Chapter Seven of the Horizontal Guidelines in which it is stated that co-operation that leads to the creation of a genuinely new market will in general not restrict competition.[164] After that, the *NMa* states that the uniform removal fee is used to subsidise the recycling of parts and materials that could in the absence of such subsidisation not take place profitably. Such parts and materials, so continues the *NMa*, were in the past shredded along with other materials, which it states to be environmentally undesirable.[165] From the fact that the recycling of these parts and materials is unprofitable, the *NMa* concludes that it is unlikely that these recycling activities would not be undertaken individually. According to the Authority, the collective collection and recycling means that economies of scale can be achieved which means a more efficient solution at lower costs and thus a higher coverage.[166]

In the next paragraph, the *NMa* appears to be addressing the arguments brought forward by the parties with regard to the inappreciability of the removal fee. According to the *NMa* there would only be a competition concern if the uniform removal fee would lead to a substantial standardisation of costs. According to the Authority no such substantial harmonisation takes place since the removal fee of € 45, – compared to the total costs of a car is so small that the risk of a co-ordination of prices and market behaviour by producers and importers is nil. The *NMa* explicitly mentions the fact that the producers and importers remain free with regard to all other commercial decisions including whether or not and to what extent they want to pass the removal fee on to the consumers.[167]

The decision in *ARN II* closely follows the judgment in *Pavlov.* On the basis of a combined rule of reason- (the agreement was necessary for the creation of a new market) and appreciability reasoning (only an insignificant harmonisation of costs), the *NMa* reaches the conclusion that Section 6 of the Competition Act does not apply. This is certainly a welcome development as it, on the one hand, acknowledges that the removal fee is a useful instrument to make a producer responsibility scheme work while it recognises that, on the other hand, the impact of the removal fee on competition is unimportant. Furthermore, *ARN II* is of interest because of the seeming role that the *NMa* awards to environmental protection considerations within the scope of the rule of reason. After having mentioned them in paragraph 26, the Authority is applying the Horizontal Guidelines to the facts of the case in paragraph 27. Whilst

---

[163] Joined Cases C-180/98 to C-184/98, *Pavlov*, [2000] ECR I-6451, *supra* paragraph 3.4.2.3 and 3.4.2.4.

[164] Decision of 22 October 2001 in Case 2026, *ARN II*, para. 26.

[165] *Ibid.*, para. 27.

[166] *Ibid.*, para. 28.

[167] *Ibid.* para. 29.

it could have simply stopped when it stated that the removal fee has led to the creation of a new market for the recycling of car parts that could otherwise not be profitably recycled, the *NMa* goes further. The *NMa* considers that the creation of this particular market is environmentally beneficial. What are we to think of this consideration? For one, the weight attached to this consideration is unclear. Certainly, it has nothing to do with the appreciability of either the co-ordination of environmental aspects of production or the removal fee itself. Rather, it is simply a statement that the subsidisation created not just any market but a market that is environmentally friendly. Secondly, this contemplation is superfluous from the perspective of the Horizontal Guidelines as no such test is provided in those Guidelines. Again, given the uncertainty surrounding the status of this consideration, it cannot be said whether the *NMa* has indeed departed from the Horizontal Guidelines. Thirdly, it is gratuitous as there will hopefully not be many producer responsibility organisations that are involved in environmentally unfriendly activities. However, should a producer responsibility organisation, for example, fail to use state of the art recycling techniques, then this consideration could possibly allow the *NMa* to come to a different conclusion with regard to the appreciability. Concluding, these environmental considerations have played only a very small role – if at all – in the competitive analysis in *ARN II*. Any substantial role for environmental protection requirements, such as to, for example, influence the appreciability, is not to be welcomed as it will in fact introduce elements into this competitive appraisal that do not belong there.[168] Indeed, the *NMa* could have certainly also come to the conclusion that the uniform removal fee did not constitute an appreciable restriction of competition without this consideration.

The Decision in *ARN II* leads to a number of interesting questions with regard to other schemes involving a removal fee. In this respect, we need to take into account that *ARN II* is the most recent decision of the *NMa* concerning the legality of a removal fee. In all other preceding decisions, the *NMa* has come to the conclusion that the decision to fix a uniform removal fee represents an appreciable restriction of competition. Does *ARN II* in fact mean that the *NMa* has radically changed its approach to the removal fee? In order to answer this question, we have to take into account that all the preceding cases involved a uniform removal fee that had to be fully passed on to consumers and separately mentioned on the invoice. The latter two requirements were absent in the *ARN II* case. Could it, for example, be said that if the uniform removal fee itself is not an appreciable restriction of competition, the decision to pass it on and separately invoice is also inappreciable? The answer must most probably be in the negative. As the parties have argued and the *NMa* has decided in *ARN II*, fixing the removal fee can be characterised as cost fixing. The decision to fully pass

[168] *Supra*, paragraph 3.4.2.4.

these costs on to consumers and the accompanying obligation to mention the fee as a separate item on the invoice actually turns this cost fixing into price fixing. Nevertheless, the underlying logic – the removal fee is negligible compared to the total costs of a car – employed by the Authority can certainly be applied analogously to the price fixing situation. In fact it could probably be applied *a fortiori* as the relative importance of the removal fee is even smaller in view of the consumer price (rather than the producer's costs) of a car. However, as we have seen above, the *NMa* is quite resolute in its refusal to accept such reasoning with regard to price fixing. Environmental agreements that contain a removal fee that has to be passed on and separately mentioned on the invoice will thus restrict competition within the meaning of Section 6 of the Competition Act. This means that such producer responsibility organisations are basically only left with the possibility of an exemption pursuant to Section 17 as a means to legalise such an agreement.

With regard to the possibility of such an exemption, the *NMa* maintains the distinction between the collective agreement fixing the removal fee per product category on the one hand and the agreement to pass the removal fee on its entirety and separately mention it on the invoice on the other.

For example, in its decision in *Wit- en Bruingoed*, the *NMa* stated that 'it is plausible that the collective co-operation (sic!) yields economic advantages'.[169] Furthermore, it states that the prevention of environmental damage is cheaper than cleaning it up once it has occurred. Finally, the *NMa* considers that environmental improvements, in combination with the economic advantages mentioned above, constitute an element that contributes to improving production or distribution and to promoting technical or economic progress.[170] These advantages arise, so holds the *NMa*, from the co-operation and the collective fixing of a uniform fee. With regard to the passing through and separate billing of the removal fee, the *NMa* states that it has not been shown that this contributes in any way to attaining these advantages.[171] The same pattern – accepting the collective fixing of the removal fee and rejecting the passing through and separate billing – recurs throughout the decision and other decisions.[172] With regard to, for example, the requirement of a fair share for consumers, the Authority holds that passing though the removal fee cannot possibly constitute a benefit for the consumer.[173] In similar vein the *NMa* refuses to accept the indispensability or necessity of the agreement to pass the fee on to consumers.[174]

[169] Decision of 18 April 2001 in Case 1153, *Wit- en Bruingoed*, para. 87.

[170] *Ibid.*, para. 89.

[171] *Ibid.*, para. 91.

[172] *Cf.*, more extensively: Vedder 2002, p. 118 *et seq.* and Vedder 2001C, p. 256 *et seq.*

[173] *E.g.* Decision of 18 December in Case 51, *Stibat*, para. 66.

[174] *E.g.* Decision of 18 April 2001 in Case 1153, *Wit- en Bruingoed*, paras. 91, 95.

Finally, the *NMa* contends itself with a mere statement that the conclusion that there is sufficient residual competition does not apply to the mandatory passing through of the removal fee without giving any reasoning.[175]

As was shown above, there is certainly a case to be made for a removal fee that is fixed per product category and must be passed on and mentioned separately. This case is primarily built on the fact that producer responsibility schemes will be dealing with historical (and orphaned) waste initially. This issue is also addressed by the *NMa* in the *Wit- en Bruingoed* case. According to the *NMa* the historical waste problem does not actually exist because there have been more new appliances sold than old appliances have been collected.[176] Apart from the fact that the observation that more new appliances are sold than old ones have been collected says nothing about the amount of historical waste,[177] this reasoning ignores the very essence of the competition problems associated with historical waste.

In its decision upon administrative appeal in *Wit- en Bruingoed*, the *NMa* has granted an exemption for the obligation to pass the collectively decided removal fee on to consumers.[178] Basically, this change of heart is the result of the WEEE-Directive, which explicitly allows for a passing through of the removal fee for the period in which the historical waste is collected.[179] More specifically, the *NMa* qualifies the environmentally friendly removal of appliances that were marketed before 13 August 2005[180] as an economic benefit. This conclusion is nowhere substantiated. Furthermore, the fact that the producers in the Netherlands have already been taking back and recycling waste appliances for several years does not result in a different cut-off date even though the volume of historical waste in the Netherlands can well be said to be smaller compared to other member states.[181] According to the *NMa* there is a fair share for consumers in the economic benefit thus identified in that they can hand in all waste appliances regardless of the brand or age whereas the consumer will also know for certain that these appliances will be treated in an environmentally friendly manner.[182] Apparently, the economic benefit identified as part of the first requirement for

[175] *Ibid.*, para. 99.

[176] *Ibid.*, para. 96 where the historical waste is referred to as *'Altlast'*.

[177] It is, for example, perfecty possible that the Mum and Dad's old television set has not broken down and is in fact only replaced for a better one while the old one is transferred to the children's bedroom. In this case the amount of historical waste remains unchanged while new appliances are indeed bought.

[178] Decision upon administrative appeal of 19 June 2003 in Case 2495, *Wit- en Bruingoed*.

[179] *Ibid.*, paras. 97-101 where the *NMa* refers to Article 8 of the WEEE Directive.

[180] This is the cut-off date provided by the Directive. All the appliances marketed after this date are considered not to constitute historical waste.

[181] Decision upon administrative appeal of 19 June 2003 in Case 2495, *Wit- en Bruingoed*, para. 104.

[182] *Ibid.*, para. 106.

an exemption does have some ecological aspects to it. The *NMa* then goes on to address the issue of the removal fee and its seemingly difficult relation with the requirement of a fair share for consumers. We have submitted above that this should not be problematic at all and indeed the *NMa* appears to also consider this. According to the *NMa*, the passing through of the removal fee will facilitate the visibility and usefulness of the system for consumers. As a result, the collection rates are likely to increase to that the increased environmental efficiency can lead to a reduction in the removal fee. Moreover, the *NMa* recognises that the WEEE Directive provides for this share of the burden between industry and consumers.[183] However, a further consideration reveals that de *NMa* does not accept the fundamental reasoning with regard to a removal fee according to which the collective fixing is to qualified as necessary only during the transitional phase whereas the pass through obligation will help bring about the internalisation even after the transitory phase.[184] In considering the necessity of the restrictions the reasoning of the *NMa* can be characterised as rather unclear and implicit.[185] The *NMa* appears to rely primarily on the arguments that have resulted in the adoption of the special provision for the historical waste (Article 8) in the WEEE Directive. As a result, the *NMa* can be said to have accepted the solidarity reasoning that was suggested in paragraph 16.5.3 above. Logically, the *NMa* reiterates that the removal fee may only cover the costs involved in taking care of the historical waste.[186] As regards the last condition for an exemption, the *NMa* considers that the agreement concerning the removal fee does not entail any consequences for all the other aspects of production and products with regard to which the parties still compete.[187] Moreover, the *NMa* does not consider there to be any legal barriers that stand in the way of multiple collection systems alongside each other.[188] It submitted that this fails to recognise that legal barriers and the exit regulations of producer responsibility organisations are not what keeps multiple systems from existing alongside each other. On the contrary, the economies of scale involved make it more than likely that the system set up by the *Stichting Witgoed* and the *Stichting Bruingoed* will remain the only system.[189]

---

[183] *Ibid.*, para. 107.

[184] See further infra paragraph 16.6 and Vedder 2002, p. 126 *et seq.*

[185] Decision upon administrative appeal of 19 June 2003 in Case 2495, *Wit- en Bruingoed*,paras. 110-112.

[186] *Ibid.*, paras. 113-114.

[187] *Ibid.*, para. 116.

[188] *Ibid.*, para. 117.

[189] See further *supra* paragraph 9.6.

## 16.6 Interim conclusion with regard to the external perspective

What, then, may we conclude from the above overview? In this paragraph we will come to some interim conclusions with regard to chapter 10. These conclusions will be divided according to the environmental and the competition point of view. Firstly, we will address the role that competition plays in the member state's environmental legislation.

With regard to this role a number of general remarks may be made. For one, the theory behind producer responsibility as an ideal means to internalise the external costs associated with the waste stage of production and consumption is widely acknowledged. Nearly all the explanatory memoranda to producer responsibility legislation boast about producer responsibility being an incentive for design for recycling or eco-design. While, however, this theory is explicitly recognised and given a central role in the rationale underlying these laws, practice is in many ways flawed. As we have seen, with the exception of the UK, the imposition of producer responsibility has lead to large-scale monopolistic producer responsibility organisations. The interim conclusion in this respect was that the emergence of such monopolistic systems can for a large part be traced back to the fact that a *product* rather than true *producer* responsibility has been imposed. This conclusion was validated by the experiences in the Netherlands where product responsibility for a wide range of products (packaging, old tyres, cars, electronical and electrical equipment, batteries etc.) has resulted in such monopolistic systems. Furthermore, the emergence of a market rather than one monopolistic system cannot, in our opinion, be traced back to the size and population of the member states concerned. If size and population were the major factors for success in Britain, then why were similarly populous and large states such as France[190] and Germany unable to create a market? Furthermore, the fact that the different schemes in the UK are not only territorially defined but also distinguished on the basis of the type of packaging covered shows that the geographical area is not the only factor with regard to which competition is possible. Even though the UK producer responsibility solution is from this perspective to be preferred over the product responsibility approach at least one remark must be made. A comparison of the German and UK recovery goals shows that Germany aims at and achieves a degree of collection and recycling that is much higher than that applying in the UK.[191] It remains to be seen whether incorporation of higher collection and recovery standards and the ensuing higher costs would not increase sunk costs to such a level that the economies of scale will also lead to monopolistic solutions or at least a concentration on the UK market for producer responsibility solutions.

---

[190] Where a product responsibility resulted in the creation of Eco-Emballages that covers approximately 75% of all packaging.

[191] *Cf.* Bastians 2002, p. 145 *et seq.*

Nevertheless, the conclusion that product responsibility is very likely to lead to monopolistic product responsibility organisations is primarily of significance for the legislature for he is responsible for drafting effective legislation. Can it, however, also be said that the effectiveness of the producer responsibility mechanism is inherently impaired when such responsibility is accepted through monopolistic systems? In Part One the mutually reinforcing relation between competition and environmental protection has already been described. Without doubt, producer responsibility as a means to internalise the external costs of the waste stage requires the presence of competition. Producer responsibility and the resulting costs of collecting and recycling the waste will remain nothing more than an incentive if there is no competitive pressure to react to this incentive. Only in the presence of the need to compete will this incentive be transformed into actual design for recycling and thus lead to less waste.[192] How, then, does the emergence of monopolistic producer responsibility organisations affect this effectiveness? At a glance it would seem that the fact that these systems are effectively monopolists rules out competition. Indeed, this has been the primary concern of both the Commission and the *Bundeskartellamt* with regard to DSD. It is, however, submitted that this view centres very much on external competitive pressure i.e. the emergence of actual competitors. It thereby fails to recognise internal competitive pressure within these monopolistic systems.

DSD's institutional structure has been analysed to find that the representation of both upstream and downstream industries provide for a good 'balance of power' and the presence of some competition. The users of packaging will want to minimise the costs associated with the waste stage of the packaging (*i.e.* the license fee in the DSD system) whereas the presence of the packaging and collection industry in DSD will ensure that this minimisation will take place through better design for recycling and not through other means.

Nevertheless, such internal checks and balances are not present in the product responsibility schemes in the Netherlands. These are operated purely by the producers made responsible. Indeed, DSD's institutional architecture with the representation of both up- as well as downstream industries is a result of an unforeseen financial crisis.[193] However, in the Netherlands, the intervision by upstream and downstream industries is replaced by supervision by the Minister for the Environment. As with all forms of government supervision, the effectiveness and efficiency of this solution compared to supervision through market forces can be doubted.

Another environmental mechanism with competition implications was identified in relation to the Dutch practice of financing product responsibility organisations by means of removal fees. We have seen that the uniform, fixed character of the removal fee together with the requirement that these are to be

[192] This is of course not to say that there are no other incentives to eco-design products.

[193] See, for further details: Bastians 2002, p. 59, 60.

passed on to consumers in their entirety effectively rules out competition pressure within one such producer responsibility system.

However, two remarks need to be made in this respect. Firstly, it must be taken into account that the goods for which producer responsibility has been accepted are primarily durable (consumption) goods. As a result it is more than likely that the goods actually being collected and recycled right now have been designed, produced and marketed years ago, before the entry into force of the producer responsibility in the first place. The conclusion must therefore be that producer responsibility is simply impossible to function as a means to internalise environmental costs associated with the waste stage. This for the simple reason that the producer cannot alter the product that he has already designed, manufactured and marketed. The fact, therefore, that producer responsibility actually concerns 'historical waste' rules out the usefulness of competitive pressure and producer responsibility.

Secondly, and this follows directly from what has been said above, once the historical waste has been dealt with and products that have been designed and marketed after the entry into force are being collected, competition is possible and should be allowed to play its role. How, then, is competition to play its part in making producer responsibility effective? With regard to the removal fee essentially two different restrictions of competition can be identified. On the one hand the fact that a uniform removal fee has been agreed upon per product group. On the other hand the agreement to pass this removal fee on to consumers in its entirety together with the obligation to mention this removal fee separately on the invoice. We have seen how the Netherlands Competition authority is willing to exempt the fixing of a uniform removal fee but remains unwilling to legalise the agreement to pass the fee on to consumers as well as the separate invoicing.[194] Thus, the *NMa* holds that competition should play its role with regard to the passing through of the removal fee.

It is submitted that, contrary to the opinion of the *NMa*, the best point of attack for competition would be the uniform character of the removal fee and not the agreement that it should be fully passed on and separately invoiced to consumers. There are two interrelated reasons for this.

Firstly, the requirement that the removal fee is to be passed on to consumers completely and must be mentioned separately on the invoice improves the transparency of the market with regard to the amount the removal fee and thus the environmental impact of the product once it reaches the waste stage. The amount of the removal fee thus directly reflects the impact of the product once it becomes waste. Secondly, this, of course, works to the advantage of the producer responsibility only if the removal fees can differ between products. On other words: a fridge that is easier to recycle should have a lower removal fee than one that is more difficult to recycle. These relative amounts should, however, not

[194] See, however, Decision upon administrative appeal of 19 June 2003 in Case 2495, *Wit- en Bruingoed.*

differ between the shops where the fridges can be bought. Only in this scenario would competition be able to play its beneficial role without additional distorting factors being present. If, for example, certain retailers would be able to negotiate the relinquishing of the obligation to fully pass on the removal fee for the difficult to recycle fridge, the result would be that consumers might be led to think that this fridge is actually better to recycle. As a result consumer choice cannot be steered with the help of the market mechanism in the direction of more environmentally friendly products.

This solution has in fact been adopted in Flanders.[195] The product responsibility enacted for electronics waste there envisages a mandatory environment fee (*milieubijdrage*).[196] This environment fee must be passed on to consumers and mentioned separately on the invoice in order to increase awareness among consumers.[197] At the same time, the agreement explicitly envisages that the fee must be adjusted on the basis of the recyclability of the products.[198]

The practicability of this approach to producer responsibility should not present us with any insurmountable hurdles. The recyclability of products can probably be determined rather easily when testing conformity of the product with (European) norms by simply dismantling it and checking how much this costs. Standardising this should not be any more difficult than standardising any other testing procedure. Furthermore, modern electronic accounting and stock administration systems should have no problems with the passing through obligation.

What may present us with some difficulties is the fact that the amount of the removal fee thus determined per product may very well not differ that much between the products. This is caused by two factors. Firstly, a significant part of the costs can be traced back to the logistics of the collection and transportation.[199] These costs (and therefore the fee) are only marginally influenced by the recyclability of a product (rather, volume and weight would appear to be of importance). Secondly, it may be expected that the difference in costs will not be that large so as to effectively influence consumer behaviour. At the moment, the uniform removal fee in the Netherlands for a car is € 45. If this amount is an average and the most difficult to recycle car is assumed to be three times as expensive to recycle as the cheapest one (€ 0), the removal fee for that car would have to be € 135. It may indeed be wondered whether a price differential of € 135

---

[195] See, for further details: Vedder 2002, p. 169 *et seq.*

[196] This product responsibility has been implemented though a co-called Environmental policy agreement (*Milieubeleidsovereenkomst*) between the Flemish government and the industry. This agreement has been published in the Belgian Statute Book (*Staatsblad*) of 31 May 2001.

[197] *Ibid.*, Section 8(1) and (4).

[198] *Ibid.*, Section 8(1), second sentence.

[199] According to the NVMP, logistics account for approximately 23% of the total costs. ARN devotes approximately 20% of its costs to logistics.

on the price of a new car is going to have any effect at all on consumer choice. In this respect, we refer back to our considerations with regard to the qualitative concept of appreciability within Article 81(1). It may be recalled that we have argued above that an agreement covering only a minor part of the price cannot be said to appreciably affect competition.

These – albeit important – practical considerations aside, the fact remains that the price mechanism and competitive pressure need not be completely ruled out even within large scale monopolistic systems funded by removal fees that are fully borne by consumers. Once the historical waste has been dealt with, removal fees should at least allow for a differentiation to reflect the actual costs of the recycling of a particular product. This should be accompanied by the obligation to pass this fee on to consumers in its entirety.

As far as the competition point of view is concerned, we have seen a number of different solutions. In Germany, the unsatisfactory situation in which DSD was tolerated has resulted in the insertion of a dedicated exemption clause in the Act Against Restrictions of Competition. This clause, Section 8 of the Act, has however, never been used and its use in the future is unlikely in view of its restrictive wording. In the Netherlands, the *NMa* has gathered quite a lot of experience in dealing with the competitive impact of environmental agreements. We have seen how it is beyond doubt that the Netherlands Competition authority allows environmental concerns to play a role in the application of the exemption clause (Section 17 of the Competition Act). This role, however, appears to be varying over time and shows signs of conceptual uncertainty from the part of the *NMa*. Despite these drawbacks, the practical experience accumulated by the *NMa* over the course of its short existence is in many respects an example for the Commission.

Despite the totally different approaches to the integration of environmental and competition concerns in the Netherlands and Germany, the fact remains that neither solution allows for a true integration of environmental concerns and competition. In both jurisdictions, competition is placed at the forefront and it is not recognised that an integration may very well require that competition takes a step back or at least shifts its focus from assuring short term consumer benefits (no removal fee) to the longer term (bringing about a competition for the environment). Indeed, the case law of the *NMa* and the German legislation very much reflect a traditional competition law approach to environmental concerns. An integration of competition and environmental protection would require a more innovative approach in which environmental improvements could of themselves warrant an exemption. In determining whether such an exemption should be granted, the competition authorities would have to try to achieve a competition for the environment. Particularly with regard to producer responsibility, the problem of the historical waste would have to lead to the conclusion that competition is simply not always possible to the extent that a traditional competition law approach may have dictated.

CHAPTER 17

# The Semi-External Perspective

## A Study of the Role of Environmental Considerations in the EC Internal Market Rules

## 17.1 Introductory remarks

Environmental protection and competition are, as we have seen in Part One, connected through the fact that the environment represents an external cost from an economic perspective. This means that measures that aim to protect the environment will also have the effect of (partly) internalising these environmental costs. Such internalisation as a result of actions on any other than a world level will inevitably result in a deterioration of the competitive position of the industry with regard to which that action is taken. In more practical terms: if, for example, the Netherlands government imposes extra environmental standards upon the companies in its territory, these companies will face extra costs and thus an immediate deterioration of their competitive position. A number of reactions are possible to this change in the relative competitive position. Basically, industry may itself try to defer these environmental costs (passing them on to a third party) or it may try to share these costs and thereby minimise the deterioration of the competitive situation. This is likely to bring industry into contact with the Treaty's competition rules addressed at undertakings as we have seen in Part Two. Alternatively, the government may want to act in order to protect the environment while also preventing a deterioration of the competitive positions of its industry. We have seen in Part Two how and under which conditions the member states of the European Union may grant state aids to industry with this objective in mind. Governments may, however, also want to enact legislation for environmental purposes. Indeed, the *Dusseldorp* and *Sydhavnens Sten & Grus* cases both concerned member state legislation that was relevant with regard to both the free movement as well as the competition rules of the Treaty. The framework by which compatibility with Community law was judged in those cases was twofold. It is thus interesting to compare these two frameworks and how they relate to environmental considerations; how they take them into account, if at all.

The Treaty contains free movement rules for goods (Articles 28-30 EC), persons (Articles 39 and 43 EC), Services (Article 49 EC) and capital (Article 56 EC). Of these four freedoms, the free movement of goods is probably the best established. Moreover, since the legal tests that are undertaken pursuant to these four freedoms have grown towards each other, the case law concerning the free movement of goods can function as an example for the other freedoms.[1] Furthermore, the rules on the free movement of goods have generated most case law involving environmental concerns, which shows that it is simply the most relevant of the four freedoms for the purpose of this study. Below, we will thus concentrate on the role of environmental protection requirements and the free movement of goods. As part of this we will address the Treaty provisions on so-

1 This is referred to as the assimilation of the four freedoms, *cf.* Mortelmans 2001.

called tariff as well as non-tariff restrictions on the free movement of goods and the most important provisions concerning harmonisation. We will thus examine the role of environmental concerns in Articles 25 and 90 EC, Articles 28-30 and, finally, Articles 95 and 176 EC. This body of legislation and case law will be referred to as the internal market rules.[2]

## 17.2 Relevance

A hint of why this may be relevant was already given in the introductory section of this chapter. Is certainly possible that one single environmental action by a member state may be subject to both the competition as well as the free trade rules in the EC Treaty.[3] In these cases, we need not so much check whether the reactions of these two sets of rules are compatible with each other but rather compare these reactions themselves. Even though the outcome of the compatibility test may differ between the free movement and the competition rules, we will thus need to look at the tests themselves in order to establish the role played by the environmental considerations.[4] We have, for example, seen that environmental concerns are allowed only an indirect role in the Community's competition rules addressed at enterprises. According to the Commission, they are a factor that can certainly be taken to contribute to the advantages listed in Article 81(3). They can, however, justify of themselves the granting of distorting state aids. It is therefore interesting to see whether and – if so – how they can also of themselves warrant an impediment of the free movement.

Another factor that makes the rules on the free movement of goods of interest is the fact there is a rather well established case law concerning the role of environmental protection requirements. There is, in other words, enough to compare the role of environmental concerns and competition law with.

Finally, the internal market rules are relevant because they have the market integration objective in common with the Community's competition rules but importantly lack the ubiquitous presence of economics as a framework for analysis. As we have seen above, the Commission is more and more 'economising' its analysis of situations that may be relevant for the competition rules.[5] Moreover, the Court's jurisprudence contains similar tendencies. In taking this more economic view, the Commission also views environmental concerns from

2 Article 176 – although of course a provision from the environment title of the EC Treaty – is nonetheless included in this list because is does entail an obvious internal market aspect, CF. the application of then Article 130T by the ECJ in Case C-206/96, *Dusseldorp*, [1998] ECR I-4075, paras. 38, 39.

3 See, in general with regard to this issue: Mortelmans 2001.

4 *Cf.* the 'seamless web-approach' advocated by Gyselen 1994.

5 *Cf.* Vogelaar 2002, p. 20 *et seq.*

this economic perspective. As we have seen above, this can lead to, on the one hand, an economisation of the environmental benefits that clutters the role of environmental considerations. On the other hand, the Commission appears to be unwilling to adopt an economic approach in connection with, for example, the appreciability of an agreement that concerns prices. Its approach in those cases can be characterised as a legalistic one.

Contrary to this, the application of the internal market rules is essentially a legal operation without any apparent economic analysis. As a result no economisation of the environmental benefits is possible. It is therefore interesting to see how an environmental protection is made to fit in the framework for analysis and problem solving in the area of the free movement rules. By thus excluding the economisation while remaining aware of the close connection between EC competition and free movement law in terms of the market integration objective, this paragraph will allow us to further identify the methodology used to take environmental considerations into account in EC internal market law.

## 17.3 Environmental protection and Articles 25 and 90 EC

So-called tariff and non-tariff barriers can impede the free movement of goods. With regard to the former, the Treaty contains Articles 25 and 90 EC. Article 25 prohibits customs duties and all charges having equivalent effect. The Court has held that there is no justification possible for a customs duty or charge having equivalent effect.[6] A charge levied upon the crossing of a border can only be allowed under Community law if it is not a customs duty or charge having an equivalent effect. For the purpose of this research the most interesting provision is Article 90 EC that deals with internal taxation.[7]

According to the Court, Article 25 and 90 EC are mutually excluding provisions. If a charge is levied on both national as well as imported or exported products, the measure is an internal taxation scheme and only subject to the non-discrimination rule laid down in Article 90 EC. Since the non-discrimination rule does not oppose treating different products in an unlike manner, the Court has allowed tax-differentiation under Article 90 EC. In *Outokumpu*, the Court was requested by a Finnish judge to rule on the compatibility with Article 90 of a Finnish eco-taxation scheme.[8] This scheme entailed an eco-tax on energy carriers according to their environmental impact. The Court came to the conclusion that, as Community law then stood, tax differentiation on the basis of objective criteria such as the nature of the raw materials used or

6 Case 29/72, *Marimex*, [1972] ECR 1309.

7 See for a general overview of these exceptions: Jans 2000, p. 224 *et seq.*

8 Case C-213/96, *Outokumpu*, [1998] ECR I-1801.

the production processes employed, was allowed if the objectives thus pursued were in accordance with the Treaty and secondary legislation.[9] On the basis of *Outokumpu*, tax differentiation on the basis of environmental considerations is certainly allowed provided that the tax is non-protectionist and the neutrality of tax burdens is ascertained.[10]

## 17.4 Environmental protection and Articles 28-30 EC

In order to show the developments that have taken place so as to be able to better understand the current state of the law, the following paragraph is set up along historical lines. As far as non-tariff restrictions on the free movement of goods are concerned, Articles 28 – 30 of the Treaty are relevant. In this triptych, Article 28 concerns restrictions on the importation of goods whereas Article 29 is concerned with export restrictions and Article 30 provides a list of justifications for such restrictions. Article 28 of the EC Treaty prohibits all quantitative restrictions on the imports of goods and – more importantly – all measures of equivalent effect. Particularly the latter concept has generated an abundance of case law primarily because of its very wide scope. The Court has, using wording reminiscent of *Consten & Grundig*, explained this concept as encompassing all government measures 'which are capable of hindering directly or indirectly, actually or potentially, intra-Community trade'.[11] Thus measures that distinguish between nationally produced and imported products and measures that apply without any distinction at all, fall within the prohibition of Article 28 as soon as they hinder free trade. As far as the Treaty is concerned, the only way for a measure that falls within the scope of Article 28 to escape from the prohibition is to qualify for one of the justifications listed in Article 30 EC. A reading of that provision will quickly reveal that environmental protection is not listed among the grounds that may justify disapplication of Article 28 EC. Probably 'protecting the life and health of humans animals and plants' comes closest to protecting the environment. However, as common sense would already seem dictate, the Court has held that there will first be a danger for the environment before there is a danger for the health and life of humans animals and plants. The Court reached this conclusion with regard to waste in the *Walloon Waste* case. This case involved a prohibition on the import of waste by the Walloon government.[12] According to the Court, unsustainable imports of waste will constitute a danger to the environment before they cause a danger to the life

9 *Ibid.*, para. 30.

10 *Cf.* Jans 2000, p. 230.

11 Case 8/74, *Dassonville*, [1974] ECR 837, para. 5.

12 Case C-2/90, *Commission* v. *Belgium* (*Walloon Waste*), [1992] ECR I-4431, para. 31.

and health. This reasoning can probably be applied outside the context of waste as well as the underlying logic is that human health is simply a more narrowly defined interest than the environment. Moreover, in interpreting Article 30 EC, we need to take into account the basic rule for the interpretation of Community law according to which the exceptions from the general rule are always interpreted narrowly.[13] In the more recent *Bluhme*[14] and *PreussenElektra*[15] cases, however, the Court appears to widening the scope of Article 30 EC. In *Bluhme* the Court considered that a Danish measure that sought to protect a species of bee with recessive genes from extinction through crossbreeding was justified since it protected the life and health of animals. Interestingly, the bees themselves were at no risk at all from the crossbreeding. Only the continued existence of the species – in other words: biodiversity – was protected by the Danish rule.[16] Similarly, in *PreussenElektra* the Court considered that a German rule that wanted to encourage the generation of renewable energy and thus reduce the greenhouse effect was partly justified because it protected the life and health of humans, animals and plants.[17] This despite the fact that the effects on life and health of global warming are rather indirect and would appear to be of primary significance for the environment.[18] Despite these possible shifts in the Court's case law the point of departure is still that grounds of environmental protection will not allow for a justification on the basis of Article 30 EC.

The effect of this narrow scope of Article 30 EC together with the sweeping Dassonville-formula has been that a large number of relatively 'innocent' measures, that were not designed to hinder imports, fell within the scope of Article 28 EC.

An example of such an innocent measure was the prohibition to sell products at a loss. This gave rise to the so-called *Keck* exemption for selling arrangements. According to this exception rules that govern sales modalities as opposed to product rules will not fall within the scope of Article 28 insofar as they apply to all market parties and do not discriminate in law or in fact between national and imported products.[19] This exception, though arguably of limited value in the environmental context,[20] has now given rise to the *Sapod Audic* case.[21] In this

13 *E.g.* Case 29/72, *Marimex*, [1972] ECR 1309, para. 4.

14 Case C-67/97, *Bluhme*, [1998] ECR I-8033.

15 Case C-379/98, *PreussenElektra*, [2001] ECR-2099.

16 Case C-67/97, *Bluhme*, [1998] ECR I-8033, para. 33.

17 Case C-378/98, *PreussenElektra*, [2001] ECR-2099, para. 72 *et seq.*

18 See for a critical note on the Court's reasoning in this case: Bronckers & Van der Vlies 2001, p. 467, 468.

19 Joined cases C-267/91 and C-268/91, *Keck & Mithouard*, [1993] ECR I-6097, para. 16.

20 *Cf.* Temmink 2000, p. 75, who had, at the time of writing, to apply *Keck* to a hypothetical case.

21 Case C-159/00, *Sapod Audic*, [2002] ECR I-5031

case the Court held that a general obligation to identify packaging that takes part in a producer responsibility scheme could constitute a sales modality.[22]

Another example of such a measure that had to deal with Article 28 was a Danish rule concerning a deposit and return system for glass bottles that gave rise to the (in)famous *Danish Bottles* case.[23] This Danish legislation had the objective of reducing curbside waste and basically consisted of two rules. Firstly, anyone wanting to market drinks in glass containers had to establish a deposit and return system. Secondly, only a limited number of approved containers would be allowed on the market.[24] The latter rule was considered necessary to keep the system workable, as many different types of container would mean that retailers would have to reserve more space for them and thus would be less willing to co-operate. Without explicitly addressing the question whether these rules actually hindered free trade, the Court went on to the question of the applicability of the so-called mandatory requirements. In earlier cases, the Court had held established, in the absence of Community harmonisation measures and provided that they were applicable without distinction and proportionate, national rules necessitated by mandatory requirements fell outside the scope of Article 28.[25] Referring to the earlier *ADBHU* case,[26] the Court held that environmental protection could constitute a mandatory requirement that could limit the application of Article 28 EC.[27] The Court then addressed the proportionality of the Danish measures. With regard to the requirement that a deposit and return system needed to be established before marketing was allowed the Court held that this 'is an indispensable element of a system intended to ensure the re-use of containers and therefore appears necessary to achieve the aims pursued by the contested rules.'[28] The second requirement, limiting the number of types of containers allowed on the market, befell a different fate. The Court observed that:

---

22 *Ibid.*, para. 73.

23 Case 203/86, *Commission* v. *Denmark* (*Danish Bottles*), [1988] ECR 4607.

24 An exception was made for small batches (up to 3000 hectoliters/year/producer) for market research purposes.

25 Case 120/78, *Cassis de Dijon*, [1979] ECR 649. It has been argued that this case law can be traced back to the *Dassonville* case where the Court held that reasonable rules would constitute measures of equivalent effect (para. 6). This, in turn, has led doctrine to baptise the exception for mandatory requirements as the 'rule of reason'. For the purpose of this research, the term rule of reason will be used only to refer to the balancing of pro- and anticompetitive effects as part of Article 81(1) EC. The exception for rules necessitated by mandatory requirements will be referred to as '*Cassis* exception' or 'exception for mandatory or imperative requirements' in accordance with the wording used by the Court.

26 Case 240/83, *Procureur de la République* v. *Association de Défense des Brûleurs d'Huiles Usagées* (*ADBHU*), [1985] ECR 531.

27 Case 203/86, *Danish Bottles*, [1988] ECR 4607, para. 9.

28 *Ibid.*, para. 13.

*'It is undoubtedly true that the existing system for returning approved containers ensures a maximum rate of re-use and therefore a very considerable degree of protection of the environment since empty containers can be returned to any retailer of beverages. Non-approved containers, on the other hand, can be returned only to the retailer who sold the beverages, since it is impossible to set up such a comprehensive system for those containers as well.*

*Nevertheless, the system for returning non-approved containers is capable of protecting the environment and, as far as imports are concerned, affects only limited quantities of beverages compared with the quantity of beverages consumed in Denmark owing to the restrictive effect that the requirement that containers should be returnable has on imports. In those circumstances, a restriction of the quantity of products which may be marketed by importers is disproportionate to the objective pursued.'*

The Court did not address the non-discriminatory nature of the Danish legislation or the question whether there was a Community harmonisation measures in any detail. *Danish Bottles*, and many other judgments, confirm that environmental considerations can without doubt of themselves justify a limitation of a basic Treaty provision, Article 28 EC. Interestingly, the Court appears to be applying two versions of the proportionality test. With regard to the obligation to set up a deposit and return system, the Court uses a necessity test whereby it examines the indispensability of the means in the light of the objective of the Danish measure. The second obligation, however, is subjected to a proportionality test whereby the free movement objective of Article 28 EC is directly balanced with the environmental objective of the Danish legislation. In practical terms, these two tests mean that with regard the first obligation, the Court accepts the level of protection chosen by the Danish government. In relation to the second obligation, the Court weighs the free movement and environment objectives to come to the conclusion that the Danish government should accept a lower level of environmental protection because the high level that it originally aimed for would be unduly restrictive of the free movement of goods.

It must be pointed out that the Court's approach to the proportionality of national measures is somewhat inconsistent in that it sometimes uses the true proportionality test whereas on other occasions it opts for the necessity test.[29] In yet other cases, the proportionality of the measure is left completely unaddressed.[30] However, *grosso modo* the underlying idea identified by doctrine appears to be that the Court will first check whether there are no less restric-

---

[29] See for an overview of the case law and doctrinal discussion: Jans 2000, p. 258 *et seq.* and Wiers 2002, p. 72 *et seq.* and p. 102 *et seq.*

[30] *E.g.* Case C-2/90, *Commission* v. *Belgium* (*Walloon Waste*), [1992] ECR I-4431 and Case C-379/98, *PreussenElektra*, [2001] ECR-2099.

tive alternative means available and only then eventually move on to an extra true proportionality test in cases where the member state applies rules that are stricter than exist on the Community level.[31]

Article 29 EC prohibits quantitative restrictions of exports and measures of equivalent effect. Apart from the fact that is refers to exports rather than imports;[32] the wording of Article 29 is identical to that of Article 28 EC. However, the Court, for reasons unknown to us, decided that the concept of a measure of equivalent effect is to be interpreted more narrowly under Article 29 than under Article 28 of the Treaty. According to the Court only measures that, firstly, distinguish between products destined for the national market and those that will be exported and, secondly, intend to confer a special benefit on the national industry will qualify as a measure of equivalent effect.[33] Contrary to Article 28, only discriminatory measures fall within the scope of Article 29 EC. This has a number of important consequences. For one, non-discriminatory measures simply fall outside the scope of Article 29 and are therefore perfectly legal. This actually implicitly incorporates, to a large extent, the exception for mandatory requirements into Article 29. A further two effects are the inapplicability of the *Cassis* and *Keck* exceptions to measures that do constitute measures of equivalent effect within the meaning of Article 29. A national measure that falls within the scope of Article 29 EC can therefore only be justified on the basis of Article 30 EC. As environmental protection is listed only among the *Cassis* exceptions and cannot be interpreted into Article 30, this means that an environmental export restriction will always be prohibited.

Initially, this narrower scope of the concept of a measure of equivalent effect in Article 29 and its consequences seemed of little importance. In whose interest can it possibly be to restrict exports? It may be gleaned from recent case law that it can be in the interest of the environment, or rather the interest of having a well-functioning waste management infrastructure in every member state. Indeed, ever since waste had to be treated to a high environmental standard, member states have sought ways to minimise the costs arising from this obligation. One of the best ways to do this is to try to achieve economies of scale. Moreover, despite considerable advances at bringing about the internal market, the member state governments apparently still think about achieving such economies of scale at the national level only.

Of course, the best way to bring about economies of scale is for the government to simply hand out statutory monopolies or special or exclusive rights. The first case involving such a situation to come before the Court of Justice was *Inter-Huiles*.[34] This case concerned a French law according to which all waste

---

31 Case C-350/97, *Monsees*, [1999] ECR I-2921, paras. 28-30., *Cf.* Wiers 2002, p.109, 110 and 142.

32 And some commas.

33 Case 15/79, *Groenveld*, [1979] ECR 3409, paras. 6, 7.

34 Case 172/82, *Inter-Huiles*, [1983] ECR 555.

oils had to be brought to approved waste companies. This had, impliedly, the effect of restricting exports. The French government attempted to justify the legislation on the basis of Article 5 of the (then) Waste Oils Directive according to which the member states had to set up a waste management infrastructure.[35] According to the Court, however, that provision of the Waste Oils Directive did not allow for the restriction of exports that followed from the obligation to hand over the waste to approved waste oil treatment undertakings only. This case law was confirmed in a number of later cases but probably reached its apogee in the *Dusseldorp* and *Sydhavnens Sten & Grus* cases.[36]

As both cases were by and large treated in parallel in Part Two we will look at them in a similar way in this paragraph. The facts and backgrounds of both cases were quite similar in that both concerned a situation where a member state wanted to ascertain the profitable functioning of a waste treatment installation. In *Dusseldorp* this concerned the incinerator operated by AVR for dangerous wastes. *Sydhavnens Sten & Grus* concerned a recovery installation for non-dangerous building and demolition wastes in Grøften. In both cases the wish to ascertain the profitability of the installation had resulted in legislation that sough to maximise the inflow of waste into that one installation. However, *Dusseldorp* that took the form of an obligation to hand over the waste to AVR unless the treatment abroad was to a higher environmental standard. The restriction of exports in *Dusseldorp* was as clear-cut as it could be and Article 29 EC was held to be applicable.[37] Whether or not there was restriction of exports in *Sydhavnens Sten & Grus* is unclear as the referring judge and the parties in the national proceedings were divided over the issue. The Court thus leaves this for the national judge to decide.

Up till then, both cases merely confirmed what we already knew from *Inter-Huiles* and other cases. Interestingly, both governments sought to justify the measure on the basis of Article 30 EC and, alternatively, tried to invoke the *Cassis* exception. As regards Article 30, the Court came to the conclusion that there was no (evidence of) any danger to the health or life of humans, animals and plants in the cases at hand. In *Dusseldorp*, the Netherlands government did not demonstrate that the transport of the waste oil filters over a longer distance or their processing in Germany caused any danger in this respect.[38] This applied *a fortiori* in *Sydhavnens Sten & Grus* as the waste in that case was harmless to health.[39]

---

35 *Ibid.*, para. 9 *et seq.*

36 Respectively Case C-203/96, *Dusseldorp*, [1998] ECR I-4075 and Case C-209/98, *Sydhavnens Sten & Grus*, [2000] ECR I-3743.

37 Case C-203/96, *Dusseldorp*, [1998] ECR I-4075, paras. 40-42.

38 *Ibid.*, para. 46.

39 Case C-209/98, *Sydhavnens Sten & Grus*, para. 46

The Court addressed the possibility of relying on the *Cassis* exception. In *Dusseldorp* the Netherlands government had argued that mandatory processing by AVR together with an export prohibition unless the treatment abroad was to a higher standard was necessary to ensure AVR's profitability. AVR's environmental activities would be hampered if it would have to buy expensive replacement fuels instead of the waste oil filters for its incinerator. The Court appears to reject this attempt to invoke the *Cassis* exception on two grounds. For one, it classified the Netherlands measure as an economic one and thus incapable of justifying a breach of Article 29.[40] Secondly, the Court appeared to have its reservations about the necessity of the measure. The result was that the Netherlands profitability reasoning was rejected despite the fact that it obviously sought to ultimately protect the environment, or rather the existence of a well functioning waste management structure, in the Netherlands.

With regard to the possibility to uphold an export restriction on environmental grounds, the Danish authorities befell a similar fate in *Sydhavnens Sten & Grus*. According to the Court:

> *'[T]he justification based on the protection of the environment, and in particular the principle referred to in Article 130R(2) [Now Article 174(2) EC] of the Treaty that environmental damage should as a priority be rectified at source, it must be pointed out that the protection of the environment cannot serve to justify any restriction on exports, particularly in the case of waste destined for recovery (see, to that effect, Case C-203/96 Dusseldorp and Others [1998] ECR I-4075, paragraph 49). That is so a fortiori where, as in the case before the national court, environmentally non-hazardous building waste is involved. Nowhere in the documents before the Court is it argued that the waste in question is harmful to the environment.'*
>
> *In those circumstances, restrictions on exports contrary to Article 34 [Now Article 29 EC] of the Treaty, such as those alleged in the main proceedings, cannot be justified by the need to protect the environment, in particular by application of the principle referred to in Article 130R(2) of the Treaty that environmental damage should as a priority be rectified at source.'*

Particularly the first consideration by the Court where it states that environmental protection 'cannot serve to justify *any* restriction on exports', seems rather far going. However, a comparison of the language versions teaches us that the Court probably meant to say that environmental protection could not justify *all* restrictions on exports.[41] Indeed, this would seem to even more true with regard to non-dangerous wastes destined for recovery abroad. The basic conclusion

40 Case C-203/96, *Dusseldorp*, [1998] ECR I-4075, para. 44.

41 German: 'nicht *jede* Ausfuhrbeschränkung:, French 'ne permet pas de justifier *toute* restriction aux exportations', Dutch: 'niet *alle* uitvoerbeperkingen'.

must in any case be that the outcome with regard to this issue in *Sydhavnens Sten & Grus* can be, just as in *Dusseldorp*, traced back to the facts of the case. Despite this rejection of the Danish environmental protection arguments in connection with the free movement provisions, we may recall that the court was quite willing to allow the invocation on identical grounds of Article 86(2) by the Danes.[42]

This brings us to the interesting issue of the role of economic analysis within the free trade rules. *Dusseldorp* confirms the Court's traditional case law according to which economic considerations can never justify a restriction of the free movement of goods. However, the Court has at times been willing to look beyond the economics and identified an underlying 'non-economic' objective.[43] Whether or not the Court will thus identify and acknowledge the underlying objective probably depends on whether it is convinced of the causality and necessity of the economic means to the non-economic end. *Sydhavnens*, however, introduced the additional difficulty of Article 86(2) EC. It may be noted that the referring judge enquired about the compatibility of the Danish measure with Article 29 as well as 82 in connection with 86 EC. The Court decided to split up the question and addressed the issue involving Article 86(2) only in connection with Article 82 EC.

We are thus still left with the question what happens to a measure that falls foul of Article 29 (and is not justified by Article 30 or saved by the *Cassis* exception) but nevertheless qualifies for a justification on the basis of Article 86(2) EC. This question comes down to whether or not Article 86(2) can also provide for the disapplication of Treaty provisions other than those in the Competition Title. It is submitted that this question is to be answered in the affirmative. For one the text of Article 86(2) refers to the 'rules contained in this Treaty' without any qualifications and explicitly mentions 'the rules on competition' as a body of Treaty rules 'in particular'. Opponents of this view often refer to the *Campus Oil* case where the Court stated that Article 86(2) was of no avail to the Irish government.[44] The Court did however in later cases explicitly investigate the applicability of Article 86(2) in cases that involved a restriction of the free movement of goods (Article 31 EC).[45] Finally, those who argue that Article 86(2) applies only with regard to the competition rules will invoke the Court's case law according to which economic considerations will not save a restriction of the free movement of goods. This, it is submitted, fails to recognise the fact that the concept

---

42 *Supra*, paragraph 7.6.

43 *E.g.* Case 118/86, *Nertsvoederfabriek*, [1987] ECR 3883, paras. 14, 15 and Case C-324/93, *Evans Medical*, [1995] ECR I-563, paras. 34-39.

44 Case 72/83, *Campus Oil*, para. 19, See further: Buendia Sierra 1999, p. 292 *et seq.*

45 *E.g.* Case C-175/94, *Commission* v. *Netherlands* (Netherlands Electricity) [1997] ECR I-5699 and Case C-159/94, *Commission* v. *France* (French Gas and Electricity), [1997] ECR I-5815 and Franzen.

'services of general economic interest' in Article 86(2) refers to economic services as a means to ascertain the performance of a non-economic objective.[46]

Thus, the Court could have easily answered this question in *Sydhavnens* by stating that in certain cases economic means (ascertaining sufficient inflow to ensure profitability) are necessary to reach a non-economic goal (recycling capacity leading to environmental protection). On the basis of this reasoning the exclusive right as well as an export restriction could have been held to fall within the *Cassis* exception. The more recent *DaimlerChrysler* case confirms this.[47] In this case the Court held that the principle of self-sufficiency may, as the Court puts it 'in theory' justify environmental legislation that results in a restriction of the free movement if this is necessary to ascertain the profitability of the waste treatment installations in order to maintain sufficient waste treatment capacity.[48]

What do the above three cases allow us to conclude with regard to the applicability of the *Cassis* exception to measures of equivalent effect within the meaning of Article 29 EC? In principle not that much. Basically, we are left with an *a contrario* reasoning according to which the fact that the Court in *Sydhavnens Sten & Grus* or *Dusseldorp* did not explicitly rule out the possibility of relying on the mandatory requirements in those cases constitutes an implicit recognition that it is possible to rely on *Cassis* in Article 29-cases. This, however, is far from satisfactory. Moreover, the addition of the words 'in theory' in *DaimlerChrysler* does not add to the clarity either. The underlying problem is submitted to be the utter lack of justification for the fact that the reliance on the mandatory requirements is subject to an extra requirement *vis a vis* a plea based on Article 30 EC. At this point there is little more to do than join the widely voiced call for an explicit and well-reasoned change in the Court's case law in this respect.[49]

In the absence of such a change, the fact remains that the Court appears quite willing to go to considerable lengths in stretching its traditional case law so as to be able to uphold national measures even when it has to adopt – in A-G Jacobs' words – 'tortuous reasoning'.[50] It must, therefore, not be excluded that the Court will be able to uphold an export restriction on environmental grounds if the facts of the case allow it to do so.

---

[46] *Cf. supra* paragraph 7.5.

[47] Case C-324/99, *DaimlerChrysler* v. *Land Baden-Württtemberg* (DaimlerChrysler), [2001] ECR I-9897.

[48] *Ibid.*, paras. 61, 62.

[49] *E.g.* Opinion of A-G Jacobs in Case C-378/98, *PreussenElektra*, [2001] ECR-2099, paras. 215 *et seq.*

[50] Opinion of A-G Jacobs in Case C-203/96, *Dusseldorp*, [1998] ECR I-4075, para. 90.

## 17.5 Environmental concerns and harmonisation

Closely connected to the free movement articles are the provisions on harmonisation. In fact, the free movement articles only apply insofar as a matter has not been harmonised by the Community. As soon as a given area of law has been harmonised, the harmonisation measure provides the framework by which the legality of a national rule is judged.[51] In cases of harmonisation on the basis of Article 95, hereafter referred to as 'internal market harmonisation', this basically means that the provisions of the secondary legislation are of importance. However, even if these do not allow more stringent national measures but provide for total or complete harmonisation, member states may still have recourse to the fourth and fifth paragraph of Article 95 EC.[52]

On the basis of Article 95(4) EC, member states may maintain existing measures that go beyond the harmonisation measure on grounds of protection of the environment, the working environment or the grounds listed in Article 30 EC. Even more interesting is Article 95(5), which allows a member state to introduce new stricter legislation even after harmonisation has occurred. Such legislation is allowed only to protect the environment or the working environment and may be introduced only after new scientific evidence has been brought forward pertaining to a problem that is specific to the member state and that has arisen after harmonisation has taken place. Both Article 95(4) as well as 95(5) measures must be approved by the Commission who will examine whether or not they constitute an arbitrary discrimination or a disguised restriction of free trade and do not constitute an obstacle to the functioning of the common market (Article 95(6) EC). The Commission has in the meantime applied Article 95(4) and 95(5) to a number of cases.[53] In doing so, it has allowed such stricter measures on environmental grounds through a direct balancing of environmental and internal market concerns. In this respect it is interesting to see how the Commission has interpreted the requirement that the stricter measure may not constitute 'an obstacle to the functioning of the internal market'. By definition, any national measure that goes beyond what Community harmonisation demands constitutes such an obstacle for the simple reason that it goes directly against the very essence of harmonisation. The Commission has considered that this literal interpretation of the said requirement would completely rob Article 95(4) and (5) of their meaning. Thus, it has interpreted this requirement as entailing a direct balancing of, on the one hand, the need to protect a certain

---

51 Case C-324/99, *DaimlerChrysler*, [2001] ECR I-9897, para. 32.

52 See, with regard to these provisions, Sevenster 2000. See for a recent case involving Article 95: Case C-512/99, *Germany* v. *Commission* (Mineral Wool), judgment of 21 January 2003, n.y.r.

53 The so-called October decisions that were taken on 26 October 1999 and all published in the OJ L 329 of 22 December 1999 in order to meet the deadline, See Jans, Sevenster & Vedder 2000, p. 161 *et seq.*

interest in a member state with, on the other, the impact of the measure on free trade.[54]

Article 176 is much less outspoken and clear in this respect. A simple comparison of the Treaty provisions learns us that Article 176 contains no procedure and does not go beyond a statement that the more stringent national measures must be compatible with the EC Treaty. This lack of clarity does not obscure the fact that Article 176, just as Article 95(4) and (5) allows for a direct balancing of the interests involved in harmonising a certain area of law with the environmental interests brought forward by the member state that wants to maintain or introduce more stringent measures.

## 17.6 Interim conclusions with regard to the semi-external perspective

Throughout the overview of the legislation and case law in this chapter we have seen how, despite the considerable differences between the provisions and their interpretations, the overarching theme is one where environmental protection requirements can justify an exception to the internal market considerations. Whether it takes place within the *Keck* or *Cassis* exceptions, environmental considerations have warranted an impediment of the free movement of goods. This takes place within a purely legal cadre without any economisation of the environmental considerations. Essentially only one aspect of this area of Community law that was investigated could give rise to any assertions that the role of environmental concerns in Community internal market law is less than wholly satisfactory. This is the fact that according to the Court's traditional case law concerning the mandatory requirements only non-discriminatory measures fall within the scope of the *Cassis* exception.

This effectively limits the scope of the mandatory requirements as a means to legalise member state actions that impede the free movement of goods compared to Article 30 EC. This cannot be logically explained. There is no reason why, for example, the protection of the life and health of animals could justify a discriminatory measure whereas grounds of environmental protection can only uphold measures that apply without distinction. This limitation will however not pose an insurmountable hurdle in most cases as environmental protection will almost never lead to or require a discriminatory measure. Moreover, we have seen how the Court is willing to go great lengths to nonetheless uphold such measures even if a strict application its very own traditional case law would not allow it to do so. Thus, the fact that environmental protection has

[54] *E.g.* Decision 2002/398, *Finish rules on cadmium in fertilisers*, OJ 2002 L 138/15, para. 51.

not been enshrined in the Treaty as a ground that can justify a restriction on the free movement of goods did not keep the Court, Commission or Community legislature from treating it as equal to the objective of bringing about the internal market.

CHAPTER 18

# Interim Conclusions on the Comparison

# 18 Interim conclusions on the comparison

What has this exercise in comparative legal research learned us? Has it indeed contributed to our understanding; our objectivity of the relation between competition and environmental protection?

To start with the environmental point of view on the relation between competition and environmental protection. In Part One we have concluded that competition or, in other words, the market mechanism is in many respects the best instrument to achieve an efficient and effective economic order. This holds true for the particular area of environmental protection as well provided that the environmental costs are internalised. The problem is that on numerous occasions attempts to internalise these external costs have actually sidetracked competition. An internalisation of environmental costs without the presence of competition will probably lead to increased environmental protection in the short term (instant recycling). It is, however, unlikely to result in the more dynamic effects associated with an integration of environmental and competition considerations. High levels of innovation, for example, are not to be expected.

We have seen how many of these competition problems arising from environmental legislation and policy can be traced back to the fact that this legislation provides for a product rather than true producer responsibility. In Germany and the Netherlands the relevant legislation takes the form of a product responsibility and has lead to large-scale monopolistic product responsibility organisations. This propensity towards monopolistic structures can in turn be traced back to the large sunk costs arising from the infrastructure that a product responsibility demands.

The United Kingdom government adopted an economically more efficient approach when it handed down the Producer Responsibility Regulations. By laying down a partially non-material specific producer responsibility it has succeeded in creating a market for collection and recycling services. Whether the current number of competitors will continue to exist when the collection and recycling quota go up and the effort and thus costs will also rise remains to be seen. For the moment, however, the conclusion must be that large-scale monopolistic product responsibility organisations are all but the necessary consequence of environmental legislation.

Some of the differences between the UK (true producer responsibility) approach and the product responsibility approach are also reflected in the involvement of the competition authorities. In the UK, the competition authority conducts a preventive competition scrutiny (*ex ante*) on the basis of the environmental legislation. In Germany and the Netherlands, the government – to put it bluntly – basically left it to the market to sort out the problems with the competition authorities (*ex post*). Germany later changed this amending the Act against

Restrictions of Competition to explicitly allow for an exemption for product responsibility organisations.

This brings us to the competition point of view on the matter. How does competition law deal with environmental considerations? In Part Two we have seen that the role of environmental protection requirements in the application of Article 81 and 82 EC is at best subservient to that of competition. Such environmental benefits are taken into account only after they have been economised. Even after this economisation, the importance of these benefits can only be characterised as secondary whereas there is still a considerable amount of uncertainty surrounding the actual role. With regard to the competition rules addressed at the member states, the result looks much better. Commission and Court practice pursuant to both Article 86 and 87 EC provides for a direct and unambiguous role for environmental considerations. Competition and environmental protection are thus treated as equals with the environmental benefits being taken into account as such and not after having been economised.

This is confirmed by the research done in this Part. With regard to the internal market rules we have seen how environmental protection requirements – albeit through various methods – can directly and of themselves warrant an impediment of free trade or a distortion of the internal market. The relevant Treaty provisions are addressed at the member states and not at private enterprises. For some reason, governments are allowed more leeway by the Treaty rules to attain environmental objectives than are private companies. Can we explain this? Not from a strictly legal perspective. If we compare Article 81(3) on the one hand with Article 87(3) and 28 on the other, the conclusion must be that none of them even mentions environmental protection. The Commission has been willing to interpret Article 81(3) and 87(3) to also apply to environmental protection. In doing this, the Commission adopted a far more environmentally friendly approach under Article 87(3) than with regard to Article 81(3) EC. The Court has of course not addressed the issue of environmental protection as part of Article 81 but its case law concerning environmental considerations and Article 87(3) and 28 EC shows that it directly balances environmental protection against, respectively, the need to have undistorted competition and free movement of goods. Thus, in provisions that are quite comparable from a legal point of view, the Community institutions are more reluctant to environmental protection to play a role if private companies rely on this compared to the situation where a member state invokes such considerations. An explanation for this tendency could be the fact that the Commission, in applying the Treaty's antitrust rules is traditionally antagonistic and perhaps even cynical with regard to industry and the arguments forwarded in order to uphold restrictions of competition. Then again, the Commission may be expected to adopt a similar attitude towards member states that grant state aids.

Even though it cannot be compared with the authorities' attitudes towards government-induced distortions of competition, we have seen that the competition authorities of the member states have adopted a similar approach to environmental considerations as part of the antitrust rules. These are at best awarded a secondary role and may warrant an exemption if accompanying economic benefits are demonstrated. This secondary role together with the economisation of environmental benefits is likely to lead to methodological difficulties as we have identified in the decision-making practice of the *NMa*. With regard to Germany Section 8 of the Act against Restrictions of Competition shows similar conceptual weaknesses that make its practical value uncertain.

These weaknesses can to a large extent be traced back to the fact that there is no integration of environmental and competition considerations within the meaning of the model of integration developed in Part One. We have seen how such integration is impossible with regard to cultural considerations and competition law. Moreover, we have observed how the reaction from the side of competition law (notably Article 87 EC) is in line with this impossibility to integrate. If we compare the reaction of EC competition law to cultural considerations with the reaction of EC and national competition laws to environmental protection requirements we see that the non-integration of environmental concerns and the competition rules directed at private enterprises lead to comparable reactions. The role of cultural considerations in EC competition law is ascertained only through the express introduction of a Treaty provision (Article 87(3)(d) EC). Similarly, the role of environmental concerns in German competition initially boiled down to the highly unsatisfactory practice of '*Duldung*'. The toleration of DSD is in many ways comparable to the Commission's approach to Book price cartels. We have seen how the Commission will tolerate such cartels as long as they remain national and only involve cross-border effects insofar as is necessary to avoid U-turns. The *Bundeskartellamt* ended up doing much the same *vis a vis* DSD: allowing it to continue its current activities but consistently refusing it to expand into new markets.

The toleration-practice of the *Bundeskartellamt* has, to a certain extent, been replaced with the introduction of Section 8 into the Act against Restrictions of Competition. Again, we see a parallel with cultural considerations and EC state aid law whereby only the introduction of an express provision could ascertain a role for such considerations. Similarly, the Netherlands legislator in enacting the Competition Act contemplated the introduction of a clause that expressly mentions environmental considerations as a reason to justify an exemption. In the end, this was not put through and the job was left to the *NMa*. The *NMa*, as we have seen, has adopted a varying approach to environmental considerations but has always steered clear of integrating environmental concerns and competition law. This point is evidenced best by the decisions relating to the funding of product responsibility organisations though a removal fee.

In sum, Part Three has shown us how many of the inconsistencies and problems of the current case law concerning competition and the environment can be traced back to the fact that there is no integration of the two. This lack of integration is particularly prominent with regard to the competition provisions directed at private enterprises. For no apparent reason (legal, political or economic), environmental arguments brought forward by them cut much less ice than do similar arguments forwarded by the member state governments.

CHAPTER 19

# Concluding Remarks and Recommendations

## Competition and environmental protection growing toward a mutually reinforcing relation

From a legal perspective the inclusion of Article 6 EC in the Treaty begs a number of questions. The main question is of course what exactly this 'integration' required by Article 6 EC means. Strictly legal reasoning cannot provide an answer to this question, as it will only lead to tautological answers along the lines that it means that environmental considerations must be taken into account. An answer to the question of what integration means could be discovered with the help of the concepts of, firstly, external costs and, secondly, internalisation of external costs. Both are essentially economic concepts that have found their way into law.

The external nature of environmental costs means that they are not taken into account in the decisions made by economic actors. In theory, an actor will pollute the environment because there are no costs arising from this whereas he can most probably save money. An internalisation of environmental costs will mean that environmental degradation will in fact entail direct and quantifiable costs for the polluter just as problems with product quality will also involve costs in terms of consumers switching to competitors. This signifies the role of the perhaps most important player in the process of internalisation: the consumer.

It is submitted that a successful internalisation of environmental costs depends more on changing consumer preferences rather than producer preferences. Producers will not mind changing their products or production processes as long as they feel that the market can bear the extra costs that will inevitably arise from this internalisation of external costs. A certain number of consumers may certainly be willing to bear these costs and indeed pay more for a greener product. This, however, does not yet mean that a full internalisation of all environmental costs on the consumption side of the economy has indeed taken place. Many consumers will simply not 'feel' the external costs whilst actually making them feel these costs will involve disproportionately large costs because of the sheer number of consumers involved. As consumers, we must ask our self what exactly it is that makes us pay more for ecologically sound products and why other people will, or rather will not, pay this extra amount? An internalisation of external costs will, in our demand-led market, first and foremost involve changing consumer preferences

Precisely because the internalisation of environmental costs is still far from complete on the production as well as the consumption side of the economy, the process of internalising environmental costs meets with opposition from the side of industry for the following reasons.

Efficiency considerations often lead to environmental costs being assigned to the production side of a market, again because of the far larger number of actors on the consumption side that would otherwise need to be supervised. The still incomplete internalisation will, however, mean that the competitive position of that industry will deteriorate *vis a vis* other producers that will not have to internalise these costs. This deterioration of the competitive position will in turn result in reactions from the side of the industry or governments in order to minimise or compensate the deterioration. This, in turn, will bring these governments or industry members within the scope of the competition laws.

With regard to these competition law cases Article 6 EC requires an integration of environmental protection requirements in particular with a view to promoting sustainable development. The integration required by Article 6 EC has been given a more precise meaning with the help of the model of integration.

According to the model of integration competition law should allow restrictions or distortions of competition insofar as they are necessary to bring about the internalisation of environmental costs. The intermediate objective of the application of the competition rules to competition cases involving environmental protection must therefore be the improved internalisation of environmental costs. This for the two interrelated reasons that as a result there will be more environmental protection whilst competition will also be intensified. The level of environmental protection will be higher because a more complete internalisation means that more consumers and producers will try to cut back on their use of the environment. They will be able to do this because producers will start to compete on the environmental characteristics of their products or production processes precisely because consumers will ask this. The result is the introduction of a new element with regard to which competition is possible. The application of the model of integration, it is submitted, is the only way in which competition law can really contribute to the objective of achieving sustainable development.

An overview of the competition law and policy with regard to cultural considerations confirms the validity of the model of integration. Precisely because of the non-existence (and even impossibility) of a principle that works analogously to the polluter pays principle, a role for cultural concerns similar to that awarded to environmental concerns on the basis of the model of integration is unattainable. The result is that the relation between competition law and cultural considerations is confined to the legislative arena because it is impossible for competition authorities to apply the competition provisions in a way that will allow for a symbiosis between competition and culture. The model of integration – being limited to the exercise of discretionary powers by competition authorities – is thus simply inoperative with regard to cultural considerations.

The application of the model of integration becomes particularly important with regard to cases where the producer responsibility principle is involved. Traditionally this principle is understood to refer to instances where producers are made responsible for the environmental impact of their products once these products reach their end of life. It is submitted that the concept of producer responsibility can be understood in a much wider sense and lends itself for application with regard to a wider array of environmental problems. The government could, for example, prescribe environmental goals to be met by industry with regard to energy efficiency, certain production methods and many other environmental aspects relating to production and products. Producer responsibility is an instrument that will internalise environmental costs and assign them to the industry without the disadvantages that are inherent in the either the pigovian- or the command-and-control approaches.

The fact that producer responsibility is an instrument aimed at achieving better internalisation of external environmental costs already shows that the internalisation is actually a process under way. During the transitory phase during which environmental considerations are being internalised, distortions of competition will arise. The reactions of governments and industry to these distortions should be dealt with by competition law according to the model of integration.

The applicability of the model of integration is not restricted to any particular system of competition law. As it only requires as replacement of the short-term objective of maintaining competition with a longer term objective of protecting effective competition, there need not be insurmountable problems concerning the objectives of competition law and policy.

The model of integration may seem to be addressed only at the competition side of the integration of environmental concerns. While this view is logical because the model of integration has its most far-reaching effects with regard to competition law, it is not justified since the model of integration also imposes demands upon the environmental side of the matter. More specifically, it demands that environmental policy instruments are chosen in order to facilitate the internalisation of external environmental costs. Only then can the mutually reinforcing relation between competition and environmental protection that lies at the foundations of the model of integration come about and will sustainable development become an option. As a result of this observation, it is suggested that legislators need to be more careful about choosing environmental policy instruments. In this respect we may point at drive to achieve 'instant recycling'. This has led to *product responsibility* schemes that, compared to *true producer responsibility* schemes, are more likely to lead to competition problems.

The model of integrations is – as the name already shows – nothing more than a model. As such it can only function as a guideline for the exercise of discretionary powers in cases that involve environmental considerations. Whether and to what extent is has been applied in practice is investigated in the second part.

## Environmental protection and EC competition law

The role played by environmental concerns in EC competition law differs widely between the various provisions. There are a number of reasons for this. The most mundane being the relative abundance or lack of cases concerning environmental protection.

With regard to Article 81 EC the Commission has already decided a relative wealth of cases. The majority of these cases have concerned producer responsibility schemes. These cases either not involved serious objections from the side of competition law or have been dealt with in a rather standard manner.

The 'green dot' cases, for example, primarily raised competition problems because of foreclosure issues. The foreclosure problems were dealt with in a way that is not different from the way in which the Commission has solved this type of restriction outside the field of environmental agreements. A further group of cases involved agreements the restrictiveness of which could be doubted in the first place. A number of agreements to cut back and energy usage or emissions on an industry-wide basis were – hardly surprisingly – found not to restrict or distort competition in the first place. These two groups of cases did not allow for an application of the model of integration for the simple reason that it was unnecessary to make a trade-off between the maintenance of competition and the furthering of the internalisation. A standard application of the competition rules is in these cases perfectly satisfactory.

One case in which a trade-off needed to be made was *VOTOB*. In this case the Commission opted for a standard competition law approach that has now been codified in the Guidelines on Horizontal Agreements. According to this approach, agreements that involve hard-core restrictions such as price-fixing will always restrict competition and therefore always fall foul of Article 81(1) EC. Furthermore, an exemption is highly unlikely according to the Commission. Despite the fact that the absence of a formal decision in *VOTOB* is probably indicative of the lack of serious consideration of the relation between competition law and environmental protection, is does appear to be functioned as a model for many more recent cases notably those involving removal or environmental fees.

Even though the model of integration does not in itself require a change of the Commission's policy in this respect, the general 'economic approach' to competition law could be taken to mean that the appreciability of an agreement involving that passing through of a minimal (environmental) fee can be doubted.

In general the role of the model of integration with regard to the first paragraph of Article 81 EC is minor. This is so because the model of integration deals primarily with the exercise of discretion, *i.e.* the moment where a trade-off between competition and environmental protection or the internalisation is to be made. Since Article 81(1) EC is essentially a legal clause governing the scope of the competition provisions, the model of integration has no role to play. This is different only where the intensification of competition that will result from the application of the model of integration is to be expected on a relatively short term. In such a case it could be held that the short-term restriction of competition must, in a rule of reason, be balanced with the increase of competition on a longer term.

This is different with regard to the third paragraph of Article 81. This provision allows the Commission to exempt agreements from the prohibition and therefore involves the exercise of a discretionary power to balance competition consideration with other considerations. The Commission's policy in this regard is far from clear. What is certain is that environmental considerations can and actually do play a role in the Commission's exemption policy. The following statement from the 1995 Competition Report is exemplary in this respect.

*'In particular, improving the environment is regarded as a factor which contributes to improving production or distribution or to promoting economic or technical progress.'*

The model of integration requires that the Commission exempts an agreement that restricts or distorts competition insofar as this is necessary in the light of achieving an internalisation. This will as a first step require the Commission to acknowledge that environmental concerns can, of themselves or in connection with economic considerations, warrant an exemption. Following this first step, the model of integration requires little more than a standard application of the exemption clause. Since environmental benefits inherently accrue to the society at large, the requirement that consumers receive a fair share in the benefit should not prove problematic. Moreover, the environmental aspects of products or production are only one of many aspects with regard to which competition is possible so that the final requirement for an exemption should not lead to problems either. The actual balancing of the environmental protection and internalisation in the one hand and the need to ensure effective competition on the other, should take place as part of the proportionality requirement.

Current Commission practice, as already becomes apparent from the above quote, hardly complies with the model of integration. Rather, the Commission appears to mention environmental considerations in a haphazard manner without according any real weight to them. A 'light at the end of the tunnel' can in this respect be found in the *DSD* (Article 81) decision. There, the Commission appears to be granting an exemption on what are primarily environmental grounds. Nevertheless, this increased role for environmental concerns is accompanied by a remaining uncertainty as to what exactly the role for these environmental concerns has been. This is disappointing for a number of reasons. For one, it is not in keeping with the Commission's role that follows from the fact that it is at this moment the only institution empowered to apply Article 81(3) EC. Following the Commission's plans for a decentralised application of that provision, guidance by the Commission will be much needed. This will hold all the more true with regard to the complex issues involved in integrating environmental and competition considerations with regard to producer responsibility schemes. Moreover, the Commission has on multiple occasions shown itself to be pleased with the spontaneous harmonisation of the competition laws of the member states after the Community model. Thus, the application and interpretation of analogous provisions of national competition law will depend on the practice of the Commission. In these circumstances the non-existence of a sufficiently established and consistent practice and thereby the lack of guidance becomes all the more pressing. This lack of guidance is only augmented by the commonly lamented Commission practice of issuing comfort letters.

This lack of clear guidance will lead to risks with regard to the uniform interpretation of Article 81(3) when this provision becomes directly applicable. It is submitted that national authorities that apply Article 81(3) EC, can also, on the basis of Article 6 EC, integrate environmental protection requirements. The relatively unimportant role awarded to environmental concerns in the Commission's practice makes it quite probable that a national authority may consider itself obliged to 'go beyond' what the Commission has already done. These risks to the uniform interpretation, it is suggested, should not be addressed through a rule according to which national authorities may not apply Article 81(3) in a manner that runs counter to Commission decisions. Rather, Commission practice should sufficiently clear, authoritative and 'integrative' that it is no longer necessary for any national authority to depart from the Commission's practice or distinguish the case before it from one in which the Commission has already decided.

Last, but certainly not least, the Commission's practice is to be lamented for the simple reason that it fails to apply the model of integration. By opting for a standard competition law-approach, the Commission forgoes the possibility to apply Article 81(3) with the longer-term objective of achieving sustainable development in mind. It is submitted that Article 6 EC but also Articles 2 and 3 EC read in conjunction require the Commission to do this. Moreover, the model of integration suggests that an application of Article 81(3) in accordance with this model may prove to be beneficial for both the intensity and undistortedness of competition as well as the protection of the environment.

Commission practice with regard to Article 82 EC is similarly disappointing. In the only case, *DSD*, that has involved environmental considerations to this date; the Commission has managed to completely ignore the environmental aspects. In a rather formulaic approach, the Commission decision remains completely silent with regard to the issue of the producer responsibility induced distortions of the competitive situation. It was argued that many of the abuses identified by the Commission could in fact be traced back to and explained by the producer responsibility enacted by the German government. The model of integration would require the Commission to also take these considerations into account when deciding whether or not the abusive practices were actually objectively justified on environmental grounds. The Commission has completely refused to do so. The degree of solidarity and collectivism that is inherent in producer responsibility is completely left unaddressed by the Commission. This is considered to be a missed opportunity because the monopolistic nature of DSD can, in the author's opinion, be traced back to the environmental policy of the German government. As such, DSD could have been used not only to better define competition policy in the waste sector but also to better define environmental policy in the waste sector.

As was already alluded to above, it is submitted that most examples of producer responsibility legislation actually contain a product responsibility. A degree of solidarity and collectivism are not just inherent in product responsibility, they are corollary. Enacting a producer responsibility in the form of a product responsibility whereby the basic obligation is one to take back the products that have been marketed will invariably lead to large-scale producer responsibility organisations and thus the competition problems that come with monopolies. Preventing such problems from arising in the first place is the responsibility of the environmental legislator. That an environmental market may actually successfully be created is shown by the British implementation of the Packaging Directive.

Once a monopolistic take back and recycling system has come about, the competition problems should not be exaggerated. Again, *DSD* can be used as an example. The representation of both up- and downstream industries in the governing board of DSD as well as the specific way in which this representation has been regulated will ensure a balance of power. As a result, the chances of DSD being used as a vehicle for abuse by either industry are greatly reduced. Again, the Commission does not address this issue. It is thus suggested that the competition authorities recognise the environmental difficulties (as well as reduced economic efficiency) that are likely to result when more than one take back recycling system exist alongside each other. Moreover, these authorities should take into account the institutional structure and its capability to prevent a take back and recycling from being abused. However, apart from the competition authorities, the environmental authorities should also take these effects of the institutional structure into account when they decide to opt for a product- rather than a true producer responsibility.

With regard to the Merger Regulation the conclusion can be succinct. It does not allow for an integration of environmental considerations if this would involve 'an obstacle to competition.' It is submitted that the model of integration would not require such a merger to be given the go-ahead for the simple reason that a healthy competition is most probably the best recipe for a good internalisation of environmental costs. If, however, during the transitory phase certain concentrations are deemed necessary from an environmental perspective, the environmental policy instruments will most likely be of the product responsibility type. The competition problems in those cases can thus be said to be the result of the environmental legislation. It is submitted that a different application of concentration control is not necessary and not called for in order to remedy these defects in the environmental legislation. This absence of a need to apply the concentration control regimes in a different manner may seem to fit in rather difficultly with the changed that are demanded with regard to the interpretation of Article 82 EC as concerns large scale take back and recycling systems. In this respect it must be taken into account that the Merger Regulation is an ex ante instrument that is primarily concerned with the market structure. Article 82, on the other hand, is an instrument that comes into play only after the market structure is already less than satisfactory from a competition perspective and abusive behaviour occurs. The structure-based character of the Merger Regulation, as opposed to the conduct-based character of Article 82, makes it uncalled for to widen the scope of concentration control regimes in order to remedy failures by the environmental legislator. In such cases a second intervention by the same public authorities that laid down the product responsibility seems more apt.

As far as the competition rules addressed at undertakings are concerned, the result as regards the model of integration or any other approach concerning competition and environmental protection for that matter, is not too positive. A consistent Commission practice can hardly be said to exist. The experience that has been gathered does not comply with the model of integration or with any other well thought through vision on the relation between competition and environmental protection. This is remarkably different with regard to the competition rules addressed at the member states.

A first and striking difference follows from the fact that environmental concerns are accorded a clear and well-defined role with regard to those competition rules. With regard to both Article 876(2) and Article 87 EC, environmental considerations are explicitly recognised to warrant and exemption or justification. In *Sydhavnens*, the Court has stated that environmental considerations may indeed warrant the application of Article 86(2) EC. As part of the proportionality test on the basis of this provision, the Court conducts a test that comes close to the test required by the model of integration. By considering that an exclusive right may be necessary for the duration of the amortisation of new installations and investments, the Court appears to be including reasons related to the internalisation of external costs in its judgment. The Commission's practice with regard to environmental subsidies provides us with an even better example of the role of environmental concerns. Firstly, these concerns can allow for an exemption on the basis of Article 87(3)(c) EC. Secondly, notably with regard to operating aids, the Commission practice is clearly aimed at bringing about an internalisation. This is done by firstly recognising that some compensation of the deterioration of the competitive position may be necessary to make this internalisation acceptable to the industry in the first place. The second step is the limited duration of this compensation and the fact that is may be degressive.

Apart from this clarity, another major improvement from the perspective of the model of integration is the fact that environmental benefits can of themselves warrant an exemption. Only with regard to the useful effect rule is this unclear, primarily because of the absence of a well-established case law. This view that environmental considerations are awarded a clear role in the competition rules addressed at the member states is confirmed by an examination of other rules in the EC Treaty addressed at the member state institutions. With regard to the rules on the free movement of goods and the rules concerning more stringent national measures after harmonisation,[1] the conclusion was that these rules certainly allow for an environmental justification.

The remarkable difference between the Commission's approach to environmental considerations forwarded by undertakings and the approach by the Court and Commission to environmental justifications brought forward by member states cannot be explained with the help of the model of integration or any legal, economic or political argumentation. The model of integration requires that all reactions – whether of private undertakings or public institutions – to the internalisation of environmental costs be judged on the basis of their contribution to the internalisation. This, as was shown above, requires that environmental considerations be awarded a clear and unambiguous role in the first place. Secondly, this role must be such that environmental considerations can of themselves warrant a justification or an exemption. Legal arguments for willingness of the Court and Commission to take environmental considerations into account in applying the competition rules addressed at member states do not exist either. Suffice in this respect that fact that the absence of any reference to environmental considerations in Article 87(3) EC has not kept the Commission from exempting state aids on environmental grounds alone.

Indeed, it seems that, contrary to what the model of integration would seem to require, this difference can be traced back to a perception by the Commission of environmental policy. According to this perception environmental policy is to be conducted by the member state authorities and is not primarily the matter of private companies. As a result the Commission is reluctant to take environmental considerations seriously if they are advanced by private undertakings as arguments for an exemption. This perception of environmental policy, of course,

1 Articles 95(4) and (5) and 176 EC

completely ignores the essence of the producer responsibility principle. Moreover, producer responsibility is endorsed by the Commission as is evidenced by a number of recent legislative initiatives that have all embraced the producer responsibility principle as a mainstay.[2]

The Court's case law contains some evidence indicating that it may be willing to extend its case law with regard to environmental considerations brought forward by the member states. *Nestlé/Perrier* is an example of case where the Court of First Instance took a wider view of the factors that are to be included in the appraisal on the basis of competition law. In this respect, the judgment in *DSD* is anxiously awaited.[3]

All in all, much is still uncertain with regard to the relation between competition law and environmental protection as far as the competition rules addressed at the member states are concerned. This uncertainty can also be seen in the member states. In Germany the toleration by the *Bundeskartellamt* of *DSD* has in the meantime partly been addressed by the legislator in the form of an amendment to the German competition law. In the Netherlands much experience has been gathered with regard to the application of the competition rules to environmental agreements. Although it is slightly more consistent than the Commission's, the case law of the *NMa* still lacks the clarity that is needed to be able to speak of a well thought through vision of the relation between competition law and environmental protection. Moreover, the case law concerning removal fees shows that the *NMa* is unwilling to apply the model of integration that was developed in this book.

A first step in the right direction would appear to be the recognition by the competition authorities that industry has a major part to play in bringing about an internalisation of environmental costs and thus environmental protection. There are a number of different methods to reach this goal. As the example of Germany shows, an option is to change the competition legislation so as to include an environmental justification *expressis verbis*. It is submitted that this is unnecessary even though it may be preferable from the perspective of the democratic legitimacy of such a choice. A far less bothersome alternative would be to simply apply the model of integration in the exercise of discretionary powers by the competition authorities.

How this already works in practice can be seen by looking at the Commission's practice with regard to environmental state aids. How this could work in practice can be shown with the help of the removal fee. Essentially, the removal fee consists of two elements that are relevant as far as competition law is concerned. Firstly, the removal fee is fixed for a certain category of products

---

[2] *E.g.* Directive 2002/96 (WEEE), OJ 2003 L 37/24.

[3] Three recent judgments in the field of competition law (Merger Regulation) have shown that the Court of First Instance is more than willing to closely and critically examine the Commission's decisions.

on a horizontal basis. Secondly, the removal fee most be passed on to consumers visibly and in its entirety. Current practice is to grant an exemption for fixing of the removal fee but to categorically refuse such an exemption for the pass through obligation. The model of integration would require this to be exactly the other way around. An exemption should certainly be possible for the pass through obligation because this aids the internalisation of external costs with the consumers whereas the exemption for the collective horizontal fixing of the removal fee should be temporary and limited only to the time span during which the historical waste is dealt with. As a result, consumers are made aware of the environmental costs of their purchases and will thus internalise the environmental costs. Only if such internalisation takes place do we stand a chance of bringing about sustainable development. In the end we must ask ourselves what undistorted competition is worth if there is nothing left to compete for.

# Bibliography

**The names and year in bold print refer to the short citation in the footnotes**

Aberle, G., *Wettbewerbstheorie und Wettbewerbspolitik* (Stuttgart: Kohlhammer 1980)

**Akyürek-Kievits 1998**, Akyürek-Kievits, H.E., *Tussen protectie en concurrentie* (Deventer: Kluwer 1998)

Amato, G., *Antitrust and the Bounds of Power* (Oxford: Hart 1997)

Andreae, C.A., 'Umweltschutz und Marktwirtschaft', *WuW* (1971) 11/12, p. 753-758

Andreae, C.M., Kirchhoff, J. & Pfeiffer, G. (eds.), *Wettbewerb als Herausforderung und Chance* (Köln: Carl Heymanns Verlag 1989)

Areeda, Ph., *Antitrust Analysis, problems, text cases* (Boston: Little, Brown and Company 1974)

**Arnull 1996**, Arnull, A., 'Case note on cases T-96/92 and T-12/93', *CML Rev.* (1996) 33, p. 319-335

**Bain 1968**, Bain, J.S., *Industrial Organization* (New York: John Wiley & Sons 1968)

Baldi, M., *Die freistellung vom EWG-Kartellverbot* (Bern: Stämpfli Verlag 1972)

Barents, R., *The Agricultural Law of the EC* (Deventer, Kluwer Law International 1994)

Barnikel, H.-H. (ed.), *Theorie und Praxis der Kartelle* (Darmstadt: Wissenschaftliche Buchgesellschaft 1972)

Bartling, H., 'Grüner Punkt: Reform wettbewerblicher Rahmenbedingungen', *WuW* (1995) 3, p. 183-196

**Bartling 1980**, Bartling, H., *Leitbilder der Wettbewerbspolitik* (München: Vahlen 1980)

Bartling, H., 'Schlußfolgerungen aus Entwicklungstendenzen der Wettbewerbstheorie für die Wettbewerbspolitik', *WuW* (1993) 1, p. 16-30

**Basedow 1995**, Basedow, J.,'Zielkonflikte und Zielhierarchien im Vertrag über die Europäische Gemeinschaft', in: Due, O., Lutter, M. & Schwarze, J.,(eds.), *Festschrift für Ulrich Everling*, (Baden-Baden: Nomos 1995)

**Bastians 2002**, Bastians, U., *Verpackungsregulierung ohne den Grünen Punkt?* (Baden-Baden: Nomos 2002)

Baudenbacher, C., 'Kartellrechtliche und Verfassungsrechtliche Aspekte gesetzesersetzender Vereinbarungen', *JZ* (1988) 14, p. 689-697

**Baquero Cruz & Castillo de la Torre 2001**, Baquero Cruz , J. & Castillo de la Torre, F., 'Note on PreussenElektra', *E.L.Rev.* (2001) 26, p. 489-501

**Blanco & Houtte 1996**, Blanco, L.O.& Houtte, B. van, *EC Competition Law in the Transport Sector*, (Oxford: Clarendon Press 1996)

**Becker-Schwarze 1997**, Becker-Schwarze, K., *Steuerungsmöglichkeiten des Kartellrechts bei Umweltschützenden Unternehmenskooperationen* (Baden-Baden: Nomos 1997)

**Bellamy & Child 2001**, Bellamy & Child, *European Community Law of Competition*, Roth, P.M. (ed.) (London: Sweet & Maxwell 2001)

**Bender & Rinne 1998**, Bender, K.W. & Rinne, A., Wettbewerbsrechtliche Grenzen der Entsorgungswirtschaft', *WuW* (1998) 5, p. 439-448

**Benzler et al. 1995**, Benzler, G., Halstrick-Schwenk, M., Klemmer., P., Löbbe, K., *Wettbewerbskonformität von Rücknahmeverpflichtungen im Abfallbereich* (Essen, Rheinisch-Westfälischen Institut für Wirtschaftsforschung 1995)

**Berg 2000**, Berg, W., 'Neue Entscheidungen des EuGH zur anwendung des EG-Kartellrechts im bereich der sozialen Sicherheit', *EuZW* (2000) 6, p. 170-181

Bittlingmayer, G., 'Die wettbewerbspolitischen Vorstellungen der Chicago School', *WuW* (1986) 9, p. 709-718

Blum, F. & Logue, A., *State Monopolies Under EC Law* (Chichester: John Wiley & Sons 1998)

Bock, M., 'Entsorgung von Verkaufsverpackungen und Kartellrecht', *WuW* (1996) 3, p. 187-203

Bock, M., 'Umweltrechtliche Prinzipien in der Wettbewerbsordnung der Europäischen Gemeinschaft', *EuZW* (1994) 2, p. 47-52

**Bogdandy 2000**, Bogdandy, A. Von, in: Grabitz/Hilf, *Kommentar zum EWG-Vertrag*, Art. 2 EGV, (München: Verlag C.H. Beck 1992)

**Bonus 1981**, Bonus, H., 'Theoretisch-empirische Analyse umweltpolitischer Instrumente und ihre Wettbewerbspolitische Implikationen', in: H. Gutzler (ed.), *Umweltpolitik und Wettbewerb* (Baden-Baden: Nomos Verlag 1981)

**Bonus 1997**, Bonus, H., 'Umweltschutz und Wettbewerb aus ökonomische Sicht', in Marburger, P., Reinhardt, M. & Schröder, M.,(eds.), *Umweltschutz und Wettbewerb* (Berlin: Erich Schmidt Verlag 1997)

**Borchardt & Fikentscher 1957**, Borchardt, K. & Fikentscher, W., *Wettbewerb Wettbewerbsbeschränkung Marktbeherrschung* (Stuttgart: Ferdinand Enke Verlag 1957)

**Bork 1978**, Bork, R.H., *The Anti-trust Paradox – A Policy at War with Itself* (New York, Basic Books 1978)

Bouterse, R.B., *Competition and Integration – what goals count* (Deventer: Kluwer 1994)

Brandt, U., 'Einige grundsätzliche Bemerkungen über Umwelt- und Wettbewerbsschutz', *WuW* (1977) 9, p. 582-584

**Bredimas 1978**, Bredimas, A., *Methods of Interpretation and Community Law*, (Amsterdam: North Holland 1978)

**Bronckers & Van der Vlies 2001**, Bronckers, M. & Van der Vlies, R., 'The European Court's PreussenElektra Judgment: Tensions between E.U. Principles and National Renewable Energy Initiatives', *ECLR* (2001) 10, p. 458-468

Brown, L.N., Kennedy, T., *The Court of Justice of the European Communities* (London: Sweet & Maxwell 1994)

**Buendia Sierra 1999**, Buendia Sierra, J.L., *Exclusive Rights and State Monopolies in EC Law* (Oxford: Oxford University Press 1999)

Bundeskartellamt, *Quo Vadis, Wettbewerbspolitik?* Dokumentation einer Grundsatzdiskussion ordnungspolitischer und kartellrechtlicher Fragen, Berlin: Bundeskartellamt 1988

Bundesministerium für Wirtschaft, *Möglichkeiten der Wettbewerbskonformen Erfüllung von Rücknahmen- und Verwertungverpflichten (Kriterienkatalog)*, Bundesministerium für Wirtschaft 1994, Dokumentation Nr. 360

**Bundesministerium für Umwelt, Naturschutz und Reaktorsicherheit 2001**, *Informationen zur Batterieverordnung* (Bonn, June 2001, WA II 3–30 114-4/4)

Bundesverband der Deutschen Industrie, *Kartellrecht und Umweltschutz –Konflikte und Lösungsansätze-* Dokumentation einer BDI-infomationsveranstaltung am 21. Februar 1995, Köln: Bundesverband der Deutschen Industrie 1995

**Chamberlin 1962**, Chamberlin, E.H., *The Theory of Monopolistic Competition* (Cambridge: Harvard University Press 1962)

**Clark 1940**, Clark, J.M., 'Toward a Concept of Workable Competition', *AER* (1940) 30, p. 241-256

Clark, J.M., 'Zum Begriff eines funktionsfähigen Wettbewerbs', in: K. Herdzina, *Wettbewerbstheorie* (Köln: Kiepenheuer & Witsch 1975)

**Clark 1961**, Clark, J.M., *Competition as a Dynamic Process* (Washington: Brookings Institution 1961)

**Coase 1960**, Coase, R.A., 'The Problem of Social Cost', *Journal of Law and Economics* October 1960, p. 1-44

Cockborne, J.E. de, 'Les règles communautaires de concurrence applicables aux entreprises dans le domaine agricole', *Rev. trim. dr. europ.* (1988) 24 (2), p. 293-321

**Collier 1996**, Collier, J.F., 'Politiek leiderschap en rechtsverandering in Zinacantan', in: Griffiths, J., (ed.), *De sociale werking van het Recht* (Nijmegen: Ars Aequi Libri 1996)

Commission, *Communication from the Commission to the Council and the European Parliament on Environmental Agreements*, COM (96) 561 final of 27.11.1996

**Commission 2001**, Commission of the European Communities, *European Packaging Waste Management Systems – Main Report* (final report February 2001, DG XI.E.3, available online on the Commission d-g environment website <www.europa.eu.int>)

**Commission 2003**, Commission of the European Communities, Communication from the Commission "Towards a thematic strategy on the prevention and recycling of waste" COM (2003) 301 final (available online on the Commission d-g environment website <www.europa.eu.int>)

**Cornes & Sandler 1996**, Cornes, R., Sandler, T., *The Theory of Externalities, Public Goods and Club Goods* (New York: Cambridge University Press 1996)

**Cox 1981**, Cox, H., 'Kartelle – Strukturanalyse, Wettbewerbswirkungen und wettbewerbspolitische Behandlung', in: Cox, H., *et al.* (eds.) *Handbuch des Wettbewerbs* (München: Vahlen 1981)

**Cox & Hübner 1981**, Cox, H., & Hübner, H., 'Eine Einführung in die Wettbewerbstheorie und Wettbewerbspolitik', in: Cox H., *et al.* (eds.) *Handbuch des Wettbewerbs* (München: Vahlen 1981)

**CPB/SCP 2002**, Centraal Planbureau and Sociaal en Cultureel Planbureau, *Boek en Markt – Effectiviteit en efficiëntie van de vaste boekenprijs* (Den Haag, Centraal Planburau en Sociaal en Cultureel Planbureau 2002)

**De Gaay Fortman 1966**, De Gaay Fortman, B., *Theory of Competition Policy* (Amsterdam: North Holland 1966)

**Delvaux 2003**, Delvaux, B., 'The EC State Aid Regime regarding Renewables : Opportunities and Pitfalls' (2003) *EELR* 4, p. 103-112

**Denys 1999**, Denys, C., 'ECJ Case Report on Case C-203/96, Dusseldorp', (1999) *EELR* 1 p. 21-30

**De Pree 1999**, De Pree, J.K., 'Het merkbaarheidsbegrip in artikel 6 Mw.', (1999) *NTER* 12, p. 305-311

**De Vries 2001**, Vries, S., de, 'Cultuur en mededinging: harmonie of dissonantie?' in: Gronden, J.W. van de, Mortelmans, K.J.M. (eds.), *Mededinging en niet-economische belangen* (Deventer: Kluwer 2001).

**Dhondt 2002**, Dhondt, N.M.L., 'Environmental law Principles and the Case Law of the Court of Justice', in: Sheridan, M., Lavrysen, L. (eds.) *Environmental Law Principles in Practice* (Brussel: Bruylant 2002)

**Dhondt 2003**, Dhondt, N., *Integration of Environmental Protection into other EC Policies* (Groningen: Europa Law Publishing 2003)

**Dhondt & Uylenburg 2000**, Dhondt, N., Uylenburg, R., 'Het beginsel van externe integratie', *M en R* (2000), 5, p. 120-128

**Doherty 1999**, Doherty, M., 'The Status of the Principles of EC Environmental Law', *JEL* (1999) 2, p. 354-386

**Dowding et al. 2000**, Dowding K., John, P., Mergoupis, T. & Vugt, M. van, 'Exit, voice and loyalty: Analytic and empirical developments', *European Journal of Political Research* (2000) 37, p. 469-495

**D'sa 1998**, D'Sa, R. M., *European Community Law on State Aid* (London: Sweet & Maxwell 1998)

Dunné, J.M. van (ed.), *Environmental Contracts and Covenants* (Lelystad: Vermande 1993)

Edwards, C.D., *Maintaining Competition* (New York: McGraw-Hill 1949)

**Ehle 1996**, Ehle, D., *Die Einbeziehung des Umweltschutzes in das Europäische Kartellrecht* (Köln: Carl Heymanns Verlag 1996)

Ehlermann, C.D., *Zukunftige Entwicklungen des Europäischen Wettbewebsrechts*, EuZW (1994) 21, p. 647-659

**Ehlermann & Laudati 1998**, Ehlermann, C.D., Laudati, L. L. (eds.), *The European Competition Law Annual 1997: Objectives of Competition Policy* (Oxford: Hart 1998)

**EIM 2001**, EIM, *De vaste boekenprijs, een internationale 'quick scan' in opdracht van: CPB/SCP*, (Zoetermeer, EIM 2001)

Elshorst, D., *The certification of Specialised Disposal Enterprises under German Waste Law*, EELR (1998) 4 , p. 112-117

Emmerich, V., *Kartellrecht* (München: Beck 1988)

**Engel 1998**, Engel, Ch., *Selbstregulierung im Bereich der Produktverantwortung – Instrumente und deren Ausgestaltung*, Preprints aus de Max-Planck-Projektgruppe Recht der Gemeinschafsgüter, Bonn 1998/7

Esch, B. van der, 'Der Stellenwert des unverfälschten Wettbewerbs in der Rechtsprechung des Europäischen Gerichtshofes und der Verwaltungspraxis der Kommission', *WuW*, (1988) 7 & 8, p. 563-575

**Esty 1999**, Esty, D.C., *Toward Optimal Environmental Governance*, 74 NYULR ( December 1999), p. 1495-1574

**Eucken 1960**, Eucken, W., *Grundsätze der Wirtschaftspolitik* (Tübingen: J.C.B. Mohr 1960)

European Foundation for the Improvement of Living and Working Conditions, *Industrial relations and Environmental Protection in Europe*, Luxembourg 1994

Everling, U.,' Zur Wettbewerbskonzeption in der neueren Rechtsprechung des Gerichtshofs der Europäischen Gemeinschaften', *WuW* (1990) 12, p. 995-1009

**Everling 1997**, Everling, U., *Buchpreisbindung im deutschen Sprachraum und Europäisches Gemeinschaftsrecht* (Baden-Baden: Nomos 1997)

**Fesenmaier 1996**, Fesenmaier, J, *Öffentliche Dienstleistungsmonopole im europäischen Recht* (Berlin: Berlin Verlag Arno Spitz; Baden-Baden: Nomos 1996)

**Franssen et al. 2000**, Franssen, E.J.A., Jacobs, A.T.J.M., Jaspers, A. Ph.C.M. & Mortelmans, K.J.M., 'Cao's en mededingingsrecht', *SMA* (2000) 7/8, p. 324-337

Freitag, D., *et al.*, *Umweltschutz und Wettbewerbsordnung* (Frankfurt am Main: Athenäum Verlag 1973)

**Friedrich 1977**, Friedrich, M., *Möglichkeiten und kartellrechtliche Grenzen Umweltschutzfördernder Kooperation zwischen Unternehmen – zugleich ein Beitrag zur Problematk einer Restriktion des § 1 GWB* (Bamberg: Schadel 1977)

Frenz, W., *Nationalstaatlicher Umweltschutz und EG-Wettbewerbsfreiheit* (Köln: Carl Heymanns Verlag 1997)

**Gabriel 1971**, Gabriel, S.L., 'Überlegungen zu einer Theorie der Organisation des Marktes', *WuW* (1971) 11 & 12, p. 802-806

Gayk, A, *Restriktionen des Tatbestandes des Art. 85 Abs. 1 EWG Vertrag: Anwendungsfälle einer Rule of Reason in der Entscheidungspraxis des Gerichtshofes der Europäischen Gemeinschaften* (Darmstadt: Dissertations druck 1991)

**Geradin 2001**, Geradin, D., 'EC Competition Law and Environmental Protection', in: Somsen, H. (ed. in chief), *Yearbook of European Environmental Law* (Volume II), Oxford: Oxford University Press 2001)

**Gerber 1998**, Gerber, D.J., *Law and Competition in Twentieth Century Europe – Protecting Prometheus* (Oxford: Clarendon Press 1998)

**Gerven 1991**, Gerven, W. van, 'Het evenredigheidsbeginsel: en beginsel met een groot verleden en een grote toekomst', in: Nieskens-Isphording et al. (eds.), *In het nu, wat worden zal, Liber Amicorum* prof. mr. H.C.F. Schoordijk (Deventer: Kluwer 1991)

**Gerven 1997**, Gerven, W. van, Gyselen, L., Maresceau, M. & Stuyck, J., *Kartelrecht II, Europese Gemeenschap* (Zwolle: W.E.J. Tjeenk Willink 1997)

Giesel, H.B., *Unternehmungswachstum und Wettbewerb* (Baden-Baden: Nomos Verlag 1975)

Glaesner, H.J., 'Die Einheitliche Europäische Akte', *EuR* (1986) 2, p. 119-146

**Goyder 1998**, Goyder, D.G., *EC Competition Law* (Oxford: Clarendon Press 1998)

Grabitz, E., *Kommentar zum EWG-Vertrag* (München: Beck 1992)

Greaves, R., *EC Block Exemption Regulations* (Chichester: Chancery Law 1994)

**Grimeaud 2000**, Grimeaud, D., 'The Integration of Environmental Concerns into EC Policies: A Genuine Policy Development?', *EELR* (2000) 7, p. 207-218

**Groeben, Thiesing & Ehlermann 1991**, Groeben, H. von der, Thiesing, J. &

Ehlermann, C.-D. (eds.), *Kommentar zum EWG-Vertrag, Band 2* (Baden-Baden: Nomos Verlag 1991)

**Groeben, Thiesing & Ehlermann 2000**, Groeben, H. von der, Thiesing, J. & Ehlermann, C.-D. (eds.), *Kommentar zum EWG-Vertrag, Band 2* (Baden-Baden: Nomos Verlag 2000)

Günther, E., 'Wettbewerbspoltik in einer freien Gesellschaft', *WuW* (1965) 2, p. 111-120

Gutzler, H. (ed.), *Umweltpolitik und Wettbewerb* (Baden-Baden: Nomos Verlag 1981)

**Gyselen 1994**, L., *The Emerging Interface between Competition Policy and Environmental Policy in the EEC*, paper presented at the 1994 IBA conference, published in: Cameron & May, Trade and the Environment (London: Cameron & May 1994)

**Gyselen 2000**, Gyselen, L., 'Case note on case C-76/96, Albany', *CML Rev.* (2000), 37 p. 425-448

**Hancher, Ottervanger & Slot 1999**, Hancher, L., Ottervanger, T. & Slot, P.J., *E.C. State Aids* (London: Sweet & Maxwell 1999)

Hansen, K., 'Wettbewerbspolitik und Strukturpolitik – das beispiel des GWB', *WuW* (1989) 5, p. 376-383

Hansen, K., 'Zur Aktualität des "Freiburger Imperativs"'. *WuW* (1991) 4, p. 287-290

Hayek, F.A., 'The Meaning of Competition', in: F.A. Hayek, *Individualism and Economic Order* (London: Routledge 1949)

**Heidenhain, Satzky & Stadler 1999**, Heidenhain, M., Satzky, H. & Stadler, Ch., *German Antitrust Law* (Frankfurt am Main: Fritz Knapp 1999)

**Hildebrand 1998**, Hildebrand, D., *The Role of Economic Analysis in the EC Competition Rules* (Den Haag: Kluwer Law International 1998)

**Hildebrand 2001**, Hildebrand, D., *The Role of Economics(sic) Analysis in the EC Competition Rules – The European School* (Den Haag, Kluwer Law International 2001)

**Herdzina 1975**, Herdzina, K. (ed.), *Wettbewerbstheorie* (Köln: Kiepenheuer & Witsch 1975)

**Hesse 1984**, Hesse, K., Grundzüge des Verfassungsrechts der Bundesrepublik Deutschland (Heidelberg: C.F. Müller Juristischer Verlag 1984)

Heuss, E., *Allgemeine Markttheorie* (Tübingen: J.C.B. Mohr 1965)

**Hirschman 1970**, Hirschman, A. O., *Exit, voice and loyalty: Responses to decline in firms, organizations and states* (Cambridge Mass., Harvard University Press 1970)

**Hoffman 1990**, Hoffman, A.B., 'Anti-competitive Sate Legislation Condemned Under Articles 5, 85 and 86 of the EEC Treaty: How Far Should the Court Go After Van Eycke?', (1990) *ECLR* 1, p. 11-27

**Hoppmann 1966**, Hoppmann, E., 'Das Konzept der optimalen Wettbewerbsintensität', *JbNSt* (1966) 179, p. 286-323

**Hoppmann 1967**, Hoppmann, E., *Wettbewerb als Norm der Wettbewerbspolitik*, Ordo (1967) 18, p. 77-94

Hoppmann, E., *Das Konzept der wirksamen Preiswettbewerb*, Tübingen, J.C.B. Mohr 1979, RuS (1978) 484/485, p. 1-42

Hoppmann, E., 'Die Funktionsfähigkeit des Wettbewerbs – Bemerkungen zu Kantzenbachs Erwiderung', *JbNSt* (1967) 181, p. 251-256

Hoppmann, E., *Von der Preistheorie zur Wettbewerbstheorie*, Ordo (1966) 17, p. 369-381

Hübner, K., *Außerkartellrechtliche Einschränkungen des Kartellverbotes*, FIW-schriftenreihe 59 (Köln, Carl Heymanns Verlag 1971)

**Hussen 2000**, Hussen, A.M., *Principles of Environmental Economics* (London, Routlegde 2000)

**Immenga 1976**, Immenga, U., 'Politische Instrumentalisierung des Kartellrechts?', Tübingen: J.C.B. Mohr 1967, *RuS* (1976) 461, p. 1-26

**Immenga & Mestmäcker 2001**, Immenga, U., Mestmäcker, E.-J., *GWB Kommentar zum Kartellgesetz* (München, Beck 2001), p. 307-313

*Integration oder Desintegration der europäischen Wettbewerbsordnung?*, referate des XVI. FIW-Symposiums (Köln: Carl Heymanns Verlag 1983)

**Jacobs 1993**, Jacobs, R., 'EEC Competition Law and the Protection of the Environment', *LIEI* (1993) 1, p. 37-67

**Jans 1995**, Jans, J.H., *European Environmental law* (Den Haag: Kluwer 1995)

**Jans 2000**, Jans, J.H., *European Environmental Law* (Groningen: Europa Law Publishing 2000)

**Jans, Sevenster & Vedder 2000**, Jans, J.H., Sevenster, H.G. & Vedder, H.H.B. (eds.), *Europees milieurecht in Nederland* (Den Haag: Boom Juridische Uitgevers 2000)

Jestaedt, T. & Budde, M., 'Beihilfen für den Umweltschutz im Rahmen des EG-Vertrages', *WuW* (1995) 3, p. 196-204

**Joliet 1967**, Joliet, R., *The Rule of Reason in Antitrust Law* (Den Haag: Martinus Nijhoff, 1967)

**Jones & González-Díaz 1992**, Jones, Ch., González-Díaz, F. E., *The EEC Merger Regulation* (London: Sweet & Maxwell 1992)

**Jones & Sufrin 2001**, Jones, A. & Sufrin, B., *EC Competition Law* (Oxford: Oxford University Press 2001)

Kaiser, J.H., 'Industrielle Absprachen im öffentlichen Interesse', *NJW* (1971) 14, p. 585-588

Kalffass, H.H., 'Die Chicago School – Eine Skizze des "neuen" Amerikanischen Ansatzes für die wettbewerbspolitik', *WuW* (1980) 9, p. 596-601

**Kantzenbach 1966**, Kantzenbach, E., *Die funktionsfähigkeit des Wettbewerbs* (Göttingen: Vandenhoeck & Ruprecht 1966)

**Kantzenbach 1967**, Kantzenbach, E., 'Das Konzept der optimalen Wettbewerbsintensität – Eine Erwiderung', *JbNSt* (1967/1968) 181, p. 193-241

**Kapteyn & VerLoren van Themaat 1998**, Kapteyn, P.J.G. & VerLoren van Themaat, P., *Introduction to the Law of the European Communities*, edited by L.W. Gormley (London: Kluwer Law International 1998)

**Kartte 1969**, Kartte, W., *Ein neues Leitbild für die Wettbewerbspolitik*, FIW-schriftenreihe 49 (Köln: Carl Heymanns Verlag 1969)

Kaysen, C. & Turner, D.F., *Antitrust Policy – An Economic and Legal Analysis* (Cambridge: Harvard University Press 1959)

Kaufer, E., 'Kantzenbachs Konzept des funktionsfähigen Wettbewerbs – Ein Kommentar', *JbNSt* (1966) 179, p. 481-492

Kaufer, E., 'Nochmals: Von der Preistheorie zur Wettbewerbstheorie', *Ordo* (1967) 18, p. 95-114

Kloepfer, M., 'Absprachen im Umweltrecht der Bundesrepublik Deutschland', *M en R* (1991) 1, p. 2-11

**Kloepfer 1980**, Kloepfer, M., 'Umweltschutz als Kartellprivileg?', *JZ* (1980) 23/24 p. 718-790

Kneese, A. V. & Schultze, Ch. L., *Pollution, Prices and Public Policy* (Washington: The Brookings Institution 1975)

Knöpfle, R., *Der Rechtsbegriff "Wettbewerb" und die Realität des Wirtschaftslebens* (Köln: Carl Heymanns Verlag 1966)

**Koenig & Sander 2000**, Koenig, Ch. & Sander, C.,'Zur Vereinbarkeit des Festbetragssystems für Arzneimittel mit dem EG-Wettbewerbsrecht', *WuW* (2000) 10, p. 975-987

**Krämer 2000**, Krämer, L., *EC Environmental Law* (London: Sweet & Maxwell 2000)

Krings, M., 'Umwelt und Wettbewerb', *DVBl.* 1.12.1996, p. 1361-1365

Küsters, H.J., *Die Gründung der Europäischen Wirtschaftsgemeinschaft*, Baden-Baden: Nomos 1982

**Lehman 2000**, Lehman, M.A., *Voluntary Environmental Agreements and Competition Policy – The Case of Germany's Private System for packaging Waste Recycling*, Fondazione Eni Enrico Mattei, Nota di Lavoro 78.2000 (available online: www.feem.it)

Lenel, H.O., 'Walter Euckens ordnungspoltischer Konzeption, die wirtschaftspolitische Lehre in der Bundesrepublik und die Wettbewerbstheorie van heute', *Ordo* (1975) 26, p. 22-78

**Lichtwer 1981**, Lichtwer, L., 'Differenzierender Wirkungen des Umweltschutzes auf die Wettbewerbsstellung kleiner und mittlerer Unternehmen und auf Konzentrationstendenzen, in: Loewenheim, U., Umweltschutz und Antitrustrecht', *WuW* (1977) 1, p. 5-18

**Lofaro & Ridyard 2002**, Lofaro, A., Ridyard, D., 'Beyond Bork: New Economic Theories of Exclusion in Merger Cases, *ECLR* (2002) 3, p. 151-153

**Loozen 1999**, Loozen, E.M.H., 'CAO's, bedrijfspensioenfondsen en het EG-mededingingsrecht', *NTER* (1999) 11, p. 274-285

**Loozen 2000**, Loozen, E.M.H., 'Pavlov en Van der Woude: meer dan een Pavlov-reactie', *NTER* (2000) 12, p. 301-307

**Lotze & Pape 2003**, Lotze, A. & Pape, U.-D., 'Kartell- en vergaberechtliche Aspekte der Neuausschreibung der DSD-Leistungsverträge', *WuW* (2003) 4, p. 364-373

**Louri 2002**, Louri, V., 'Undertaking' as a jurisdictional element for the Application EC Competition Rules, *LIEI* (2002) 2, p. 143-176

**Lutz 1956**, Lutz, F.A., 'Bemerkungen zum Monopolproblem', *Ordo* (1956) 8, p. 19-43

**Maks 2002**, Maks, H., 'The "New" Horizontal Agreements Approach in the EU: an "Economic" Assessment', *Intereconomics* (2001) 1, p. 28-35

**Martínez-López 2000**, Martínez-López, M., 'Horizontal agreements on energy efficiency of appliances: a comparison between CECED and CEMEP' *Competition Policy Newsletter* (2000) 2, p. 24-25

McLachlan, D.L. & Swann, D., *Competition Policy in the European Community* (London: Oxford University Press 1967)

**Mestmäcker 1971**, Mestmäcker, E.-J., *Europäisches Wettbewerbsrecht* (München, Beck, 1971)

Meyring, B., 'Silvano Raso: When is a Statutory Monopoly Contrary to the E.C. Treaty?', *E.L.Rev* (1998) 23, p. 364-370

Miert, K. van, *Environment protection and competition policy two complementary actions*, speech 7 juni 1993

Miert, K. van, 'The role of competition policy today', *Competition Policy Newsletter* (1994) 3, p. 1-4

Miert, K. van, 'Die Wettbewerbspolitik der neuen Kommission', *Competition Policy Newsletter* (1995) 5, p. 1-6

Miert, K. van, 'La conference intergouvernementale et la politique communautaire de concurrence', *Competition Policy Newsletter* (1997) 2, p. 1-5

**Mok 1995**, Mok, M.R., *Kartelrecht I Nederland*, Zwolle: W.E.J. Tjeenk Willink 1995

**Mok 1998**, Mok, M.R., *Kartelrecht I Nederland*, Zwolle: W.E.J. Tjeenk Willink 1998

Mok, M.R. 'Mededinging en mededingingsrecht', *TVVS* 9 (1993) p. 218-222

Montagnie, Y., 'Verticale prijsbinding: moet kunnen', *SEW* 5 (1998) mei p. 196-201. Met naschrift Mok

**Monti 2002**, Monti, G., 'Article 81 EC and Public Policy', *CML Rev.* (2002) 39, p. 1057-1099

**Mortelmans 1999**, Mortelmans, K.J.M., 'Niet-economische belangen en de Mededingingswet', *NJB* 27 (1999) p. 1244-1250

**Mortelmans 2001**, Mortelmans, K., 'Towards Convergence in the Application of the Rules on Free Movement and on Competition?', *CML Rev.* (2001) 38, p. 613-649

**Möschel 1981**, Möschel, W., 'Zur wettbewerbstheoretischen Begründbarkeit von Ausnahmebereichen', *Ordo* (1981) 31, p. 85-102

**Möschel 1995**, Möschel, W., 'Subsidiaritätsprinzip und europäisches Kartellrecht', *NJW* (1995) 5, p. 281-285

Müller-Graff, P.-C., 'Die freistellung vom Kartellverbot', *EuR* (1992) 1, p. 1-40

Muller, J.Z., *Adam Smith in his time and ours: designing the decent society* (New York: The Free Press 1993)

**Neergaard 1998**, Neergaard, U.B., *Competition and Competences – the tension between European competition law and anti-competitive measures by the member states* (Copenhagen: DJØF Publishing 1998)

Niemeyer, H.-J., 'Die Anwendbarkeit der Art. 85 und 86 auf staatliche Maßnahmen', *WuW* (1994) 9, p. 721-731

**Nihoul**, *Les Télécommunications en Europe : Concurrence our Organisation de Marché* (Published by the Université Catholique de Louvain)

**Odudu 2001A**, Odudu, O., 'Interpreting Article 81(1): object as subjective intention', *E.L.Rev.* 26 (2001), p. 60-75

**Odudu 2001B**, Odudu, O., 'Interpreting Article 81(1) : demonstrating retrictive effect', *E.L. Rev.* 26 (2001), p. 261-274

**Odudu 2002**, Odudu, O., 'Article 81(3), Discretion and Direct Effect', *ECLR* (2002) 23(1), p. 17-25

Organisation for Economic Co-operation and Development, *Competition Policy and Environment*, (Paris: Organisation for Economic Co-operation and Development 1996)

**Onida 2002**, Onida, M., *Challenges and Opportunities in EC Waste Management: Perspectives on the Problem of End of Life Vehicles*, in: H. Somsen (ed.), Yearbook of European Environmental Law Vol. I (Oxford: Oxford University Press 2000)

**Ottervanger 1990**, Ottervanger, T.R., 'Antitrust and Agriculture in the Common Market', in: Hawk, B. E., (ed.), *1989 Annual Proceedings of the Fordham Corporate Law Institute*, (New York: Transnational Juris Publications 1990)

**Paschke 1997**, Paschke, M., 'Umweltschutz und Wettbewerb aus Kartellrechtlicher Sicht', in: Marburger, P., Reinhardt, M. & Schröder, M., (eds.), *Umweltschutz und Wettbewerb* (Berlin: Erich Schmidt Verlag 1997)

Pernice, I., 'Rechtlicher Rahmen der europäischen Unternehmenskooperation im umweltbereich unter besonderer Berücksichtigung von art. 85 EWGV', *EuZW* (1992) 5, p. 139-143

**Pijnacker-Hordijk 1999**, Pijnacker-Hordijk, E.H., 'Towards the tenth anniversary of the EC merger regulation; an interim report', *SEW* (1999) 4, p. 118-143

**Portwood 1994**, Portwood, T., *Competition law & the Environment* (London: Cameron May 1994)

**Posner 1992**, Posner, R.A., *Economic Analysis of Law* (Boston: Little, Brown and Company 1992)

Posner, R.A., 'The Chicago School of Antitrust Analysis', University of *Pennsylvania Law Review* (1979) 127, p. 925-948

**Rabe & Schütte 1988**, Rabe, D. & Schütte, M., 'Die erste Verordnung des Rates zur Anwendung des EWG-Kartellrechts (art. 85 und 86 EWGV) auf den Seeverkehr', *RIW* 1988, 9, p. 701-705

Reich, N., *Förderung und Schutz diffuser Interessen durch die Europäischen Gemeinschaften* (Baden-Baden: Nomos Verlag 1987)

Rengeling, H.-W. (ed.), *Umweltschutz und andere Politiken der Europäischen Gemeinschaft* (Köln: Carl Heymanns Verlag 1993)

**Ritter, Braun & Rawlinson 1991**, Ritter, L., Rawlinson, F. & Braun, W. D., *EEC Competition Law – a Practitioner's Guide*, (Deventer: Kluwer Law and Taxation Publishers 1991)

**Ritter, Braun & Rawlinson 2000**, Ritter, L., Rawlinson, F. & Braun, W. D., *EC Competition Law – a Practitioner's Guide*, (The Hague: Kluwer Law International 2000)

**Robinson 1948**, Robinson, J., *The Economics of Imperfect Competition* (London: Macmillan 1948)

**Ross 2000**, Ross, M., 'Article 16 E.C. and Services of General Interest: From Derogation to Obligation', 25 *E.L. Review.* (2000), p. 22-28

Sandhovel, A., 'Instruments of Self Regulation', *EELR* (1998) 3, p. 83-84

Sauter, W., *Competition Law and Industrial Policy in the EU* (Oxford: Clarendon Press 1997)

**Schaub 1998**, Schaub, A., Working Paper VIII, in: Ehlermann, C. D., Laudati, L. L. (eds.), *European Competition Law Annual 1997: Objectives of Competition Policy* (Oxford: Hart 1998)

**Scherer & Ross 1990**, Scherer, F.M. & Ross, D., *Industrial Market Structure and Economic Performance* (Boston: Houghton Mifflin Company 1990)

**Schermers & Waelbroeck 1992**, Schermers, H.G. & Waelbroeck, D.F., *Judicial Protection in the European Communities*, (Deventer: Kluwer Law and Taxation Publishers 1992)

**Schina 1987**, Schina, D., *State Aids Under the EEC Treaty Articles 92 to 94*, (Oxford: ECR Publishing 1987)

Schlarmann, J., 'Die kartellrechtliche Behandlung von Selbstbeschränkungsabkommen', *NJW* (1971) 32, p. 1394-1395

Schmidt, I., 'Europäische Industriepolitik – ein Widerspruch zur Wettbewerbsordnung', *WuW* (1995) 12, p. 971-985

**Schmidt 1966**, Schmidt, I., 'Neuere Entwicklungstendenzen in der Wettbewerbsheorie unter Berücksichtigung wachstumspolitischer Zielsetzungen', *WuW* (1966) 9, p. 699-731

**Schmidt 1993**, Schmidt, I., *Wettbewerbspolitik und Kartellrecht* (Stuttgart, Gustav Fischer Verlag 1993)

**Schmidt & Rittaler 1989**, Schmidt, I. & Rittaler, J.B., *A Critical Evaluation of the Chicago School of Antitrust Analysis* (Dordrecht, Kluwer, 1989)

**Schröter 1991**, Schröter, H., 'Wettbewerbsregeln', in: Groeben, H. von der, Thiesing, J. & Ehlermann, C.-D., (eds.) *Kommentar zum EWG-Vertrag, Band 2* (Baden-Baden: Nomos Verlag 1991)

**Schröter 1999**, Schröter, H., 'Wettbewerbsregeln', in: Groeben, H. von der, Thiesing, J. & Ehlermann, C.-D., (eds.) *Kommentar zum EU-/EG-Vertrag, Band 2* (Baden-Baden: Nomos Verlag 1999)

**Schumacher 2002**, Schumacher, K., 'Sonstige Kartelle, Section 7, und Umweltschutzkartelle', *WuW* (2002) 2, p. 121-131

Sevenster, H.G., *Milieubeleid en gemeenschapsrecht* (Deventer: Kluwer 1992)

Sevenster, H.G., 'De geoorloofdheid van milieubeleidsafspraken in Europees perspectief', in: Aalders, M.V.C. & Acht, R.J.J., (eds.), *Afspraken in het milieurecht* (Zwolle: W.E.J. Tjeenk Willink 1992)

**Sevenster 2000**, Sevenster H.G., 'The Environmental Guarantee after Amsterdam: Does the Emperor Have New Clothes?', in: H. Somsen (ed.), *Yearbook of European Environmental Law Vol. I* (Oxford: Oxford University Press 2000)

**Smith 1994**, Smith, A., *An Inquiry in to the Nature and Causes of the Wealth of Nations*, edited by E. Cannan (New York: Random House 1994)

Smith, A., *The Theory of Moral Sentiments*, edited by D.D. Raphael & A.L. Macfie (Oxford: Clarendon Press 1976)

Steinbeck, A.V., 'Umweltvereinbarungen und europäisches Wettbewerbsrecht', *WuW* (1998) 6, p. 554-566

**Staaten 1998**, Straaten, J. van der, 'Sustainable Development and Public Policy', in: S. Faucheux, M. O'Connor and J. van der Straaten (eds.) *Sustainable Development: Concepts, Rationalities and Strategies* (Dordrecht, Kluwer Academic Publishers 1998)

**Stuyck et al. 2000**, Stuyck, J., Waelbroeck, M., Reeken, B.L.P. van, Noë, S.B., *Competition Law in the EU and the Netherlands* (Edited by F.O.W. Vogelaar) (Deventer: W.E.J. Tjeenk Willink 2000)

Swaak, Ch.R.A. & Woude, M.H. van der, *De Nederlandse Mededingingswet: deel 1 Teksten* (Deventer: Kluwer 1997)

**Temmink 2000**, Temmink, H., 'From Danish Bottles to Danish Bees: The Dynamics of Free Movement of Goods and Environmental Protection – a Case Law Analysis', in: H. Somsen (ed.), *Yearbook of European Environmental Law Vol. I* (Oxford: Oxford University Press 2000)

**Tolksdorf 1980**, Tolksdorf, M., 'Stand und Entwicklungstendenzen der Wettbewerbstheorie', *WuW* (1980) 12, p. 785-803

Tuchtfeldt, E., 'Über die staatsfunktionen bei Adam Smith', *Ordo* (1976) 27, p. 29 *et seq.*

**Turner 1970**, Turner, D.F., 'The Scope of Antitrust and Other Economic Regulatory Policies', in: J.W. Markham & G.F. Papanek (eds.), *Industrial Organization & Economic Development*, (Boston: Houghton Mifflin Company, 1970)

Ulmer, P., 'Muß der leistungswettbewerb stärker geschützt werden?', *WuW* (1987) 9, p. 701-705

**Van de Gronden 2001**, Gronden, J.W. van de, 'Milieu en mededinging: is milieubescherming alleen een publieke taak of ook onderdeel van de producentenverantwoordelijkheid?', in: Gronden, J.W. van de, Mortelmans, K.J.M. (eds.), *Mededinging en niet-economische belangen* (Deventer: Kluwer 2001)

**Van de Gronden & Mortelmans 2001**, Gronden, J.W. van de & Mortelmans, K.J.M., 'Het mededingingsrecht en niet-economische belangen', in: Gronden, J.W. van de, Mortelmans, K.J.M. (red.), *Mededinging en niet-economische belangen* (Deventer: Kluwer 2001).

**Van den Bergh 1993**, Van den Bergh, R., *Economische analyse van het mededingingsrecht: een terrein verkenning* (Arnhem: Gouda Quint 1993)

Van den Bergh, R.J. & Camesasca, P.D., 'De zesde Duitse Kartelwet-Novelle: hoe ver is Brussel van Berlijn?', *SEW* (1999) 2, p. 48-56

**Van den Bergh & Camesasca 2000**, Van den Bergh, R.J. & Camesasca, P.D., 'Irreconcilable Principles? The Court of Justice Exempts Collectieve Labour Agreements from the Wrath of Antitrust', *E.L.Rev* (2000), 25, p. 492-508

**Van der Meulen 2000**, Meulen, B.M.J. van der, 'Belangenafweging', *M & M* (2000) 5, p. 196-198

**Rossem & Vedder 2000**, Rossem, A. van, & Vedder, H.H.B., 'Sydhavnens: Dusseldorp revisited?', *NTER* (2000) nr. 9, p. 209-216

Väth, A., *Die Wettbewerbskonzeption des Europäischen Gerichtshofs: Eine wettbebwerbstheoretische Analyse der rechtsprechung des höchsten europäischen Gerichts anhand ausgewählter Entscheidungen* (Bayreuth: P.C.O. Verlag 1987)

**Vedder 2000**, Vedder, H.H.B.. 'Mededinging en milieubescherming', in: Jans, J.H., Sevenster, H.G., Vedder, H.H.B., *Europees milieurecht in Nederland* (Den Haag: Boom Juridische Uitgevers 2000)

**Vedder 2001**, Vedder, H.H.B., *Mededinging en milieu – knelpunten en kansen*, (Alphen a/d Rijn, Samsom 2001)

**Vedder 2001A**, Vedder, H.H.B., 'Environmental Protection and Free Competition: A new Balance?', *LIEI* (2001) 1, p. 105-116

**Vedder 2001B**, Vedder, H.H.B., 'Het Europese recht en de stimulering van duurzame energie – Duitse windhandel', *NTER* (2001) 6, p. 147-155

**Vedder 2001C**, Vedder, H.H.B., 'Case Note on Stichting Wit- en Bruingoed, zaaknr. 1153', *M & M* (2001) 7, p. 254-258

**Vedder 2002**, Vedder, H.H.B., *Competition Law, Environmental Policy and Producer Responsibility – Experiences in the Netherlands from a European perspective* (Groningen: Europa Law Publishing 2002)

**Vedder 2003**, Vedder, H.H.B., 'Recente ontwikkelingen in het Europese Afvalstoffenrecht' Forthcoming in *SEW*.

**Velte 1999**, Velte, R., *Duale Abfallentsorgung und Kartellverbot* (Baden-Baden: Nomos 1999)

**Viscusi, Vernon & Harrington 2000**, Viscusi, W.K., Vernon, J.M., Harrington, J.E., *Economics of Regulation and Antitrust* (Cambridge MA: The MIT Press 2000)

**Vogelaar 1995**, Vogelaar, F.O.W., 'Towards an Improved Integration of EC Environmental Policy and EC Competition Policy: An Interim Report', in: B. Hawk (ed.), *Annual Proceedings of the Fordham Corporate Law Institute 1994*, (Den Haag: Kluwer Law International 1995)

**Vogelaar 2000**, Vogelaar F.O.W., *Marktwerking moet!*, (Inaugural address held on 19 April 2000) (Amsterdam: Vossiuspers AUP 2000)

**Vogelaar 2002**, Vogelaar, F., 'Modernization of EC Competition Law, Economy and Horizontal Cooperation between Undertakings', *Intereconomics* (2002) 1, p. 19-27

**Waelbroeck & Frignani 1997**, Waelbroeck, M. & Frignani, A., *Commentaire J. Megret, 4, Concurrence* (Bruxelles, Editions de l'Université de Bruxelles 1997)

**Wasmeier 2001**, Wasmeier, M., 'The Integration of Environmental Protection as a General Rule for Interpreting Community Law', *CML Rev.* (2001) 38, p. 15- 177

**Wesseling 2000**, Wesseling, R., *The Modernisation of EC Antitrust Law* (Oxford: Hart Publishing 2000)

**Wettbewerbskommission und Preisüberwacher 1996**, Wettbewerbskommission und Preisüberwacher, *Veröffentlichungen der Schweizerischen Kartellkommission und des Preisüberwachters, (2) Berichte Januar bis Juni 1996 der Kartellkommission* (Bern: Eidgenossische Drucksachen- und Materialzentrale 1996)

**Whish 2001**, Whish, R., *Competition Law* (London: Butterworths 2001)

**Wiers 2002**, Wiers, J., *Trade and Environment in the EC and the WTO* (Groningen: Europa Law Publishing 2002)

Wille, F. & Gläser, M., 'Staatsaufgaben bei Adam Smith, eine Würdigung unter Allokationsaspekten', *Ordo* (1977) 28, p. 34-

Willemsen, A., *Wettbewerbstheorie – Wettbewerbspolitik und die kartellrechtlichen bestimmungen des EWG-Vertrages und des EFTA-Vertrages* (Bern: Stämpfli 1971)

Willgerodt, H., 'Fehlurteile über vielzahligen Wettbewerb', Ordo (1975) 26, p. 97-130

Willimsky, S.M., 'The Concept(s) of Competition', *ECLR* (1997) 1, p. 54-57

**Wilt 2002**, Wilt, C.J. van der, 'Het Convenant bodemsanering bedrijfsterreinen', *M en R* (2002) 2, p. 26-32

**Wolf 1997**, Wolf, D., *Die Erwartungen des Bundeskartellamts an de 6. GWB-Novelle – Mehr Konvergenz mit europäischem Recht ?*, speech for XVII International Forum EC Competition law of the Studievereniging Kartelrecht, Brussels 15/16 May 1997

Wolf, D., *Wo liegen die Chancen und Risiken/Grenzen von freiwilligen Selbstverpflichtungen für Gesellschaft und Unternehmen?*, speech for SPD-group in Bavaria 1 July 1997

**Zohlnhöfer 1981**, W. Zohlnhöfer, 'Umweltschutz und Wettbewerb – grundlegende Analyse -,' in: H. Gutzler (ed.), *Umweltpolitik und Wettbewerb* (Baden-Baden: Nomos Verlag 1981)

**Zweigert & Kötz 1998**, Zweigert, K., Kötz, H., *Introduction to Comparative Law* (Oxford: Clarendon Press 1998).

# Abbreviations

| | |
|---|---|
| *AER* | The American Economic Review |
| *CFI* | Court of First Instance |
| *CML Rev.* | Common Market Law Review |
| *DVBl.* | Deutsches Verwaltungsblatt |
| *ECLR* | European Competition Law Review |
| *EELR* | European Environmental Law Review |
| *EC* | European Community |
| *ECJ* | European Court of Justice |
| *ECSC* | European Coal and Steel Community |
| *EEC* | European Economic Community |
| *E.L.Rev.* | European Law Review |
| *EuR* | EuropaRecht |
| *Euratom* | European Atomic Energy Community |
| *EuZW* | Europäisches Zeitschrift für Wirtschaftsrecht |
| *EWG* | Europäische Wirtschaftsgemeinschaft (EEC) |
| *FAZ* | Fankfurter Allgemeine Zeitung |
| *GWB* | Gesetz gegen Wettbewerbsbeschränkungen (German act against restraints of competition) |
| *JbNSt* | Jahrbuch für Nationalökonomie und Statistik |
| *JEL* | Journal of Environmental Law |
| *JZ* | Juristenzeitung |
| *LIEI* | Legal Issues of Economic Integration (previously: Legal Issues of European Integration |
| *M & M* | Markt en Mededinging |
| *M en R* | Milieu en Recht |
| *Mw* | Mededingingswet (Dutch competition act) |
| *NJB* | Nederlands juristenblad |
| *NJW* | Neue Juristische Wochenschrift |
| *NYULR* | New York University Law Review |
| *ORDO* | ORDO Jahrbuch für die Ordnung von Wirtschaft und Gesellschaft |
| *Rev. trim. dr. Europ.* | Revue trimestriel droit Europeen |
| *rn* | Randnummer |
| *RIW* | Recht der Internationalen Wirtschaft |
| *RTDE* | Revue trimestrielle de droit européen |
| *RuS* | Recht und Staat in Geschichte und Gegenwart |
| *SEW* | Sociaal economische wetgeving |
| *SMA* | Sociaal Maandblad Arbeid |
| *Stb* | Staatsblad (Statute book) |
| *Stcrt* | Staatscourant (State Gazette) |
| *TVVS* | Tijdschrift voor vennootschappen, verenigingen en stichtingen |
| *WEEE* | Waste of Electronic and Electrical Equipment |
| *Wem* | Wet economische mededinging (Dutch act on economic competition) |
| *WuW* | Wirtschaft und Wettbewerb |

# Index

# Samenvatting

## Inleiding

Dit boek bevat een onderzoek naar de integratie van milieubelangen en het mededingingsrecht van de EG. In eerste instantie was de aanleiding voor dit onderzoek gelegen in het integratiebeginsel dat is te vinden in artikel 6 EG. Volgens dit beginsel dienen de eisen inzake milieubescherming te worden geïntegreerd in de omschrijving en uitvoering van het beleid en het optreden van de Gemeenschap [...] in het bijzonder met het oog op het bevorderen van duurzame ontwikkeling. De vraag is dan wat precies "integreren" inhoudt. Een puur juridische poging tot beantwoording van deze vraag leidt vaak tot tautologische antwoorden in de trant van: integreren betekent rekening houden met. Aldus moest het integratiebeginsel op andere wijze worden geduid.

## Deel een: de zoektocht naar een model voor integratie

*Het vervuiler betaalt beginsel en producentenverantwoordelijkheid en de internalisatie van het milieu*

Met behulp van een combinatie van juridisch redeneren en economische inzichten kan het integratiebeginsel wel een beter omlijnde inhoud worden gegeven wat betreft de rol die milieuoverwegingen moeten spelen in het mededingingsrecht. Deze economische inzichten zijn voor een groot deel terug te voeren op het vervuiler betaalt beginsel. Volgens dit beginsel zou de vervuiler moeten betalen voor de schade die hij het milieu berokkent. Daarmee poogt het beginsel het probleem van de externe kosten aan te pakken. Volgens de economische theorie kan milieuvervuiling worden verklaard aan de hand van het feit dat een aantasting van het milieu vaak geen kosten met zich meebrengt voor degene die verantwoordelijk is voor de milieuaantasting. Wanneer alle milieukosten maar worden geïnternaliseerd, heeft alle gebruik van het milieu (bijvoorbeeld om in te lozen, te bouwen of om er grondstoffen aan te onttrekken) een prijs. Doordat een bepaalde activiteit een intensiever gebruik (misbruik) van het milieu dan een hogere prijs met zich meebrengt zal dit ook resulteren in een hogere prijs op de markt voor de desbetreffende activiteit. Een hogere prijs resulteert in minder gebruik van deze activiteit en daardoor minder milieubelasting. Traditioneel werd voor het aanwijzen van de vervuiler meteen naar de aanbodzijde van de markt gekeken. Producenten werden geacht de vervuilers te zijn. In dit boek worden echter de consumenten ten minste even verantwoordelijk gehouden voor de verslechtering van het milieu. Kan immers niet worden gesteld dat in een vrije markteconomie als de onze, de producenten niet meer doen dan datgene produceren in een hoeveelheid en kwaliteit waar de consument om vraagt? Schijnbaar wil een grote groep consumenten eenvoudigweg niet meer betalen voor scharrelvlees, schonere bezine of een treinkaartje in plaats van de auto. Nu de waarheid omtrent wie de werkelijke vervuiler is - als altijd - in het midden ligt, dient te worden onderzocht waarom de kosten dan toch vaak aan de aanbodzijde van de markt worden geïnternaliseerd.

Aan de hand van het beginsel van de producentenverantwoordelijkheid is getracht een antwoord te geven op deze vraag. Daarbij werd duidelijk dat het gehele "probleem" van mededinging en milieu samenkomt in dit beginsel. Volgens het beginsel van de producentenverantwoordelijkheid zijn de fabrikanten verantwoordelijk voor de milieuvriendelijke inname en verwerking van het afval dat hun producten worden nadat de consument ze heeft afgedankt. De aanname hierachter is dat op dit moment de afvalfase van de productie en consumptiecyclus geen rol speelt (hiervoor is immers de gemeente feitelijk en financieel verantwoordelijk). Aldus bestaat er bij de producenten weinig aanleiding om bij het ontwerpen en vervaardigen van hun producten rekening te houden met de recyclebaarheid van deze producten. Het resultaat zijn twintig verschillende plastics, moeilijk los te halen klikverbindingen en moeilijk te verwerken materialen die de kosten van de recycling doen stijgen en daarmee zorgen voor een nog lager recyclingpercentage. Door de producenten verantwoordelijk te maken voor de afvalfase, ontstaat er voor hen een directe aanleiding om de kosten die zijn gemoeid met deze afvalfase te verminderen (door bijvoorbeeld het aantal verschillende plastics te reduceren of de hoeveelheid verpakking terug te brengen). Op dit moment wordt de vraag naar de werkelijke verantwoordelijke weer actueel. Er kan van worden uitgegaan dat de keuze voor de meerdere soorten plastics in de eerste plaats is ingegeven uit kostenbesparingsoverwegingen. Dit betekent dat het beter te recyclen product waarschijnlijk duurder zal zijn. Daarbij komt dat het ophalen en recyclen van de afgedankte producten eveneens geld kost. Geld dat consumenten eerder schijnbaar niet bereid waren te betalen om de eenvoudige reden dat zij evengoed de vervuilers zijn in dit opzicht. Toch maakt de producentenverantwoordelijkheid alleen de producenten verantwoordelijk. Dit kan worden verklaard aan de hand van de noodzaak om de zaken zo efficiënt mogelijk te regelen. Ten eerste pleiten handhavingsredenen voor het verantwoordelijk maken van de producenten. Als een bepaalde groep geconfronteerd wordt met extra kosten dan zal een deel van die groep pogen om deze kosten te ontduiken (wildstorten). In dit licht is het slim om de groep die moeten worden gecontroleerd teneinde de ontduiking tegen te gaan zo klein mogelijk te houden. Het is immers eenvoudiger om honderd producenten en importeurs te controleren dan zestien miljoen Nederlanders. Ten tweede zal de milieueffectiviteit groter zijn wanneer de producenten de kosten dragen van de milieubelasting. De omvang van de kosten voor hen is vele malen groter (zij dragen dan immers de kosten voor hun gehele productie) en dus beter voelbaar zodat het eerder tot een vermindering van de milieubelasting zal leiden. Veel belangrijker is echter de mogelijkheid die de producenten hebben om te innoveren ten aanzien van de milieubelasting van hun producten.

Wanneer kosten ontstaan in de afvalfase, ontstaat niet alleen een prikkel om deze kosten omlaag te brengen maar ontstaat ook een prikkel om onderzoek te doen naar mogelijkheden om deze kosten verder omlaag te brengen dan op grond van de huidige stand der techniek mogelijk is. Deze prikkel tot innovatie op milieugebied is onmisbaar om duurzame ontwikkeling te verkrijgen. Alleen wanneer de gehele economie er niet alleen op is gericht om de milieubelasting hier en nu te beperken maar ook probeert om de milieubelasting structureel te reduceren door onderzoek naar nieuwe technieken, is er ook maar een kans dat er duurzame ontwikkeling ontstaat.

Wat betreft de milieubescherming verklaart het bovenstaande waarom het beginsel van producentenverantwoordelijkheid centraal staat in de relatie tussen mededinging en milieubescherming. Ook wat betreft het mededingingsrecht komt het aan op dit beginsel.

Aan de mededingingszijde van het centrale onderwerp van dit onderzoek speelt allereerst het begrip concurrentieverstoring een grote rol. De licht euforische toon hierboven verdekt immers niet dat volledige internalisatie van alle externe milieukosten en duurzame ontwikkeling op dit moment helaas grotendeels theoretisch zijn. Er hoeft maar een land te zijn dat het minder nauw neemt met het milieu en het invoeren van een producentenverantwoordelijkheid (of welke andere milieumaatregel ook) zal onmiddellijk leiden tot een concurrentieverstoring. De extra kosten hoeven immers niet te worden gedragen door het land met de kortzichtige regering. Verder kan worden herinnerd aan het feit dat een grote groep consumenten even kortzichtig is zodat een milieuvriendelijk maar duurder alternatief op dit moment altijd een niche product zal zijn. Wanneer deze beperkte omzet voor dit milieuvriendelijke product onvoldoende blijkt te zijn verdwijnt het product weer van de markt en is er geen milieuwinst. Deze verstoringen van de concurrentie kunnen worden teruggevoerd op de gebrekkige internalisatie van milieukosten op dit moment. Een aantal actoren op de markt heeft de milieukosten wel geïnternaliseerd maar een minstens even grote groep geeft niet steeds te weinig om het milieu. In deze overgangsfase, waarbij een paar regeringen en ondernemingen hun kop boven het maaiveld uitsteken en milieuvriendelijker proberen te wezen, voelt deze voorhoede een verslechtering van de concurrentiepositie.

Bij het compenseren van deze verslechtering van de concurrentiepositie speelt het mededingingsrecht zijn rol. Een compensatie zou immers plaats kunnen vinden doordat de ondernemingen die worden geconfronteerd met extra milieukosten subsidies ontvangen. Ook komt het voor dat ondernemingen gaan samenwerken om het milieuprobleem beter aan te kunnen pakken. Een laatste voorbeeld is een wettelijk monopolie uitgedeeld door de regering om te verzekeren dat het milieuvriendelijke bedrijf verzekerd is van voldoende klandizie om uit de kosten te komen. Deze drie voorbeelden bevatten optreden van de overheid en ondernemingen dat in strijd is met de mededingingsbepalingen van het EG verdrag. Bij de vraag of ze zouden moeten worden toegestaan, speelt het model van integratie een rol.

*Het model voor integratie*

Volgens dit model voor integratie zou de toepassing van het mededingingsrecht moeten zijn gericht op het vergemakkelijken en totstandbrengen van de internalisatie van milieukosten. Alleen bij een volledige internalisatie, zo is hierboven aangetoond, is er een kans dat we een duurzame ontwikkeling krijgen. In de praktijk betekent dit dat milieuvriendelijke initiatieven van koplopers moeten worden gestimuleerd. Waar mededingingsbeperkingen noodzakelijk zijn ter compensatie van een concurrentieverstoring, dienen deze te worden toegestaan door het mededingingsrecht. Waar de noodzaak van een compensatie niet (langer) aanwezig is, dient het mededingingsrecht echter onverbiddelijk iedere mededingingsbeperking tegen te gaan. De afwezigheid van een concurrentieverstoring wijst er immers op dat de er een volledige internalisatie heeft plaatsgevonden. Op dat moment dient de onverstoorde mededinging zijn tuchtigende werking op de markt te hebben zodat een concurrentie ten aanzien van het milieu ontstaat. Zijn immers alle milieukosten volledig geïnternaliseerd, dan zal een consument meer moeten betalen voor een vervuilend product dan voor een milieuvriendelijk product, hetgeen hij niet zal willen zodat het vervuilende product verdwijnt. Bovendien zal hij, waar de milieuvriendelijke producten nog steeds duurder zijn dan de milieuonvriendelijke alternatieven bereid zijn om deze hogere prijs te betalen aangezien hij weet dat het andere product hem minstens evenveel zal kosten als hij de milieubelasting in aanmerking neemt. De aldus vergroende markt zal leiden tot een strijd om zo milieuvriendelijk mogelijk te produceren en te consumeren.

Dit model voor integratie is, zoals hierboven blijkt, weliswaar ontstaan met betrekking tot artikel 6 EG, maar alles behalve beperkt tot het EG mededingingsrecht. De onderliggende economische redenering is universeel en kan worden toegepast op ieder stelsel van mededingingsregels. Een juridisch bezwaar tegen de toepassing van dit model zou kunnen zijn dat het tot gevolg heeft dat milieubescherming een doel van het mededingingsrecht wordt. Voor wat betreft de mededingingsregels van de EG doet dit juridische bezwaar al geen opgeld vanwege artikel 6 EG dat een plicht tot integratie bevat voor alle beleid en optreden van de Gemeenschap, inclusief het mededingingsrecht en de toepassing daarvan. Andere stelsels van mededingingsrecht kennen echter niet dergelijke integratiebepalingen. Voor deze stelsels is daarmee geen onoverkomelijke barrière opgeworpen die in de weg staat aan de toepassing van het model van integratie. Het model van integratie leidt er immers op de langere termijn toe dat de concurrentie minder wordt verstoord doordat het een vollediger internalisatie tot gevolg heeft. Daarmee zijn milieubescherming en een bescherming van de mededinging op de langere termijn wederzijds versterkende doelstellingen die geenszins in strijd zijn met de doelstellingen van het mededingingsrecht. Juridisch en economisch gezien zijn er geen bezwaren tegen de toepassing van het model voor integratie. Wel zullen de mededingingsautoriteiten er een langere termijn visie op na moeten gaan houden wat betreft het doel van de bescherming van de onverstoorde mededinging.

Nu het model voor integratie is ontwikkeld kan worden gekeken of het model ook wordt toegepast in de toepassing van het EG mededingingsrecht

## Deel twee: EG mededingingsrecht en milieubescherming

*Inleiding*

In dit deel wordt het volledige mededingingsrecht van de EG onderzocht op de rol die milieubelangen hebben gespeeld in de toepassing van deze regels. Daarbij wordt ook bekeken of de rol die aan milieuoverwegingen is toegekend overeenkomt met het model voor integratie. Allereerst komen de beginselen van het EG mededingingsrecht aan de orde (hoofdstuk 7). Daarna wordt de toepassing van artikel 81 EG (het kartelverbod) onderzocht in hoofdstuk 8. De toepassing van het verbod op misbruik van een economische machtspositie (artikel 82 EG) komt daarna aan de orde in hoofdstuk 9. Als laatste van de tot ondernemingen gerichte mededingingsregels wordt in hoofdstuk 10 de Concentratiecontrole Verordening onderzocht. In hoofdstuk 11 komt de nuttig effect regel (artikel 10 juncto 81 EG) aan de orde terwijl in hoofdstuk 12 de toepassing van artikel 86 EG (publieke ondernemingen) wordt besproken. De toepassing van het verbod van staatssteun in artikel 87 EG is hekkensluiter.

In alle gevallen vangt het hoofdstuk aan met een algemene bespreking van de desbetreffende bepalingen waarna meer specifiek wordt gekeken naar de toepassing met betrekking tot milieubescherming.

*Beginselen van EG mededingingsrecht*

Onder de beginselen worden verstaan de rol van het mededingingsrecht in het Verdrag en de werkingssfeer van de mededingingsregels. Ten aanzien van de rol van de mededingingsregels in het Verdrag kan worden vastgesteld dat behalve de verzekering van een bepaalde mate of intensiteit van de mededinging, de marktintegratie eveneens een belangrijk doel is. Het Hof legt de mededingingsregels dan ook teleologisch uit hetgeen (grote) gevolgen heeft voor de toepassing van de regels. De mededingingsregels van de EG dienen, net als alle andere beleid en optreden van de EG te worden gezien in het licht van de doelstellingen van de EG zoals die zijn neergelegd in artikel 2 EG. De mededingingsregels van de EG zijn in principe van toepassing op de gehele economie. Alleen ten aanzien van de landbouw-, transport- en defensie-industrie bestaan bijzondere regels. Deze regels worden, als uitzonderingen op de regel, beperkt geïnterpreteerd en laten dan ook geen ruimte voor een toepassing van het model voor integratie. De personele werkingssfeer van het Europese mededingingsrecht valt samen met het begrip onderneming. Alleen ondernemingen, dat wil zeggen, entiteiten die marktactiviteiten verrichten, vallen onder de mededingingsregels. Entiteiten die dus een niet-economische activiteit verrichten zijn uitgezonderd van de toepassing van het mededingingsrecht. Uit de jurisprudentie kunnen twee soorten van niet-economische activiteiten worden afgeleid met de daarbij horende tests: de overheidsprerogatieven-test en de markteconomie-test. De overheidsprerogatieven-test is al eens gebruikt om een entiteit die milieubeschermingsactiviteiten uitvoert, uit te sluiten van het ondernemingsbegrip. De precieze inhoud van de markteconomietest is onduidelijk maar het is niet uit te sluiten dat op grond van de onderliggende solidariteitsgedachte, ook bepaalde milieuactiviteiten worden buiten de werkingssfeer van het mededingingsrecht vallen. Ten aanzien van de territoriale werkingssfeer heeft het onderzoek zich beperkt tot het constateren dat er snel sprake zal zijn van een invloed op de intracommunautaire handel.

*Artikel 81 EG*

In verband met artikel 81 EG wordt allereerst de Albany-exceptie onderzocht. Volgens deze uitzondering vallen collectieve arbeidsovereenkomsten, ondanks hun mededingingsbeperkende effecten, niet onder het verbod van artikel 81 EG aangezien het EG verdrag hun totstandkoming aanmoedigt. Een nader onderzoek wijst uit dat de juridische onderbouwing van de Albany-exceptie een analoge toepassing op collectieve milieuovereenkomsten uit sluit. Wat betreft het vereiste van artikel 81 dat de afspraak tot doel of tot gevolg moet hebben dat de mededinging wordt beperkt, wordt een tendens tot een economische uitlegging van artikel 81(1) gesignaleerd. Zo speelt de vraag of een mededingingsbeperking wel merkbaar is, eens steeds grotere rol. Ook lijkt uit de rechtspraak een *rule of reason*, op grond waarvan de mededingingsbeperkende en mededingingsversterkende effecten tegen elkaar moeten worden afgewogen, te kunnen worden afgeleid. In het kader van deze twee aspecten kunnen milieuoverwegingen een rol spelen. Vaak zal de conclusie moeten zijn dat een afspraak tussen fabrikanten ten aanzien van bepaalde milieuaspecten van het productieproces of de producten geen merkbare mededingingsbeperking tot gevolg hebben aangezien zij op veel meer (en belangrijker) aspecten concurreren dan de milieuprestaties alleen (prijs, kwaliteit etc.) Ook kan een afspraak ten aanzien van de milieubescherming noodzakelijk zijn voor het creëren van een nieuwe markt. Met name op het terrein van de afvalverwerking is dit mogelijk. In dit soort gevallen kunnen de positieve effecten voor de mededinging de negatieve effecten voor de mededinging meer dan compenseren zodat er als netto resultaat niet kan worden gesproken van een beperking (veeleer een versterking) van de concurrentie. In de literatuur is wel een Europese *rule of reason* ontwaard in de rechtspraak van het Hof. Volgens deze opvatting zou ieder dwingend vereiste de toepassing van artikel 81(1) op de mededingingsbeperkingen die inherent zijn aan dit dwingend vereiste, uitsluiten. Aangezien milieubescherming is geaccepteerd als dwingend vereiste, kan deze uitzondering worden ingeroepen. Evenwel zou een dergelijke uitlegging van artikel 81(1), in tegenstelling tot de (niet-Europese) *rule of reason*, wel degelijk artikel 81(3) overbodig maken. Legalistische redeneringen op grond waarvan de effecten op de mededinging niet langer behoeven te worden vastgesteld wanneer een mededingingsbeperkend doel is vastgesteld worden (niet alleen vanuit het oogpunt van het model voor integratie) afgekeurd. In het kader van het onderzoek naar artikel 81 EG wordt ook vastgesteld dat in een aantal gevallen wellicht kan worden gesproken van een (economisch) dwangkartel op milieugronden. De omstandigheden die de overheid dan creëert zijn zodanig dat er geen ruimte meer is voor concurrentie; samenwerking is dan de enige economisch rationele optie. Ten aanzien van het eerste lid van artikel 81 EG is de conclusie dat het model voor integratie niet noopt tot meer dan een economisch verantwoorde toepassing. Een grotere rol (bijvoorbeeld uitsluiten van artikel 81(1) ondanks dat er wel een mededingingsbeperking is) voor milieuoverwegingen druist tegen het model voor integratie in aangezien dit model er juist van uit gaat dat, na internalisatie, de mededinging zijn nuttige werk moet doen.

Binnen artikel 81 EG lijkt het model voor integratie zijn rol dan ook voornamelijk te moeten spelen met betrekking tot het derde lid van deze bepaling. Op grond van deze bepaling kunnen mededingingsbeperkende afspraken worden toegestaan wanneer zij voldoen aan vier cumulatieve vereisten. Het model voor integratie eist dat milieuvoordelen rechtstreeks, zonder dat deze worden omgezet in economische voordelen, worden geaccepteerd als voordelen die kunnen leiden tot een toepassing van deze bepaling. Verder komen milieuvoordelen inherent ten goede aan een open groep personen zodat aan het tweede vereiste voor de toepassing van artikel 81(3) is voldaan. In het kader van de onmisbaarheid van de afspraak om de voordelen te behalen kan worden afgewogen of de afspraak noodzakelijk is in het licht van de stand van zaken wat betreft de internalisatie en eventuele noodzaak om verstoringen van de concurrentie te compenseren. Het laatste vereiste voor een toepassing van artikel 81, lid 3, zal geen problemen opleveren aangezien de milieuaspecten slechts een element zijn ten aanzien waarvan concurrentie plaatsvindt. Voldoende restconcurrentie zal er dus blijven.

De huidige praktijk van de Commissie is teleurstellend in dit opzicht. Niet alleen is de Commissie onduidelijk waar het gaat om het gewicht dat aan milieuvoordelen wordt toegekend, de rol die milieuvoordelen spelen lijkt niet te voldoen aan de eisen van het model van integratie. De onduidelijkheid van het beleid van de Commissie kan tot grote problemen leiden wanneer artikel 81, lid 3, rechtstreeks werkend wordt verklaard. Vanaf dat moment kan immers iedere rechter deze bepaling toepassen. Ondanks dat dit voor de toepassing van het model voor integratie niets uitmaakt, bestaan er wel degelijk gevaren voor de eenvormige toepassing van artikel 81(3) door de gehele Gemeenschap. De oplossing die de Commissie lijkt voor te staan (een gedeeltelijke continuering van haar uitleggingsmonopolie) zal in dit verband niet helpen. Evenmin zal het reduceren van de toepassing van artikel 81, lid 3, tot puur economische overwegingen helpen aangezien een nationale rechter bij de toepassing van artikel 81(3) EG gebonden is aan het integratiebeginsel en zich dus geroepen kan voelen om aan milieuvoordelen een zeker gewicht toe te kennen. Het belang van een duidelijk beleid van de Commissie ten aanzien van milieuoverwegingen in het kader van artikel 81(3) kan dus niet worden onderschat.

*Artikel 82 EG*

Met betrekking tot artikel 82 EG, het verbod van misbruik van een economische machtspositie, wordt eerst de rol van milieuoverwegingen op de marktafbakening onderzocht. Artikel 82 is totnogtoe slechts in een milieuzaak toegepast. De uitkomst van de DSD zaak is als onbevredigend gekarakteriseerd. Op grond van het model voor integratie had meer rekening moeten worden gehouden met de bijzondere vereisten die de Duitse milieuregelgeving oplegt. Deze hadden hun rol kunnen spelen in het kader van de mogelijkheid van de zogenaamde objectieve rechtvaardiging. Verder werd gesteld dat deze bijzondere vereisten zeer wel kunnen leiden tot de karakterisering van DSD (en zijn lotgenoten) als natuurlijk monopolie of universele diensten verrichter. Dit is onbevredigend vanuit het perspectief van het model voor integratie aangezien daarmee moet worden aanvaard dat de markt is beperkt tot een aanbieder. Zinvolle concurrentie is dan niet mogelijk. Het ontstaan van een dergelijk natuurlijk monopolie valt in eerste instantie de milieuregelgever te verwijten. Door te kiezen voor een voor iets dat in werkelijkheid neerkomt op een *productverantwoordelijkheid* in plaats van een *echte producentenverantwoordelijkheid*, verspeelt hij de kans op het creëren van een functionerende markt. Het toepassen van het misbruikverbod in deze omstandigheden is niet meer dan een lapmiddel waarmee de structurele fouten niet kunnen worden rechtgezet. Veeleer zal de aandacht zich moeten richten op de institutionele structuur van de monopolist waarbij deze zodanig moet zijn dat deze niet kan verworden tot vehikel waarmee de oprichtende of deelnemende ondernemingen hun invloed kunnen uitoefenen. In het geval van DSD is de institutionele structuur zodanig dat DSD niet kan worden misbruikt door de benedenstroomse of bovenstroomse industrie om toetreders te weren uit de benedenstroomse of bovenstroomse markten. Verder zal deze structuur eveneens voorkomen dat DSD zich abusief gaat gedragen op de markt waarop het zelf actief is.

*Concentratiecontrole*

Met betrekking tot concentratiecontrole kan de samenvatting kort zijn: de Concentratiecontrole Verordening staat het terzijde zetten van mededingingsoverwegingen op grond van milieuoverwegingen niet toe. De toepassing van het model voor integratie is dan ook onmogelijk. Dit is evenwel geen probleem aangezien de Concentratiecontrole Verordening een structureel instrument is. Het valt niet in te zien waarom een verandering in de marktstructuur die de mededinging beperkt noodzakelijk zou zijn vanuit milieuperspectief. De internalisatie van milieulasten is in het einde het best gediend met de aanwezigheid van mededinging. Het toestaan van een mededingingsbeperkende concentratie op milieugronden zou neerkomen op het accepteren van het ontstaan van natuurlijke monopolies zoals dat hierboven (in verband met artikel 82) werd gezien als teleurstellend gevolg van weinig doordachte milieuregelgeving.

*Nuttig effect regel*

Ter zake van de nuttig effect regel bestaat nog veel onduidelijkheid. In ieder geval kan de nuttig effect regel als lex generalis ten opzichte van artikel 86 worden gekwalificeerd. Dat brengt met zich mee dat de gevolgen van en voorwaarden voor een uitzondering op de nuttig effect regel gelijk moeten met die voor wat betreft artikel 86 EG. Uit de rechtspraak kan worden afgeleid dat de nuttig effect regel niet van toepassing is op de goedkeuring van een afspraak als die "onderliggende" afspraak zelf niet in strijd is met artikel 81 EG. De mogelijkheden voor uitzonderingen op artikel 81 EG wegens milieugronden spelen daarmee eveneens een rol binnen de nuttig effect regel. Verder dient de nuttig effect regel – teneinde de parallellie met artikel 86 te bewaren – een uitzondering naar analogie van artikel 86(2) EG te bevatten. Met de uitzondering voor het algemeen belang zoals het Hof die lijkt te hebben gecreëerd, is dit het geval. Deze uitzondering is weliswaar nog niet toegepast in een milieucontext, maar dit lijkt zonder meer mogelijk. Het model voor integratie kan aldus worden toegepast in het kader van de nuttig effect regel aangezien deze een rechtstreekse afweging van milieudoelstellingen en mededingingsbescherming toestaat.

*Artikel 86 EG*

Artikel 86 EG bestaat uit twee regels. In het eerste lid is een verbod te vinden op grond waarvan lidstaten niet het nuttig effect aan de regels van het Verdrag mogen ontnemen wanneer zij wettelijke monopolies uitvaardigen. Het tweede lid verklaart de regels van het Verdrag buiten toepassing voor zover dit noodzakelijk is voor het uitvoeren van een taak van algemeen economisch belang. Uit de rechtspraak in verband met artikel 86 kan worden afgeleid dat het Hof de milieubeschermingsoverwegingen die door lidstaten te berde worden gebracht, kritisch benadert. Vrij recent heeft het Hof een wettelijk monopolie toegestaan op milieugronden. Daarbij overwoog het in het kader van de evenredigheidstoets dan het monopolie noodzakelijk was voor het totstandbrengen van een voldoende recycling capaciteit Daarbij hield het Hof rekening met de noodzaak om de desbetreffende onderneming te beschermen voor de duur van de afschrijving van de investeringen. In een eerdere zaak wees het Hof een vergelijkbaar beroep op het verzekeren van de rentabiliteit af. Milieuoverwegingen lijken dit opmerkelijke verschil te kunnen verklaren Vanuit het perspectief van het model voor integratie is deze rechtspraak zonder meer toe te juichen. Door milieubeschermingsoverwegingen rechtstreeks in aanmerking te nemen en door duidelijk te erkennen dat een uitzondering op de mededingingsregels noodzakelijk is in verband met de internalisatie, draagt het Hof met zijn toepassing van artikel 86 EG bij tot het internaliseren van milieulasten.

*Artikel 87 EG*

Artikel 87 EG vertoont qua structuur een grote overeenkomst met artikel 81 EG: een ruim geformuleerd verbod gekoppeld aan de mogelijkheid van een uitzondering voor bepaalde vormen van staatssteun. De parallel met artikel 81 bestaat ook in de uitlegging en met name de recente ontwikkelingen daarbij. Waar het eerste lid van artikel 81 recentelijk ook beperkter wordt geïnterpreteerd, legt het Hof in het recente arrest PreussenElektra het eerste lid van artikel 87 eveneens beperkt uit. Het resultaat is dat het de verplichting tot afname van duurzame energie tegen een prijs boven de marktwaarde, ondanks dat dit wel een voordeel voor de duurzame stroomproducenten oplevert, niet onder het verbod van artikel 87(1) valt. Vanuit milieubeschermingsoverwegingen lijkt deze uitspraak zeer wenselijk. Verder laat het beleid van de Commissie met betrekking tot de toepassing van de vrijstellingen in het derde lid van artikel 87 EG ook zien dat milieuoverwegingen een grote rol spelen. Zeker in verband met de toepassing van het derde lid kan zonder meer worden gesproken van een toepassing van het model voor integratie. De Commissie staat bijvoorbeeld zeer mededingingsverstorende bedrijfssteun toe voor zover dit noodzakelijk is om de concurrentieverstoringen als gevolg van onvolledige internalisatie te compenseren. Milieuoverwegingen en met name de noodzaak om tot een internalisatie te komen, rechtvaardigen aldus rechtstreeks een tijdelijke uitzondering op de mededingingsregels.

*Tussenconclusie*

Op grond van het bovenstaande is de tussenconclusie dat er eer niet te verklaren verschil is tussen de rol die milieubelangen spelen in de mededingingsregels die zijn gericht tot ondernemingen en de rol die zij spelen in de tot overheden gerichte mededingingsregels. Wat betreft de mededingingsregels gericht tot ondernemingen is de rol beperkt en indirect. Bovenal kan niet worden gesproken van een toepassing van het model voor integratie. De toepassing van de tot overheden gerichte regels laat echter een volledig ander beeld zien. Milieuvoordelen kunnen zonder meer een uitzondering rechtvaardigen en bij de toepassing van deze uitzondering wordt uitdrukkelijk rekening gehouden met de noodzaak om internalisatie te bewerkstelligen. Het model voor integratie wordt zonder meer toegepast.

## Deel drie: een vergelijking

*Inleiding*

Teneinde de bevindingen van de voorgaande twee delen te verifiëren (het model voor integratie en zijn al dan niet toepassing in het EG mededingingsrecht) vindt in het derde deel een vergelijking plaats. Daarbij wordt vanuit drie perspectieven gekeken naar de rol die milieubelangen spelen in het EG mededingingsrecht. Ten eerste het interne perspectief waarbij de rol van cultuurbelangen in het EG mededingingsrecht wordt bestudeerd. Als tweede het externe perspectief waarbij vanuit de ervaringen met milieubelangen in een drietal andere stelsels van mededingingsrecht wordt gekeken naar de eerdere bevindingen. Als laatste het semi-externe perspectief waarbij de rol die milieubelangen hebben gespeeld in de andere interne marktregels de maatstaf wordt.

*Het interne perspectief*

Maar al te vaak worden de zogenaamde niet-economische doelen op één hoop geveegd. De wederzijds versterkende relatie zoals die hierboven werd geschetst voor mededinging en milieubescherming bestaat echter niet voor alle andere niet-economische doelstellingen. Met betrekking tot cultuur, bijvoorbeeld, bestaat er geen beginsel naar analogie van het beginsel dat de vervuiler betaalt. Daarbij komt dat uiteindelijk de doelstellingen van cultuurbeleid en mededingingsbeleid fundamenteel tegengesteld zijn. Op grond van deze uitgangspunten zou het dus onmogelijk moeten zijn om een model voor integratie te ontwikkelen voor cultuurbelangen. Verder zou het dus ook onmogelijk moeten zijn om de mededingingsregels van de EG te interpreteren op een wijze die in deel twee is gekwalificeerd als een toepassing van het model voor integratie. Een onderzoek van de toepassing van het EG mededingingsrecht met betrekking tot zaken waarin cultuurbelangen een rol spelen heeft dit bevestigd. Cultuurbelangen spelen geen rol zoals milieubelangen die wel spelen bij de toepassing van het EG mededingingsrecht in die zin dat cultuurbelangen niet hebben geleid tot het tijdelijk ter zijde zetten van de mededingingsregels. Waar cultuurbelangen wel een rol spelen is dat het rechtstreekse gevolg van ingrijpen van de wetgever. Cultuurbelangen spelen hun in het mededingingsrecht op een wijze die niet analoog is aan de manier waarop milieubelangen volgens het model voor integratie wel degelijk hun rol spelen.

*Het externe perspectief*

In dit deel werd de relatie tussen mededinging en milieubescherming onderzocht voor wat betreft Duitsland, het Verenigd Koninkrijk en Nederland in een traditionele rechtsvergelijkende exercitie. Daarbij werd zowel naar de "mededingingskant" (wat is de rol van milieubelangen in het mededingingsrecht?) als naar de "milieukant" (welk belang wordt aan mededinging toegekend in het milieubeleid?) van de medaille gekeken. Wat betreft de toepassing van het mededingingsrecht in milieuzaken, is het beeld grotendeels gelijk aan dat wat al met betrekking tot de toepassing van de EG mededingingsregels voor ondernemingen werd vastgesteld. De rol van milieuoverwegingen is onduidelijk en als zij tot een besluit leiden dan is hun belang vaak indirect. Wat betreft de milieukant van de medaille bleek uit een vergelijking van de oplossing die in het Verenigd Koninkrijk is gekozen voor de implementatie van de Verpakkingsrichtlijn met de Duitse aanpak ten aanzien van verpakkingsafval dat het opleggen van producentenverantwoordelijkheid niet onherroepelijk tot monopolistische systemen hoeft te leiden. De Britse oplossing kan worden gekarakteriseerd als een echte producentenverantwoordelijkheid waarbij de producent verantwoordelijk is voor het (doen) inzamelen en recyclen van een bepaalde hoeveelheid materiaal die hij als verpakkingen heeft gebruikt. De continentale aanpak van het verpakkingsafval kan echter als productverantwoordelijkheid worden gekenmerkt waarbij de producent verantwoordelijk is voor zijn eigen verpakkingen. Deze verschillende invalshoek leidt ertoe dat bij een productverantwoordelijkheid de schaalvoordelen dermate groot zijn dat een natuurlijk monopolie wordt gecreëerd. De onwenselijkheid van een onmogelijkheid van mededinging behoeft in het licht van het model voor integratie weinig toelichting. In dit opzicht bevat het model voor integratie dus niet alleen een aanwijzing voor de mededingingsautoriteiten maar evengoed voor de milieuregelgevers.

*Het semi-externe perspectief*

In het semi-externe perspectief werd de rol die milieubelangen hebben gespeeld in de EG mededingingsregels vergeleken met het belang dat een milieubelangen is toegekend in het kader van de andere marktintegratie bepalingen uit het EG Verdrag. Daaruit blijkt dat milieubelangen rechtstreeks kunnen leiden tot een inperking van deze bepalingen. Zo heeft het Hof beperkingen op het vrije verkeer van goederen (art. 28 EG) toegestaan om milieuredenen. Verder bevat het EG Verdrag zelf een mogelijkheid tot afwijking van harmoniserende regels vanwege milieuoverwegingen (art. 95 EG). Verder is dit perspectief interessant omdat volgens de vaste rechtspraak van het Hof beperkingen op het basisvrijheden niet mogelijk zijn om economische redenen. De duidelijke en vergaande rol die milieubelangen spelen in de andere interne markt regels bevestigen, wat ook al bleek in deel twee, dat milieubelangen een grotere rol spelen in het kader van de regels die zijn gericht tot overheden dan in de regels die zijn gericht tot ondernemingen.

*Conclusies en aanbevelingen*

Naar aanleiding van het onderzoek wordt aanbevolen om het model van integratie toe te passen. De manier waarop milieubelangen worden meegewogen in het kader van de tot de overheden gerichte mededingingsregels kan in dit opzicht als voorbeeld functioneren.

Met betrekking tot artikel 81 speelt het model voor integratie zijn voornaamste rol in het kader van de toepassing van het derde lid. In dit verband zouden milieuvoordelen direct en als zodanig moeten kunnen leiden tot een toepassing van deze bepaling zonder dat daarvoor een economisering noodzakelijk is. In verband met artikel 82 zou de mogelijkheid van objectieve rechtvaardiging moeten worden toegepast in het licht van de milieuoverwegingen. Ten aanzien van de toepassing van de Concentratiecontrole verordening en de mededingingsregels die zijn gericht tot overheden kan worden vastgesteld dat de huidige praktijk in overeenstemming is met het model van integratie. Ten slotte bevat het model voor integratie een belangrijke vingerwijzing voor de milieuregelgever om bij het ontwerpen van regels inzake producentenverantwoordelijkheid rekening te houden met de mogelijkheid van mededinging.

Alleen dan kan het krachtige instrument van de mededinging worden aangewend om de internalisatie te bevorderen en zo een concurrentie om het milieu mogelijk te maken. De mededingingsautoriteiten zullen moeten inzien dat de bescherming van de mededinging daarbij tijdelijk op een lager pitje moet worden geplaatst. Op de langere termijn is zowel de bescherming van het milieu als de onvervalste concurrentie hiermee gediend. Tijdelijk wat minder concurrentie is een aanvaardbaar offer voor een kans op duurzame ontwikkeling. Immers, wat is mededinging waard als er niets is dat het waard is om voor te concurreren?